MW00717177

LEGAL ENVIRONMENT OF BUSINESS

Public law and regulation

LEGAL ENVIRONMENT
of
BUSINESS

Public law and regulation

JOHN D. BLACKBURN, J.D.
College of Administrative Science
The Ohio State University

ELLIOT I. KLAYMAN, J.D., LL.M.
College of Administrative Science
The Ohio State University

MARTIN H. MALIN, J.D.
IIT/Chicago-Kent College of Law

1982

RICHARD D. IRWIN, INC.
Homewood, Illinois 60430

Irwin-Dorsey Limited
Georgetown, Ontario L7G 4B3

© RICHARD D. IRWIN, INC. 1982

All rights reserved. No part of this publication may be
reproduced, stored in a retrieval system, or transmitted,
in any form or by any means, electronic, mechanical,
photocopying, recording, or otherwise, without the prior
written permission of the publisher.

ISBN 0-256-02480-4

Library of Congress Catalog Card No. 81–81550

Printed in the United States of America

1 2 3 4 5 6 7 8 9 0 K 8 7 6 5 4 3 2 1

To Our Parents

PREFACE

This book is designed to fill the need for quality teaching material for the course on the legal environment of business. It consists of 19 chapters organized into 6 parts. Part One, Legal Framework of Business, introduces the student to the legal system and presents the administrative and constitutional framework of government regulation of business. Parts Two through Five discuss the major areas of government regulation. Part Two, Antitrust Law, discusses economic regulation affecting a business's relations with its competitors and distributors. It includes a chapter on franchising in addition to chapters on restraints of trade, monopolization, mergers, and price discrimination. Part Three, Consumer Law, reflects the increased legislation and litigation inaugurated by the consumer movement. It includes chapters on product safety, advertising, and debtor-creditor relations. Part Four, Securities Law, discusses regulation of issuing and trading securities. Part Five, Labor Law, includes a chapter on labor standards and employee safety and a chapter on equal employment opportunity in addition to the chapter on traditional labor relations law. Part Six, Social Environment of Business, examines business's responsibility to society. A chapter on environmental law is included as illustrative of regulation designed to protect the community from the consequences of commercial activity. Special attention is given to the ethical and social influences upon managerial decision making in the chapter on business ethics and corporate social responsibility.

There is nothing sacred about the book's organization. Each part and each chapter has been written to stand by itself, thus allowing the instructor to rearrange the sequence of the contents without harm. Some instructors may even wish to omit entire parts or chapters from their course coverage to suit their time constraints or subject preferences.

This book is a legal environment of *business* book, but it may also serve in engineering, agricultural, and general education programs. Cases with a business fact pattern are included to illustrate the legal dynamics of managerial decision making. The book's managerial perspective is also exemplified by Chapter 4, Constitutional Law, which discusses business-related constitutional law.

The materials are current and teachable. Most of the cases represent current legal trends. Cases were not included simply on the basis of their decision date, however. The pedagogical properties of a case determined its selection. Landmark precedents are included where their pedagogical quality is consistent with their precedental value. The teachability of the book is enhanced by the inclusion of questions after the cases, discussion problems at the end of each chapter, and part review problems at the end of each part. Thus a building-block approach is provided with questions and problems whereby the student is challenged to recall and analyze legal principles through the case questions, apply what has been learned in the chapter discussion problems, and synthesize and evaluate the various areas of law in the part review problems. The pedagogical value is enhanced also by a discussion of policy considerations. Such policy discussion is designed to provide food for thought for students and instructors who wish to consider the policy implications of legal developments. A glossary of legal terms used throughout the text is also included. Students should not need to purchase a legal dictionary. Appendixes of selected statutes are provided for easy reference to important statutory sources.

We have had considerable help in writing this book. We wish to thank our colleagues at The Ohio State University, Indiana University, the Wharton School, and IIT/Chicago-Kent College of Law for their support and encouragement. We also wish to especially thank professors Edwin Epstein of the University of California at Berkeley, Jeffrey Gale of the University of Washington, Nancy Hauserman of the University of Iowa, and Barry Roberts of the University of North Carolina at Chapel Hill who read the manuscript and offered many helpful suggestions. Special thanks also to Carol D'Laine Ditzhazy Vogel of IIT/Chicago-Kent College of Law, who lent her expertise to the environmental law chapter. A number of law students deserve special mention for their very capable research assistance: Marcia Clegge, Louis A. Goodman, Janice Linn, John Neueuschwander, and Timothy K. Williams. Portions of these materials have been class-tested with both undergraduate and graduate students at The Ohio State University, Indiana University, and the Wharton School. We wish to thank our students for their helpful comments and suggestions. Several typists have had a hand in producing an accurate and readable manuscript: Dolly Bakitis, Hazel Blankenship, Kay Hechesky, Joyce Klayman, Geraldine Mohr, and Helene Robinson. We also wish to extend a special and very sincere note of appreciation to our editor Gerald W. Saykes for his patience, encouragement, and collegiality. Finally, we wish to thank our families for their patience while we were writing this book. None of these people is responsible for the views expressed or materials used. Any errors are our own.

John D. Blackburn
Elliot I. Klayman
Martin H. Malin

CONTENTS

obtaining judicial review. *Standing. Reviewability. Exhaustion of administrative remedies.* Policy considerations.

The historical context of the U.S. Constitution. Federal authority to regulate commerce. *The original meaning of the Commerce Clause. Early Supreme Court interpretation of the Commerce Clause. Supreme Court restrictions of congressional commerce power. Depression-era decisions. The present position.* The relationship between state and federal regulation. *The Commerce Clause. The Supremacy Clause.* First Amendment freedoms. *Sunday blue laws. Freedom of speech and press.* Property rights and economic regulation. *The substantive due process doctrine. Impairment of property values and eminent domain.* Constitutional protections in administrative procedures. *Administrative investigations.* Policy considerations.

PART TWO: ANTITRUST LAW

Antitrust administration and enforcement. *Justice Department enforcement. Federal Trade Commission enforcement. Private enforcement.* Section 1 of the Sherman Act. *Contract, combination, or conspiracy. Restraints of trade—the rule of reason.* Horizontal restraints. *Price-fixing. Divisions of territories, customers, and markets.* Vertical restraints. *Resale price maintenance. Territorial, customer, and market restraints. Exclusive dealing contracts—section 3 of the Clayton Act. Tying devices.* Concerted refusals to deal. The Sherman Act in action: Limitations on trade association activities. *Membership qualifications. Statistical reporting and price exchanges. Product standardization. Codes of ethics. Activities aimed at customers or suppliers.* Policy considerations.

Monopolization and section 2 of the Sherman Act. *The relevant market. Assessing power in the relevant market. Intent to monopolize.* Oligopolies. Attempts to monopolize. Conspiracies to monopolize. Policy considerations.

Determining the relevant market. Horizontal mergers. *Rebutting the presumption of illegality. Using postmerger evidence.* Vertical mergers. Conglomerate mergers. The failing company defense. Remedies. Policy considerations.

The early Clayton Act. Seller discrimination. *Price difference. Two sales. Commodities. Like grade and quality. Competitive injury. Commerce.* Defenses. *Cost justification. Meeting competition. Changing conditions.* Buyer discrimination. Brokerage payments. Promotional allowances and services. Enforcement. Policy considerations.

The FTC franchise rule. *The rule's coverage. Required disclosure. Earning predictions. Violations of the rule.* Section 3 of the Clayton Act. *Exclusive dealing. Tie-in devices.* Other antitrust considerations. *Covenants not to compete. Franchisor-franchisee competition.*

Territorial and customer restraints. Promotions and advertising. Termination of the franchise relationship. Policy considerations.

PART THREE: CONSUMER LAW

Product liability. *Negligence. Warranties. Strict liability.* The Magnuson-Moss Warranty Act. *Disclosure. Full and limited warranty. Limitation of disclaimer. Remedies.* The Consumer Product Safety Act. *Structure of the Consumer Product Safety Commission. Consumer product. Information gathering. Rules and bans. Imminent hazards. Substantial product hazard. Remedies.* The National Highway Traffic and Motor Vehicle Act. *Remedies.* Policy considerations.

Private remedies for false advertising. *Consumer remedies. Competitor remedies.* Administrative regulation of false advertising. *Regulation of advertising by the FTC.* Policy considerations. *The role of advertising. The need for governmental regulation. Regulatory reform.*

The Truth in Lending Act. *Creditor. Consumer credit. Disclosure. TILA interpretation. Credit advertising. Cancellation of credit agreements. Consumer leasing. Penalties. Credit cards.* The Fair Credit Reporting Act. *Permissible purposes. Obsolete information. Compliance. Investigative consumer reports. Disclosure. Disputes. Requirements on users of reports. Remedies.* The Fair Credit Billing Act. The Equal Credit Opportunity Act. Debt collection. *Common law.* The Fair Debt Collection Practices Act. *Postjudgment collection.* Uniform Consumer Credit Code. The Bankruptcy Reform Act. *Liquidation. Reorganization. Adjustment of debts for individuals with regular income.* Policy considerations.

PART FOUR: SECURITIES LAW

Business organizations. *Sole proprietorship. Partnership. Corporation.* Introduction to securities regulation. Federal securities laws. *The Securities Act of 1933. The Securities Exchange Act of 1934. Other securities legislation.* The Securities and Exchange Commission. Definition of a security. *Common enterprise. Expectation of profit. Derivation of profits.* Registration. *Prefiling period. Waiting period. Posteffective period.* Marketing securities. *Firm commitment. Best efforts.* Exemptions. *Persons other than issuer. Private placements. Intrastate offerings. Small offerings. Integration.* Private remedies. *Misrepresentation in registration statement. Failure to file registration statement. Misrepresentation and fraud in sale of security.* Public remedies. *Stop orders. Injunction. Criminal penalties.* State laws. *Registration of securities. Exemptions. Remedies.* Policy considerations.

Securities markets. *Securities exchanges. Over-the-counter markets.* Registration and reporting. Control of corporate insiders. *Director. Officer. Ten percent beneficial owner.*

Filing. Recovery of profits. Valuation of profits. Defense. Proxy rules. *Liability. Proposals by security holders.* Takeover bids. Broker-dealer registration. *Churning. Scalping. Disclosure. Financial responsibility.* Remedies. *Express remedies. Implied remedies.* Policy considerations.

PART FIVE: LABOR LAW

PART SIX: SOCIAL ENVIRONMENT OF BUSINESS

Introduction

Legal study differs from other business study. Thus business students need an orientation to the nature of legal study before they turn to the substantive subjects of the business legal environment. This introduction provides a frame of reference from which business students can analyze, apply, synthesize, and evaluate the various areas of law affecting business. The discussion explores the objectives of legal study by business students before explaining the nature of legal study.

OBJECTIVES OF LEGAL STUDY BY BUSINESS STUDENTS

It is particularly appropriate at the beginning to inquire into the educational objectives of a book or course on the legal environment of business. Thus the following discussion focuses on the rationale and the objectives of legal study by business students.

Why study law in a business school?

It is generally assumed that law is a subject taught to aspirant attorneys in a professional program within the law school. Historically, however, law has been considered a subject particularly important to the lay public. In earlier days, legal study was considered part and parcel of a liberal education. Today, legal study outside the law school is gaining renewed interest. This trend is a manifestation of a simple fact of modern life: that law is too important to be left to the lawyers.

Business colleges have long recognized the importance of legal study in the business curriculum. Business managers must be aware that their business relations are also legal relations. Thus a contract manifests both a legal and an economic relationship. The performance or breach of a contract carries both legal and economic consequences.

In today's world of government growth, it is particularly important that business students be exposed to material on public law and regulation. The

1

plethora of regulations emanating from various government agencies mandates that today's manager acquire some familiarity with the rudiments of government regulation. Today's manager deals not only with suppliers and customers but with an array of state and federal agencies. A list of the acronyms of these agencies (e.g., SEC, NLRB, FTC, OSHA, and EEOC) sounds more like an alphabet soup than a collection of government entities. Woe to the uninitiated manager who does not even know what these abbreviations stand for, let alone the shorthand jargon (e.g., "affirmative action," "stop order") of the bureaucrats who work for those agencies. Today the language of business includes not only the items of the balance sheet but the legalese of government regulations.

What are the objectives of a course on the legal environment of business?

A course on the legal environment of business has many objectives. Some are general and resemble the objectives of other business law courses. Others are more specific and are particularly germane to a course on the legal environment of business. The following list includes both types. Two points should be noted: (1) the list is not meant to be exhaustive; and (2) the formulation of course objectives should not be an exercise which a text author or an instructor does alone, but should be a cooperative effort involving the text authors, the instructor, and the students. The following list is offered as the authors' contribution toward such an effort. A course on the legal environment of business should help the student to:

1. Develop the ability to apply conceptual knowledge to real-world problems. A principal goal of legal environment courses is to teach conceptual knowledge for future use in decision-making situations. This is accomplished by communicating the concepts in a case-oriented setting and by giving the student practice in applying the concepts to case problems.

2. Become more effective in coping with all challenges in an orderly manner. The use of case study makes the student sort out relevant and important facts, determine the issues involved, and reach conclusions based on known rules, regulations, standards, and principles.

3. Acquire a vocabulary of terms and concepts that will make it possible to understand further communications and so facilitate a continuation of learning beyond the limits of the classroom.

4. Develop the principles of inquiry, restraint, objectivity, and regard for considerations of public policy. Understanding the "legal method" of resolving conflicts helps a person to develop restraint by not reaching conclusions too quickly on the basis of narrow thinking, to be more objective, and to consider not only the immediate issue but also the broader considerations of economic and social benefit.

5. Develop an understanding of the terms and concepts of the legal environment of business in order to understand better the sources that business

people read every day. These sources include business papers and periodicals, technical journals, and financial reports.

6. Develop an understanding of the philosophy underlying the legal rules and regulations controlling business activity. This will result in an awareness of the individual's role in the improvement of the legal and regulatory system. Legislative bodies, administrative agencies, and courts should insure that the legal and regulatory system reflects the consensus of public thought. Therefore, everyone should think critically about the present system and the desirability of change.

7. Facilitate interdisciplinary communication in business. Accountants, financial executives, marketing experts, and other business specialists must constantly communicate with one another. Frequently the subject matter will involve legal concepts with which all of them must be familiar (e.g., price discrimination, bona fide occupational qualification, tombstone ads).

8. Develop an understanding of the principal areas of law and regulation affecting business transactions in order to do a better business management job. Legal rules and regulations affect almost every business activity. Ignorance of these rules and regulations leaves a large void in the formal education of a business manager. The fact that there is a professional field of law practice does not free managers from the need to know about the legal environment of business. Many will not have lawyers on retainer, and even those who do cannot rely on their lawyers to instruct them on every business matter in which law is involved. Almost every business decision is affected in some ways by existing rules of law.

9. Develop an awareness of legal pitfalls so that professional legal assistance can be sought before losses occur.

10. Satisfy the intellectual curiosity that drives every person to learn more about the principles and concepts that give meaning to observations and experiences. Legal environment courses show how law and regulation fit into the business sector of the social order and give the student a better understanding of the relationship between business practice and social development.

LEGAL STUDY

The peculiar feature of legal study is the inclusion of selected legal cases in the text. These cases are unlike the business cases usually included in business school case courses. Legal cases are not really cases at all, but are legal opinions written by a judge, usually on an appellate court, which resolve the legal issues in the dispute brought before the court. It is such written legal opinions that constitute the cases presented in this book. The cases are designed to illustrate the application of the principles of law (provided in the textual material preceding each case) to particular legal disputes.

These cases, plus the text and the discussion by the instructor either in answering specific questions or in further exploring points of law, form the standard substance from which the student will set out to learn about the legal environment of business.

The cases selected have been chosen by the text authors for teaching purposes. Various criteria have been used in selecting these cases. Some cases have been selected because they proceed on unsound assumptions or somehow fail to meet the problems at hand. Such cases provide the maximum opportunity for class discussion and criticism. Other cases have been included because they are the great landmark cases. From these cases the student will learn "sound law" and come into contact with dominant ideas. Some recent cases, illustrating trends in the law, have also been selected. These permit the student and instructor to evaluate the decision against the background of their own current experience.

Reading cases

The first thing the student is expected to do is to read the textual material immediately preceding a case. This material presents the fundamental legal principles in a general manner. After this, the student must read the case following the textual presentation. This does not mean reading the case as you would read a novel, skimming lightly for the thread of the plot. It means reading the case as carefully as you would read a page of statistics, accounting, or finance. You should read each word, looking up the unknown words in the glossary or a legal dictionary. The old proverb "To read many times is not necessarily to understand" is worth cherishing, plain as it is.

In reading cases, it is necessary to bear in mind the points of law which you are seeking. It does not suffice to read legal opinions merely as a narrative. The cases are presented to illustrate particular areas of the law, and your legal analysis of the cases should be structured to make your reading profitable. You not only must know what you are looking for; you ought also to have a method that will help you in your search. As the learned Justice Cardozo has said, "Cases do not unfold their principles for the asking. They yield up their kernel slowly and painfully."[1]

Your reading of these cases, then, must be done systematically, keeping in mind that an appellate judge does not always write his or her opinion with an eye toward functional, simple, orderly legal analysis. Our American legal system is one of the few in the world in which people are not specifically trained to become judges. Our judges have usually been trained to become lawyers (though even this is not always a prerequisite). Then, depending on the particular judicial procedure, some of these lawyers are either elected to a judgeship or appointed to this office of honor and power. When people

---

[1] B. Cardozo, *The Nature of the Judicial Process* 29 (1921).

become judges, lightning does not strike them with the knowledge and expertise necessary to write meaningful (or even lucid) legal opinions. They sometimes experience great difficulty in formulating their decisions. However, important decisions may be made in such instances. Problems in case selection arise when an important decision is contained in an opinion written by a judge who may have had great difficulty in committing his or her thoughts to paper. Often, the authors have included such cases within the text. In such instances your analysis may be impeded by obscure language. Also, many of the legal opinions in your text have been edited to conform to necessary space limitations or so that a case which in its entirety illustrates many points of law could be used to illustrate a single point.

Briefing cases

You may be expected to prepare what is called a *brief* of the case. This is a digested version of the case. Almost every instructor has his or her own idea of what a well-formed brief should be. Sometimes your instructor will tell you how to brief cases in an introductory lecture. More frequently, you will learn what your instructor expects through criticisms of your own products in class.

Even so, let us approach the problem of briefing by examining the functions which it is to perform for you. If a brief performs these functions, then it is a useful one. The brief is intended to remind you in class of the salient facts and points of law raised and decided in the case. One timeworn request of instructors is to ask you to "state" a given case, and here a well-drawn brief will help refresh your memory. If your brief is too long, you will lose the salient points in the verbiage.

A further function of the brief is to serve as an aid in reviewing the course for examinations. Instead of attempting to accomplish the impossible task of rereading all the cases, you can recall the problems to mind by referring to your briefs. Hence, these briefs should contain enough details to recall for you the problems and the pertinent approaches advanced in class discussion.

What follows is an annotated outline of a suggested briefing format. Some of the points described may not be relevant to a particular case, and these points will seldom appear in the order in which they are presented here. However, the format is a useful means for reaching the central ideas contained within the case material.

A suggested brief

Parties.   Who is suing whom? Who is the plaintiff? Who is the defendant?

Legal proceedings.   In order to ascertain the nature of the legal proceedings, ask yourself: Is the litigation civil or criminal? What remedies are being sought? What was the result in the trial court? If the case was reviewed before it reached the reported appellate court, what was the result of that review? How did the case come before the appellate court?

Facts. What happened? This requires, not a recitation of all the details which can be learned, but a selection of those relevant to the decision.

Legal provision. What rules of law are applicable?

Issues. What issue or issues are presented for decision? The court must decide the legal issues involved in the case. These can often be presented in terms of a series of questions. Sometimes a case involves only a single issue. Other times a complicated series of transactions by the parties results in a multitude of issues. In either case the court will attempt to resolve the issue or issues presented before it.

Arguments. As an aid in understanding the dilemmas confronted by the court in resolving the legal issues, an analysis of the arguments which were presented is helpful. The legal resolution of disputes within a court of law is most often resorted to when all other forms of conciliation (or reconciliation) have failed. Business managers use the courtroom only when all other means of solving the problem have been exhausted, since litigation is expensive and time consuming. When a problem does ripen into a legal controversy, the parties have argued themselves into a polarization rather than into a compromise of their differences. Starting with the arguments of the contending parties is thus sometimes a useful way of discovering the issues of the particular controversy presented, and many judges will include the arguments of the parties in their written decision.

Decision. How are the issues decided? Who won, and what did he or she win? The decision in the case is, simply, the answer to the issues.

Rule of the case. What general rule does the case lay down?

Reasons. What explanation does the court give to justify its decision? Within a conscious framework of legal reference, the court makes a decision based on an appraisal of the issues presented. On the appellate level, where these legal opinions are often presented in a formal, written format, the judges usually feel compelled to back up their decision with what they consider to be the reasons for it. The appellate court looks not only to further appellate review of its opinion (if this is possible) but also to the principle of legal precedent. In an important case a court will realize that the ramifications of its decision may be far reaching and that the case may set a precedent for decades to come. Realizing the importance of such a powerful act, a court often feels compelled to explain why the decision was reached—thus the reasons for the decision.

Concurring and dissenting opinions. If there are any concurring and/or dissenting opinions, what do they say?

Legal terminology. Legal terms, such as *ex parte* or *scienter,* must be looked up in the glossary or a law dictionary because the definitions in an ordinary dictionary are not sufficient. Law dictionaries by Ballentine and Black are in most college libraries.

General comment. Class discussion may not always or even usually follow this outline, and students may not be required to utilize it. The important thing is the result, understanding the cases, and not the technique by which that result is attained. However, it is believed that an understanding of any case requires an understanding of the items listed and that students will profit by following the outline at least until they are able to devise alternatives.

PART ONE

Legal framework of business

CHAPTER 1

Nature of law

Jurisprudence is the name given to the study of legal philosophy. At first blush this subject is not attractive to many practical-minded people. Philosophical subjects are not normally studied by today's pragmatic student. However, it is appropriate that an introductory chapter focus on fundamental aspects of the subject to be studied, leaving for later chapters the treatment of more practical matters. Some foundation is needed to provide a frame of reference for that treatment. The following discussion focuses on a fundamental philosophical topic: the nature of law.

VARIOUS MEANINGS GIVEN TO LAW

"What is law?" is a favorite question used by law professors to start discussion of their subject. Each person seems to have his or her own answer to the question. Some think of law as a body of rules. Others see it as a means of restricting human conduct. Still others see it as an instrument for protecting basic freedoms. A historian may regard law as a reflection of a society's mores at a particular time. A sociologist may regard it as a particular social institution. Thus law is different things to different people, and perhaps like other fundamental concepts applicable to human behavior it is susceptible to several definitions. Perhaps the definition provided reveals more about the person who provides it than about the subject defined.

Just because law has been defined in many ways does not mean that the attempts to define it have been frustrating exercises in futility. Scholars through the ages have sought to define law. From Aristotle, the Greek philosopher, and Cicero, the Roman senator, to Jerome Frank, a federal circuit court judge, and Karl Llewellyn, a law school professor, highly intelligent men and women have wrestled with this problem. An examination of their efforts reveals that law is a fundamental part of any civilization, from the simplest agrarian societies to the most complex industrial states, and that its functions reflect the fundamental objectives of the society it serves. The

11

simple question "What is law?" leads to a complex answer which reveals the many-faceted nature of the subject of this book.

Ideal conceptions: Natural law

Natural law philosophers think of law as ordained by nature. For them, law consists of a body of higher principles existing independently of human experience. It exists as an ideal condition that is either inherent in human nature or derived from a divine source.

People cannot create natural law, but they can discover its principles through the application of reason. Knowledge of natural law is thus an informed intuition of what is fair and just. The principles of natural law, discoverable by reason, are universally valid. Thus natural law is a body of principles of right and justice existing for all peoples irrespective of time and culture. It transcends Man-made notions of what is right and just. The following excerpt from Cicero's work *The Republic* is perhaps the earliest and most quoted statement of the natural law philosophy.

Cicero, The Republic
211 (C. W. Keyes trans. 1928)

True law is right reason in agreement with nature; it is of universal application, unchanging and everlasting; it summons to duty by its commands and averts from wrongdoing by its prohibitions; and it does not lay its commands or prohibitions upon good men in vain, though neither have any effect on the wicked. It is a sin to try to alter this law, nor is it allowable to attempt to repeal any part of it, and it is impossible to abolish it entirely. We cannot be freed from its obligations by senate or people, and we need not look outside ourselves for an expander or interpreter of it. And there will not be different laws at Rome or at Athens, or different laws now and in the future, but one eternal and unchangeable law will be valid for all nations and all times, and there will be one master and ruler, that is, God, over us all, for He is the author of this law, its promulgator, and its enforcing judge. Whoever is disobedient is fleeing from himself and denying his human nature, and by reason of this very fact he will suffer the worst penalties, even if he escapes what is commonly considered punishment.

Positive conceptions: Rules of a sovereign

In a word-association exercise the word *law* might frequently evoke the response "Rules." Most people think of law in terms of rules, regulations, statutes, commandments, and the like. In his *Commentaries,* Blackstone defined law as "a rule of civil conduct, prescribed by the supreme power in a state, commanding what is right and prohibiting what is wrong."[1] Blackstone saw law as consisting of a general body of rules which are addressed by

---

[1] W. Blackstone, 1 *Commentaries on the Laws of England* 38 (1771).

the rulers of a political society to its members and which are generally obeyed. In jurisprudential terms this is the positive conception of law.

The positivist school of jurisprudence regards law as a body of rules imposed by a sovereign. The term *positive* stems from the root word *posit*, which means to place, put, or lay down something. A positive law is a law laid down by the duly constituted authority. Early attempts to codify rules include the Code of Hammurabi and the Justinian Code.

Early statements of the positive conception of law reflected an element of injustice in that positive law was defined as arbitrary. Thus Justinian's *Institutes* defined law with the Latin phrase *Quad principi placuit, legis habet vigorem* ("Whatever has pleased the prince, has the force of law").[2] Similarly, in *The Science of Law* Sheldon Amos stated, "A law . . . is a command proceeding from the supreme political authority of a state, and addressed to the persons who are subjects of that authority."[3] While at first appearing to be a disadvantage, the arbitrariness reflected in these statements in fact has the advantage of expediency. Although arbitrary, positive law sets standards for regulating society; it facilitates decision making; it helps get things done.

Positive law and natural law are not the same thing. Natural law embodies justice and fairness. Positive law can embrace fairness and justice, but it does not have to. The distinction between natural law and positive law was pointed out by Thomas Hobbes, an English social philosopher who upheld the supreme authority of the sovereign, in his 17th-century political treatise *Leviathan*. He wrote: "These dictates of reason, men used to call by the name of laws, but improperly: for they are but conclusions, or theorems concerning what conduceth to the conservation and defence of themselves; whereas law, properly is the word of him, that by right hath command over others."[4]

Historical conceptions

To define law as the command of a political sovereign may be criticized as ignoring a large number of rules which have bound people in the past. It may be argued that law is often older than the state and that the state is an incidental product of the more mature legal systems rather than the distinguishing characteristic of all law.

The historical school of jurisprudence defines law as the embodiment of a society's customs. Historical jurisprudence holds that custom is the chief manifestation of law and that law develops with social development. For the historical school, law is the spirit of the people.

Custom may influence and become the basis of positive law. Thus an interaction of custom and positive law occurs as a society's most compelling

---

[2] Justinian, 2 *Institutes* 9 (T. Cooper trans. 1812).

[3] S. Amos, *Science of Law* 48 (8th ed. 1896).

[4] T. Hobbes, *Leviathan* 104–5 (M. Oakeshott ed., 1946).

cultural values rise to the level of formal positive law. As customs and cultural values change, the direction of positive law may be expected to follow. Thus custom often becomes the basis for positive law because laws patterned after custom are likely to meet with greater social acceptance.

The following excerpt is by the earliest advocate of the historical conception of law, Friedrich Karl von Savigny, a German nobleman. When he wrote, the area that became the nation of Germany comprised many independent states. Savigny's opinions were quite popular because at this time the German states were moving toward a transformation into a unified nation which was more consonant with the common characteristics of their people.

F. K. von Savigny, Of the Vocation of Our Age for Legislation and Jurisprudence
24, 27 (A. Hayward trans., London 1831)

In the earliest times to which authentic history extends, the law will be found to have already attained a fixed character, peculiar to the people, like their language, manners and constitution. Nay, these phenomena have no separate existence, they are but the particular faculties and tendencies of an individual people inseparably united in nature, and only wearing the semblance of distinct attributes to our view. That which binds them into one whole is the common conviction of the people, the kindred consciousness of an inward necessity, excluding all notion of an accidental and arbitrary origin. . . .

But this organic connection of law with the being and character of the people, is also manifested in the progress of the times; and here again, it may be compared with language. For law, as for language, there is no moment of absolute cessation; it is subject to the same movement and development as every other popular tendency; and this very development remains under the same law of inward necessity, as in its earliest states. Law grows with the growth, and strengthens with the strength of the people, and finally dies away as the nation loses its nationality.

Sociological conceptions

Closely associated with the historical conception is the sociological conception of law. The sociological conception defines law in terms of present human conduct. Thus law is not just what the lawbooks permit but what human behavior provides. The similarity between the historical conception and the sociological conception is obvious. Both rely on human conduct as the source of law. However, the historical conception embodies a long-range perspective, whereas the sociological conception focuses on more immediate experience.

The sociological conception of law is not necessarily in conflict with the positive conception, because positive law may reflect current human conduct. However, where human conduct is not in accord with a formal proposition of law, those adhering to the sociological conception would change the law to bring it into line with human conduct. Stretched to its limits, this logic would reduce formal law to its lowest level if people chose to ignore it. The following selection from Eugen Ehrlich's *Fundamental Principles of the Sociology of Law* summarizes the sociological conception.

E. Ehrlich, Fundamental Principles of the Sociology of Law 483 (W. Moll trans., Cambridge, Mass. 1936)

It is often said that a book must be written in a manner that permits of summing up its content in a single sentence. If the present volume were to be subjected to this test, the sentence might be the following: At the present as well as at any other time, the center of gravity of legal development lies not in legislation, nor in juristic science, nor in judicial decision, but in society itself. This sentence, perhaps, contains the substance of every attempt to state the fundamental principles of the sociology of law.

This then is the *living* law in contradistinction to that which is being enforced in the courts and other tribunals. The living law is the law which dominates life itself even though it has been posited in legal propositions. The source of our knowledge of this law is, first the modern legal documents; secondly, the direct observation of life, of commerce, of customs and usages, and of all associations, not only of those that the law has recognized but also of those that it has overlooked and passed by, indeed even of those it has disapproved.

Realist conceptions

A conception of law which is closely allied to the sociological school is the realist conception. Realism is a school of jurisprudence which looks beyond the allusions of logic and reasoning and examines what actually occurs in the legal process. A realist thus would agree with Justice Holmes' statement that "the life of the law has not been logic; it has been experience."[5] Both sociological and realist jurisprudence view life experiences as affecting legal development. However, the realist conception focuses primarily on the social influences affecting the judicial process. It views law as the impact of various social influences on official discretion. Jerome Frank, a federal circuit court judge and a leading realist, thus defined law by saying: "From the point of view of the judge, the law may fairly be the judging process or the power to pass judgment."[6] Karl Llewellyn, a law professor, went beyond the judging process and included other official conduct in the realist definition of law when he wrote: "This doing of something about disputes, this doing of it reasonably, is the business of the law. And the people who have the doing of it in charge, whether they be judges or clerks or jailers or lawyers, are officials of the law. *What these officials do about disputes is, to my mind, the law itself.*"[7]

[5] O. Holmes, *Common Law* 6 (1881).

[6] J. Frank, *Law and the Modern Mind* 126 (1926).

[7] K. Llewellyn, *The Bramble Bush* 12 (1950).

The realist school flourished in the 1920s and 1930s. Its impact on legal study is still being felt. Legal study according to a realist involves more than book learning based on appellate court opinions; it also includes examination of the legal process by court visitation and the study of trial court and agency transcripts and examination of the social, economic, and political influences that affect court and agency decision making.

Summary

From this review of the various conceptions held by the fundamental schools of jurisprudence, it can be seen that many meanings have been given to the term *law*. One cannot simply use the ordinary dictionary definition. For example, the second edition of *Webster's New International Dictionary* contains six entries for the term *law*, the first of which covers 13 separate meanings. As shown by the preceding discussion, law may be viewed as a field of forces, with no one theory encompassing the whole field. One's conclusions about the nature of law follow from one's assumptions about the social order. *Law* is necessarily an abstract term, and the definer is free to choose a particular level of abstraction.

SOURCES OF LAW

It is frequently stated that the legislative branch of the government makes the laws, the executive branch enforces them, and the judicial branch interprets them. While this is a valid outline of the separation of powers among the three branches of government, it is not entirely accurate. In reality, each branch "makes law." Moreover, administrative agencies, which collectively have come to be called "the fourth branch of government," are sometimes given rulemaking authority, investigative and enforcement powers, and adjudicative responsibilities. The following discussion focuses on the sources of law.

The legislature: Statutes

One source of law was established with the creation of the legislature. A legislature is an organized body of persons having the authority to make laws for a political unit and often exercises other functions, such as the control of government administration.

The creation of a legislature is a development of an organized society. Early legislatures were councils consisting of aristocrats who were appointed by royal rulers to provide them with financial assistance and advice. In the 18th century, the power of legislative bodies grew in comparison with that of the royal rulers. In the 19th century, legislatures took on a republican character; that is, members of legislatures were elected by their constituencies rather than appointed by the ruler.

The legislative bodies existing today are either offshoots of the English Parliament or have been established in imitation of it. In this country the federal and state legislative bodies have been constitutionally created. Thus Article I, Section 1, of the U.S. Constitution provides: "All legislative Powers herein granted shall be vested in a Congress of the United States, which shall consist of a Senate and House of Representatives."

Laws created by a legislature are called statutes, enactments, acts, or legislation. Such law is sometimes described as written law.

The legislative process. The term *legislation* refers either to the process by which a statute is enacted or to the result of that process, an enacted law. Legislative acts become laws only after passing through certain formal steps in the legislature and, usually, after having received later approval of the executive (i.e., a governor or the president). The procedure by which Congress enacts a statute is typical of legislative procedures. A federal statute begins as a bill introduced in either the House of Representatives or the Senate. Many bills are introduced by sponsors who realize that the bills have little or no chance of passage. Such sponsors may use the bills to satisfy constituent demands or to call public attention to particular issues.

After a bill has been introduced, it is referred to the appropriate committee. Most bills die in committee from inaction. Those which receive serious consideration result in public hearings and, not infrequently, studies by the committee staff. The committee then meets in executive session to "mark up" the bill, that is, to go over it line by line, reviewing and rewriting it. Finally, the committee sends the bill to the floor of a house of Congress. The bill is accompanied by a committee report which details the policy reasons for the bill and explains the bill's intended effect on existing law. A minority report may also be included, if members of the committee disagree with the majority view. Following debate, the bill is voted on. If it receives the support of those voting, it is sent to the other house of Congress, where it undergoes similar treatment.

If both houses pass similar but different bills, a conference committee consisting of members of both houses is established. This committee attempts to agree upon a bill that will be acceptable to both houses. The conference committee's bill is then submitted to each house, where it is voted upon.

Bills that have passed both houses of Congress are forwarded to the president for his signature. Pursuant to Article I, Section 7, of the U.S. Constitution, the president may sign the bill into law or may return it to the house in which it originated (i.e., veto it). If the president takes no action within 10 days following the bill's transmittal, the bill becomes law "unless the Congress by their Adjournment prevent its Return, in which Case it shall not be a Law." Thus, if Congress adjourns after transmitting a bill to the president, the president may "pocket-veto" the bill by simply doing nothing.

State laws are enacted through similar procedures which are specified in state constitutions. All state laws are subject to the prohibitions of the

U.S. Constitution. State laws must also comply with the applicable state constitution.

Legislative interpretation. Although the legislature has the primary lawmaking function, the meaning of a statute is not fully known until the statute is interpreted by the courts in deciding cases involving its application. Thus the judicial process of legislative interpretation is another major source of law.

The courts have developed rules of legislative interpretation to determine the meaning of statutes. The purpose of these rules is to determine the legislative intent. However, the legislature may not have envisioned the particular controversy before a court, and therefore the legislative intent may be nonexistent. In such a case the court attempts to determine what the legislature would have intended to be the application of the statute in the given case.

The most obvious indicia of the legislative intent are the statute's language. Where the statutory language is clear and a particular application would not be patently absurd or render the statute unworkable, a court will apply the plain meaning of the legislative language. This is known as the plain meaning rule. That is to say, where the language of a statute is clear, a court will not go beyond the plain meaning of its words to determine what the statute means. However, a court will not apply a statute literally where doing so produces an absurd result or renders the statute unworkable.

The plain meaning rule is a rule of judicial self-restraint. Courts are not free to delve into a morass of nonstatutory material to determine the meaning of a statute whose intent is clear.

In the absence of a plain meaning, courts look to other indicia of the legislative intent. One approach is to examine the context of the statutory language. Another is to look to the legislative history, that is, the historical context of the statute's enactment along with any documents of the legislative debate. When the statutory and historical contexts fail to reveal the legislative purpose, courts use legal reasoning and apply the statute to effectuate its underlying policy.

In examining the statutory context, a court considers the statute as a whole and not merely the particular clause at issue in the case. In this way the court avoids considering a particular statutory clause out of context. Thus courts do not divorce a single phrase or section of a statute from its other portions. Legislative intent is determined, not by viewing a word or clause apart from its statutory setting, but by considering it in the context of the entire statute.

Where the context of the statutory language fails to reflect the legislative intent, courts frequently consider legislative history. This involves considering the social conditions that gave rise to the legislative response and any legislative documents, such as committee reports and proceedings and records of legislative debates. For example, knowing the history of race relations in the United States before 1964 is helpful in understanding the legislative purposes of the federal Civil Rights Act of 1964.

Frequently the committee that reports a bill to the floor of the legislature will attempt to express the legislative purpose and intent in the committee report included with the bill. At the state level, this is usually not done. However, in much of the model and uniform legislation drafted by the National Conference of Commissioners on Uniform State Laws and offered to the state legislatures as proposals for legislative reform, a "drafter's comment" on the statute's meaning is appended to each section of the proposed statute. When these model laws are enacted, the comment is frequently included with them, not as binding law, but as an indication of the legislative intent. Formal committee reports are found more frequently in the legislative history of federal statutes. These reports and published proceedings of committee hearings are frequently used by courts to fathom the congressional will. Congressional committee reports for enacted laws are published in the *U.S. Congressional News and Administrative Report.* Proceedings of congressional committee hearings are published by the U.S. Government Printing Office and may be found in libraries that are repositories of government documents.

Occasionally a congressional enactment is unaccompanied by a committee report. This occurred with the 1964 Civil Rights Act, which was considered by several committees. For that act, the only evidence of the legislative history is the congressional debates which, like all federal legislative debates, were published in the *Congressional Record.* This is published daily.

Legislative history is an imprecise but often used instrument of legislative interpretation. The imprecision of the documentation reflecting a statute's legislative history may be seen from the common practice among congressional members of editing their remarks for the record. Members of Congress may edit their remarks on the floor of Congress before the remarks are published in the *Congressional Record.* Such editing often adds to the remarks or changes their nature entirely. Of course, the editing may merely clarify what the individual speaker intended his or her remarks to convey. However, to say that such edited legislative remarks may have persuaded other members of Congress to vote one way or another may be to overstate the importance of the remarks.

Frequently the *Congressional Record* includes remarks that are simply not relevant to the interpretation of a particular statute. In the case of the 1964 Civil Rights Act, its opponents filibustered against its enactment. If one were to refer to the entire record of their filibuster, one would find an occasional poem and several recipes for Southern cooking.

Where both the statutory context and the legislative history are incomplete, courts use logic and legal reasoning and apply the statute to best effectuate the statute's judicially determined policy objectives.

Constitutional limitations. The legislature's authority to make law is limited by constitution. State legislatures are limited by both the pertinent state constitution and the U.S. Constitution. Congress is limited by the U.S. Constitution.

Congressional legislative authority is prescribed by Article I, Section 8, of the U.S. Constitution. That section empowers Congress to, among other things, lay and collect taxes, provide for the common defense and general welfare, regulate commerce, and "make all Laws which shall be necessary and proper for carrying into Execution the foregoing Powers, and all other Powers vested by this Constitution in the Government of the United States, or in any Department or Officer thereof."

The Constitution also contains certain proscriptions against congressional legislation. Most of these are contained in the first 10 amendments, commonly known as "the Bill of Rights." For example, the First Amendment provides: "Congress shall make no law respecting an establishment of religion, or prohibiting the free exercise thereof; or abridging the freedom of speech, or of the press; or the right of the people peaceably to assemble, and to petition the Government for a redress of grievances."

If Congress or a state legislature enacts a statute which violates the Constitution, the courts may declare that statute to be unconstitutionally void. In an early decision the U.S. Supreme Court, in a unanimous opinion delivered by Chief Justice John Marshall, found that the Supreme Court had the power to declare acts of Congress void when, in its view, the acts were in conflict with the Constitution.[8]

Although judicial review of the constitutionality of legislation is a tradition in this country, this is not the case in other countries. In England, for example, the supreme judicial tribunal, the House of Lords has no power to declare acts of Parliament void. Not only does England not have a written constitution, but Parliament is considered the supreme sovereign. Thus the English courts cannot overrule the will of Parliament. This is generally true in other countries as well. Thus the Supreme Court of the Netherlands cannot review the constitutionality of the acts of Parliament, though it can review the constitutionality of statutes enacted by the provincial and municipal authorities.

Judicial review of the constitutionality of U.S. legislation is not expressly provided by the Constitution. Since Congress is subordinate to the law of the Constitution, and members of Congress take an oath not to pass any legislation that violates the Constitution, it might be argued that legislation which Congress determines is constitutional should be binding on the other two branches of government. Nevertheless, the Supreme Court's decision in *Marbury* v. *Madison* has established the Court as the final arbiter of the Constitution's meaning as it relates to legislation.

The executive

Article II of the U.S. Constitution provides that "the executive Power shall be vested in a President." The executive branch of the government consists of the president, the Cabinet, and the agencies and bureaus which

---

[8] *Marbury* v. *Madison,* 5 U.S. (1 Cranch) 137 (1803).

operate under the president's authority. The executive branch is often over-looked as a source of law. However, legal realists such as the late Karl Llewellyn see the exercise of official discretion as a source of law. In addition, the Constitution gives the president limited authority to make law in foreign and domestic affairs. The president's treaty powers make the executive branch a source of law regarding the country's international relations. This is particularly important to businesses doing business abroad or facing foreign competition in domestic markets. Furthermore, the president's executive orders serve as a source of domestic law.

Presidential authority over foreign affairs. The president's power to make law regarding foreign affairs derives from the President's position as commander in chief of the nation's armed forces and the president's power, subject to the advice and consent of two thirds of the Senate, to make treaties. The president's power as commander in chief of the armed forces is limited by the constitutional war powers of Congress. Under Article I of the U.S. Constitution, only Congress can declare war, raise and support the Army and Navy, and make rules for the government and regulation of the armed forces. Thus Congress, not the president, is the source of military law.

However, Article II also gives the president power to make treaties with foreign nations, by and with the advice of the Senate, provided two thirds of the senators concur. Although the treaty power is shared with the Senate, the president is the primary source for its exercise. It should be noted that although Congress shares its lawmaking power with the president (legislation needs presidential approval to become law), the president shares the treaty power with the Senate only.

By virtue of the Supremacy Clause in Article XI, treaties confirmed by the Senate become part of the supreme law of the land, along with the Constitution and congressional enactments. Judges of every state are bound by a treaty notwithstanding any state law or state constitution to the contrary. Thus any state statute or state constitutional provision which conflicts with the treaty provision is invalid. The treaty controls regardless of whether its ratification precedes or follows the enactment of state law.

Presidential authority over domestic affairs. The president's authority over domestic affairs also serves as a source of law, albeit a more limited source than exists with regard to foreign affairs. Executive lawmaking in domestic affairs is exemplified by the executive orders issued and implemented by presidents throughout U.S. history.

Although presidents have issued executive orders over the years, their power to make law in this way has been limited by the Supreme Court's interpretation of the Constitution. In *Youngstown Sheet and Tube Co.* v. *Sawyer,*[9] President Truman's executive order directing seizure of the nation's steel mills to prevent a threatened strike during the Korean War was held invalid

---

[9] 72 S. Ct. 863 (1952).

by the Court because there was no constitutional basis for such an executive order and because Congress had rejected the conferring of such authority upon the president. The Court stated that the president's power to issue an executive order must stem from an act of Congress or from the Constitution itself.

Currently many executive orders are in operation. Executive orders germane to the business community pertain to providing affirmative action in equal employment opportunity. A long series of executive orders dating from 1938 has recognized the necessity of expending federal funds in a manner consistent with the nation's equal employment opportunity objectives. Thus Executive Order No. 11246 requires that government contractors take "affirmative action" to insure that their hiring and promotion of employees will be on a nondiscriminatory basis. Several lower courts have upheld the constitutionality of this executive order. However, the U.S. Supreme Court has not decided the question, and scholarly commentary on the issue is mixed. The subject is explored in more detail in Chapter 17. The topic is discussed here to illustrate that the president frequently makes law by issuing executive orders which affect the large and growing segment of American business which does business with the government.

The judiciary: Judicial lawmaking

Courts are also a source of law. When a court decides a dispute it makes law. Through the application of general legal principles to actual controversies, these principles are refined and shaped into a more precise statement of law. A court's interpretation of a statute and its application of that interpretation to a particular pattern of facts give meaning to the statute. In the absence of legislative guidance a court will decide a dispute by applying to the present controversy the reasoning of past judicial decisions in similar factual contexts. Sometimes a court must decide an issue where no statute or prior judicial decision exists to guide its determination. When this occurs, the court is faced with what is called a "case of first impression." A court confronted with such a novel situation must determine what the law should be. The court is truly creating new law when it decides such cases.

The doctrine under which past judicial decisions are applied to decide a present controversy is called *stare decisis* ("let the decision stand"). A rule of law decided by the highest court of a jurisdiction is binding on all lower courts within that jurisdiction. It is also binding on the same court's later decisions unless that court overrules its earlier decision. The decision is followed in future cases presenting the same legal issue. The decision is not binding on courts in other jurisdictions, though they may find its reasoning persuasive and may follow it when considering the issue in disputes arising within their jurisdictions. For example, although the Supreme Court of California is not bound by the decisions of the Supreme Court of Pennsylvania, it may find the Pennsylvania court's reasoning persuasive on a point in the case before it and may adopt that reasoning in making its decision. The purpose of *stare decisis* is to provide stability and discipline in the judicial system. Lower court judges are prevented from arbitrary decision making by the doctrine because they are bound to follow the decisions of the appellate courts in their jurisdictions or face reversal in a higher court.

Similarly, some consistency in judicial lawmaking is provided by the fact that the same appellate court must generally follow its previous decisions in later cases presenting the same issue. This prevents vacillation that might otherwise result from changes in court personnel. However, the court may overrule an earlier decision of its own where there is good reason for doing so. For example, technological change or changes in social conditions may dictate that changes be made in the law to prevent stagnation in legal development, or events occurring after an earlier decision may prove that the earlier decision was wrong. It would be quite ironic if appellate courts, which are empowered to correct the errors of lower courts, were to lack the power to correct their own errors. Thus appellate courts can correct the erroneous precedents of their predecessors. If this were not the case, the law would cease to grow.

When an appellate court decides a case it usually states the reasons for its decision. This process of stating the reasoning behind judicial decision making—the process of issuing opinions—subjects the appellate court's decision making to public criticism. Opinions are issued and published in virtually every decision of an appellate court, so that any interested person can ascertain what the appellate court decided and its rationale for the decision.

The utility of *stare decisis* as a check against arbitrary judicial behavior was expressed by Justice Cardozo in the following excerpt from *The Nature Of The Judicial Process*.

B. Cardozo, The Nature of the Judicial Process
33–34 (1921).

I must be logical, just as I must be impartial, and upon like grounds. It will not do to decide the same question one way between one set of litigants and the opposite way between another. If a group of cases involves the same point, the parties expect the same decision. It would be a gross injustice to decide alternate cases on opposite principles. If a case was decided against me yesterday when I was defendant, I shall look for the same judgment today if I am plaintiff. To decide differently would raise a feeling of resentment and wrong in my breast; it would be an infringement, material and moral, of my rights. Everyone feels the force of this sentiment when two cases are the same. Adherence to precedent must then be the rule rather than the exception if litigants are to have faith in the evenhanded administration of justice in the courts. A sentiment like in kind, though different in degree, is at the root of the tendency of precedent to extend itself along the lines of logical development.

Stare decisis is important to the public generally and to the business community in particular because of the reliance which this doctrine places on judicial decision making. Because earlier decisions of a court will be followed by that same court or by a lesser court within its jurisdiction in cases presenting the same issue, the business manager can rely on these court decisions in conducting his or her affairs.

Administrative agencies

Administrative agencies, like courts and legislatures, have the power to take action that affects the rights of private parties. Administrative agencies are housed in the executive branch of the government but are created by the legislature. An administrative agency may have functions which are traditionally executive, such as investigating, administering, and prosecuting, but it may also have functions which are traditionally legislative or judicial, such as rulemaking and adjudication.

Later chapters discuss lawmaking by administrative agencies in more detail. However, it is helpful to an understanding of that discussion to realize that administrative agencies may make law in much the same way that the legislative, executive, and judicial branches do. For example, if Congress confers rulemaking authority upon an agency, that agency's duly authorized rules and regulations create law as if Congress had acted on the matters.

Interaction among the various sources of law

The various sources of law in the United States do not operate in a vacuum. There is frequent interaction among the three branches of government. Although the U.S. govermental structure is often described as embodying a separation of powers, there is interaction among the three branches that is also described as providing a system of checks and balances. As already noted, a congressional enactment needs presidential approval to become law, and a treaty negotiated by the executive branch needs Senate ratification.

It is often thought that the judiciary stands isolated from the other two branches and that it has the final word on any issue. Students frequently read appellate court opinions in their casebooks as the final word on what the law is. However, the purpose of this discussion is to point out the dynamic interaction that occurs between the judiciary and the other branches of government. The objective is to show the reader that the judicial opinions contained in the text should be carefully critiqued rather than blindly accepted as the final word. The student should query not only what the law is but what it should be.

The supremacy of legislation. The legislative branch has the power to change centuries of judge-made case law by simply enacting a statute. Statutes control over case law. It is true that courts ultimately interpret legislation, but if a legislature considers a particular case to be an incorrect interpretation of its statute, the legislature can amend the statute to repudiate the interpretation. And while the judiciary has the power to review the constitutionality of legislation, a particular judicial decision can be nullified through the process of constitutional amendment.

The following case and statutory note illustrate the interaction that sometimes occurs between the legislative and judicial branches of government. In *General Electric Co.* v. *Gilbert,* the Supreme Court was presented with an issue of statutory interpretation. The Court's decision made law with regard to the statute's application. Feminist groups which supported the unsuccessful litigants took the litigants' cause to Congress. The statute which follows the Court's opinion is the legislative response to the Court.

General Electric Co. v. *Gilbert*
429 U.S. 125 (1976)

Gilbert (appellee) brought suit against General Electric (petitioner), alleging that the company's exclusion of disabilities arising from pregnancy from its disability plan violated Title VII of the Civil Rights Act of 1964, which prohibits sex discrimination in employment. The district court found for Gilbert, and the Court of Appeals for the Fourth Circuit affirmed. The Supreme Court reversed.

Mr. Justice Rehnquist: As part of its total compensation package, General Electric provides nonoccupational sickness and accident benefits to all employees under its Weekly Sickness and Accident Insurance Plan (the "Plan") in an amount equal to 60 percent of an employee's normal straight-time weekly earnings. These payments are paid to employees who become totally disabled as a result of a nonoccupational sickness or accident. Benefit payments normally start with the eighth day of an employee's total disability (although if an employee is confined earlier to a hospital as a bed patient, benefit payments will start immediately), and continue up to a maximum of 26 weeks for any one continuous period of disability or successive periods of disability due to the same or related causes. . . .

Following trial, the District Court made findings of fact, conclusions of law, and entered an order in which it determined that General

Electric, by excluding pregnancy disabilities from the coverage of the Plan, had engaged in sex discrimination in violation of § 703 (a)(1) of Title VII, 42 U.S.C. 2000e–2(a)(1). The District Court found that normal pregnancy, while not necessarily either a "disease" or an "accident," was disabling for a period of six to eight weeks, that approximately "ten per cent of pregnancies are terminated by miscarriage, which is disabling," and that approximately 10 percent of pregnancies are complicated by diseases which may lead to additional disability. The District Court noted the evidence introduced during the trial, a good deal of it stipulated, concerning the relative cost to General Electric of providing benefits under the Plan to male and female employees, all of which indicated that, with pregnancy-related disabilities excluded, the cost of the Plan to General Electric per female employee was at least as high, if not substantially higher, than the cost per male employee.

The District Court found that the inclusion of pregnancy-related disabilities within the scope of the Plan would "increase G.E.'s [disability benefits plan] costs by an amount which, though large, is at this time undeterminable." The District Court declined to find that the present actuarial value of the coverage was equal as between men and women, but went on to decide that even had it found economic equivalence, such a finding would not in any case have justified the exclusion of pregnancy-related disabilities from an otherwise comprehensive nonoccupational sickness and accident disability plan. Regardless of whether the cost of including such benefits might make the Plan more costly for women than for men, the District Court determined that "[i]f Title VII intends to sexually equalize employment opportunity, there must be this one exception to the cost differential defense."

The ultimate conclusion of the District Court was that petitioner had discriminated on the basis of sex in the operation of its disability program in violation of Title VII. An order was entered enjoining petitioner from continuing to exclude pregnancy-related disabilities from the coverage of the Plan, and providing for the future award of monetary relief to individual members of the class affected. Petitioner appealed to the Court of Appeals for the Fourth Circuit, and that court by a divided vote affirmed the judgment of the District Court.

Between the date on which the District Court's judgment was rendered and the time this case was decided by the Court of Appeals, we decided *Geduldig* v. *Aiello,* 417 U.S. 484 (1974), where we rejected a claim that a very similar disability program established under California law violated the Equal Protection Clause of the Fourteenth Amendment because that plan's exclusion of pregnancy disabilities represented sex discrimination. The majority of the Court of Appeals felt that *Geduldig* was not controlling because it arose under the Equal Protection Clause of the Fourteenth Amendment, and not under Title VII. The dissenting opinion disagreed with the majority as to the impact of *Geduldig.* We granted certiorari to consider this important issue in the construction of Title VII.

Section 703(a)(1) provides in relevant part that it shall be an unlawful employment practice for an employer "to discriminate against any individual with respect to his compensation, terms, conditions, or privileges of employment, because of such individual's race, color, religion, sex, or national origin," 42 U.S.C. §2000e–2(a)(1).

While there is no necessary inference that Congress, in choosing this language, intended to incorporate into Title VII the concepts of discrimination which have evolved from court decisions construing the Equal Protection Clause of the Fourteenth Amendment, the similarities between the congressional language and some of those decisions surely indicate that the latter are a useful starting point in interpreting the former. Particularly in the case of defining the term "discrimination," which Congress has nowhere in Title VII defined, those cases afford an existing body of law analyzing and discussing that term in a legal context not wholly dissimilar from the concerns which Congress manifested in enacting Title VII. We think therefore, that our decision in *Geduldig* v. *Aiello, supra,* dealing with a strikingly similar disability plan, is quite relevant in determining whether or not the pregnancy exclusion did discriminate on the basis of sex. In *Geduldig,* the disability insurance system was funded entirely from contributions deducted from the wages of participating employees, at a rate of 1 percent of the employee's salary up to an annual maximum of $85. In other relevant respects, the operation of the program was similar to General Electric's disability benefits plan.

We rejected appellee's Equal Protection challenge to this statutory scheme. We first noted that:

> We cannot agree that the exclusion of this disability from coverage amounts to invidious discrimination under the Equal Protection Clause. California does not discriminate with respect to the persons or groups which are eligible for disability insurance protection under the program. The classification challenged in this case relates to the asserted underinclusiveness of the set of risks that the State has selected to insure.

This point was emphasized again, when later in the opinion we noted that

> [T]his case is thus a far cry from cases like *Reed* v. *Reed,* 404 U.S. 71 (1971), and *Frontiero* v. *Richardson,* 411 U.S. 677 (1973), involving discrimination based upon

gender as such. The California insurance program does not exclude anyone from benefit eligibility because of gender but merely removes one physical condition—pregnancy—from the list of compensable disabilities. While it is true that only women can become pregnant, it does not follow that every legislative classification concerning pregnancy is a sex-based classification like those considered in *Reed, supra,* and *Frontiero, supra.* Normal pregnancy is an objectively identifiable physical condition with unique characteristics. Absent a showing that distinctions involving pregnancy are mere pretexts designed to effect an invidious discrimination against the members of one sex or the other, lawmakers are constitutionally free to include or exclude pregnancy from the coverage of legislation such as this on any reasonable basis, just as with respect to any other physical condition.

The lack of identity between the excluded disability and gender as such under this insurance program becomes clear upon the most cursory analysis. The program divides potential recipients into two groups—pregnant women and nonpregnant persons. While the first group is exclusively female, the second includes members of both sexes.

The quoted language from *Geduldig* leaves no doubt that our reason for rejecting appellee's equal protection claim in that case was that the exclusion of pregnancy from coverage under California's disability benefits plan was not in itself discrimination based on sex.

We recognized in *Geduldig,* of course, that the fact that there was not sex-based discrimination as such was not the end of the analysis, should it be shown "that distinctions involving pregnancy are mere pretexts designed to effect an invidious discrimination against the members of one sex or the other."

The Court of Appeals was therefore wrong in concluding that the reasoning of *Geduldig* was not applicable to an action under Title VII. Since it is a finding of sex-based discrimination that must trigger, in a case such as this, the finding of an unlawful employment practice under § 703(a)(1), 42 U.S.C. § 2000e–2(a)(1), *Geduldig* is precisely in point in its holding that an exclusion of pregnancy from a disability benefits plan providing general coverage is not a gender-based discrimination at all. . . .

The instant suit was grounded on Title VII rather than the Equal Protection Clause, and our cases recognize that a prima facie violation of Title VII can be established in some circumstances upon proof that the *effect* of an otherwise facially neutral plan or classification is to discriminate against members of one class or another. For example, in the context of a challenge, under the provisions of § 703(a)(2), to a facially neutral employment test, this Court held that a prima facie case of discrimination would be established if, even absent proof of intent, the consequences of the test were "invidiously to discriminate on the basis of racial or other impermissible classification," *Griggs* v. *Duke Power Co.,* 401 U.S. 424, 431 (1971). Even assuming that it is not necessary in this case to prove intent to establish a prima facie violation of § 730(a)(1), the respondents have not made the requisite showing of gender-based effects.

As in *Geduldig, supra,* respondents have not attempted to meet the burden of demonstrating a gender-based discriminatory effect resulting from the exclusion of pregnancy-related disabilities from coverage. Whatever the ultimate probative value of the evidence introduced before the District Court on this subject in the instant case, at the very least it tended to illustrate that the selection of risks covered by the Plan did not operate, in fact, to discriminate against women. . . . The "package" going to relevant identifiable groups we are presently concerned with—General Electric's male and female employees—covers exactly the same categories of risk, and is facially nondiscriminatory in the sense that "[t]here is no risk from which men are protected and women are not. Likewise, there is no risk from which women are protected and men are not." As there is no proof that the package is in fact worth more to men than to women, it is impossible to find any gender-based discriminatory effect in this scheme simply because women disabled as a result of pregnancy do not receive benefits; that is to say, gender-based discrimination does not result simply because an employer's disability benefits plan is less than all-inclusive. For all that appears, pregnancy-related disabilities constitute an *additional* risk, unique to women, and the failure to compensate them for this risk does not destroy the presumed parity of the benefits, accruing to men and women alike, which results from the facially evenhanded *inclusion* of risks. To hold otherwise would endanger the common-sense notion that an employer who has no disability benefits program at all does not violate Title VII even though the "underinclusion" of risks impacts, as a result of pregnancy-related disabilities, more heavily upon one gender than upon the other. Just as there is no facial gender-based discrimination in that case, so, too, there is none here.

* * * * *

We therefore agree with petitioner that its disability benefits plan does not violate Title VII because of its failure to cover pregnancy-related disabilities. The judgment of the Court of Appeals is *Reversed.*

CASE NOTE

In 1978 Congress enacted the Pregnancy Discrimination Act, an amendment to the Civil Rights Act of 1964:

701(k) "The terms 'because of sex' or 'on the basis of sex' include, but are not limited to, because of or on the basis of pregnancy, childbirth or related medical conditions; and women affected by pregnancy, childbirth, or related medical conditions shall be treated the same for all employment-related purposes, including receipt of benefits under fringe benefit programs, as other persons not so affected but similar in their ability or inability to work, and nothing in section 703(h) of this title shall be interpreted to permit otherwise."

Case questions

1. What is the basis of the Court's holding that excluding pregnancy from GE's disability plan is not a violation of Title VII?

2. Why did the Court address the constitutional case law in interpreting Title VII, a statute?

3. Did Congress repudiate *Gilbert* when it enacted the Pregnancy Discrimination Act? Explain.

4. Could men successfully argue that the Pregnancy Discrimination Act is unconstitutional? Why?

Classification of law

For descriptive purposes, law is sometimes classified into several categories. Among the major categories are: statutory law and common law, substantive law and procedural law, criminal law and civil law, and private law and public law.

Statutory law and common law. As previously discussed, statutory law is law enacted by a legislature. It is written law. It is legislation. It is contained in the code books.

Common law is judge-made law or case law. Following the Norman conquest of England, William the Conquerer sent his court officials throughout the realm to keep the king's peace. The court officials decided disputes. Disputes were resolved by the application of custom. William's purpose was to bring the various parts of his newly conquered country under one law, a common law. Thus there developed in England a body of judicial decisions that constituted the country's "common law." Without a Parliament (which did not come into existence until later) and without a written constitution, these decisions became the law of England. Thus, long before statutes existed, England developed a body of judge-made law called the common law. Today the term *common law* refers to those areas of law that have been principally developed by the courts and are not the product of legislative enactments. More and more, statutes are supplanting the common law. However, several areas of law are still primarily the product of judicial decision making, such as the law of contracts and the law of torts.

Substantive law and procedural law. Substantive law is law which is concerned with rights and duties. An example of substantive law is contract law, which concerns the rights and duties of contracting parties. Procedural law, sometimes called adjective law, concerns the process by which substantive rights and duties are enforced. Rules of court procedure and rules of evidence are examples of procedural law.

Criminal law and civil law. Criminal law defines offenses against the state and provides for their punishment. In most states, crimes are defined by statute. Only the state may bring a criminal proceeding against an alleged offender of the criminal code. Thus a prosecutor will bring the case against the defendant on behalf of the state, and the claim will be described as "the State versus the defendant." If the defendant is found guilty, the state imposes punishment in the form of a fine or imprisonment, or both. The defendant pays the fine to the state, not to the victim.

Civil law exists for the redressing of claims brought by private litigants. For example, the victim of a crime may be able to bring a civil action against the criminal and recover a monetary award compensating him or her for the injuries and damages incurred as a result of the crime. Thus civil law serves to redress private claims.

Private law and public law. Private law is concerned with the relations of persons and organizations to each other. Public law is concerned with the relations of persons and organizations with organized society, or the state. Examples of private law are the law of contracts, tort law, and property law. Examples of public law are constitutional law, administrative law, and the various areas of government regulation. Although this book includes areas of private law where this is necessary to understand fully an area of public law, it concentrates primarily upon public law areas.

Summary. As can be seen, the differences among the categories of law described above are sometimes quite subtle. The breakdown given here represents common attempts to classify law into major categories. It should be viewed as important for descriptive purposes only.

Review problems

1. The Declaration of Independence provides in pertinent part: "When in the Course of human events it becomes necessary for one people to dissolve the political bands which have connected them with another, and to assume among the powers of the earth, the separate and equal station to which the Laws of Nature and of Nature's God entitle them, a decent respect to the opinions of mankind requires that they should declare the causes which impel them to the separation. We hold these truths to be self-evident, that all men are created equal, that they are endowed by their Creator with certain unalienable Rights, that among these are Life, Liberty and the pursuit of Happiness." What conception of law is embodied in this statement?

2. In 1973 the U.S. Supreme Court was called upon to decide the constitutionality of a state statute making it a crime to obtain an abortion. In deciding that the statue was unconstitutional, the Court stated: "We forthwith acknowledge our awareness of the sensitive and emotional nature of the abortion controversy, of the vigorous opposing views, even among physicians, and of the deep and seemingly absolute convictions that the subject inspires. One's philosophy, one's experiences, one's exposure to the raw edges of human existence, one's religious training, one's attitudes toward life and family and their values, and the moral standards one establishes and seeks to observe, are all likely to influence and to color one's thinking and conclusions about abortion. . . .

"Our task, of course, is to resolve the issue by constitutional measurement free of emotion and predilection."

What conception of law best describes the Court's statement? Do you think that the Court can resolve the issue "by constitutional measurement free of emotion and predilection"?

3. What did Holmes mean when he wrote: "The life of the law has not been logic; it has been experience"?

4. Arthur and Ava Strunk have two sons, Tommy, age 28, and Jerry, age 27. Tommy is married, employed, and a part-time college student. He suffers from a fatal kidney disease and is being kept alive by frequent treatment on an artificial kidney, a procedure which cannot be continued much longer. Jerry is incompetent, and through proper legal proceedings has been committed to a state institution for the mentally retarded. He has an IQ of approximately 35, which corresponds to a mental age of approximately six years. He is further handicapped by a speech defect that makes it difficult for him to communicate with persons who are unacquainted with him. When it was determined that Tommy, in order to survive, would need a kidney transplant, the doctors looked for a donor. Possible donors include cadavers as well as live persons. Because of compatibility of blood type and tissue, the only acceptable live donor is Jerry. The parents petitioned a court for authority to proceed with the operation. No statute exists to guide the court's determination. Likewise, no prior case law exists. In short, the case is one of first impression. How should the court decide?

5. What classification of law does the case in the preceding problem fall under? Explain.

6. Employer grants sick pay to employees disabled by nonoccupational sickness or injury but not to employees disabled by pregnancy. Further, Employer denies accumulated seniority to female employees returning to work following disability caused by childbirth. Does Employer's personnel policies violate Title VII?

7. The Federal Trade Commission, a federal agency, brings action against Conglomerate Car Company as a result of a complaint filed with the commission by Bigdome Car Company. After reviewing the complaint, the commission concludes that Conglomerate is guilty of monopolization in violation of the Sherman Act. The commission's opinion provides its reasons for reaching this conclusion. Is the commission's opinion law? Explain.

8. The president of the United States concludes a commercial treaty with the Soviet Union. The treaty is subsequently ratified by the U.S. Senate. After ratification, a group of citizens file a lawsuit in a federal court attacking the treaty as unconstitutional. Will the citizens win? Explain. *no, Supreme law of land*

9. Julius Smith throws a brick through Penelope Jones's window. Penelope calls the police and files a complaint against Julius. Julius is arrested and brought to trial by the prosecutor for the state. What classification of law does the case fall under? Explain. *criminal law*

10. Suppose that in the preceding problem Penelope went to her lawyer, who filed a complaint on her behalf in a court of common pleas, seeking reimbursement from Julius for the damage done to her property. What classification of law does the case fall under now? Explain.

civil law

CHAPTER 2

Business and the legal system

Now that the nature and sources of law have been examined, it is appropriate to explore further the legal context within which business operates. A general description of the judicial and regulatory systems is first provided. Then the more specific aspects of the lawyer-client relationship and the business firm's interaction with government are treated.

THE JUDICIAL SYSTEM

The judicial system in the United States consists of the federal system and the judicial systems of the 50 states. This means that there are 51 distinct judicial systems. It is not unusual for a firm to do business in a number of states and hence to be potentially subject to the federal judicial process as well as the judicial processes of the various states. It thus behooves the business manager to understand the workings of the federal and state systems.

The federal system

The federal judicial system derives from Article III of the U.S. Constitution, which provides that "the judicial Power of the United States shall be vested in one supreme Court, and in such inferior Courts as the Congress may from time to time ordain and establish." Pursuant to Article III, Congress has created 94 district courts and 11 circuit courts of appeal.

All federal courts are courts of limited jurisdiction; they may exercise jurisdiction only over cases strictly defined by congressional statutes. The basic federal trial court is the U.S. district court. There is at least one district in every state and territory. Many states are divided into more than one district, depending on size, population, and amount of litigation.

The district court's jurisdiction is defined by several statutes. The two most important statutes provide for federal question and diversity jurisdiction. Federal question jurisdiction includes any claim arising under a federal statute, a treaty, or the U.S. Constitution. Hence, it is proper for a federal district court to hear a case which involves a substantial issue of federal law.

Diversity jurisdiction extends to controversies between citizens of different states where the amount in contest exceeds $10,000. A corporation is considered a citizen of the state in which it is incorporated and in which it has its principal place of business. Hence, for purposes of diversity jurisdiction a corporation holds dual citizenship.

Assume that eight individual plaintiffs join together in a suit against ABC, Inc., seeking damages incurred because wastes dumped by ABC, Inc., into a waterway ultimately pollute the plaintiffs' property. Seven of the plaintiffs are citizens of Ohio, while the eighth is a citizen of Michigan. ABC, Inc., is incorporated under the law of Delaware and has its principal place of business in Michigan. Here, diversity of citizenship is not present as a basis for federal jurisdiction since a plaintiff and a defendant are citizens of Michigan. If the Michigan plaintiff was eliminated from the suit, then diversity jurisdiction would be present, assuming that the jurisdictional amount was met. Since there are multiple plaintiffs, each must claim in good faith damages exceeding $10,000. Although the plaintiffs in this case could then bring the suit in the federal district court, they are not required to and may elect to file suit in a proper state court. This is because in diversity of citizenship cases the district court has concurrent jurisdiction as opposed to exclusive jurisdiction. However, if the plaintiffs instituted suit in a state court, ABC, Inc., could file a petition having the case removed to the appropriate federal district court. The district court has removal jurisdiction over any cases which could have originally been brought in the district court.

The federal system also contains specialized trial courts. The Court of Claims (Trial Division) hears contract claims brought against the federal government. Other specialized courts are the Tax Court and the Customs Court.

Appeals from district courts and the Tax Court are heard by the circuit courts of appeal. Appeals from the Trial Division of the Court of Claims are heard by the Court of Claims, while appeals from the Customs Court are heard by the Court of Customs and Patent Appeals. Further review may then be sought in the U.S. Supreme Court. The circuit courts of appeal also hear appeals from administrative agency decisions, discussed later in this chapter and more fully treated in Chapter 3.

Sitting atop the federal legal system is the U.S. Supreme Court. Review in the Supreme Court is usually not automatic. Parties seeking review must file a petition for a *writ of certiorari,* that is, a request that the Court hear the case. The Court has absolute discretion to grant or deny the writ. It rarely gives a reason for such a denial. The denial of certiorari has no precedential value. Certiorari is likely to be granted when a constitutional issue of national importance is posed or when an issue has been decided in a conflicting manner by the circuit courts of appeal. A few types of cases are reviewed in the Supreme Court by appeal rather than certiorari. In these cases the Court has no discretion but must decide the merits of the appeal. In rare instances the Supreme Court sits as a court of original jurisdiction, that is, it serves as a trial court. It has original and exclusive jurisdiction over all controversies between two or more states and over cases where a foreign ambassador is sued. In a few other types of cases the Supreme Court has original but not exclusive jurisdiction. One such type comprises cases in which a state sues the citizens of another state or aliens.

Ohio v. *Wyandotte Chemicals Corp.*
401 U.S. 493 (1971)

Ohio filed a motion seeking to invoke the original jurisdiction of the Supreme Court. Ohio's complaint was against Wyandotte Chemicals Corp. (Wyandotte), Dow Chemical Co. (Dow America), and Dow Chemical Company of Canada, Ltd. (Dow Canada). Wyandotte is a citizen of Michigan; Dow America is a citizen of Delaware and Michigan; and Dow Canada is a citizen of Ontario, Canada. Ohio alleged that mercury dumped by the defendants into streams ended up in Lake Erie and contaminated the lake's waters, fish, vegetation, and wildlife. Ohio sought an injunction preventing the defendants from polluting Lake Erie, as well as damages and other relief for harm to the lake, fish, wildlife, vegetation, and citizens and inhabitants of Ohio. The Supreme Court declined to exercise jurisdiction.

Mr. Justice Harlan: That we have jurisdiction seems clear enough. Beyond doubt, the complaint on its face reveals the existence of a genuine "case or controversy" between one State and citizens of another, as well as a foreign subject. Diversity of citizenship is absolute. Nor is the nature of the cause of action asserted a bar to the exercise of our jurisdiction. . . .

Ordinarily, the foregoing would suffice to settle the issue presently under consideration: whether Ohio should be granted leave [permission] to file its complaint. For it is a time-honored maxim of the Anglo-American common-law tradition that a court possessed of jurisdic-tion generally must exercise it. Nevertheless, although it may initially have been contemplated that this Court would always exercise its original jurisdiction when properly called upon to do so, it seems evident to us that changes in the American legal system and the development of American society have rendered untenable, as a practical matter, the view that this Court must stand willing to adjudicate all or most legal disputes that may arise between one State and a citizen or citizens of another, even though the dispute may be one over which this Court does have original jurisdiction.

*   *   *   *   *

This Court is, moreover, structured to perform as an appellate tribunal, ill-equipped for the task of factfinding and so forced, in original cases, awkwardly to play the role of factfinder without actually presiding over the introduction of evidence. Nor is the problem merely our lack of qualifications for many of these tasks potentially within the purview of our original jurisdiction; it is compounded by the fact that for every case in which we might be called upon to determine the facts and apply unfamiliar legal norms we would unavoidably be reducing the attention we could give to those matters of federal law and national import as to which we are the primary overseers.

Thus, we think it apparent that we must recognize "the need [for] the exercise of a sound discretion in order to protect this Court from an abuse of the opportunity to resort to its original jurisdiction in the enforcement by States of Claims against citizens of other States." . . .

*   *   *   *   *

In applying this analysis to the facts here presented, we believe that the wiser course is to deny Ohio's motion for leave to file its complaint.

Two principles seem primarily to have underlain conferring upon this Court original jurisdiction over cases and controversies between a State and citizens of another State or country. The first was the belief that no State should be compelled to resort to the tribunals of other States for redress, since parochial factors might often lead to the appearance, if not the reality, of partiality to one's own. The second was that a State, needing an alternative forum, of necessity had to resort to this Court in order to obtain a tribunal competent to exercise jurisdiction over the acts of nonresidents of the aggrieved State.

Neither of these policies is, we think, implicated in this lawsuit. The courts of Ohio, under modern principles of the scope of subject matter and *in personam* jurisdiction, have a claim as compelling as any that can be made out for this Court to exercise jurisdiction to adjudicate the instant controversy, and they would decide it under the same common law of nuisance upon which our determination would have to rest. . . .

Our reasons for thinking that, as a practical matter, it would be inappropriate for this Court to attempt to adjudicate the issues Ohio seeks to present are several. History reveals that the course of this Court's prior efforts to settle disputes regarding interstate air and water pollution has been anything but smooth. . . .

The difficulties that ordinarily beset such cases are severely compounded by the particular setting in which this controversy has reached us. For example, the parties have informed us, without contradiction, that a number of official bodies are already actively involved in regulating the conduct complained of here. A Michigan circuit court has enjoined Wyandotte from operating its mercury cell process without judicial authorization. The company is, moreover,

currently utilizing a recycling process specifically approved by the Michigan Water Resources Commission and remains subject to the continued scrutiny of that agency. Dow Canada reports monthly to the Ontario Water Resources Commission on its compliance with the commission's order prohibiting the company from passing any mercury into the environment.

Additionally, Ohio and Michigan are both participants in the Lake Erie Enforcement Conference, convened a year ago by the Secretary of the Interior pursuant to the Federal Water Pollution Control Act, as amended. The Conference is studying all forms and sources of pollution, including mercury, infecting Lake Erie. The purpose of this Conference is to provide a basis for concerted remedial action by the States or, if progress in that regard is not rapidly made, for corrective proceedings initiated by the Federal Government. And the International Joint Commission, established by the Boundary Waters Treaty of 1909 between the United States and Canada, issued on January 14, 1971, a comprehensive report, the culmination of a six-year study carried out at the request of the contracting parties, concerning the contamination of Lake Erie. That document makes specific recommendations for joint programs to abate these environmental hazards and recommends that the IJC be given authority to supervise and coordinate this effort.

In view of all this, granting Ohio's motion for leave to file would, in effect, commit this Court's resources to the task of trying to settle a small piece of a much larger problem that many competent adjudicatory and conciliatory bodies are actively grappling with on a more practical basis.

The nature of the case Ohio brings here is equally disconcerting. It can fairly be said that what is in dispute is not so much the law as the facts. And the factfinding process we are asked to undertake is, to say the least, formidable. We already know, just from what has been placed before us on this motion, that Lake Erie suffers from several sources of pollution other than mercury; that the scientific conclusion that mercury is a serious water pollutant is a novel one; that whether and to what extent the existence of mercury in natural waters can safely or reasonably be tolerated is a question for which there is presently no firm answer; and that virtually no published research is available describing how one might extract mercury that is in fact contaminating water. Indeed, Ohio is raising factual questions that are essentially ones of first impression to the scientists. The notion that appellate judges, even with the assistance of a most competent Special Master, might appropriately undertake at this time to unravel these complexities is, to say the least, unrealistic. . . . Other factual complexities abound. For example, the Department of the Interior has stated that eight American companies are discharging, or have discharged, mercury into Lake Erie or its tributaries. We would, then, need to assess the business practices and relative culpability of each to frame appropriate relief as to the one now before us.

*   *   *   *   *

Ohio's motion for leave to file its complaint is denied without prejudice to its right to commence other appropriate judicial proceedings.

[Mr. Justice Douglas dissented.]

Case questions

1. What issue does this case present?

2. What were the original reasons for conferring jurisdiction upon the Supreme Court in a case such as this? Why are those reasons not convincing in this case?

3. For what other reasons did the Court decline jurisdiction? Do you think they are good reasons? (Apparently Justice Douglas did not.)

4. What courts can Ohio now turn to in order to adjudicate the controversy?

The state system

State trial courts consist of courts of general and limited jurisdiction. A court of general jurisdiction is usually empowered to hear any type of case unless specifically prohibited by statute. Thus many cases which can be brought in the federal district courts may also have been properly commenced in a state court. Among the exceptions are admiralty, bankruptcy, and patent infringement actions, which may only be brought in federal court. Most state trial courts of general jurisdiction are organized at the county level. Their names vary from state to state. The most popular names are circuit court, court of common pleas, and superior court.

State trial courts of limited jurisdiction are only empowered to hear specific cases. A probate court cannot hear a divorce case; a mayor's court cannot try a felony case. Some courts can only hear disputes up to a maximum monetary ceiling.

Most states have intermediate courts of appeals, similar to the federal circuit courts. Following decision by the court of appeals, review may be sought in the state supreme court, which, like the U.S. Supreme Court, reviews most cases by certiorari. In the smaller and less populous states, appeals from the trial court are taken directly to the state supreme court, since there is no intermediate court of appeals.

The state supreme court is the highest authority on the law of the state in which it sits. The U.S. Supreme Court has no power to decide issues of state law. State supreme court decisions interpreting federal statutes, treaties, and the U.S. Constitution are, however, subject to Supreme Court review. An overview of the federal and state judicial systems is provided in Figure 2–1.

Jurisdiction

Jurisdiction is the power of a court to hear and decide a controversy. In order to possess that power, a court must have jurisdiction over both the subject matter of the dispute and the parties to the dispute. Jurisdiction over the subject matter is accomplished by selecting a court empowered to hear the type of dispute that it is called upon to decide. State courts of general jurisdiction are usually empowered to hear any type of dispute. The federal courts, as previously observed, have limited subject matter jurisdiction.

Jurisdiction over the person may be accomplished by serving the defendant with notice of the suit, called a summons, within the state in which the court is located. Personal service was the only authorized method in the early days of our court system. This required a process server to slap the summons in the defendant's hand. Nothing short of that was deemed good service. There are harrowing stories about heroic process servers who climbed tall buildings and shuffled along windowsills in order to serve the defendant with process. There are other stories of not so brave process servers who did not take to the cat-and-mouse sport. The personal service requirement

Figure 2–1

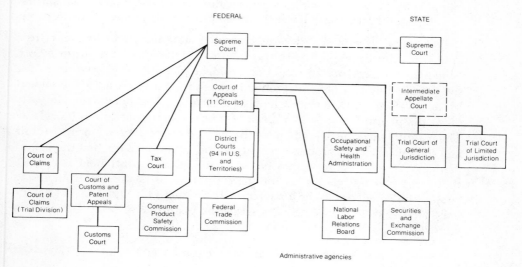

Administrative agencies

encouraged "sewer service," that is, filing an affidavit of return of service stating that the defendant had been served when in fact the process server had been unable to locate the defendant. In response, states adopted other methods of service designed to inform the defendant within the state of the suit. Residential service and certified mail service are two of the more common methods. Residential service occurs when the process server leaves the summons with a responsible person at the defendant's residence. Sending the summons by certified mail to the defendant's address has been adopted more recently as a way of effecting service. Under certain circumstances publication in a newspaper is an acceptable means of securing service over a defendant.

The requirement that the process be served on the defendant in the state in which the court was located posed a severe limitation. Suppose a defendant who lived in Alaska and was visiting Florida struck a Florida pedestrian while operating a motor vehicle. If the Alaskan resident returned to Alaska, then the injured pedestrian would be forced to sue in Alaska. To combat this inequity states enacted long arm statutes. A long arm statute is a means of gaining service over an out-of-state defendant. Most states have long arm statutes that subject an out-of-state defendant to the jurisdiction where the defendant is doing business or has committed a civil wrong. Long arm statutes are subjected to constitutional due process scrutiny. The landmark decision of *International Shoe Co.* v. *Washington*[1] in considering the application of a long arm statute said:

> . . . [D]ue process requires only that in order to subject a defendant to a judgment in personam, if he be not present within the territory of the forum, he must have certain minimum contacts with it such that the maintenance of the suit does not offend traditional notions of fair play and substantial justice. . . . Whether due process is satisfied must depend rather upon the quality and nature of the activity in relation to the fair and orderly administration of the laws which it was the purpose of the due process clause to insure.

Not every attempted service of an out of state defendant pursuant to a long arm statute complies with the due process standard laid out in *International Shoe*. In one reported case a nonresident plaintiff attempted to invoke the jurisdiction of a North Carolina court against a nonresident defendant by application of that state's long arm statute.[2] The defendant allegedly owed the plaintiff money as a result of a business transaction in Maryland. The plaintiff sued the defendant for the amount of the debt in North Carolina and sought service of process over the defendant on the basis that the defendant owned real estate within North Carolina. The court held that since the realty had no relation to the debt, there were insufficient contacts to subject the defendant to the jurisdiction. In another case a nonresident defendant who sold 25 bags of grass seed to the plaintiff's agent in Illinois was

---

[1] 326 U.S. 310 (1945).

[2] *Balcon, Inc.* v. *Sadler*, 36 N.C. App. 322, 244 S.E.2d 164 (1978).

sued by the plaintiff (an Illinois resident) alleging that the grass was full of "noxious weed." The court held that one isolated sale was insufficient contact to subject the out-of-state defendant to its jurisdiction.[3]

Venue

Jurisdiction must be distinguished from *venue*. Whereas jurisdiction relates to the power of a court to hear an action, venue is concerned with the geographic locality within the state (e.g., county or district) where an action should be tried. Within a particular state many courts may have jurisdiction; however, not all may meet the venue requirements specified by statute. For example, venue may require that the case be heard in the county where the defendant resides or where the property that is the subject of the action is located. When there are multiple defendants, several geographic localities may be proper, and the plaintiff may be authorized to make the selection. When the trial of a cause would result in an inconvenience and a hardship, the doctrine of *forum non conveniens* permits a defendant to transfer the case to another geographic location where venue is proper.

Case or controversy

A dispute must involve a *case or controversy* before a court will adjudicate it. Courts neither engage in the resolution of hypothetical situations nor act upon matters when there is no real dispute. Otherwise they would be embroiled in unnecessary litigation. Courts are best equipped to decide a case when the parties have a real personal stake in the outcome of a dispute and may be adversely affected by it. Under these circumstances each party has the incentive to expend its best efforts in prosecuting or defending its case. This is the adversary system. In this adversarial environment, courts are in the best position to examine the arguments, find the truth, and apply justice.

An overview of a legal dispute

The overwhelming majority of the cases are disposed of at the trial level of the judicial system. The parties are brought into a court, and both sides present their evidence and examine witnesses in front of a judge and jury (or simply in front of a judge, if no jury is requested by the parties). This trial court, the bottom level of the judicial system, hears the evidence, listens to the witnesses, and renders a decision based on the information brought before the court, as applied to the relevant law. The court considers what the witnesses have said (called *testimony*) and other evidence, such as business records, photographs, or other tangible objects (called *exhibits*). The judge

---

[3] *Morgan* v. *Heckle,* 171 F. Supp. 482 (E.D.Ill. 1959).

decides what testimony and exhibits are proper for the given case, using the available law as a guide to admitting or excluding certain offered evidence. If the judge decides that the evidence can properly be brought before the court, it is then the job of the jury (or the judge in the absence of a jury) to decide what evidence to believe.

Quite often, witnesses have conflicting versions of a particular event, based on their own memory and perception of it. The jury, then, really decides what, in *fact,* to believe. If there is no jury, then the judge, in addition to ruling on matters of law, also decides as a matter of fact what evidence is closest to the truth. Finally, at the end of the trial the jury (or the judge if there is no jury) renders its *decision,* in terms of what the judicial system will do in order to solve the problem at hand. The substance of this decision will vary according to the type of case which has been presented before the court. In the American legal system, as well as the legal systems of many other countries, the judicial system actually performs a dual role; this duality is determined by the two types of cases brought into this single system.

One type of case involves basically *private* disputes. These disputes may involve problems between people in their business or personal relationships, or the claim that one party has been injured in some way by another party. Disputes of this type are called *civil* cases. The other type of case involves situations in which someone has overstepped the social conduct prescribed by society and society seeks a way to punish the offender. These are called *criminal* cases. One incident may have both civil and criminal ramifications. For example, suppose that a person, while driving a car, fails to heed a red light, runs through the light, and smashes into another person's car. This chain of events may result in criminal sanctions for failing to stop for the red light and may also result in a separate, civil claim by the person whose car has sustained damage. However, these two legal problems will be tried separately. Though the same legal system will take care of both cases, the outcome in one case is not dependent upon the outcome in the other. The distinction between a criminal law case and a civil law case is graphically illustrated in Figure 2–2.

The decision of the court, then, must take into account exactly what type of problem it has been asked to solve. Courts are not boundless in their power; they take into the system only those situations which the law recognizes as legal problems. For example, the little boy next door to you may stand out on the sidewalk in front of your house and make faces at you. This behavior may annoy you greatly, but it would be fruitless to look to the legal system for an answer to your problem. The little boy has not really overstepped the social bounds of behavior, so no criminal sanction is available. The type of annoyance you suffer is not of such a degree that you can legally claim to have experienced a civil wrong. Some other method might be available to halt the little boy's conduct, but the legal system simply does not extend that far. The wrong you complain of

Figure 2–2

	Civil	Criminal
Who institutes the action?	Individual or business enterprise	Sovereign
Who has been wronged?	Individual or business enterprise	Society
What is the burden of proof?	Preponderance of the evidence*	Beyond a reasonable doubt†
What is the remedy?	Damages, injunction, or other private relief	Punishment (fine and/or imprisonment)

* By the greater weight of the evidence.

† To satisfy this burden the trier of the facts (judge or jury) must have an abiding conviction amounting to a moral certainty of the guilt of the accused. This is a greater burden of proof than "preponderance of the evidence."

is not a legal wrong, and the legal system only attempts to provide relief for legal wrongs.

The court's decision must also consider the available answers that the court can provide for your problem, and these answers (called *remedies*) are also limited. Suppose that instead of simply standing at the edge of the sidewalk in front of your house and making faces at you, the little boy takes a brick and throws it through your picture window, breaking the glass. You now have a situation which the legal system can handle, by both criminal and civil sanctions. Society does not allow its constituents to ruin other people's property, and you, as a private individual, have been injured by another private individual's conduct. In terms of the criminal conduct of the little boy, however, remedies available to the court are extremely limited. The court certainly will not order that the little boy be shot or branded on his forehead for breaking your window. The court may have no stronger available legal remedy for the criminal wrong than a reprimand for him. If his unsocial behavior continues, the court may order him to be sent to a place of confinement. In terms of a civil remedy, the resources of the court are also limited. The court could order the boy to pay for the window (damages), but that would probably not be a practical answer, since it is doubtful that he has enough money. The court could order him to refrain from throwing bricks at your windows in the future (an *injunction*). However, this would not pay for your present damages. In some states the court could order the boy's parents to pay for the window, and that might be a sufficient civil remedy (as long as the parents have enough money.)

What is being explained is the limitation in solving problems that has been placed upon our legal system. There must be evidence of a legal wrong for which the court can provide some available legal remedy. Even more, the court must consider legal wrong and legal remedy in the context of the person seeking legal relief. If the boy had broken your friend's window across the street, your friend would have to seek civil relief from the court, since the legal wrong was committed against your friend and not you. Your friend has *standing* to sue, but you do not. In essence, then, the court's decision will be based on the legal wrong which has been shown, on available legal remedies, and on whether or not the complaining party can demonstrate that the legal wrong has happened to him or her. If these prerequisites are fulfilled, then the legal system will be available to solve the problem at hand.

THE CIVIL PROCESS

The pleading stage

A lawsuit begins when the suing party, or *plaintiff*, files a *complaint* with the court. The complaint is a document which identifies the parties and states the basis for the court's jurisdiction, the facts comprising the plaintiff's cause of action, and the remedy the plaintiff seeks.

When the complaint is filed, the clerk of the court issues a *summons*. The summons notifies the defendant of the suit and generally informs the defendant what must be done to contest the action. The summons and complaint are then served on the *defendant*.

The defendant must then file an answer. The answer will admit, deny, or state an inability to admit or deny the particular allegations of the complaint. The defendant may also list *affirmative defenses* to the action, in the complaint. The defendant may assert a *counterclaim* against the plaintiff in the answer. If there are two or more defendants, any defendant may assert a *cross claim* against another defendant for any action he or she may have against that defendant. Defendants may also *implead* persons not original parties to the suit who they believe are liable. In a proper case a person not named as a party to the suit may *intervene.* When the answer sets up a counterclaim, the plaintiff must normally *reply* by admitting, denying, or stating an inability to admit or deny the particular allegations in the counterclaim.

During the pleading stage each party (plaintiff or defendant) may make *motions* in an attempt to win the case. Motions are requests to the court to rule on questions of law. Three common motions interposed at this stage are:

1. Motion to dismiss. This motion is filed by the defendant. It argues that even if the allegations of the complaint were true, the defendant would be entitled to judgment as a *matter of law.* Assume that the plaintiff files suit in a federal district court against a defendant, alleging diversity of citizenship and a debt of $5,000 owed by the defendant to the plaintiff. Defendant's motion to dismiss plaintiff's complaint would be granted since the complaint fails to allege an amount in controversy exceeding $10,000. Hence the district court lacks jurisdiction over the subject matter and, as a matter of law, the defendant must prevail.

2. Motion for judgment on the pleadings. This motion may be filed by either party after all the pleadings have been filed. It argues that on the face of the pleadings the moving party is entitled to judgment as a matter of law.

3. Motion for preliminary injunction. Usually a party will sue for money damages. Frequently a plaintiff will ask the court for an injunction, that is, an order compelling the defendant to do something or refrain from doing something. The plaintiff will not be entitled to a permanent injunction until the end of the case. However, the plaintiff may, in a proper case, obtain a preliminary injunction by demonstrating that the plaintiff is very likely to win on the merits of the case and will suffer irreparable harm if the preliminary injunction is not issued, that the injunction will not be unjustly harsh on the defendant, and that the injunction is in the public interest.

The discovery stage

Prior to trial the parties participate in discovery proceedings. Each party seeks to obtain information under the control of the other. In this way the parties become better able to evaluate the strengths and weaknesses of both their opponent's case and their own. This knowledge is helpful in settlement negotiations. Discovery may be accomplished by *interrogatories* (written questions addressed to the other party, who must answer the questions in writing under oath), *requests for documents,* and *requests to admit specific facts.* A *request for a physical* or *mental examination* is permitted when the physical or mental condition of the party is at issue. One of the more frequently used and flexible discovery tools is the *deposition.* Potential witnesses (including the parties) are examined under oath by the parties before a court reporter. The testimony may be transcribed. It gives the parties an idea of how the witness will testify at trial and may be used at trial to impeach the credibility of a witness whose testimony varies from that given at the deposition.

During the discovery stage it is not uncommon for a party to make a motion to the court for *summary judgment.* This motion argues that there are no disputed issues of material fact and therefore there is no need for a trial. It contends that the moving party is entitled to judgment as a matter of law.

Before trial, there is normally a *pretrial conference.* The judge meets with the attorneys representing the parties, and they discuss the issues that must be tried, the length of trial, and the possibility of settlement.

The trial stage

If the plaintiff is seeking *legal relief,* that is, money damages, the parties are ordinarily entitled to a trial by jury. They may waive this right and try the case to the court. If the plaintiff is seeking *equitable relief,* such as an injunction or other court order, the parties are not entitled to a jury trial.

The plaintiff has the burden of proving the case by a preponderance of the evidence. To sustain that burden of proof the plaintiff must establish that it is more probable than not that the facts are as the plaintiff alleges.

After selection of the jury (if a jury trial is proper and not waived), counsel for the plaintiff makes an *opening statement,* telling the court or the jury what he or she intends to prove. Defense counsel may then make an opening statement or reserve the opening statement until the close of plaintiff's case. Plaintiff then presents its *case-in-chief* by calling witnesses and presenting evidence. The defendant is given the opportunity to cross-examine the plaintiff's witnesses. The admissibility of the evidence is decided by the judge, based on the law of evidence. The plaintiff rests after completing his or her case-in-chief.

The defendant frequently makes a *motion for directed verdict,* after the plaintiff's case-in-chief, arguing that, as a matter of law, the defendant must prevail since on the basis of the plaintiff's case reasonable minds cannot differ as to the outcome. If the motion is granted, then the defendant wins. This motion is, however, rarely granted. If it is denied, the defendant proceeds with the opening statement, if previously reserved, and presents his or her case-in-chief. When all the evidence has been offered, the defendant may renew the motion for directed verdict. The plaintiff may make a similar motion, arguing that reasonable minds cannot differ as to the outcome and that the plaintiff is entitled to judgment as a matter of law. If these motions are denied, the parties make closing arguments. The *closing arguments* attempt to persuade the trier of the facts (judge or jury) by reasoning from the evidence.

If the case was tried to the court, the judge finds the facts, applies the law, and renders judgment. If the case was tried to a jury, the judge *instructs the jury* on the applicable law and tells the jury to resolve the factual issues and apply the law to reach a verdict.

Following the jury's verdict, the losing party may move for *judgment notwithstanding the verdict,* (sometimes referred to in the Latin form as *judgment non obstante verdicto,* or abbreviated *judgment n.o.v.*) again arguing that the movant is entitled to judgment as a matter of law. The losing party may also move for a *new trial,* arguing that the verdict is against the clear weight of the evidence. If, however, reasonable minds could reach the same conclusion as the jury, the verdict will not be set aside. The judge then enters a *judgment* in accordance with the verdict.

James Gibbons Co. v. Hess
407 A.2d 782 (Md. Ct. App. 1979)

Grady Garland was employed by the James F. Gibbons Company (appellant). During the course of his employment he sustained an accident that resulted in his death. Shirley Hess (claimant) instituted a workers' compensation action against Gibbons on behalf of her two children, who were born out of wedlock to Garland and Hess. The Workmen's Compensation Commission denied benefits on the basis that the children were not dependents of the decedent. Hess appealed from that finding to the Baltimore City Court, where the ques-

tion of "dependency" was heard by a jury. At the end of Hess' case Gibbons made a motion for direct verdict, which was denied. The case was submitted to the jury, which found that the children were "wholly dependent upon the deceased." Gibbons thereafter made a motion for judgment notwithstanding the verdict and new trial, which the court overruled. Gibbons appealed those rulings. The Maryland Court of Special Appeals affirmed.

* * * * *

Liss, Judge: The issue raised by this appeal is: Whether the Baltimore City Court erred in denying the employer and insurer's motions for a directed verdict and allowing to stand the jury's verdict that the claimants were wholly dependent upon the deceased at the time of his accidental injury and death.

To a substantial extent, the facts in the case are undisputed. Shirley Hess and the deceased, Grady Garland, were never married, but they were the parents of two children, Angela, born on July 20, 1968, and Grady Scott, born on June 22, 1975. These two children, Mrs. Hess, and Mrs. Hess's four other children from a previous marriage lived with the deceased from 1967 to 1975. In September of 1975, after an argument between Mrs. Hess and Mr. Garland, Mr. Garland left the home to live with his sister. It is undisputed that from September of 1975 until Garland's death on December 16, 1976 the parties did not live together.

The evidence presented at trial showed that Shirley Hess and Grady Garland entered into a paternity agreement in September of 1975 by which Garland agreed to pay the sum of $15.45 per week for the support of each of the children, a total payment of $138.27 per month. A decree was entered evidencing this agreement. Mrs. Hess was then receiving a grant from the Department of Social Services in the amount of $308.00 for the support of the members of her family. As a condition for the continuation of her Social Services grant, Mrs. Hess was required to sign a "form 80" allowing the agency to receive support payments on her behalf, the payments to come out of the weekly payments to be made by

the deceased pursuant to the paternity decree. The evidence also indicated that during the period of the deceased's separation from his children he would visit them two or three times a week, and on those occasions Mr. Garland and Mrs. Hess would "go shopping for groceries, medicine, if the children needed them, anything that they needed," and "Mr. Garland also brought the children clothing, birthday presents . . . generally anything . . . that they needed."

A number of payments were made pursuant to the decrees, and at the time of his death the decedent was in arrears on the required payments. An agent for the Maryland Parole and Probation Department testified that the Department of Social Services grant was made subject to the understanding that when Garland made any payments pursuant to the paternity decree, these funds would be paid to the Social Services Department without any increase or decrease in the grant.

* * * * *

There was additional testimony by Mrs. Hess that there was a possibility that she and Mr. Garland might resume living together, but she conceded there were "a few little problems we had yet, and besides, he was living in Reisterstown." In any case, no date had been set for the resumption of their previous living arrangement.

In reviewing the propriety of the trial judge's action in denying a directed verdict or judgment n.o.v., we are required to resolve all conflicts in the evidence in favor of the plaintiff, to assume the truth of all credible evidence presented in support of the plaintiff, and to accept as true all inferences naturally and legitimately arising from the evidence which tend to support the plaintiff's right to recover. If there is competent evidence, however slight, tending to support the plaintiff's right to recover, the case should be submitted to the jury and the motion for judgment n.o.v. denied.

Appellant urges that the trial court erred in denying appellant's motions for a directed verdict and by allowing the jury's verdict that the claimants were wholly dependent on the deceased to stand.

Maryland Code . . . provides: "In all cases,

questions of dependence, in whole, or in part, shall be determined by the Commission in accordance with the facts in each particular case existent at the time of the injury resulting in death of such employee. . . ." Appellant argues that this section requires the Commission to consider only the facts existent at the time of the injury and to determine from those facts whether the claimant was actually receiving the necessities of life from the decedent. . . .

There [are], however, . . . cases that [suggest] that dependency may be found when the facts existent at the time of injury reveal that the claimant had in the past substantially received the necessities of life from the workman, that a temporary lapse had occurred in the workman's support of the claimant, and that a reasonable probability existed that the support of the claimant would resume in the near future. . . .

* * * * *

It is our function in this case to determine whether there was evidence legally sufficient to be submitted to the jury. We are convinced that there was. We conclude that based on the evidence in this case the question of dependency was a question of fact, not of law. There was evidence from which the jury might have found that the deceased after separation remained in the area at a known address and phone number; that he continued to be employed in the immediate area; that he regularly visited the children; that in addition to signing a paternity decree in which he obligated himself to pay support fot the children on a monthly basis, he regularly purchased groceries, clothing, medicine and other needs of the children; that the deceased made regular payments on the order in the paternity cases from November 24, 1975 until February 3, 1976, though he was substantially in arrears when he died in December, 1976; that deceased did not marry anyone or arrange to live with another woman; that at the time of his death the deceased and Mrs. Hess were actively engaged in discussing a reestablishment of their family. These facts were sufficient to require the trial court to deny appellant's motion for directed verdict and to deny its motion for judgment n.o.v. or for a new trial.

* * * * *

Case questions

1. What issue does this case present?

2. Does the court's concept of "dependency" line up with yours? Explain. What was the claimant's legal theory? What facts supported that theory?

3. What would this court have done if the jury in this case had returned in favor of Gibbons? What do motion for directed verdict and a motion for judgment notwithstanding the verdict have in common?

4. How could you modify the facts in this case so that the appellant's motions should be granted?

Appeals

Once a decision has been made at the trial level, the parties consider whether they feel that the trial court has committed a serious error in the conduct of the trial. The basis of such an error might be that the judge's ruling on a motion was wrong or that the judge's instruction to the jury misstated the law. The legal system provides an opportunity for a party to ask a higher court to review a case for error. The courts which review trial court decisions are called *appellate courts.* These courts review the trial record to determine whether or not a party's claim that a serious error was made is true. An appellate court does *not* hold a new trial, nor does it hear additional evidence; it merely reviews the record of the trial held previously and listens to the arguments of the party (called the *appellant*) claiming some serious error in that trial. The appellate court also listens to the arguments of the opposing party (called the *appellee*), who may be claiming that no serious error occurred. After reviewing the record of the trial and the arguments of the parties involved, the appellate court has several alternatives. It can (1) *affirm* the verdict of the trial court, that is, accept it as is and change nothing; or (2) *reverse* the verdict, which is to decide that the outcome of the trial was wrong; or (3) *modify* the legal remedy provided by the trial court; or (4) *remand* the case to the trial court level for a new trial.

The great majority of trial cases never reach the appellate level, since the parties involved simply accept the verdict of the trial court. When cases are appealed, the appellate court judges often decide to write down the reasons for their decision, as a guide to the parties involved and also as a guide to anyone who may have a similar problem in the future. These written decisions create precedent.

The appeal is decided by at least three appellate judges. A majority vote decides the issues. One judge is usually assigned to write the majority's opinion, which constitutes the *opinion of the court.* A judge may disagree with the majority by writing a *dissenting opinion.* A *concurring opinion* may be written by a judge who agrees with the result but for different reasons. It is such written legal opinions which constitute the cases presented in this book. The opinions illustrate the many points of law which are presented, the application of legal principles, and the extent of the answers, or remedies, which were available to the people involved and will be available to anyone else who might be faced with similar problems in the future.

THE CRIMINAL PROCESS

The criminal process begins when a sworn affidavit is filed with the court charging a defendant with the commission of a crime. Depending upon the nature of the offense charged, the defendant will be arrested (if not already in custody) or merely summoned to appear in court to answer the charge. When arrested, the defendant is given an opportunity to appear before a judicial officer who sets a bail bond for the defendant's release. Some offenses have *station house bond,* a predetermined amount listed according to the offense. Under our criminal justice system the defendant is presumed innocent until proven guilty. The only purpose of bond is to insure the defendant's appearance at trial; it is not designed to punish the accused. If the defendant posts the bond with the court, it will be returned to the defendant at the conclusion of the case. A bonding company is often enlisted to aid a defendant. For a fee (usually 10 percent) the bonding company posts the bond for the defendant. Some jurisdictions permit the defendant to place an *appearance* bond with the court. Here, the defendant posts a percentage of the bond (usually 10 percent) with the court and after trial receives a return of the full amount posted. A failure to appear results in a forfeiture of the amount posted plus an obligation to pay the remainder. If the judge is convinced that a bond is not necessary to insure the defendant's appearance, the judge may release the defendant on his or her own recognizance.

In felony cases many states provide for a *preliminary hearing* to determine whether there is probable cause to bind the defendant over to the grand jury. The grand jury usually consists of 15 to 23 jurors, depending upon the locality, who sit to determine whether there is sufficient evidence to require the defendant to stand trial. Absent sufficient evidence, the grand jury will *ignore* the case and the defendant will go free. If the grand jury determines that there is sufficient evidence, then it will *indict,* and the defendant must stand trial. A defendant can waive the grand jury procedure and request the prosecution to proceed on a *bill of information.* After indictment or a bill of information the defendant is arraigned before a judge. At that time the defendant is called upon to enter a *plea.* The most common pleas are guilty, not guilty, and not guilty by reason of insanity. Some states recognize the plea of nolo contendere (no contest), a plea that admits the facts in the indictment but questions whether the defendant is guilty under those facts.

If a plea of guilty is entered, then the judge will *sentence* the defendant. Many states provide for a *presentence report.* The presentence report is compiled by the probation department or other office of the court. It contains a profile of the defendant and aids the judge in providing detailed information about the defendant. If a nolo contendere plea is entered, then the judge must decide whether the facts as contained in the indictment constitute the crime as charged. If a plea of not guilty or not guilty by reason of insanity has been entered, then the defendant will be afforded a full trial.

The format of the criminal trial is very similar to that of the civil trial. A defendant is entitled to a jury trial unless this has been waived.[4] The prosecutor has the burden of proof to show the defendant's guilt beyond a reasonable doubt. This is accomplished through the presentation of testimony and tangible evidence. At the end of the prosecutor's case-in-chief the defendant may move for a *judgment acquittal* on the basis that the prosecutor failed to produce sufficient evidence to sustain a conviction. If the motion is overruled, then the defendant has an opportunity to present evidence. The defendant does not have to testify because of the constitutional privilege against self-incrimination. In fact the jury is instructed by the judge not to draw an unfavorable inference from the failure of the defendant to take the stand. After the defendant's case-in-chief, closing arguments, and instructions to the jury, the jury retires to deliberate. In most states

---

[4] States do not have to afford a jury trial for minor misdemeanors.

the verdict of the jury must be unanimous. If a jury cannot reach a verdict, then the jury is referred to as *hung* and the defendant must be retried or the case dismissed. Normally the jury deliberates and reaches a verdict of acquittal or conviction. If convicted, the defendant will be sentenced. The conviction is subject to review by the appellate courts.

THE REGULATORY PROCESS

Both the federal government and state government perform various functions delegated to them by the people. Those functions include regulating private conduct. Government employs the administrative process and administrative agencies to accomplish this end. An administrative agency is not a court, yet it often possesses the power to make law by deciding cases. An administrative agency is not a legislative body, yet it is often empowered to promulgate rules and regulations. An administrative agency is established by the legislative or executive branch of government, and as such it is an agent of its creator. In many instances it is vested with the power to enforce statutes and agency rules through criminal and civil sanctions.

Administrative agencies run the gamut from those that exact taxes, such as the Internal Revenue Service, to those that disburse monies, such as the Social Security Administration. In between are the administrative agencies that have been created to regulate certain activities and industries. Price-fixing, the issuing of securities, pollution, creditor practices, and product safety are but a few of the areas regulated by specific administrative agencies.

Administrative agencies are established to perform specialized tasks. They usually employ large numbers of personnel who are organized along hierarchical lines. These agencies are well suited for their assigned tasks because of the expertise they employ and the expertise they develop from experience in their particular fields. For example, the millions of claims which the Social Security Administration disposes of every year constitute many times the number of cases that are heard by all the federal courts combined. The Environmental Protection Agency analyzes highly technical data involving the impact of various potential pollutants and activities on the environment. The agency's expertise in this area is greater than that of the courts or Congress; hence, presumably, it can do the work more efficiently. The regulatory process via administrative agencies is detailed in Chapter 3 and will be considered throughout the remainder of this book.

THE FIRM AND ITS ATTORNEY

With the advent of increased government regulation, businesses have become more apt to call upon lawyers to assist them through the "red tape." In the past a business usually did not contact lawyers until a problem arose, for example, when it was sued or when a distributor would not pay an outstanding debt. However, more and more businesses are concerned with preventive law, in attempts to avoid the unfavorable consequences that accompany uninformed business practices. Business managers today have a more ongoing relationship with the lawyers than they had in the past and thus need to know exactly how lawyers function.

Lawyers have a common base of training: law school. In law school the lawyer receives generalized training enabling him or her to adapt to a wide range of tasks. The average person thinks lawyers know the law. It is more accurate, however, to say that lawyers are generally versed in an array of legal principles and that they know how to find the relevant law and to apply it to particular circumstances. It is this general training and ability that equip a lawyer for various specialized tasks.

Counselor

The lawyer practices preventive law by counseling the business client. Wise counsel can avoid a host of problems; for example, advising a corporation regarding the legal consequences of a merger might avert potential antitrust problems. As a counselor, the business lawyer must be imaginative and perceive the range of alternative courses of action and foresee the probable legal consequences that attach to each. To do this the business lawyer must be versed in the multidimensional operations and activities of the business firm.

Investigator

The role of investigator is often preliminary to the role of counselor or advocate. The lawyer needs to accumulate potentially useful information and then to extract the data pertinent to the particular task. This takes cooperation with the business client who knows the intrafirm operations and where to find specific documents. During the course of the investigation the attorney may uncover damaging information or even evidence of criminal activity. The attorney owes an allegiance to the client. Although an attorney is deemed an officer of the court and cannot counsel a client to participate in illegal activities, nonetheless the canons of ethics, as constituted at present, do not require the attorney to "blow the whistle."

Drafter

The business lawyer drafts documents for the firm. Contracts, deeds, corporate instruments, and securities registration statements are just a few of the documents that are commonly prepared by lawyers. Good drafting is important to avoid adverse legal consequences. In this respect drafting is a form of preventive law.

Negotiator

The lawyer possesses negotiating skills. The role of the negotiator is akin to that of the advocate. The lawyer presents the client's strongest arguments in order to achieve the best result possible. Negotiation may be necessitated by a dispute with a regulatory agency, another business, or the customer. Successful negotiation resulting in a settlement often avoids costly suits, work stoppages, and other undesirable economic consequences.

Advocate

In the capacity of an advocate, the lawyer is called upon to represent the client's interest. This may occur in a court, before an administrative agency or a legislative body, or in another arena. The lawyer's duty, as an advocate, is to present the facts and the law in the light most favorable to the client. Of course, the opponent's lawyer will be doing the same. This is the adversary system which enables the judge or other hearing officer to examine the full range of arguments before arriving at a reasoned decision.

Selecting a lawyer

No lawyer is an expert in all of the above roles or in every substantive area of the law. Some lawyers concentrate their practice in the area of counseling, while others develop and utilize specialized skills in advocacy. Some attorneys concentrate on antitrust law, while others specialize in tax law. For these reasons, it might seem desirable for the corporate client to choose a lawyer based on the specific problem that arises. However, this is not always feasible. First, lawyers do not normally "hang specialty shingles," and in most states they are prohibited from doing so. Consequently it is difficult for the business manager to know whom to call upon among the ranks of the specialists. Second, specialists have a narrow focus on their specialty and lack a perception of the big picture. Selecting a generalist as corporate counsel has its advantages. The general practitioner can effectively handle most of the routine problems that confront a business firm. When a problem arises that necessitates a specialist, the general corporate practitioner is in a position to refer the client to one. The general practitioner will then be in a position to assist the client by briefing the specialist on the problem, thus saving valuable time.

Large companies hire lawyers and establish their own inside law firm. In-house lawyers have the advantage of being closer to and more familiar with the business firm. They are hence in a better position than outside counsel to quickly identify and react to potential legal pitfalls and to render on-the-spot advice. When a problem necessitates specialized attention, it can be referred to outside counsel.

Communicating with lawyers

A lawyer is not permitted to solicit clients by direct contact. A person needing a lawyer's services must take the initiative and should contact counsel early and not wait until the problem intensifies. It is better to have a lawyer draft a contract than to call in a lawyer to remedy a problem arising from a contract poorly drafted by the client. If a firm has retained counsel or has an ongoing professional relationship with counsel, then that counsel can take the initiative when aware of an activity or law that will affect the firm's business. This is not deemed solicitation since a lawyer-client relationship already exists.

It is important that the client make a full disclosure of the facts relevant to the given question or problem. If an attorney's opinion is based on anything less, the opinion is incomplete. A general understanding of the law affecting the business will help a business client to detail the material facts and avoid irrelevancies when communicating with a lawyer. Understanding the lawyer's role will facilitate communications. For example, a lawyer's questioning when seeking information from a client may sometimes seem accusatory. This questioning is deliberate, however, and it may be designed to prepare a client for intensive cross-examination at a court trial. The informed business client does not take offense at such questioning and recognizes that when the time for advocacy occurs, the lawyer will exert his or her skills toward defending the client.

The client should not take a passive role but should be actively engaged in assisting the lawyer's search for solutions. The business client needs to clearly inform the lawyer of the business purpose so that the lawyer will seek solutions compatible with that purpose. Finally, the client should expect high-quality service from counsel and should communicate that expectation. After all, the client is paying the bill.

The attorney-client privilege

The law encourages clients to fully communicate with their counsel by protecting such communication from disclosure to a third person. The attorney-client privilege gives the client the right to conceal matters relating to his or her counsel's advice. The canons of ethics do not permit an attorney to disclose communications regarding legal advice to the client. The client may, however, waive the privilege and authorize the attorney to make disclosure. The privilege only applies to confidential communications. Communications made to an attorney in the presence of third parties other than the client's agents or employees are not privileged.

The work-product doctrine, akin to the attorney-client privilege, protects notes, summaries, and other written data prepared in connection with the client's consultation on a case.

The attorney-client privilege and the related work-product doctrine are examined in the following case.

Upjohn Co. v. United States
49 U.S.L.W. 4093 (Jan. 13, 1981)

Upjohn (petitioner) sells pharmaceuticals. During an audit it was discovered that one of the petitioner's foreign subsidiaries made payments to officials of foreign governments in order to obtain government business. The accountants communicated this finding to Gerald Thomas, the petitioner's vice president, secretary, and general counsel. Thomas contacted outside counsel, and an internal investigation began. The attorneys drafted a questionnaire and sent it to the relevant managers. The questionnaire was designed to compile full information on the extent of the payments made to foreign governmental officials. As part of the investigation, Thomas and the outside counsel interviewed the questionnaire recipients and 33 other officers and employees.

The company disclosed its findings of "questionable payments" to the Securities and Exchange Commission and the Internal Revenue Service (IRS). The IRS began its own investigation and issued a summons to Upjohn demanding "all files relative to the investigation conducted under the supervision of Gerald Thomas," including the questionnaires and the notes of interviews. The company refused to comply with the summons, maintaining that those items were protected from disclosure by the attorney-client privilege and the work-product doctrine. The United States sought enforcement in the district court, which determined that the petitioner must comply with the summons. The petitioner appealed to the court of appeals, which held that under the "control group test" the attorney-client privilege was not applicable to communications made by persons "not responsible for directing [petitioner's] actions in response to legal advice." The court also held that the work-product doctrine was inapplicable. The Supreme Court reversed and remanded.

Mr. Justice Rehnquist: . . . The attorney-client privilege is the oldest of the privileges for confidential communications known to the common law. Its purpose is to encourage full and frank communication between attorneys and their clients and thereby promote broader public interests in the observance of law and administration of justice. The privilege recognizes that sound legal advice or advocacy serves public ends and that such advice or advocacy depends upon the lawyer being fully informed by the client. . . .

The Court of Appeals, however, considered the application of the privilege in the corporate context to present a "different problem," since the client was an inanimate entity and "only the senior management, guiding and integrating the several operations, . . . can be said to possess an identity analogous to the corporation as a whole." The first case to articulate the so-called "control group test" adopted by the court below . . . reflected a similar conceptual approach. . . . Such a view, we think, overlooks the fact that the privilege exists to protect not only the giving of professional advice to those who can act on it but also the giving of information to the lawyer to enable him to give sound and informed advice. . . .

* * * * *

The control group test adopted by the court below thus frustrates the very purpose of the privilege by discouraging the communication of relevant information by employees of the client to attorneys seeking to render legal advice to the client corporation. The attorney's advice will also frequently be more significant to non-control group members than to those who officially sanction the advice, and the control group test makes it more difficult to convey full and frank legal advice to the employees who will put into effect the client corporation's policy.

The narrow scope given the attorney-client privilege by the court below not only makes it difficult for corporate attorneys to formulate sound advice when their client is faced with a specific legal problem but also threatens to limit the valuable efforts of corporate counsel to ensure their client's compliance with the law. In light of the vast and complicated array of regulatory legislation confronting the modern corporation, corporations, unlike most individuals, "constantly go to lawyers to find out how to obey the law," . . . particularly since compliance with the law in this area is hardly an instinctive matter. . . . The test adopted by the court below is difficult to apply in practice, though no abstractly formulated and unvarying "test" will necessarily enable courts to decide questions such as this with mathematical precision. But if the purpose of the attorney-client privilege is to be served, the attorney and client must be able to predict with some degree of certainty whether particular discussions will be protected. . . .

*   *   *   *   *

The Court of appeals declined to extend the attorney-client privilege beyond the limits of the control group test for fear that doing so would entail severe burdens on discovery and create a broad "zone of silence" over corporate affairs. Application of the attorney-client privilege to communications such as those involved here, however, puts the adversary in no worse position than if the communications had never taken place. The privilege only protects disclosure of communications; it does not protect disclosure of the underlying facts by those who communicated with the attorney. . . .

. . . [W]e conclude that the narrow "control group test" sanctioned by the Court of Appeals in this case cannot, consistent with "the principles of the common law as . . . interpreted . . . in light of reason and experience," govern the development of the law in this area.

Our decision that the communications by Upjohn employees to counsel are covered by the attorney-client privilege disposes of the case so far as the responses to the questionnaires and any notes reflecting responses to interview questions are concerned. The summons reaches further, however, and Thomas has tes-

tified that his notes and memoranda of interviews go beyond recording responses to his questions. To the extent that the material subject to the summons is not protected by the attorney-client privilege as disclosing communications between an employee and counsel, we must reach the ruling by the Court of Appeals that the work-product doctrine does not apply to [IRS] summonses. . . .

The Government concedes, wisely, that the Court of Appeals erred and that the work-product doctrine does apply to IRS summonses. . . . While conceding the applicability of the work-product doctrine, the Government asserts that it has made a sufficient showing of necessity to overcome its protections. The magistrate apparently so found. . . .

*   *   *   *   *

We do not decide the issue at this time. It is clear that the magistrate applied the wrong standard when he concluded that the Government had made a sufficient showing of necessity to overcome the protections of the work-product doctrine. The magistrate applied the "substantial need" and "without undue hardship" standard. . . . The notes and memoranda sought by the Government here, however, are work product based on oral statements. If they reveal communications, they are, in this case, protected by the attorney-client privilege. To the extent they do not reveal communications, they reveal the attorneys' mental processes in evaluating the communications. . . . [S]uch work product cannot be disclosed simply on a showing of substantial need and inability to obtain the equivalent without undue hardship.

While we are not prepared at this juncture to say that such material is always protected by the work-product rule, we think a far stronger showing of necessity and unavailability by other means than was made by the Government or applied by the magistrate in this case would be necessary to compel disclosure. [The government attempted to show necessity on the basis that interviewees are scattered inconveniently throughout the world.—Ed.] Since the Court of Appeals thought that the work-product protection was never applicable in an enforcement proceeding such as this, and since the magistrate whose recommendations the District Court adopted applied too lenient a standard of protection, we think the best procedure with respect to this aspect of the case would be to reverse the judgment of the Court of Appeals for the Sixth Circuit and remand the case to it for such further proceedings in connection with the work-product claim as are consistent with this opinion.

Case questions

1. What is the difference between the attorney-client privilege and the work-product doctrine?

2. What is the purpose of the attorney-client privilege? Why did the High Court reject the "control group test"?

3. What is the purpose of the work-product doctrine?

4. Assume in *Upjohn* that more than one half of the interviewees were no longer employed by the company and could not be located. Assume further that of the 33 other officers and employees, 25 were awaiting trial on charges relevant to the illegal bribery. What arguments could the government make for obtaining the attorneys' work product? What are the counterarguments?

THE FIRM'S INTERACTION WITH GOVERNMENT

Corporate activities which are perceived as socially undesirable frequently provoke governmental regulatory responses. Businesses therefore frequently attempt to influence government action.

Efforts to influence political campaigns and elections

Many state governments have enacted laws regulating political campaigns in general and political contributions in particular. These laws apply to state and local election campaigns and are as varied as the state governments which have enacted them.

Federal elections are governed by the Federal Election Campaign Act of 1971, as amended in 1974. The act specifically prohibits federal election campaign contributions by national banks, federally chartered corporations, and labor unions. It further prohibits such contributions by businesses and others that enter into or are negotiating contracts with the federal government.

All other persons and businesses are limited in the amount of the federal campaign contributions they can make. Individual contributions may not exceed $1,000 to any one candidate and $25,000 in total during any calendar year. The 1974 amendments also prohibited individuals, including candidates, from spending on their own, as opposed to contributing, more than specified amounts on political campaigns during a calendar year. This limitation was declared unconstitutional by the Supreme Court.[5] The Court deter-

[5] *Buckley* v. *Valeo*, 424 U.S. 1 (1976).

mined that the limitation did not significantly deter corrupt election practices but did severely limit individual freedom of expression.

Lobbying

Efforts to influence the legislature are called lobbying. The Federal Regulation of Lobbying Act defines lobbyists as those who, for pay, attempt to influence the passage or defeat of legislation before Congress. The act does not cover individuals who engage in lobbying on their own behalf or who confine their lobbying activities to testifying before Congress. It also does not cover individuals who are uncompensated for their lobbying activities.

Every lobbyist is required to register with the clerk of the House of Representatives and the secretary of the Senate. The registration must include the lobbyist's name and address, the lobbyist's employer, the amount and source of the lobbyist's compensation and expense account, the types of expenses that the employer reimbursed, and the duration of the lobbyist's employment. Each lobbyist is also required to file quarterly reports with the clerk and the secretary detailing all monies received and expended during the preceding quarter, the recipients and purposes of these payments, the names of any publications in which the lobbyist has caused editorials or articles to be published, and the specific pieces of legislation which the lobbyist has been employed to oppose or support.

Persons and corporations or other organizations that solicit contributions for use in support of or in opposition to legislation pending before Congress are also required to file detailed reports. These reports are also filed quarterly, and they must include the name and address of each person making a contribution of $500 or more, the total amount of contributions received for the calendar year, the name and address of each person receiving $10 or more during the calendar year, the amount of the expenditures made for that person, and the amount of all expenditures during the calendar year.

The First Amendment to the Constitution guarantees the freedom of speech and press. Underlying these freedoms is the right to petition the government for the redress of grievances. Many activities designed to influence governmental action, which might otherwise be illegal, are protected by the First Amendment. The degree of this protection is well illustrated by the following case.

Eastern Railroad Presidents Conference v. *Noers Motor Freight, Inc.*
365 U.S. 127 (1961)

Eastern Railroad Presidents Conference (defendant-appellant) is an association that represented 24 railroads. The appellant hired a public relations firm to conduct a publicity campaign against the trucking industry. The campaign was designed to promote the adoption and retention of laws and enforcement procedures that hampered the truckers from competing with the railroads in the long-distance freight business. The campaign was also designed to injure the truckers' goodwill. Toward that end the public relations firm utilized the third-party technique, "whereby material prepared and produced by the public relations firm was made to appear as spontaneously expressed views of independent persons." Noers Motor Frieght, Inc. (plaintiff-appellee), a member of the trucking industry, instituted suit against the defendant-appellant. The lower court held in favor of Noers on the basis that Eastern Railroad's activities unreasonably restrained trade and thus violated the Sherman Antitrust Act. The court of appeals affirmed. The Supreme Court granted certiorari and reversed.

Mr. Justice Black: We accept, as the starting point for our consideration of the case, the same basic construction of the Sherman Act adopted by the courts below—that no violation of the Act can be predicated upon mere attempts to influence the passage or enforcements of laws.

We think it equally clear that the Sherman Act does not prohibit two or more persons from associating together in an attempt to persuade the legislature or the executive to take particular action with respect to a law that would produce a restraint or a monopoly. Although such associations could perhaps, through a process of expansive construction, be brought within the general proscription of "combination[s] . . . in restraint of trade," they bear very little if any resemblance to the combinations normally held violative of the Sherman Act, combinations ordinarily characterized by an express or implied agreement or understanding that the participants will jointly give up their trade freedom, or help one another to take away the trade freedom of others, through the use of such devices as price-fixing agreements, boycotts, market-division agreements, and other similar arrangements. . . .

In the first place, such a holding would substantially impair the power of government to take actions through its legislature and executive that operate to restrain trade. In a representative democracy such as this, these branches of government act on behalf of the people and, to a very large extent, the whole concept of

representation depends upon the ability of the people to make their wishes known to their representatives. To hold that the government retains the power to act in this representative capacity and yet hold, at the same time, that the people cannot freely inform the government of their wishes would impute to the Sherman Act a purpose to regulate, not business activity, but political activity, a purpose which would have no basis whatever in the legislative history of that Act. Secondly, and of at least equal significance, such a construction of the Sherman Act would raise important constitutional questions. The right of petition is one of the freedoms protected by the Bill of Rights, and we cannot, of course, lightly impute to Congress an intent to invade these freedoms. . . .

. . . For these reasons, we think it clear that the Sherman Act does not apply to the activities of the railroads at least insofar as those activities comprised mere solicitation of governmental action with respect to the passage and enforcement of laws. We are thus called upon to consider whether the courts below were correct in holding that, notwithstanding this principle, the Act was violated here because of the presence in the railroads' publicity campaign of additional factors sufficient to take the case out of the area in which the principle is controlling.

The first such factor relied upon was the fact, established by the finding of the District Court, that the railroads' sole purpose in seeking to influence the passage and enforcement of laws was to destroy the truckers as competitors for the long-distance freight business. But we do not see how this fact, even if adequately supported in the record, could transform conduct otherwise lawful into a violation of the Sherman Act. . . . The right of the people to inform their representatives in government of their desires with respect to the passage or enforcement of laws cannot properly be made to depend upon their intent in doing so. It is neither unusual nor illegal for people to seek action on laws in the hope that they may bring about an advantage to themselves and a disadvantage to their competitors.

* * * * *

The second factor relied upon by the courts below to justify the application of the Sherman

Act to the railroads' publicity campaign was the use in the campaign of the so-called third-party technique. The theory under which this factor was related to the proscriptions of the Sherman Act, though not entirely clear from any of the opinions below, was apparently that it involved unethical business conduct on the part of the railroads. As pointed out above, the third-party technique, which was aptly characterized by the District Court as involving "deception of the public, manufacture of bogus sources of reference, [and] distortion of public sources of information," depends upon giving propaganda actually circulated by a party in interest the appearance of being spontaneous declarations of independent groups. . . . Insofar as that Act sets up a code of ethics at all, it is a code that condemns trade restraints, not political activity, and, as we have already pointed out, a publicity campaign to influence governmental action falls clearly into the category of political activity. The proscriptions of the Act, tailored as they are for the business world, are not at all appropriate for application in the political arena. . . .

* * * * *

There may be situations in which a publicity campaign, ostensibly directed toward influencing governmental action, is a mere sham to cover what is actually nothing more than an attempt to interfere directly with the business relationships of a competitor and the application of the Sherman Act would·be justified. But this certainly is not the case here. No one denies that the railroads were making a genuine effort to influence legislation and law enforcement practices. Indeed, if the version of the facts set forth in the truckers' complaint is fully credited, as it was by the courts below, that effort was not only genuine but also highly successful. Under these circumstances, we conclude that no attempt to interfere with business relationships in a manner proscribed by the Sherman Act is involved in this case.

In rejecting each of the grounds relied upon by the courts below to justify applications of the Sherman Act to the campaign of the railroads, we have rejected the very grounds upon which those courts relied to distinguish the campaign conducted by the truckers. In doing so, we have restored what appears to be the true nature of the case—a "no holds-barred fight" between two industies both of which are seeking control of a profitable source of income. Inherent in such fights, is the possibility, and in many instances even the probability, that one group or the other will get hurt by the arguments that are made. In this particular instance, each group appears to have utilized all the political powers it could muster in an attempt to bring about the passage of laws that would help it or injure the other. But the contest itself appears to have been conducted along lines normally accepted in our political system, except to the extent that each group has deliberately deceived the public and public officials. And that deception, reprehensible as it is, can be of no consequence so far as the Sherman Act is concerned. That Act was not violated by either the railroads or the truckers in their respective campaigns to influence legislation and law enforcement.

* * * * *

Case questions

1. Did the Court base its ruling on the Sherman Act or the First Amendment to the Constitution? Explain.

2. Why did the Court reject the district court's finding that the defendant's use of the third-party technique could form the basis of their liability?

3. Do you agree with the Court's characterization of our political system as a "no-holds-barred fight"? Explain.

4. What outcomes do you think Noers will encourage? What limitations did the Court place upon attempts to influence governmental action? Formulate a publicity campaign that you feel would be prohibited under Noers.

Other business efforts to influence government action

The federal criminal code establishes two types of offenses—bribery and gratuities—for the giving of money or anything else of value to government employees. A person convicted of bribery is subject to a maximum penalty of 15 years in prison; a fine of $20,000 or three times the amount of the bribe, whichever is greater; or both. A person convicted of offering or giving a gratuity is subject to a maximum penalty of two years in prison, a $10,000 fine, or both. Similar penalties are imposed upon government employees convicted of soliciting or receiving bribes and gratuities.

The bribery and gratuity prohibitions encompass the giving or promising of anything of value to a government employee. The difference between the two is that a bribe must be a payment or promise which is corruptly made; that is, bribery occurs where the payment or promise is intended as a quid pro quo for official action that might otherwise not be undertaken. A gratuity is any payment or promise, regardless of whether it is specifically designed to procure official action. Thus gratuities encompass payments made to administrative officials to speed up the approval of applications which would have been approved anyway.

Prohibitions against outright gifts do not eliminate the opportunities for more subtle influences upon government officials. Consequently other regulatory and statutory provisions have been designed to bolster the antibribery law. It is a criminal offense for a former government employee to represent a client (other than the United States) in a matter before any agency, department, committee, or court (involving the United States) in which that employee participated personally and substantially while so employed. Violation of this provision subjects the former employee to a prison sentence of up to two years, a fine of up to $10,000, or both. A partner of a former government employee is subject to similar prohibitions. The partner may be imprisoned up to one year and fined up to $5,000.

It is a civil offense for any elected or appointed official or any employee of any branch of the government to accept an honorarium of more than $2,000 for a speaking engagement or to accept honoraria totaling more than $25,000 in any calendar year.

Efforts to influence foreign governments

In response to many disclosures of corporate acts of foreign bribery, Congress enacted the Foreign Corrupt Practices Act of 1977. The act specifies accounting methods and disclosures to be made by companies which the Securities and Exchange Commission regulates.

The act also criminalizes certain corrupt practices in foreign countries and in dealings with foreigners. Specifically prohibited are the giving of anything of value to any foreign official for the purpose of influencing any official action by a foreign government or to any foreign political party or candidate for the purpose of influencing the outcome of a foreign election, where the motivation behind the payment is to obtain or retain business or to direct business to anyone. The act also restricts the class of illegal payments to those made to foreign officials, rather than all employees of foreign governments, and to those intended to influence the performance of official acts. The act does not appear to prohibit "grease" payments to speed up routine matters.

POLICY CONSIDERATIONS

In recent years there has been an explosion in the number of lawsuits. Both federal and state judicial structures are being overtaxed. The Supreme Court of the United States receives about 4,000 new filings per year and selects less than 200 cases to hear. The circuit courts of appeal receive more than three times that number and do not normally have the discretion to deny hearing a case. Over the last 10 years, federal trial court dockets increased every year at a staggering rate. In some state courts the docket control problem has been even greater.

One reason that has been suggested for the increase in litigation is the increase of population. The population of the United States increased from about 130 million in 1940 to about 215 million in 1980. Although the population growth rate appears to have declined, population increases are still expected. The increase in the number of people also increases the potential for conflict.

The passage of new legislation is another reason that has been offered to explain increased litigation. New laws afford people increased rights and new causes of action. For example, the Consumer Credit Protection Act, Fair Credit Reporting Act, Consumer Product Safety Act, and many other recent legislative enactments have given consumers expanded substantive rights.

An increase in the availability of legal services has been another contributing factor to the expanding quantity of litigation. The federal government provides grants to private corporations that serve clients through legal assistance programs at nearly 700 offices throughout the United States. Nonprofit public interest law firms have been increasing in number. These firms concentrate on litigation involving such public policy concerns as environmental and consumer protection, land and energy use, health care, welfare benefits, and corporate responsibility. Through their efforts more and more people have become conscious of their legal rights, and hence have engaged in more litigation. Traditionally the cost of attorney fees was borne by each individual litigant, and this discouraged some potential litigants from instituting suits. However, statutory authorization of attorney fees to victorious plaintiffs has become common. The Fair Labor Standards Act, the Securities Act of 1933, and the Fair Debt Collection Practices Act are a few of the acts that extend this right to plaintiffs. This increases the incentive to litigate.

One possible solution to the impending litigation crisis is to expand the judiciary. However, there are obstacles to this solution. For example, the funds for additional judges may be unavailable.

Another possible solution is to expand the use of available dispute resolution procedure outside the court system. One such procedure is the use of neighborhood mediation centers through which local residents could handle their local disputes. Mediation, although assisting the parties in reconciling a dispute, has no power to force a solution.

Another possible means for relieving the pressure on the judicial system is compulsory and binding arbitration. An arbitrator acts like a judge, decides a dispute, and binds the parties to the judgment. Courts could delegate the resolution of cases to private arbitration panels. Arbitration has the benefit of being swifter and less costly than the use of courts. Rules of evidence are relaxed, and the proceedings are normally less formal than those employed by a judge. Arbitrators can be selected on the basis of their particular areas of expertise. An alternative procedure is to require arbitration in certain cases (for example, cases involving a controversy of less than $50,000) as a prerequisite to invoking the judiciary; any dissatisfied party could proceed to the proper court. At present, voluntary arbitration is available through the American Arbitration Association and other private arbitration associations. The use of this service could be increased by making its availability better known.

Some have suggested that administrative tribunals be established to curb the rising tide of cases. These tribunals would hear cases that involve repetitious factual issues arising out of specialized legislation. The tribunals could maintain flexibility by conducting hearings informally and without counsel when feasible. Appeals from the tribunals' decisions could be processed by the appellate courts in the same manner that they now process appeals from administrative agency decisions. The tribunals would gain expertise in handling complex factual issues that recur in cases dealing with, for example, energy, safety, and health. This would free courts of their overload.

Some have advocated eliminating the diversity jurisdiction of the federal courts. This measure could eliminate up to 50 percent of a given district court's case load. Although the measure would result in an increased case load for the state courts, its impact would be spread over many state courts, so that the diversion would hardly be noticeable.

Perhaps the resolution of the growing litigation crisis lies not in any one of the above methods but in a combination thereof.

Review problems

1. Trans-Bay Engineers and Builders, Inc., a California corporation, is engaged in construction and general contracting work in the San Francisco Bay area. In 1971 Trans-Bay entered into an agreement to build a 231-unit housing project in Oakland, California, for low- and moderate-income families. The construction contract was made with a nonprofit, community-based California corporation, More Oakland Residential Housing, Inc. (MORH).

MORH, the owner of the project, also entered into a mortgage and building loan agreement in the amount of $6 million with Advance Mortgage Corporation, a Delaware corporation whose principal place of business is in Michigan. In addition, the secretary of HUD, a Washington, D.C., citizen, agreed that HUD would insure the mortgage between Advance and MORH. Trans-Bay completed the construction work on time and applied to HUD for release of $467, 301 retained during periodic construction advances pursuant to the contract. Shortly after Trans-Bay's request for payment, Advance assigned the outstanding mortgage between Advance and MORH to HUD because of the default of MORH. Due to financial complications Trans-Bay has not been paid. In an attempt to obtain the funds due it under the contract, Trans-Bay has brought suit against HUD and Advance for breach of contract. Trans-Bay would like to have its case heard by a federal district court judge. Can Trans-Bay bring its action in the federal district court? Under what theory? Explain.

2. Ohio and Michigan are involved in a dispute over the ownership of a portion of Lake Erie. The resolution of the dispute involves complex factual issues that require inquiry into thousands of pages of historical documents, treaties, and laws. It is projected that a trial would involve months of exhaustive presentation of a plethora of witnesses and mounds of exhibits. Ohio institutes suit in the U.S. Supreme Court. Does the Court have the discretion to deny jurisdiction? Why or why not? What are the policy arguments in favor of your answer.

3. Harry and Kay Robinson purchased a new Audi in New York. The Robinsons, who were residents of New York, thereafter left the state, in their Audi, for a new home in Arizona. While they were passing through the state of Oklahoma, their Audi was rear-ended by another automobile. Mrs. Robinson and her two children were severely burned in the accident. The Robinsons brought suit against the Audi manufacturer (Audi), its importer (Volkswagen), its regional distributor (Worldwide), and its dealer (Seaway), claiming that the injuries resulted from a defective design and placement of Audi's gas tank. Audi is a foreign corporation. Volkswagen, Worldwide, and Seaway are incorporated and have their principal place of business in New York. None of the defendants do business in Oklahoma, ship or sell any products to that state, or advertise in any media calculated to reach Oklahoma. What is the outcome of the suit and why?

4. A prison inmate had been living with a paramour before he was incarcerated. He intended to return to her after his release. He was married with four children and had not provided any support for his wife or children during his incarceration (two years). Before he was killed, as a result of an accident while working as a day laborer for the prison, he sent a letter to his wife expressing his love and concern for his family. He was due to be paroled after serving one more year. The wife (claimant) filed a death benefit workers' compensation claim for herself and the children. The workers' compensation statute awards benefits to "dependents" of a decedent who is injured or dies due to a job-related accident. After the claimant's case-in-chief the defendant (prison) made a motion for directed verdict. What should be the result? Explain.

5. Professor Ephraim Cross is employed by New York University to teach French, Spanish, and Romance linguistics. In June 1954 he and his wife sailed from New York for France via Portugal, Morocco, Algeria, and Italy. Upon arriving in Marseilles, they split up. Mrs. Cross continued to tour, and Mr. Cross, though not pursuing a formal course of study, visited schools, courts of law, churches, book publishers, and restaurants; read magazines; listened to radio broadcasts; conversed with students and teachers; and attended political meetings. Cross and his wife returned to New York in September, in time for Cross to resume his teaching schedule at NYU. In 1955 Cross filed his income tax return and deducted the full cost of the trip he and his wife took to Europe. Cross contended that the deduction was pursuant to the Internal Revenue Code provision which allows deductions for all expenses incurred in carrying on a trade or business. The IRS objected to the deduction and brought suit against Cross, demanding payment of the amount he withheld. Cross presented affidavits of other professors which indicated the desirability and necessity of foreign travel for a professor of foreign languages. He then motioned for a summary judgment. Cross contended that the summary judgment was appropriate under the circumstances.

Do you agree? What is the criterion for granting a summary judgment? What if Cross listed separately the expenses incurred by his wife and himself and sought to deduct only his own expenses? Would additional information still be required?

6. Al Ladin, attorney for Spray Lawn, Inc., suspected that two of Spray Lawn's lower echelon employees were diverting the corporation's funds to their own use. Ladin confronted the employees with his suspicions, and they both confessed. At Ladin's insistence the employees wrote a detailed account of their activities involving the diversion of company funds. Their employment was then terminated. Subsequently the IRS conducted an audit of Spray Lawn, Inc., and issued a summons for the written statements in Ladin's possession. Must Ladin produce the summons? Explain. Could the IRS derive the desired information in any other way?

7. American Cyanamid Company is suing Hercules Powder Company for infringement of its Daniel Patent No. 2,595,935. American alleges that Hercules' sales of resin products under its Keim patents infringe the Daniel patent. Each party is attempting to obtain documents from the other; however, each is also resisting the discovery of the other by invoking the attorney-client privilege. Hercules asserts that communications from Peverill, a lawyer in its employ, are protected by the privilege. The documents in question were prepared by Peverill; however, they do not pertain to legal matters, but contain information regarding prior patents and the manufacture of certain resins. American contends that letters received by it

from Hoxie and Kelton, two New York lawyers working as outside counsel for American, are protected from disclosure by the attorney-client privilege. The letters, prepared for American prior to the sale of its Keim patent resins, concern an analysis of whether the employment of these resins in producing paper infringes the claims of the Daniel patent.

Are the communications between American and its lawyers and between Hercules and its lawyer protected by the attorney-client privilege? Explain.

8. In 1971 McDonald's Corporation, which then operated two restaurants in San Francisco, applied for licenses for the operation of three more restaurants in the city. The permits were granted by the San Francisco Department of Public Works; however, they were subsequently revoked by the San Francisco Board of Permit Appeals. According to McDonald's, the revocation resulted from the efforts of an association of two groups of restaurant and hotel employees and a labor union which acted in concert to advance their own interests at the expense of McDonald's. Individual members of the association had appeared before the Board of Permit Appeals and opposed each and every permit granted to McDonald's by the Department of Public Works. In its campaign to defeat the issuance of the permits to McDonald's, the association threatened to withdraw its political support from board members and other city officials who supported the McDonald's applications. McDonald's complained that the actions were intended to, and in fact did, injure and suppress McDonald's competitiveness in the San Francisco market. Because of the injurious effects of the association's activities, McDonald's has brought suit against it to prevent similar activity by the association in the future and to collect damages for the association's past activities.

Did the association engage in illegal activities? Explain.

9. Trucking Unlimited (plaintiff) sued California Motor Transport Company and others (defendants), alleging that defendants, competing trucking companies, conspired to restrain trade in violation of the Sherman Act. Plaintiff alleged that as part of the conspiracy, defendants instituted proceedings before courts and administrative agencies to defeat plaintiff's applications for route operating rights. The proceedings were allegedly instituted regardless of defendants' belief in their merits, for the sole purpose of running plaintiff out of business. Do you think the complaint states a cause of action? Explain.

10. What are the short- and long-term consequences of an overtaxed judiciary? Analyze each of the proposed solutions to the problem contained in the "Policy Considerations" section, and rank each solution on a 10-point scale in terms of effectiveness. Can you develop any other solution?

CHAPTER 3

Administrative procedures

As recently as the mid-1950s the areas of major governmental regulatory responsibility were limited to communications, antitrust, transportation, and financial institutions. By 1976 the federal bureaucracy had mushroomed to encompass 77 regulatory agencies. The *Federal Register*, daily federal government publication containing agency announcements, regulations, and orders, has in recent years exceeded 75,000 pages annually. The federal courts process upward of 200,000 cases annually. By comparison, some agencies, such as the IRS and the Social Security Administration, process claims numbering in the millions.

The rise of the administrative agency may be linked to increased congressional regulatory activities. In a complex technological society it is inefficient, and perhaps impossible, for Congress to immerse itself in the intricacies of each regulated activity. Congress has neither the time nor the expertise to do so. It therefore sets general goals and policies and delegates the task of applying them to administrative agencies composed of experts in the regulated areas.

An administrative agency is a governmental body other than a court or legislature which takes action that affects the rights of private parties. Agencies may be called boards, commissions, agencies, administrative departments, or divisions. They may consist of single individuals, or they may be large bureaucratic structures employing hundreds of persons. Administrative agencies have specialized functions in implementing government policy in specifically defined fields. Much of the maze of government regulations with which business must contend emanates from administrative agencies. This chapter will focus on the structure, creation, and general procedures of administrative agencies.

AGENCY STRUCTURE AND POWERS

Administrative agencies exist at all levels of government. State and local governments have agencies which perform strictly local functions, such as zoning boards and liquor control commissions. Other agencies on the state and local levels, such as state environmental protection agencies, are counterparts to federal agencies. This chapter, however, will concentrate primarily on federal administrative agencies.

Many administrative agencies exist within the Executive Office of the President or within the executive departments which are comprised by the president's Cabinet. Congress has given the president general authority to delegate to subordinate officials functions vested in him by law. Cabinet officials receive authority delegated to them by the president or by statutes which Congress enacts. These Cabinet officials frequently redelegate such functions to agencies under their command. Other agencies under their command are established by Congress to administer particular statutes.

The independent regulatory agencies

Much of the administrative regulation with which businesses must deal emanates from the independent regulatory agencies. The first administrative agency was created by Congress on July 31, 1789, but it was not until 1887 that the Interstate Commerce Commission was established as the first independent regulatory agency. This was done because Congress was reluctant to vest the regulatory authority in President Benjamin Harrison, who had formerly been a railroad lawyer. The ICC has served as a model for the numerous other independent regulatory agencies which have followed.

The independent agency is usually headed by a board or commission whose members are appointed for a term of years by the president with the advice and consent of the Senate. During their tenure these commissioners or board members may be removed only for statutorily defined cause. No more than a bare majority of a commission or board may come from the same political party.

Agency structure and organization

An agency's structure and organization vary with its functions and powers. Because all agencies have specialized functions, they develop bureaucratic hierarchies to implement and monitor regulations within their jurisdictions. Set forth in Figure 3–1, to provide a flavor of this bureaucracy, is the organizational structure of the Federal Trade Commission. The FTC was selected because it regulates many of the substantive areas covered in later chapters of this book. These include antitrust, advertising, consumer credit, and product safety.

Agency functions and powers

The functions and powers of agencies are as varied as the agencies themselves. Many agencies are authorized to promulgate regulations which have the force and effect of law. This process is known as rulemaking. Agencies may also conduct administrative proceedings, known as adjudications, to

Figure 3–1: The Federal Trade Commission

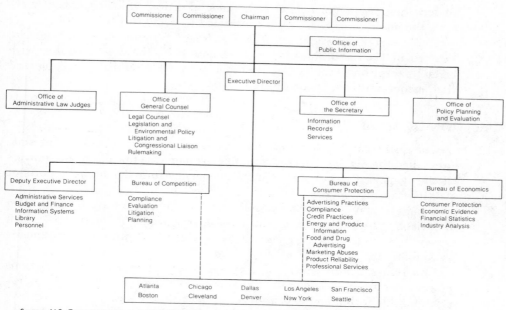

Source: *U.S. Government Manual, 1979–80* (Washington, D.C.: U.S. Government Printing Office, 1979), p. 556

determine whether a particular individual or corporation has violated a statute or regulation. Some agencies also administer licensing systems. For example, radio and television broadcasters must obtain licenses from the Federal Communications Commission.

Most administrative activities are informal. Agencies administer grants-in-aid and other assistance programs. They undertake investigations, gather and analyze data, issue reports, and provide advice to governments and private parties. The ability to give informal advice is one of the strongest powers an agency has. For example, if an inspector from the Occupational Safety and Health Administration suggests that a particular condition at a plant is unsafe, the employer, fearing a citation and fine, will be very reluctant to ignore the suggestion. Similarly, broadcasters hesitate to ignore informal suggestions from the FCC because they fear that their actions may harm them when their licenses must be renewed. All agencies are subject to the following statutes, which will be considered in greater detail later in the chapter but are summarized here for introductory purposes.

The Administrative Procedure Act (APA). Enacted in 1946, the APA was a congressional response to criticism of the vast discretion and power afforded numerous agencies. The act specifies the procedural formalities with which agencies must comply and establishes standards and prerequisites for judicial review of agency action.

The National Environmental Policy Act (NEPA). Enacted in 1970, NEPA requires all agencies to formulate environmental impact statements before undertaking any major federal governmental action which significantly affects the environment. NEPA is considered in detail in Chapter 18.

The Freedom of Information Act (FOIA) and the Government in the Sunshine Act. Enacted in 1966 and amended in 1974 and 1976, these acts require, with certain exceptions, that agency documents be made publicly available and that agency proceedings be open.

CREATION OF AN AGENCY

Congress creates an administrative agency by passing a statute. The statute, called the *enabling legislation,* specifies the name, composition, and powers of the agency. It frequently requires the agency to make annual reports of its activities to Congress.

Congress may, at any time, overturn an agency's ruling by amending the enabling legislation. Each house has agency oversight committees which review the work of the agencies, hold hearings, and propose amendments to enabling legislation.

Congress can also control agency activities through its appropriations powers. For example, Congress has at times considered riders to FTC appropriation bills forbidding expenditures on particular cases.

Two other methods of congressional oversight have received increased use in recent years. Sunset legislation provides that an agency's authority shall expire on a given date unless Congress extends it. The legislative veto provides that an agency's regulations shall not take effect for a specified period of time following promulgation, usually 60 or 90 days. During that time Congress may pass a resolution of disapproval vetoing the regulation or a resolution of reconsideration returning the regulation to the agency, which may repromulgate, modify, or withdraw it. Some legislative veto provisions require the resolution to be passed by both houses of Congress, while others allow either house to act unilaterally.

Legislative vetoes differ from amendments to the enabling legislation because they need not be presented to the president for signature and because in some cases they need be approved by only one house. These differences have resulted in a heated debate over the constitutionality of the legislative veto. Opponents contend that Congress may only act through legislation, that is, by passing a bill in both houses and presenting it to the president. Defenders counter that the legislative veto is authorized by the Necessary and Proper Clause because it enables Congress to control the agencies it creates pursuant to its other enumerated powers.

Constitutional status of administrative agencies

Administrative agencies have been referred to as "the fourth branch of government." This is because agencies frequently engage in activities typical of the other three branches. When an agency investigates, administers, or prosecutes, it acts like an executive. When it promulgates regulations, it acts like a legislature. When it engages in adjudication, it resembles a court.

The Constitution separates the executive, legislative, and judicial functions among three equal branches of government. The delegation of judicial and legislative functions to administrative agencies has been challenged as violating this separation of powers. At one time this challenge posed a significant problem for Congress. Congress could not delegate legislative authority to administrative agencies in such a broad manner as to indicate that it was abdicating its policymaking function.

In theory, Congress states in general terms what activity is prohibited or in what manner a class of activities is to be regulated. It is the agency's function to determine whether particular situations are specific instances of the general activity Congress sought to regulate or prohibit. Although such fact-finding may be the product of quasi-legislative rulemaking or quasi-judicial adjudication, it does not transgress the Constitution's separation of powers if the delegation enables the courts, the public, and Congress to determine whether the agency has exceeded its authority.

At one time Congress was required to provide very specific standards and guidelines for the exercise of agency discretion. For example, the Emergency Price Control Act of 1942 was upheld against constitutional attack, even though it delegated to the Office of Price Administration the power to set maximum rents and commodity prices. The act directed that prices be based on those prevailing at a specific date and enumerated the factors which the agency could consider in deviating from those levels.[1]

Some states still require their legislatures to provide rigid guidelines for the exercise of administrative discretion. Federal courts and most states, however, have stretched the requirement of standards and guidelines to sustain very broad delegations of power, such as those by which the Federal Trade Commission can prohibit "unfair methods of competition" and the Federal Communications Commission licenses radio broadcasters to operate in the "public interest, convenience and necessity."

The current approach views delegation as requiring Congress to express an "intelligible principle" to which an agency must adhere. Thus, whereas the 1942 Emergency Price Control Act specified base dates and a detailed list of factors to justify deviating from them, the Economic Stabilization Act of 1970 simply delegated to the president the power to "issue such orders and regulations as he may deem appropriate to stabilize prices, rents, wages and salaries at levels not less than those prevailing on May 25, 1970." It also authorized the president to redelegate the task to any subordinate officer or agency that he might deem appropriate. The courts had little trouble in sustaining the statute's constitutionality.[2]

---

[1] *Yakus* v. *United States*, 321 U.S. 414 (1944).

[2] *Amalgamated Meat Cutters* v. *Connolly*, 337 F. Supp. 737 (D.D.C. 1971).

JUDICIAL REVIEW OF AGENCY ACTION

Administrative agencies possess no inherent power, but derive their authority exclusively from their enabling legislation. They are, in effect, agents of Congress, implementing congressional policies in specific situations. Their procedures must facilitate an accurate and evenhanded application of those policies. The procedures must also facilitate oversight which insures that the agencies not exceed the scope of the congressional delegation.

Although oversight of administrative agencies occurs in Congress and among the general public, the primary task of insuring agency compliance with congressional dictates has fallen on the courts. The availability and timing of judicial review will be explored later in the chapter. When a case is properly brought, a court may overturn an agency's action for any of the following reasons:

1. The agency failed to comply with the procedures detailed in its enabling legislation, the APA, or NEPA.

2. The agency's action conflicts with its enabling legislation and therefore exceeds the scope of its authority. To determine whether the agency acted within the scope of its authority, the court must interpret the enabling legislation to ascertain the intent of Congress. The traditional tools of statutory construction detailed in Chapter 1 are employed.

3. The agency's decision is premised on an erroneous interpretation of the law. Courts are never bound by agency legal interpretations, though they may find such interpretations persuasive.

4. The agency's action conflicts with the Constitution. For example, a regulation prohibiting a certain type of advertising may violate the First Amendment's guarantee of free speech, or an inspection by an administrator who lacks a search warrant may violate the Fourth Amendment's protection from unreasonable searches and seizures. The Constitution's limitations on government regulation of business are explored in Chapter 4.

5. The agency erred in the substance of its action. The APA contains several standards which courts may apply in reviewing the substance of an agency's action. These standards vary in strictness and in the degree of discretion they afford the agency.

The strictest standard employed by a court is de novo review. The court is not bound by the agency's findings of fact, but instead holds an entirely new hearing and makes independent findings. If an agency's enabling legislation subjects the agency's findings to de novo review, it may also provide that these findings are prima facie evidence of the agency's position. Courts engaging in de novo review may also find the agency's decision persuasive, particularly on matters within the agency's expertise.

Statutes frequently provide that agency findings of fact must be supported by substantial evidence on the record as a whole. In applying this standard, a reviewing court will not receive new evidence, but will canvass the record and weigh the evidence supporting an agency's finding against the evidence contradicting it. If the contradictory evidence substantially outweighs the supporting evidence, the finding will be set aside.

The standard affording agencies the widest degree of discretion provides that agency findings not be set aside unless they are arbitrary and capricious. In applying this standard, a court must determine whether the agency considered all relevant factors and whether it made a clear error in judgment.

One of the most difficult problems facing the judiciary has been the appropriate extent of its involvement in reviewing informal agency action. Courts do not wish to handcuff administrators with requirements of procedural formality which might impede their day-to-day operations. However, courts must be wary of allowing administrators unfettered discretion in determining how to exercise their power. Similarly, in reviewing an agency's action, courts must avoid substituting their judgment for that of the agency and at the same time must avoid abdicating the review function. The following case deals with these issues.

Citizens to Preserve Overton Park v. *Volpe*
401 U.S. 402 (1971)

In 1969 the Secretary of Transportation, John Volpe, approved a plan to extend Interstate 40 into Memphis, Tennessee. The six-lane, high-speed expressway was designed to bisect Overton Park, a 342-acre city park near the center of Memphis, so that the zoo would be severed from the remainder of the park, which contained a golf course, an outdoor theater, and nature trails. Petitioners, a coalition of environmentalist groups, sued to enjoin the Department of Transportation (DOT) from financing the completion of Interstate 40. They contended that approval of the route violated the Federal-Aid Highway Act, DOT's enabling legislation, which prohibited the use of federal funds for highway construction through a public park if a "feasible and prudent alternative" existed. Where there was no such alternative, funding was permissible only after "all possible planning to minimize harm" to the park. Based on affidavits of DOT personnel, the district court granted defendant's motion for summary judgment. The court of appeals affirmed. The U.S. Supreme Court reversed.

Mr. Justice Marshall: In April 1968, the Secretary [of Transportation] announced that he concurred in the judgment of local officials that I-40 should be built through the park. And in September 1969 the State acquired the right-of-way inside Overton Park from the city. Final approval for the project—the route as well as the design—was not announced until November 1969. . . . Neither announcement approving the route and design of I-40 was accompanied by a statement of the Secretary's factual findings. He did not indicate why he believed there were no feasible and prudent alternative routes or why design changes could not be made to reduce the harm to the park.

Petitioners contend that the Secretary's action is invalid without such formal findings and that the Secretary did not make an independent determination but merely relied on the judgment of the Memphis City Council. . . .

The District Court and the Court of Appeals found that formal findings by the Secretary were not necessary and refused to order the deposition of the former Federal Highway Administrator because those courts believed that probing of the mental processes of an administrative decision-maker was prohibited.

. . . We agree that formal findings were not required. But we do not believe that in this case judicial review based solely on litigation affidavits was adequate.

* * * * *

In all cases agency action must be set aside if the action was "arbitrary, capricious, an abuse of discretion, or otherwise not in accordance with law" or if the action failed to meet statutory, procedural, or constitutional requirements. In certain narrow, specifically limited situations, the agency action is to be set aside if the action was not supported by "substantial evidence." And in other equally narrow circumstances the reviewing court is to engage in a de novo review of the action and set it aside if it was "unwarranted by the facts."

Petitioners argue that the Secretary's approval of the construction of I-40 through Overton Park is subject to one or the other of these latter two standards of limited applicability. . . . Neither of these standards is, however, applicable.

Review under the substantial-evidence test is authorized only when the agency action is taken pursuant to a rulemaking provision of the Administrative Procedure Act itself, or when the agency action is based on a public adjudicatory hearing. The Secretary's decision to allow the expenditure of federal funds to build I-40 through Overton Park was plainly not an exercise of a rulemaking function. And the only hearing that is required by either the Administrative Procedure Act or the statutes regulating the distribution of federal funds for highway construction is a public hearing conducted by local officials for the purpose of informing the community about the proposed project and eliciting community views on the design and route. The hearing is nonadjudicatory, quasi-legislative in nature. It is not designed to produce a record that is to be the basis of agency action—the basic requirement for substantial-evidence review.

Petitioners' alternative argument also fails.

De novo review of whether the Secretary's decision was "unwarranted by the facts" is authorized in only two circumstances. First, such *de novo* review is authorized when the action is adjudicatory in nature and the agency factfinding procedures are inadequate. And, there may be independent judicial factfinding when issues that were not before the agency are raised in a proceeding to enforce nonadjudicatory agency action. Neither situation exists here.

Even though there is no *de novo* review in this case and the Secretary's approval of the route of I-40 does not have ultimately to meet the substantial-evidence test, the generally applicable standards require the reviewing court to engage in a substantial inquiry. Certainly, the Secretary's decision is entitled to a presumption of regularity. But that presumption is not to shield his action from a thorough, probing, in-depth review.

The court is first required to decide whether the Secretary acted within the scope of his authority. This determination naturally begins with a delineation of the scope of the Secretary's authority and discretion. As has been shown, Congress has specified only a small range of choices that the Secretary can make. Also involved in this initial inquiry is a determination of whether on the facts the Secretary's decision can reasonably be said to be within that range. The reviewing court must consider whether the Secretary properly construed his authority to approve the use of parkland as limited to situations where there are no feasible alternative routes or where feasible alternative routes involve uniquely difficult problems. And the reviewing court must be able to find that the Secretary could have reasonably believed that in this case there are no feasible alternatives or that alternatives do involve unique problems.

Scrutiny of the facts does not end, however, with the determination that the Secretary has acted within the scope of his statutory authority. Section 706(2) (a) requires a finding that the actual choice made was not "arbitrary, capricious, an abuse of discretion, or otherwise not in accordance with law." To make this finding the court must consider whether the decision was based on a consideration of the relevant factors and whether there has been a clear error of judgment. Although this inquiry into the facts is to be searching and careful, the ultimate standard of review is a narrow one. The court is not empowered to substitute its judgment for that of the agency.

The final inquiry is whether the Secretary's action followed the necessary procedural requirements. Here the only procedural error alleged is the failure of the Secretary to make formal findings and state his reason for allowing the highway to be built through the park.

Undoubtedly, review of the Secretary's action is hampered by his failure to make such findings, but the absence of formal findings does not necessarily require that the case be remanded to the Secretary. Neither the Department of Transportation Act nor the Federal-Aid Highway Act requires such formal findings. Moreover, the Administrative Procedure Act requirements that there be formal findings in certain rulemaking and adjudicatory proceedings do not apply to the Secretary's action here. And, although formal findings may be required in some cases in the absence of statutory directives when the nature of the agency action is ambiguous, those situations are rare. Plainly, there is no ambiguity here; the Secretary has approved the construction of I-40 through Overton Park and has approved a specific design for the project.

* * * * *

. . . Moreover, there is an administrative record that allows the full, prompt review of the Secretary's action that is sought without additional delay which would result from having a remand to the Secretary.

That administrative record is not, however, before us. The lower courts based their review on the litigation affidavits that were presented.

These affidavits were merely "post hoc" rationalizations, which have traditionally been found to be an inadequate basis for review.

* * * * *

Thus it is necessary to remand this case to the District Court for plenary review of the Secretary's decision. That review is to be based on the full administrative record that was before the Secretary at the time he made his decision. But since the bare record may not disclose the factors that were considered or the Secretary's construction of the evidence, it may be necessary for the District Court to require some explanation in order to determine if the Secretary acted within the scope of his authority and if the Secretary's action was justifiable under the applicable standard.

The court may require the administrative officials who participated in the decision to give testimony explaining their action. Of course, such inquiry into the mental processes of administrative decision-makers is usually to be avoided. And where there are administrative findings that were made at the same time as the decision, . . . there must be a strong showing of bad faith or improper behavior before such inquiry may be made. But here there are no such formal findings and it may be that the only way there can be effective judicial review is by examining the decision-makers themselves.

The District Court is not, however, required to make such an inquiry. It may be that the Secretary can prepare formal findings . . . that will provide an adequate explanation for his action. Such an explanation will, to some extent, be a "post hoc rationalization" and thus must be viewed critically. If the District Court decides that additional explanation is necessary, that court should consider which method will prove the most expeditious so that full review may be had as soon as possible.

Case questions

1. Under what circumstances will a court review an agency's findings de novo? When will it use the substantial evidence test? When will it use the arbitrary and capricious test?

2. How did the Court define the phrase "arbitrary and capricious"?

3. If an agency is not required to keep a formal record for informal decisions, how can a court review the agency's proffered justifications?

ADJUDICATION

The APA defines adjudication as any process, including licensing, which results in an order. An *order* is defined as a final disposition other than a regulation. From this cryptic definition, adjudication has developed as a primary means of enforcing agency statutes and regulations. The agency prosecutes an alleged violator and affords the violator a trial before it. Having the same agency serve as prosecutor and judge presents obvious problems. The APA attempts to deal with these problems by requiring agencies to separate their prosecutorial and judicial functions.

The separation of functions in the adjudication process

The adjudicatory hearing is presided over by an agency employee known as an administrative law judge (ALJ). The APA prohibits ALJs from consulting ex parte any person or party involved in the proceeding. It also requires that ALJs not be responsible to or subject to the supervision or direction of any persons in the prosecutorial or investigative divisions of the agency.

The APA thus attempts to split the agency into somewhat autonomous judging and prosecutorial divisions. For example, the chart on Figure 3–1 shows that the FTC's administrative law judges are structurally separate from the enforcement sections of the Bureaus of Competition and Consumer

Protection. Agency prosecutorial and investigative powers are frequently formidable. Agencies often can subpoena business records and require companies being investigated to present evidence of their compliance with the law. Generally, however, agency subpoenas are not self-enforcing. If an individual refuses to comply with a subpoena, the agency must ask a court to order compliance. Following such an order, an individual who persists in noncompliance may be prosecuted for contempt of court.

A typical adjudication

The National Labor Relations Board is fairly typical of an agency with adjudicatory enforcement powers. For example, the XYZ Widget Corporation employed Harold Worker as a stock clerk. Harold had been very active in attempting to unionize the employees of XYZ. He had also been late for work on a few occasions, and once he called in sick when he was actually not ill. He was fired from his job. Section 8(a)(1) of the National Labor Relations Act prohibits employer restraint, interference, or coercion with regard to employees exercising their rights to organize and bargain collectively. It was Harold's belief that he had been fired because of his union activities and, he believed that, therefore, his firing had violated section 8(a)(1).

The prosecutorial division of the NLRB is headed by the general counsel, who is appointed by the president. The general counsel has final authority over all prosecutions. Under his supervision are the regional directors and their staffs.

The board itself consists of five persons who serve staggered five-year terms after appointment by the president and confirmation by the Senate. The board appoints administrative law judges. They may be removed only after a hearing by the Civil Service Commission at which good cause for removal must be established.

If Harold wishes to prosecute the XYZ Widget Corporation, he must file a charge with the regional director, whose staff will investigate the complaint. If the regional director finds reasonable cause to believe a violation has occurred, he will so advise XYZ and will try to settle the matter informally. Such settlements are entered in the form of "consent decrees" or "consent orders." Frequently they provide that the respondent denies the alleged violation but agrees to take the action demanded by the agency. If a settlement is unattainable, the regional director must file a complaint with the board.

The complaint is served on XYZ, which may file an answer admitting or denying the allegations. The case is assigned to an ALJ. Then there are prehearing proceedings. These are similar to pretrial court proceedings, but less formal and with less extensive discovery.

The matter comes to trial before the ALJ. The trial is less formal than a court trial. For example, the rules of evidence are relaxed. Hearsay and other types of evidence frequently not admissible in court are admissible before the ALJ.

The parties may present both written and oral arguments to the ALJ, who then examines the hearing transcript and prepares a decision which includes findings of fact, conclusions of law, and a recommended order. The losing party may appeal to the full board.

Enforcement and judicial review

Orders of the NLRB and some other agencies are not self-enforcing. A party may violate them without penalty. If a party refuses to comply voluntarily, the agency must seek an order enforcing its decision from the appropriate court. Usually the party refusing to comply will cross-petition the court to overturn the agency's decision. If the court enforces the order, continued refusal to comply can result in punishment for contempt.

The orders of most agencies are self-enforcing. Violations of these orders are punishable in contempt proceedings. A party seeking to appeal such an order to the courts must either comply with the order or obtain a stay pending appeal from either the agency or the reviewing court.

A few agency adjudications are reviewable in the U.S. district courts. The most significant are orders of the Social Security Administration denying claims for disability benefits. Most agency orders, however, are reviewable in the circuit courts of appeal.

The orders of a few agencies may be reviewed in only one circuit. For example, orders of the FCC may be reviewed only in the D.C. Circuit. Most agency orders, however, may be reviewed in that circuit or any other circuit in which the responding party resides or conducts business. Thus, all respondents except those found only in the District of Columbia, have a choice of at least two circuits. Firms doing business nationwide may choose any circuit court they wish. Parties, therefore, tend to shop around for the circuit court they think will be most favorable to them.

Although the agency enforcement division operates autonomously from the ALJs and the board members, the same agency is prosecutor and judge. Therefore, it may appear to be something less than impartial. For this reason, and because the agency rules of evidence and procedure are less formal than the court rules, courts use the substantial evidence test in reviewing adjudication.

In applying this test, the court will defer to the agency on matters peculiarly within its expertise. If the ALJ and the board disagree, the court considers the disparity in their findings in assessing the evidence. The court is particularly suspicious of board reversals of ALJ findings where the key issue is the credibility of the witnesses. This is because the ALJ is in an excellent position to observe and compare the demeanors of the witnesses.

Assume, for example, that Harold Worker's complaint comes to trial before the ALJ. Assume further that both the ALJ and the board conclude that Harold was fired for his poor work habits rather than his union activities. If the record only established that he was active in the union, that he was frequently tardy and abused his sick leave, the board's findings would probably be affirmed. They would probably also be affirmed if the board had found that the employer's motivation for firing Harold was his union activity and ordered him reinstated.

If, however, the record also established that several other employees who opposed the union had worse attendance records and worse abuses of sick leave but were never disciplined, the reviewing court would probably reverse.

RULEMAKING

The APA defines a *rule* as "an agency statement of general or particular applicability and future effect designed to complement, interpret or prescribe law or policy." Rulemaking is the process of promulgating rules. In other words, rulemaking is the enactment of regulations that will be generally applicable in the future. All such regulations are compiled in the *Code of Federal Regulations.*

Interpretive and procedural rules

Interpretive and procedural rules are exempt from the procedural requirements of the APA. Procedural rules set forth the regulations governing practice before the agency.

Interpretive rules are statements containing agency interpretations of the statutes it administers. These rules are intended to advise the public of the agency's positions on particular issues. They are not legally binding on the agency, the courts, or the public. Nevertheless, when courts construe the underlying legislation, they frequently find such agency interpretations persuasive. This is because the agency is usually the body closest to the legislation and has developed a particular expertise in interpreting it. Agency interpretations are given considerable weight if, after they have been issued, Congress reenacts the statute without disapproving the interpretations. Congress is then presumed to have been aware of the interpretations and, by its silence, to have endorsed them.

Inconsistent interpretive rules are not persuasive. Inconsistencies may arise within an agency. They may also arise where two or more agencies are charged with administering the same or similar statutes. This situation occurred in administering the prohibitions against sex discrimination in employment contained in the 1964 Civil Right Act and the Equal Pay Act.

The Equal Employment Opportunity Commission's interpretive rules prohibited an employer that offered health insurance benefits from excluding coverage for hospitalization due to pregnancy. Similar Labor Department regulations did not prohibit such exclusion. When called upon to resolve the conflict, the Supreme Court found EEOC's position unpersuasive. This was due in part to EEOC inconsistency. Initially EEOC agreed with the Labor Department's interpretation, but it reversed its position several years later.[3]

Legislative rules

Legislative rules must be enacted in accordance with the APA. When such rules are consistent with the APA, NEPA, the enabling legislation, and the Constitution, they have the force and effect of law. As such, they are binding on the agency, the courts, and the public.

The APA sets forth two methods for rulemaking: informal and formal. Informal rulemaking is used by most agencies. Formal rulemaking is only used when an agency's enabling legislation requires that its rulemaking be conducted "on the record." Each method is considered in detail below.

Informal rulemaking. Informal, or "notice and comment," rulemaking is begun when an agency publishes a "Notice of Proposed Rulemaking" in the *Federal Register*. The notice must contain a statement of the time, place, and nature of the proceedings, the legal authority, usually a citation to the enabling legislation, under which the rule is proposed; and either the terms of the proposed regulation or a description of the subjects or issues involved. The notice provides interested members of the public sufficient information to enable them to participate in the proceedings. It need not parrot the language of the regulation eventually enacted. The agency need not even have any particular wording in mind. A simple, brief description of the subject matter is all that is uaually required.

An example of a notice of proposed rulemaking follows.

Federal Register
Vol. 43 p. 9488

NONDISCRIMINATION IN FINANCIAL ASSISTANCE PROGRAMS OF SMALL BUSINESS ADMINISTRATION-EFFECTUATION OF POLICIES OF FEDERAL GOVERNMENT AND SBA ADMINISTRATOR

Proposed inclusion of the Nondiscrimination Sanctions Contained in Section 504 of the Rehabilitation Act of 1973, as Amended, and the Addition of Federal Financial Assistance Programs Which Are Covered by This Part to Appendix A.

---

[3] *General Electric Co.* v. *Gilbert,* 429 U.S. 125 (1976).

AGENCY: Small Business Administration.

ACTION: Notice of proposed rulemaking.

SUMMARY: This proposed revision would put into effect the requirements of Section 504 of the Rehabilitation Act of 1973, as amended, by making it unlawful for any recipient or subrecipient of Federal financial assistance to discriminate against a qualified handicapped person, on the basis of handicap, in employment or the receipt of services. It also adds to the listing of the types of Federal financial assistance programs which are covered by this part.

DATE: Comments must be received on or before April 7, 1978.

ADDRESS: 1441 L Street N.W., Suite 1200, Vermont Building, Washington, D.C. 20416.

FOR FURTHER INFORMATION CONTACT:
J. ARNOLD FELDMAN, Chief, Compliance Division, Office of Equal Employment Opportunity and Compliance, 202–653–6054.

SUPPLEMENTARY INFORMATION: Copies of this proposal are available in braille and tape by contacting the above office.

Dated: February 17, 1978.
Patricia M. Cloherty,
Acting Administrator

The remainder of the notice contained the text of the proposed regulation. Following publication of the notice of proposed rulemaking, the agency provides a period of time during which interested parties may submit written comments. The agency may hold public hearings, but it is not required to do so.

Many agencies grant licenses allowing individuals to engage in particular activities. For example, the Federal Communications Commission licenses radio and television broadcasters, and the Nuclear Regulatory Commission licenses nuclear power plants. Agency regulations detail the requirements for obtaining a license, the activities in which the licensee may engage, and the restrictions placed on the license. Most of the statutes that provide for licensing also empower the agency to modify or revoke the licenses; such provisions require that the licensee be personally notified and afforded a hearing prior to revocation or modification. Courts have generally interpreted these provisions as being designed to protect individual licensees from punitive agency action aimed at particular individual licensees. Therefore, even if a proposed regulation would modify existing licenses, an agency need not hold a hearing on the regulation if it uses informal rulemaking.

Many interested parties may wish to participate in the rulemaking proceeding. For example, the SBA Notice of Proposed Rulemaking probably drew responses from small businesses, trade associations, organizations seeking improved conditions for the handicapped, employment agencies, and labor unions.

After the agency receives and considers the comments, it may publish the final version of the regulation in the *Federal Register* or discontinue proceedings. The agency must include a summary and discussion of the major comments received. However, it is not restricted to considering only the evidence produced in a formal manner. In addition to the comments received, it may consider information in its files, literature and general knowledge in the field, material prepared by other agencies, and its own expertise. Where the agency intends to rely upon outside documents, it should so indicate in the *Federal Register* and make them available for inspection by interested parties. The regulation may take effect no sooner than 30 days following its publication.

About one year after the SBA's Notice of Proposed Rulemaking was published, the final version of the regulation appeared in the *Federal Register*.

Federal Register
Vol. 44 p. 20067

SMALL BUSINESS ADMINISTRATION
13 CFR Part 113

NONDISCRIMINATION IN FINANCIAL ASSISTANCE PROGRAMS OF SMALL BUSINESS ADMINISTRATION—EFFECTUATION OF POLICIES OF FEDERAL GOVERNMENT AND SBA ADMINISTRATOR: INCLUSION OF NONDISCRIMINATION SANCTIONS CONTAINED IN SECTION 504 OF THE REHABILITATION ACT OF 1973, AS AMENDED, AND THE ADDITION OF A FEDERAL FINANCIAL ASSISTANCE PROGRAM WHICH IS COVERED BY THIS PART OF APPENDIX A

AGENCY: Small Business Administration

ACTION: Final Rule

SUMMARY: This revision will put into effect the requirements of Section 504 of the Rehabilitation act of 1973, as amended, making it unlawful for any recipient or subrecipient of Federal financial assistance administered by the Small Business Administration to discriminate against a qualifed handicapped person on the basis of handicap, in employment or the receipt of services.

It also adds to the listing of the types of Federal financial assistance programs which are covered by this part.

EFFECTIVE DATE: April 4, 1979.

FOR FURTHER INFORMATION CONTACT:
Mr. J. Arnold Feldman, Chief, Compliance Division, 1441 L Street, N.W., Suite 1200, Vermont Building, Washington, D.C. 20416, (202) 653–6054.

SUPPLEMENTAL INFORMATION: On March 8, 1978, the Small Business Administration published in the *Federal Register* notice of proposed changes in our Rules and Regulations, 13 CFR Part 113, regarding nondiscrimination against qualified handicapped persons on the basis of handicap, in employment or receipt of services.

This revision also listed another type of Federal assistance program which is covered by this part.

Interested parties were given 30 days to submit comments, suggestions, or objections regarding this revision. In response to requests from some groups interested in the problems of the handicapped, an additional 30 days was allowed for comment. Many comments were received from these groups. Most of the comments dealt with the nondiscrimination subsections of the regulation, 113.3, 113.3–1, and 113.3–3. Suggestions were made concerning the expansion and clarification of those subsections dealing with employment, accessibility, and usability of recipient businesses. Suggestions were also made concerning the clarification and interpretation of the concept of reasonable accommodation. In response to these suggestions, some sections of the nondiscrimination subsections have been changed to expand and clarify them.

Dated: March 17, 1979.

The text of the regulation followed. A comparison of the final regulation with the proposed rule would reveal several changes which were probably prompted by the comments received by the SBA. Among them are the following:

1. The final version of subsection 113.3 prohibits companies receiving SBA assistance from contracting with employment agencies, unions, or others in a manner that discriminates against the handicapped in recruitment, employment, promotion, tenure, layoff, termination, compensation, job assignments and classifications, leaves, fringe benefits, selection and support for training, and social and recreational activities. It sets standards for employment tests, preemployment physical examinations, and preemployment inquiries concerning physical handicaps.

2. Revised subsection 113.3–1 provides that recipients of SBA assistance must make reasonable accommodation to known handicaps of its employees unless this would impose an undue hardship on the operation of the business. It specifies the factors to be considered in evaluating the hardship.

3. Revised subsection 113.3–3 sets a timetable for making structural changes to accommodate handicapped employees and clients.

Regulations promulgated through informal rulemaking are subject to judicial review. The reviewing court will strictly scrutinize the rulemaking proceeding to insure that the agency has not violated the Constitution, its enabling legislation, or the procedural requirements of NEPA and the APA. The court will defer to the agency's expertise when reviewing the substance of the regulation. It will not substitute its judgment on the wisdom of a rule for the judgment of the agency. However, it will set aside a rule which it finds arbitrary or capricious. The following decision provides a good example of informal rulemaking and judicial control of the process.

Home Box Office, Inc. v. FCC
567 F.2d 9 (D.C. Cir. 1977)

The Federal Communications Commission (respondent) promulgated regulations prohibiting cable television stations from broadcasting feature films more than 3 but less than 10 years old, sports events shown on broadcast television during the past 5 years, more than a specified number of other sports events, and all series programs. Home Box Office, Inc. (petitioner), appealed the regulations to the D.C. Circuit Court of Appeals, which reversed.

The FCC contended that the regulations were necessary to prevent siphoning by cable television companies. Siphoning was said to occur when an event currently shown on free television was purchased by a cable operator. The FCC feared that this practice would delay the program's showing on free television or render the program unavailable to free television.

Per Curiam:

*   *   *   *   *

Standard of review

*   *   *   *   *

Because the statute does not otherwise indicate, this rulemaking is also informal rulemaking governed by Section 4 of the Administrative Procedure Act (APA).

*   *   *   *   *

It is axiomatic that we may not substitute our judgment for that of the agency. Yet our review must be "searching and careful," and we must ensure both that the Commission has adequately considered all relevant factors and that it has demonstrated a "rational connection between the facts found and the choice made."

*   *   *   *   *

Equally important, an agency must comply with the procedures set out in Section 4 of the APA. The APA sets out three procedural requirements: notice of the proposed rulemaking, an opportunity for interested persons to comment, and "a concise general statement of [the] basis and purpose " of the rules ultimately adopted. As interpreted by recent decisions of this court, these procedural requirements are intended to assist judicial review as well as to provide fair treatment for persons affected by a rule.

*   *   *   *   *

To this end there must be an exchange of views, information, and criticism between interested persons and the agency.

*   *   *   *   *

Consequently, the notice required by the APA, or information subsequently supplied to the public, must disclose in detail the thinking that has animated the form of a proposed rule and the data upon which that rule is based.

*   *   *   *   *

Moreover, a dialogue is a two-way street: the opportunity to comment is meaningless unless the agency responds to significant points raised by the public.

*   *   *   *   *

First, an agency proposing informal rulemaking has an obligation to make its views known to the public in a concrete and focused form so as to make criticism or formulation of alternatives possible. Second, the "concise and general" statement that must accompany the rules finally promulgated must be accommodated to the realities of judicial scrutiny, which do not contemplate that the court itself will, by a laborious examination of the record, formulate in the first instance the significant issues faced by the agency and articulate the rationale of their resolution. . . . [The record must] enable us to see what major issues of policy were ventilated by the informal proceedings and why the agency reacted to them as it did.

*   *   *   *   *

Applying the standard

The need for regulation. At the outset, we must consider whether the Commission has made out a case for undertaking rulemaking at all since a "regulation perfectly reasonable and appropriate in the face of a given problem may be highly capricious if that problem does not exist." . . . Here the Commission has framed the problem it is addressing as how cablecasting can best be regulated to provide a beneficial supplement to over-the-air broadcasting without at the same time undermining the continued operation of that "free" television service. . . . To state the problem this way, however, is to gloss over the fact that the Commission has in no way justified its position that cable television must be a supplement to, rather than an equal of, broadcast television. Such an artificial narrowing of the scope of the regulatory problem is itself arbitrary and capricious and is ground for reversal. . . . Moreover, by narrowing its discussion in this way the Commission has failed to crystallize what is in fact harmful about "siphoning." Sometimes the harm is characterized as selective bidding away of programming from conventional television. . . . and sometimes [perhaps] the financial collapse of conventional broadcasting. . . . As a result, informed criticism has been precluded and formulation of alternatives stymied.

Setting aside the question whether siphoning is harmful to the public interest, we must next ask whether the record shows that siphoning will occur. The Commission assures us that siphoning is "real, not imagined." . . . We find little comfort in this assurance, however, because the Commission has not directed our attention to any comments in a voluminous record which would support its statement. Moreover, whatever evidence the Commission thought it had was self-admittedly insufficient to give it a "clear picture as to the effects of subscription television upon conventional broadcasting."

* * * * *

The Commission did not consider whether conventional television broadcasters could pay more for feature film and sports material than at present without pushing their profits below a competitive return on investment and, consequently, it could not properly conclude that siphoning would occur because it could not know whether or how much broadcasters, faced with competition, would increase their expenditures by reducing alleged monopoly profits.

* * * * *

We have similar difficulties with the second cardinal assumption of the Commission, i.e., that "siphoning" would lead to loss of film and sports programming for audiences not served by cable systems or those too poor to subscribe to pay cable. . . . [T]o reach such a conclusion the Commission must assume that cable firms, once having purchased exhibition rights to a program, will not respond to market demand to sell the rights for viewing in those areas that cable firms do not reach. We find no discussion in the record supporting such an assumption. Indeed, a contrary assumption would be more consistent with economic theory since it would *prima facie* be to the advantage of cable operators to sell broadcast rights to conventional television stations in regions of the country where no cable service existed.

Case Questions

1. What is the function of the notice of proposed rulemaking? What must it contain?

2. Why did the court conclude that the regulation was arbitrary and capricious? Did the FCC fail to consider any relevant factors? Did it make a clear error in judgment?

3. Compare the review of the FCC's decision to that given the secretary of transportation's decision in *Overton Park.* Is one review more stringent than the other?

The principal advantage of informal rulemaking is its efficiency. The lack of required hearings minimizes the opportunities for delay. Such efficiency is obtained at a great cost: members of the public have only minimal opportunity to be heard on the desirability of the proposed regulations.

The opportunity to be heard is particularly important in legitimizing a regulation. Individuals who have been afforded that opportunity are less likely to view the regulation as being forced upon them and consequently are more likely to comply voluntarily. A much greater opportunity to be heard is afforded interested parties when an agency is required to use formal rulemaking.

Formal rulemaking. Like informal rulemaking, formal, or "on the record," rulemaking begins when the agency publishes a Notice of Proposed Rulemaking in the *Federal Register.* The notice must set a date, time, and place for public hearings. The agency must hold formal trial-type hearings where it must present all the evidence with which it intends to justify the proposed regulation. Interested parties have the right to examine the agency's exhibits and to cross-examine its witnesses. They may also introduce their own exhibits and call their own witnesses. These exhibits and witnesses are subject to examination and cross-examination by the agency and all other interested parties. The agency must then make formal findings justifying the regulation. The findings must be in writing and must be based on the evidence adduced at the hearings. The court of appeals for the appropriate circuit may review the findings and may set them aside if they are not supported by substantial evidence in the record as a whole.

The requirement of formal hearings enables parties that might be adversely affected by a proposed regulation to delay its implementation. Opportunities to do this exist at every stage of the rulemaking process. Such parties frequently flood the agency with issues they claim should be considered at the adjudicatory hearings. During prehearing conferences designed to simplify the issues and the trial, these parties can raise countless trivial procedural issues. Finally, they can drag the hearings out for years by cross-examining agency witnesses and by parading a seemingly endless supply of their own witnesses before the agency.

The most notorious example of such delays occurred when the FDA proposed a regulation requiring that peanut butter contain at least 90 percent peanuts. The peanut butter industry resisted the regulation, insisting that the appropriate amount was 87 percent. The rulemaking began in 1959 and did not end until 1968. The industry sought judicial review, and the Third Circuit Court of Appeals approved the regulation in 1970. The matter was finally laid to rest in late 1970, when the Supreme Court denied certiorari.

Congress has experimented with various procedures in a search for the proper balance between public input and efficient government. Most recently, it has created a hybrid of formal and informal methods. It has required this procedure in the enabling legislation of the Occupational Safety and Health Administration and the Federal Trade Commission.

Hybrid rulemaking. In hybrid rulemaking, the agency publishes a notice of proposed rulemaking and allows for a period of public comment. It must then hold public hearings. The type of hearings required depends on the type of issues considered.

If the issues concern general matters of public policy or general facts and characteristics (known as legislative facts), the agency need only hold hearings of a legislative type. These hearings allow participants to give oral testimony and present exhibits but do not provide for cross-examination or other formal trial procedures.

If the issues involve adjudicative facts—that is, if they entail inquiries to determine which specific actors did what, where, when, how, why, and with what motive and intent—the agency must hold trial-type hearings.

For example, suppose that the FTC were to propose a regulation requiring nursing homes to make certain disclosures in their advertisements, but exempting government-run establishments from the requirement. The issue of whether such a distinction is necessary, proper, or reasonable raises questions of general legislative policy and would not require an adjudicatory hearing. The issue of whether specific advertisements of particular public nursing homes were misleading, however, would require a trial-type hearing.

Findings of legislative fact are reviewed under the arbitrary and capricious test. Findings of adjudicative fact, however, are reviewed under the substantial evidence test.

The choice between rulemaking and adjudication

Adjudication enables an agency to make law and policy on a case-by-case basis in much the same way as a court. Adjudication gives an agency considerable flexibility in developing an area of regulation. Rulemaking, on the other hand, results in regulations of greater certainty and consistency and allows for broader public input.

An agency may use adjudication even where it wishes to announce new principles or to overturn prior decisions. The choice between rulemaking and adjudication is initially at the agency's discretion, and a court will overturn the agency's choice only where the agency has been arbitrary or capricious. A court is most likely to overturn the agency's choice where the agency has used adjudication to impose new liability on individuals for past actions undertaken in reliance on prior agency adjudications and pronouncements.

PUBLIC DISCLOSURE OF AGENCY INFORMATION

Concern over secretive agency operations has led Congress to enact two statutes that require public disclosure of agency activities. These are the Freedom of Information Act and the Government in the Sunshine Act.

The Freedom of Information Act (FOIA)

The FOIA requires all federal administrative agencies to make all agency documents publicly available upon request unless the documents qualify for one of nine specific exemptions. The act provides for indexing certain documents, sets time limits and uniform fees for handling requests for documents, and subjects any agency employee to disciplinary action for arbitrarily refusing such a request. Agency refusals to provide material are subject to de novo review in the U.S. district courts. A successful litigant may be entitled to recover attorney fees from the agency.

The specific exemptions of the FIOA are as follows:

1. Documents classified by the president in the interest of national security. The act, however, gives a federal district judge discretion to view such documents in camera and to order their disclosure if the president has abused his classifying authority.
2. Documents related to an agency's internal personnel practices. This exemption relieves agencies of the burden of maintaining for public inspection documents concerning such matters as parking privileges and lunch hours, in which the public has no reasonable interest.
3. Documents whose disclosure is prohibited by other statutes.
4. Documents containing "trade secrets or commercial and financial information obtained from a person and privileged or confidential." This exemption has been construed as applying where disclosing the information would injure the competitive position of the party who provided it.
5. Interagency and intraagency memoranda which contain advisory opinions or recommendations or otherwise reflect the deliberative process of policy formulation. If, however, the memorandum contains only factual information or can be redacted so that only factual information remains, it must be disclosed.
6. Personnel, medical, and similar files if the disclosure "would constitute a clearly unwarranted invasion of privacy." The invasion of privacy must be severe, and it must be incapable of being avoided by redacting the individual's name.
7. Law enforcement records where disclosure would interfere with enforcement proceedings, jeopardize an individual's right to a fair trial, reveal a confidential source, disclose confidential sources or investigative techniques, or endanger the lives of law enforcement personnel.
8. Documents regarding the operation of financial institutions.
9. Geological and geophysical maps and data.

The FOIA has been used by businesses to obtain sensitive information about competitors. Information of this type may often be found in agency files because of the numerous reports that companies are required to file. An FOIA request is directed to an agency. The act provides for judicial review of the agency's denial of the request but does not state whether the party which supplied the information may prevent the agency from disclosing it. This issue is considered in the following case.

Chrysler Corp. v. Brown
60 L.Ed.2d 273 (1980)

In order to be eligible for a federal government contract, Chrysler Corporation was required to furnish the Defense Logistics Agency (DLA) with reports on its affirmative action programs and on the general composition of its work force at several plants. Executive Orders 11246 and 11375 empowered the secretary of labor to request and evaluate such reports to insure that government contract holders were providing equal employment opportunity regardless of race or sex. When the DLA informed Chrysler that it was about to release this information to third parties who had requested it under the Freedom of Information Act, Chrysler objected and secured a temporary restraining order in federal district court. At trial, Chrysler argued that disclosure was barred by the Freedom of Information Act, inconsistent with the Trade Secrets Act (18 USC, section 1905), and an abuse of agency discretion. Although the district court held that both the FOIA and the Trade Secrets Act did bar release of some of the Chrysler material, the Third Circuit Court of Appeals reversed. The U.S. Supreme Court vacated this reversal.

Mr. Justice Rehnquist:

* * * * *

In contending that the FOIA bars disclosure of the requested equal employment opportunity information, Chrysler relies on the Act's nine exemptions and argues that they require an agency to withhold exempted material. In this case it relies specifically on Exemption 4:

(b) [FOIA] does not apply to matters that are . . . (4) trade secrets and commercial or financial information obtained from a person and privileged or confidential. . . .

Chrysler contends that the nine exemptions in general, and Exemption 4 in particular, reflect a sensitivity to the privacy interests of private individuals and nongovernmental entities. That contention may be conceded without inexorably requiring the conclusion that the exemptions impose affirmative duties on an agency to withhold information sought. In fact, that conclusion is not supported by the language, logic or history of the Act.

The organization of the Act is straightforward. Subsection (a) places a general obligation on the agency to make information available to the public and sets out specific modes of disclosure for certain classes of information. Subsection (b), which lists the exemptions, simply states that the specified material is not subject to the disclosure obligations set out in subsection (a). By its terms, subsection (b) demarcates the limits of the agency's obligation to disclose; it does not foreclose disclosure.

That the FOIA is exclusively a disclosure statute is, perhaps, demonstrated most convincingly by examining its provision for judicial relief. Subsection (a) (4) (B) gives federal district courts "jurisdiction to enjoin the agency from withholding agency records and to order the production of any agency records improperly withheld from the complainant." That provision does not give the authority to bar disclosure, and thus fortifies our belief that Chrysler, and courts which have shared its view, have incorrectly interpreted the exemption provisions to the FOIA. The Act is an attempt to meet the demand for open government while preserving workable confidentiality in governmental decisionmaking. Congress appreciated that with the expanding sphere of governmental regulation and enterprise, much of the information within Government files has been submitted by private entities seeking Government contracts or responding to unconditional reporting obligations imposed by law. There was sentiment that Government agencies should have the latitude, in certain circumstances, to afford the confidentiality desired by these submitters. But the congressional concern was with the agency's need or preference for confidentiality; the FOIA by itself protects the submitters' interest in confidentiality only to the extent that this interest is endorsed by the agency collecting the information.

* * * * *

Chrysler contends, however, that even if its suit for injunctive relief cannot be based on the FOIA, such an action can be premised on the Trade Secrets Act, 18 USC §1905. The Act provides:

> Whoever, being an officer or employee of the United States or of any department or agency thereof, publishes, divulges, discloses, or makes known in any manner or to any extent not authorized by law any information coming to him in the course of his employment or official duties or by reason of any examination or investigation made by, or return, report or record made to or filed with, such department or agency or officer or employee thereof, which information concerns or relates to the trade secrets, processes, operations, style of work, or apparatus, or to the identity, confidential statistical data, amount or source of any income, profits, losses, or expenditures of any person, firm, partnership, corporation, or association; or permits any income return or copy thereof or any book containing any abstract or particulars thereof to be seen or examined by any person except as provided by law; shall be fined not more than $1,000 or imprisoned not more than one year, or both; and shall be removed from office or employment.

* * * * *

We reject, however, Chrysler's contention that the Trade Secrets Act affords a private right of action to enjoin disclosure in violation of

that statute. This Court has rarely implied a private right of action under a criminal statute, and where it has done so "there was at least a statutory basis for inferring that a civil cause of action of some sort lay in favor of someone." Nothing in §1905 prompts such an inference. . . . [T]here is no indication of legislative intent to create a private right of action. Most importantly, a private right of action under §1905 is not "necessary to make effective the congressional purpose," for we find that review of DLA's decision to disclose Chrysler's employment data is available under the APA.

While Chrysler may not avail itself of any violations of the provisions of §1905 in a separate cause of action, any such violations may have a dispositive effect on the outcome of judicial review of agency action pursuant to §10 of the APA. Section 10(a) of the APA provides that "[a] person suffering legal wrong because of agency action, or adversely affected or aggrieved by agency action . . . , is entitled to judicial review thereof."

* * * * *

Both Chrysler and the Government agree that there is APA review of DLA's decision. They disagree on the proper scope of review. Chrysler argues that there should be *de novo* review, while the Government contends that such review is only available in extraordinary cases and this is not such a case.

* * * * *

We believe any disclosure that violates §1905 is "not in accordance with law." *De novo* review by the District Court is ordinarily not necessary to decide whether a contemplated disclosure runs afoul of §1905. The District Court is this case concluded that disclosure of some of Chrysler's documents was barred by §1905, but the Court of Appeals did not reach the issue. We shall therefore vacate the Court of Appeals' judgment and remand for further proceedings consistent with this opinion in order that the Court of Appeals may consider whether the contemplated disclosures would violate the prohibition of §1905. Since the decision regarding this substantive issue—the scope of §1905—will necessarily have some effect on the proper form of judicial review pursuant to §706(2), we think it unnecessary, and therefore unwise, at the present stage of this case for us to express any additional views on that issue.

Vacated and remanded.

Case questions

1. Was Chrysler able to obtain judicial review under the FOIA? the Trade Secrets Act? the APA? If review was not available under one or more of these statutes, are the statutes irrelevant to the outcome of the case? Explain.

2. What standard of review will a court apply to an agency's decision to release information? Explain.

3. How did Chrysler learn that the agency intended to release the information? Will all companies know beforehand that information about them is to be released?

4. The EEOC has charged that Willie's Widget Works refused to hire an applicant because she was female. Willie's claims that the applicant did not meet specified qualifications for the job. The EEOC subpoenas Willie's book of job descriptions. Willie's complains that the book is confidential and resists the subpoena. The parties settle, Willie's agreeing to turn over the book and the EEOC agreeing not to copy it, to keep it confidential, and to return it when it is no longer needed. Can Willie's competitors use the FOIA to obtain the book while it is in the EEOC's possession?

The Government in the Sunshine Act

Enacted in 1976, the Sunshine Act requires that all meetings of an agency headed by two or more persons appointed by the president and confirmed by the Senate be open to the public unless the agency, by majority vote, decides to close a meeting and the meeting qualifies for one of the following exemptions:

1. National security or foreign policy meeting.
2. Internal personnel rules.
3. Exempted by another statute.
4. Concerns trade secrets or confidential commercial information.
5. Would be a clearly unwarranted invasion of privacy.
6. Would disclose law enforcement records.
7. Concerns financial institutions.
8. Involves censoring an individual or accusing that individual of a crime.
9. Involves rulemaking or litigation.
10. Would frustrate contemplated action because of premature disclosure.

Agency decisions to close their meetings are also subject to de novo review in the U.S. District courts.

PREREQUISITES TO OBTAINING JUDICIAL REVIEW

Not all complaints about agency action receive judicial attention. To challenge agency action in court, a party seeking judicial review must take the initiative. Such a party must meet threshold requirements of standing, reviewability, and exhaustion of administrative remedies.

Standing

Article III of the Constitution limits the jurisdiction of the federal courts to actual "cases and controversies." Thus a federal court has no power to act except when this is necessary to resolve a dispute. It may not render an advisory opinion or entertain a case which has become moot as a result of subsequent events. A federal court which acted in the absence of a live dispute would intrude into the provinces of the executive and legislative branches, thereby violating the principle of separation of powers.

Similarly, a court case must be brought by a party that actually has a dispute with the defendant. Such a party is said to have standing. The requirement of standing also insures that the court will have two parties that are sufficiently antagonistic to develop a full record and present full arguments. Thus standing is usually thought of as requiring the party seeking judicial review of agency action to have a stake in the outcome.

Standing is rarely a concern when judicial review of adjudication is sought. A respondent which loses before the agency will be ordered to do something or to cease and desist its prior illegal practice. The respondent clearly has standing to appeal the agency's decision.

Rulemaking and informal actions pose more difficult problems of standing. For example, consider the SBA regulation prohibiting recipients of SBA assistance from discriminating against the handicapped. It is clear that a small businessperson receiving SBA assistance who, in the absence of judicial review, would have to comply with the regulation, has standing to challenge the regulation in court. It is equally clear that the small businessperson's next-door neighbor, who is not receiving SBA assistance lacks standing. Between these extremes are a potential employee who feels threatened by having to compete with handicapped persons for a job with an SBA-assisted company; a customer who is concerned that the company's prices will rise because of the expense of such alterations as installing ramps and making curb cuts to provide handicapped persons access to the premises; and a local civic group which has no handicapped members but is currently promoting a "hire the handicapped" campaign.

Initially courts responded to the issue of standing to challenge agency action by requiring litigants to demonstrate a legal interest in the action. A party seeking judicial review thus had to show that the action infringed a right granted that party by the Constitution, a statute, or the common law.

As agency regulation expanded, courts became more liberal in finding standing. The current test requires a party challenging an agency action to allege a resulting injury tolling within the zone of interests protected by the statute or the constitutional provision which the action is claimed to contravene. The most concrete type of injury is an economic loss resulting from the action. Less concrete injuries, however, will suffice. Thus the harm may be emotional, spiritual, environmental, or aesthetic. But a mere interest in the subject matter of the action is not sufficient to confer standing.

For example, the Sierra Club challenged a decision by the secretary of the interior granting Walt Disney Enterprises a use permit to develop a ski resort in the Mineral King Valley of the Sequoia National Forest.[4] The Sierra Club alleged that it was interested in preserving Mineral King in its undeveloped state, but the club did not allege that any of its members used Mineral King or would suffer any specific injury from the development of the ski resort. This strong interest, by itself, was held insufficient to confer standing on the Sierra Club.

On the other hand, the Students Challenging Regulatory Agency Procedures (SCRAP) challenged an Interstate Commerce Commission ruling permitting a 2.5 percent across-the-board increase in railroad freight rates. SCRAP alleged that the action would increase the transportation costs for recycled goods and that this in turn would increase the price of recyclable goods relative to disposable goods, increasing solid wastes and virgin source extraction; and cause harm to mountains, rivers, streams, and forests used by SCRAP members for recreation. The Court held that these allegations were sufficient to establish SCRAP's injury and, consequently, its standing.[5]

An agency action may be attacked on the ground that it violates a statute or the Constitution. When the action is alleged to be arbitrary and capricious, the party seeking review is claiming that the action violates the APA. When the action is challenged as being beyond the scope of the agency's authority, the party making the challenge is claiming that the action violates the enabling legislation.

An injury's relation to the statutory or constitutional grounds for challenging the action must be very remote for the court to hold that the injury fails to come within the zone of protected interests. For example, assume that an Occupational Safety and Health Administration regulation imposes new and extensive record-keeping requirements on any employer engaged in interstate commerce. This causes the president of XYZ Company to spend an additional 10 hours per week at the office. Consequently the president's spouse experiences increased loneliness. Although that loneliness is an injury caused by the regulation, the injury does not come within the zone of interests protected by the APA. Thus the spouse would not have standing to challenge the regulation as arbitrary and capricious. The following case illustrates the standing concept.

---

[4] *Sierra Club* v. *Morton,* 405 U.S. 727 (1972).
[5] *United States* v. *SCRAP,* 412 U.S. 669 (1973).

Tax Analysts and Advocates v. Blumenthal
566 F.2d 130 (D.C. Cir. 1977)

Tax Analysts and Advocates, a tax reform organization, and its executive director, Thomas F. Field (appellants), sought judicial review of IRS regulations allowing tax credits for payments made to foreign nations in connection with oil extraction and production. They claimed that the regulations violated the Internal Revenue Code. Field claimed standing because he owned a currently producing domestic oil well and competed with those companies which were granted tax credits.

Wilkey, Circuit Judge:

*   *   *   *   *

Appellant alleges two injuries in his capacity as a competitor. As the first injury appellant Field alleges that the IRS rulings "result in his obtaining lower prices for his oil production than he would receive if the international companies could only deduct and not credit their oil production related payments." The rulings at issue in this case enable the international companies to pay far less income tax to the United States than if these payments were merely deductible. A substantial portion of the oil produced in Saudi Arabia, Libya, Kuwait, Iran and Venezuela by United States companies is exported to the United States. The prices charged by the international companies largely determine the market price for uncontrolled crude oil received by independent producers such as appellant Field. According to appellants, the lower taxes paid by the international companies allow these companies to sell their foreign oil in the United States at lower prices than would prevail if the companies could only deduct and not credit their foreign income tax payments. Thus, as a consequence, appellant Field contends that the IRS rulings result in competitive injury due to the loss of potential income in the sale of his domestically produced oil.

The second injury of a competitive nature alleged by appellant Field concerns the impact of the challenged rulings on the value of his operating interest in his domestic oil well. According to appellant Field, the challenged IRS rulings increase the net income from foreign oil production over what it would be if the foreign payments could only be deducted from gross income for federal tax purposes. Thus, as a result of the rulings, foreign oil production yields higher investment returns and investors are more willing to invest in foreign oil production than they would be if the rulings had not been promulgated. The value of foreign oil well investments is therefore increased relative to similar domestic investments, to the alleged competitive detriment of appellant Field.

*   *   *   *   *

The standing doctrine has two sources: the "case or controversy" requirement of Article III of the Constitution, and judicially imposed rules of self-restraint known as "prudential limitations." The Article III constitutional requirement is one of "injury in fact, economic or otherwise"; such injury is the "irreducible constitutional minimum which must be present in every case." If a court finds that there is no injury in fact, "no other inquiry is relevant to consideration of . . . standing." The vast majority of the case law on standing at all levels of the federal court system has been directed at defining this constitutionally based concept of injury in fact.

Prudential limitations, on the other hand, are not constitutional requirements; these limitations are developed and imposed by the Supreme Court in its supervisory capacity over the federal judiciary. . . . The first of these limitations to be enunciated . . . is the so-called "zone test": "whether the interest sought to be protected by the complainant is arguably within the zone of interests to be protected or regulated by the statute or constitutional guarantee in question.". . .

1. Injury in fact. We conclude that appellant Field has suffered injury in fact in his capacity as a competitor. Although appellant's economic injury is relatively small in magnitude, this does not negate our finding of injury in fact. Appellant Field has alleged "a distinct and palpable injury to himself" which meets the requirements of Article III of the Constitution; given that the constitutional hurdle has been surmounted, we must now proceed to examine appellant's claim in light of the zone test.

2. Zone of interests. . . . The zone test admittedly presents the courts with an ambiguous and imprecise standard to apply. . . .

The zone test serves no independent purpose but, rather, constitutes one method to ensure that the basic purposes and policies of the standing doctrine itself are effectuated. . . . The first purpose, or basic policy, is to ensure the complete adversarial presentation of the issues before the court. The second purpose concerns the "proper—and properly limited—role of the courts in a democratic society." That is, the standing doctrine can be employed to define the proper judicial role relative to the other major governmental institutions in the society. As the Court has stated, the "prudential rules of standing . . . serve to limit the role of the courts in resolving public disputes."

We believe that the zone test is particularly suited to the task of furthering the second stated purpose of the standing doctrine relating to the role of the federal judiciary. The zone test, by its very language, implicates the relationship between the legislative and judicial branches as the predominant factor in its operation—"the zone of interests to be protected or regulated by the statute . . . in question." Thus, the zone test serves the purpose of allowing courts to define those instances when it believes the exercise of its power at the instigation of a particular party is not congruent with the mandate of the legislative branch in a particular subject area.

By its choice of language, the Supreme Court has indicated that the zone test is a quite generous standard; on the other hand, the test is obviously meant to serve as a limitation on those who can use the federal courts as a forum for grievances emanating from agency action taken pursuant to a particular statutory mandate. These competing considerations serve to frame the bounds of a court's discretion in applying the zone test. The discretion of a court to deny standing on the basis of the zone standard is not undefined; the zone test limitation is grounded in Congressional action as embodied in statute. The zone test therefore cannot be used arbitrarily to deny access to the courts; it is based on discerned Congressional purpose, a purpose which can be more clearly or differently defined as Congress wishes.

*   *   *   *   *

APPLICATION OF ZONE TEST TO APPELLANT FIELD

Having described what we believe to be the purpose of the zone test and the manner in which it should operate, it is now possible to formulate with precision the relevant zone test inquiry with respect to appellant Field's standing as a competitor: did Congress arguably legislate with respect to competition in Section 901 of the Code so as to protect the competitive interests of domestic oil producers?

We answer the posed query in the negative for the following reasons. The purpose of the tax credit provision of Section 901 of the Code is to prevent the double taxation of any United States companies operating abroad. This purpose is clear from the face of the statute itself, and has been consistently confirmed in the case law dealing with this particular provision in other contexts. The tax credit envisioned in Section 901 is also available to U.S. companies operating outside the sphere of oil extraction and production, with the same purpose of avoiding the double taxation of United States taxpayers, whether such companies have domestic competition or not. Given this purpose, it is obvious that the protective intent of the statutory section extends to all those U.S. companies doing business abroad and paying foreign income taxes.

In addition it cannot be said that parties in the position of appellant Field are arguably intended to be regulated by the provision granting tax credits; that is, appellant Field cannot be said to fall within the regulatory field of concern without stretching the concept of regulation to implausible limits. Therefore, we conclude that the interests being asserted by appellant Field as a competitor are not the interests arguably intended to be protected by the tax credit provision of Section 901 which is the statutory basis for the challenge in this case. The congruence between the purpose of the statute (to prevent the double taxation of particular parties) and the interests asserted by appellant (competitive interest in fairness) is not sufficient to invoke the federal judicial power.

*   *   *   *   *

. . . Every decision by a government agency generates consequences and various forms of impact on a wide range of valid interests held by a diverse range of parties. There is no doubt that the decisions embodied in the challenged revenue rulings have had an impact on appellant Field. But the concepts of consequence and impact are not the proper guideposts to define the relevant zone of interests; reference

to these concepts does not aid greatly to determining whether a protected interest exists, but rather serves as part of the vocabulary in defining the relationship between an alleged injury and an asserted interest.

*   *   *   *   *

We recognize that as the result of our decision in this case it is likely that the revenue rulings at issue in the case may go unchallenged in federal court due to the lack of a proper party to sue. This eventuality does not, however, operate in favor of granting standing to the parties in this case. The standing doctrine should not be manipulated to guarantee that there is a party to bring any action in court that some persons may think desirable to have adjudicated. Since we cannot conclude that appellants have standing under the current framework of analysis provided by the Supreme Court, the order of the District Court is this case is

Affirmed.

Case questions

1. What was Field's injury? Why did it not come within the zone of protected interests?

2. What is the difference between the injury requirements and the zone of interests requirements? What functions do these requirements serve?

3. Does a rule which gives standing to SCRAP but denies it to Field serve the purposes of a standing requirement?

4. Who might be injured by the IRS regulation and have standing to challenge it?

Reviewability

The APA creates a strong presumption that final agency action is subject to judicial review. That presumption may be overcome if Congress specifies that a particular action shall be exempt from judicial review if this is required by reasons of public policy. Congress must be clear and specific in indicating its intent to preclude judicial review. Similarly, policy considerations precluding review must clearly outweigh those favoring review.

Decisions by the U.S. attorney not to bring criminal charges against an individual are not subject to judicial review. A contrary result would involve judicial intrusion into an executive function. The U.S. attorney's decision may be motivated by long-range law enforcement goals. For example, the

U.S. attorney may decline prosecution because the suspect has agreed to aid other, more extensive law enforcement investigations.

Exhaustion of administrative remedies

Administrative agencies are created when Congress believes that a particular type of activity must be regulated by an expert body. In reviewing agency action, courts have therefore deferred to agency expertise in technical matters. Courts also frequently rely on agency views in interpreting enabling legislation.

To insure having the benefit of agency expertise, courts require that an agency action be in final form before it is subjected to judicial review. Courts also require that a party seeking judicial review first exhaust the available administrative remedies. Thus a small businessperson reading the SBA's notice of a proposed rule to prohibit discrimination against the handicapped could not have the rule enjoined. That person would first have to present his or her objections to the SBA, and could obtain judicial review only after publication of the final version of the rule.

The exhaustion requirement generally applies even though the complaining party contends that the agency has exceeded its authority. For example, section 5 of the Federal Trade Commission Act empowers the FTC to order persons employing unfair or deceptive trade practices or unfair methods of competition to cease and desist using such practices, where such an order is in the public interest. If FTC complaint counsel charges a party with violating section 5, that party must file an answer, proceed to trial before an administrative law judge, and appeal to the full commission before the matter will be subject to judicial review. This is so even though the respondent claims that the action is not in the public interest. The court will want the benefit of the agency's expertise on this jurisdictional issue as well as its expertise on the substantive violation. However, if the agency's action is plainly beyond its jurisdiction and there is no need for the agency's expert opinion, the court will dispense with the exhaustion requirement.

POLICY CONSIDERATIONS

Administrative agencies have received considerable criticism from representatives of the entire political and economic spectrum. Some of these critics believe that agencies are ineffective in carrying out their regulatory missions because they draw many of their highly specialized employees from the industries they regulate. Those who hold this view claim that agency administrators may be biased in favor of the companies they regulate because they hope to leave the agencies for more lucrative positions with the regulated companies. These critics demand stiff requirements that administrators disclose any interests in regulated companies and that they be prohibited from working for those companies for a period of time after leaving the agency.

A related criticism is that regulated industries are vigorously represented by their trade associations and their lobbyists, while representation of consumer interests before administrative agencies is sporadic and uncoordinated. A bill to create an office that would represent consumer interests in regulatory proceedings was defeated in Congress in 1975.

The regulatory process has also been criticized as wasteful and inefficient. Proponents of this view advocate greater reliance on market mechanisms. This criticism has been received more favorably by Congress in recent years. In 1978 Congress voted to gradually deregulate the airline industry. It followed with similar deregulation of interstate trucking. The short-term dislocations and long-term effects of these measures remain to be seen.

Review problems

1. The Natural Resources Defense Council (NRDC), an environmental group, asked the Securities and Exchange Commission to promulgate regulations pursuant to the Securities Act of 1933 and the Securities and Exchange Act of 1934, requiring corporations to include in any prospectus or annual report detailed discussions of the environmental impact of their activities. The SEC held hearings on the request, determined that such information was not generally used by investors in evaluating the quality of investments, and refused to issue the requested regulations. Can the NRDC secure judicial review of the SEC's action? Will the reviewing court compel the SEC to issue the regulations? Explain.

2. You are the president of a restaurant trade association. The FTC issued a notice of proposed rulemaking which stated that its studies had found that many restaurants misrepresented the food they served. Dishes described on menus and in advertising as "veal" often contained substantial amounts of beef and soy. "Hamburgers" contained large percentages of soy and similar additives, and "fresh vegetables" were often frozen. The notice proposed regulations detailing specific requirements when these and similar terms were used on menus or in ads. The association's members oppose the proposed regulations. How will you respond to the notice?

3. You are the personnel manager for XYZ Corporation. The company president has given you a copy of a complaint served on the company by the regional director of the NLRB. The complaint charges that the company fired two employees because they were involved in union organizing activities. Your records show that both employees were active union organizers but that they were fired because each had 15 unexcused absences over the past year. Prepare a memorandum for the president outlining the procedures which the NLRB will use in processing the complaint and recommending a course of action.

4. The Economic Development Administration is empowered to award communities with high unemployment rates grants for use in community projects designed to create jobs. To fund a project that will compete with local private businesses, EDA must find that there is sufficient demand to support the funded project as well as the local businesses. EDA, relying on data from the Department of Labor which show a 15 percent unemployment rate in and around Duluth, Minnesota, makes a substantial grant to the city of Duluth for operation of a ski resort at nearby Spirit Mountain. EDA projects future demand by using a formula based on an average of demand for the preceding five years. It therefore refuses to consider reports from the National

Weather Service predicting an abnormally warm winter in the upper Great Lakes region. It also makes a mathematical error in applying its formula, resulting in an underestimation of the demand. If the competing private ski resorts sue EDA and the city of Duluth, will they succeed in having the grant set aside?

5. The National Bank Act requires approval by the comptroller of the currency before a national bank is organized. A group led by Pitts sought such approval for a new bank in Huntsville, South Carolina. The act does not require the comptroller to hold a hearing or to provide formal findings regarding such applications. It requires the comptroller to ascertain whether the applicant is lawfully qualified to operate a bank. The qualifications involve the capital account, the directors' identity, the amount of capital stock owned by each director, and similar matters. Upon finding the applicant qualified, "the comptroller shall give to [the applicant] a certificate [of approval]. But the comptroller may withhold . . . his certificate" when he has reason to believe that the applicant's objectives are not legitimate.

The comptroller's consistent practice has been to consider the need for a new banking facility in evaluating applications. The comptroller denied Pitts's application, stating, "We have concluded that the factors in support of a new National Bank in this area are not favorable." Pitts sought reconsideration. The comptroller again denied the application, stating that he found no need for a new bank and listing the existing banks in the area and their deposits. If Pitts sues to overturn the comptroller's decision, what standard of review will the court apply? With what result?

6. The National Motor Vehicle Safety Act empowers the secretary of transportation to issue regulations establishing practicable standards that meet the need for motor vehicle safety. The secretary proposes a regulation requiring that all retread tires contain permanent labeling of tire size, maximum inflatable pressure, ply rating, tubeless or tube type, and bias belted or radial construction. During the notice and comment period, tire retreaders seek modification of the proposal to eliminate the requirement of permanency. They claim that two thirds of all the tire casings they receive either lack labels or have labels which are obliterated during the retread process. They further argue that furnishing permanent labels will require the use of mold plates. Unlike a tire manufacturer who mass-produces large batches of tires to the same specifications, retreaders deal with small batches of different sizes and construction. This means that the mold plates will have to be changed frequently by employees working with hand tools at temperatures up to 300° F. The retreaders produce a study showing that the labeling process is 80 percent effective and adds 30 percent to the cost of retreads. If the secretary promulgates the regulation, will it be sustained in court?

7. The Clean Air Act authorizes the Environmental Protection Agency to regulate gasoline additives whose emissions "will endanger the public welfare." EPA promulgates regulations requiring a stepwise reduction of the lead content of gasoline. Scientific and clinical evidence shows that high concentrations of lead in the body are toxic, that lead can be absorbed from ambient air, and that 90 percent of the lead in the air comes from automobiles. However, air is only one of several lead sources absorbed by the body. Furthermore, since all humans breathe the same air, it is impossible to conduct a controlled experiment. Consequently it is impossible to identify the precise level of airborne lead that will endanger human health, and no single dispositive study fully supports the EPA's position. Will a court overturn the rule? Explain.

8. When a union attempts to organize a company's employees, it asks them to sign cards authorizing the union to act as the collective bargaining representative. If the union signs up at least 30 percent of the employees, it may submit the cards to the National Labor Relations Board, which will then conduct an election to determine whether a majority of the employees desire the union. The United

Widget Workers has signed up 60 percent of the employees at Willie's Widget Works and given the cards to the NLRB. If Willie's requests copies of the cards from the NLRB, may the union prevent disclosure?

9. A local builders' association seeks to challenge a zoning ordinance which limits construction in an area to single-family housing. The association's members are builders who construct multifamily units. They claim that the ordinance is designed to keep blacks from moving into the community and therefore violates the 1964 Civil Rights Act. Does the association have standing?

10. Consider the impact of deregulation of the airline and trucking industries. Should greater reliance be placed on market mechanisms rather then bureaucratic regulation? Explain.

CHAPTER 4

Constitutional law

The U.S. government derives its power to regulate business from the Constitution of the United States. This document establishes the structure and power of the federal government. It is the foundation of all federal regulation of business. Thus a preliminary question underlying any attempt to regulate business is whether the regulatory effort is constitutional. This chapter explores the constitutional issues inherent in government regulation of business.

THE HISTORICAL CONTEXT OF THE U.S. CONSTITUTION

Before the American Revolution, the 13 colonies exhibited a degree of autonomy. Although created by crown charters and governed by royal governors, the colonies developed substantial experience in self-governance through their legislative assemblies.

When difficulties between Great Britain and the colonies developed in June 1774, the Massachusetts and Virginia assemblies called for an intercolonial meeting of delegates from all the colonies. That September the first Continental Congress met in Philadelphia. After fighting started in Lexington, the Continental Congress became a de facto revolutionary government, coordinating the colonial military effort and declaring independence from Britain in 1776. After this declaration the Congress began preparing a formal plan of government. In 1778 a plan of confederation was approved by the states. The plan was contained in the Articles of Confederation. By this plan the 13 states joined in a "firm league of friendship," and little more.

Weaknesses in the Articles of Confederation soon became apparent. For example, Congress could not levy taxes, enact legislation without the concurrence of nine states, or amend the Articles without unanimous state approval. Among the weaknesses of the Articles of Confederation was the lack of congressional authority to regulate foreign or interstate commerce. Legislation in this area was left to the individual states. Disputes arose between states having a common interest in the navigation of certain rivers and

99

bays. One such dispute, between Virginia and Maryland in 1785 over navigation of the Potomac River, led to the appointment of commissioners by both states to resolve the issue. At Mount Vernon the commissioners agreed upon navigation of the Potomac and, more important, submitted to their respective states a report favoring a convention of all the states "to take into consideration the trade and commerce" of the Confederation. This proposal led to a convention in Annapolis in 1786, at which only nine states were represented. Because of the disappointing attendance, the conferees did not conduct any business but called for another convention to meet in Philadelphia. In May 1787, with congressional approval and with all the states sending delegates, the Constitutional Convention met in Philadelphia. Although charged to revise the Articles of Confederation, the Convention reported a new Constitution to Congress, in September 1787. State ratification followed, in 1788, with Massachusetts, New Hampshire, and New York recommending that a bill of rights be appended.

The U.S. Constitution was a response to the weaknesses inherent in the Articles of Confederation. One such weakness was the lack of congressional authority over commerce. In place of a loose confederation of states with no central authority over commerce arose a plan for a strong federal government with power "[t]o regulate Commerce with foreign Nations, and among the several States."

FEDERAL AUTHORITY TO REGULATE COMMERCE

The U.S. government is a government of enumerated powers. Every power exercised by the government must be authorized by the Constitution. Thus, whenever the federal government seeks to regulate business activity, the first issue posed is: What is the constitutional basis for the regulation? The Constitution's Commerce Clause provides the most significant regulatory power of Congress.

Article I, Section 8, of the Constitution enumerates the various powers of the federal government. Clause 3 provides that Congress shall have power "[t]o regulate Commerce with foreign Nations, and among the several States." Foreign commerce concerns imports from and exports to foreign nations. The following paragraphs concentrate on congressional power to regulate domestic commerce, that is, commerce "among the several States."

The original meaning of the Commerce Clause

Although the Commerce Clause is frequently said to regulate "interstate commerce," meaning that its scope is confined to commerce between states, nowhere in the clause do the terms *interstate* or *between* appear. The Constitution provides Congress with power to regulate "commerce among the several States," *not* "interstate* commerce."

In his book *Politics and the Constitution*, Professor William Crosskey explored the 18th-century meaning of the language in the Commerce Clause. He sought to examine the content of the Constitution in the context of its time. That is, he wanted to know what its words meant to the 18th-century mind. In this way he hoped to discover the original meaning of the clause.

Crosskey found that the verb *to regulate,* as it was used in the 18th-century, was synonymous with "to govern," and it meant this in a general way. "Commerce" included all areas of gainful activity, all transactions in manufacture, transportation, marketing, finance, and agriculture. The preposition *among,* as used by the Constitution's drafters, and as understood by the people, or the state ratifying conventions, was not synonymous with "between." Rather, the term meant "in the midst of" or "intermingled with" discrete groups of persons. The term *State* in 1787 meant *'the people* of a state," not the territory or government of a state. Thus, as understood at the time of its drafting, the Commerce Clause provided Congress with the power "to govern generally every species of gainful activity carried on by Americans in the midst of the states of their own country." According to Crosskey, the clause provided Congress with complete authority to regulate all commerce conducted in the United States, not an incomplete power to regulate only interstate trade.

Early Supreme Court interpretation of the Commerce Clause

In the landmark decision of *Gibbons* v. *Ogden,*[1] Ogden, the assignee of a New York State grant of exclusive rights to operate steamboats between New York City and New Jersey, obtained an injunction against Gibbons's operation of steamboats on the same route. The Supreme Court reversed, as Gibbons had licensed and enrolled his boats pursuant to a federal statute. In sustaining the constititionality of this statute, Chief Justice Marshall wrote:

> Commerce, undoubtedly, is traffic, but it is something more: it is intercourse. It describes the commercial intercourse between nations, and parts of nations, in all its branches, and is regulated by prescribing rules for carrying on that intercourse.
>
> * * * * *
>
> . . . The word "among" means intermingled with. . . . Commerce among the States cannot stop at the external boundary line of each State, but may be introduced into the interior.
>
> * * * * *
>
> . . . This power [to regulate interstate commerce] . . . is complete in itself, may be exercised to its utmost extent, and acknowledges no limitations other than are prescribed in the Constitution.

Marshall, however, recognized one limitation upon congressional power under the Commerce Clause. He excluded commerce that was completely

---

[1] 22 U.S. (9 Wheat) 1 (1824).

internal to one state and had no effect on other states. Marshall added this important dictum:

> . . . It is not intended to say that these words comprehend that commerce which is completely internal, carried on between man and man in a State, or between different parts of the same State, and which does not extend to or affect other States. Such a power would be inconvenient, and is certainly unnecessary. Comprehensive as the word "among" is, it may very properly be restricted to that commerce which concerns more states than one. . . . The completely internal commerce of a State, then, may be considered as reserved for the State itself.

This dictum opened the door for the Supreme Court to later distinguish between interstate and intrastate commerce.

Despite the generally broad interpretation of *Gibbons* v. *Ogden*, Congress rarely exercised its powers under the Commerce Clause until 1887, when it passed the Interstate Commerce Act. This was followed by the Sherman Antitrust Act in 1890. Subsequent expanded use of the Commerce Clause did not meet with the favor of the Supreme Court.

Supreme Court restrictions of congressional commerce power

Toward the turn of the 20th-century the Supreme Court restricted the scope of congressional power under the Commerce Clause. It did this by holding that the word *among* was a synonym for "between" and by limiting the definition of *commerce* to mean only "transportation." By redefining these words, the Court limited congressional power to regulate business.

The case of *Hammer* v. *Dagenhart*[2] (The Child Labor Case) represents the Court's most restrictive view of the Commerce Clause. A federal statute prohibited the interstate transportation of goods made in factories that employed children. Although couched in terms of prohibiting the transportation of goods made by child labor, the statute left no doubt that its real purpose was to suppress child labor. The Court held the statute unconstitutional by finding that manufacturing was an internal state affair not subject to regulation under the Commerce Clause. This position dominated the Court until the administration of Franklin D. Roosevelt.

Depression-era decisions

With the economic depression of the 1930s, there emerged increased public pressure for federal solutions. Congress responded by passing legislation regulating business activity and labor-management relations. The National Industrial Recovery Act of 1933 (NIRA) provided for industry codes of

---

[2] 247 U.S. 251 (1918).

self-regulation of production, prices, wages, and work hours. The National Labor Relations Act of 1935 (NLRA) forbade unfair labor practices.

In *Schechter Poultry Corp.* v. *United States*[3] (The Sick Chicken Case), the Court held that the NIRA, as applied to New York poultry slaughterhouses, was unconstitutional. This resulted in President Roosevelt's unsuccessful effort to "pack" the Court. Roosevelt called for legislation to allow for an additional appointment whenever a Supreme Court justice reached the voluntary retirement age but refused to retire. Because six members of the Court were past the voluntary retirement age, this would have given Roosevelt six new appointments. Although the "Court-packing" plan failed to get congressional approval, Roosevelt's influence was felt. Chief Justice Hughes, worried about a potential confrontation with the executive branch, lobbied two justices to change their positions.

By 1937 the Court's majority had changed. That year the Court decided *NLRB* v. *Jones & Laughlin Steel Corp.*,[4] which upheld the constitutionality of the NLRA. In what represented a turning point in Commerce Clause interpretation, the Court rejected the argument that manufacturing was not commerce, holding instead that congressional power was no longer limited to commerce moving across state lines, but included all activities, even those that might be intrastate in character when considered alone, "if they have a close and substantial relation to interstate commerce."

In 1941 *Hammer* v. *Dagenhart*[5] was formally overruled in *United States* v. *Darby*, where the Court upheld the constitutionality of the Fair Labor Standards Act (FLSA), a statute establishing minimum wages and maximum hours for employees producing goods in interstate commerce. Addressing the point that the statute's real purpose was to set certain wage and working standards, rather than to regulate the transportation of goods across state lines, the Court stated: "Whatever their motive and purpose, regulations of commerce which do not infringe some constitutional prohibition are within the plenary power conferred on Congress by the Commerce Clause."

The present position

In *Darby* the Court upheld the FLSA as applied to an employer whose sole activity was the production of goods, some of which were later shipped in interstate commerce. The Court decided that the production of goods "affected" interstate commerce, even though the activity took place entirely within one state. Thus the modern view is what is called the affectation doctrine. Congress has the power to regulate any activity, whether it be interstate or intrastate, if it has any appreciable effect upon interstate commerce, whether that effect is direct or indirect. As one commentator concluded:

---

[3] 295 U.S. 495 (1935).
[4] 301 U.S. 1 (1937).
[5] 312 U.S. 100 (1941).

The whole point about the present law is that these activities can no longer be considered alone. If they have an effect upon interstate commerce, they concern more than one state and come within the Commerce Clause.

The key question thus becomes: Does the subject of regulation affect interstate commerce? An affirmative answer compels the conclusion that it is within federal power.[6]

The affectation doctrine has been applied to: (1) purely intrastate marketing of local products that compete with similar products moving in interstate commerce, (2) price-fixing for commodities, (3) regulation of branding, (4) regulation of manufacturing, and (5) regulation of farm production. Under the commerce power the Court has upheld statutes aimed at barring racial discrimination in activities connected with interstate commerce. In *Heart of Atlanta Motel, Inc.* v. *United States* the Court upheld provisions of the 1964 Civil Rights Act which forbade racial discrimination in public accommodations (e.g., theaters, hotels, restaurants).[7] The Court held that however local their operations might appear, such places of business might be open to interstate travelers, they might purchase their supplies from out of state, and discrimination in them might affect interstate commerce.

The following case shows the Court applying the affectation doctrine.

McLain v. *Real Estate Board of New Orleans*
100 S. Ct. 502 (1980)

James McLain and others (petitioners) brought a class action on behalf of real estate sellers and purchasers against real estate trade associations, real estate firms, and a class of real estate operators in the Greater New Orleans area (respondents), claiming that the respondents had violated federal antitrust laws during the four years before the complaint was filed. Petitioners alleged that respondents had engaged in a price-fixing conspiracy in violation of the Sherman Antitrust Act. The district court discussed the complaint, finding that the respondents' activities involving real estate were purely local in nature and did not substantially affect interstate commerce. The court of appeals affirmed. The Supreme Court reversed.

The pertinent allegations of the complaint were: (1) that the activities of respondents were "within the flow of interstate commerce and have an effect upon that commerce"; (2) that the services of respondents were employed in connection with the purchase and sale of real estate by "persons moving into and out of the Greater New Orleans area"; (3) that respondents "assist their clients in securing financing and insurance involved with the purchase of real estate in the Greater New Orleans area," which "financing and insurance are obtained from sources outside the State of Louisiana and move in interstate commerce into the State of Louisiana through the activities of the [respondents]"; and (4) that respondents had engaged in an unlawful restraint of "interstate trade and commerce in the offering for sale and sale of real estate brokering services."

Mr. Chief Justice Burger: The broad authority of Congress under the Commerce Clause

---

[6] B. Schwartz, *Constitutional Law* 97–98 (1972).

[7] 379 U.S. 241 (1964).

has, of course, long been interpreted to extend beyond activities actually *in* interstate commerce to reach other activities, while wholly local in nature, nevertheless substantially *affect* interstate commerce.

* * * * *

On the record thus far made, it cannot be said that there is an insufficient basis for petitioners to proceed at trial to establish Sherman Act jurisdiction. It is clear that an appreciable amount of commerce is involved in the financing of residential property in the Greater New Orleans area and in the insuring of titles to such property. The presidents of two of the many lending institutions in the area stated in their deposition testimony that those institutions committed hundreds of millions of dollars to residential financing during the period covered by the complaint. The testimony further demonstrates that this appreciable commercial activity has occurred in interstate commerce. Funds were raised from out-of-state investors and from interbank loans obtained from interstate financial institutions. Multistate lending institutions took mortgages insured under federal programs which entailed interstate transfers of premiums and settlements. Mortgage obligations physically and constructively were traded as financial instruments in the interstate secondary mortgage market. Before making a mortgage loan in the Greater New Orleans area, lending institutions usually, if not always, required title insurance, which was furnished by interstate corporations. Reading the pleadings, as supplemented, most favorably to petitioners, for present purposes we take these facts as established.

At trial, respondents will have the opportunity, if they so choose, to make their own case contradicting this factual showing. On the other hand, it may be possible for petitioners to establish that, apart from the commerce in title insurance and real estate financing, an appreciable amount of interstate commerce is involved with the local residential real estate market arising

out of the interstate movement of people or otherwise.

To establish federal jurisdiction in this case, there remains only the requirements that respondents' activities which allegedly have been infected by a price-fixing conspiracy be shown "as a matter of practical economics" to have a not insubstantial effect on the interstate commerce involved. It is clear, as the record shows, that the function of respondent real estate brokers is to bring the buyer and seller together on agreeable terms. For this service the broker charges a fee generally calculated as a percentage of the sale price. Brokerage activities necessarily affect both the frequency and the terms of residential sales transactions. Ultimately, whatever stimulates or retards the volume of residential sales, or has an impact on the purchase price, affects the demand for financing and title insurance, those two commercial activities that on this record are shown to have occurred in interstate commerce. Where, as here, the services of respondent real estate brokers are often employed in transactions in the relevant market, petitioners at trial may be able to show that respondents' activities have a not insubstantial effect on interstate commerce.

It is axiomatic that a complaint should not be dismissed unless "it appears beyond doubt that the plaintiff can prove no set of facts in support of his claim which would entitle him to relief." This rule applies with no less force to a Sherman Act claim, where one of the requisites of a cause of action is the existence of a demonstrable nexus between the defendants' activity and interstate commerce. Here what was submitted to the District Court shows a sufficient basis for satisfying the Act's jurisdictional requirements under the effect of commerce theory so as to entitle the petitioners to go forward. We therefore conclude that it was error to dismiss the complaint at this stage of the proceedings. The judgment of the Court of Appeals is vacated and the case is remanded for further proceedings consistent with this opinion.

Case questions

1. The Court states in *McLain* that "[t]o establish federal jurisdiction in this case, there remains only the requirement that respondents' activities which allegedly have been infected by a price-fixing conspiracy be shown 'as a matter of practical economics' to have a not insubstantial effect on the interstate commerce involved." How would this be done?

2. In light of the Court's current posture regarding the Commerce Clause, is any activity not capable of being reached by the power of Congress to regulate "commerce among the several States"? Explain.

THE RELATIONSHIP BETWEEN STATE AND FEDERAL REGULATION

The previous discussion focused on the federal regulatory power in national and local matters. Now the discussion turns to the power of the states to regulate business. The individual states have a strong interest in legislating to protect the health, safety, and morals of their people. When they enact such legislation they are said to be exercising their police power. That power, though broad, is not unlimited, as it may not be exercised in a manner contrary to the Constitution.

Some state activity is specifically prohibited by the Constitution. For example, only the federal government has the power to coin money, declare war, and impose tariffs. Other provisions of the Constitution impliedly limit state action. The following discussion focuses on two such provisions: the Commerce Clause and the Supremacy Clause.

The Commerce Clause

When Congress chooses not to exercise its commerce power over a particular area of interstate commerce, can the states attempt to fill the void created by the silence of Congress and regulate the activity through state legislation? The answer to this question is not to be found on the face of the Constitution's Commerce Clause. However, the Commerce Clause not only contains an affirmative grant of federal power over interstate commerce, but by negative implication it limits the authority of states to regulate in a manner that unduly restricts the free flow of interstate commerce. Without the Commerce Clause, individual states could establish regulatory barriers against interstate commerce in order to give local commercial interests an economic advantage. This is precisely the sort of economic Balkanization that the Constitution sought to end.

When Congress remains silent and a state enacts legislation on a subject of interstate commerce, the Supreme Court sits as the umpire of the competing national and state interests. In distinguishing between legitimate exercises of a state's police power and unconstitutional restraints upon interstate commerce, the Court balances the need for national uniformity in law against the state's interest in protecting its people from health and safety hazards.

On some occasions the court has carved out areas of exclusive federal control, and on other occasions it has struck down state statutes that discriminate against or obstruct interstate commerce.

Areas exclusively federal. Generally, when Congress remains silent on a subject of interstate commerce, the states are free to exercise their police power in that area. Thus the states possess a residuum of power to make laws governing matters of local concern which in some measure affect interstate commerce. Congress may remove this permissible area of state regulation by exercising its commerce power and enacting legislation. However, some subjects of interstate commerce are such that state regulation is unconstitutional even in the absence of congressional legislation. An area where national uniformity in regulation is necessary is one of exclusive federal control. Congress possesses exclusive power over this area of interstate commerce. No state will be permitted to regulate in the area. If regulation in the area is needed, the regulatory effort can come only from Congress.[8]

Most of the cases raising the issue of federal exclusivity have involved state transportation regulation. For example, in *Southern Pacific Co. v. Arizona*[9] the Court struck down an Arizona law making it illegal to operate within Arizona a train of more than 14 passenger cars or 70 freight cars. Although the statute was a safety measure designed to reduce railroad accidents, the Court concluded that the length of trains was an area in which national uniformity was indispensable. Efficient interstate train operation would be impeded if trains were forced to stop and reassemble upon entering and leaving each regulating state.

Obstructions of and discrimination against interstate commerce. Even though an area of interstate commerce is not exclusively federal, a state is nevertheless not free to use its regulatory authority to obstruct interstate commerce. Similarly, a state may not enact discriminatory laws designed to protect or aid local business in its competition with interstate commerce. For example, license fees that are required only from nonresidents or from businesses bringing in goods from outside the state have been held to contravene the Commerce Clause as undue impediments to the free flow of interstate commerce.

In the following case, the court examines the constitutionality of a state takeover statute under the Commerce Clause.

Great Western United Corp. v. Kidwell
577 F.2d 1256 (5th Cir. 1978)

Tom McEldowney (appellant), director of finance of the Idaho Finance Department, ap- *pealed a district court judgment declaring that the Idaho takeover statute was unconstitu-*

---

[8] 53 U.S. (12 How.) 299 (1851).

[9] 325 U.S. 761 (1945).

tional. The order of the district court was af-firmed.

The Idaho statute regulated corporate takeover bids through a tender offer. A tender offer is a public invitation, usually announced in a newspaper advertisement, to all share-holders of a targeted corporation to tender their shares for sale at a specified price. To induce the shareholders to sell, the price usu-ally includes a premium over the current mar-ket price of the target company's shares. A tender offer may be used to gain control of a company.

The Idaho statute prevented the making of tender offers in the state until the offeror met the statute's requirements, which in-cluded filing a statement with a state official, disclosure to the targeted company of the offeror's intent to make a tender offer, and participation in any hearings required by a state agency. The Williams Act, an amend-ment to the federal Securities Exchange Act of 1934, contains restrictions on the making of tender offers, disclosure requirements, and a provision against fraud.

In March 1977 Great Western (appellee) decided to make a tender offer for 2 million shares of the Sunshine Mining and Metal Com-pany, whose principal place of business was in Idaho. Great Western filed a Schedule 13D with the federal Securities and Exchange Com-mission, disclosing information specified by the Williams Act. Great Western also at-tempted to comply with the Idaho statute, but received communications from the then director of the Idaho Department of Finance, Melvin Baptie, raising objections to the disclo-sures Great Western had made and asking for amendments. After delays were encountered, Great Western filed suit in the Idaho federal district court and obtained a declaratory judg-ment that the Idaho statute was unconstitu-tional.

Wisdom, Circuit Judge:

* * * * *

The commerce clause, U.S. Const., art. I, § 8, grants to Congress the power to regulate foreign and interstate commerce. This affirma-tive grant also imposes limits upon state power to regulate commerce over which Congress has primary responsibility. Nevertheless, not every exercise of state power with some impact on interstate commerce is invalid. "Rather, in areas where activities of legitimate local concern overlap with the national interests expressed by the Commerce Clause—where local and na-tional powers are concurrent—the Court in ab-sence of congressional guidance is called upon to make 'delicate adjustment of the conflicting state and federal claims.' "

* * * * *

B. THE PIKE TEST

Because Congress has not settled the com-merce clause issues raised in this case, we must look to the numerous Supreme Court decisions on the commerce clause for guidance. Fortu-nately, the Court has recently undertaken a re-statement and distillation of its cases. In *Pike v. Bruce Church, Inc.,* 1970 397 U.S. 137, a unanimous Court adopted the following state-ment of the law:

Although the criteria for determining the validity of state statutes affecting interstate commerce have been variously stated, the general rule that emerges can be phrased as follows: where the statute regulates even-handedly to effectuate a legitimate local public interest, and its effects on interstate commerce are only incidental, it will be up-held unless the burden imposed on such commerce is clearly excessive in relation to the putative local benefits. If a legitimate lo-cal purpose is found, then the question be-comes one of degree. And the extent of the burden that will be tolerated will of course depend on the nature of the local intent in-volved, and on whether it could be pro-moted as well with a lesser impact on inter-state activities.

1. Legitimate local purposes

The district judge concluded that the imme-diate purpose of the Idaho takeover law is to protect incumbent management. The district judge further ruled that this purpose is not a legitimate one for state regulation and that no other legitimate local purpose for the Idaho law could be found. McEldowney strongly condemns these findings as a usurpation of the Idaho legislature's functions. We agree with him that at this stage of its analysis the district court too quickly dismissed possible legitimate local interests served by the Idaho takeover law.

It is true that the Idaho law helps incumbent management. One purpose of this favoritism may be to prevent the removal of local business to other states. This purpose would be unacceptable. Indeed, statutes *requiring* business operations to be performed in the home state that could more efficiently be performed elsewhere impose a burden on commerce that is *per se* illegal. Idaho's law does not require any business to remain in Idaho; at worst, it hinders relocation. Nevertheless, the purpose of preserving local industry cannot support the legislation. Nor can that effect be ignored.

McEldowney advances a different state interest in helping incumbent management. He points out that a corporation can influence local lifestyle through such means as charitable contributions or civil involvement and the depth of its commitment to issues such as pollution control or job safety. He contends that this interest in benevolent management is a legitimate reason for Idaho to regulate the means by which outsiders can change management. We accept this as a legitimate local interest.

McEldowney argues that the true purpose of the Idaho takeover statute is to protect investors. This is certainly a legitimate purpose. Since we are not concerned at this step of our analysis with the relationship between the legitimate purpose and the means of regulation, we also consider this interest. We note, however, that Idaho has little reason to protect shareholders of other states, if their securities transactions do not take place within that state or substantially affect Idaho shareholders. . . . In this case, only about two percent of Sunshine's shareholders reside in Idaho. That there are even that many is by chance. Idaho's law would have applied even if no shareholders had resided in Idaho and no securities transactions had taken place within Idaho. Moreover, the

business realities of tender offers make it unlikely that there will be many offers for corporations held predominately by Idahoans (or citizens of any other narrow geographic area). Investment bankers know that local owners are characteristically loyal to management. Therefore, corporations with widespread stock ownership are more promising tender offer targets.

2. Impact on interstate commerce

Rather than establishing interference with commerce that occurred in connection with the Great Western offer for Sunshine, much of the evidence in this case consisted of disputed expert opinions about the general impact Idaho's law would be likely to have on the making of interstate offers and the functioning of national securities markets. One of the effects mentioned at trial is the disruption of the normal securities markets that state-mandated advance notification or announcement of an offer can cause. Another is a change in strategy by offerors. For instance, an offeror anticipating a battle during the delay caused by a state law might deliberately make a low initial offer so that it can raise its offer to meet that of a competitor. There was also testimony that state statutes such as Idaho's have a general effect of discouraging tender offers. . . .

To some extent this evidentiary situation was unavoidable. State takeover laws can have numerous effects on a tender offeror's plans. It would be unusual for each of those effects to be felt in a single offer. Nevertheless, we would hesitate to agree with the district court that the evidence shows a substantial effect on interstate commerce if the record contained only speculation about the effect of Idaho's statute and of state takeover laws in general. The record contains more. Baptie's letter of March 21, 1977 delayed an interstate tender offer that would otherwise have gone forward. That action in itself not only had a substantial impact on interstate commerce, it *stopped* over 31 million dollars of interstate commerce. An executive of Great Western testified that after Baptie's letter the company doubted it could ever satisfy Idaho's requirements.

In addition, except in the rare tender offer

made entirely within Idaho, Idaho's extraterritorial approach to tender offer regulation has an inherent impact on interstate commerce. Idaho's law is designed to alter the disclosure made in securities transactions between Idaho and another state, two other states, and even entirely within another state. Idaho's law can also change the time when, if ever, those non-Idaho securities sales will occur.

* * * * *

3. The balance of the burden and the benefit

The final step under *Pike* is to determine whether the legitimate local purposes served by Idaho's takeover statute justify the law's substantial impact on interstate commerce. . . .

. . . We are interested in the substantiality of both the local interest itself and the link between the interest and the Idaho takeover law. Finally, we note that the challenged regulations are not examples of the kind of safety regulations the Court has been particularly reluctant to strike down.

One state interest to consider is that of protecting investors. The strength of this interest is substantially diluted because Idaho has little reason to protect the large majority of the shareholders affected by the takeover act. In addition, as the district court pointed out, the benefits to investors from the Idaho takeover statute are not certain. McEldowney asserts that during the state imposed delay of a tender offer, the original offeror may be forced to raise the offer, or another more advantageous competing offer may be made. Nothing in the Idaho statute guarantees those benefits. Indeed, shareholders could be *harmed* by the delay if during the waiting period the offeror reduces the offer or abandons altogether a bid shareholders would want to accept if they had a chance.

The additional disclosure required by Idaho's statute may assist some shareholders. It may confuse others. Moreover, additional disclosure from the offeror is not likely to be of great use to a shareholder making economic judgments about the desirability of a tender offer. The key relationship is that between the price offered and the value of the target under current management. Incumbent management is more likely to possess information about the current value of the target than is the offeror.

Another interest asserted by the appellant is that of encouraging civic responsibility by the management of local corporations. No doubt this can be a substantial interest. We question, however, whether it is advanced more than incidentally by the statute challenged in this lawsuit. Surely it cannot be true that all incumbent managers are model corporate citizens or that all tender offerors are vandals. The record certainly contains no support for such a conclusion. Yet, the Idaho takeover statute imposes the same handicaps on all offerors and the same advantages on all incumbent managers.

There is, of course, some relation between the Idaho takeover law and the interest in responsible management. The increased disclosure required by state law might help interested shareholders to determine whether a tender offeror is civically responsible. But that information would be of no help if it is never disclosed because the burdensome state requirements discourage a responsible offeror from ever making an offer for an Idaho corporation. Nor would the state law help if civically irresponsible incumbents are able to force an officer to abandon his bid by invoking time consuming hearing processes or litigating the adequacy of the immaterial disclosures required by the Idaho statute. Moreover, disclosure will not be an effective means of encouraging corporate civic responsibility if the shareholders concentrate more on the economics of an offer than the civic attitudes of the offeror. This economic bias seems particularly likely when, as here, most of the shareholders are not Idahoans.

Idaho could encourage good corporate citizenship with legislation more focused on that purpose. Health and safety regulations can be enacted. Tax incentives can encourage charitable contributions. Programs to involve local businessmen in civic problems can be created. These approaches would be likely to have a more direct impact on corporate behavior than increased disclosure in tender offers. They would also impose a substantially smaller burden on interstate commerce than the Idaho takeover law.

Against this uncertain protection for the small percentage of Sunshine shareholders in whom Idaho has a substantial legitimate local interest, and the, at best, indirect and incidental preservation of corporate civic responsibility provided by fuller disclosure, we must weigh our conclusions about the impact of Idaho's takeover statute on interstate commerce. Idaho's extraterritorial regulation of tender offers interferes with securities transactions all over the country. In this case, Idaho's law halted over 31 million dollars of interstate commerce.

In addition, Idaho's statute would have compelled a non-Idaho offeror to make burdensome disclosures beyond those required by federal law to Sunshine shareholders all over the world.

We conclude that these burdens are disproportionate to the legitimate benefits the Idaho takeover law provides. This conclusion is strengthened because another effect—perhaps unintended—of the Idaho statute is to hinder the movement of local businesses to other states. As a result, we agree with the district court that the Idaho takeover law is invalid under the commerce clause.

Case questions

1. The circuit court used a tripartite framework for determining the constitutionality of the Utah regulation of tender offers set out in *Pike v. Bruce Church, Inc.* What three inquiries did the court focus on, and what conclusions did the court reach?

2. If the Commerce Clause does not expressly prohibit state regulation in all areas of commerce, how can a court conclude that a state tender offer statute is unconstitutional?

3. Would the application of the Idaho statute to a tender offer made entirely within Idaho violate the Commerce Clause?

4. Suppose that Great Western had introduced evidence that New York also had a statute regulating tender offers and that if New York had asserted jurisdiction over the Sunshine offer, its legal requirements would have contradicted Idaho's. What effect would that have had on the court's decision?

5. Would the case have turned out differently if a large percentage of Sunshine shareholders were Idaho residents? Explain.

The supremacy clause

The Constitution's Supremacy Clause provides that "[t]his Constitution, and the Laws of the United States which shall be made in Pursuance thereof . . ., shall be the supreme Law of the land." From this clause has evolved what is called the preemption doctrine. Under this doctrine, to the extent that Congress has acted, the federal power is exclusive and no conflicting state regulation is permitted. Where a state statute is in conflict with a federal law, the federal law controls and preempts the state statute. Thus Congress may, under the Supremacy Clause, preempt state regulation of an area. Sometimes Congress specifically declares state regulation to be preempted. For example, it has done this in the Employee Retirement Income Security Act (1974 Pension Reform Act). At other times Congress specifically declares that it does not intend to preempt state regulation. When Congress is silent, courts must determine whether the state and federal statutes are in conflict. To the extent that they are, federal law prevails. Because of the judicial presumption of the constitutionality of legislation, the basic approach favors sustaining state regulation wherever possible. Thus a state law is superseded because of conflict with federal law only where the conflict is so direct that the state and federal regulations cannot be reconciled. In determining whether the preemption doctrine applies, courts consider the following factors: (1) the historical or conventional classification of the subject matter, (2) the completeness of the federal scheme of regulation, (3) the similarity between the federal and state statutes, (4) the dominance of federal interest in the field, and (5) the interest in uniform, national regulation—the most important factor.

The following case is a continuation of the *Kidwell* opinion.

Great Western United Corp. v. *Kidwell*
577 F. 2d 1256 (5th Cir. 1978)

Wisdom, Circuit Judge: No simple, mechanical formula can summarize the analysis necessary to determine whether a state statute is void under the supremacy clause, U.S. Const. art. I, § 10. The nature of a court's inquiries as to this question has been established in earlier cases. The Supreme Court summarized these inquiries in *Jones* v. *Rath Packing Co.,*

The first inquiry is whether Congress, pursuant to its power to regulate commerce, U.S. Const. Art. 1 § 8, has prohibited state regulation of the particular aspects of commerce involved in this case. . . . [W]hen Congress has "unmistakably . . . ordained," that its enactments alone are to regulate a part of commerce, state laws regulating that aspect of commerce must fall. This result is compelled whether Congress' command is explicitly stated in the statute's language or implicitly contained in its structure and purpose.

Congressional enactments that do not exclude all state legislation in the same field nevertheless override state laws with which they conflict. The criterion for determining whether state and federal laws are so inconsistent that the

state law must give way is firmly established in our decisions. Our task is "to determine whether, under the circumstances of this particular case, [the state's] law stands as an obstacle to the accomplishment and execution of the full purposes and objectives of Congress." This inquiry requires us to consider the relationship between state and federal laws as they are interpreted and applied, not merely as they are written.

. . . We rely . . . on the principles in the second paragraph quoted from *Jones,* and hold that the particular takeover law before us cannot stand because it conflicts with the federal statute. . . .

*   *   *   *   *

B.   THE CONFLICT BETWEEN THE IDAHO TAKEOVER STATUTE AND THE WILLIAMS ACT

The underlying purpose of the Williams Act is to protect investors. Congress chose this goal in the Williams Act and adopted a distinct means of achieving it. Essentially, Congress relied upon a "market approach" to investor protection. The function of federal regulation is to get information to the investor by allowing both the offeror and the incumbent managers of a target company to present fully their arguments and then to let the investor decide for himself. In identical language the Senate and House Reports explained, "This bill is designed to make the relevant facts known so that shareholders have a fair opportunity to make their decision.". . .

The reason for this approach was congressional recognition that tender offers often benefit an investor and that a statute preventing tender offers could harm, rather than protect, investors. The original bill to amend the 1934 Act, introduced in 1965, sought to protect investors by making it difficult for tender offers to succeed. This approach attracted considerable opposition, including that of the SEC.

As a result, Congress amended the draft bill to make it less burdensome to offerors. A cornerstone of the revised approach to investor protection was the law's deliberate neutrality among the contestants in a tender offer. The Senate Report explained:

The committee has taken extreme care to avoid tipping the balance of regulation either in favor of management or in favor of the person making the takeover bid. The bill is designed to require full and fair disclosure for the benefit of investors while at the same time providing the offeror and management equal opportunity to fairly present their case.

*   *   *   *   *

Of course, this language does not mean Great Western has a right under the Williams Act to complete its tender offer successfully. Instead, it creates the investor's right to hear a fair presentation of the offeror's proposal. This investor's right can be carried out, however, only by avoiding regulation that puts the offeror at a disadvantage to incumbent management. Congress recognized that delay can seriously impede a tender offer. It rejected legal requirements, such as precommencement review by the SEC, that could delay offers unnecessarily. Such delay could prevent the offeror from fairly presenting its case.

*   *   *   *   *

There is no real dispute that the Idaho statute—like most of the state takeover laws—increases a target company's ability to defeat a tender offer. The Idaho law helps target companies primarily through provisions not found in the Williams Act that give them advance notice of a tender offer and the ability to delay the commencement of an offer, by means such as insisting on a hearing. Most observers of takeover battles agree that time is among the most effective weapons available to a company resisting a tender offer. The Idaho statute favors the target in other ways, as well. Idaho's regulation of defensive efforts by a target is significantly weaker than Idaho's regulation of an offeror's activities. Finally, the Idaho statute gives the target corporation board the power to exclude an offer from state regulation by approving the offer.

The district court concluded that these pro-management provisions evidenced a legislative purpose "to inhibit tender offers for the benefit of management." The district court further reasoned that this purpose conflicted with the Williams Act's purpose of protecting investors, and that this conflict meant the Williams Act preempted Idaho's statute.

McEldowney strenuously objects to the district court's characterization of the purpose of the Idaho takeover law. He contends that Idaho, like Congress, legislated to protect investors. He explains the pro-management provisions not as an attempt to prevent tender offers, but as a means of involving the directors and officers of the target in the evaluation of a tender offer. With the advance warning and additional time provided by the state law, so he argues, target directors have an opportunity to fulfill their fiduciary duties to shareholders by studying the offer and either negotiating better terms or making a recommendation based on the shareholders' interests. McEldowney also explains that management has the power to exclude an offer from Idaho regulation because presumably management will do so only when it already has had an opportunity to study the offer thoroughly and to negotiate fully a takeover.

We need not probe the minds of Idaho legislators to determine whether the true purpose of the Idaho takeover law was to protect investors or to protect incumbent management. Even if we accept the appellant's interpretation of the legislature's purpose, it is still true that Idaho chose to protect investors differently from the way Congress protected investors. Instead of relying upon investors' decisions after full disclosure, Idaho relies upon the business judgment of corporate directors with a fiduciary duty to their shareholders. Idaho's "fiduciary approach" to investor protection may be one way to protect shareholders, but it is an approach Congress rejected.

Idaho's statute is preempted, because the market approach to investor protection adopted by Congress and the fiduciary approach adopted by Idaho are incompatible. . . . Congress intended for the investor to evaluate a tender offer; Idaho asks the target company management to make that decision on behalf of the shareholders. That Congress rejected provisions very similar to some of those in the Idaho takeover statute does not mean the state law is automatically preempted. In this situation, however, Congress rejected those provisions to preserve the neutral regulatory stance that gives each side of a tender offer an equal opportunity to persuade the investor. When Idaho enacted those rejected provisions it hampered an offeror's ability to express and explain its position directly to investors. In doing so, Idaho disrupted the neutrality indispensable for the proper operation of the federal market approach to tender offers regulation. The Idaho takeover statute "stands as an obstacle to the accomplishment and execution of the full purposes and objectives" of the Williams Act.

The Idaho statute requires substantially more disclosure than the Williams Act. In that respect, as the SEC points out, it also interferes with federal regulation. McEldowney argues that Congress had the express desire to get information to investors. Idaho's more demanding disclosure requirements, he contends, only go further in the same direction, thereby carrying out rather than frustrating the purposes and objectives of Congress.

Superficially Idaho's extensive disclosure requirements appear compatible with a market approach to tender offer investor protection. In reality, in the area of financial disclosure it can be true that "less is more." Disclosure of a mass of irrelevant data can confuse the investor and obscure relevant disclosures. Management may also be able to halt an offer because some immaterial information required by excessive disclosure standards is missing or inaccurate. Those excessive requirements would cut off an offeror's opportunity to present the material information that investors need to make their decisions.

In § 13(d) of the Williams Act Congress delegated to the SEC the task of specifying what data is material to an investor considering a tender offer. The SEC has attempted to write disclosure requirements that provide enough material information without producing reports so detailed and complicated that few shareholders would want to read them. That judgment is a legislative one. Idaho's effort to second guess that judgment cannot stand. This is particularly true because Idaho's additions to the federal disclosure requirements reduce the utility of federally required disclosure and produce an obstacle to the accomplishment of the federal objective to enable investors to make an informed choice about a tender offer.

* * * * *

Case questions

1. What basic principles guided the circuit court's decision?

2. How did the circuit court characterize the underlying purpose of the Williams Act? Would it have made any difference if Congress

had provided that the purpose of the Williams Act was "solely" to protect investors?

3. How was the circuit court's decision affected by the fact that Congress, when enacting the Williams Act, rejected approaches resembling the Idaho statute's approach to tender offer regulation?

4. Why should the states not be permitted to require more stringent standards on tender offers than does Congress so as to protect their

people from making hasty and uninformed decisions when such offers are made?

5. Suppose Congress had expressly consented to state tender offer regulation. What effect would that have had on the circuit court's decision?

FIRST AMENDMENT FREEDOMS

The First Amendment of the U.S. Constitution provides:

> Congress shall make no law respecting an establishment of religion, or prohibiting the free exercise thereof; or abridging the freedom of speech, or of the press; or the right of the people peaceably to assemble, and to petition the Government for a redress of grievances.

Although the First Amendment is phrased as a prohibition against congressional encroachment upon the freedoms of religion, speech, press, and association, the Supreme Court has applied its protection to state impairments of these freedoms. The Court has done this by finding that the 1st Amendment freedoms are among those fundamental personal rights and liberties protected by the Due Process Clause of the 14th Amendment, which is a limitation upon state action. The Court has thus absorbed the 1st Amendment freedoms into the 14th's Due Process Clause. This is known as the absorption doctrine or the incorporation doctrine. Those fundamental liberties guaranteed by the first 10 amendments (the Bill of Rights) against federal infringement—liberties that the Court finds to be fundamental and necessary to the ordered liberty of a free society—are incorporated into the 14th's Due Process Clause—and thus made applicable against the states.

Sunday blue laws

Many states have Sunday closing laws, sometimes called Sunday blue laws, prohibiting the conduct of business on Sunday. Although these laws do not interfere with religious beliefs or observances, their enforcement does occasion economic loss to nonconformists and members of religious minorities whom the laws prevent from doing business on Sundays. Conceding that these laws might have had religious origins, the Supreme Court nevertheless sustained their constitutionality in *McGowan* v. *Maryland*,[10] concluding that they now served the secular purpose of providing society with a uniform day of rest and recreation.

---

[10] 366 U.S. 420 (1961).

Freedom of speech and press

The First Amendment guarantees of the freedoms of speech and press, have not been considered by the Supreme Court to be absolute. As Justice Holmes said in *Schenck* v. *United States,* "The most stringent protection of free speech would not protect a man in falsely shouting fire in a theatre and causing panic."[11] What speech, then, is protected by the Constitution, and what speech may be prohibited or punished? These questions have not been easy ones for the Court.

Although frequently thought of in connection with speech in a political context, the First Amendment also applies to speech in a commercial context. The following discussion focuses on one area of commercial speech: advertising.

Advertising and the First Amendment. The First Amendment to the Constitution protects freedom of speech and freedom of the press from infringement by the government. As the advertising industry expanded, courts faced the issue of whether these protections extended to advertising.

In 1942 the Supreme Court decided *Valentine* v. *Chrestensen.*[12] Chrestensen distributed a handbill advertising a submarine he operated as an amusement attraction. He was advised that an ordinance prohibited the distribution of commercial material in the street. Chrestensen revised the handbill, printing his advertisement on one side and a protest against the ordinance on the other. He was restrained from distributing the handbill. The Court upheld the prohibition, reasoning that Chrestensen's purpose in printing the protest was to avoid the ordinance. The Court sustained the constitutionality of the ordinance, holding that commercial speech was not entitled to First Amendment protection.

Although *Chrestensen* was a unanimous opinion, several state supreme courts interpreted their state constitutions as protecting commercial speech.[13] Subsequently the *Chrestensen* decision was limited as the Court held that paid political advertisements [14] and abortion advertisements[15] were protected by the Constitution.

In *Virginia Pharmacy Board* v. *Virginia Citizens Commerce Council,* the Supreme Court was again confronted by a claim that purely commercial speech was protected by the Constitution.[16] A Virginia statute prohibited licensed pharmacists from advertising their prices for prescription drugs. The Commerce Council, a consumer group, challenged the law's constitutionality. The Court examined the interests of the parties to the advertisement. It noted that

---

[11] 249 U.S. 47 (1919).

[12] 316 U.S. 52 (1942).

[13] *Preir* v. *White,* 132 Fla. 1, 180 So. 247 (1938): *Orangeburg* v. *Farmer,* 181 S.C. 143, 186 S.E. 783 (1938).

[14] *New York Times* v. *Sullivan,* 376 U.S. 255 (1964).

[15] *Bigelow* v. *Virginia,* 421 U.S. 809 (1975).

[16] 425 U.S. 746 (1976).

the advertiser's motivation was purely economic. However, after reviewing decisions rendered after *Chrestensen,* it concluded that this did not necessarily disqualify the advertisement from constitutional protection.

The Court then focused on the consumer's interests, interests which were not represented before the Court in *Chrestensen* 24 years earlier. The consumer's interest in the free flow of commercial information was at least as strong as the consumer's interest in political debates. Information about drug prices facilitated the intelligent, well-informed private economic decisions responsible for allocating resources in a predominantly free enterprise economy. The consumer's interests, although not considered in *Chrestensen,* were also protected by the First Amendment. Thus the Virginia statute was declared unconstitutional.

The Court indicated, however, that reasonable restrictions on the time, place, and manner of commercial speech are permissible where such restrictions are justified by a significant governmental interest and where ample alternative channels of communication remain available. By this qualification the Court in *Virginia Pharmacy* indicated that there was still life in the commercial speech doctrine. Lest any doubt remain, however, the Court applied the doctrine two years later in *Ohralik* v. *Ohio State Bar Association,* upholding the suspension of an attorney's license to practice law where the attorney solicited clients.[17]

The following case illustrates the constitutional analysis involved in commercial speech cases.

Central Hudson Gas and Electric Corp. v. Public Service Commission of New York
100 S. Ct. 2343 (1980)

Central Hudson Gas and Electric (appellant) brought suit in a New York State court to challenge the constitutionality of a regulation of the New York Public Service Commission (appellee) which completely barred promotional advertising by the utility. The regulation prohibited private electric utilities from engaging in promotional advertising intended to stimulate sales. The order was necessary, the commission maintained, to further energy conservation and to forestall pricing inequities among consumers ascribable to a rate structure that subsidized the costs of incremental units of electricity. The regulation was upheld by the trial court and at the inter- *mediate appellate level. On appeal by the utility the New York Court of Appeals sustained the regulation. The U.S. Supreme Court reversed.*

Mr. Justice Powell:

* * * * *

The Commission's order restricts only commercial speech, that is, expression related solely to the economic interests of the speaker and its audience. The First Amendment, as applied to the States through the Fourteenth Amendment, protects commercial speech from unwarranted governmental regulation. Commercial expression not only serves the eco-

---

[17] 436 U.S. 447 (1978).

nomic interest of the speaker, but also assists consumers and furthers the societal interest in the fullest possible dissemination of information. In applying the First Amendment to this area, we have rejected the "highly paternalistic" view that government has complete power to suppress or regulate commercial speech. "[P]eople will perceive their own best interests if only they are well enough informed, and . . . the best means to that end is to open the channels of communication rather than to close them.". . .

Nevertheless, our decisions have recognized "the 'commonsense' distinction between speech proposing a commercial transaction, which occurs in an area traditionally subject to government regulation, and other varieties of speech." The Constitution therefore accords a lesser protection to commercial speech than to other constitutionally guaranteed expression. The protection available for particular commercial expression turns on the nature both of the expression and of the governmental interests served by its regulation.

The First Amendment's concern for commercial speech is based on the informational function of advertising. Consequently, there can be no constitutional objection to the suppression of commercial messages that do not accurately inform the public about lawful activity. The government may ban forms of communication more likely to deceive the public than to inform it, or commercial speech related to illegal activity.

If the communication is neither misleading nor related to unlawful activity, the government's power is more circumscribed. The State must assert a substantial interest to be achieved by restrictions on commercial speech. Moreover, the regulatory technique must be in proportion to that interest. The limitation on expression must be designed carefully to achieve the State's goal. Compliance with this requirement may be measured by two criteria. First, the restriction must directly advance the state interest involved; the regulation may not be sustained if it provides only ineffective or remote support for the government's purpose. Second, if the governmental interest could be served as well by a more limited restriction on com-

mercial speech, the excessive restrictions cannot survive.

* * * * *

The second criterion recognizes that the First Amendment mandates that speech restrictions be "narrowly drawn." The regulatory technique may extend only as far as the interest it serves. The State cannot regulate speech that poses no danger to the asserted state interest, nor can it completely suppress information when narrower restrictions on expression would serve its interest as well. . . .

In commercial speech cases, then, a four-part analysis has developed. At the outset, we must determine whether the expression is protected by the First Amendment. For commercial speech to come within that provision, it at least must concern lawful activity and not be misleading. Next, we ask whether the asserted governmental interest is substantial. If both inquiries yield positive answers, we must determine whether the regulation directly advances the governmental interest asserted, and whether it is not more extensive than is necessary to serve that interest.

The Commission does not claim that the expression at issue either is inaccurate or relates to unlawful activity. Yet the New York Court of Appeals questioned whether Central Hudson's advertising is protected commercial speech. Because appellant holds a monopoly over the sale of electricity in its service area, the state court suggested that the Commission's order restricts no commercial speech of any worth. The court stated that advertising in a "non-competitive market" could not improve the decisionmaking of consumers. The court saw no constitutional problem with barring commercial speech that it viewed as conveying little useful information.

This reasoning falls short of establishing that appellant's advertising is not commercial speech protected by the First Amendment. Monopoly over the supply of a product provides no protection from competition with substitutes for that product. Electric utilities compete with suppliers of fuel oil and natural gas in several markets, such as those for home heating and industrial power. . . . Each energy source continues to offer peculiar advantages and disadvantages that may influence consumer choice. For consumers in those competitive markets, advertising by utilities is just as valuable as advertising by unregulated firms.

Even in monopoly markets, the suppression of advertising reduces the information available for consumer decisions and thereby defeats the purpose of the First Amendment. The New York court's argument appears to assume that the providers of a monopoly service or product are willing to pay for wholly ineffective advertising. Most businesses—even regulated monopolies—are unlikely to underwrite promotional advertising that is of no interest or use to consumers. Indeed, a monopoly enterprise legitimately may wish to inform the public that it has developed new services or terms of doing business. A consumer may need information to aid his decision whether or not to use the monopoly service at all, or how much of the service he should purchase. In the absence of factors that would distort the decision to advertise, we may assume that the willingness of a business to promote its products reflects a belief that consumers are interested in the advertising. Since no such extraordinary conditions have been identified in this case, appellant's monopoly position does not alter the First Amendment's protection for its commercial speech.

The Commission offers two state interests as justifications for the ban on promotional advertising. The first concerns energy conservation. Any increase in demand for electricity— during peak or off-peak periods—means greater consumption of energy. The Commission argues, and the New York court agreed, that the State's interest in conserving energy is sufficient to support suppression of advertising designed to increase consumption of electricity. In view of our country's dependence on energy resources beyond our control, no one can doubt the importance of energy conservation. Plainly, therefore, the state interest asserted is substantial. [The Court's discussion of the second state interest is omitted.—Ed.]

* * * * *

Next, we focus on the relationship between the State's interests and the advertising ban. . . .

. . . [T]he State's interest in energy conser-

vation is directly advanced by the Commission order at issue here. There is an immediate connection between advertising and demand for electricity. Central Hudson would not contest the advertising ban unless it believed that promotion would increase its sales. Thus, we find a direct link between the state interest in conservation and the Commission's order.

We come finally to the critical inquiry in this case: whether the Commission's complete suppression of speech ordinarily protected by the First Amendment is no more extensive than necessary to further the State's interest in energy conservation. The Commission's order reaches all promotional advertising, regardless of the impact of the touted service on overall energy use. But the energy conservation rationale, as important as it is, cannot justify suppressing information about electric devices or services that would cause no net increase in total energy use. In addition, no showing has been made that a more limited restriction on the content of promotional advertising would not serve adequately the State's interests.

Appellant insists that but for the ban, it would advertise products and services that use energy efficiently. These include the "heat pump," which both parties acknowledge to be a major improvement in electric heating, and the use of electric heat as a "back-up" to solar and other heat sources. Although the Commission has questioned the efficiency of electric heating before this Court, neither the Commission's Policy Statement nor its order denying rehearing made findings on this issue. In the absence of authoritative findings to the contrary, we must credit as within the realm of possibility the claim that electric heat can be an efficient alternative in some circumstances.

The Commission's order prevents appellant from promoting electric services that would reduce energy use by diverting demand for less efficient sources, or that would consume roughly the same amount of energy as do alternative sources. In neither situation would the utility's advertising endanger conservation or mislead the public. To the extent that the Commission's order suppresses speech that in no way impairs the State's interest in energy conservation, the Commission's order violates the

First and Fourteenth Amendments and must be invalidated.

The Commission also has not demonstrated that its interest in conservation cannot be protected adequately by more limited regulation of appellant's commercial expression. To further its policy of conservation, the Commission could attempt to restrict the format and content of Central Hudson's advertising. It might, for example, require that the advertisements include information about the relative efficiency and expense of the offered service, both under current conditions and for the foreseeable future. In the absence of a showing that more limited speech regulation would be ineffective, we cannot approve the complete suppression of Central Hudson's advertising.

Our decision today in no way disparages the national interest in energy conservation. We accept without reservation the argument that conservation, as well as the development of alternate energy sources, is an imperative national goal. Administrative bodies empowered to regulate electric utilities have the authority—and indeed the duty—to take appropriate action to further this goal. When, however, such action involves the suppression of speech, the First and Fourteenth Amendments require that the restriction be no more extensive than is necessary to serve the state interest. In this case, the record before us fails to show that the total ban on promotional advertising meets this requirement.

* * * * *

Case questions

1. Was Justice Powell correct in asserting that "[t]he Commission's order restricts *only* commercial speech"? (Emphasis added.)

2. Suppose the commission's order prohibited more than mere proposals to engage in certain kinds of commercial transactions. How would that fact alter the Court's approach in deciding the case?

3. Suppose the Public Service Commission of New York adopts a regulation prohibiting "utilities from using bill inserts to discuss political matters, including the desirability of future development of nuclear power." Would such a regulation be constitutional?

4. Should the Court give commercial speech treatment different from that accorded to political speech?

PROPERTY RIGHTS AND ECONOMIC REGULATION

Economic regulation frequently restricts the use of property or lessens its value. Resort to the Constitution is often made to prevent such impairment of "property rights." The discussion now turns to an examination of these economic liberties.

The substantive due process doctrine

Both the 5th and 14th amendments provide that no person shall be "deprived of life, liberty, or property, without due process of law." These due process clauses were originally intended to assure procedural safeguards when life, liberty, or property were the subjects of governmental action. However, the Supreme Court later used the Due Process Clause to examine the constitutional validity of legislation affecting life, liberty, or property.

Using the Due Process Clause to scrutinize the substance of such legislation became known as the substantive due process doctrine. From 1890 until the 1930s the Court embarked on a path now considered to have been erroneous in which it applied the Due Process Clause to invalidate a substantial number of statutes dealing with social and economic matters. Although the substantive due process doctrine is of only historical significance today, a review of its application is presented to provide some perspective on the Court's current posture.

The primacy of legislation: In 1877 the Court upheld the constitutionality of a state statute fixing maximum prices for storing grain in warehouses. The Court stated:

> Rights of property which have been created by the common law cannot be taken away without due process; but the law itself . . . may be changed at the will, or even at the whim, of legislatures, unless prevented by constitutional limitations. . . . For protection against abuses by legislatures the people must resort to the polls, not the courts.[18]

At this time, however, a treatise by Thomas Cooley entitled *Constitutional Limitations Which Rest upon the Legislative Power of the States of the American Union* was also quite popular. In this treatise Cooley advocated that the Due Process Clause be used to strike down legislative enactments which interfered with vested property rights. Cooley argued that due process of law was synonymous with the law of the land, which was the general law or the general rules governing a society. He went so far as to say that "a legislative enactment is not necessarily the law of the land."[19]

Due process becomes due substance. By the turn of the 20th-century the Supreme Court's personnel had changed. Most of the new justices had been corporate lawyers before coming to the bench, and they were firmly wedded to Cooley's notion that courts might invalidate statutes under the theory of substantive due process. Using the Due Process Clause, the Court struck down statutes that it considered unreasonable.

Substantive due process hit its high-water mark with the case of *Lochner* v. *New York,* in which the Court invalidated a state statute setting a maximum workweek of 60 hours.[20] The Court reasoned that such a law restricted the liberty of an employer and an employee to contract to work more hours than the law allowed.

Justice Holmes' dissenting opinion in *Lochner* laid the foundation for future Court opinions. Holmes stated:

> I think that the word "liberty" in the Fourteenth Amendment is perverted when it is held to prevent the natural outcome of a dominant opinion, unless it can be said that a rational and fair man necessarily would admit that the

---

[18] *Munn* v. *Illinois,* 94 U.S. 113 (1877).
[19] T. Cooley, *Constitutional Limitations* 353 (3d ed. 1874).
[20] 198 U.S. 45 (1905).

statute proposed would infringe fundamental principles as they have been understood by the traditions of our people and our law.

The decline of substantive due process. The substantive due process doctrine fell into disfavor when the Court applied it during the economic depression of the 1930s to invalidate innovative legislation designed to address that crisis. Roosevelt's Court-packing plan, discussed earlier with reference to Supreme Court decisions regarding federal power to regulate the economy under the Commerce Clause, also influenced the Court's subsequent shift away from substantive due process.

Impairment of property values and eminent domain

All governments have historically enjoyed the right of eminent domain, which is the right of a government to take, or to authorize the taking of, private property for public use. The Fifth Amendment recognizes this basic governmental right but requires that just compensation be given to the owner. It provides that private property may not "be taken for public use, without just compensation." Thus, if government wants to convert a privately owned building into a post office or to build a dam that will flood nearby land, it must compensate owners for the losses resulting from these activities.

As the scope of governmental regulation grows, the economic impact of governmental regulation upon business requires examination of whether such regulation has resulted in a governmental taking of private property calling for just compensation to be paid to the owners. Concern with environmental quality and land use has made this a major issue in modern society. Regulation of environmental quality and land use has increased in recent years. Environmental protection regulations and zoning laws often disproportionately affect the property rights of a few community members. Compensating these property owners may make the price of obtaining environmental quality and land use control politically impractical. The conflict between public need and private loss thus arises as the forces of social change come into conflict with established economic interests. Hence, the issue is when the public should be required to compensate private property owners who suffer from a diminution of property values as a result of government regulations.

Under the Supreme Court's interpretation of the Fifth Amendment, compensation is required only for a governmental taking of property and not for losses occasioned by mere regulation. However, the general rule is that while property may be regulated to a certain extent, regulation which goes too far will be recognized as a taking. Where a regulation does not constitute a taking of private property, the Court has held that the Constitution permits outright condemnation or a complete impairment of property without compensation. Thus, government may not have to pay a penny when it prohibits the continuation of a business which has been established for a long time;

or outlaws certain businesses altogether, with ensuing total or near total destruction of values; or prohibits the use of land for any of the purposes which give it substantial economic value. Where government engages in such business regulation, courts usually decide that the economic loss suffered by the private citizen is merely an incident of the lawful exercise of police power and not compensable.

The following case presents the Supreme Court's current approach to government's right of eminent domain. The Court's approach in deciding whether a particular governmental action has effected a taking is to balance the character of the action against its economic impact. The test appears to be whether the property owner has been singled out to endure financial hardship for no rational reason.

PruneYard Shopping Center v. *Robins*
100 S. Ct. 2034 (1980)

Michael Robins (appellee) and his high school classmates sought to solicit support for their opposition to a United Nations resolution. One Saturday afternoon they set up a table in a corner of the PruneYard Shopping Center's central courtyard. PruneYard (appellant) is a privately owned shopping center which contains over 75 commercial establishments and is open to the public. Soon after the students had begun soliciting signatures, a security guard informed them that they would have to leave. The students left the premises immediately. Later they filed suit against PruneYard, seeking to enjoin it from denying them access to the shopping center for the purpose of circulating their petitions. The trial court decided against the students. However, the California Supreme Court reversed, holding that the California constitution protected petitioning, reasonably exercised, in shopping centers even when the centers were privately owned. PruneYard appealed to the U.S. Supreme Court, which affirmed the California Supreme Court's decision.

Mr. Justice Rehnquist:

* * * * *

Appellants . . . contend that a right to exclude others underlies the Fifth Amendment guarantee against the taking of property without just compensation and the Fourteenth Amendment guarantee against the deprivation of property without due process of law.

It is true that one of the essential sticks in the bundle of property rights is the right to exclude others. And here there has literally been a "taking" of that right to the extent that the California Supreme Court has interpreted the state constitution to entitle its citizens to exercise free expression and petition rights on shopping center property. But it is well-established that "not every destruction or injury to property by governmental action has been held to be a 'taking' in the constitutional sense." Rather, the determination whether a state law unlawfully infringes a landowner's property in violation of the Taking Clause requires an examination of whether the restriction on private property "forc[es] some people alone to bear public burdens which, in all fairness and justice, should be borne by the public as a whole." This examination entails inquiry into such factors as the character of the governmental action, its economic impact, and its interference with reasonable investment backed expectations. When "regulation goes too far it will be recognized as a taking."

Here the requirement that appellants permit appellees to exercise state-protected rights of free expression and petition on shopping center property clearly does not amount to an unconstitutional infringement of appellants' property rights under the Taking Clause. There is nothing to suggest that preventing appellants from prohibiting this sort of activity will unreasonably impair the value or use of their property as a shopping center. The PruneYard is a large commercial complex that covers several city blocks, contains numerous separate buiness establishments, and is open to the public at large. The decision of the California Supreme Court makes it clear that the PruneYard may restrict expressive activity by adopting time, place and manner regulations that will minimize any interference with its commercial functions. Appellees were orderly and they limited their activity to the common areas of the shopping center. In these circumstances, the fact that they may have "physically invaded" appellants' property cannot be viewed as determinative.

*   *   *   *   *

. . . A State is, of course, bound by the Just Compensation Clause of the Fifth Amendment, but here appellants have failed to demonstrate that the "right to exclude others" is so essential to the use or economic value of their property that the State-authorized limitation of it amounted to a "taking."

There is also little merit to appellants' argument that they have been denied their property without due process of law. In *Nebbia* v. *New York,* this Court stated that

> [Neither] property rights nor contract rights are absolute. . . . Equally fundamental with the private right is that of the public to regulate it in the common interest. . . . [T]he guaranty of due process, as has often been held, demands only that the law shall not be unreasonable, arbitrary or capricious, and that the means selected shall have a real and substantial relation to the objective sought to be [obtained].

Appellants have failed to provide sufficient justification for concluding that this test is not satisfied by the State's asserted interest in promoting more expansive rights of free speech and petition than conferred by the Federal Constitution.

*   *   *   *   *

Case questions

1. What test did the Court use in determining whether there had been an unconstitutional taking of private property?

2. What factors did the Court isolate in determining whether permitting the students to petition on shopping center property would unreasonably impair the value of the property as a shopping center?

3. Suppose the shopping center consisted of only five commercial establishments and the students wished to solicit support for their petition at the only entrance to the center. Would the case have been decided differently?

CONSTITUTIONAL PROTECTIONS IN ADMINISTRATIVE PROCEDURES

Thus far, much of the discussion regarding the constitutional background of administrative regulation has pertained to the constitutional issues raised by the legislative process. However, most governmental regulation of business is accomplished through administrative agencies. Administrative agencies are established by the legislature, which delegates to them the authority to pursue the public interest as it is legislatively defined. In this way the legislature frees itself from the day-to-day aspects of economic regulation by empowering agencies staffed by experts to administer legislatively defined regulatory objectives.

Increasing governmental regulation has made the relationship between administrative power and individual rights more important in modern society. Thus the following discussion focuses on the rights of individual members of the business community vis-à-vis the administrative process. The discussion examines agency efforts to acquire information about the subjects of their regulation.

Administrative investigations

Administrative agencies need information in order to exercise their rulemaking and enforcement powers intelligently.[21] Access to information is necessary to effect the administration of governmental regulation of business. Regulation of businesses cannot be intelligently undertaken unless the regulators have access to information that only the regulated businesses can supply. Indeed, private parties supply most of the information that agencies acquire for these rulemaking and enforcement activities. For example, there is an enormous flow of information to the Internal Revenue Service in the form of tax returns and to the Securities and Exchange Commission in the form of registration statements. Nevertheless, some protection against governmental meddling is provided by the Fourth Amendment's prohibition against "unreasonable searches and seizures" and by the Fifth Amendment's prohibition against compelling any person "in any criminal case to be a witness against himself."

Agencies obtain information through (1) record-keeping and reporting requirements, (2) the inspection of records and premises, and (3) the subpoena of witnesses and documents.

Record-keeping and reporting requirements. In a country where regulation is a fundamental fact of economic existence, record-keeping and reporting requirements span the entire business spectrum. An agency generally requires a regulated business to keep records and further requires the business to file reports with the agency so that the agency can be kept apprised of its compliance with the law. The requirements that certain records be kept and certain reports filed are necessary and incidental to any agency's regulatory activities.

The Supreme Court has held in *Shapiro* v. *United States* that records required to be kept by law are to be considered public records and hence are not shielded from agency inspection by the Fifth Amendment.[22] Any records required to be kept in connection with a regulated activity are thus public records. Under the Court's approach, private business records become public

---

[21] Some agencies are authorized to promulgate rules which have the force of law. This rulemaking power is discussed in more detail in Chapter 3.

[22] 335 U.S. 1 (1948).

as soon as they are required to be kept. For regulated businesses the effect of this approach is to remove the protection against self-incrimination contained in the Fifth Amendment with regard to any relevant records that a regulating agency might require them to keep.

Similarly, the Court has held that the Fifth Amendment does not protect a business against a report requirement.[23] Under the Court's present approach, the public interest in obtaining information outweighs the private interest in opposing disclosure.

Administrative inspections. Inspection is an indispensable aspect of any agency's enforcement procedures. The major issue with regard to administrative inspection of business premises pertains to the Fourth Amendment's prohibition against warrantless, unreasonable searches and seizures.

In *See* v. *City of Seattle* the Court recognized the constitutional right of a business premise not to be subjected to an administrative inspection without a search warrant.[24] When he was convicted for refusing to permit a fire inspector to enter his warehouse without a warrant, Norman See, a Seattle businessman, appealed to the Supreme Court. As a result, the conviction was overturned. In ruling that commercial property merited the same Fourth Amendment protection as residential property, the Court stated: "The businessman, like the occupant of a residence, has a constitutional right to go about his business free from unreasonable official entries upon his private commercial property."[25]

In 1970, in *Colonnade Catering Corp.* v. *United States,* the Court carved out an exception to the *See* warrant requirement, holding that it was not applicable to a closely regulated business, such as a liquor establishment.[26] In such a business the legislature may validly authorize warrantless inspections by relevant regulatory agencies. If the legislature is not restricted in the area of liquor regulation, it might be presumed that it is likewise unrestricted in other fields of economic activity subjected to pervasive regulation. However, as is shown by the following case, *Marshall* v. *Barlow's, Inc.,* the Court refused to expand the *Colonnade* exception to the warrant requirement.

Marshall, Secretary of Labor v. Barlow's, Inc.
436 U.S. 307 (1978)

Section 8(a) of the Occupational Safety and Health Act of 1970 (OSHA or act) empowers agents of the secretary of labor (secretary) to search the work area of any employment facility within the act's jurisdiction. The purpose of the search is to inspect for safety hazards and violations of OSHA regulations. No search warrant or other process is expressly required under the act.

On the morning of September 11, 1975,

---

[23] *Byers* v. *California,* 402 U.S. 424 (1971).

[24] 387 U.S. 541 (1967).

[25] *Id.* at 542–43.

[26] 397 U.S. 72 (1970).

an OSHA inspector entered the customer service area of Barlow's, Inc. (appellee), an electrical and plumbing installation business in Pocatello, Idaho. The president and general manager, Errol B. Barlow, was on hand. After showing his credentials, the OSHA inspector informed Barlow that he wished to conduct a search of the working areas of the business. Barlow asked whether any complaint had been received about his company. The inspector answered no, explaining that Barlow's, Inc., had simply turned up in the agency's selection process. The inspector again asked for permission to enter the nonpublic area of the business. Barlow responded by asking the inspector whether he had a search warrant. The inspector had none. Thereupon, Barlow refused to allow the inspector to enter the employee area of his business. Barlow said he was relying on his rights as guaranteed by the Fourth Amendment of the U.S. Constitution.

Three months later the secretary of labor petitioned the U.S. district court for the district of Idaho to issue an order compelling Barlow to admit the inspector. The requested order was issued on December 30, 1975, and was presented to Barlow on January 5, 1976. Barlow again refused admission, and he then sought injunctive relief against the warrantless searches assertedly premitted by OSHA. On December 30, 1976 a three-judge district court ruled in Barlow's favor. It held that the Fourth Amendment required a warrant for the type of search involved here and that the statutory authorization for warrantless inspections was unconstitutional. The court also entered an injunction against searches or inspections pursuant to section 8(a). The secretary of labor (appellant) appealed to the U.S. Supreme Court, which affirmed the district court's judgment.

Mr. Justice White: The Secretary urges that warrantless inspections to enforce OSHA are reasonable within the meaning of the Fourth Amendment. Among other things, he relies on §8(a) of the Act, . . . which authorizes inspection of business premises without a warrant and which the Secretary urges represents a congres-

sional construction of the Fourth Amendment that the courts should not reject. Regrettably, we are unable to agree.

This Court has already held that warrantless searches are generally unreasonable, and that this rule applies to commercial premises as well as homes. In *Camara* v. *Municipal Court* . . . we held:

> [E]xcept in certain carefully defined classes of cases, a search of private property without proper consent is "unreasonable" unless it has been authorized by a valid search warrant.

On the same day, we also ruled:

> As we explained in *Camara,* a search of private houses is presumptively unreasonable if conducted without a warrant. The businessman, like the occupant of a residence, has a constitutional right to go about his business free from unreasonable official entries upon his private commercial property. The businessman, too, has that right placed in jeopardy if the decision to enter and inspect for violation of regulatory laws can be made and enforced by the inspector in the field without official authority evidenced by a warrant.

These same cases also held that the Fourth Amendment prohibition against unreasonable searches protects against warrantless intrusions during civil as well as criminal investigations. . . . The reason is found in the "basic purpose of this amendment . . . which is to safeguard the privacy and security of individuals against arbitrary invasions by government officials.". . . If the government intrudes on a person's property, the privacy interest suffers whether the government's motivation is to investigate violations of criminal laws or breaches of other statutory or regulatory standards. It therefore appears that unless some recognized exception to the warrant requirement applies, *See* v. *Seattle* would require a warrant to conduct the inspection sought in this case.

The Secretary urges that an exception from the search warrant requirement has been recognized for "pervasively regulated business-

[es],''. . . and for ''closely regulated'' industries ''long subject to close supervision and inspection.''. . . These cases are indeed exceptions, but they represent responses to relatively unique circumstances. Certain industries have such a history of government oversight that no reasonable expectation of privacy . . . could exist for a proprietor over the stock of such an enterprise. Liquor and firearms are industries of this type; when an entrepreneur embarks upon such a business, he has voluntarily chosen to subject himself to a full arsenal of governmental regulations.

Industries such as these fall within the ''certain carefully defined classes of cases.''. . . The element that distinguishes these enterprises from ordinary businesses is a long tradition of close government supervision, of which any person who chooses to enter such a business must already be aware. ''A central difference between those cases . . . and this one is that businessmen engaged in such federally licensed and regulated enterprises accept the burdens as well as the benefits of their trade, whereas the petitioner here was not engaged in any regulated or licensed business. The businessman in a regulated industry in effect consents to the restrictions placed upon him.''

* * * * *

The critical fact in this case is that entry over Mr. Barlow's objection is being sought by the Government agent. Employees are not being prohibited from reporting OSHA violations. What they observe in their daily functions is undoubtedly beyond the employer's reasonable expectation of privacy. The Government inspector, however, is not an employee. Without a warrant he stands in no better position than a member of the public. What is observable by the public is observable, without a warrant, by the Government inspector as well. The owner of a business has not, by the necessary utilization of employees in his operation, thrown open the areas where employees alone are permitted to the warrantless scrutiny of Government agents. That an employee is free to report, and the Government is free to use, any evidence of noncompliance with OSHA that the employee observes furnishes no justification for federal agents to enter a place of business from which the public is restricted and to conduct their own warrantless search.

* * * * *

The Secretary submits that warrantless inspections are essential to the proper enforcement of OSHA because they afford the opportunity to inspect without prior notice and hence to preserve the advantages of surprise. While the dangerous conditions outlawed by the Act include structural defects that cannot be quickly hidden or remedied, the Act also regulates a myriad of safety details that may be amenable to speedy alteration or disguise. The risk is that during the interval between an inspector's initial request to search a plant and his procuring a warrant following the owner's refusal of permission, violations of this latter type could be corrected and thus escape the inspector's notice. To the suggestion that warrants may be issued *ex parte* and executed without delay and without prior notice, thereby preserving the element of surprise, the Secretary expresses concern for the administrative strain that would be experienced by the inspection system, and by the courts, should *ex parte* warrants issued in advance become standard practice.

We are unconvinced, however, that requiring warrants to inspect will impose serious burdens on the inspection system or the courts, will prevent inspections necessary to enforce the statute, or will make them less effective. In the first place, the great majority of businessmen can be expected in normal course to consent to inspection without warrant; the Secretary has not brought to this Court's attention any widespread pattern of refusal. . . .

Whether the Secretary proceeds to secure a warrant or other process, with or without prior notice, his entitlement to inspect will not depend on his demonstrating probable cause to believe that conditions in violation of OSHA exist on the premises. Probable cause in the criminal law sense is not required. For purposes of an administrative search such as this, probable cause justifying the issuance of a warrant may be based not only on specific evidence of an existing violation but also on a showing that ''reasonable legislative or administrative standards for conducting an . . . inspection are satisfied with respect to a particular [establishment]." . . . A warrant showing that a specific business has been chosen for an OSHA search on the basis of a general administrative plan for the enforcement of the Act derived from neutral sources such as, for example, dispersion of employees in various types of industries across a given area, and the desired frequency of searches in any of the lesser divisions of the area, would protect an employer's Fourth Amendment rights. We doubt that the consumption of enforcement energies in the obtaining of such warrants will exceed manageable proportions.

* * * * *

Nor do we agree that the incremental protections afforded the employer's privacy by a warrant are so marginal that they fail to justify the administrative burdens that may be entailed. The authority to make warrantless searches devolves almost unbridled discretion upon executive and administrative officers, particularly those in the field, as to when to search

and whom to search. A warrant, by contrast, would provide assurances from a neutral officer that the inspection is reasonable under the Constitution, is authorized by statute, and is pursuant to an administrative plan containing specific neutral criteria. Also, a warrant would then and there advise the owner of the scope and objects of the search, beyond which limits the inspector is not expected to proceed. These are important functions for a warrant to perform, functions which underlie the Court's prior decisions that the Warrant Clause applies to inspections for compliance with regulatory statutes. . . . We conclude that the concerns expressed by the Secretary do not suffice to justify warrantless inspections under OSHA or vitiate the general constitutional requirement that for a search to be reasonable a warrant must be obtained.

We hold that Barlow's was entitled to a declaratory judgment that the Act is unconstitutional insofar as it purports to authorize inspections without warrant or its equivalent and to an injunction enjoining the Act's enforcement to that extent. . . .

Case questions

1. Is it true that after *Barlow's* most employers will consent to an OSHA inspection without requiring a warrant? What "reasonable legislative or administrative standards" for conducting an inspection would constitute probable cause for issuing a warrant? Who pays the ultimate price for the Court's decision? Must an OSHA official who observes a serious OSHA violation in the public area of an employer's premises first obtain a warrant before inspecting the remainder of the premises or causing a citation to be issued?

2. Which would you prefer: to feel safe in your home or to feel safe on your job? Explain.

3. Suppose a magistrate issues a batch of warrants to an inspector, leaving blank the description of the premises to be searched. If refused consent to an inspection, may the inspector on the spot fill in the blanks of the warrant and thereby compel entry?

4. Does the warrant requirement significantly hamper inspectors? Does it significantly protect employers?

5. Does a business premise have the same privacy interest as a residential premise?

The subpoena power. Administrative investigatory power is supported by the authority to issue a subpoena. A subpoena is an official order commanding an individual to appear and testify or to produce specified documents. However, by itself an agency subpoena is merely a piece of paper. It has no legal effect until it is enforced by a court.

The constitutional concept of separation of powers requires that an agency apply to a court for enforcement of a subpoena. If an agency vested with the subpoena power issues a subpoena and the subject of the subpoena fails to appear or to produce the required documents, the agency must apply for a court order, whose violation is punishable as a contempt of court.

POLICY CONSIDERATIONS

The Constitution is written in general terms and uses such words as *due process* without definition. Thus it should not be surprising that individual Supreme Court justices have differed in their constructions of the Constitution. The Constitution's framers and the state ratifying conventions debated the meaning of the Constitution's various provisions, and the Supreme Court has continued that debate to this day. Indeed the Supreme Court has been characterized as a continuing constitutional convention.

Although many judicial philosophies have been represented on the Court over the years, the popular press has generally failed to educate the public regarding the nature of Court conflicts. An individual justice is often described as being either a liberal or a conservative on the Court or is labeled as either a strict constructionist or an expansionist with regard to constitutional interpretation. Such characterizations are often incorrect or simplistic.

Individual judicial philosophies are not easily stereotyped. The voting records of the Court reveal that, contrary to what many people believe, the justices do not engage in bloc voting. Although individual justices may frequently concur with certain of their brethren in similar cases, each justice is free to view each issue as an individual and to write a separate opinion on it. Thus the Court cannot generally be said to have a conservative bloc or a liberal bloc.

The diversity of judicial opinion is often confusing to the lay public. However, it should not seem so surprising that the justices of the Court have disagreed about the meanings of such terms as *due process* and *commerce.* If one were to examine other disciplines, such as internal medicine or psychiatry, one would find that practitioners of these disciplines frequently disagree on the diagnosis of individual cases. If nine psychiatrists or nine practitioners of internal medicine were asked to diagnose a particular case, it would not be surprising if they disagreed regarding either the diagnosis or the cure. If disagreement is to be expected in the natural sciences, it should almost certainly be expected when the meaning of Man-made constitutional language is involved.

One thing is sure, however. The Constitution's framers drafted a general document with a view to the future. They did not seek to specify in detail a constitutional solution to every social problem. Rather, they provided general constitutional contours for a society based on ordered liberty. They expected the Constitution to be an instrument capable of evolving as the American society itself evolved.

Review problems

1. Congress passed the Agricultural Adjustment Act of 1938 in an effort to stablize agricultural production so that farmers could obtain reasonable minimum prices. With regard to wheat, the secretary of agriculture issued an annual proclamation of a national acreage allotment which was apportioned among the states and ultimately among individual farms. Filburn was a small farmer who kept chickens and dairy cattle and raised a small amount of winter wheat, some of which was sold but most of which was used by his family or as feed for his livestock. Filburn's quota for 1941 was set at 11.1 acreas. However, he sowed and harvested 23 acres. The secretary of agriculture fined him $117.11. Filburn brought suit against the secretary, seeking an injunction against enforcement of the penalty. He claimed that the regulation was beyond the reach of the Commerce Clause, since the production of wheat for farm and family use was a purely local activity. Is Filburn right?

2. Under New York City law, advance approval must be obtained from the New York City Landmarks Preservation Commission before exterior changes can be made on property that is designated a landmark. In 1967 the commission designated Grand Central Terminal a landmark. The Penn Central Transportation Company, which owned the terminal, sought permission in 1968 to construct a 55-story office building above it. Penn Central submitted two plans, one requiring that a cantilevered building rest on the terminal's roof, the other necessitating the destruction of the terminal's south facade. Both plans were rejected. Because full development of the terminal site was prohibited, Penn Central was entitled to exceed zoning maxima on other parcels of land. Penn Central challenged the Landmarks Preservation Law, alleging that its property had been taken without just compensation in violation of the 5th and 14th amendments. Is Penn Central correct?

3. The First National Bank of Boston planned to incur expenditures for a campaign against a proposed amendment to the state constitution submitted to the voters in 1976; the amendment would have authorized the Massachusetts legislature to impose a graduated tax on individual income. The bank was constrained, however, by a Massachusetts statute prohibiting a corporation from making contributions or expenditures to influence the referendum vote on questions which did not materially affect the corporation's business or property. The statute specifically proscribed corporate expenditures to affect referenda "solely concerning the taxation of the income, property or transactions of individuals." The bank filed suit to obtain a judgment declaring the statute unconstitutional. Will the bank obtain the judgment?

4. The state of Minnesota required all power plants in the state to obtain a waste disposal permit from the Minnesota Pollution Control Agency. To obtain such a permit, a power company had to comply with the state's regulations regarding maximum levels of pollutant emissions. The limits imposed by the state on radioactive emissions were more stringent than those imposed by the federal Atomic Energy Commission (AEC). Northern States Power Co. was licensed by the AEC to operate a nuclear power plant on the Mississippi River in Minnesota. It complied with the state regulation and then sued to have the regulation declared unconstitutional. Will Northern succeed?

5. Should the Supreme Court have the power to declare Acts of Congress unconstitutional?

6. The Hospital Building Company, which operates a proprietary hospital, Mary Elizabeth, in Raleigh, North Carolina, brought an antitrust action against the Rex Hospital, a private tax-exempt hospital, and its officers. It claimed that they had violated the Sherman Act by conspiring to block the expansion of Mary Elizabeth in order to enable Rex to monopolize the business of providing hospital services in Raleigh. The Hospital Building Company alleged that a substantial portion of its medicines and supplies came from out-of-state sellers; that a large portion of its revenue came from out-of-state insurance companies; that it paid a management service fee to its parent company, a Georgia-based Delaware corporation; and that the planned expansion would be largely financed through out-of-state lenders. Rex moves to dismiss the complaint, arguing that the Hospital Building Company's business is strictly local and that Rex's alleged conduct only incidentally and insubstantially affected interstate commerce. Will the district court dismiss the case?

7. Mr. and Mrs. Goldfarb contracted to buy a home in Fairfax County, Virginia, and the lender who financed the purchase required them to obtain title insurance. This necessitated a title examination that could be performed legally only by a member of the Virginia State Bar. The Goldfarbs unsuccessfully tried to find a lawyer who would examine the title for less than the fee prescribed in a minimum-fee schedule published by the Fairfax County Bar Association. They then brought a class action against the bar association, alleging that the minimum-fee schedule constituted a price-fixing agreement in violation of the Sherman Act. The bar association moved the court to dismiss the suit, claiming that real estate title examinations are a purely local activity. The Goldfarbs argued that interstate commerce is involved because the title searches are tied to the financing of home purchases. Who is right?

8. Ranch Acres Liquors, an Oklahome liquor retailer, sued under the Sherman Act to enjoin a statewide division of territories by Oklahoma liquor wholesalers. There are no distilleries in Oklahoma. Out-of-state liquor is shipped in substantial volume to wholesalers' warehouses and held there until purchased by retailers. The wholesalers claim that interstate commerce is not involved. Are they right?

9. Title VII of the Civil Rights Act of 1964 prohibits employers from discriminating according to race, color, sex, national origin, or religion in any employment advertisement. Is this statutory restriction on employment advertising constitutional?

10. A local zoning commission changed the zoning of an area from commercial use to residential use due to the influx of more residents into what had previously been an industrial area. Does this change constitute a taking under the Fifth Amendment?

PART I: REVIEW PROBLEMS

1. The Consumer Product Safety Act empowers the Consumer Product Safety Commission (CPSC) to promulgate regulations setting safety standards which are reasonably necessary to prevent consumer injuries or reduce their likelihood. The CPSC has for some time been studying hunting rifles. Recently the following appeared in the *Federal Register:*

Notice of Proposed Rulemaking—Consumer Product Safety Commission

The Consumer Product Safety Commission has for two years studied consumer use of rifles. The CPSC has found that 500 persons are killed annually and another 50,000 wounded due to accidents in the home involving rifles. The CPSC believes that prohibiting individual ownership of rifles will prevent needless death and injury. Accordingly, the CPSC proposed to prohibit all sales of rifles to individuals, said prohibition to take effect three years following publication of the final regulation. The CPSC also proposes to prohibit all advertising of rifles beginning 60 days following the publication of the final regulation.

The notice also contained a citation to the CPSA and advised of a 90-day period for comments. You are the director of a trade association of gun dealers and manufacturers. How will you react?

2. The following notice recently appeared in the *Federal Register:*

Notice of Proposed Rulemaking—Federal Trade Commission

The FTC staff has conducted an initial study of real estate sales personnel and has found that many salespersons are incompetent. The use of incompetent salespersons has harmful effects on consumers who rely on these persons for information concerning the law, the market, and what to look for in buying a house. Accordingly, the commission proposes the following regulation:

Section 1. Authority for this regulation may be found in section 5 of the Federal Trade Commission Act which empowers the FTC to enact regulations designed to prevent unfair methods of competition and unfair and deceptive trade practices in interstate commerce.

Section 2. The Commission finds that the use of inadequately trained real estate salespersons is an unfair and deceptive trade practice which affects interstate commerce.

Section 3. No person may sell real estate anywhere in the United States unless he or she has obtained an FTC Real Estate Sales License (RESL).

Section 4. To apply for a RESL, an individual must hold at least an Associate of Arts degree in real estate from an accredited university, college, or junior college. The applicant's program of study must include courses in real estate law, real estate finance, the real estate market, and elementary architecture.

Section 5. Each applicant, upon passing a comprehensive examination with a score of 65 percent or higher, will be issued a license. The license will be subject to renewal five years after it is issued. A licensee must pass a renewal examination at that time. Interested persons may submit comments until March 15th. A hearing will be held at FTC headquarters in Washington, D.C., on March 19 at 9:00 A.M.

You are the president of the American Real Estate Trade Association (ARETA). The membership of your association is vehemently opposed to this new regulation. You must prepare a report to the membership. In your report, be sure to include the following:

1. What action, if any, should ARETA take to oppose the proposed regulation? How far can ARETA legally go in lobbying the FTC against the proposed regulation?

2. If the regulation is enacted, can ARETA challenge it in court? How should ARETA do this?

3. If ARETA challenges the regulation in court, is it likely to succeed? Consider the following: Is the regulation authorized by the statute? If so, is the statute consistent with the U.S. Constitution? What standard of review will the court apply to the FTC's finding that the regulation is needed?

PART TWO

Antitrust law

CHAPTER 5

Restraints of trade

In the post–Civil War period, disparities in the distribution of wealth widened markedly. By many, whether they subscribed to laissez-faire economics or not, the new inequality was received with displeasure and suspicion. For example, farmers had to sell their crops at prewar prices or less but had to buy commodities at inflated prices. Much anger was focused on the corporations which were receiving substantial land grants and other lucrative privileges in exchange for developing the railroads. The shifts in the distribution of wealth were also blamed on "trusts," which had arisen in oil, sugar, linseed oil, and whiskey.

A trust is a legal arrangement which secures property or other assets for beneficiaries by placing legal title and usually management responsibility in a trustee. In the late 19th century, however, trusts were used as covert devices to eliminate competition. Participating corporations pooled their stock, placing it under the control of trustees whom they selected. In return, they received trust certificates and were paid dividends. Since no corporate entity was involved, the participants in trusts projected a public image of independent companies competing with one another. In reality, the designated trustees made all crucial industry decisions: prices were fixed, supplies manipulated, and exclusive territories carved out. Thus competition among member companies ceased and outside competition was choked off.

A number of states passed "antitrust" statutes, designed specifically to outlaw the trust device. But when it was revealed that many trusts had received secret rebates from the railroads, Congress responded to citizen furor by enacting, in 1890, the Sherman Anti-Trust Act. Although the trust device of the late 19th century is gone, the Sherman Act, Clayton Act, and Federal Trade Commission Act still function to protect the public from monopolistic control of the economy and to facilitate but regulate competition. Table 5–1 is intended to introduce and highlight the significant provisions of the Sherman, Clayton, and Federal Trade Commission acts, which will be discussed in depth in this and the four following chapters.

137

Table 5–1: An overview of the antitrust laws

Statute	Provision
Sherman Act	
Section 1	Prohibits contracts, combinations, and conspiracies which restrain trade.
Section 2	Prohibits single-firm monopolization, attempts to monopolize, and conspiracies to monopolize.
Clayton Act	
Section 2	As amended by the Robinson-Patman Act of 1936, forbids discrimination in price, brokerage, advertising or promotional allowances, or services where the effect may be to injure or prevent competition with the buyer, the seller, or customers of either.
Section 3	Prohibits conditioning the sale or lease of commodities on the buyer's agreement not to purchase or lease competing commodities where the effect may be to substantially lessen competition or to tend to create a monopoly. As interpreted, the section applies to exclusive dealing agreements and tie-in devices.
Section 7	Prohibits mergers, whether consummated by stock or asset acquisition, where the effect may be to substantially lessen competition or to tend to create a monopoly.
Section 8	Prohibits interlocking corporate directorates.
Federal Trade Commission Act	
Section 5	Prohibits unfair methods of competition and unfair or deceptive trade practices. Violations of the Sherman and Clayton acts are also violations of the Federal Trade Commission Act, although the prohibitions of the latter are far broader.

ANTITRUST ADMINISTRATION AND ENFORCEMENT

Violations of the Sherman Act may be prosecuted civilly or criminally, whereas violations of the Clayton and FTC acts are limited to civil enforcement. Civil enforcement may be undertaken by the U.S. Department of Justice, the Federal Trade Commission and private parties, but only the Justice Department may bring criminal charges. Final judgments won by the Justice Department in civil or criminal proceedings are admissible as prima facie evidence of the defendant's liability in subsequent private actions.

Justice Department enforcement

The Antitrust Division is one of the most active sections of the Department of Justice. It employs over 500 attorneys. At any given time it has between 650 and 800 investigations pending. Table 5–2 documents Justice Department antitrust enforcement activity.

Violations of the Sherman Act are felonies, with individual violators subject to three years' imprisonment and a fine of $100,000 and corporate violators subject to a fine of $1 million. These criminal provisions are enforced in the same way as all other federal criminal laws. Before a defendant may be called to answer for its actions, a grand jury must find that there is probable cause to believe the defendant committed the alleged violation. Upon such a finding, the grand jury returns an indictment which gives the defendant notice of the pending charges.

The government has the burden of proving the defendant guilty beyond a reasonable doubt, and the defendant is presumed innocent until proven guilty. Few criminal antitrust cases proceed to trial. Most terminate in bargained pleas of nolo contendre, in which the defendant does not admit guilt but chooses not to contest the pending charges.

The Justice Department enforces the Sherman and Clayton acts with civil suits seeking injunctive orders designed to remedy violations. Such orders may simply prohibit anticompetitive business practices or may require the defendant to take affirmative action, such as divesting itself of assets, divisions, or subsidiaries.

Prior to filing a civil antitrust complaint, the Justice Department usually invites the prospective defendant to negotiate a consent decree. This is an order agreed to by the parties which prescribes or prohibits actions by the defendant. There is strong incentive for a defendant to accept a consent decree or to plead nolo contendre. This is because consent decrees and no-contest pleas are exceptions to the rule that final judgments in Justice Department actions are prima facie evidence of the defendant's liability in subsequent private civil damage suits. Until 1975, consent decree negotiations were usually shrouded in secrecy. Since then, however, a 1974 amendment to the Clayton Act has required that all proposed consent decrees be published in the *Federal Register* at least 60 days before they become effective. The publication must include a competitive impact statement summarizing

Table 5–2: Justice Department antitrust investigations

Year	Investi-gations	Year	Investi-gations
1967	644	1972	773
1968	692	1973	776
1969	710	1974	715
1970	678	1975	701
1971	758		

Source: *Economic Offenses: Recommendations of the A.B.A.* (Washington, D.C.: American Bar Association, 1977), p. 32.

the proceeding, the rationale for the remedy, and the remedies available to private parties damaged by the alleged violations. Summaries of these documents must appear in the newspapers published where the case is filed, and interested parties must be afforded an opportunity to comment on the proposed decree. After a hearing allowing interested persons to participate, the court must determine whether the proposed decree is in the public interest.

Justice Department civil enforcement actions begin with the filing of a complaint and proceed in the same way as any other civil action. Prior to 1975 the losing party in a civil action brought by the Justice Department had the right to appeal an antitrust decision directly from the district court to the Supreme Court. Currently all such actions must follow the normal route of appeal to the circuit court of appeals, with review in the Supreme Court by certiorari.

Federal Trade Commission enforcement

The Federal Trade Commission enforces section 5 of the Federal Trade Commission Act, which prohibits unfair methods of competition and unfair or deceptive trade practices. Unfair or deceptive trade practices are discussed in Chapter 11. Violations of the antitrust laws are unfair methods of competition forbidden by section 5. This prohibition is far broader than the antitrust laws, however, and it reaches conduct not specifically covered by the Sherman or Clayton acts. For example, although section 7 of the Clayton Act is limited to mergers of two or more corporations, the FTC may, pursuant to section 5, take action against a corporation acquiring businesses that are not incorporated.[1] The FTC proceeds by administrative adjudication, utilizing the methods discussed in Chapter 3.

The Hart-Scott-Rodino Antitrust Improvements Act of 1976 amended the Clayton Act to include a 30-day premerger notification program administered by the FTC. The purpose of the premerger notification is to allow the FTC and the Justice Department to enjoin mergers which they believe have anticompetitive effects. If the acquiring company has sales or assets of $100 million or more and the company to be acquired has sales or assets of $10 million or more, they must inform the FTC of the proposed merger 30 days before the merger is scheduled to take place. During the 30-day period the FTC may request additional data from the parties.

Private enforcement

Section 4 of the Clayton Act allows persons injured in their trade or business to sue alleged violators of the antitrust laws. Such persons may recover treble damages, court costs, and attorney fees and may also obtain injunctive relief. Alleged injuries to plaintiffs' trade or business are a frequent subject of litigation. Most courts require proof of a direct relationship be-

---

[1] See, e.g., Beatrice Foods Co., Trade Reg. Rep. [CCH] ¶17, 244 (FTC 1965).

tween such an injury and an antitrust violation or require that the plaintiff be within the target area of the economy affected by the violation. Thus a competitor injured by an antitrust violation clearly may sue. The competitor's shareholders, suppliers, creditors, and employees may also be injured by the violation. Their injuries, however, are derived from the injuries sustained by the competitor. Most courts consider injured shareholders and the like to be too remote from the violation to bring suit. The Court of Appeals for the Sixth Circuit has interpreted "an injury to trade or business" more liberally. This court allows plaintiffs to sue if they are injured in fact and come within the zone of interests protected by the antitrust laws.[2]

Consumers are protected by the antitrust laws in two ways. First, under appropriate circumstances they may sue the violators. Second, under the Hart-Scott-Rodino amendments state attorneys general may bring actions on behalf of all natural persons residing in their states for injuries sustained by them.

A problem which has plagued the courts is which purchasers, if any, may recover damages from sellers of raw materials where antitrust violations have resulted in higher prices for the materials. The immediate purchaser will probably use the materials in fabricating another product. This product will probably be sold to another manufacturer which may use it in making a consumer good that will be sold to a wholesaler, then to a distributor, then to a retailer, and finally to a consumer. Each purchaser probably passes on a portion of the overcharge in the price it charges. For example, assume that because of a price fix a steel company overcharges a manufacturer of lawn mower carburetors and that when prorated, the amount of the overcharge is $1 per carburetor. Table 5–3 illustrates how this overcharge might be passed on.

Table 5–3

Steel Company
  ↓ $1.00 overcharge for steel

Carburetor manufacturer
  ↓ $0.85 overcharge for carburetor

Lawn mower manufacturer
  ↓ $0.75 overcharge for lawn mower

Lawn mower wholesaler
  ↓ $0.70 overcharge

Distributor
  ↓ $0.70 overcharge

Retailer
  ↓ $0.65 overcharge

Consumer

---

[2] *Malamud* v. *Sinclair Oil Corp.* 521 F. 2d 1142 (6th Cir. 1975).

The Supreme Court has held that the original purchaser may recover the full amount of the overcharge, all or part of which has been passed on.[3] Subsequent purchasers, however, may not recover.[4] This ruling has been criticized as particularly harsh on the ultimate purchaser, frequently a consumer, who has probably paid most of the overcharge.

SECTION 1 OF THE SHERMAN ACT

Section 1 of the Sherman Act prohibits every contract, combination, and conspiracy in restraint of trade in interstate or foreign commerce. The requirement that the restraint of trade involve interstate commerce is typical of federal regulatory legislation and was discussed in detail in Chapter 4. The other two elements of a Sherman Act violation are a contract, combination, or conspiracy and a restraint of trade. These are discussed below.

Contract, combination, or conspiracy

A contract is an agreement between two or more parties to do things that they were previously not obligated to do. A conspiracy conjures up visions of clandestine meetings and elaborate plans. A combination seems less sinister than a conspiracy and less formal than a contract.

In antitrust legislation, however, "contract, combination, or conspiracy" is a term of art meaning joint or concerted action. Section 1 of the Sherman Act prohibits two or more entities from pooling their economic power to restrain trade. Unilateral action does not violate section 1 even though the identical action taken jointly would be illegal. The requirement of joint action will be discussed in relation to intraenterprise conspiracy and conscious parellelism.

Intraenterprise conspiracy. The requirement of an agreement between two separate entities raises questions affecting a corporation's internal structure. If a corporation organizes separate departments into wholly owned subsidiaries, these subsidiaries are independent legal entities capable of conspiring with the parent company. If, however, the corporation maintains its departments as divisions within the same company, there is only one entity and no conspiracy or agreement can result. Similarly, a corporation cannot conspire with its own officers or other employees where they are acting within the scope of their employment.

The need for two separate entities as a precondition for conspiracy in restraint of trade is dramatically illustrated by considering the experience of Joseph E. Seagram & Sons, Inc. At one time Seagram marketed its liquor through wholly owned subsidiaries. The Supreme Court held that a price-

---

[3] *Hanover Shoe, Inc.* v. *United Shoe Machinery Corp.,* 329 U.S. 481 (1968).
[4] *Illinois Brick Co.* v. *Illinois,* 429 U.S. 1087 (1977).

fixing agreement between two of these subsidiaries violated section 1, and it rejected Seagram's claim that the subsidiaries were mere instrumentalities of a single merchandising unit.[5] However, when Seagram reorganized and marketed its merchandise through divisions rather than subsidiaries, it was found to not have violated section 1 because the divisions were not separate legal entities.[6]

Conscious parallelism. Oligopolistic markets are highly concentrated markets dominated by a small number of large producers. A change in the output of any one dominant firm will affect the market price substantially. Consequently, many oligopolistic industries are characterized by conscious parallelism, in which most competitors follow the actions of the dominant leader. Such consciously parallel behavior most frequently affects price: competitors follow the leader's announcement of price increases or cuts with similar announcements.

When all or most competitors raise prices by similar amounts, the question raised is whether the price increases were arrived at unilaterally or were the product of an agreement. The existence of a contract, combination, or conspiracy is an issue of fact. Where only consciously parallel behavior is shown, as a matter of law there is no section 1 violation because no evidence of an agreement has been introduced. Circumstantial evidence may exist, however, which will allow a jury to infer that what appears to be consciously parallel behavior is actually the result of an agreement. This evidence includes meetings or other communications among competitors, parallel action which would benefit any one competitor only if all others took the same action, and a particularly complex series of consciously parallel steps.

Restraints of trade—the rule of reason

No law is passed in a vacuum. A statute can be interpreted only by looking beyond its surface expressions to its roots. In construing the Sherman Act, the U.S. Supreme Court said that "where words are employed in a statute which had at the time a well-known meaning at common law or in the law of this country, they are presumed to have been used in that sense unless the context compels to the contrary."[7]

At common law, courts refused to enforce contracts which were illegal or contrary to public policy. Parties frequently argued that their contracts should not be enforced because they restrained trade and were thus contrary to public policy. Two views developed on the enforceability of restraints of trade. Under one view, if the restraint was the primary agreement, it

---

[5] *Kiefer-Stewart Co.* v. *Joseph E. Seagram & Sons, Inc.,* 340 U.S. 211 (1957).

[6] *Hawaiian Oake Liquors Ltd.* v. *Joseph E. Seagram & Sons, Inc.,* 416 F. 2d 71 (9th Cir. 1969), certiorari denied, 390 U.S. 1062 (1970).

[7] *Standard Oil Co.* v. *United States,* 221 U.S. 1, 59 (1911).

was not enforceable. However, if the restraint was an ancillary portion of a broader agreement, the court would enforce it, provided the restraint was reasonable. Under the other view, this rule of reason was applied regardless of the primary or ancillary nature of the restraint.

Courts which analyzed the reasonableness of restraints inquired into their purposes and effects. To be reasonable a restraint must have been jusitifed by a legitimate business purpose and must not have had an anticompetitive effect.

The restraint of trade most frequently encountered by courts prior to the passage of the Sherman Act was the covenant not to compete. The following example provides an understanding of this covenant. Assume that a buyer purchased a restaurant. In addition to paying for the tangible assets of the business, the buyer also paid for its goodwill. This purchase of goodwill would have been meaningless if the seller could establish a competing restaurant across the street. The buyer would have sought protection by obtaining a promise not to compete from the seller.

If the covenant not to compete prohibited the seller from establishing a restaurant in another state, where there would have been no danger to the buyer's goodwill, the covenant would have been broader than its legitimate business purpose. Similarly, if the covenant had bound the seller not to compete for five years, it would have been overbroad, because within five years the buyer's efforts rather than the seller's name would account for the buyer's goodwill. Courts refused to enforce overbroad covenants not to compete and covenants not to compete which had no legitimate business purpose.

It was against this background that Congress used the term *restraint of trade*. Common-law policing of restraints of trade proved inadequate. Restraints were brought before courts only when one party sought to enforce them against another. Many of the most anticompetitive restraints, such as agreements fixing prices or allocating markets, were never challenged because the parties voluntarily adhered to them. In passing the Sherman and Clayton acts, Congress authorized the government and private parties to challenge these restraints, but it incorporated the rule of reason. Every contract binds its parties and thus "restrains trade" to some extent. It is necessary to determine whether the questionable restraint promotes or suppresses competition, that is, whether it is reasonable.

The rule of reason requires that a restraint be scrutinized for its purpose, effect, and intent and the power it confers upon the parties. To be reasonable a restraint must be used to achieve a procompetitive business purpose and not have an effect beyond that purpose. A restraint is unreasonable if the parties intended to unlawfully suppress competition even though they could not or did not achieve that goal. A restraint is also unreasonable if it confers upon the parties the power to substitute their judgment for the judgment of the marketplace.

The following case, one of the earliest to apply the rule of reason, remains the classic example of section 1 analysis.

Chicago Board of Trade v. United States
246 U.S. 231 (1918)

Sales of grain on the Chicago Board of Trade fell into three categories: futures were orders for delivery at a much later date; spot sales were orders for grain already in Chicago; sales to arrive were orders for harvested grain in transit to Chicago. The board adopted a Call rule which established a fixed period of time for trading in grain to arrive. The rule barred Board of Trade members from purchasing or offering to purchase grain to arrive between the close of the Call and the next business day at a price other than the price bid at the close of the Call. The district court held the rule violated the Sherman Act. The Supreme Court reversed.

Mr. Justice Brandeis:

* * * * *

In 1913 the United States filed suit against the Board to enjoin the enforcement of the Call rule, alleging it to be in violation of the Anti-Trust Law.

* * * * *

. . . The case rested upon the bald proposition, that a rule or agreement by which men occupying positions of strength in any branch of trade, fixed prices at which they would buy or sell during an important part of the business day, is an illegal restraint of trade under the Anti-Trust Law. But the legality of an agreement or regulation cannot be determined by so simple a test, as whether it restrains competition. Every agreement concerning trade, every regulation of trade, restrains. To bind, to restrain, is of their very essence. The true test of legality is whether the restraint imposed is such as merely regulates and perhaps thereby promotes competition or whether it is such as may suppress or even destroy competition. To determine that question the court must ordinarily consider the facts peculiar to the business to which the restraint is applied; its condition before and after the restraint was imposed; the nature of the restraint and its effect, actual or probable. The history of the restraint, the evil

believed to exist, the reason for adopting the particular remedy, the purpose or end sought to be attained, are all relevant facts. This is not because a good intention will save an otherwise objectionable regulation or the reverse; but because knowledge of intent may help the court to interpret facts and to predict consequences. . . . The evidence admitted makes it clear that the rule was a reasonable regulation of business consistent with the provisions of the Anti-Trust Law.

First: The nature of the rule: The restriction was upon the period of price-making. It required members to desist from further price-making after the close of the Call until 9:30 A.M., the next business day: but there was no restriction upon the sending out of bids after close of the Call. Thus it required members who desired to buy grain "to arrive" to make up their minds before the close of the Call how much they were willing to pay during the interval before the next session of the Board. . . .

Second: The scope of the rule: It is restricted in operation to grain "to arrive." It applies only to a small part of the grain shipped from day to day to Chicago, and to an even smaller part of the day's sales: members were left free to purchase grain already in Chicago from anyone at any price throughout the day. It applies only during a small part of the business day; members were left free to purchase during the sessions of the Board grain "to arrive," at any price, from members anywhere and from non-members anywhere except on the premises of the Board. It applied only to grain shipped to Chicago: members were left free to purchase at any price throughout the day from either members or non-members, grain "to arrive" at any other market. . . .

Third: The effects of the rule: . . . The rule had no appreciable effect on general market prices; nor did it materially affect the total volume of grain coming to Chicago. But within the narrow limits of its operation the rule helped to improve market conditions thus:

(a) It created a public market for grain "to arrive." . . .

(b) It brought into the regular market hours of the Board sessions more of the trading in grain "to arrive."

(c) It brought buyers and sellers into more direct relations; because on the Call they gathered together for a free and open interchange of bids and offers.

(d) It distributed the business in grain "to arrive" among a far larger number of Chicago receivers and commission merchants than had been the case there before.

(e) It increased the number of country dealers engaging in this branch of the business; supplied them more regularly with bids from Chicago; and also increased the number of bids received by them from competing markets.

(f) It eliminated risks necessarily incident to a private market, and thus enabled country dealers to do business on a smaller margin. In that way the rule made it possible for them to pay more to farmers without raising the price to consumers.

(g) It enabled country dealers to sell some grain to arrive which they would otherwise have been obliged either to ship to Chicago commission merchants or to sell for "future delivery."

(h) It enabled those grain merchants of Chicago who sell to millers and exporters to trade on a smaller margin and, by paying more for grain or selling it for less, to make the Chicago market more attractive for both shippers and buyers of grain.

(i) Incidentally it facilitated trading "to arrive" by enabling those engaged in these transactions to fulfill their contracts by tendering grain arriving at Chicago on any railroad, whereas formerly shipments had to be made over the particular railroad designated by the buyer.

Case questions

1. What is the true test of the legality of a restraint of trade?

2. What factors should a court consider in applying the test?

3. What specific findings convinced the Supreme Court that the Call rule, as adopted and implemented by the Chicago Board of Trade, was permissible?

4. Is a rule which prohibits members of a professional association of engineers from negotiating prices with a customer until the customer has made an initial selection of a project engineer an illegal restraint of trade?

Per se violations. When the rule of reason is applied to determine whether a restraint violates the Sherman Act, the court is required to examine the intricate details of the industry and the economy. However, certain restraints have been held to be per se unreasonable. When such a restraint is involved, the court need only find that the restraint exists to find a violation of section 1. In this way the court bypasses a rigorous inquiry into the restraint's reasonableness.

Per se unreasonable restraints are those whose effect on competition is so pernicious that they are beyond justification. Particular restraints are declared to be per se unreasonable only after courts have gained sufficient experience with them to be able to generalize about their competitive effects. If courts believe that a restraint necessarily substitutes the judgment of the parties for the judgment of the marketplace, they will hold the restraint per se illegal.

The per se rule serves a number of important functions. First, by declaring certain restraints per se illegal, the rule sets a standard of unreasonableness against which other restraints may be measured. This spares courts the necessity of performing complex economic analyses, for which they are ill-suited. Second, a standard of unreasonableness tends to promote the stability and predictability necessary for business planning.

It is very tempting to label all restraints as requiring analysis under either the rule of reason or the per se rule. However, such a breakdown would be misleading because the per se rule is a specific application of the rule of reason. Restraints which at first may not appear to be per se unreasonable may, after preliminary analysis, prove identical with per se violations.

With this background, specific restraints will now be examined. These will be divided into three categories: horizontal restraints, vertical restraints, and group boycotts. Each of these categories will be examined in relation to section 1 of the Sherman Act. Vertical restraints will also be considered in relation to section 3 of the Clayton Act.

HORIZONTAL RESTRAINTS

A horizontal restraint is one in which two or more competitors agree to avoid competing with one another. The most common horizontal agreements are those fixing prices and those dividing territories, customers, or markets. Such restraints are per se violations of section 1 even if the parties are free to set their own prices in their designated territories and regardless of whether the agreement is between sellers of the same brand or competing brands of merchandise. These restraints are called horizontal because they occur across competitors, for the benefit of competing retailers, distributors, or franchisees. When they occur among sellers of different brands they are said to suppress interbrand competition. When they occur among sellers of the same brand they are said to suppress intrabrand competition.

Price-fixing

The restraint that was first declared to be per se illegal was the price fix. In a free market economy, price is set by the interaction of supply and demand. When two or more competitors agree to fix the prices for their goods or services, they substitute their judgment for that of the marketplace. The Sherman Act is concerned with the power to manipulate prices as well as with the effect of artificially determined prices. Thus the reasonableness of the fixed price is irrelevant. A reasonably fixed price today may become an unreasonable price tomorrow. All price-fixing agreements are per se illegal.

Price-fixing arrangements are not limited to agreements which specify particular prices. Conspiracies to stabilize prices, set a floor under prices, or set a maximum level for prices are also per se illegal. Few restraints blatantly set forth an agreement to fix prices. Thus it is necessary to determine whether a seemingly innocuous restraint results in a price fix. If the parties to the restraint intend to set prices, then the restraint is per se illegal despite its appearance or its actual effect.

For example, a new-car dealers' association circulated a list of suggested retail prices which were higher than the manufacturer's sticker price, with the purpose of setting a starting point for dealers to use in bargaining with customers. Although most sales were made below the suggested prices, the use of the list was held to be an illegal price fix.[8]

A particularly complex example of illegal price-fixing occurred in the gasoline industry during the late 1920s and early 1930s. Most major oil companies had their own distribution facilities for entry into the retail market. But independent companies supplied 15 percent of retail gasoline, much of which was committed under long-term contracts. The uncommitted remainder of the independents' gasoline formed the spot market.

During the late 1920s and early 1930s more oil was being refined into gasoline than was demanded. Because the independents had little storage capacity, they were forced to sell their "distress oil" on the spot market. This glut on the market severely depressed prices.

The major oil companies responded with a buying program. Each "major," regardless of its needs, agreed to buy distress oil from a designated independent. Because the majors had plentiful storage capacity, they could keep the oil until a need for it developed.

Although it appeared that the majors were only seeking to purchase the gasoline on the spot market and were allowing the market to fix a price, the purpose of their buying program was to set a floor under prices and thereby to stabilize them. Purchases by the majors were timed to have maximum impact on stabilization of the spot market price. Stabilization, in turn, was compounded by pricing formulas in the long-term contracts which were based on the spot market price. The buying program was therefore held to be per se illegal.[9]

Not all business arrangements which affect prices are condemned as per se price fixes. Many arrangements which have legitimate business purposes also have incidental effects on price. For example, a group of competing sellers may organize a buying cooperative to take advantage of bulk discounts. Such an arrangement may affect price, but its effects on price are incidental to its legitimate business purpose. Similarly, the use of joint selling agents by competitors may incidentally reduce price competition while achieving its legitimate purpose, economies of scale for the participants. The following decision illustrates the process by which a court determines whether an agreement is an illegal price fix.

---

[8] *Plymouth Dealers' Association* v. *United States* 279 F.2d 128 (9th Cir. 1960).

[9] *United States* v. *Socony-Vacuum Oil Co.*, 310 U.S. 150 (1940).

Evans v. S. S. Kresge Co.
544 F.2d 1184 (3d Cir. 1976)

Kresge (defendant) operated a number of discount department stores under the trade name K mart. Defendant sought to induce independent food retailers to operate K mart Food Stores under the same roof as the department stores. Kresge licensed the Hempfield Corporation to use the trade name K mart in connection with the operation of two such food stores. The license required Hempfield, among other things, to limit nonfood merchandise to certain specified items, to refrain from using trading stamps without Kresge's permission, to maintain competitive prices, and to charge prices on items sold by it and Kresge identical with those charged by Kresge.

Hempfield alleged that these restrictions violated the Sherman Act. The district court granted defendant's motion for summary judgment on the grounds that the restraint did not involve interstate commerce and was not unreasonable. The court of appeals held that interstate commerce was involved. It then addressed the issue of the reasonableness of the restraint.

Garth, Circuit Judge:

* * * * *

Hempfield contends that the pricing and product restriction imposed by Kresge are illegal *per se* within the contemplation of the Sherman Act. Kresge, on the other hand, disputes the illegality of its admitted restrictions, claiming that these restrictions must be tested by the rule of reason and, when so measured, must be found to be reasonable and, therefore, permissible.

On its face, §1 of the Sherman Act appears to bar any combination of entrepreneurs so long as it is "in restraint of trade." Theoretically, all manufacturers, distributors, merchants, sellers, and buyers could be considered as potential competitors of each other. Were § 1 to be read in the narrowest possible way, any commercial contract could be deemed to violate it. The history underlying

the formulation of the antitrust laws . . . [indicates] that Congress did not intend to prohibit all contracts, nor even all contracts that might in some insignificant degree or attenuated sense restrain trade or competition. In lieu of the narrowest possible reading of § 1, the Court adopted a "rule of reason" analysis for determining whether most business combinations or contracts violate the prohibitions of the Sherman Act. An analysis of the reasonableness of particular restraints includes consideration of the facts peculiar to the business in which the restraint is applied, the nature of the restraint and its effects and the history of the restraint and the reason for its adoption.

While the Court has utilized the "rule of reason" in evaluating the legality of most restraints alleged to be violative of the Sherman Act, it has also developed the doctrine that certain business relationships are *per se* violations of the Act without regard to a consideration of their reasonableness.

* * * * *

It is only after considerable experience with certain business relationships that courts classify them as per se violations of the Sherman Act. . . .

For our purposes here, there is no necessity to fit this relationship into any one business category. Our only inquiry is whether there has been sufficient judicial examination of, and experience with, the hybrid business arrangement at issue here. We are satisfied that this kind of business arrangement has yet to be exposed to judicial review. . . . [W]e . . . "need to know more than we do about the actual impact of these arrangements on competition to decide whether they have such a 'pernicious effect on competition and lack . . . any redeeming virtue' and therefore should be classified as *per se* violations of the Sherman Act." Accordingly, under the circumstances presented here, we cannot subsume the challenged restraints to *per se* treatment.

. . . The restraints normally found within the *per se* category are horizontal limitations constituting "naked restraints of trade with no purpose except stifling of competition." Horizontal restraints by definition require agreements between competitors. . . . Here the relationship established by the parties demonstrates to our satisfaction that the necessary element of competition is lacking. . . .

We find that Hempfield and Kresge were not competitors. In the first place, the Kresge department stores and the Hempfield grocery supermarkets were designed to sell entirely different kinds of merchandise. That was the reason for the agreements. The fact that somewhere between 2% and 5% of merchandise sold by Hempfield was also sold by defendant's stores does not, in our view, require a finding that Hempfield and Kresge were competitors. . . .

We grant that certain non-food items were offered for sale by both Kresge and Hempfield. On the surface, this might appear to indicate that the parties were competitors in that the proceeds of each sale went into the pocket of either seller Kresge or seller Hempfield. As we view the substance of the transaction, however, both Kresge and Hempfield presented a common front under a common name to the customer. Therefore, whether the non-food item was purchased from Kresge or from Hempfield, it was as if that item had been offered for sale by Kresge alone, but at two different locations in its K-Mart establishment. Here, the fact of noncompetition is dictated by the practical business arrangement of the parties, and indeed is disclosed as their intent by uncontradicted affidavit. If for no other reason than the absence of this necessary element of "competitors," a horizontal limitation cannot be made out.

Moreover, the challenged restraint enabled Kresge to add a food component to its discount operation without causing customer confusion or threatening the low-price "K-Mart" discounting image upon which the success of K-Mart (including K-Mart Food) would depend. Therefore, far from attempting to stifle competition, the restraints had as their purpose the stimulation of business and efficiency for both the department store and the supermarket: they [the restraints] would assure that the overall operation would compete effectively in both the discount and food markets vis-à-vis other department store and food discounters. The restraints thus serve a legitimate business purpose.

Case questions

1. Why did the court conclude that Kresge's requiring Hempfield to charge the same price as Kresge charged on common merchandise was not a price fix?

2. What was the purpose of the restraints? What were the effects? Do you believe the restraints were reasonable?

3. If Hempfield had carried more than 5 percent of its goods in common with Kresge, would the restraints have been a price fix? What percentage of Kresge goods could Hempfield carry without violating the Sherman Act?

Divisions of territories, customers, and markets

When two or more competitors get together and agree to divide up territories or customers, they necessarily avoid competing with one another. Such arrangements are per se violations of section 1 even if the parties are free to set their own prices within their territories. Each competitor has eliminated the competitive forces within its territory that check its economic power.

Horizontal territorial or customer divisions are equally illegal whether they occur among sellers of competing brands or among sellers of the same brand. An agreement between two Ford dealers to divide customers is as illegal as a comparable agreement between a Ford dealer and a Chevrolet dealer. The protection of intrabrand competition from horizontal restraints has a priority equal to the protection of interbrand competition. As the following case points out, a horizontal territorial division which restrains intrabrand competition cannot be justified because it promotes interbrand competition.

United States v. Topco Associates, Inc.
405 U.S. 596 (1972)

Topco was a membership association composed of 25 independent supermarket chains. Its members owned equal amounts of Topco stock, chose Topco's directors, and completely controlled Topco's operations. Topco marketed numerous groceries under the Topco brand name. Its members were each granted a territory in which it could sell Topco products. Members were prohibited from selling Topco products beyond their territories. Most of the territories granted members were exclusive; those that were not guaranteed to be exclusive were in practice exclusive. No member was permitted to expand into the territory of another member without the consent of the other member.

The government instituted a civil action to have Topco enjoined from enforcing the exclusivity agreements. The district court entered judgment for Topco, and the Supreme Court reversed.

Mr. Justice Marshall:

* * * * *

While the Court has utilized the "rule of reason" in evaluating the legality of most restraints alleged to be violative of the Sherman Act, it has also developed the doctrine that certain business relationships are *per se* violations of the Act without regard to a consideration of reasonableness.

Antitrust laws in general, and the Sherman Act in particular, are the Magna Charta of free enterprise. They are as important to the preservation of economic freedom and our free enterprise system as the Bill of Rights is to the protection of our fundamental personal freedoms. And the freedom guaranteed each and every business, no matter how small, is the freedom to compete—to assert with vigor, imagination, devotion, and ingenuity whatever economic muscle it can muster. Implicit in such freedom is the notion that it cannot be foreclosed with respect to one sector of the economy because certain private citizens or groups believe that such foreclosure might promote greater competition in a more important sector of the economy.

The District Court determined that by limiting the freedom of its individual members to compete with each other, Topco was doing a greater good by fostering competition between members and other large supermarket chains. But, the fallacy in this is that Topco has no authority under the Sherman Act to determine the respective values of competition in various sectors of the economy. On the contrary, the Sherman Act gives to each Topco member and to each prospective member the right to ascertain for itself whether or not competition with other supermarket chains is more desirable than competition in the sale of Topco brand products. Without territorial restrictions, Topco members may indeed "[c]ut each other's throat." But we have never found this possibility sufficient to warrant condoning horizontal restraints of trade.

Mr. Chief Justice Burger dissenting: In joining in this cooperative endeavor, these small chains did not agree to the restraints here at issue in order to make it possible for them to exploit an already established line of products through non-competitive pricing. There was no such thing as a Topco line of products until this cooperative was formed. The restraints to which the cooperative's members have agreed deal only with the marketing of the products in the Topco line, and the only function of those restraints is to permit each member chain to establish and through its own local advertising and marketing efforts, [*sic*] a local consumer awareness of the trademarked family of products as that member's "private label" line. The goal sought was the enhancement of the individual members' abilities to compete, albeit to a modest degree, with the large national chains which had been successfully marketing private label lines for several years. The sole reason for a cooperative endeavor was to make economically feasible such things as quality control, large quantity purchases at bulk prices, the development of attractively printed labels, and the ability to offer a number of different lines of trademarked products. All these things, of course, are feasible for the large national chains operating individually, but they are beyond the reach of the small proceeding alone. . . .

With all respect, I believe that there are two basic fallacies in the Court's approach here. First, while I would not characterize our role under the Sherman Act as one of "rambl[ing] through the wilds," it is indeed one that requires our "examin[ation of] difficult economic problems." We can undoubtedly ease our task, but we should not abdicate that role by formulation of per se rules with no justification other than the enhancement of predictability and the reduction of judicial investigation. Second, from the general proposition that per se rules play a necessary role in antitrust law, it does not follow that the particular per se rule promulgated today is an appropriate one.

The District Court specifically found that the horizontal restraints involved here tend positively to promote competition in the supermarket field and to produce lower costs for the consumer. The Court seems implicitly to accept this determination, but says that the Sherman Act does not give Topco the authority to determine for itself "whether or not competition with other supermarket chains is more desirable than competition in the sale of Topco brand products." But the majority overlooks a further specific determination of the District Court, namely, that the invalidation of the restraints here at issue "would not increase competition in Topco private label brands." Indeed, the District Court seemed to believe that it would, on the contrary, lead to the likely demise of those brands in time. And the evidence before the District Court would appear to justify that conclusion.

There is no national demand for Topco brands, nor has there ever been any national advertising of those brands. It would be impracticable for Topco, with its limited financial resources, to convert itself into a national brand distributor in competition with distributors of existing national brands. Furthermore, without the right to grant exclusive licenses, it could not attract and hold new members as replacements for those of its present members who, following the pattern of the past, eventually grow sufficiently in size to be able to leave the cooperative organization and develop their own individual private label brands. Moreover, Topco's present members, once today's decision has had its full impact over the course of time, will have no more reason to promote Topco products through local advertising and merchandising efforts than they will have such reason to promote any other generally available brands.

Case questions

1. What is a private label? Why did offering private labels give the large national supermarkets a competitive edge over smaller regional chains? Is it possible for smaller chains to offer private labels without territorial divisions?

2. What is the basis for the majority's holding that Topco's territorial divisions were per se illegal?

3. What is the basis for the chief justice's dissent?

4. If instead of assigning exclusive territories, Topco had assigned each member primary areas of responsibility and had required each member to advertise and otherwise develop the Topco name in its area, would the restraint have violated the Sherman Act?

VERTICAL RESTRAINTS

Vertical restraints are agreements between two or more parties at different levels of the distribution process. Typically they are agreements between manufacturer and distributor or retailer or between franchisor and franchisee. Vertical restraints frequently sacrifice some intrabrand competition to further interbrand competition. Some restraints which are per se illegal in a horizontal context are treated differently in a vertical context. Others are treated in the same way regardless of their context. Two types of vertical arrangements, exclusive dealing contracts and tie-in devices, are covered by both the Sherman Act and section 3 of the Clayton Act.

Resale price maintenance

A manufacturer may wish to insure that its product is not sold at retail above a maximum price or below a minimum price. The manufacturer may wish to set a maximum retail price as part of an aggressive compaign to take customers away from competitors. It may desire to maintain a minimum price in order to give its goods an aura of high price and high quality. If the manufacturer and retailer agree to minimum or maximum resale prices, the contract is a vertical price fix and per se violative of the Sherman Act. A number of states enacted fair trade laws which specifically declared resale price maintenance to be legal. These laws conflicted with the Sherman Act, and in the absence of a congressional intent to the contrary they would have been preempted. In 1937, however, Congress enacted the Miller-Tydings Amendment, which exempted from the Sherman Act resale price maintenance agreements sanctioned by state fair trade laws. This amendment was repealed in 1975. Consequently, all state fair trade laws are now preempted by the Sherman Act.

In determining whether a program of resale price maintenance violates the Sherman Act, the major issue is whether the required contract, combination, or conspiracy exists. A contract obligating a purchaser to resell at a given price clearly violates section 1. However, where only unilateral action by the initial seller exists, there is no violation. Thus a manufacturer may lawfully maintain retail prices by suggesting retail prices and unilaterally terminating or refusing to deal with retailers that sell below the suggested prices.

Courts are quick to condemn resale price maintenance schemes whenever they find an agreement. Thus, if a manufacturer involves its distributors in policing such a scheme, a violation results. Similarly, if a manufacturer refuses to deal with a retailer because of the retailer's discount prices, but later reinstates the retailer, courts will infer an agreement fixing the resale price. Section 1 is even violated by an agreement with a third party to compete against the discounter until the discounter returns to the fixed price.

Territorial, customer, and market restraints

Manufacturers and franchisors frequently impose territorial restraints upon their distributors, retailers, or franchisees. These restraints may take the form of exclusive territories or customer divisions. Less restrictive restraints may also be used, such as assigning areas of primary responsibility or designating the location of a dealer or franchisee. Vertical territorial or customer restraints differ from horizontal restraints in that they are designed for the benefit of the manufacturer or the franchisor rather than for the benefit of the competing retailers, distributors, or franchisees.

Vertical territorial or customer divisions have received varied treatment from the Supreme Court. The issue was initially posed in *White Motor Co.* v. *United States.*[10] White Motor, a truck manufacturer, granted its distributors and dealers exclusive territories but prohibited them from selling to government agencies without its permission. The district court held these restrictions to be per se violations of section 1. The Supreme Court reversed the district court's decision and remanded the case for trial and assessment of the reasonableness of the restrictions.

At trial the district court was required to consider White Motor's proffered justification for the restrictions. White Motor contended that it was a small manufacturer struggling for survival among giants. It claimed that the territorial restraints were necessary to induce competent dealers and distributors to make the capital investment involved in selling White Motor trucks and to insure that White Motor distributors and dealers would concentrate on competing with other brands instead of with one another. The customer restraints were justified, White Motor maintained, because they insured that large fleet accounts would not be lost due to incompetent handling by dealers or distributors.

In *White Motor* the Court's view was that its experience with vertical territorial restraints was not sufficient to declare them per se illegal. In *United States* v. *Arnold Schwinn & Co.,*[11] the court concluded that it had gained enough experience to do so. There the Court held that vertical territorial divisions were per se illegal if the manufacturer parted with dominion and control of the product. Where the manufacturer retained title to the product, however, exclusive territories were not per se unreasonable.

Many manufacturers found it impossible to change their distribution systems in a manner that would insure their retention of legal title to their products. These manufacturers resorted to assigning areas of primary respon-

---

[10] 372 U.S. 253 (1963).
[11] 388 U.S. 350 (1967).

sibility and employing dealer location clauses. One such manufacturer was G.T.E. Sylvania, Inc.

Continental TV, Inc. v. GTE Sylvania, Inc.
433 U.S. 36 (1977)

Continental TV was a licensed dealer of GTE Sylvania products. Its license contained a dealer location clause which prohibited Continental from selling Sylvania products at locations other than the one specified. Continental violated the location clause by establishing a new store at another location and transferring Sylvania products from the approved location to the new location. Sylvania canceled Continental's dealership, and Continental sued, contending that the dealer location clause violated section 1 of the Sherman Act. The lower courts held for Sylvania. The Supreme Court affirmed.

Mr. Justice Powell: We turn first to Continental's contention that Sylvania's restriction on retail locations is a *per se* violation of section one of the Sherman Act as interpreted in *Schwinn.* The restrictions at issue in *Schwinn* were part of a three-tier distribution system. . . .

* * * * *

In the present case, it is undisputed that title to the television sets passed from Sylvania to Continental. . . . [W]e are unable to find a principled basis for distinguishing *Schwinn* from the case now before us.

Both Schwinn and Sylvania sought to reduce but not to eliminate competition among their respective retailers through the adoption of a franchise system. . . . In intent and competitive impact, the retail-customer restriction in *Schwinn* is indistinguishable from the location restriction in the present case. In both cases the restrictions limited the freedom of the retailer to dispose of the purchased products as he desired. The fact that one restriction was addressed to territory and the other to customers is irrelevant to functional antitrust analysis and, indeed, to the language and broad thrust of the opinion in *Schwinn.*

* * * * *

Sylvania argues that if *Schwinn* cannot be distinguished, it should be reconsidered. Although *Schwinn* is supported by the principle of *stare decisis,* we are convinced that the need for clarification of the law in this area justifies reconsideration. *Schwinn* itself was an abrupt and largely unexplained departure from *White Motor Co.* v. *United States.* . . . Since its announcement, *Schwinn* has been the subject of continuing controversy and confusion. . . . The great weight of scholarly opinion has been critical of the decision, and a number of the federal courts confronted with analogous vertical restrictions have sought to limit its reach. In our view, the experience of the past 10 years should be brought to bear on this subject of considerable commercial importance.

* * * * *

The market impact of vertical restrictions is complex because of their potential for a simultaneous reduction of intrabrand competition and stimulation of interbrand competition. . . .

Vertical restrictions reduce intrabrand competition by limiting the number of sellers of a particular product competing for the business of a given group of buyers. Location restrictions have this effect because of practical constraints on the effective marketing area of retail outlets. Although intrabrand competition may be reduced, the ability of retailers to exploit the resulting market may be limited both by the ability of consumers to travel to other franchised locations and, perhaps more importantly, to purchase the competing products of other manufacturers. None of these key variables, however, is affected by the form of the transaction by which a manufacturer conveys his products to the retailers.

Vertical restrictions promote interbrand competition by allowing the manufacturer to achieve certain efficiencies in the distribution of his products. These "redeeming virtues" are implicit in every decision sustaining vertical restrictions under the rule of reason. Economists have identified a number of ways in which manufacturers can use such restrictions to compete more effectively against other manufacturers. For example, new manufacturers and manufacturers entering new markets can use the restrictions in order to induce competent and aggressive retailers to make the kind of investment of capital and labor that is often required in the distribution of products unknown to the consumer. Established manufacturers can use them to induce retailers to engage in promotional activities or to provide service and repair facilities necessary to the efficient marketing of their products. . . . The availability and quality of such services affect a manufacturer's goodwill and the competitiveness of his product. Because of market imperfections such as the so-called "free rider" effect, these services might not be provided by retailers in a purely competitive situation, despite the fact that each retailer's benefit would be greater if all provided the services than if none did.

Economists also have argued that manufacturers have an economic interest in maintaining as much intrabrand competition as is consistent with the efficient distribution of their products. . . .

* * * * *

We revert to the standard articulated in *White Motor*. . . . Accordingly, we conclude that the *per se* rule stated in *Schwinn* must be overruled. . . .

. . . When anticompetitive effects are shown to result from particular vertical restrictions they can be adequately policed under the rule of reason, the standard traditionally applied for the majority of anticompetitive practices challenged under section one of the Act.

Case questions

1. Why did the Court conclude that Sylvania's dealer location clause was indistinguishable from Schwinn's customer restrictions?

2. What factors led the Court to conclude that *Schwinn* should be overruled?

3. What justifications exist for the conclusion that vertical territorial restraints are reasonable?

The Court's decision in *Sylvania* states that the per se rule is inapplicable to vertical territorial restraints. It further states that in assessing the reasonableness of vertical restraints, a court must compare their anticompetitive effects in the intrabrand market with their procompetitive effects in the interbrand market. This was precisely the comparison that the Court refused to make in *Topco*. Although *Topco* involved a horizontal rather than a vertical restraint, the Court's approach in *Sylvania* was very similar to that espoused in Chief Justice Burger's dissent in *Topco*. It is possible that *Topco* will be reexamined in light of *Sylvania*. Until that occurs, however, courts and businesses will have to distinguish vertical from horizontal restraints. This may be difficult where a manufacturer competes with its distributors or retailers. Territorial restraints in such situations will have both vertical and horizontal components. The manufacturer will have to establish that the restraints are intended to promote interbrand competition, thereby enabling a court to conclude that they serve a vertical rather than a horizontal purpose.

Exclusive dealing contracts—section 3 of the Clayton Act

Section 3 of the Clayton Act prohibits a party from selling or leasing goods or other commodities upon the condition that the purchaser or lessee not deal in or use the goods of a competitor of the seller or lessor. Section 3 applies only where the restraint is associated with the sale or lease of goods or commodities. It does not apply to services, trademark licenses, or extensions of credit. Two types of arrangements should be scrutinized for section 3 violations: exclusive dealing contracts and tie-ins.

Exclusive dealing agreements are contracts which obligate the buyer to purchase all of its requirements of a given commodity from the seller. Such arrangements may represent impositions of the seller's will on the buyer or may be mutually advantageous. In the latter situation the buyer is assured of a constant supply, is protected against price increases, and avoids the costs of storage, while the seller reduces its selling expenses, is protected against market fluctuations, and is afforded a predictable market for its product.

The Supreme Court has issued two significant decisions interpreting section 3 as applied to exclusive dealing arrangements. In the first case, *Standard Oil Co. of California* v. *United States,* Standard's exclusive dealing contracts with over 6,000 independent service stations, representing 16 percent of all outlets in seven western states, were challenged under section 3.[12] Standard was the leading refiner in the area, with 23 percent of the market, while its next six competitors together accounted for another 42 percent. Standard's exclusive sales contracts usually covered a period of one year, and such contracts were also employed by most other refiners. The market shares of all refiners had remained constant for a considerable period of time.

In determining what test should be applied to evaluate the legality of exclusive dealing contracts, the Court struggled with two conflicting concerns. On the one hand, the benefits which such agreements could provide both buyers and sellers seemed to require a complex economic inquiry into each contract's economic usefulness and restrictive effects. Among the subjects of that inquiry would be the reasonableness of the contract's duration in light of the industry, whether competition flourished despite the contract, and the seller's strength in the market. The Court viewed this inquiry as difficult at best. In *Standard Oil,* the refiners' market positions had remained constant and the exclusive dealing contracts were an industry-wide practice. It was virtually impossible to determine whether this indicated that the exclusive dealing contracts had had no competitive impact or had enabled the established refiners to maintain their positions and prevented the entrants from gaining more than an insignificant share of the market. The Court, therefore, rejected the complicated economic inquiry and held that exclusive dealing arrangements would violate section 3 where "competition has been

---

[12] 337 U.S. 293 (1949).

foreclosed in a substantial share of the line of commerce affected." In applying this test, the Court found that the Standard Oil contracts violated section 3.

The Supreme Court interpreted section 3 for the next and last time in *Tampa Electric Co.* v. *Nashville Coal Co.*[13] Tampa Electric contracted with Nashville Coal to supply all of Tampa's coal requirements for 20 years. The amount of commerce involved totaled $128 million. The lower courts found this substantial and held that the contract violated section 3. The Supreme Court, however, reversed.

The Court held that substantiality could not be measured in absolute quantities but must be considered in terms of the relevant market. It then engaged in an economic analysis similar to the type it had rejected in *Standard Oil*. It found the relevant market to include the entire Appalachian region and calculated the amount of commerce foreclosed by the contract as less than 1 percent of that market. The Court concluded that this was not substantial and consequently found no violation.

At first glance the rationales of *Tampa* and *Standard Oil* appear to conflict. The former employs rigorous economic analysis, while the latter rejects such analysis as impractical. The decisions can be reconciled, however, by comparing the facts of *Tampa* with those of *Standard Oil*. In *Tampa* the use of exclusive dealing contracts was not an industry-wide practice and there were not a large number of outlets with substantial sales volumes. Tampa Electric and Nashville Coal had relatively equal bargaining power, and the agreement conferred substantial benefits on both parties. It therefore did not appear that the seller was coercing an interdependent buyer. Thus exclusive dealing arrangements are more likely to be found legal where they are not imposed by a dominant party on a weaker party and where they are not industry-wide practices.

Tying devices

Tie-ins occur when a party offers to sell, lease, or license one good or service only to those who agree to purchase, lease, or accept a license for another good or service. The good which the buyer desires is called the tying product, while the good which the buyer is forced to take is called the tied product. Tying devices are per se violations of section 1 of the Sherman Act because they necessarily restrain competition in the product which the customer is forced to purchase. The customer purchases the tied product only because of the coercion applied. Price, quality, service, and other characteristics in which sellers usually compete become largely irrelevant. Three requirements must be met for a tie-in to exist. A not insubstantial amount of commerce must be affected; there must be two separate products

---

[13] 365 U.S. 320 (1961).

or services; and the defendant must possess sufficient economic power in the tying product to be able to enforce the tie-in.

Two different products. The existence of two separate products is a requirement which occasionally causes problems. Among the factors that courts consider in assessing whether a particular arrangement is a valid package of goods or an illegal tie-in are whether (1) others in the field offer the products separately, (2) the number of pieces in each package varies considerably, (3) the purchaser is charged separately for each item, and (4) some of the items are available separately to other consumers.

A situation in which two or more products must be sold together does not necessarily signal an illegal tie-in. It is clear that if the two products are totally unrelated, the two-product requirement is satisfied. It is also clear that some combinations of products do not signify the existence of a tie-in. For example, no tie-in exists even though it is impossible to purchase a new car without a spare tire. But, suppose a dealer refused to sell a car without an automatic transmission or a stereo tape deck. Is the dealer's refusal equally illegal whether he is selling a subcompact car or a full-sized luxury vehicle?

Sufficient economic power. Tie-ins only exist where the defendant possesses sufficient economic power to enforce them. No tie-in exists, for example, if a supermarket refuses to sell eggs unless the customer also purchases bacon, if the customer can buy eggs separately at a store down the street. If, however, the supermarket is the only local source of eggs, it probably possesses sufficient economic power to enforce the tie.

The presence of sufficient economic power is usually a question of fact. Where, however, the defendant has a legal monopoly on the tying product, for example, through a patent, trademark, or copyright, the defendant has the economic power to enforce the tie-in as a matter of law. The following case deals with the issue of sufficient economic power.

United States Steel Corp. v. Fortner Enterprises, Inc.
429 U.S. 610 (1977)

Fortner (respondent), a real estate development company, borrowed over $2 million from Credit Corporation, a wholly owned subsidiary of U.S. Steel (petitioner) to cover Fortner's cost of acquiring vacant land and buying and erecting prefabricated houses. The loan was conditioned on Fortner's buying the houses from U.S. Steel. Fortner alleged that this was a tie-in in violation of section 1 of the Sherman Act. At trial Fortner showed that U.S. Steel was one of the country's largest corporations, that almost all Credit Corpora-tion loans contained similar tie-in clauses, and that Fortner had paid more than the market price for the houses. Fortner also showed that because the loan covered 100 percent of its costs at a low rate to it and a high risk to the lender, comparable financing would have been unavailable from other conventional lenders. The trial court found this to be a tie-in and entered judgment for Fortner. The court of appeals affirmed. The Supreme Court reversed.

Mr. Justice Stevens:

* * * * *

Although the Credit Corp. is owned by one of the Nation's largest manufacturing corporations, there is nothing in the record to indicate that this enabled it to borrow funds on terms more favorable than those available to competing other lending institutions. . . . Instead, the affiliation was significant only because the Credit Corp. provided a source of funds to customers of the Home Division. That fact tells us nothing about the extent of petitioners' economic power in the credit market.

The same may be said about the fact that loans from the Credit Corp. were used to obtain house sales from Fortner and others. In some tying situations a disproportionately large volume of sales of the tied product resulting from only a few strategic sales of the tying product may reflect a form of economic "leverage" that is probative of power in the market for the tying product. If, as some economists have suggested, the purpose of a tie-in is often to facilitate price discrimination, such evidence would imply the existence of power that a free market would not tolerate. But in this case Fortner was only required to purchase houses for the number of lots for which it received financing. The tying product produced no commitment from Fortner to purchase varying quantities of the tied product over an extended period of time. This record, therefore, does not describe the kind of "leverage found in some of the Court's prior decisions condemning tying arrangements."

The fact that Fortner—and presumably other Home Division customers as well—paid a noncompetitive price for houses also lends insufficient support to the judgment of the lower court. Proof that Fortner paid a higher price for the tied product is consistent with the possibility that the financing was unusually inexpensive and that the price for the entire package was equal to, or below, a competitive price. And this possibility is equally strong even though a number of Home Division customers made a package purchase of homes and financing.

The most significant finding made by the District Court related to the unique character of the credit extended to Fortner. This finding is particularly important because the unique character of the tying product has provided critical support for the finding of illegality in prior cases.

. . . [T]hese decisions do not require that the defendant have a monopoly or even a dominant position throughout the market for a tying product. They do, however, focus attention on the question whether the seller has the power, within the market for the tying product, to raise prices or to require purchasers to accept burdensome terms that could not be exacted in a completely competitive market. In short, the question is whether the seller has some advantage not shared by his competitors in the market for the tying product.

Without any such advantage differentiating his product from that of his competitors, the seller's product does not have the kind of uniqueness considered relevant in prior tying-clause cases. . . .

* * * * *

Quite clearly, if the evidence merely shows that credit terms are unique because the seller is willing to accept a lesser profit—or to incur greater risks—than its competitors, that kind of uniqueness will not give rise to any inference of economic power in the credit market. Yet this is, in substance, all that the record in this case indicates.

* * * * *

Case questions

1. Were there two separate products? Which was the tying product, and which was the tied product?

2. What factors did Fortner claim supported the finding that U.S. Steel had sufficient economic power to enforce the tie? Why did the Court disagree?

3. What evidence could Fortner have introduced to support its position that this was an illegal tie-in?

4. A motion-picture company refuses to lease individual motion pictures to theaters. Instead it requires the theaters to buy packages, thereby forcing the theaters to take low-quality movies in order to get high-quality movies. Does this practice violate section 1 of the Sherman Act?

The Clayton Act. Unlike exclusive dealing arrangements, tying devices have virtually no purpose other than the suppression of competition. They are per se unreasonable under section 1 of the Sherman Act. When the tying and tied products are tangible commodities and a substantial amount of commerce is involved in the tied product, tie-ins also violate section 3 of the Clayton Act. Tie-ins are thus treated more severely than exclusive dealing arrangements. Whereas determining the legality of exclusive dealing arrangements requires a rigorous analysis to define the relevant market and to establish what percentage of that market the arrangement forecloses, tie-ins are illegal if a substantial dollar volume or number of units of commerce is foreclosed.

CONCERTED REFUSALS TO DEAL

An individual may refuse to deal with anyone without violating section 1 of the Sherman Act. Group boycotts, or concerted refusals to deal, however, are per se violations of the act.

The application of the per se rule to group boycotts arose from cases in which a group of firms at one level of the market coerced a group of firms at another level not to deal with competitors of the first group. For example, a group of retail lumber dealers circulated a black list to induce all retailers not to deal with wholesalers who also sold lumber at retail discount prices.[14] This practice was held illegal. Similarly, it was illegal for a group of automobile dealers to induce General Motors not to deal with competing discount outlets.[15]

The condemnation of group boycotts as per se illegal has serious consequences for industries which engage in self-regulation. Two Supreme Court decisions illustrate this point. In the first case, the Court found an illegal concerted refusal to deal where the defendant gas association refused to give its seal of approval to plaintiff's furnaces. Utility companies refused to supply gas to homes whose furnaces did not have the seal. The Court emphasized that there were no objective standards for determining when the seal would be withheld. Thus the charge that the seal was arbitrarily and capriciously withheld to induce a concerted refusal to deal was valid.[16]

In the second case, plaintiff, a stockbroker who was not a member of

---

[14] *Eastern States Retail Lumber Dealers Association* v. *United States,* 193 U.S. 38 (1904).

[15] *United States* v. *General Motors Corp.,* 384 U.S. 127 (1966).

[16] *Radiant Burners, Inc.* v. *Peoples Gas Light and Coke Co.,* 364 U.S. 656 (1961).

the New York Stock Exchange, sued the exchange after it had ordered its members to cut off his direct wire connection. Plaintiff needed the connection to trade in over-the-counter securities. The market for over-the-counter securities was established by traders through constant communication. The direct wire allowed an individual to learn instantly the latest offers to buy and sell.

Despite plaintiff's efforts, the exchange refused to advise him of the reason for the cutoff or to give him an opportunity to protest. The Court acknowledged the exchange's power of self-regulation, but reaffirmed the principle that such power might not be exercised arbitrarily lest a concerted refusal to deal result. It would be impossible, the Court said, to check the exercise of such power unless the plaintiff were told the reasons for the cutoff and given an opportunity to contest them. The exchange's refusal to do this converted its self-regulation into a group boycott.[17]

Thus, to avoid liability for group boycotts, industries which regulate themselves must apply objective standards. Disciplinary action must be accompanied by adequate notice of the action to be taken and the reasons therefore, and an opportunity to contest the action must be provided.

THE SHERMAN ACT IN ACTION: LIMITATIONS ON TRADE ASSOCIATION ACTIVITIES

Trade associations are organizations of competitors with common interests and business pursuits. Section 1 of the Sherman Act has had a severe impact on many trade association activities. Accordingly, trade associations are an excellent vehicle for observing the practical application of the antitrust laws. Several trade association activities are explored below.

Membership qualifications

Trade associations often provide services which assist their members' businesses and thereby enhance their abilities to compete. Consequently, their membership criteria are subject to Sherman Act scrutiny under the rule of reason. Unreasonable restraints of trade result from membership requirements not reasonably related to the functioning of the service and membership fees set so high that they raise barriers to entry.

An example of a trade association service is the multiple listing of houses maintained by most real estate associations. Each member broker lists houses for sale with the multiple listing service and has access to the houses listed by all other members. Thus a member broker assisting a prospective buyer has the competitive advantage of access to the listings of many other brokers. Simply listing the seller's house enables a broker employed by a seller to make the house available for consideration by many buyers' brokers. Denial

---

[17] *Silver* v. *New York Stock Exchange*, 373 U.S. 341 (1963).

of admission to a real estate association results in denial of access to the multiple listing service. This makes it more difficult for a nonmember broker to compete for the business of buyers and sellers. But not all denials of membership are unlawful. The criteria upon which an exclusion rests must be analyzed.

The requirements that members approve applications of prospective members, that exclude part-time brokers from membership, or that freeze membership are unrelated to the functioning of the multiple listing service. Such requirements place nonmember competitors at a disadvantage and accordingly have been found to unreasonably restrain trade. On the other hand, specific objective requirements for membership which insures the high integrity and reliability of all users of the service have been found reasonable in light of the responsibility each member takes for the actions of other members.[18]

Statistical reporting and price exchanges

Among the most important functions of American trade associations are the collection and dissemination of data providing a statistical profile of their industries. In an otherwise perfect market, greater access to information enhances competition. Data gathering activity, however, may also signal association members about pricing policies they have previously agreed upon. It is well established that a trade association may gather and disseminate information on costs, volume of production, stocks on hand, and past transactions and may meet and discuss such information, provided that no effort is made to reach any agreement as to prices, units of production, or other restraints on competition. Data gathering schemes are viewed as price fixes if they involve daily reporting, revealing the identities of participating companies and the information furnished by each, and audits to insure accurate reporting.

The maintenance of the anonymity and confidentiality of reports is a critical factor in avoiding antitrust violations. For example, the manufacturers of corrugated containers agreed that each would, upon request, provide the others with its most recent price charged or quoted. The information exchanges were infrequent and irregular. The industry, however, involved a fungible product in which competition focused on price. Demand was inelastic, as buyers placed orders only for short-term needs. Low barriers to entry caused supply to exceed demand. Upon learning a competitor's price, a manufacturer tended to match it. Consequently, the Court found that the exchange of price information produced a uniformity of prices and resulted in an unreasonable restraint of trade.[19]

---

[18] For further discussion, see Miller and Shedd, "Do Antitrust Laws Apply to the Real Estate Brokerage Industry?" 17 *Am. Bus. L.J.* 313 (1979). Malin, "Real Estate Multiple Listing Services and the Sherman Act: A Response to Miller and Shedd," 18 *Am. Bus. L.J.* 77 (1980).

[19] *United States* v. *Container Corp.*, 393 U.S. 337 (1969).

Product standardization

Product standardization campaigns can have a procompetitive effect by eliminating consumer confusion and focusing consumer attention on price. Where products are standardized, however, prices frequently tend toward uniformity. The problem posed is whether that uniformity is a natural market response to standardization or whether standardization is a method of fixing prices. A few examples will illustrate the factors viewed by the courts and the FTC in determining the legality of a standardization program.

A trade association of crown bottle cap manufacturers standardized all aspects of the product, including decoration and color. Although there was no actual agreement to charge uniform prices, the members' prices were identical. A patent license for one type of cap required licensees to observe a minimum price. The association also promoted a freight equalization program under which the price charged did not depend upon the manufacturer's distance from the customer. The court affirmed the FTC's order that the association cease and desist all of these practices. The court recognized that the standardization program by itself was not illegal. However, it held that when combined with the other practices described above, the program revealed the association's overriding desire to present prospective customers with uniform products, prices, and terms of sale.[20]

In a similar action, the court upheld an FTC order that the Milk and Ice Cream Can Institute cease and desist standardizing cans where the program was accompanied by uniform prices, a freight equalization plan, and classification.[21]

In addition to facilitating price-fixing, standardization may inhibit innovation. Generally the dgree of standardization plays a leading role in determining whether a particular program unlawfully inhibits innovation. Standards which are recommended and are confined to legitimate aims such as improved safety will usually survive antitrust attack. Where, however, a program attempts to standardize color, design, size, or similar features, or where such a program imposes sanctions for deviations, the program may stifle innovation and violate the Sherman Act.

Codes of ethics

Trade associations frequently promulgate ethical codes in an effort at industry self-regulation. Some code provisions, such as those fixing minimum fees, blatantly violate section 1. Others, such as those which merely advise against fraudulent or deceptive advertising, are clearly reasonable. Code provisions between these extremes must be assessed under the rule of reason to determine whether they violate the Sherman Act. Code provisions must

---

20 *Bond Crown & Cork Co.* v. *FTC,* 176 F.2d 974 (4th Cir. 1959).
21 *Milk and Ice Cream Can Institute* v. *FTC,* 152 F.2d 478 (7th Cir. 1946).

be justified as either procompetitive or as serving legitimate business purposes with no restraints or insubstantial restraints on competition.

Some codes of ethics are simply advisory in nature. Each association member must follow its own conscience in deciding whether it will comply. Many codes, however, contain sanctions for violations. The sanctions may range from reprimands to suspension or expulsion from the trade association. If a sanction is, in effect, a group boycott, it is a per se violation. Thus an antitrust violation may result from the enforcement of a code provision which is otherwise lawful.

Activities aimed at customers or suppliers

Some association activities dealing with customers and suppliers are per se illegal group boycotts under the Sherman Act. Sometimes boycott activity is blatant. For example, in an effort to combat style piracy, the members of an association of women's clothing designers agreed to boycott retailers that sold copies of their originals.[22] Similarly, the American Medical Association was found to have violated the Sherman Act by pressuring hospitals to boycott doctors who worked for a nonprofit health maintenance organization.[23]

Association activites not intended as group boycotts may lead individual members to boycott suppliers or customers or may imply that the concerted power of association members can coerce suppliers or customers into following association recommendations. Consequently, enforcement authorities view such activities cautiously, even where the activities may serve the interests of the association's members and the customers or suppliers.

Association activities which do not involve direct contact with customers or suppliers but are aimed at them do not violate the Sherman Act if they serve legitimate purposes and do not involve price-fixing, boycotts, or other unreasonable restraints. The most common activity of this kind is credit reporting. Many companies are too small to carry out their own credit checks economically. These companies may band together through their trade association to achieve an economy of scale which enables them to establish a credit reporting service. Credit reporting generally does not violate section 1 unless it is accompanied by agreements to fix credit terms or to deny credit to particular customers.

Joint selling and buying activities may result in price-fixing or may simply represent reasonable efforts to secure economies of scale. In the former case, section 1 of the Sherman Act has been violated, while in the latter case, as long as market forces continue to set prices, the restraints are reasonable.

---

[22] *Fashion Originators Guild* v. *FTC,* 312 U.S. 457 (1941).
[23] *American Medical Association* v. *United States,* 317 U.S. 519 (1943).

POLICY CONSIDERATIONS

While trade associations and individual businesses have coped with the pitfalls of the antitrust laws, a policy debate on the social role of antitrust laws has been taking place. One view holds that the primary purpose of the antitrust laws is the pursuit of maximum economic efficiency. This is attained by maximizing total output. Among the proponents of this view differing schools of thought have developed concerning how to attain maximum economic efficiency.

One of these schools contends that monopolizing a market is inefficient, that resources are allocated optimally in a competitive market. It sees the major barriers to entry into a market as economies of scale and government action. Markets may also be rendered noncompetitive by cartels or similar horizontal agreements. This school urges caution in the adoption and extension of per se rules, particularly with regard to vertical restraints. It presumes that manufacturers act in their self-interest and are subject to actual and potential intrabrand competition. Thus manufacturer-imposed vertical restraints such as territorial allocations and resale price maintenance enhance efficiency.

Another school recognizes other barriers to entry into a market. These barriers include high capital requirements and competition for scarce resources. Since these barriers restrict potential market entrants, vertical restraints may not be efficient but instead may raise additional barriers. Such restraints as tie-in devices necessarily foreclose portions of the market and should be per se illegal.

The view that economic efficiency is the primary goal of the antitrust laws has been criticized in a number of ways. Some challenge the assumption of objective economic analysis that each individual acts rationally to maximize wealth. These critics point to such economically irrational motives as religious beliefs, lust for power, altruism, and friendship. Critics also suggest that the antitrust laws serve important social and political goals. Among these goals they include curbing the concentration of economic power and preserving opportunities for small businesses. Per se rules may thus be justified on grounds of social policy as well as economic efficiency.

Judges generally have more expertise in dealing with social and political issues than with problems in objective economics. Numerous court decisions recognize the limits of judicial ability to employ complex economic analyses as a justification for per se rules. These decisions implicitly adopt the view that antitrust is designed to serve goals other than economic efficiency.

Review problems

1. A trade association of china manufacturers conducted a cost accounting survey of its members. The study was conducted to enable members to bring their prices more nearly in line with costs. It was intended to replace an outdated study which had been

conducted by a member of the association. The study's results were discussed at association meetings and unanimously adopted by members as their bsais for determining price. There are over 1,700 sizes, shapes, and colors of china. China prices have never tended toward uniformity. Has the association violated the Sherman Act?

2. Sealy, Inc., manufacturers box springs and mattresses. Its stock is owned by its licensees, and only licensees are eligible for seats on its board of directors. Licensees receive the right to manufacture and sell Sealy products. Sealy also provides licensees with national advertising, product development, sales training, and a means of central negotiations for selling to national retail organizations. Sealy specifies the location of each licensee's manufacturing plant and assigns each licensee an area in which it is primarily responsible for promoting Sealy products.

To deal with national retailers, Sealy developed a national accounts program. Sealy approached these retailers directly and negotiated agreements with them. Once an agreement was reached, each licensee was given the option to participate. If a licensee agreed to participate, it would supply Sealy products to the retailer's outlets in the licensee's area of primary responsibility at the prices set by Sealy and the retailer. Has Sealy violated any antitrust laws?

3. You are marketing director for a major oil company. For the past six months you have been considering requiring the retail gasoline stations that sell your brand to offer maintenance and repair services, with qualified mechanics on duty six days a week. Two months ago, one of your retailers ceased all maintenance and repair operations, converting to a "gas and go" station. The retailer passed the savings on overhead on to its customers by lowering gasoline prices six cents per gallon. Your other retailers in the area have complained to you about this. Should you adopt your original plan?

4. Your company is entering the computer toys field. You wish to promote your toys as offering the highest quality for the lowest price. To this end you wish to set a maximum retail price and insure that no one sells above it. How can you do this legally?

5. A group of coal producers agreed to use the same agent to sell their coal. All of the companies delivered their coal to the agent, which used its best efforts to sell the coal at the highest available price. No restrictions were placed on output.

Prior to the arrangement coal prices had been depressed for a number of reasons. First, many companies sold their coal through distributors who competed with one another. Thus a company's coal competed with itself. Second, companies which filled orders for coal of specific sizes dumped other sizes of coal on the market at distress prices. Finally, buyers frequently pooled their buying power. Following the use of the common sales agent, prices stabilized. Was the practice legal?

6. In 1914 a group of composers organized the American Society of Composers, Authors, and Publishers (ASCAP) because the performers of copyrighted music were so numerous and widespread, and most performances of such music so fleeting, that as a practical matter it was impossible for the many individual copyright owners to negotiate with and license the users and to detect unauthorized use. Today ASCAP sells users and performers a blanket license entitling them to use any and all compositions of ASCAP members. The licensees pay ASCAP a fee based on total revenues which does not directly depend on the amount or type of music used. Does this arrangement violate the Sherman Act?

7. Semolina wheat is used in the manufacture of macaroni. Most macaroni manufacturers use almost 100 percent semolina. Due to unexpected severe weather the semolina harvest this year was poor. If all macaroni manufacturers continue to use 100 percent semolina, demand will far outstrip supply. Can the manufacturers agree to limit the semolina content of their macaroni without violating section 1 of the Sherman Act?

8. Coca-Cola Company manufacturers and sells syrups and concentrates used in soft drink processing. It began operations around the turn of the century. At that time it produced no bottled soft drinks but licensed the Coca-Cola trademark in perpetuity to independent businesspersons who operated their own bottling and wholesaling operations with exclusive assigned territories.

Coca-Cola operates in the same way as it did when it began, with two exceptions: (1) It has repurchased the bottling rights for 27 of the territories and services those territories itself. Its territories account for 14 percent of the U.S. population. (2) It has introduced the soft drinks Tab, Sprite, Fresca, Fanta, and Mr. Pibb. These soft drinks are bottled and distributed in the same manner as Coke.

Coca-Cola's method of licensing bottlers in exclusive territories is an industry-wide practice. The territories were originally parceled out at a time when manual equipment was used in bottling facilities and bottled soft drinks were delivered in horse-drawn wagons over dirt roads. Today bottlers use automated equipment and modern delivery trucks. There has been a vast increase in the production capacity of bottling plants. Most bottlers use this increased capacity to produce and distribute the soft drinks of competing manufacturers. Other bottlers have entered into agreements to supply neighboring bottlers' requirements for certain package sizes or have by consolidations combined their territories. Do Coca-Cola's exclusive territories violate the Sherman Act?

9. The publisher of the only morning newspaper in New Orleans also publishes one of the city's two evening newspapers. The publisher will only sell advertising in a package which obligates the advertiser to place an ad in both newspapers. Has the publisher violated section 1 of the Sherman Act?

10. The British Restrictive Trade Practices Act allows price-fixing and other restrictive agreements to be enforced if they meet one of eight justifications. The justifications are evaluated by a Restrictive Practices Court which consists of 5 judges and 10 lay members selected for their expertise in commerce, industry, or public affairs. How does this system differ from American antitrust? Is it preferable?

CHAPTER 6

Monopolization

The preceding chapter considered contracts, combinations, and conspiracies which restrain trade. It dealt with the legality of two or more entities pooling their economic power. Accumulations of economic power are not confined to combinations of entities. Frequently an individual entity is able to attain vast amounts of economic power. In these cases section 2 of the Sherman Act comes into play. As Table 6–1 illustrates, many American businesses have grown to enormous size. Size alone, however, does not violate section 2 of the Sherman Act. The way in which the law treats monopolies is the subject of this chapter.

MONOPOLIZATION AND SECTION 2 OF THE SHERMAN ACT

Section 2 of the Sherman Act does not prohibit the existence of monopoly power. It prohibits the act of monopolizing. To monopolize one must have monopoly power and actively seek it. Thus, determining liability for the offense of monopolizing is a two-step process. Step 1 inquires into whether the defendant has monopoly power; step 2 asks whether the defendant acquired monopoly power with the intent to monopolize. Determining whether monopoly power exists is also a two-step process. Step 1 ascertains which markets the defendant operates in; step 2 assesses the defendant's power in those markets.

The relevant market

The relevant market is that segment of commerce in which a firm may, by becoming dominant, raise prices, exclude competitors, or generally operate independently of competitive forces. The relevant market must be defined in terms of product and geographic markets. The ultimate goal of these definitions is to establish a framework for assessing a firm's economic power. The relevant market concept applies the rule of reason to section 2 of the Sherman Act. The rule of reason in section 1 was applied because every contract by its nature restrains trade. Similarly, every producer is a monopo-

169

Table 6–1: The nation's 50 largest industrial companies as of 1980

Rank 1978	Company	Sales ($000)	Assets ($000)	Rank	Net income ($000)	Rank	Stockholder equity ($000)	Rank
2	Exxon (New York)	79,106,471	49,489,964	1	4,295,243	1	22,551,951	1
1	General Motors (Detroit)	66,311,200	32,215,800	2	2,892,700	3	19,179,300	2
4	Mobil (New York)	44,720,908	27,505,756	3	2,007,158	4	10,513,264	5
3	Ford Motor (Dearborn, Mich.)	43,513,700	23,524,600	5	1,169,300	11	10,420,700	6
5	Texaco (Harrison, N.Y.)	38,350,370	22,991,955	6	1,759,069	6	10,645,836	4
6	Standard Oil of California (San Francisco)	29,947,554	18,102,632	7	1,784,694	5	9,283,886	7
9	Gulf Oil (Pittsburgh)	23,910,000	17,265,000	8	1,322,000	9	8,688,000	8
7	International Business Machines (Armonk, N.Y.)	22,862,776	24,529,974	4	3,011,259	2	14,961,235	3
8	General Electric (Fairfield, Conn.)	22,460,600	16,644,500	10	1,408,800	8	7,362,300	10
12	Standard Oil (Ind.) (Chicago)	18,610,347	17,149,899	9	1,506,618	7	8,368,625	9
11	International Telephone & Telegraph (New York)	17,197,423	15,091,321	12	380,685	42	5,621,147	13
13	Atlantic Richfield (Los Angeles)	16,233,959	13,833,387	13	1,165,894	12	6,119,504	12
14	Shell Oil (Houston)	14,431,211	16,127,016	11	1,125,561	13	7,003,616	11
15	U.S. Steel (Pittsburgh)	12,929,100	11,029,900	15	(293,000)	492	4,894,600	16
18	Conoco (Stamford, Conn.)	12,647,998	9,311,171	17	8,15,360	17	3,783,111	21
16	E. I. du Pont de Nemours (Wilmington, Del.)	12,571,800	8,940,200	19	938,900	15	5,312,100	15
10	Chrysler (Highland Park, Mich.)	12,001,900	6,653,100	26	(1,097,300)	493	1,605,400	60
19	Tenneco (Houston)	11,209,000	11,631,000	14	571,000	24	3,345,000	24
17	Western Electric (New York)	10,964,075	7,128,324	24	635,898	21	4,021,576	19
23	Sun (Radnor, Pa.)	10,666,000	7,460,600	23	699,900	19	3,769,900	22
33	Occidental Petroleum (Los Angeles)	9,554,795	5,560,330	35	561,646	26	1,463,362	70
26	Phillips Petroleum (Bartlesville, Okla.)	9,502,775	8,518,709	21	891,121	16	4,257,227	17
20	Procter & Gamble (Cincinnati)	9,329,306	5,663,627	34	577,331	23	3,229,135	25
27	Dow Chemical (Midland, Mich.)	9,225,387	10,251,637	16	783,898	18	3,896,638	20
21	Union Carbide (New York)	9,176,500	8,802,600	20	556,200	27	4,042,500	18
32	United Technologies (Hartford, Conn.)	9,053,358	6,426,123	28	325,608	53	2,510,348	38
28	International Harvester (Chicago)	8,392,042	5,247,475	39	369,562	44	2,149,073	43
22	Goodyear Tire & Rubber (Akron, Ohio)	8,238,676	5,371,239	38	146,184	129	2,163,350	42
40	Boeing (Seattle)	8,131,000	4,897,200	45	505,400	34	1,847,500	50
25	Eastman Kodak (Rochester, N.Y.)	8,028,231	7,554,128	22	1,000,764	14	5,390,603	14
42	LTV (Dallas)	7,996,809	3,864,757	56	173,527	105	696,998	176
43	Standard Oil (Ohio) (Cleveland)	7,916,023	9,209,001	18	1,186,116	10	3,086,403	27

	Company							
24	Caterpillar Tractor (Peoria, Ill.)	7,613,200	37	5,403,300	37	491,600	28	3,065,300
35	Union Oil of California (Los Angeles)	7,567,698*	32	6,013,149	36	500,604	30	2,956,877
31	Beatrice Foods (Chicago)	7,468,373	60	3,669,095	62	261,010	51	1,836,972
30	RCA (New York)	7,454,600	33	5,990,200	58	283,800	53	1,759,800
29	Westinghouse Electric (Pittsburgh)	7,332,000	25	6,821,500	488	(73,900)	40	2,250,000
34	Bethlehem Steel (Bethlehem, Pa.)	7,137,200	40	5,165,900	59	275,700	35	2,570,400
47	R. J. Reynolds Industries (Winston-Salem, N.C.)	7,133,100	29	6,421,900	28	550,900	29	2,997,800
36	Xerox (Stamford, Conn.)	7,027,000	27	6,553,600	25	563,100	26	3,221,400
49	Amerada Hess (New York)	6,769,941	44	4,899,237	33	507,116	48	1,900,209
38	Esmark (Chicago)	6,743,167	99	2,389,872	193	92,423	150	833,774
52	Marathon Oil (Findlay, Ohio)	6,680,597	50	4,321,133	54	323,222	55	1,688,787
44	Ashland Oil (Russell, Ky.)	6,473,867	70	3,113,214	29	526,253	126	967,501
37	Rockwell International (Pittsburgh)	6,466,100	53	4,127,600	61	261,100	63	1,539,200
39	Kraft (Glenview, Ill.)	6,432,900	93	2,523,300	93	188,100	79	1,324,400
51	Cities Service (Tulsa)	6,276,500	47	4,773,000	48	347,500	41	2,227,400
45	Monsanto (St. Louis)	6,192,600	36	5,539,100	50	331,000	32	2,781,800
46	Philip Morris (New York)	6,144,091	30	6,378,852	32	507,881	39	2,470,955
41	General Foods (White Plains, N.Y.)	5,472,456	92	2,565,312	71	232,149	81	1,320,987

Source: Fortune, May 5, 1980, p. 276. Reprinted with permission.

list of its own product. The sole source of Coca-Cola is the Coca-Cola Company. However, Coca-Cola competes with Pepsi-Cola, Royal Crown Cola, and other colas. Undoubtedly there are persons whose loyalty to Coke is so strong that they would not consider switching to another brand. They are in a distinct minority. If the Coca-Cola Company raises the price of Coke, most persons will switch to Pepsi, RC, or some other brand, Thus, although the Coca-Cola Company is the sole source of Coke, it does not possess the power to operate independently of market forces. It is therefore not a monopolist.

The relevant product market. To understand the problems involved in defining the relevant product market, consider the Coca-Cola example. It is clear that if the price of Coke increases, many persons will switch to other cola brands. Thus these brands compete with Coke and should be included in the relevant product market. If Coke dominated the cola market, would it be able to raise prices without concern for the response of producers of other soda pop flavors? If not, then the product market should include all soda pop. Soda pop, however, competes with noncarbonated beverages such as lemonade and ice tea. These compete with fruit juices, which in turn compete with milk, coffee, and hot tea. Soft drinks also compete with beer and wine, which in turn compete with hard liquors. How far should this analysis be carried before a line is drawn? It is difficult to think of milk and vodka as being in the same market. The process can be carried to an even greater extreme by hypothesizing a situation in which all beverage prices are raised so much that consumers decide to drink water and spend their money on other items.

The courts have focused on the concept of substitutability in determining whether products should be included in the relevant market. Substitutability may be viewed from the perspective of either the producer or the consumer. From the producer's perspective inquires into whether price increases substitutability in one product will cause producers of other products to shift production and enter the market. The factors to be considered include whether the producers employ similar technologies and whether they could surmount the barriers to entry into the market. Where producers are substitutable, their potential competition checks the ability of a firm already in the market to raise prices.

Most section 2 cases focus on substitutability from the consumer's viewpoint. Products are substitutable for each other if, considering price, quality and use, they are reasonably interchangeable. However, some products which are of similar price, quality, and function and will substitute easily for other products may not be chosen by consumers who are resistant to change. On the other hand, there may be functionally very different products which consumers are willing to substitute for each other. For example, an individual may have $8,000 to spend and may be planning to spend it on a vacation. If hotel or transportation costs rise, the consumer might decide to spend the money on a new car instead.

Cross-elasticity of demand is one measure of substitutability. Demand is defined as the various amounts of a particular good or service which buyers will purchase in a given period of time at all possible prices, all things remaining constant. Elasticity of demand is a measure of the responsiveness of the amount demanded to changes in the price of the good or service. Cross-elasticity of demand is a measure of the relation of the demand for two different goods or services. It measures consumer willingness to switch from one product or service to another.

Economists define cross-elasticity of demand as the percentage change in the demand of one product divided by the percentage change in the price of another product. Thus, the cross-elasticity of demand for products X and Y would be defined as the ratio of change in the demand for X to the change in the price of Y. For example, suppose that products X and Y are interchangeable goods, that they both sell for $1, and that the demand for X is 100. Because of material shortages, the price of Y has just been raised to $1.10; some Y buyers have shifted to X, raising demand for X to 105. Here, the cross-elasticity between X and Y is the percent change in X demand (5 percent, from 100 to 105) divided by the percent change in Y's price (10 percent, from $1 to $1.10). Thus, the cross-elasticity of demand is 5 percent divided by 10 percent, or ½.

If cross-elasticity of demand is negative, the products are complements; that is, as the price of Y decreases, demand for X increases. For example, cars and tires are complements; a decrease in the price of cars will probably cause an increase in the number of tires demanded. If cross-elasticity of demand is positive and high, the products are considered close substitutes. In the example in the preceding paragraph, a firm dominating the market in product Y cannot raise prices because customers will switch to product X. Thus, the relevant product market should include both X and Y. An example of two products with a positive and high cross-elasticity of demand is butter and margarine, as these are substitute products.

Cross-elasticity of demand is difficult for economists to calculate precisely because conditions other than demand for X and the price of Y do not remain constant. The best that can be hoped for is a probable estimate. Courts are even less able to measure cross-elasticity of demand. Few judges are trained economists. Judges must almost always rely on the testimony of experts called by the parties. Expert opinions will differ, with each expert emphasizing the factors that support the position of the party for which the expert is testifying. A court must combine the economic testimony with common sense to arrive at a market definition.

The leading Supreme Court decision dealing with the method of determining relevant product market is *United States* v. *E. I. du Pont de Nemours & Co.*[1] The government charged Du Pont with monopolizing cellophane. The evidence showed that Du Pont produced 75 percent of the nation's cellophane

---

[1] 351 U.S. 377 (1950).

and 20 percent of all flexible packaging materials. The Supreme Court affirmed the trial court's finding that the relevant market included all flexible packaging materials. The Court relied on evidence showing that for bakery products cellophane accounted for only 7 percent of the wrappings; for candy, 25 percent; for snacks, 32 percent; for nuts and poultry, 35 percent; for crackers and biscuits, 27 percent; for fresh produce, 47 percent; for frozen food, 34 percent; and for cigarettes, 75–80 percent. Thus, only in the wrapping market for cigarettes was cellophane dominant. Other users were willing to employ substitutes for cellophane. Furthermore, the Court found that except for permeability to gases, cellophane's qualities were shared by many other wrapping materials. It found that at various points in time Du Pont had lost business to other materials, including substantial losses in meat packaging to Pliofilm and greased paper. Finally, the Court found that Du Pont had taken the prices of waxed paper, glassine, greaseproof paper, vegetable parchment, and similar materials into consideration when pricing cellophane. It had reduced its prices on several occasions and had succeeded in attracting customers away from other materials.

On the other hand, the Court has also affirmed trial court findings of very narrow relevant markets. In one case, the Court found a relevant market limited to championship boxing matches and rejected the defense contention that the market should encompass all prizefights.[2] In another case, the government charged the defendants with monopolizing a market of central station protection services. The Court rejected the defendants' contention that the relevant market included other protection devices. Providers of central station services installed hazard-protecting devices on the customer's premises and monitored these devices in a central station which was staffed 24 hours a day. When an alarm was received, station operators would dispatch guards and notify police, fire departments, and other appropriate authorities. Other protection systems had defects which made them poor substitutes. Security guards were less reliable, and on-site alarms might be inoperable without being detected or might not attract needed help. Direct hookups to police stations were generally not available in cities served by central stations. Furthermore, insurance companies usually offered discounts to central station customers which were unavailable to users of other protective devices.[3]

The use of cross-elasticity of demand and substitutability as criteria for delineating the relevant market has been the subject of frequent criticism. The most common criticism is that cross-elasticity fails to consider the price at which the alleged monopolist's product is selling. Even a firm with monopoly power is unable to raise prices astronomically without incurring competition from poor substitutes. If a monopolist raises its prices far above the

---

[2] *International Boxing Club of New York, Inc.,* v. *United States* 358 U.S. 242 (1959).
[3] *United States* v. *Grinnell Corp.,* 384 U.S. 563 (1963).

prices it would have charged in the competitive marketplace, the cross-elasticity of demand between its goods and poor substitutes will be high. This criticism highlights the need, recognized by courts, to treat the concept of cross-elasticity of demand as only a starting point in defining the relevant market. The purpose of defining the relevant market—to assess an alleged monopolist's power—should always be kept in mind. When measures of cross-elasticity alone will not provide an accurate gauge of economic power, such measures should not be the sole determinant of the relevant market.

For example, in *United States* v. *Aluminum Company of America* the government charged that Alcoa, the only domestic producer of virgin aluminum ingot, monopolized that market.[4] Alcoa sold its virgin ingot to aluminum fabricators which processed it into rolls and sheets. Alcoa also used some of the ingot itself to fabricate aluminum that it sold. The court included the aluminum fabricated by Alcoa in the relevant market because all ingot was used to fabricate intermediate or end products. Consequently, the court reasoned, all aluminum fabricated by Alcoa pro tanto reduced the demand for ingot.

The virgin ingot produced by Alcoa competed with secondary ingot recycled from scrap by many other companies. The prices of the two products were comparable, and many users of virgin ingot could just as easily use secondary ingot. Nevertheless, the court did not include secondary ingot in the relevant market. The court reasoned that because Alcoa was the sole domestic supplier of virgin ingot and could predict what portion of the virgin would be recycled as secondary, Alcoa could control the amount of the secondary with which it would have to compete. Consequently, including the secondary ingot in the relevant market would distort the true picture of Alcoa's economic power.

Other instances in which substitutability alone has not been used to determine the relevant market are those in which the alleged monopolist offers a cluster of goods or services. Consider the soft drink manufacturer which makes cola. That manufacturer may diversify into other flavors, but it may also make such items as glass and party trays bearing its trademark. It may use these items as premiums or special offers to attract customers to its soft drinks. Although different, its products are related because they can be used by the same customer and can be marketed by the same methods.

Courts have taken a pragmatic approach in deciding whether to group such clusters in a single market. The particular facts and circumstances of each case are considered, with the views of consumers and producers given most emphasis. Where all producers tend to offer the same cluster of products or where consumers tend to view the cluster as a whole, the entire product line is likely to be included in the relevant market. The interplay of economic concepts, legal standards, and common sense is illustrated in the following decision.

---

[4] 148 F.2d 416 (2d Cir. 1945).

Telex Corp. v. International Business Machines Corp.
510 F.2d 894 (10th Cir. 1975)

Telex (plaintiff) sued IBM (defendant), alleging that IBM monopolized peripheral data processing devices. The trial court held that the relevant market was peripheral devices plug compatible with IBM central processing units (CPUs). It entered judgment for Telex. The Tenth Circuit Court of Appeals reversed.

The data processing equipment industry consisted of central processing units and peripheral devices which could be connected to the central processing unit. Peripheral devices included information storage components such as magnetic tape drives, magnetic disc drives, magnetic drums, and magnetic strip files; terminal devices such as printers; memory units; and specialized storage units. Peripheral devices were said to be plug compatible with the central processing units that they fitted.

Per Curiam:

* * * * *

The threshold issue is whether the court erred in its findings as to the scope and extent of the relevant product market for determination whether there existed power to control prices or to exclude competition, that is, whether there was monopoly power. [T]he court determined that the relevant product market was limited to peripheral devices plug compatible with IBM central processing units together with particular product submarkets; magnetic tape products, direct access storage products, memory products, impact printer products and communication controllers, all of which were plug compatible with an IBM CPU. IBM had sought a determination that the relevant product market consisted of electronic data processing systems together with the products which are part of such systems or at least that the relevant product market should consist of all peripheral products and not be limited to those currently attached to IBM systems.

The trial court's initial approach to the prob-

lem was restricted to consideration of whether the market "may be realistically subdivided in the time frame 1969–1972 to focus on and encompass only those parts of current product lines which are respectively attached to IBM systems rather than all those products which actually have similar uses in connection with other systems." The court recognized that inasmuch as every manufacturer, originally at least, has 100 percent of its own product, including the peripherals, the likelihood of finding monopolization in this area increases as the circumscribing products market is more circumscribed.

The trial court also recognized that the cost of adaptation of peripherals to the CPUs of other systems is roughly the same with respect to every system, that is, the cost of the interface, the attachment which allows the use of peripherals manufactured by one system to be used on another central processing unit is generally about the same. But these practical interchange possibilities did not deter the court in reaching a conclusion that the products market was practically restricted. A factor which influenced the trial court was the commitment of Telex to supplying peripherals plug compatible with IBM systems. The court appeared to disregard the interchangeability aspect of the peripherals manufactured by companies other than IBM, giving emphasis to the fact that Telex, for example, had not chosen to manufacture such peripheral products of the kind and character manufactured by companies other than IBM. The trial court did, however, recognize the presence of interchangeability of use and the presence of cross-elasticity of demand. The court thought, however, that the presence of these factors were [*sic*] not sufficiently immediate.

We recognize that market definition is generally treated as a matter of fact and that findings on this subject are not to be overturned unless clearly erroneous. Our question is, therefore, whether it was clearly erroneous for the court to exclude peripheral products of systems other than IBM such as Honeywell, Univac, Burroughs, Control Data Corp. and others, together with peripheral products plug compatible with the system and, indeed, whether the systems themselves manufactured by the companies are to be taken into account. It is significant, of course, that peripheral products constitute a large percentage of the entire data processing system, somewhere between 50 and 75 percent.

Inasmuch as IBM's share of the data processing industry as a whole is insufficient to justify any inference or conclusion of market power in IBM, the exclusion from the defined market of those products which are not plug compatible with IBM central processing units has a significant impact on the court's decision that IBM possessed monopoly power.

* * * * *

In dealing with the issue whether peripehral products non-compatible with IBM systems ought to be considered, the court said in Finding 47 that as a practical matter there is no direct competition between IBM peripherals and the peripherals of other systems manufacturers. However, this finding is out of harmony with other findings which the court made. See, for example, Finding 38, wherein the court said that "It cannot be gainsaid that indirectly at least and to some degree the peripheral products attached to non-IBM systems necessarily compete with and constrain IBM's power with respect to peripherals attached to IBM systems." The court also stated in Finding 38 that:

. . . [S]uppliers of peripherals plug compatible with non-IBM systems could in various instances shift to the production of IBM plug compatible peripherals, and vice versa, should the economic rewards in the realities of the market become sufficiently attractive and if predatory practices of others did not dissuade them. In the absence of defense tactics on the part of manufacturers of CPU's, the cost of developing an interface for a peripheral device would generally be about the same regardless of the system to which it would be attached, and such cost

has not constituted a substantial portion of the development cost of the peripheral device.

* * * * *

[A Telex senior vice president testified] that the engineering costs of developing interfaces was [*sic*] minimal and that he had advocated modifying interfaces so that Telex products could be used with systems other than IBM. Another example of ease of interface design is shown by the fact that following RCA's decision to abandon the computer systems business and turn it over to Univac, Telex recognized a marketing opportunity and it began marketing its 6420 tape unit, the plug compatible equivalent of IBM's 3420 Aspen tape unit, as a plug compatible unit with RCA CPUs. . . .

Still another exhibit in the record recognizing the practicability of interface change on peripheral equipment is a February 4, 1972, memorandum of R. M. Wheeler, Chairman of the Board of Telex, requesting a letter for his signature which could be sent to systems manufacturers. This letter was to be sent to systems manufacturers. It offered to sell peripheral equipment plug compatible with the central processing units of the manufacturers. Specific reference was made to the 6420 tape unit, among others, which would normally be compatible to IBM's central processing unit. The Wheeler letter stated that Telex would be willing to interface their equipment at no cost to the purchaser.

Manufacturers of peripherals were not limited to those which were plug compatible with IBM CPUs. The manufacturers were free to adapt their products through interface changes to plug into non-IBM systems. It also followed that systems manufacturers could modify interfaces so that their own peripheral products could plug into IBM CPUs. Factually, then, there existed peripheral products of other CPU manufacturers which were competitive with IBM peripherals and unquestionably other IBM peripherals were capable of having their interfaces modified so that their peripheral products would plug into non-IBM's CPU.

The fact that Telex had substantially devoted itself to the manufacture of peripheral products which were used in IBM CPUs and which competed with IBM peripheral products cannot control in determining product market since the legal standard is whether the product is reasonably interchangeable.

This standard was laid down by the Supreme Court in the famous case of *United States* v. *E. I. duPont de Nemours & Co.* The Supreme Court determined that if one product may substitute for another in the market it is "reasonably interchangeable." On this the Court stated:

> [W]here there are market alternatives that buyers may readily use for their purposes, illegal monopoly does not exist merely because the product said to be monopolized differs from others. If it were not so, only physically identical products would be a part of the market.

One evidence of cross-elasticity is the responsiveness of sales of one product to price changes of another. But a finding of actual fungibility is not necessary to a conclusion that products have potential substitutability. . . .

It seems clear that reasonable interchangeability is proven in the case at bar and hence the market should include not only peripheral products plug compatible with IBM CPUs, but all peripheral products, those compatible not only with IBM CPUs but those compatible with non-IBM systems. This is wholly justifiable because the record shows that these products, although not fungible, are fully interchangeable and may be interchanged with minimal financial outlay, and so cross-elasticity exists within the meaning of the DuPont decision.

Case questions

1. How did the trial court define the relevant market? How did it justify this definition? How did the court of appeals define the relevant market? What evidence did it point to in support of its definition?

2. Did the court of appeals examine substitutability from the producer's view or the consumer's view?

3. Why were all peripheral data service devices clustered in a single market and the central processing units excluded from the market?

4. Do you agree with the court of appeals that a product should be included in the relevant market where it is shown to be potentially substitutable although not actually fungible?

The relevant geographic market. Questions concerning the relevant geographic market arise less frequently than those involving the relevant product market. When such questions do occur they can be very troubling. A restaurant located in the downtown section of a central city may draw its customers from all parts of the city and its suburbs. The restaurant competes for patrons with similar establishments in the far eastern suburbs and the far western suburbs. The restaurants of the eastern suburbs, however, probably do not compete at all with their counterparts in the western suburbs.

The courts have taken a practical approach to defining the relevant geographic market. The most important factors are the views and actions of consumers and producers. Do producers regard particular cities or regions as separate markets, or do they plan, sell, advertise, and operate nationally? Over what distances do most consumers travel to comparison-shop? The answers to these questions will depend on the size of the purchase and the needs of the consumer. For example, an individual living in a suburb of a large city may not be willing to travel more than a mile to find a Laundromat. That same individual will probably shop in the city and neighboring suburbs when buying a washer and dryer, while the Laundromat may shop regionally for the best buy on its fleet of washers and dryers. The manufacturers of the washers and dryers probably shop nationally for materials and component parts.

Factors in addition to producer and consumer actions which are frequently considered include transportation costs, availability of distribution networks, and legal restrictions such as licensing requirements and zoning laws. Sometimes a national geographic market may be useful for assessing monopoly power but must yield to more refined definitions when a remedy is being devised. For example, a national market may be used to assess monopoly power where most competitors operate nationally, use national price lists, and are affected by other national factors, even though the service is essentially local. In such a case, however, the national market must be refined into regional submarkets in order to devise a remedy.

Assessing power in the relevant market

A company has monopoly power within the relevant market if it is capable of raising prices and excluding competitors, that is, if it is capable of operating independently of market forces. Absolute independence is impossible to achieve, for there will always be poor substitutes which will compete effectively when the price of the monopolist's product is raised sufficiently. Thus, only relative ability to raise prices is required.

The starting point for determining market power is to determine the alleged monopolist's market share, expressed as a percentage of production, units sold, or revenue. This is frequently the end point as well. The court in *Alcoa* inferred from Alcoa's 90 percent share of the market that Alcoa had monopoly power. The court indicated that a two-thirds share of the market would be a questionable case and that a one-third share would clearly not amount to monopoly power. Although other opinions have used slightly different figures, it is clear that a firm possessing a market share between 85 percent and 100 percent will be deemed conclusively to have monopoly power, while a firm whose share is less than 50 percent will be found to lack such power. The range in between forms a gray area in which courts must examine the specific circumstances of the case. Factors beyond percentage share of the market must be considered. These factors include the structure of the market, barriers to entry into the market, and the strength of the alleged monopolist's competitors. Conduct inconsistent with a competitive marketplace, such as the imposition of one-sided contract terms upon customers or suppliers, is further evidence of monopoly power. Prices charged or profits made, however, are generally not relevant to the determination. The Sherman Act is concerned with the existence and acquisition of monopoly power, not with the reasonableness of its exercise. Just as the reasonableness of the prices charged by parties to a price-fixing conspiracy is irrelevant under section 1, so too the reasonableness of the prices charged or profits made by a monopolist is irrelevant under section 2.

Intent to monopolize

The mere existence of monopoly power does not violate section 2 of the Sherman Act. It is not illegal per se to be too big. The alleged monopolist must have acted with the intent to monopolize. The intent component of a section 2 violation draws upon the criminal law generally and upon its standards of culpability. At one extreme, certain offenses are considered strict liability offenses. A person who does the prohibited act is guilty regardless of intent. For example, an individual driving at an excessive speed commits an offense even though that individual's speedometer is broken and the individual believes the car is traveling at a lawful speed. At the other extreme are specific intent offenses. A person is not guilty unless the prohibited act has been done with a specific intent. For example, the crime of larceny consists of taking property of another with the specific intent of permanently depriving the owner of that property. A person who steals a car for the purpose of joyriding and intends to return the car does not commit the crime of larceny.

Most offenses fall between the two extremes and require a showing of general intent. In these cases one is presumed to intend the natural and foreseeable consequences of one's actions. Monopolizing under section 2 of the Sherman Act is a general intent offense. Where the natural and foreseeable consequences of a firm's actions are to confer monopoly power upon that firm, the firm is presumed to have intended to monopolize. These actions are not limited to predatory, immoral, or unfair practices. They encompass actions which, in the absence of monopoly power, would generally be regarded as good business practices. For example, Alcoa was found to have monopolized aluminum ingot because it anticipated increases in demand and expanded production to meet those increases before other companies were able to enter the market.

When a firm achieves monopoly power without intending to, it is said to be a passive beneficiary of monopoly, or monopoly is said to have been thrust upon it. Such legal monopolies exist when the government confers a monopoly upon a firm, as in the case of public utilities and patents. In some cases a market is so small that only one firm can efficiently and profitably serve it. For example, a movie theater owner in a town whose population will support only one movie theater is the passive beneficiary of a monopoly. In other cases, changes in taste may drive out all but one producer or a producer may develop a new product or a new technology and be the only firm in the market until other producers enter it. Finally, the alleged monopolist may have achieved its position as a result of a superior product or superior business acumen. In these instances, where as a result of superior skill, foresight, and industry one firm is the sole survivor of a group of active competitors, that firm is not viewed as a monopolist.

The line between a firm which has engaged in practices whose natural and foreseeable consequences are monopoly power and a firm which has achieved monopoly power as a result of superior skill is often a fine one. The policy which enables courts, attorneys, and businesses to draw that line recognizes that monopolies may be tolerated in order to preserve competitive incentives. The following decision illustrates this point.

United States v. *United Shoe Machinery Corp.*
110 F. Supp. 205 (D. Mass. 1953)

The United States (plaintiff) sued United Shoe Machinery Corporation (defendant), charging that it monopolized the market for shoe machinery. Judgment for the United States.

United Shoe Machinery Corporation was formed by the merger of several smaller companies. It supplied over 75 percent of the demand for shoe machines. It was the only manufacturer offering a full line of shoe machines and the only manufactures of shoe machines with an extensive research and development operation. It leased machines under 10-year leases and provided maintenance and repair service free of additional charge. It refused to sell its machines. It required lessees to operate its machines at full capacity whenever possible.

Wyzanski, District Judge:

* * * * *

On the foregoing facts, the issue of law is whether defendant in its shoe machinery business has violated that provision of §2 of the Sherman Act. . . .

* * * * *

. . . The facts show that (1) defendant has, and exercises, such overwhelming strength in the shoe machinery market that it controls that market, (2) this strength excludes some potential, and limits some actual competition, and (3) this strength is not attributable solely to defendant's ability, economies of scale, research,

natural advantages, and adaptation to inevitable economic laws.

In estimating defendant's strength, this Court gives some weight to the 75 plus percentage of the shoe machinery market which United serves. But the Court considers other factors as well. In the relatively static shoe machinery market where there are no sudden changes in the style of machines or in the volume of demand, United has a network of long-term, complicated leases with over 90 percent of the shoe factories. These leases assure closer and more frequent contacts between United and its customers than would exist if United were a seller and its customers were buyers. Beyond this general quality, these leases are so drawn and so applied as to strengthen United's power to exclude competitors. Moreover, United offers a long line of machine types, while no competitor offers more than a short line. Since in some parts of its line United faces no important competition, United has the power to discriminate, by wide differentials and over long periods of time, in the rate of return it procures from different machine types. Furthermore, being by far the largest company in the field, with by far the largest resources in dollars, in patents, in facilities, and in knowledge, United has a marked capacity to attract offers of inventions, inventors' services, and shoe machinery businesses. And, finally, there is no substantial substitute competition from a vigorous secondhand market in shoe machinery.

To combat United's market control, a competitor must be prepared with knowledge of shoemaking, engineering skill, capacity to invent around patents, and financial resources sufficient to bear the expense of long developmental and experimental processes. The competitor must be prepared for consumers' resistance founded on their long-term, satisfactory relations with United, and on the cost to them of surrendering United's leases. Also, the competitor must be prepared to give, or point to the source of, repair and other services, and to the source of supplies for machine parts, expendable parts, and the like. Indeed, perhaps a competitor who aims at any large-scale success must also be prepared to lease his machines. These considerations would all affect *potential* competition, and have not been without their effect on *actual* competition.

Not only does the evidence show United has control of the market, but also the evidence does not show that the control is due entirely to excusable causes. The three principal sources of United's power have been the original constitution of the company, the superiority of United's products and services, and the leasing system. The first two of these are plainly beyond reproach. The original constitution of United in 1899 was judicially approved. It is no longer open to question, and must be regarded as protected by the doctrine of *res judicata,* which is the equivalent of a legal license. Likewise beyond criticism is the high quality of United's products, its understanding of the techniques of shoemaking and the needs of shoe manufacturers, its efficient design and improvement of machines, and its prompt and knowledgeable service. . . .

But United's control does not rest solely on its original constitution, its ability, its research, or its economies of scale. There are other barriers to competition, and these barriers were erected by United's own business policies. Much of United's market power is traceable to the magnetic ties inherent in its system of leasing, and not selling, its more important machines. The lease-only system of distributing complicated machines has many "partnership" aspects, and it has exclusionary features such as the 10-year term, the full capacity clause, the return charges, and the failure to segregate

service charges from machine charges. Moreover, the leasing system has aided United in maintaining a pricing system which discriminates between machine types.

* * * * *

In one sense, the leasing system and the miscellaneous activities just referred to (except United's purchases in the secondhand market) were natural and normal, for they were "honestly industrial." They are the sort of activities which would be engaged in by other honorable firms. And, to a large extent, the leasing practices conform to long-standing traditions in the shoe machinery business. Yet, they are not practices which can be properly described as the inevitable consequences of ability, natural forces, or law. They represent something more than the use of accessible resources, the process of invention and innovation, and the employment of those techniques of employment, financing, production, and distribution, which a competitive society must foster. They are contracts, arrangements, and policies which, instead of encouraging competition based on pure merit, further the dominance of a particular firm. In this sense, they are unnatural barriers; they unnecessarily exclude actual and potential competition; they restrict a free market. While the law allows many enterprises to use such practices, the Sherman Act is now construed by superior courts to forbid the continuance of effective market control based in part upon such practices. Those courts hold that market control is inherently evil and constitutes a violation of § 2 unless economically inevitable, or specifically authorized and regulated by law.

* * * * *

So far, nothing in this opinion has been said of defendant's *intent* in regard to its power and practices in the shoe machinery market. . . . Defendant intended to engage in the leasing practices and pricing policies which maintained its market power. That is all the intent which the law requires when both the complaint and the judgment rest on a charge of "monopolizing," not merely "attempting to monopolize." Defendant, having willed the means, has willed the end.

* * * * *

Case questions

1. What factors led the court to conclude that United possessed monopoly power?

2. What three factors produced United's monopoly position? How did the court evaluate each of these?

3. Did United intend to monopolize? Explain.

Monopoly power not otherwise unlawful may violate section 2 if it was improperly obtained or is improperly used or maintained. For example, a patent obtained by fraud is invalid, and the resulting monopoly violates section 2 of the Sherman Act. Similarly, a firm may enter and compete for a market which can only support one company, but it will violate section 2 if it uses predatory or unfair methods. Illustrative of this situation is *Union Leader Corp.* v. *Newspapers of New England, Inc.*[5] The controversy revolved around a battle between two newspapers for the business of Haverhill, Massachusetts, a town which was capable of supporting only one newspaper. When workers at the *Haverhill Gazette* went on strike, a rival publisher of other Massachusetts newspapers began publishing a paper in Haverhill. The rival publisher continued publishing after the strike was settled. It made payments to members of the labor union which had struck in order to create the appearance that organized labor supported it. It also gave secret payments, discounts, and kickbacks to advertisers that refused to do business with the *Gazette.* The court held that Union Leader's use of these predatory tactics in competing for a natural monopoly violated section 2 of the Sherman Act. Interestingly, the *Gazette* fought back with kickbacks and discounts of its own. The court held that as long as the *Gazette* confined such tactics to those necessary to meet the competition, no violation of the Sherman Act would result from them.

A company which obtains its monopoly legally may still violate section 2 if it acts intentionally to maintain or extend its monopoly power. For example, in *United States* v. *Griffith* a chain of movie theaters in Oklahoma, Texas, and New Mexico owned theaters in 85 towns.[6] Some of the towns were natural monopolies, that is, their populations were so small that they could support only one theater. The Griffith chain used its legally attained monopoly position in these towns to extract from distributors exclusive rights to motion pictures in towns where it faced competition. The court held that this use of a natural monopoly violated section 2. It indicated that monopoly power in one market might not be used to foreclose competition, or even to gain a competitive advantage, in another market.

In some instances a firm with a lawfully acquired monopoly may be

---

[5] 284 F.2d 582 (1st Cir. 1960), *certiorari denied,* 365 U.S. 833 (1961).

[6] 334 U.S. 100 (1948).

required not only to refrain from using its power to gain a competitive advantage in another market but also to give its competitors access to its monopoly. Illustrative is *United States* v. *Terminal Railroad Association*.[7] Because of its geography, St. Louis could accommodate only one railroad terminal. Several railroads combined to form the Terminal Railroad Association, which owned and operated the city's sole terminal. The association required the unanimous consent of its members to allow nonmember railroads access to the facility. The court held it violative of section 2 for the association to refuse proper and equal use of the terminal by nonmember companies. The following case raises similar issues of misuse of monopoly power.

Official Airline Guide, Inc. v. FTC
No. 80–4028 (2d Cir. Sept. 18, 1980)

Official Airline Guide, Inc. (OAG), the successor to the Reuben H. Donnelley Corp. (appellant), appealed an order of the Federal Trade Commission (appellee) which required it to list the connecting flights of commuter airlines in its Official Airline Guide. *The Court of Appeals for the Second Circuit reversed the FTC.*

OAG and Donnelley published the Guide, *which became the primary reference for airlines and travel agents in booking passengers on flights. The* Guide *listed both the direct and connecting flights of certified airlines but only the direct flights of commuter airlines. Thus a person seeking passage between two cities which were not serviced by a direct flight could determine at a glance which certified airlines connected to which other certified airlines to compete the route. To determine how to complete a route by using a commuter airline, a person would have to consult a separate section of the* Guide *to find what cities the commuter airlines provided direct service to and then turn to the certified airlines direct service section to find a connecting flight. This hampered the commuter airlines' ability to compete.*

Oakes, Circuit Judge:

*   *   *   *   *

We turn then to the crucial issue in the case, whether Donnelley as a monopolist had some

duty under section 5 of the FTC Act not to discriminate unjustifiably between the competing classes of carriers so as to place one class at a significant competitive disadvantage. In other words, does the FTC Act authorize the Commission to find unlawful the type of challenged activity engaged in by petitioner? The Commission itself recognized that "[t]he question we are presented with is outside the mainstream of law concerning monopolies and monopolization."

On the other hand, the petitioner refers us to the principle that

> [i]n the absence of any purpose to create or maintain a monopoly, the [Sherman Act] does not restrict the long-recognized right of a trader or manufacturer engaged in an entirely private business, freely to exercise his own independent discretion as to parties with whom he will deal.

The Commission did not find in the present case "any purpose to create or maintain a monopoly." . . .

The Commission's brief, however, refers us to two lines of cases with which it claims its decision is consistent. The first line recognizes limitations that may be placed upon a monopolist's rights to affect competition. . . . Though recognizing the general right of a private business to select its customers, the Court [has] held that the exercise of this right for the pur-

---

[7] 284 U.S. 383 (1912).

pose of monopolization violates the Sherman Act. . . . The Commission similarly argues that its position is supported by [decisions in which] the Court held that a monopolist may not abuse its monopoly power in one market to gain an improper advantage or to destroy threatened competition in an adjacent market in which it also operates. But as the Commission itself pointed out, the instant case "differs from ordinary monopolization cases where challenged acts or practices were engaged in to benefit the monopolist competitively, either in the market in which the monopoly power existed or in some adjacent market into which the monopolist had extended its operations." Donnelley, though possibly a monopolist in the airline schedule publishing industry, admittedly had no anticompetitive motive or intent with respect to the airline industry and is engaged in a different line of commerce from that of the air carriers.

The second line of cases relied upon in the Commission's brief recognizes the duty that the joint owners of a scarce resource have to make the resource available to all potential users on nondiscriminatory terms. Thus . . . in *United States* v. *Terminal Railroad Association,* the Court held that an association of railroad companies controlling access to the city's only terminal facilities had to make them available to nonmembers on reasonable, nondiscriminatory terms. And in *Silver* v. *New York Stock Exchange,* the Court held that the New York Stock Exchange and its members violated section 1 of the Sherman Act when they jointly denied nonmember broker-dealers access to private wire services with certain Exchange members. Each of these cases, however, involved joint refusals to deal resulting in injury to the *defendants'* competitors, while the instant case involves only unilateral behavior by Donnelley which allegedly has affected competition among air carriers, a business in which Donnelley is not engaged.

* * * * *

Conceding in effect that there is no case precisely in point, the Commission suggested in oral argument that it was but a "small step" that we would be taking were we to uphold

their decision. Of course, we are reminded by the line of cases that "[w]hile the final word is left to the courts, necessarily 'we give great weight to the Commission's conclusion . . .' " as to what is an "unfair method of competition" or "an unfair act or practice" within the meaning of section 5 of the FTC Act. We note that the FTC with some justification states that the arbitrary refusal of a monopolist to deal leaves the disadvantaged competitor, even though in another field, with no recourse to overcome the disadvantage, and the Commission wants us to take the "small step" in terms of "the fundamental goals of antitrust."

But we think enforcement of the FTC's order here would give the FTC too much power to substitute its own business judgment for that of the monopolist in any decision that arguably affects competition in another industry. Such a decision would permit the FTC to delve into, as the Commission itself put the extreme case, "social, political, or personal reasons" for a monopolist's refusal to deal. Professors Areeda and Turner give examples of a monopolist theater which refuses to admit men with long hair or a monopolist newspaper which refuses to publish advertising from cigarette manufacturers. The Commission says that neither of these examples would trigger antitrust scrutiny because there is no competition among persons who attend movies, and refusing to publish advertisements for all cigarette companies would not place any of them at a disadvantage vis-à-vis a competitor. Nevertheless, the Commission's own example of a monopolist newspaper refusing to take advertisements from a particular cigarette company because of the style of prior advertisements or the political views of its president shows just how far the Commission's opinion could lead us. What we are doing, as the Commission itself recognized, is weighing benefits to competition in the other field against the detrimental effect of allowing the Commission to pass judgment on many business decisions of the monopolist that arguably discriminate among customers in some way. Thus, if the only supermarket in town decides to stock Birdseye vegetables but not Green Giant vegetables, the FTC would be able to require it to stock Green Giant vegetables if it were to find Green Giant competitively disadvantaged.

. . . "[I]t has always been the prerogative of a manufacturer to decide with whom it will deal." . . . We think that even a monopolist, so long as he has no purpose to restrain competition or to enhance or expand his monopoly, and does not act coercively, retains this right. . . .

* * * * *

Case questions

1. How did OAG's and Donnelley's alleged misuse of monopoly power differ from other cases in which defendants were found to have violated section 2?

2. Why did the court refuse to defer to the FTC's expertise?

3. In this case OAG and Donnelley did not refuse to deal with the commuter airlines but dealt with them on terms less favorable than the terms given the certified airlines. The court considered this to be the same as a refusal to deal. Do you agree?

OLIGOPOLIES

Oligopolistic industries are industries dominated by a small number of large firms. Usually none of the firms individually possesses sufficient market power to render it liable to attack under section 2. Oligopolistic industries are usually marked by conscious parallelism and price leadership. However, as noted in Chapter 5, consciously parallel action does not amount to a contract, combination, or conspiracy. Thus oligopolistic markets are generally not subject to attack under section 1 of the Sherman Act.

Some individuals and authorities have suggested a theory of shared monopoly which would apply section 2 to oligopolies. Pursuant to this theory, where two or more companies act in an interdependent manner resulting in anticompetitive effects, the companies would be considered a single entity for section 2 purposes. The concept of shared monopoly currently exists in theory only and has yet to be tested before any court.

A complaint filed by the FTC against Kellogg Company, General Mills, Inc., General Foods Corporation, and Quaker Oats Company illustrates the theory.[8] The complaint alleged that together these companies accounted for 90 percent of the ready-to-eat (RTE) cereal market. It charged that the companies acted interdependently to proliferate RTE cereal brands through intensive, and at times deceptive, advertising aimed primarily at children, and to control shelf space in retail grocery stores. It contended that these actions raised artificial barriers to entry into the RTE cereal market. It urged that the companies' shared monopoly power was evidenced by price leadership, restricted use of trade deals and trade-directed promotions, limited use of consumer-directed promotions, artifically inflated prices, profits in excess of those obtainable in a competitive market, substitutions of product imitation for product innovation, and blocks to entry into the market. This

[8] *In re Kellogg Co.,* Antitrust and Trade Reg. Repr. No. 547 (BNA) at A–3 (Jan. 24, 1972).

complaint and a similar complaint filed against the major oil companies were still pending before the FTC as of the publication date of this book.

ATTEMPTS TO MONOPOLIZE

The offense of attempting to monopolize, in violation of section 2 of the Sherman Act, differs little conceptually from other attempt offenses in the general criminal laws. Whereas completed offenses require varying degrees of culpability ranging from strict liability to specific intent, the offense of attempt always requires a specific intent to perform the attempted act.

One person may fantasize a murder but take no steps to carry out the fantasy. Another person may shoot but miss the intended victim. The former person would have committed no crime, but the latter would clearly be guilty of attempted murder. The law has often had to draw a line between these two extremes. The general rule is that an individual is guilty of an attempt where there is a dangerous probability that the attempt will ripen into the accomplished act.

Finally, the law has recognized a defense of impossibility to the crime of attempt. The impossibility must be legal rather than factual. For example, a person cannot be charged with the attempted murder of another who is already dead because it is legally impossible to murder a dead person. On the other hand, a person can be charged with attempting to murder another who was out of town on the day of the attempt, as the murder was only factually impossible.

When these general concepts are applied to attempted monopolization, many problems arise. The requirement of a specific intent to monopolize necessitates an inquiry into the defendant's subjective state of mind. This inquiry may be less difficult where the defendant is a corporation rather than an individual, as intracompany memoranda and minutes of meetings will frequently be available as evidence. However, most evidence usually consists of inferring subjective intent from objective conduct. Thus companies are often called upon to justify prior conduct in the guise of an inquiry into intent.

A complex factual issue arises when an effort is made to determine what point a company must reach to come dangerously close to monopoly. Closely aligned to this inquiry and the defense of impossibility is whether the relevant market must be established to prove attempted monopolizing. The weight of authority supports requiring its establishment, but some cases, most notably in the Ninth Circuit, have taken the opposite view.[9]

CONSPIRACIES TO MONOPOLIZE

Conspiracy to monopolize is a separate offense under section 2 of the Sherman Act. It requires proof that two or more entities conspired with

---

[9] *See Lessig* v. *Tidewater Oil Co.,* 327 F.2d 439 (9th Cir.), certiorari denied, 377 U.S. 993 (1964).

the specific intent of monopolizing. Providing such conspiracy is no different from proving conspiracy under section 1 of the Sherman Act, while proving such intent is no different from proving intent in attempted monopolization cases.

POLICY CONSIDERATIONS

At the beginning of this chapter it was emphasized that the Sherman Act prohibits monopolization rather than monopoly. A firm possessing monopoly power does not violate section 2 if it obtained that power as a result of superior skill or business acumen, government grant, or historical accident. A monopolist must actively seek, maintain, or expand monopoly power to violate section 2.

Much of the recent criticism of the current law under section 2 has been focused on the requirement of examining a monopolist's conduct. Proposals have been advanced which would outlaw no fault monopolies. These proposals generally provide that where a firm has held monopoly power in a relevant market for a long, continuous period of time, the firm should be restructured into smaller firms unless this would impede its efficiency.

Proponents of the no-fault approach to monopoly argue that it would greatly reduce the costs of Sherman Act litigation. They suggest that in major monopolization cases, proof of the defendant's conduct consumes 30–45 percent of the time involved in the litigation. They further contend that the reasons for the defendant's monopoly position are not relevant to the evils section 2 was designed to remedy. Monopoly is undesirable because it misallocates resources, discourages innovation, and limits consumer choice. Even where a firm has achieved its monopoly power through superior performance, that power may survive long after the firm's original advantages have disappeared. Rivals may not challenge the firm because of their ineptness or their indifference to the market or because of barriers to entry. Thus proponents urge that the relevant inquiry would focus not on how the monopoly developed but on how to get rid of it. That is, the inquiry would focus on how the market could be made more competitive.

Opponents of the no-fault concept urge that its application would discourage entrepreneurs from competing aggressively. They contend that firms would be reluctant to undertake actions which might turn them into "monopolists" and subject them to dismemberment. They further argue that consideration of conduct is relevant to the evils the Sherman Act was designed to remedy. They hold that monopoly may be attributed to one of four factors: government grants, mergers, predatory actions, or superior efficiency. Mergers are governed by the Clayton Act. Government grants reflect a policy decision that monopoly is desirable. It is therefore only predatory conduct that section 2 should be concerned with.

Opponents of the no-fault proposal also consider it unfair to break up a company which has achieved a dominant position in the market through positive conduct. They regard such a breakup as particularly unfair to the firm's investors whom it would deprive of part of the returns to which they are entitled.

Review problems

1. The Eastman Kodak Company is the world's largest manufacturer of film. Since 1952 its annual film sales have always exceeded 82 percent of the national volume and 88 percent of the national revenues. Kodak also produces instant-loading cameras designed for the mass market. Between 1954 and 1973 it never enjoyed less than 61 percent of the annual unit sales or less than 64 percent of the annual dollar volume, and in the peak year of 1964, Kodak cameras accounted for 90 percent of market revenues. Much of this success has been due to the firm's history of innovation.

In 1963 Kodak first marketed the 126 Instamatic instant-loading camera, and in 1972 it came out with the much smaller 110 Pocket Instamatic. These small, light cameras employ film packaged in cartridges that can simply be dropped in the back, thus obviating the need to load and position a roll of film manually. The introduction of these cameras triggered successive revolutions in the industry. Amateur still camera sales in the United States averaged 3.9 million units annually between 1954 and 1963, with little annual variation. In the first full year after Kodak's introduction of the 126, industry sales leaped 22 percent, and they took an even larger jump when the 110 came to market. Other camera manufacturers, copied both of these cameras, but for several months after each was introduced, those who wished to buy one had to purchase a Kodak.

When Kodak introduced the 110 Instamatic it also introduced Kodacolor II film, which it marketed as a "remarkable new film" producing better pictures. Kodak made conscious decisions to introduce the new camera and film together, not to make the film available in the 126 format for 18 months, and not

to provide its competitors with advance notice of the innovations. Kodak has also followed a consistent policy of refusing to make film available for formats other than those in which it makes cameras. Has Kodak violated section 2?

2. The Otter Tail Power Company sold electric power to 465 communities in Minnesota and North and South Dakota. It functioned pursuant to municipally granted franchises of 10 to 20 years' duration. Several municipalities chose not to renew Otter Tail's franchises, deciding to replace the power company with municipally owned systems. Otter Tail responded by refusing to sell power at wholesale to the new municipal systems and by refusing to transport over its lines power which the municipal systems had purchased from other sources. Did Otter Tail violate section 2?

3. Cargill, Inc., operates a grain elevator in the Port of Baton Rouge. It is the only grain elevator in Louisiana and 1 of 15 in the Gulf area of the lower Mississippi. Grain is transported by barge to the elevator. About 40 percent is transported in barges owned by Cargo Carriers, Inc., a wholly owned subsidiary of Cargill. Towboats can haul 30 or more barges at a time. Barges are parked in an area known as a fleet while they wait to be unloaded. Small harbor towboats move the barges into and out of the fleet. This operation is known as switching.

The Hutton Company provided all fleeting and switching services for grain barges in Baton Rouge until customer dissatisfaction over delays in handling caused Cargo to commence fleeting and switching operations. Cargo was more efficient, and eventually it took almost all of Hutton's business. Hutton went bankrupt, leaving Cargo as the only firm providing fleeting and switching services for grain barges in Baton Rouge. (A second firm provided similar services for petrochemical barges.) The volume handled is too small to support more than one grain-fleeting and - switching company if the companies are not engaged in other businesses as well.

Last year Clark Marine, Inc., began to compete with Cargo in fleeting and switching grain barges. It also operates a boat repair and service business. It is a very efficient fleeter and switcher and has taken many customers away from Cargo. However, its boat repair business has been failing. Losses on its boat repairs are threatening Clark's existence. If Clark folds, does Cargo face a Sherman section 2 problem?

4. The chrysanthemum industry was internally specialized. Breeders created new varieties and sold them to propagators. The propagators distributed cuttings to growers, who sold them to retail florists. Yoder Brothers, Inc., a breeder and propagator, was charged with monopolizing. If the relevant market was chrysanthemums, Yoder had monopoly power, but if it was all ornamental flowers, Yoder did not have monopoly power. The ultimate consumer tended to accept any of several ornamental flowers. Market demand at the consumer level fluctuated with the prices of various ornamental flowers. Grower demand responded to consumer demand. Many growers handled a wide variety of ornamental flowers. However, factors such as greenhouse space and layout, watering systems, and use of lights made it inconvenient and somewhat costly for a grower to switch from one ornamental flower to another. Define the relevant market.

5. IBM, facing stiff competition from newcomers to the market for peripheral data processing devices, announced a series of price reductions designed to eliminate that competition. It also announced that it would lease peripheral devices for a fixed term of years instead of allowing customers to cancel leases on 30 days' notice. The fixed term leases were for periods of up to two years, shorter in duration than those offered by IBM's competitors. If these changes allow IBM to capture a monopolist's share of the market, has IBM violated section 2 of the Sherman Act?

6. Plaza Theaters, Inc., owns all of the movie theaters in a city with a population of 50,000. A rival corporation from the other end of the state has announced plans to build a new theater which will complete with Plaza. Plaza warns the potential competitor: "If you open a theater here, Plaza will compete vigorously. It will go after all the first-run films and will offer them at the lowest possible prices. Plaza will make it impossible for you to survive in this town." If the rival cancels its plans to open the theater, has Plaza violated section 2?

7. Klearflax Linen Looms, Inc., was the sole domestic manufacturer of linen rugs. It sold rolls of linen rug material to distributors which would cut them into required sizes, finish them by binding the cut edges, and sell them to retail stores. Klearflax also cut and finished some rugs at its factory. For several years Klearflax was the sole bidder on federal government contracts to supply linen rugs. One year a Klearflax distributor also bid on the contract. The distributor's bid was lower, and it was awarded the contract. Klearflax then refused to supply the distributor with linen rug material. Did Klearflax violate section 2?

8. The Providence Fruit and Produce Building, Inc. (PFPBI), was a corporation owned by local produce wholesalers who also used part of the Providence Produce Building. The sole purpose of the corporation was to own and operate the building, which provided the most favorable storage, selling, and shipping facilities for wholesalers because of its location along the trunk of the New Haven Railroad. Gamco, Inc., a wholesaler, was ac-

quired by a Boston firm. Gamco had leased space in the building. PFPBI refused to renew Gamco's lease because of its policy of leasing only to Rhode Island companies. Other usable premises were available to Gamco, but they were less conveniently located than the Produce Building. Did PFPBI violate section 2?

9. Describe the concept of shared monopoly. Should this concept be recognized under section 2 of the Sherman Act?

10. Discuss the arguments in favor of and against a no-fault monopoly law. What is your opinion in this issue?

CHAPTER 7

Mergers

A merger combines two corporations into one. This may be accomplished by combining both companies into a single new company, by having one company acquire the assets of the other company, or by having one company acquire the stock of the other. Figure 7–1 shows recent fluctuations in merger activity.

During the early history of the Sherman Act, attacks on mergers had sporadic success. In one case the Supreme Court held lawful a merger of sugar refiners which placed 98 percent of the nation's output of refined sugar in the hands of a single corporation.[1] In another case the Court held unlawful a combination of railroads which gave a single company control over all railroad routes to the West.[2] Congressional concern over mergers resulted in the inclusion of section 7 in the Clayton Act, which was enacted in 1914. That provision prohibited one corporation from acquiring the stock of another where the effect might be to lessen competition between them or to tend to create a monopoly. The Clayton Act was ineffective in blocking mergers. Companies were able to avoid it entirely by structuring their mergers as asset acquisitions rather than stock acquisitions. Furthermore, courts placed a strict interpretation on the anticompetitive effect necessary to make a stock acquisition illegal, rendering section 7 little different from section 1 of the Sherman Act. Thus, from 1914 to 1950 only 15 mergers were successfully attacked under section 7, and 10 of these were also successfully attacked under the Sherman Act.

In 1950 the Celler-Kefauver Act amended section 7 of the Clayton Act, expanding it to encompass all mergers, regardless of their form. The prohib-

---

[1] *United States* v. *E. C. Knight Co.*, 156 U.S. 1 (1895).
[2] *Northern Securities Co.* v. *United States*, 193 U.S. 197 (1904).

ited effects of mergers were also amended to include those mergers which might tend to lessen competition or tend to create a monopoly in any line of commerce in any section of the country. Congress made clear its intent that section 7 be a prophylactic measure designed to nip anticompetitive

Figure 7–1: Number of corporate mergers and acquisitions valued at $100 million or more

Source: *Twentieth Annual Antitrust Law Institute,* (New York: Practicing Law Institute, 1979), 2:843. Reprinted with permission.

activity in the bud. Congress also expressed concern over the growing levels of concentration in American industry.

Mergers may be classified as horizontal, vertical, and conglomerate. Horizontal mergers involve firms selling the same good or service at the same level of distribution. Vertical mergers involve firms at different levels of distribution—usually a supplier and a customer. Conglomerate mergers involve firms whose products or services are not directly related. Mergers cannot be analyzed in a vacuum. As with monopolies, the relevant markets must be defined to provide a framework for analysis.

DETERMINING THE RELEVANT MARKET

The relevant market determination for section 7 of the Clayton Act is broader than that for section 2 of the Sherman Act. Under section 2, concern is focused on finding a market capable of being monopolized. That concern is also present under section 7, for it prohibits mergers which may tend to create a monopoly. Section 7 also prohibits mergers which may substantially lessen competition; that is, it prohibits mergers which may create conditions fostering anticompetitive practices such as other mergers or violations of section 1 of the Sherman Act. These effects may occur in markets which cannot be monopolized. Thus a relevant market may have several submarkets. Section 7 is also concerned with protecting potential competition. This includes interindustry competition. A relevant market may thus be composed of two or more markets or submarkets.

Courts take a very practical approach to market definition in merger cases. They do not determine relevant product markets and submarkets only by examining substitutability and cross-elasticity of demand. They also refer to such factors as industry or public recognition of a market as a separate economic entity and the existence of peculiar product characteristics, unique production facilities, distinct customers or prices, sensitivity to price changes, and specialized vendors.

The judicial approach to the geographic market in merger cases is equally practical. The geographic market must correspond to commercial realities and be economically significant and may include submarkets. The wide flexibility employed in considering geographic markets is demonstrated by *Brown Shoe Co.* v. *United States.*[3] In reviewing a district court finding that a merger between Brown and G. R. Kinney Company, two national chains of shoe retailers, violated section 7, the Supreme Court approved the trial judge's definition of the relevant geographic markets as every city with a population exceeding 10,000 and its immediate contiguous suburbs. The Court recognized that different cities might produce different patterns of competition and that competition existed between smaller communities within standard metropolitan areas. Nevertheless, it found the trial court's definition workable because that definition included the most important competitors—downtown business districts and suburban shopping centers. The Court also approved the trial judge's method of analyzing the competitive effects in the geographic markets. The trial judge had analyzed the St. Louis market in detail, had made a statistical analysis of market share in a representative sampling of cities, and had generalized to draw conclusions about all cities. The following case illustrates the judicial approach to relevant market in Clayton Act section 7 cases.

---

[3] 370 U.S. 294 (1961).

RSR Corp. v. FTC
602 F.2d 1317 (9th Cir. 1979)

RSR Corporation (appellant) appealed an order of the FTC (appellee) which found that a merger of RSR and Quemetco, Inc., violated section 7 of the Clayton Act and required RSR to divest itself of three lead smelting plants acquired in the merger. RSR contended that the FTC erred in finding secondary lead to be the relevant product market and in finding the nation as a whole to be the relevant geographic market. The Ninth Circuit Court of Appeals affirmed the FTC.

RSR produced secondary lead from smelting plants in Dallas and Newark. Quemetco operated similar plants in Seattle, Indianapolis, and City of Industry, California, and it was completing a fourth plant in Wallkill, New York. After the merger RSR closed its Newark plant. Secondary lead is lead recycled from scrap automobile batteries. Primary lead is lead processed from lead ore.

Pergerson, District Judge: The parties first disagree over whether the overall lead market (including both primary and secondary lead) or the secondary lead market alone is the relevant product market for testing the RSR/Quemetco merger under Section 7. RSR contends that substantial competition exists between primary and secondary producers in the production of soft lead; thus, the overall lead market must be considered. The FTC, relying on distinctions between the primary and secondary lead markets, argues that the secondary lead market alone is the relevant product market.

The factors used to determine the relevant product market in an antitrust case were set out by the Supreme Court in *Brown Shoe Co. v. United States.* The Court stated that the outer boundaries of a product market can be determined by the "reasonable interchangeability of use or the cross-elasticity of demand between the product itself and substitutes for it." The Court observed that well-defined submarkets

may also exist which, in themselves, can constitute product markets for antitrust purposes, and suggested that determining the boundaries of such a submarket could be done "by examining such practical indicia as industry or public recognition of the submarket as a separate economic entity, the product's peculiar characteristics and uses, unique production facilities, distinct customers, distinct prices, sensitivity to price changes, and specialized vendors."

* * * * *

We have considered each of the *Brown Shoe* indicia separately and find that substantial evidence supports the FTC's determination that the secondary lead market is the relevant product market for testing the RSR/Quemetco merger. We have briefly summarized some of this evidence below.

Industry or public recognition of the submarket as a separate economic entity. Evidence was presented to show that the lead industry distinguishes between primary and secondary lead in terms of the products and their producers. RSR contends that this recognition signifies only that the industry is aware of the different raw material source for each type of lead. Nevertheless, evidence indicated that consumers and lead producers, as well as national production reports, distinguish between the two types of lead.

Product's peculiar characteristics. Secondary lead is derived from recycling other lead products, not from smelting raw lead ore. As a result, secondary lead as a rule contains impurities (primarily metals) not found in primary lead. Secondary lead, although it can be purified almost to the degree of pure lead, is generally used as hard or metallic lead. Primary lead, since it is pure and free of hardening metals, is generally used as soft lead. Soft lead and hard lead are generally not used for the same purposes. Primary and secondary soft lead can sometimes be interchanged, as can primary and secondary hard lead, but certain uses require either primary lead, while other uses require secondary lead. Moreover, it is usually not economical for a primary producer to manufacture hard lead. Secondary producers obtain some soft lead as a by-product of the manufacture of antimonial lead; due to impurities, this soft lead is generally not suitable for most industrial soft lead uses.

Distinct customers. At the time of the FTC hearing, hard lead was chiefly used for automobile battery posts and grids, while soft lead was used for battery oxides and tetraethyl lead, an antiknock additive to gasoline. Battery manufacturers were thus the major customers of both primary and secondary lead producers. Evidence was presented to show that some customers specify not only that they require hard or soft lead but also that they want primary or secondary lead.

Distinct vendors. Most of the lead produced by primary producers is pure or soft lead. Although metal can be added to the pure lead to harden it, the evidence shows that it is not economical to do so. Moreover, casting characteristics of artificially hardened lead make it unsuitable for battery grids and posts. Thus, primary producers generally restrict their production to soft lead. Secondary producers, on the other hand, chiefly produce hard lead. During the production of antimonial lead, a hard lead, some soft lead is also produced. At the time of the merger, secondary producers were using most of this soft lead in their internal operations rather than selling it to manufacturers of battery oxides.

*   *   *   *   *

Distinct prices. RSR presented evidence that only one worldwide price is set for lead: no distinctions between primary and secondary lead are made on the London Exchange. But the evidence showed and the FTC found that, although both primary and secondary producers discount the price of lead, secondary lead customarily sells for about 10 percent less than primary lead.

Sensitivity to price changes. Because secondary lead is generally shipped over shorter distances than primary lead, secondary producers customarily ship by truck while primary producers ship by rail. Evidence was presented to show that trucking costs vary more widely than rail costs, causing secondary lead prices to vary accordingly.

*   *   *   *   *

As its second contention, RSR strenuously argues that the relevant geographic market to be used in testing the RSR/Quemetco merger for a Section 7 violation should not be the entire United States. Nonetheless, RSR does not suggest an alternate market.

The parties agree that, due to high trucking costs, secondary lead producers attempt to ship their products to customers located within a few hundred miles of the plants. Since the RSR and Quemetco plants are located in different areas of the country, RSR argues that Quemetco and RSR were not actually competing anywhere in the country. Alternatively, RSR argues that the only place in which there might have been competition was in the Midwest market, which could be served by both Quemetco's Indianapolis plant and RSR's Dallas plant.

*   *   *   *   *

Although the FTC recognized that high trucking costs cause secondary producers to ship most of their product to customers within a few hundred miles, evidence was presented to show that the distances over which secondary lead producers were willing to ship products varied according to economic and market conditions, including plant size, secondary lead prices in a certain region, and fluctuations in transportation costs. RSR relies heavily on data showing that Quemetco, in 1971 and 1972, shipped lead to less than one third of the states. But the evidence also showed that the states into which Quemetco shipped its lead were the states where most of the lead was consumed. Furthermore, the evidence showed that many of the major battery manufacturers, the primary consumers of antimonial lead, are concentrated in the Midwest, with smaller groups in the Northeast and in Southern California.

Thus, the fact that RSR and Quemetco did not compete in every state is of little relevance when many states generate little or no demand for secondary lead. Finally, evidence was also presented showing that regional pricing patterns for secondary lead are interrelated.

Evidence on the pre-merger competition between RSR and Quemetco, coupled with evidence of pricing interdependence nationwide and evidence of the ability of secondary producers to ship lead into states in which most secondary lead is consumed, is substantial. That evidence is sufficient to support the FTC's factual findings on the relevant geographic market issue.

*   *   *   *   *

Case questions

1. What was the relevant product market? What factors did the court rely on?

2. What were RSR's arguments concerning the relevant geographic market? Why did the court reject them?

3. If RSR had merged with a firm which produced only primary lead, would this case have precluded finding a market of all lead?

HORIZONTAL MERGERS

Horizontal mergers have the most consistent and immediate anticompetitive potential because they replace two competitors with a single, stronger firm. Consequently, when the industry in which such a merger occurs is concentrated and the merger results in a company with an "undue market share," a rebuttable presumption arises that the merger is illegal. The levels of concentration and market share necessary to trigger this presumption are not very great. They are particularly small where the industry has experienced a trend toward further concentration. Courts have reasoned that the Clayton Act is designed to stop anticompetitive practices in their incipiency and have feared that permitting even a small merger in an increasingly concentrated market will trigger further mergers of other anticompetitive activity.

Illustrative of the low levels necessary to invoke the presumption of illegality is *United States* v. *Von's Grocery Co.*[4] The action challenged the merger of Von's and Shopping Bag Food Stores, two supermarket chains in the

---

[4] 384 U.S. 270 (1966).

Los Angeles metropolitan area. These chains ranked third and sixth, respectively, with 4.7 percent and 4.2 percent of the market. The top four firms had only 28.6 percent of the market, and there were thousands of competitors. Nevertheless, the Court held the merger presumptively illegal because the evidence showed a trend toward increased concentration. Specifically, the number of competitors had declined from 5,365 to 3,590 in a 13-year period.

Rebutting the presumption of illegality

Statistical evidence of concentration and market share is only the starting point in analyzing a horizontal merger. It may be the end point as well if there is no evidence that rebuts the presumption of substantial anticompetitive effects. The rebuttal must focus on the characteristics and structure of the market concerned. It should emphasize structural characteristics of the market which contradict the conclusion that a merger of two significant firms in a concentrated market is likely to trigger additional mergers, foreclose significant markets to competitors, or otherwise injure competition. The significance of the postmerger market share and concentration levels is lessened if barriers to entry are low and potential entrants are strong and likely to enter. Additional facts which would further rebut the presumption include evidence of readily available substitutes for the defendant's product and evidence of consumers' willingness to switch to substitutes if prices vary slightly.

It is clear that a presumption of illegality cannot be rebutted by showing that the merger will have no competitive effects in another market. For example, when the second and third largest commercial banks in Philadelphia merged, the Court refused to allow the banks to rebut the presumption of anticompetitive effects in metropolitan Philadelphia by showing that they could compete more effectively against banks from other major cities for national accounts.[5] In the following case the defendant successfully rebutted the presumption of illegality.

---

[5] *United States* v. *Philadelphia National Bank,* 374 U.S. 321 (1963).

United States v. General Dynamics Corp.
415 U.S. 486 (1974)

The government (appellant) sued General Dynamics (appellee), the successor to Material Service Corporation, a deep-mining coal producer, complaining that Material Service's acquisition of United Electric Coal Companies, a strip-mining coal producer, violated section 7 of the Clayton Act. The trial court entered judgment for General Dynamics, and the government appealed. The Supreme Court affirmed.

The government's case consisted of production statistics showing that in specified geographic markets the number of coal producers had been declining, that the markets for coal were concentrated, and that the acquisition substantially increased Material Service's market share. In finding that the merger would not substantially lessen competition, the trial court relied on evidence showing that United Electric's long-term reserves were almost depleted.

Mr. Justice Stewart: In prior decisions involving horizontal mergers between competitors, this Court has found prima facie violations of § 7 of the Clayton Act from aggregate statistics of the sort relied on by the United States in this case. . . .

The effect of adopting this approach to a determination of a "substantial" lessening of competition is to allow the Government to rest its case on a showing of even small increases of market share or market concentration in those industries or markets where concentration is already great or has been recently increasing, since "if concentration is already great, the importance of preventing even slight increases in concentration and so preserving the possibility of eventual deconcentration is correspondingly great."

While the statistical showing proffered by the government in this case . . . would under this approach have sufficed to support a finding of "undue concentration" in the absence of other considerations, the question before us is whether the District Court was justified in finding that other pertinent factors affecting the coal industry and the business of the appellees mandated a conclusion that no substantial lessening of competition occurred or was threatened by the acquisition of United Electric. We are satisfied that the court's ultimate finding was not in error.

*   *   *   *   *

Much of the District Court's opinion was devoted to a description of the changes that have affected the coal industry since World War II. . . . First, it found that coal had become increasingly less able to compete with other sources of energy in many segments of the energy market. . . .

Second, the court found that to a growing extent since 1954, the electric utility industry has become the mainstay of coal consumption. . . .

Third, and most significantly, the court found that to an increasing degree, nearly all coal sold to utilities is transferred under long-term requirements contracts, under which coal producers promise to meet utilities' coal consumption requirements for a fixed period of time, and at predetermined prices. . . .

Because of these fundamental changes in the structure of the market for coal, the District Court was justified in viewing the statistics relied on by the Government as insufficient to sustain its case. Evidence of past production does not, as a matter of logic, necessarily give a proper picture of a company's future ability to compete. . . .

In the coal market, . . . statistical evidence of coal production was of considerably less significance. The bulk of the coal produced is delivered under long-term requirements contracts, and such sales thus do not represent the exercise of competitive power but rather the obligation to fulfill previously negotiated contracts at a previously fixed price. The focus of competition in a given time frame is not on the disposition of coal already produced but on the procurement of new long-term supply contracts. . . . A more significant indicator of a company's power effectively to compete with other companies lies in the state of a company's uncommitted reserves of recoverable coal. . . .

The testimony and exhibits in the District Court revealed that United Electric's coal reserve prospects were "unpromising." . . . Many of the reserves held by United had already been depleted at the time of trial, forcing the closing of some of United's midwest mines. Even more significantly, the District Court found that of the 52,033,304 tons of currently mineable reserves in Illinois, Indiana, and Kentucky controlled by United, only four million tons had not already been committed under long-term contracts. United was found to be facing the future with relatively depleted resources at its disposal, and with the vast majority of those resources already committed under contracts allowing no further adjustment in price. In addition, the District Court found that "United Electric has neither the possibility of acquiring more [reserves] nor the ability to develop deep coal reserves," and thus was not in a position to increase its reserves to replace those already depleted or committed.

. . . Irrespective of the company's size when viewed as a producer, its weakness as a competitor was properly analyzed by the District Court and fully substantiated that court's conclusion that its acquisition by Material Service would not "substantially . . . lessen competition. . . ."

*   *   *   *   *

Case questions

1. What was the basis for the government's case that the merger might substantially lessen competition?

2. Was the government's evidence sufficient to raise a presumption that the merger was illegal?

3. What was the basis for rebutting the presumption?

Using postmerger evidence

Generally a merger is challenged after it has taken place. Frequently several years pass before the case comes to trial. During the period between the merger and the trial the market will respond to the merger. Evidence of the market's response would appear to be the most significant evidence of the merger's competitive effects. Courts, nevertheless, view such evidence with extreme caution and are rarely swayed by postmerger evidence of lack of competitive injury.

In rejecting postmerger evidence, courts have emphasized that section 7 requires an assessment of the probable effects of a merger rather than its actual effects. Thus the fact that anticompetitive effects have not manifested themselves by the date of trial is no guarantee that such effects will not become apparent in the future. Furthermore, courts are reluctant to even imply that a merger did not adversely affect competition prior to trial because they find it impossible to deduce what would have happened had the merger not been consummated. Finally, courts are concerned that if they adopted a rule which considered postmerger evidence, the defendant would postpone aggressive or anticompetitive actions until after the trial was completed.

On the other hand, postmerger evidence which indicates that a merger initially thought to lack anticompetitive effects has actually adversely affected competition may form the basis for attacking the merger several years later. The merged companies may not seek refuge in the statute of limitations, for it does not begin to run until the anticompetitive effects of the merger become apparent. Thus a company which has acquired other companies must watch its behavior long after the acquisition to avoid possible section 7 attack.

VERTICAL MERGERS

A vertical merger is a merger of firms that deal in the same product but at different distribution levels. A widget manufacturer's acquisition of a retail widget chain would be a vertical merger. Vertical mergers may reflect a desire to realize economies in distribution, to insure the availability of supplies, or to insure retail distribution for a manufacturer's product.

Vertical mergers are more difficult to evaluate than horizontal mergers because the same number of competitors remain in both the supplier and customer markets. Not every vertical merger results in a violation of section 7. Nevertheless, a vertical merger may have anticompetitive effects on the markets of the supplier or the customer. The degree of market foreclosure is the starting point in analyzing any vertical merger. The larger the market that the merger forecloses to the competitor of one of the merging firms, the greater is the likelihood that the merger will be held illegal. The intent of the parties to the merger is another important consideration. The level of concentration in the merging firms' markets and trends toward increasing concentration in either market can also prompt a finding that the merger is illegal. The concern of courts is particularly acute where there is a trend toward vertical integration. Firms that merge vertically are frequently potential competitors in each other's markets. This is frequently a factor causing a court to invalidate a vertical merger.

Section 7 does not apply to corporations purchasing stock in other corporations "solely for investment and not using [the stock] by voting or otherwise to bring about, or in attempting to bring about, the substantial lessening of competition." This is known as the "solely for investment purposes defense."

The following case represents the leading Supreme Court pronouncement regarding the regulation of vertical mergers.

United States v. E. I. du Pont de Nemours & Co.
353 U.S. 586 (1957)

Du Pont (appellee) acquired 23 percent of the stock in General Motors during 1917–19. The U.S. government (appellant) brought suit in 1949 challenging the acquisition under sec- -tion 7 of the Clayton Act. The district court dismissed the action, and the government appealed directly to the Supreme Court, which reversed.

Mr. Justice Brennan: The primary issue is whether du Pont's commanding position as General Motors' supplier of automotive finishes and fabrics was achieved on competitive merit alone, or because its acquisition of the General Motors' stock, and the consequent close intercompany relationship led to the insulation of most of the General Motors' market from free competition, with the resultant likelihood, at the time of suit, of the creation of a monopoly of a line of commerce. . . .

Section 7 is designed to arrest in its incipiency not only the substantial lessening of competition from the acquisition by one corporation of the whole or any part of the stock of a competing corporation, but also to arrest in their incipiency restraints or monopolies in a relevant market which, as a reasonable probability, appear at the time of suit likely to result from the acquisition by one corporation of all or any part of the stock of any other corporation. The section is violated whether or not actual restraints or monopolies, or the substantial lessen-

ing of competition, have occurred or are intended. Acquisitions solely for investment are excepted, but only if, and so long as, the stock is not used by voting or otherwise to bring about, or in attempting to bring about, the substantial lessening of competition.

We are met at the threshold with the argument that §7, before its amendment in 1950, applied only to an acquisition of the stock of a competing corporation, and not to an acquisition by a supplier corporation of the stock of a customer corporation—in other words, that the statute applied only to horizontal and not to vertical acquisitions. . . .

The first paragraph of §7, written in the disjunctive, plainly is framed to reach not only the corporate acquisition of stock of a competing corporation, where the effect may be substantially to lessen competition between them, but also the corporate acquisition of stock of any corporation, competitor or not, where the effect may be either (1) to restrain commerce in any section or community, or (2) tend to create a monopoy of any line of commerce. . . .

We hold that any acquisition by one corporation of all or any part of the stock of another corporation, competitor or not, is within the reach of the section whenever the reasonable likelihood appears that the acquisition will result in a restraint of commerce or in the creation of a monopoly of any line of commerce. Thus, although du Pont and General Motors are not competitors, a violation of the section has occurred if, as a result of the acquisition, there was at the time of suit a reasonable likelihood of a monopoly of any line of commerce. . . .

Appellees argue that there exists no basis for a finding of a probable restraint or monopoly within the meaning of §7 because the total General Motors market for finishes and fabrics constituted only a negligible percentage of the total market for these materials for all uses, including automotive uses. It is stated in the General Motors brief that in 1947 du Pont's finish sales to General Motors constituted 3.5% of all sales of finishes to industrial users, and that its fabrics sales to General Motors comprised 1.6% of the total market for the type of fabric used by the automobile industry.

Determination of the relevant market is a necessary predicate to a finding of a violation of the Clayton Act because the threatened monopoly must be one which will substantially lessen competition "within the area of effective competition." Substantiality can be determined only in terms of the market affected. The record shows that automotive finishes and fabrics have sufficient peculiar characteristics and uses to constitute them products sufficiently distinct from all other finishes and fabrics to make them a "line of commerce" within the meaning of the Clayton Act. Thus, the bounds of the relevant market for the purposes of this case are not coextensive with the total market for finishes and fabrics, but are coextensive with the automotive industry, the relevant market for automotive finishes and fabrics.

The market affected must be substantial. Moreover, in order to establish a violation of §7 the Government must prove a likelihood that competition may be "foreclosed in a substantial share of . . . [that market]." Both requirements are satisfied in this case. The substantiality of a relevant market comprising the automobile industry is undisputed. The substantiality of General Motors' share of that market is fully established in the evidence.

General Motors is the colossus of the giant automobile industry. It accounts annually for upwards of two-fifths of the total sales of automotive vehicles in the Nation. In 1955 General Motors ranked first in sales and second in assets among all United States industrial corporations and became the first corporation to earn over a billion dollars in annual net income. In 1947 General Motors' total purchases of all products from du Pont were $26,628,274, of which $18,938,229 (71%) represented purchases from du Pont's Finishes Division. . . . Expressed in percentages, du Pont supplied 67% of General Motors' requirements for finishes in 1946 and 68% in 1947. In fabrics du Pont supplied 52.3% of requirements in 1946, and 38.5% in 1947. Because General Motors accounts for almost one-half of the automobile industry's annual sales, its requirements for automotive finishes and fabrics must represent approximately one-half of the relevant market for these materials. Because the record clearly shows that quantitatively and percentagewise du Pont supplies the largest part of General Motors' requirements, we must conclude that du Pont has a substantial share of the relevant market.

The appellees argue that the Government could not maintain this action in 1949 because §7 is applicable only to the acquisition of stock and not to the holding or subsequent use of the stock. This argument misconceives the objective toward which §7 is directed. The Clayton Act was intended to supplement the Sherman Act. Its aim was primarily to arrest apprehended consequences of intercorporate relationships before those relationships could work their evil, which may be at or any time after the acquisition, depending upon the circumstances of the particular case. . . .

To accomplish the congressional aim, the Government may proceed at any time that an acquisition may be said with reasonable probability to contain a threat that it may lead to a restraint of commerce or tend to create a monopoly of a line of commerce. Even when the purchase is solely for investment, the plain language of §7 contemplates an action at any time the stock is used to bring about, or in attempting to bring about, the substantial lessening of competition. . . .

Related to this argument is the District

Court's conclusion that 30 years of nonrestraint negated "any reasonable probability of such a restraint" at the time of the suit. While it is, of course, true that proof of a mere possibility of a prohibited restraint or tendency to monopoly will not establish the statutory requirement that the effect of an acquisition "may be" such restraint or tendency, the basic facts found by the District Court demonstrate the error of its conclusion.

The du Pont Company's commanding position as a General Motors supplier was not achieved until shortly after its purchase of a sizable block of General Motors stock in 1917. At that time its production for the automobile industry and its sales to General Motors were relatively insignificant. General Motors then produced only about 11% of the total automobile production and its requirements, while relatively substantial, were far short of the proportions they assumed as it forged ahead to its present place in the industry. . . .

. . . [T]he trial court expressly found that ". . . reports and other documents written at or near the time of the investment show that du Pont's representatives were well aware that General Motors was a large consumer of products of the kind offered by du Pont," and that John J. Raskob, du Pont's treasurer and the principal promoter of the investment, "for one, thought that du Pont would ultimately get all that business. . . ."

Raskob foresaw the success of the automobile industry and the opportunity for great profit in a substantial purchase of General Motors stock. On December 19, 1917, Raskob submitted a Treasurer's Report to the du Pont Finance Committee recommending a purchase of General Motors stock in the amount of $25,-000,000. That report makes clear that more than just a profitable investment was contemplated. A major consideration was that an expanding General Motors would provide a substantial market needed by the burgeoning du Pont organization. Raskob's summary of reasons in support of the purchase includes this statement: "Our interest in the General Motors Company will undoubtedly secure for us the entire paint and varnish business of those com-

panies, *which is a substantial factor.*" (Emphasis added.)

This thought, that the purchase would result in du Pont's obtaining a new and substantial market, was echoed in the Company's 1917 and 1918 annual reports to stockholders. In the 1917 report appears: "Though this is a new line of activity, it is one of great promise and one that seems to be well suited to the character of our organization. *The motor companies are very large consumers of our . . . paints and varnishes.*" (Emphasis added.) The 1918 report says: "The consumption of paints, varnishes and fabrikoid in the manufacture of automobiles gives another common interest."

This background of the acquisition, particularly the plain implications of the countemporaneous documents, destroys any basis for a conclusion that the purchase was made "solely for investment." Moreover, immediately after the acquisition, du Pont's influence growing out of it was brought to bear within General Motors to achieve primacy for du Pont as General Motors' supplier of automotive fabrics and finishes. . . .

The fact that sticks out in this voluminous record is that the bulk of du Pont's production has always supplied the largest part of the requirements of the one customer in the automobile industry connected to du Pont by a stock interest. The inference is overwhelming that du Pont's commanding position was promoted by its stock interest and was not gained solely on competitive merit. We agree with the trial court that considerations of price, quality and service were not overlooked by either du Pont or General Motors. Pride in its products and its high financial stake in General Motors' success would naturally lead du Pont to try to supply the best. But the wisdom of this business judgment cannot obscure the fact, plainly revealed by the record, that du Pont purposely employed its stock to pry open the General Motors market to entrench itself as the primary supplier of General Motors' requirements for automotive finishes and fabrics.

Similarly, the fact that all concerned in high executive posts in both companies acted honorably and fairly, each in the honest conviction that his actions were in the best interests of his own company and without any design to overreach anyone, including du Pont's competitors, does not defeat the Government's right to relief. It is not requisite to the proof of a violation of §7 to show that restraint or monopoly was intended.

The statutory policy of fostering free competition is obviously furthered when no supplier has an advantage over his competitors from an acquisition of his customer's stock likely to have the effects condemned by the statute. We repeat, that the test of a violation of §7 is whether, at the time of suit, there is a reasonable probability that the acquisition is likely to result in the condemned restraints. The conclusion upon this record is inescapable that such likelihood was proved as to this acquisition. It burned briskly to forge the ties that bind the General Motors market to du Pont, and if it has quieted down, it remains hot, and, from past performance, is likely at any time to blaze and make the fusion complete.

The judgment must therefore be reversed and the cause remanded to the District Court for a determination, after further hearing, of the equitable relief necessary and appropriate in the public interest to eliminate the effects of the acquisition offensive to the statute.

* * * * *

Case questions

1. What was the probable effect of the merger and how did the Supreme Court go about ascertaining the probable effect?

2. What does *du Pont* reveal about the "solely for investment purposes defense"?

3. How could the government legally wait 30 years to attack this merger?

CONGLOMERATE MERGERS

Conglomerate mergers pose the smallest immediate threat to competition. Mergers which involve firms in similar or related industries may, nevertheless, have anticompetitive effects which violate section 7. Those which have been recognized by the courts are as follows.

Elimination of potential competition. If the acquiring company is producing goods related to those produced by the acquired company and has considered entering the market on its own, the merger has the effect of eliminating that potential competition. The loss of potential competition must be evaluated from the viewpoint of the potential entrant and of those already in the market. This requires assessing the likelihood that the potential entrant would enter the market independently were the merger not allowed and assessing the effect of that potential entry on the activities of those already in the market.

Reduction in interindustry competition. Sometimes a merger involves firms in different industries which serve similar functions. The merger may be unlawful if it reduces competition between the industries. For example, the Supreme Court held that a merger between the second leading producer of cans and the third leading producer of bottles violated section 7 because it lessened competition between the two types of containers.[6]

Potential for reciprocity. If company X produces a good whose market includes suppliers of company Y, a merger between X and Y may violate section 7 because suppliers of Y may purchase from X out of fear that they will lose Y as a customer.

FTC v. *Consolidated Foods Co.* illustrates the problem of reciprocity.[7] Consolidated, which owned food processing plants and a network of wholesale and retail food stores, acquired Gentry, Inc., a manufacturer of dehydrated onions and garlic. Because food processors which sold to Consolidated gave their onion and garlic business to Gentry for purposes of reciprocity, the Court held that the merger violated section 7.

Entrenchment. If a larger, wealthier firm acquires a smaller firm which is dominant in its market, the acquisition may have the effect of entrenching the smaller firm's position. The following case presents a "product extension merger," which is often described as a form of conglomerate merger.

FTC v. Procter & Gamble Co.
386 U.S. 568 (1967)

The Federal Trade Commission (appellant) held that the acquisition by Procter & Gamble (appellee) of Clorox Chemical Company violated section 7 of the Clayton Act. At the time of the acquisition Clorox was the leading producer of household bleach, with 48.8 percent of the market. The top four firms accounted for 80 percent of the market, with the remaining 20 percent divided among 200 small producers. Clorox was the only company operating nationwide. Procter & Gamble (P&G) did not produce bleach, but it accounted for 54.4 percent of all packaged detergent sales. The top three firms controlled 80 percent of that market.

The FTC found that P&G's huge assets and advertising budget combined with Clorox's dominant position would dissuade potential entrants and that the merger eliminated P&G as a potential competitor. It also found that the merger gave P&G the potential to underprice Clorox so as to drive out competitors

and to use its dominant position in household detergents so as to obtain preferred shelf space from retailers for Clorox. The FTC ordered divestiture. The Sixth Circuit Court of Appeals reversed the FTC, labeling its findings as speculation and relying on postmerger evidence that competitors had not been eliminated. The Supreme Court reversed the Sixth Circuit and instructed the circuit court to enforce the FTC's order.

Mr. Justice Douglas:

* * * * *

Section 7 of the Clayton Act was intended to arrest the anticompetitive effects of market power in their incipiency. The core question is whether a merger may substantially lessen competition, and necessarily requires a prediction of the merger's impact on competition, present and future. This section can deal only with probabilities, not with certainties. And there is certainly no requirement that the anticompetitive power manifest itself in anticom-

---

[6] *United States* v. *Continental Can Co.*, 378 U.S. 441 (1964).

[7] 380 U.S. 592 (1965).

petitive action before §7 can be called into play. . . .

All mergers are within the reach of §7, and all must be tested by the same standard, whether they are classified as horizontal, vertical, conglomerate or other. As noted by the Commission, this merger is neither horizontal, vertical, nor conglomerate. Since the products of the acquired company are complementary to those of the acquiring company and may be produced with similar facilities, marketed through the same channels and in the same manner, and advertised by the same media, the Commission aptly called this acquisition a "product extension merger.". . .

*   *   *   *   *

The liquid bleach industry was already oligopolistic before the acquisition, and price competition was certainly not as vigorous as it would have been if the industry were competitive. Clorox enjoyed a dominant position nationally, and its position approached monopoly proportions in certain areas. The existence of some 200 fringe firms certainly does not belie that fact. Nor does the fact, relied upon by the court below, that, after the merger, producers other than Clorox "were selling more bleach for more money than ever before." In the same period, Clorox increased its share from 48.8% to 52%. The interjection of Procter into the market considerably changed the situation. There is every reason to assume that the smaller firms would become more cautious in competing due to their fear of retaliation by Procter. It is probable that Procter would become the price leader and that oligopoly would become more rigid.

The acquisition may also have the tendency of raising the barriers to new entry. The major competitive weapon in the successful marketing of bleach is advertising. Clorox was limited in this area by its relatively small budget and its inability to obtain substantial discounts. By contrast, Procter's budget was much larger; and, although it would not devote its entire budget to advertising Clorox, it could divert a large portion to meet the short-term threat of a new entrant. Procter would be able to use its volume discounts to advantage in advertising Clorox.

Thus, a new entrant would be much more reluctant to face the giant Procter than it would have been to face the smaller Clorox.

Possible economies cannot be used as a defense to illegality. Congress was aware that some mergers which lessen competition may also result in economies, but it struck the balance in favor of protecting competition.

The Commission also found that the acquisition of Clorox by Procter eliminated Procter as a potential competitor. . . . The evidence clearly showed that Procter was the most likely entrant. Procter had recently launched a new abrasive cleaner in an industry similar to the liquid bleach industry, and had wrested leadership from a brand that had enjoyed even a larger market share than had Clorox. Procter was engaged in a vigorous program of diversifying into product lines closely related to its basic products. Liquid bleach was a natural avenue of diversification since it is complementary to Procter's products, is sold to the same customers through the same channels, and is advertised and merchandised in the same manner. . . . Procter's management was experienced in producing and marketing goods similar to liquid bleach. Procter had considered the possibility of independently entering but decided against it because the acquisition of Clorox would enable Procter to capture a more commanding share of the market.

It is clear that the existence of Procter at the edge of the industry exerted considerable influence on the market. First, the market behavior of the liquid bleach industry was influenced by each firm's predictions of the market behavior of its competitors, actual and potential. Second, the barriers to entry by a firm of Procter's size and with its advantages were not significant. There is no indication that the barriers were so high that the price Procter would have to charge would be above the price that would maximize the profits of the existing firms. Third, the number of potential entrants was not so large that the elimination of one would be insignificant. Few firms would have the temerity to challenge a firm as solidly entrenched as Clorox. Fourth, Procter was found by the Commission to be the most likely entrant. These

findings of the Commission were amply supported by the evidence.

The judgment of the Court of Appeals is

reversed and remanded with instructions to affirm and enforce the Commission's order.

*   *   *   *   *

Case questions

1. Is there a distinction between a conglomerate merger and a product extension
merger?

2. What factors led the Court to conclude
that the merger would have the probable effect
of reducing competition?

3. Why did the Court discount the postmerger evidence.

4. How did the Court evaluate P&G as a
potential competitor of Clorox?

5. If P&G had acquired one of the 200
small firms comprising the bottom 20 percent
of the market, would the merger have violated
section 7?

THE FAILING COMPANY DEFENSE

A merger which might otherwise violate section 7 is considered lawful
if one of the companies is failing. For this defense to apply, the failing
company must be about to die, with no reasonable hope of survival short
of merger. The acquiring company must either be the only company interested in purchasing the failing company, or if other companies are interested,
it must be the company which poses the least threat to competition. Finally,
it must be shown that methods to save the failing company short of merger
have been tried and have failed or that such methods would be futile.

REMEDIES

Like all other antitrust laws, section 7 may be enforced by government
and private actions. Private section 7 lawsuits have often been used by a
company's incumbent management in efforts to defeat another company's
tender offer. A tender offer is a publicly announced offer to purchase the

stock of a target company's shareholders for a stated price contingent upon the offeror's obtaining sufficient shares to control the target company. Tender offers are discussed in detail in Chapter 14.

The officers of a target company may seek to defeat a tender offer because they view it as bad for the company and because they fear they will lose their jobs if it succeeds. Officers of target companies have often challenged tender offers under section 7, contending that the resulting acquisition would reduce competition. This tactic has met with varying success.

Most section 7 actions are brought by the government. Where the government is able to show that it is likely to prevail on the merits and that allowing the merger to proceed will result in irreparable harm to competition, courts have entered a preliminary injunction restraining the merger. Courts have also issued a preliminary injunction which permitted the merger to occur but required that the formerly independent companies continue to maintain their separate identities.

Where the government has not obtained preliminary injunctive relief or a merger has been consummated prior to the government's challenge, the court's task upon finding a violation is to unscramble the merger and restore market conditions to what they would have been had the merger not occurred. This is extremely difficult to do. The starting point is an order requiring the acquiring firm to divest itself of the acquired firm. However, such an order is often insufficient to restore preexisting competitive conditions. For example, assume that a family owns a small but aggressive and innovative competitor. The owners, wishing to retire, sell the company to the dominant firm in the market. If the acquisition is found to violate section 7, the dominant firm will be ordered to divest itself of the smaller firm. However, the owners who provided the smaller firm's aggressive, innovative method of operation will no longer be available to manage the business. It is very likely that the firm will be sold to another large corporation, albeit one which is not now competing in the market. This may have the ironic effect of raising additional barriers to new entries into the market. Even if not purchased by another large concern, the divested firm will probably face many of the start-up costs and recognition problems of a new entrant. The following case deals with a court's power to order relief beyond divestiture.

Ford Motor Co. v. United States
405 U.S. 562 (1972)

Ford (appellant) acquired the assets of Electric Autolite Company's Autolite Spark Plug division. The trial court held that the acquisition violated section 7 and ordered Ford to divest itself of the division. It also enjoined Ford from manufacturing spark plugs for 10 years, ordered Ford to purchase at least one half of its annual spark plug requirements from the divested firm for 5 years, and prohibited Ford from using its own trade names on spark *plugs for 5 years. Ford appealed, and the Supreme Court affirmed.*

Prior to the merger there were three major brands of spark plugs, of which two—Autolite and Champion—were independent. The third, AC, was owned by General Motors. Spark plug manufacturers sold their product to the auto companies at very low prices for use as original equipment (OE). They made their profits in the replacement market, known as the aftermarket. Mechanics servicing automobiles tended to replace OE plugs with plugs of the same brand. The trial court found that Ford's acquisition of Autolite eliminated Ford as a potential entrant into the spark plug market and foreclosed it as a purchaser of 10 percent of the industry's output. The Supreme Court affirmed the finding of violation and proceeded to consider the remedy.

Mr. Justice Douglas:

* * * * *

The main controversy here has been over the nature and degree of the relief to be afforded.

* * * * *

The relief in an antitrust case must be "effective to redress the violations" and "to restore competition." The District Court is clothed with "large discretion" to fit the decree to the special needs of the individual case.

Complete divestiture is particularly appropriate where asset or stock acquisitions violate the antitrust laws.

Divestiture is a start toward restoring the pre-acquisition situation. Ford once again will then stand as a large industry customer at the edge of the market with a renewed interest in securing favorable terms for its substantial plug purchases. Since Ford will again be a purchaser, it is expected that the competitive pressures that existed among other spark plug producers to sell to Ford will be re-created. The divestiture should also eliminate the anticompetitive consequences in the *aftermarket* flowing from the second largest automobile manufacturer's entry through acquisition into the spark plug manufacturing business.

* * * * *

A word should be said about the other injunctive provisions. They are designed to give the divested plant an opportunity to establish its competitive position. The divested company needs time so it can obtain a foothold in the industry. The relief ordered should "cure the ill effects of the illegal conduct, and assure the public freedom from its continuance," and it necessarily must "fit the exigencies of the particular case." . . .

. . . The ancillary measures ordered by the District Court are designed to allow Autolite to re-establish itself in the OE and replacement markets and to maintain it as a viable competitor until such time as forces already at work within the marketplace weaken the OE tie. Thus Ford is prohibited for 10 years from manufacturing its own plugs. But in five years it can buy its plugs from any source and use its name on OE plugs.

* * * * *

The requirement that, for five years, Ford purchase at least half of its spark plug requirements from the divested company under the Autolite label is to give the divested enterprise an assured customer while it struggles to be re-established as an effective, independent competitor.

. . . Ford's own studies indicate that it would take five to eight years for it to develop a spark plug division internally. A major portion of this period would be devoted to the development of a viable position in the aftermarket. The five-year prohibition on the use of its own name and the 10-year limitation on its own manufacturing mesh neatly to allow Ford to establish itself in the *aftermarket* prior to becoming a manufacturer while, at the same time, giving Autolite the opportunity to re-establish itself by providing a market for its production. . . .

. . . Forces now at work in the marketplace may bring about a deconcentrated market structure and may weaken the onerous OE tie. The District Court concluded that the forces of competition must be nurtured to correct for Ford's illegal acquisition. We view its decree as a means to that end. * * * *

Mr. Chief Justice Burger (concurring in part and dissenting in part):   In addition to requiring divestiture of Autolite, the District Court made ancillary injunctive provisions that go far beyond any that have been cited to the Court. . . .

An understanding of the District Court's findings as to the spark plug market shows three reasons why it was in error in requiring Ford to support Autolite. First, the court did *not* find that the weakness of an independent Autolite's competitive position resulted from Ford's acquisition. Rather, a reading of its findings makes apparent that the precariousness of Autolite's expected post-divestment position results from pre-existing forces in the market. Therefore, the drastic measures employed to strengthen Autolite's position at Ford's expense cannot be justified as a remedy for any wrong done by Ford. Second, the remedy will perpetuate for a time the very evils upon which the District Court based a finding of an antitrust violation. Third, the court's own findings indicate that the remedy is not likely to secure Autolite's competitive position beyond the termination of the restrictions. Therefore, there is no assurance that the judicial remedy will have the desired impact on long-run competition in the spark plug market.

*   *   *   *   *

The remedial provisions are unrelated to restoring the *status quo ante* with respect to the two violations found by the District Court, the ending of Ford's status as a potential entrant with a moderating influence on the market and the foreclosure of a significant part of the plug market. Indeed, the remedies may well be anticompetitive in both respects. First, the District Court's order actually undercuts the moderating influence of Ford's position on the edge of the market. It is the possibility that a company on the sidelines will enter a market through internal expansion that has a moderating influence on the market. By prohibiting Ford from entering the market through internal expansion, therefore, the remedy order wipes out, for the duration of the restriction, the pro-competitive influence Ford had on the market prior to its acquisition of Autolite. Second, the Court's order does not fully undo the foreclosure effect of the acquisition. Divestment alone would return the parties to the *status quo ante*. Ford would then be free to deal with Autolite or another plug producer or to enter the market through internal expansion. Yet the Court has ordered Ford to buy at least half its requirements from Autolite for five years. Thus, the order itself forecloses part of Ford's need from the forces of competition.

*   *   *   *   *

The findings of the District Court indicate that Autolite's precarious position did not result from its acquisition by Ford. Prior to the acquisition both Champion and Autolite were in a continually precarious position in that their continued large share of the market was totally dependent on their positions as OE suppliers to auto manufacturers. The very factor that assured that they faced no serious competition in the short run also assured that in the long run their own position was dependent on their relationship with a large auto manufacturer. Thus, the threat to Autolite posed by a simple divestiture is the same threat it had lived with between 1941 and 1961 as an independent entity: it might be left without any OE supply relationship with a major auto manufacturer, and therefore its market position based on this relationship might decline drastically.

*   *   *   *   *

In the final analysis it appears to me that the District Court, seeing the immediate precariousness of Autolite's position as a divested entity, designed remedies to support Autolite without contemplating whether it was equitable to restrict Ford's freedom of action for these purposes or whether there was any real chance of Autolite's eventual survival. I fear that this is a situation where the form of preserving competition has taken precedence over an understanding of the realities of the particular market. Therefore I dissent from today's affirmance of the District Court's harshly restrictive remedial provisions.

*   *   *   *   *

Case questions

1. What relief in addition to divestiture did the district court order? Why was this relief justified?

2. What is the basis for Chief Justice Burger's dissent?

3. How would Justice Douglas answer the criticisms made by Chief Justice Burger?

4. If one company illegally acquires the stock of another company, can the court effectively remedy the acquisition by ordering the acquiring company to distribute the acquired stock to its shareholders?

POLICY CONSIDERATIONS

Interpretations under section 7 of the Clayton Act have made horizontal and vertical mergers very risky for all but tiny, insignificant firms. Conglomerate mergers of firms producing complementary or otherwise related products are somewhat less vulnerable to section 7 attack but still face a substantial risk of being found illegal. Consequently, much of the merger activity in recent years has been "pure conglomerate"; that is, the acquired company has been in a field totally unrelated to that of the acquiring company. Merger activity is particularly high when firms with large cash surpluses see "bargains," firms whose stock is selling only slightly above or below the value of their assets.

Many scholars and policymakers view the trend toward large conglomerate acquisitions with alarm. They contend that such mergers are difficult to attack under section 7 because the mergers usually do not lessen competition in any specific market. They are concerned because large conglomerate mergers substantially increase the political power and influence of the acquiring firms. When firms merge, the number of political actors is reduced. Two formerly independent firms with potentially diverse views on political issues, candidates, and referenda are replaced by one united front. The large diversified firm further increases its political power by effecting economies of scale in lobbying and other political activities and by gaining access to the resources of the formerly independent firm for use in furthering its own political interests. Thus a car manufacturer that acquires a pharmaceutical company may use the latter's resources to lobby on issues affecting the auto industry. Prior to the merger the pharmaceutical company would have had no concern with auto industry issues.

Individuals concerned about conglomerate mergers also suggest that such mergers increase management's discretionary power, that is, management's power to make decisions with aims other than the aim of profit maximization. The exercise of this discretionary power in such areas as location of the enterprise, charitable contributions, and hiring and promotion policies can have substantial social impact. The concentration of these decisions in the hands of fewer corporate decision makers increases that impact.

Finally, persons who wish to stem the tide of conglomerate mergers contend that such mergers reduce organizational flexibility and diminish innovation. These persons have proposed legislation to prohibit mergers where the resulting firm's sales or assets would exceed a certain level ($2 billion is a frequently cited figure) unless the acquiring firm simultaneously divests itself of a division whose size is comparable to that of the acquired firm.

Those who oppose this approach argue that its proponents exaggerate corporate political power. They contend that corporate political power is balanced by the power of other interest groups, such as labor unions and consumer organizations. Further, many Americans view the exercise of corporate political influence very skeptically, and this in turn reduces that influence.

These individuals also suggest that prohibiting conglomerate mergers would be inefficient. They note that many firms become attractive acquisitions because of poor management. When a large conglomerate acquires such a firm, it is able to supply competent managers who restore the firm to a healthy business position. Conglomerate mergers also promote efficiency by allowing the merged firms to combine research and development, advertising, and marketing skills and resources. Moreover, mergers achieve economies of scale in raising capital by reducing legal fees and underwriting costs.

Finally, these individuals are against prohibiting conglomerate mergers for philosophical reasons. They hold that the antitrust laws are intended to protect competition and thereby to insure the operation of a free market economy. They oppose government intervention which is not directed toward this goal. They view outright prohibitions of mergers as unrelated to the protection of competition.

Review problems

1. Black & Decker Manufacturing Company was the leading manufacturer of portable electric power tools and accessories. It acquired the McCulloch Corporation, the leading manufacturer of gasoline-powered chain saws. Prior to the merger the two largest producers of gasoline-powered chains saws accounted for 54.3 percent of the market; the top four, for 77.5 percent; and the top eight, for 93.5 percent. During the years preceding the merger, demand for these saws rose substantially and a number of new firms entered the market. Meanwhile, the market for porta-

ble electric power tools became saturated and Black & Decker began looking for areas into which it might expand. It made a detailed study of the gasoline-powered tool market but it lacked sufficient expertise in gasoline technology to enter that market on its own. Did the acquisition violate section 7?

2. Falstaff Brewing Company, the fourth largest beer producer in the country, acquired Narrangansett, the largest seller of beer in New England. Falstaff did not previously sell beer in the northeast. Falstaff's management

was unwilling to enter the Northeast except by acquisition. Did the acquisition violate section 7?

3. General Motors Corporation, the nation's largest automobile manufacturer, decided to enter the snowmobile industry. It did this by creating a wholly owned subsidiary. Previously the snowmobile market had been characterized by low concentration and small firms. GM's subsidiary, backed by GM's massive advertising budget, offered its snowmobiles at an average price $50 below that of comparable models. In its first year of operation it gained 60 percent of the market. Did this violate section 7?

4. Widgets are an essential ingredient in the production of gizmos. The top seven widget firms control 90 percent of the market. The remaining 10 percent is divided among 25 small firms. Ace Gizmo Company is the leading manufacturer of gizmos, with 45 percent of the market. Ace accounts for 40 percent of the total domestic demand for widgets. Its needs have been supplied by a combination of large and small widget producers. Wonderful Widgets, Inc., is the 17th-largest widget manufacturer, with 0.3 percent of the market. Its sole customer has been Ace. Wonderful has run into cash flow difficulties and is unable to pay its bills as they come due. Creditors have threatened to file involuntary bankruptcy proceedings against it. Wonderful has proposed selling all its assets to Ace, paying its bills, and liquidating. Should Ace accept the deal?

5. The publisher of the *Los Angeles Times,* the largest daily newspaper in southern California, acquired the largest local daily paper in San Bernardino County, which borders Los Angeles on the east. The *Times* provided detailed coverage of state, national, and international news, while the local newspaper focused on county news. The *Times* San Bernardino circulation was mostly in the western part of the county, while the local paper's circulation was mostly in the eastern part. Approximately 25 percent of their circu-

lation overlapped. Define the relevant markets.

6. The XYZ Widget Company acquires the ABC Widget Company. The market for widgets is concentrated. The top firm has 25 percent, the next firm 23 percent, the third firm 20 percent, and the fourth 15 percent. XYZ is fifth, with 7 percent, and ABC is sixth, with 5 percent. XYZ believes that by acquiring ABC it will be a stronger competitor and may threaten the top four firms. Will the acquisition violate section 7?

7. Amax, Inc., and Copper Range Company merged. Prior to the merger Copper Range was the nation's seventh largest producer of copper, with 4.6 percent of the market. Amax mined copper pursuant to a joint venture with another company, and accounted for 1.4 percent of the market. All of Amax's reserves were obtained pursuant to joint ventures with other companies. Prior to the merger Amax announced its intention to expand its reserves and increase production. The copper industry was marked by high barriers to entry and high concentration, with the four largest companies holding 66 percent and the eight largest, 90 percent. Did the merger violate section 7?

8. Kennecott Copper Corporation, the largest copper producer in the country, accounting for 33 percent of the market, acquired Peabody Coal Company, the nation's largest coal producer, with 10 percent of the market. Due to dwindling copper reserves Kennecott liquidated some of its assets, thus obtaining a large amount of cash. It used this cash to buy Peabody. Kennecott made the purchase to diversify its operations in anticipation of the exhaustion of its copper reserves. Several years before the merger Kennecott had acquired a small coal company in order to supply its own needs for coal. The coal market was not highly concentrated, but it did have very high barriers to entry. Did the merger violate section 7?

9. CPS Industries, Inc., was the oldest and largest company in the gift wrap industry.

Due to poor management it began suffering substantial losses. It was then acquired by Papercraft Corporation, the second largest company in the industry. Papercraft's management turned CPS around, restoring its profitability. The FTC found that the merger violated section 7 and ordered divestiture. It further ordered Papercraft not to deal with any parties which, during the two years before the merger, had been CPS customers. This prohibition was to last for three years. If Papercraft appeals the remedy, will it be successful?

10. Compare the arguments for and against prohibiting conglomerate mergers. What is your opinion on this issue?

CHAPTER 8

Price Discrimination

Antitrust activity in the early 1900s focused on the anticompetitive efforts of trusts and monopolies. But during this era price discrimination was another practice which was perceived as adversely affecting competition. Price discrimination occurs when a seller gives a more favorable price treatment to one buyer over another. Price discrimination was a familiar practice of large producers. They were in a position to remove competitors and dissuade potential entrants by selective territorial price discrimination. They achieved this result by lowering their prices in geographic areas where competition was heavy. Meanwhile, these large producers could offset their profit concession by maintaining higher prices in geographic markets where their position was secure.

THE EARLY CLAYTON ACT

In 1914 Congress sought to neutralize the practice of price discrimination by enacting the Clayton Act. Section 2 of that act made it unlawful to "discriminate in price between different purchasers of commodities . . . where the effect of such discrimination may be *substantially to lessen competition* or tend to create a monopoly in any *line of commerce*" (emphasis added).

The act proved only partly successful in preventing price discrimination and its injurious effects. The phrase "line of commerce" was interpreted to confine the application of section 2 to a lessening of competition at the seller's level of distribution (primary-line injury). According to early judicial pronouncements, injury to competition at the buyer's level (secondary-line injury) was not encompassed by the statute.[1] Nonetheless, large purchasers were in a position to extract favorable discounts from their suppliers. This caused injury to competing purchasers that were not large enough to command such price concessions. In addition, judicial construction of section

---

[1] In 1929 *Van Camp & Sons Co.* v. *American Can Co.*, 278 U.S. 245 (1929), deviated from the traditional understanding of Clayton and extended its application to reach competitive injury at the buyer's rung.

216

2 was especially restrictive in its interpretation of "substantially to lessen competition." Only large firms were deemed within the scope of the language, as small firms rarely experienced sufficient injury to satisfy this statutory language.

The Clayton Act provided for exemptions. Its effectiveness was hampered by one exemption in particular: quantity discounts. Historically section 2 was intended to reach only the effect of price discrimination on the seller's competitors. Volume discounts were not understood to be a threat, since all sellers would realize an equal reduction of costs on volume sales and would supposedly be in an equal position to reduce their prices accordingly. However, under the act even a small variation in quantity justified a large price differential. Large chain stores, by avoiding the middle link in the normal distribution system, were able to extract larger discounts from the manufacturer than those obtained by smaller purchasers. This resulted in secondary level injury to the smaller purchasers.

These loopholes were large enough to protect the discriminatory policies of the large chain stores. By the 1920s these stores possessed a great advantage over the independent stores, which were forced to continue buying through the conventional distribution system in lesser volume than the chains. The larger the retail chain, the more leverage it possessed to extract additional discounts or other concessions from the manufacturer.[2] Chain stores were increasing rapidly in number and were altering the complexion of the American retail market. By 1933 they accounted for 25 percent of the market. Special concern mounted in the grocery industry when the independent "Ma and Pa" groceries began to disappear. Consequently, the wholesalers that customarily sold to the corner groceries were declining. To reverse this threatening trend, retail and wholesale grocers banded together in associations to increase their economic and political strength. The associations turned to Congress, which responded with the Robinson-Patman Act in 1936.

SELLER DISCRIMINATION

The Robinson-Patman Act is an amendment to the Clayton Act. It was designed to remove the shortcomings of the original Clayton Act in the area of price discrimination. The crux of the amendment is section 2(a), which makes it unlawful to discriminate in price between pruchasers of commodities of like grade and quality, where interstate commerce is involved and where such discrimination results in competitive injury.

Price Difference

A discrimination in price is simply a difference in price. Price is computed on the basis of the purchaser's actual cost. A supplier may set up a price

---

[2] Concessions might take the form of promotional payments for advertising the supplier's product in the retail stores.

scheme whereby wholesalers, retailers, and consumers pay the same price. This is not deemed discriminatory as distributors at higher functional levels of distribution are not entitled to a lower price. Not all price differentials are apparent. The Robinson-Patman Act equally prohibits indirect and direct price discrimination. Sometimes the buyer's actual costs must be adjusted by deducting various allowances and rebates. Other, more subtle terms may necessitate an adjustment in order to arrive at the purchaser's actual net price. Discriminatory terms of sale may be a means for effecting price discrimination and may thus constitute a violation of section 2(a). There are many ways in which one customer may be favored over another. Offering favored customers a 30-day option to purchase a product at the existing prices in a rising market is an unlawful indirect discrimination in price. Similarly, variations in the terms regarding delivery, sales returns, discounts for cash payment, and warehousing are all subject to the act's prohibitions. Any discrimination in price, direct or indirect, that results from differences in the treatment of customers may be viewed as a violation.

Two sales

For a violation on the Robinson-Patman Act to occur, there must be at least two completed sales. A sale to customer X for $1 and an offer to sell to customer Y for 80 cents is insufficient to meet the two-sale requirement. Only when the offer to Y has been accepted will the two-sale requirement be met. There must be an enforceable contract in existence before a sale has occurred for purposes of the Robinson-Patman Act. The mere quotation of different prices to different buyers or the dissemination of discriminatory price lists does not violate the act. Generally, a sale to one purchaser combined with a refusal to sell to another purchaser does not bring the act into play. Sellers are free to select "their own customers in bona fide transactions." However, as discussed in Chapter 5, a refusal to deal may be prohibited by the Sherman Act under section 1 if that refusal has been decided in concert with another. Moreover, in certain cases a Sherman Act section 2 violation occurs where the seller perpetuates a monopoly power by refusing to deal.

Consignments are not considered sales under the Robinson-Patman Act. A consignment occurs when one party delivers goods to a second in order to have the second party sell the goods. The party which delivers the goods is referred to as the consignor, while the party to which the goods are delivered is referred to as the consignee. What may be characterized as a consignment, however, may in reality be a sale. In a bona fide consignment the consignor retains title to the product until the ultimate sale to the consumer. If the incidents of title pass to the consignee, then the transaction is a sale.

Gifts are not considered sales under the act. However, one may not avoid the prohibitions of the act by disguising a sale as a gift. For example, a supplier may not circumvent the act by selling 100 tires to Tire, Inc., at

$20 per tire while selling 50 tires to Tire, Inc.'s competitor, Whitewall, Inc., at $20 per tire, but coupling that sale with a gift of 50 tires to Whitewall, Inc.

Close in time. The Robinson-Patman Act comes into operation only when the two sales are reasonably close in time. What is defined as close in time is determined by the circumstances. Where sales of a high-cost, low-volume product such as a jet engine are involved, a time differential of a year may be considered contemporaneous. Yet rapid shifts in market conditions may negate the contemporaneous nature of two sales made in close succession. Where what is involved are smaller items that trade in high volume with great fluctuations in supply and demand, such as food commodities, an interval of hours may not satisfy the requirement of a sale close in time.

Sales for future delivery may differ in price from sales for immediate delivery without running afoul of the act. A seller, in January, may sell corn to be delivered to one buyer in March for a price that differs from the same seller's price to another buyer for immediate delivery. However, if a seller contracts with buyer 1 to deliver March futures corn for $3 per bushel and with buyer 2 to deliver March futures corn for $3.50 per bushel, a price discrimination exists.

Same seller. The two sales must of course originate from the same seller before the Robinson-Patman Act applies. It is normally easy to discern whether this requirement has been met. The question becomes more difficult when a parent corporation and its subsidiary sell the same product at different prices to competing customers. The determining factor is often the degree of control exercised over the subsidiary by the parent corporation. The fact that the subsidiary is wholly owned and that the boards of the parent and the subsidiary have directors in common does not automatically result in a finding that they are the same seller for purposes of the Robinson-Patman Act. As long as the parent and the subsidiary are independent entities in their pricing and distribution policies, they will be deemed autonomous. In one reported case the plaintiff operated a retail store that purchased its products from Philco Distributors, Inc., a wholly owned subsidiary of Philco, with common officers. Philco, the parent corporation, sold the same products for less to a competitor of the plaintiff. The plaintiff brought an action against Philco, alleging price discrimination. Since there was no evidence to show that Philco established prices for its subsidiary, the parent and the subsidiary were treated as two distinct sellers and no violation existed.[3]

Commodities

The Robinson-Patman Act only applies to sales of commodities. Commodities are movable or tangible property. They do not encompass intangibles

---

[3] *Baim & Blank, Inc.* v. *Philco Distributors, Inc.,* 148 F. Supp. 541 (D.C.N.Y. 1957).

such as services or leasehold interests. The sale of news information services, bus tickets, mutual fund shares, and advertising; the licensing of a patented proofreading process; and the extension of loans are all outside the scope of the act's applicability. When a sale involves both commodities and services, the dominant nature of the transaction determines whether it falls within the act. For example, in one case a builder allegedly sold bricks at a discriminatory price in connection with a contract to construct public housing facilities. In the contract the price of the bricks was segregated from the price of the construction services and was a significant determinant of the total contract price. The court nevertheless found the whole contract to be an indivisible construction service contract.

Like grade and quality

There can be no violation of the Robinson-Patman Act unless the products which are the subject of the alleged price discrimination are of like grade and quality. Thus truck tires can be sold at a different price than bicycle tires. Goods, however, do not have to be of exactly the same grade and quality but only of like grade and quality to satisfy that portion of the act. Slight differences in dimensions or quality will not exempt products from the act's prohibition. Juice containers that differ in size by only one-eighth inch are of like grade and quality since they are functionally similar in performance. It is clear that a strong customer preference for one product over another, even though the differences in product design are nominal, may cause the products to be dissimilar in grade and quality. This introduces the concept of commercial fungibility (interchangeability). If two products are only slightly different in physical appearance, yet consumers are generally willing to pay a higher price for one than for the other, then the products are not interchangeable and not of like grade and quality. One federal court explained this by stating:

> . . . [C]ross elasticity of demand, substitutability, physical appearance, and identity of performance, are factors to be considered in determining whether goods are of "like grade and quality.". . .
>
> [If] there are substantial physical differences in products affecting consumer use, preference or marketability, such products are not of "like grade and quality," regardless of manufacturing costs.[4]

A brand name distinction does not automatically remove a case from the like grade and quality requirement. Whether strong public demand for one brand over another negates a finding of like grade and quality is the subject of the next case, which involved the marketing of evaporated milk.

---

[4] *Checker Motors Corp.* v. *Chrysler Corp.*, 283 F. Supp. 876 at 888–89 (S.D.N.Y. 1968), affirmed, 405 F.2d 319 (2d Cir. 1969).

FTC v. Borden Co.
383 U.S. 637 (1965)

The Borden Company (defendant) sells evaporated milk under the Borden name, a nationally recognized premium brand, and under private, nonpremium labels. The nonpremium brand milk is physically and chemically identical with the premium brand milk but is marketed to Borden's customers at a price below that of the premium brand milk. There is a distinct consumer preference for the premium brand. The FTC (plantiff) found that the two brands were of "like grade and quality" and held that the price differential was discrimination in violation of section 2(a) of the Robinson-Patman Act. The court of appeals reversed the commission's decision and found that the nonpremium brand was not of the same grade and quality as the premium brand. It based its decision on the fact that "decided consumer preference for one brand over another, reflected in the willingness to pay a higher price for the well-known brand, was . . . sufficient to differentiate chemically identical products and to place the price differential beyond the reach of § 2(a)." The Supreme Court rejected the rationale of the court of appeals and reversed and remanded the case.

Mr. Justice White:

* * * * *

. . . The Commission's view is that labels do not differentiate products for the purpose of determining grade or quality, even though the one label may have more customer appeal and command a higher price in the marketplace from a substantial segment of the public. That this is the Commission's long-standing interpretation of the present Act, as well as §2 of the Clayton Act before its amendment by the Robinson-Patman Act, may be gathered from the Commission's decisions dating back to 1936. . . .

. . . Moreover, what legislative history there is concerning this question supports the Commission's construction of the statute rather than that of the Court of Appeals.

* * * * *

If two products, physically identical but differently branded, are to be deemed of different grade because the seller regularly and successfully markets some quantity of both at different prices, the seller could, as far as § 2(a) is concerned, make either product available to some customers and deny it to others, however discriminatory this might be and however damaging to competition. Those who were offered only one of the two products would be barred from competing for those customers who want or might buy the other. The retailer who was permitted to buy and sell only the more expensive brand would have no chance to sell to those who always buy the cheaper product or to convince others, by experience or otherwise, of the fact which he and all other dealers already know—that the cheaper product is actually identical with that carrying the more expensive label.

* * * * *

Our holding neither ignores the economic realities of the marketplace nor denies that some labels will command a higher price than others, at least from some portion of the public. But it does mean that "the economic factors inherent in brand names and national advertising should not be considered in the jurisdictional inquiry under the statutory 'like grade and quality' test." And it does mean that transactions like those involved in this case may be examined by the Commission under § 2(a). The Commission will determine, subject to judicial review, whether the differential under attack is discriminatory within the meaning of the Act, whether competition may be injured, and whether [the defendant has a statutory defense to the action]. . . .

* * * * *

Case Questions

1. Did the Court "ignore the economic realities of the marketplace"? What are those realities?

2. What is the difference between "like grade" and "like quality"? Give an example of two products that are of like grade but not of like quality. Now give an example of two products that are of like quality but not of like grade.

3. Who is injured, if anyone, as a result of "private branding"? Why are consumers willing to pay more for the same product under a different label?

4. After a finding of "like grade and quality," does the inquiry end? Is Borden automatically guilty of a section 2 (a) violation? Explain.

5. What if Borden produced only a small quantity of the private brand milk and the customer demand exceeded the supply? What effect might this have on competition?

On remand to the Fifth Circuit Court of Appeals in *Borden Co.* v. *FTC* the court found that no customer was favored since the nonpremium brand was available to all customers.[5] Thus the price differential between the premium and nonpremium brand created no competitive advantage for the recipients of the cheaper private brand. Without the threat of competitive injury there was no violation.

Competitive injury

In order to establish a Robinson-Patman price discrimination violation it is necessary to show only potential injury, not actual competitive injury. There are three types of illegal injury under the act. It is unlawful to discriminate in price where the effect of such discrimination (1) may be substantially to lessen competition or (2) may tend to create a monopoly in any line of commerce or (3) may injure, destroy, or prevent competition with any person who either grants or knowingly receives the benefit of such discrimination, or to customers of either of those persons. The first two types of injury involve the same kind of proof that is necessary for a Clayton section 7 merger violation: proof of a probable adverse competitive impact in the total relevant market. These types of injury are rarely invoked because of the complexity of the proof requirements. (These requirements are discussed in Chapter 7.) The third type of injury is the one usually invoked in attempts to fulfill the competitive injury portion of the act. The test of this type of injury is satisfied if there is a probability of injury to competition at certain levels of the distributive function.

Primary-line injury. Primary-line injury (or injury at the seller's level) occurs when a seller suffers injury as a result of price discrimination by a competing seller. This normally occurs when a seller cuts prices to purchasers

[5] 381 F.2d 175 (5th Cir. 1967).

in one geographic area in an attempt to drive out a local competitor. The situation is demonstrated by the accompanying diagram.

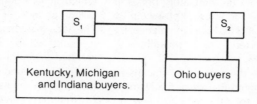

S_1 and S_2 are competitors in Ohio. If S_1 slashes its prices to Ohio buyers in an attempt to drive S_2 out of business, without a corresponding decrease in prices to its customers in Kentucky, Michigan, and Indiana, S_2 may suffer a primary-line injury. Of course, before a violation of the act can occur, S_1's economic power must be sufficient to pose a probability of injury to S_2.

In some cases such economic power is evidenced by a seller's ability to drive a competitor out of business by practicing price discrimination.

Continental Baking Co. v. Old Homestead Bread Co.
476 F.2d 97 (10th Cir. 1973)

The Old Homestead Bread Company (plaintiff-appellee) sued Continental Baking Company (defendant-appellant), Rainbo Bread Company, and Interstate Brands Corporation for violating the Robinson-Patman Act. Interstate cross-claimed against Continental. A jury returned verdicts in favor of Old Homestead and Interstate against Continental. Continental appealed. The Tenth Circuit Court of Appeals affirmed the verdict.

All of the parties were competing bread bakeries whose white bread was of like grade and quality. They sold their bread to independent grocers in Denver, Colorado, and southeastern Wyoming. Most of the grocers belonged to a buying cooperative. Members of the cooperative formed the Five States Supply Company, whose purpose was to provide them with a private label bread known as Tender Crust Bread. Continental agreed to supply Five States with Tender Crust Bread and bakery products, at a price at least one cent per loaf less than it charged for its major brand,

Wonder Bread. In return, Five States grocers agreed to give preferred shelf space to Continental products.

Seth, Circuit Judge:

* * * * *

The record shows that Continental in its Denver plants sold in 1963 about 27,700,000 pounds of bread products and lost money there in 1963, 1964, 1965, and 1966. In 1967 the operations of Continental at Denver showed a modest profit of $14,000.00 while nationally its profits were about twenty-one million dollars. In 1967 Continental had increased its sales in the Denver area to over 40,000 pounds of bread products. During the forty-month complaint period the volume of sales by Old Homestead fell sharply, until, finally on December 31, 1967, Old Homestead dropped out of the industry.

In this opinion we only give consideration to the Robinson-Patman aspect of the litigation. This case thus involves primary-line competition since Old Homestead and Interstate were in competition with Continental, the party charging the allegedly discriminatory prices. It is clear that primary-line injury is protected by the Robinson-Patman Act. For convenience, Interstate will be referred to as a "plaintiff."

* * * * *

The term "price discrimination" means no more than price differentiation, or the charging of different prices to different customers for goods of like grade and quality. It is undisputed that Continental charged one price per loaf for its product labeled "Wonder Bread" and a different price for its product labeled "Tender Crust Bread." It is also uncontroverted that both of these brands were of like grade and quality. Since the goods are of like grade and quality, the fact that they are sold under different labels will not justify what would otherwise be price discrimination under section 2(a). Therefore, the price discrimination element of this action is established by uncontroverted facts.

* * * * *

PREDATORY INTENT

Although the statute does not speak of "predatory intent," the courts have reasoned that, from a finding of predatory intent, the jury can infer that a reasonable possibility of competitive injury exists. . . .

Since the "sum total of all the evidence must be considered" to find predatory intent, there is no set formula for such a finding. . . . [P]redatory intent [can] be found from "persistent unprofitable sales below cost and radical price cuts themselves discriminatory." There is some evidence in the case before us of sales below cost during a very short period, and discriminatory price cuts represented by discounts to Tender Crust customers only. . . . [T]he Act "comes into play to regulate the conduct of price discriminators when their discriminatory prices consistently undercut other competitors.". . . . [T]his conduct [is] highly indicative of predatory intent.

There are several significant but isolated facts in the case before us which could support a finding of predatory intent. For example, in

1962, Continental built a bakery which was the largest in the Rocky Mountain Area but which at its opening operated at thirty-three million pounds, or fifty percent of its capacity. The Vice-President testified that he knew that it could not be operated profitably until it reached seventy-five per cent capacity, or fifty-two million pounds. From 1963 to 1967, Continental increased its production by fifty per cent or from thirty-three million pounds to fifty-two million pounds and at the end of the period was for the first time in the black. The seemingly impossible goal Continental set for itself in 1963 and, in view of the existing suppliers, the achievement of that goal would indicate that Continental's operations were based on something more than "fierce competitive instincts." The record also shows that the plaintiff Old Homestead ceased to do business on December 31, 1967, and on January 2, 1968, Continental raised its prices and did away with all discounts. There are other examples in the record which, when considered with those mentioned, could provide the jury with sufficient evidence from which to draw a strong inference of predatory intent on Continental's part.

* * * * *

CAUSAL CONNECTION

* * * * *

An analysis of the exhibits covering the years of 1963 and 1967 permits the following tabulation to be made:

	Sales	*Bread*
1963		
Continental	5,100,875	27,739,659
Rainbo	2,559,039	14,938,838
Interstate	2,314,000	12,850,000
Old Homestead	4,118,938	22,850,000
Total	14,092,852	78,378,497
1967		
Continental	7,319,792	40,850,512
Rainbo	3,186,818	17,521,511
Interstate	2,879,000	16,000,000
Old Homestead	906,445	5,030,000
Total	14,292,055	79,402,032

In comparing the sales in dollars for the years 1963 and 1967, assuming that these four companies represent the total independent wholesale bread market, then Continental's sales represented $5,100,875.00 of the total $14,092,852.00 or 36.2 per cent of the dollar volume of sales in 1963. In 1967, Continental's sales represented $7,319,792.00 of approximately the same total volume or 51.2 per cent. Also, these figures show that Old Homestead's losses during these years were not redistributed evenly over the remainder of the market but the relatively greatest amount went to Continental.

Comparing the sales in pounds, Continental's sales volume in 1963 was 27,739,659 of a total market of 78,378,497 or 35.4 percent. In 1967, Continental's sales volume was 40,850,512 of a total market of 79,402,023 or 51.5 per cent.

* * * * *

Case questions

1. Why did the court hold that Continental was engaging in price discrimination? What if Tender Crust Bread was wholewheat only and Wonder Bread was bleached white only?

2. Can you distinguish "fierce competitive instincts" from "predatory intent"? Why is this line of demarcation important?

3. What evidence does the court point to in order to establish competitive injury? How about causal connection?

4. What if Old Homestead was simply inefficient in its deliveries and most independents did not want to deal with the company? Would that change the complexion of the case?

5. Did you discover any other antitrust violations in this case? Discuss.

Secondary-line injury. Secondary-line injury (or injury at the buyer's level) occurs when a seller discriminates in price between two competing buyers. This injury is illustrated as follows:

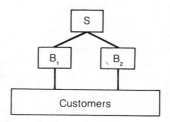

B_1 and B_2 are competing for the same customers. If S sells products at a lower price to B_1 than to B_2, then B_2 is at a competitive disadvantage and may suffer competitive injury. However, if the diagram appears as follows, no such competitive injury occurs:

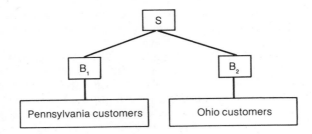

Here, since there is no competition at the buyer level, there can be no buyer-level injury based on price discrimination. In such a case S may discriminate in price between B_1 and B_2 without violating the act. Should B_1 develop customers in Ohio, then S's more favorable treatment of B_1 may cause competitive injury to B_2 and thus violate the act.

Tertiary-line injury. Tertiary-line injury occurs when a customer of a seller's favored distributor possesses a competitive advantage over a disfavored distributor. The diagram in such an instance appears as follows:

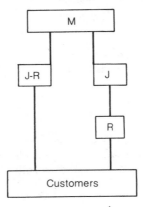

Here, assume that M sells goods at a lower price to J (Jobber) than to J-R (Jobber-Retailer). As a result J may be in a position to sell to R (retailer) at a price that enables R to give more favorable treatment in price to customers than J-R can give. Competitive injury may result on the third level, so that J-R would have a cause of action against M for price discrimination under the act.

Fourth-line injury. Fourth-line injury is illustrated in *Standard Oil Co.* v. *Perkins,* where the plaintiff, Perkins, was an independent gasoline dealer in the wholesale and retail business.[6] Perkins was the recipient of less favorable treatment than Standard Oil afforded to another wholesaler. The favored

---

[6] 395 U.S. 642 (1969).

wholesaler sold to a firm that sold to retail outlets which competed with the plaintiff. The distribution diagram appears as follows:

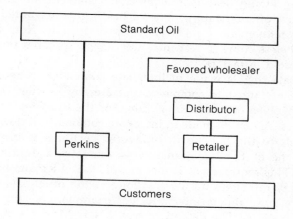

Perkins alleged and proved injury as a result of the discriminatory pricing. The Supreme Court upheld a jury verdict in favor of Perkins and put to rest the belief that the wording of the Robinson-Patman Act would not support a finding of competitive injury below the third-line level. As long as a causal relationship exists between the discrimination and the injury, the distribution level at which the injury occurs appears immaterial.

Commerce

Congress derived its power to enact the Robinson-Patman Act from the Commerce Clause. Congress did not expand its authority to regulate interstate commerce to the fullest extent permissible under the Constitution. Under section 2(a) a violation of the Robinson-Patman Act may occur only when certain interstate commerce activities occur. First, a violator must be engaged in interstate commerce. Second, discriminatory practices must occur in the course of interstate commerce. Third, either of the purchases must be made in interstate commerce.

Generally, a company that sells its goods intrastate has failed to meet the first test that it be engaged in interstate commerce. However, if that firm resells goods it received from outside the state, it may fall within the flow of interstate commerce and be treated as a firm engaged in interstate commerce. Where, for example, gasoline is refined in Indiana and sold to a supplier in Michigan for temporary storage and ultimate resale in Michigan, the gasoline is deemed within the stream of interstate commerce. The subject of the resale satisfies the interstate commerce requirement. In certain cases a different result may be reached. If the product is substantially altered after it arrives in the state before resale, then the flow of interstate commerce ends. For example, if raw oil was shipped into Michigan from Indiana and then refined in Michigan before being sold within Michigan, the act of refining would destroy the interstate character of the oil. In such a case the flow of interstate commerce has been interrupted by the intervening act of refinement. Similarly, goods shipped in from a foreign state may nonetheless come to rest intrastate, if incorporated into a finished product and resold intrastate.

A sale that is made in interstate commerce is necessarily made in the course of interstate commerce and thereby satisfies the second test if the sale involves price discrimination. For the third test to be met, one of the purchases must be made in interstate commerce. It does not matter whether the sale to the favored or unfavored customer is interstate, as long as at least one of the two transactions generates a discrimination across state lines. This requirement is met even if the objecting disfavored customer is a purely intrastate business as long as the other sale which is the subject of the complaint is interstate. For example, consider *Moore* v. *Mead's Fine Bread Company*.[7] The defendant was a New Mexico company engaged in the bread baking business in New Mexico. The company had a close marketing interrelationship with other corporations that did business in New Mexico and Texas. It also sold bread in Texas, which it serviced with a bread truck operating out of its New Mexico location. The plaintiff was engaged in a purely intrastate bakery business in New Mexico. Plaintiff alleged that the defendant cut prices to wholesalers in Texas but failed to do so in New Mexico, resulting in competitive injury. The court held that this was sufficient to satisfy the commerce requirements of the Robinson-Patman Act, since the defendant made discriminatory sales in interstate commerce.

DEFENSES

There are three basic defenses to an alleged price discrimination. They are cost justification, meeting competition, and changing market conditions.

Cost justification

Section 2(a) of the Robinson-Patman Act provides a complete defense to a seller when price discrimination is justified by a difference in cost. The particular proviso affording the defense is satisfied as long as price differences are linked to "differences in the cost of manufacture, sale, or delivery resulting from the differing methods [used] or quantities" sold. A seller is not required to give a cost break to a buyer based on a cost saving, but it may give a buyer a cost break as long as the cost saving is supported by a reliable cost study. If the seller gives a cost break to a particular buyer, the seller may not discriminate against other buyers. The cost saving must be equally available to them.

---

[7] 348 U.S. 115 (1954).

The burden of proof for establishing that a price differential is based on a difference in the cost of manufacturing, selling, or delivering rests upon the seller. This burden appears reasonable since the seller is normally in control of the information needed to establish its cost basis. Volume discounts may be justified on the basis of a cost saving effected by eliminating salespersons, travel expense, warehousing, or transportation.

Computing costs. The construction of a cost study begins with the establishment of a relevant price. The relevant price is the net price the buyer pays for the product. To arrive at the net price all discounts, rebates, and other reductions must be deducted from the selling price.

Cost justification would in most instances be impossible if not for the permissibility of placing customers in homogeneous groups in order to average the costs of selling to each group. The group classifications must be reasonable, and each group must have sufficient homogeneity so that the average costs for the whole group are fairly representative of the costs of dealing with each of its members. The cost difference which justifies less favorable pricing treatment for some customers must arise from differing methods or the differing quantities that are sold or delivered. The cost difference must be related to lower costs of manufacture, sale, or delivery. The cost study must be based on fair and consistent accounting procedures.

Distribution costs. The most popular area of cost justification is that of savings in distribution costs. Included in the distribution cost category are transportation, storage, advertising, accounting, management, clerical work, salaries, and services for the customer.

Manufacturing costs. Price discrimination based on a saving in the area of manufacturing costs is less popular because proof is more difficult. As noted by statute, justified price concessions must be related to a cost saving based on differing quantities or methods. There are two areas where such manufacturing cost savings may be more readily proved. When a customer orders quantities well in advance, a supplier may be in a position to justify charging that customer a lower price than the price charged a customer that orders for immediate needs during a rush season. A cost saving for the seller may occur in the form of cheaper off-season labor or elimination of overtime wages. Similarly, where a customer without storage facilities requires spot deliveries during the rush season for which the manufacturer must prepare and store, the manufacturer may be justified in charging that customer a higher price than the price charged another customer that orders in advance and handles the storage.

Meeting competition

The meeting competition defense is rooted in section 2(b) of the Robinson-Patman Act, which exonerates a seller that discriminates in price if the seller can show that the lower price "was made in good faith to meet an equally low price of a competitor." The burden is upon the seller to prove the elements of the defense. The statute is very clear that a seller may only discriminate in order to meet competition. Beating competition is not a defense. This concept is more difficult to apply than it sounds. A price differentiation may not be justified where the seller of a premium product reduces its prices in a geographic area to the level charged by a competitor that is selling a nonpremium product. For example, Anheuser-Busch reduced the price of Budweiser beer in the St. Louis area from $2.93 per case to $2.35 per case in response to the price charged by three regional brewers that were selling their beer at $2.35 per case. Anheuser-Busch's meeting competition defense was rejected on the basis that the reduction was not necessary to hold its customers because the effect of the reduction was to beat competition rather than meet it.[8]

The competition which this defense decidedly refers to is that of the seller's competitor and not that of the customer's competitor. A seller may not lower its price to assist its customer in meeting competition unless the reduction is made in response to competitive practices of the seller's competitor.

Inherent in the meeting competition defense is a good faith test. A seller that seeks refuge in this defense must not have a predatory intent. The motive of the discriminating seller must be based on a reasonably prudent belief that responding by reducing prices is a competitive necessity. A seller that acts in good faith, though under an erroneous belief, is protected by the meeting competition defense. However, a seller has a duty to act with reasonable care in verifying competitive offers made to its prospective customers.

Lowering prices to meet competition need not be aimed only at retaining old customers. Meeting competition may also have the effect of obtaining new customers. However, the seller must not act in bad faith and cross over from the permissible limits of meeting competition to the illegal area of driving out competition.

A discriminatory lower price which is legally in effect under the meeting competition defense may not remain legal indefinitely. It remains legal only as long as the competition of the seller remains a threat. When the seller is aware of changing conditions that might alter the competitive condition that resulted in its price reduction, the seller has a duty to investigate or test the competitor to see whether that condition still exists. And if, for example, the competitor goes out of business, the seller may no longer justify a discriminatory price by hiding under the cloak of meeting competition.

Changing conditions

A seller may reduce certain prices in response to changing conditions which affect the marketability of its goods. Those conditions include the

---

[8] 363 U.S. 536 (1960).

threatened deterioration of perishable goods, the obsolescence of seasonal goods, distress sales under court process, and discontinuance of business in specified goods.

Generally, the defense speaks of a price difference justification on the basis of a change in market conditions or in the marketability of the product. These changes are usually beyond the seller's control. The classic example of change in product marketability is provided by the automobile industry. Once automobile models for the new year become available, the old year's inventory becomes less marketable. In response, automobile manufacturers may reduce the prices of the old year's models without fear of Robinson-Patman liability.

BUYER DISCRIMINATION

Section 2(f) of the Robinson-Patman Act makes it unlawful to knowingly induce or receive a price discrimination in violation of section 2(a). This section was designed to reach the big purchasers that were in a position to extract large discriminatory price concessions from the seller.

Great Atlantic & Pacific Tea Co., Inc., v. *FTC*
440 U.S. 69 (1979)

The FTC (respondent) instituted a complaint against Great Atlantic & Pacific Tea Co., Inc. (A&P) (petitioner), which included a charge that A&P violated section 2(f) of the Robinson-Patman Act by knowingly inducing or receiving price discriminations from Borden. The FTC found that A&P knew or should have known that it was the beneficiary of unlawful price discrimination. A&P appealed the decision to the court of appeals, which affirmed the FTC. A&P sought review in the Supreme Court, which granted certiorari and reversed.

A&P was Borden's largest customer in the Chicago area. A&P wished to change from selling brand label milk to selling private label milk. It communicated this desire to Borden, which offered A&P a discount on private label milk. The offer would have saved A&P $410,000 per year. A&P then solicited offers from other dairies and received a more favorable bid from Bowman Diary. It communicated this fact to Borden but refused to reveal the details of the Bowman bid. Borden, fearing

the loss of A&P's business, responded with a new bid which would increase A&P's annual saving to $820,000. Borden stated that its new offer was designed to meet Bowman's bid. A&P accepted Borden's bid, knowing that it was better than Bowman's.

Mr. Justice Stewart: . . . The petitioner . . . argues that it cannot be liable under §2(f) if Borden had a valid meeting competition defense. The respondent, on the other hand, argues that the petitioner may be liable even assuming that Borden had such a defense. The meeting competition defense, the respondent contends, must in these circumstances be judged from the point of view of the buyer. Since A&P knew for a fact that the Borden bid beat the Bowman bid, it was not entitled to assert the meeting competition defense even though Borden may have honestly believed that it was simply meeting competition. Recognition of a meeting competition defense for the buyer in this situation, the respondent argues, would be contrary to the basic purpose of the Robinson-Patman Act to curtail abuses by large buyers.

* * * * *

In a competitive market, uncertainty among sellers will cause them to compete for business by offering buyers lower prices. Because of the evils of collusive action the Court has held that the exchange of price information by competitors violates the Sherman Act. Under the view advanced by the respondent, however, a buyer, to avoid liability, must either refuse a seller's bid or at least inform him that his bid has beaten competition. Such a duty of affirmative disclosure would almost inevitably frustrate competitive bidding and, by reducing uncertainty, lead to price matching and anticompetitive cooperation among sellers.

* * * * *

. . . Accordingly, we hold that a buyer who has done no more than accept the lower of two prices competitively offered does not violate §2(f) provided the seller has a meeting competition defense.

Because both the Commission and the Court of Appeals proceeded on the assumption that a buyer who accepts the lower of two competitive bids can be liable under section 2(f) even if the seller has a meeting competition defense, there was not a specific finding that Borden did in fact have such a defense. But it quite clearly did.

The test for determining when a seller has a valid meeting competition defense is whether a seller can "show the existence of facts which would lead a reasonable and prudent person to believe that the granting of a lower price would in fact meet the equally low price of a competitor.". . . "A good faith belief, rather than absolute certainty, that a price concession is being offered to meet an equally low price offered by a competitor is sufficient to satisfy the Robinson-Patman's section 2(b) defense."

Since good faith, rather than absolute certainty, is the touchstone of the meeting competition defense, a seller can assert the defense even if it has unknowingly made a bid that in fact not only met but beat his competition.

Under the circumstances of this case, Borden did act reasonably and in good faith when it made its second bid. The petitioner, despite its longstanding relationship with Borden, was dissatisfied with Borden's first bid and solicited offers from other dairies. . . .

* * * * *

Thus Borden was informed by the petitioner that it was in danger of losing its A&P business in the Chicago area unless it came up with a better offer. . . . In light of Borden's established relationship with the petitioner, Borden could justifiably conclude that A&P's statements were reliable and that it was necessary to make another bid offering substantial concessions to avoid losing its account with the petitioner.

Borden was unable to ascertain the details of the Bowman bid. It requested more information about the bid from the petitioner, but this request was refused. It could not then attempt to verify the existence and terms of the competing offer from Bowman without risking Sherman Act liability. Faced with a substantial loss of business and unable to find out the precise details of the competing bid, Borden made another offer stating that it was doing so in order to meet competition. Under these circumstances, the conclusion is virtually inescapable that in making that offer Borden acted in a reasonable and good faith effort to meet its competition, and therefore was entitled to a meeting competition defense.

Since Borden had a meeting competition defense and thus could not be liable under § 2(b), the petitioner who did no more than accept that offer cannot be liable under § 2(f).

Case questions

1. Under a strict reading of section 2(f), is A&P guilty? Why did the administrative law judge, the commission, and the Second Circuit Court of Appeals all hold that A&P had violated section 2(f)?

2. Do you think that Borden's desire was to just meet its competition or to beat it? Why?

3. Does the seller have any duty to make good faith attempts to ascertain its competitors before lowering the price of its goods? What if A&P had told Borden the competitor's price and then Borden and A&P had agreed on that exact price? Would there have been a Sherman Act violation? What dilemma is Borden faced with if A&P refuses to reveal the details of the Bowman bid?

4. How would A&P establish a defense to a section 2(f) violation based on cost justification?

5. Are we back where we started from, with large buyers having the power to extract discriminatory price concessions from suppliers? Discuss.

BROKERAGE PAYMENTS

Section 2(c) of the Robinson-Patman Act makes it unlawful for any person to pay or receive "a commission, brokerage, or other compensation, or any allowance or discount in lieu thereof, except for services rendered in connection with the sale or purchase of goods . . ." This section was intended to eliminate "dummy" brokerage fees that large buyer chains extracted from sellers. The results of this practice were price concessions and, in reality, unfair price discriminations for favored buyers. A seller may not give a brokerage fee to the buyer's broker since the buyer's broker does not render services to the seller. To do so would violate section 2(c).

Section 2(c) is self-containing and without reference to any other sections. As such, no cost justification, meeting competition, or changing market defenses appear to be available. A violation of section 2(c) may result from a single transaction. There is no need for two sales. No showing of competitive injury is needed. All that is required for a violation is a brokerage fee flowing from buyer to seller, or vice versa, without supportive services rendered. However, recent cases have been chipping away at the traditional approach, so that more and more of section 2(a) elements and the cost justification and meeting competition defenses are seeping into the case law.

PROMOTIONAL ALLOWANCES AND SERVICES

Price concessions are not the only way a seller may favor one customer over another. The Robinson-Patman Act also comprehends such forms of discrimination as promotional allowances, signs, displays, demonstrations, packaging, warehousing, return privileges, and a host of other merchandising services. These potential abuses are covered in sections 2(d) and 2(e). Section 2(d) requires that any payments or allowances by a seller to a buyer for promotional services be available on proportionally equal terms to competing customers. Section 2(e) requires that any services furnished by a seller to a buyer be made available on proportionally equal terms to all competing customers.

Only sellers can violate sections 2(d) and 2(e). Although there is no prohibition against a buyer inducing or receiving discriminatory promotional allowances or services, the FTC seeks to control this practice by means of section 5 of the Federal Trade Commission Act, which prohibits unfair methods of competition.

The seller must inform customers of the availability of advertising allowances and promotional services. The terms should be openly communicated to all customers by the same media to avoid the suspicion of discriminatory conduct. However, a seller need only make the allowances and services available to competing customers. Whether two customers compete must be determined primarily on the basis of geography. It is unlikely that a California customer competes with a Florida customer. However, a Queens, New York, customer may compete with a Long Island, New York, customer. In close cases a resort to market analysis and conditions may be necessary to determine whether two customers actually compete. The seller may not formulate a promotional plan that benefits only some competing customers. Each competing customer must be able to take advantage of the seller's promotional plan even if this requires tailoring the plan to fit a specific competitor's needs.

The promotional allowances or services must be made available to competing customers on "proportionally equal terms." Proportionally equal terms may be computed as a percentage of the dollar volume of goods sold or of the quantity of goods purchased. If a seller makes available to each customer an advertising allowance equal to 2 per cent of annual purchases, the proportionally equal terms requirement would be satisfied. However, if the 2 per cent allowance would not apply until a specified quantity of products were purchased, the allowance might be violative of the requirement if only a few large buyers could benefit from it. Consider the following case in which a mobile home retailer was allegedly denied "delivery services."

Purdy Mobile Homes v. Champion Home Builders
594 F.2d 1313 (9th Cir. 1979)

Purdy (plaintiff) sells mobile homes at retail. Champion (defendant) manufactures and distributes mobile homes. Purdy sued Champion for violation of section 2(e) of the Robinson-Patman Act, alleging that it had been denied promotional (delivery) services on proportionally equal terms to those of its competitors. Purdy alleged that Champion granted it the exclusive right to purchase and resell Tamarack mobile homes within a prescribed area surrounding Spokane, Washington; that Champion marketed two other lines of mobile homes, the Titan and Concord, which were substantially identical to the Tamarack; that *although Champion sold these two lines to other dealers within Purdy's exclusive territory, they were not "delivered" to Purdy for sale; and that Champion improperly terminated Purdy's franchise. The district court found that Purdy had failed to state a claim and dismissed the action. The court of appeals affirmed.*

Hug, Circuit Judge:

*   *   *   *   *

The purpose of section 2(e) and its companion section 2(d) is to strengthen the prohibition against unfair price discrimination by prohibiting price discrimination disguised in the form of advertising or promotional services provided to purchasers on a discriminatory basis. The prohibitions of section 2(e) apply only to services or facilities connected with the resale of the product by the purchaser.

The question before us is whether Champion's refusal to sell the Titan and Concord lines of mobile homes to Purdy constitutes discrimination in the furnishing of services or facilities connected with the resale of the mobile homes. We hold that it does not.

Purdy relies upon [a] decision of the Seventh Circuit . . . [which] held that a supplier engaged in discriminatory practices in violation of section 2(e) of the Robinson-Patman Act when it delivered a product in a consistently late fashion to one purchaser while making timely deliveries to other purchasers. The court concluded that delivery of a product is a "service or facility" within the meaning of section 2(e) because timely deliveries would "obviously promote and facilitate" the resale of the product. . . .

. . . Other courts have limited the definition of "services or facilities" in section 2(e) to services or materials directly related to advertising, promotions or merchandising.

. . . Even assuming that delivery is a "service" as that term is used in section 2(e), the actions of Champion do not violate that section. Purdy does not assert that Champion delivered in a discriminatory manner a product it had agreed to sell . . . rather Purdy complains that Champion refused to sell certain product lines to it and eventually terminated its dealership. It has long been recognized that the statute does not require a seller to sell to, or maintain a customer relationship with, any buyer or prospective buyer. Thus, the termination of the franchise agreement did not violate the Act. Moreover, refusal to sell a line of products to a prospective customer while maintaining sales of the product to other customers is similarly not the type of discrimination prohibited by the Robinson-Patman Act. Therefore, neither Champion's refusal to sell the Titan and Concord lines to Purdy, nor its termination of the franchise agreement, violated section 2(e).

Case Questions

1. How do you define the issue in this case?

2. How can *Purdy Mobile Homes* be used by a distributor to punish a complaining customer? What is the ultimate in discrimination?

3. The Seventh Circuit Court of Appeals in a previous case held that delivery of a product is a "service or facility" within the meaning of section 2(e). Why did Purdy not have to answer that question? What if you had to answer the question? Would it make any difference if there was a separate charge for the transportation? Explain.

4. How would you change the facts in this case to make it a section 2(d) case?

5. How could Purdy have protected itself so as to avoid the result in this case?

Cost justification and lack of competitive injury are not available defenses to a section 2(d) or section 2(e) violation. Nonetheless, they have been considered by courts in determining whether a promotional plan is discriminatory. The meeting competition defense is available in a proper section 2(d) or section 2(e) case. As with a section 2(a) price discrimination case, the seller must show that more favorable services or allowances are designed in good faith to meet, not beat, competition.

ENFORCEMENT

The Robinson-Patman Act is enforced civilly and criminally in the same manner as the other antitrust laws. A detailed discussion of enforcement procedures appears in Chapter 5. Although the Justice Department and the FTC have concurrent power to civilly enforce the statute, in practice the Justice Department usually defers to FTC jurisdiction. Exceptions occur in extraordinary cases, where, for example, the defendant's conduct also violated the Sherman Act.

Robinson-Patman violations may be prosecuted criminally by the Justice Department. Penalties of up to $5,000 and one-year imprisonment may be imposed. These sanctions are rarely invoked. The most effective enforcements are the private treble-damage actions, which proceed in the same manner as other private antitrust actions.

POLICY CONSIDERATIONS

The Robinson-Patman Act has survived criticism for over 40 years. One of the more serious indictments against the act is that its injunction against price discrimination places artificial restraints upon competition and thus actually injures competition. Critics of Robinson-Patman contend that it reduces the vigor of competition by inhibiting the competitive pricing process, encouraging price-fixing, and forcing departures from the most efficient ways of doing business. They argue that these effects and the added cost of compliance, avoidance, and in some cases evasion of the act push prices upward. The higher prices are ultimately borne by the consumer. Due in large part to these criticisms various committees, authorized to study the act over the years, have urged its reform. Some critics of Robinson-Patman advocate its outright repeal. Others opt for a compromise that would place fewer restrictions on pricing activities than the present act.

To date, the critics of Robinson-Patman have gone unheeded. The act's supporters point to the protection it affords small business and to the absence of hard-core data buttressing the contentions of its critics.

Until legislative revision occurs, the business manager needs to be concerned about the present act's application. And, although the FTC's enforcement of the act has ground down considerably over the past 20 years, the increase in private treble-damage suits should be sufficient to encourage a high level of interest in its workings.

Review problems

1. Mayer Paving & Asphalt Company was in the asphalt paving business in Skokie, Illinois. Material Service Corporation produced and distributed crushed limestone, sand, and other compounds used in the paving and construction business. It operated five quarries in Chicago and distributed its products to paving and construction contractors in Indiana and Illinois. Material Service charged Mayer Paving more for crushed stone

than it charged Mayer Paving's competitors, all of which were located in Illinois. Mayer Paving complains that Material Service has violated section 2(a) of the Robinson-Patman Act. Does the court have jurisdiction to hear the case? Explain.

2. The *Bismarck Tribune* is a daily newspaper based in Bismarck, North Dakota. The *Morning Pioneer* is a daily newspaper based in Mandan, North Dakota, which is about seven miles from Bismarck. The two newspapers have a long history of coexistence, each serving its own market area without attempting to infringe the market of the other. Recent developments have caused this amicable relationship to break down, and the *Tribune* is now waging an active campaign to capture the Mandan market. In its attempt to win the *Pioneer's* customers the *Tribune* has reduced the price of its newspaper delivered in Mandan below the Bismarck price. The *Tribune* delivered in Mandan contains older news than the *Tribune* delivered in Bismarck. Also the *Tribune* advertisements are valuable only to those persons who shop in Bismarck. The *Pioneer* has brought an action to prevent the *Tribune* from engaging in what the *Pioneer* considers illegal activity in violation of section 2(a) of the Robinson-Patman Act. What is the *Pioneer's* argument? What is the *Tribune's* counterargument?

3. JLG Industries, a Pennsylvania corporation, manufacturers self-lifting work platforms. Burress, a Virginia distributor of these platforms, purchased several of them from JLG, pursuant to a distributorship agreement. While the agreement was in force, JLG attempted to coerce Burress to enter into a new, substantially less favorable distributorship agreement. At the same time JLG was offering other companies more favorable price terms for a distributorship. Burress rejected the new agreement and continued under the old distributorship until it expired. Burress then instituted suit against JLG, alleging a price discrimination violation. Who will prevail, and why?

4. Fred Meyer, Inc., operates a chain of 13 retail supermarkets in the Portland, Oregon, area. Meyer annually conducts a four-week promotional campaign in its stores based on the distribution of coupon books to consumers. The consumer buys a book for 10 cents and surrenders the appropriate coupon when purchasing particular goods. Aside from the 10 cents paid by the consumer for the coupon book, Meyer finances the promotion by charging the supplier of each featured product a fee of at least $350 per coupon-page of advertising. In addition, some suppliers replace, at no cost, a percentage of goods sold during the campaign. The FTC has commenced action against Meyer, alleging that its scheme violates the Robinson-Patman Act. The FTC contends that Meyer's actions have put the wholesale customers of Meyer's supplier at a competitive disadvantage because the concessions granted to Meyer are not granted to the wholesalers. Do you agree with the FTC? Explain. If not, is Meyer's scheme violative of the Robinson-Patman Act in any way? Explain. What defenses may be available to Meyer?

5. Sun Oil Company (Sun), a major integrated refiner and distributor of petroleum products, markets a single grade of gasoline under the trade name Sunoco in 18 states. Gilbert McLean is the lessee-operator of a Sunoco gas station in Jacksonville, Florida. He operates in a sales territory which includes eight other Sun stations. Initially all Sun stations within McLean's territory received gasoline from Sun at the same price and obtained the same profit upon resale to the public. Four months after McLean began business, the Super Test Oil Company opened a Super Test gas station diagonally across the street from McLean and began selling its gasoline at a price far below the price at which McLean and the other Sun stations within his territory sold their gasoline. After suffering dramatic losses due to the competition of the Super Test station, McLean appealed to Sun and was granted a price reduction. This reduction was not extended to any other Sun dealers within

McLean's territory. As a result of the reduction in price McLean was able to compete with the Super Test station. McLean also succeeded in luring customers away from the other Sun stations within his sales territory. The FTC brought action against Sun, alleging a violation of the Clayton Act. What action on Sun's part would the FTC find objectionable? Can Sun justify its policy? Would the situation be different if Sun could prove that the Super Test station's supplier was offering Super Test at a reduced price?

6. Morton Salt Company manufactures and sells different brands of table salt to wholesalers and larger retail grocery chains. Its finest brand, Blue Label, is sold on a "standard quantity discount system." Blue Label purchasers pay a delivered price based on the quantities bought:

	Per case
Less than carload purchases............	$1.60
Carload purchases	1.50
5,000-case purchases in any consecutive 12 months	1.40
50,000-case purchases in any consecutive 12 months	1.35

Only five companies operating large chains of retail stores have been able to buy Blue Label at $1.35 per case. Because of the discount these companies command, they are able to sell Blue Label at retail cheaper than the wholesaler purchasers can sell it to independently operated retail stores. Many of those independently operated stores compete directly with the retail outlets of the five large chains. The FTC seeks to enjoin Morton from sales of salt under this discount system. Identify and discuss the key issues.

7. Simplicity manufactures and sells tissue patterns which are used in the home for making women's and children's wearing apparel. The patterns are sold throughout the United States to about 12,300 retailers with a total of 17,200 outlets. These customers can be divided into two categories. Department and variety stores comprise 18 per cent of Simplicity's customers but account for 70 per

cent of its total sales volume. The remaining 82 per cent of Simplicity's customers are small stores whose primary business is the sale of yard-good fabrics. While not all of the 17,200 retail outlets are in direct competition with one another, in most cities there is substantial competition between the variety and fabric stores in the sale of Simplicity patterns. Simplicity offers its patterns to its customers at a uniform price. However, it furnishes the patterns to the variety stores on a consignment basis, thus affording them an investment-free inventory. In addition, Simplicity furnishes cabinets, catalogs, and transportation to the variety stores. The fabric stores are not allowed to sell on consignment and are obliged to pay for all services offered to them by Simplicity. Simplicity justifies its actions by explaining that the cost of supplying such services to the variety stores is substantially below the cost of supplying similar services to the fabric stores. Furthermore, Simplicity contends that the fabric stores suffer no competitive injury as a result of its policies with regard to the variety stores. The FTC has commenced a suit against Simplicity in an attempt to enjoin its discriminatory practices. Has Simplicity violated any provision of the Robinson-Patman Act? Explain. Does Simplicity have a defense? Explain.

8. S. J. Greene Company wholesaled frozen and prepared seafood products. E. J. Kozin Company took over a seafood business that was in competition with Greene. Bernard Kane, Greene's sales manager and the son-in-law of Greenes president, left Greene to become a director and officer of Kozin as well as its principal shareholder. Thereafter Kane persuaded Greene officials to purchase substantial quantities of seafood from Kozin. In return he received $19,780 in sales commissions from Kozin. Greene went bankrupt, and the trustee in bankruptcy brought a treble-damage action against the Kozin Company and Kane, alleging a violation of section 2(c) of the Robinson-Patman Act. Decide the case.

9. Kroger Company operates a chain of more than 1,400 retail grocery stores located in 19 states. Its sales exceed $2 billion a year. The competitors of Kroger's Charleston Division include national and regional chains and independent supermarkets.

Beatrice Foods, a large U.S. dairy company, has $569 million in annual sales. Beatrice supplies Kroger's Charleston Division.

Kroger decided to employ private label sales in order to become more competitive. It invited companies to submit bids for bottling Kroger-label milk for its Charleston Division. Broughton submitted the first bid. Beatrice officials then met with a Kroger representative in the hope of making a successful bid for bottling Kroger's private brand milk.

When a Beatrice official said that his company would offer a 15 per cent discount, the Kroger representative replied, "Well, forget it—I've already got one at 20 per cent off the list price." Actually, Kroger had not received any bid lower than the Beatrice offer. Beatrice then offered to meet the 20 per cent discount, and Kroger accepted the offer. Is Beatrice in violation of the Robinson-Patman Act? Why or why not? Is Kroger in violation of the act? Why or why not?

10. Explain why many perceive the Robinson-Patman Act to be inconsistent with main-line antitrust philosophy.

CHAPTER 9

Franchising

The average person considering franchising is likely to think of the numerous fast-food chains commonly found along major streets. Franchising, however, encompasses a much broader segment of the marketplace. Franchises cover real estate brokerages, accounting and bookkeeping services, computer software, temporary help and other employment services, car rentals, building supplies, and a myriad of other areas. Virtually anything which has a marketing plan and can be packaged into something salable can be franchised. Two marketing and management experts have described the franchise relationship as follows:

> The basis of franchising is a contract, or franchise, by which a franchisor in return for a consideration, and the assumption of certain responsibilities by the franchisee, grants to the franchisee the right to use a trademark or copyright. Commonly, the brand or trademark applies to the system according to which business under that franchise is to be conducted as well as to the product or service which is the subject of the franchise.[1]

Franchising has expanded tremendously in recent years. It has enabled franchisors to establish national distribution networks with minimal capital outlays while enabling small local concerns to affiliate with nationally known operations. This chapter explores how the antitrust laws have affected this burgeoning method of marketing.

THE FTC FRANCHISE RULE

Chapter 5 discussed the prohibitions against unfair methods of competition and unfair or deceptive trade practices contained in section 5 of the Federal Trade Commission Act. It noted that the act encompasses the Sherman and Clayton acts but is broader than those statutes in coverage. The FTC has the authority to promulgate trade regulation rules setting basic

---

[1] Jones and Hamacher, "Franchising," in *Marketing Manager's Handbook* 765 (Britt ed. 1978).

standards of lawful business conduct. In response to widespread evidence of abuses by franchisors in the marketing of franchises, the FTC has promulgated a rule governing the offering of franchises. The rule requires that all franchisors subject to it provide a prospective franchisee with a document containing specific disclosures.

The rule's coverage

The FTC rule is designed to cover all sellers of franchises, including retail businesses, distribution rights for trademarked products, and vending machine route programs. The rule applies to franchises, which it defines as contractual relationships of either of two types. The first type has three requirements:

1. The franchisee offers, sells, or distributes goods, commodities, or services which are either identified by the franchisor's trademark, trade name, or other commercial symbol or are required to meet the franchisor's quality standards, and the franchisee operates under the trademark, trade name, or other commercial symbol of the franchisor. A McDonald's franchisee would meet both alternatives of this requirement. A McDonald's franchisee offers food for sale under such commercial symbols as Big Mac and Egg McMuffin. The franchisee is also required to meet the franchisor's standards governing the quality of food served and operates under the McDonald's name using such commercial symbols as golden arches. A Coca-Cola bottler is also covered because, although the bottler may operate under its own name, it distributes soft drinks identified by the franchisor's trademarks such as Coca-Cola, Tab, and Sprite. Finally, a franchisee operating a Century 21 real estate brokerage franchise is covered because, although it does not distribute any trademarked items, it is required to meet the franchisor's quality standards and operates under the Century 21 trademark.

2. The franchisor exercises significant control over the franchisee's methods of operation or gives the franchisee significant assistance in its methods of operation. Areas of significant control or assistance include the franchisee's business organization, promotional activities, management, or marketing plan.

3. The franchisee is obligated to pay a fee of at least $500 to the franchisor within six months after starting business.

The rule also has three requirements for the second type of franchise:

1. The franchisee offers, sells, or distributes goods, commodities, or services which are either supplied by the franchisor or are supplied by another party with which the franchisee is required to deal.

2. The franchisor secures for the franchisee retail outlets, accounts, or sites for vending machines, rack displays, or similar sales displays.

3. The franchisee is obligated to pay a fee of at least $500 to the franchisor within six months after starting business.

The first type of franchise encompasses what marketing experts have traditionally called a franchise—a marketing system centered on uniform standards and a trademark or trade name. The second type involves business opportunities such as middleperson distributorships and vending machine supply contracts which are not centered on specific trademarks or subject to uniform standards.

The FTC rule excepts employment relationships, relationships among general partners, cooperative associations, certification and testing services, and single-trademark licenses. For example, it does not apply to a distributor or vending machine supplier who is an employee of the alleged franchisor. The rule also does not cover membership cooperative associations such as Topco, Inc., whose exclusive territories were explored in Chapter 5. This is so even though all members of the association sell goods identified by the Topco trademark.

In separate rulings, oil and gasoline franchises and automobile dealerships have also been exempted by the FTC. Oil and gasoline franchises are subject to the Petroleum Marketing Practices Act, which duplicates much of the regulation contained in the rule. Automobile dealers must make large initial investments. They are usually relatively knowledgeable investors or use independent business advisers and engage in extended negotiations before entering a franchise relationship. The FTC therefore concluded that the protections provided by its rule were not needed by either gasoline or automobile franchisees.[2]

The purpose of the rule is to protect franchisees against prerule abuses. Previously franchisors received immediate payment of large sums of money from franchisees but failed to fulfill their promises to the franchisees, leaving the franchisees without any effective means of legal redress. Thus franchises are covered by the rule only when the franchisee is required to pay the franchisor $500 or more within six months after starting business. If a franchisor wishes to avoid the rule without disrupting its system, it may do so by not requiring such a payment. The $500 limit includes not only payments made for the right to have a franchise but also payments made by the franchisee for tools, equipment, promotional material, and other goods and services provided by the franchisor. For the franchisor who takes this route to avoid compliance with the FTC rule, problems may arise in connection with franchisee payments for inventory, optional franchisee payments, and franchisee payments required after the six months.

Payments for inventory.   The typical retail franchisee is required to establish an initial inventory. For example, new automobile dealerships are required to purchase an initial inventory of vehicles, parts, and accessories. Inventory purchases are not considered required payment if they are made in quantities which a reasonable entrepreneur would require and at bona fide wholesale prices.

Where inventory requirements are unreasonable in price or quantity, the FTC may view them as required payments.

---

[2] 975 ATRR (BNA) at E–1 (1980).

Optional payments. Purchases of noninventory items may be considered required payments where these items may be obtained only from the franchisor. To avoid this, franchisors can allow their franchisees to purchase equipment, tools, training and promotional materials, and other goods and services from alternative sources. This transforms required payments into optional ones. The franchisee's option to purchase from alternative sources must be realistic in light of the industry and community. The factors considered by the FTC include the franchisor's financial incentive to require payments to it for optional items, franchisor pressure on the franchisee to make such payments, and the availability of competitive sources of supply.

The FTC has indicated that it is particularly suspicious of real estate purchases and leases where the franchisor has considerable incentive to require the franchisee to use franchisor-owned property that would otherwise be unproductive. In two advisory opinions the FTC has indicated that service station leases will be considered required payments even though the franchisee has the option of leasing a station from other sources, purchasing an existing station, or constructing a new station. Traffic patterns, traffic access, and zoning restrictions give existing leases a comparative advantage over other alternatives, while the initial capital required and uncertainties in financing make the purchase or construction of a new station a dubious possibility for new franchisees.[3]

Payment required after the first six months. The FTC's franchise rule assumes that in six months the franchisee will become sufficiently familiar with the franchisor to be able to make informed judgments about the relationship. Thus payments to be made after the first six months are not counted in determining the rule's applicability. A franchisor can avoid the rule's operation by accepting a promissory note payable later than six months from the start of business. For the note to be effective the franchisor must not be able to discount it and thus destroy the franchisee's ability to assert legal defenses in the collection process.

Required disclosure

All franchisors covered by the FTC rule must furnish a disclosure document to prospective franchisees. The rule does not provide for prior review of the document by the FTC. The cover of the document must contain the following statement in boldface 12-point type:

INFORMATION FOR PROSPECTIVE FRANCHISEES
REQUIRED BY FEDERAL TRADE COMMISSION

* * *. * *

To protect you, we've required your franchisor to give you this information. *We haven't checked it, and don't know if it's correct.* It should help you make up your mind. Study it carefully. While it includes some information about your contract, don't

---

[3] FTC Franchise Advisory Opinions Nos. 17 and 18 to Sinclair Marketing, Inc., and Marathon Oil Co. (Oct. 1, 1979, and Oct. 5, 1979).

rely on it alone to understand your contract. Read all of your contract carefully. Buying a franchise is a complicated investment. Take your time to decide. If possible, show your contract and this information to an advisor, like a lawyer or an accountant. If you find anything you think may be wrong or anything important that's been left out, you should let us know about it. It may be against the law.

There may also be laws on franchising in your state. Ask your state agencies about them.

Federal Trade Commission
Washington, D.C. 20580

The document must then set forth the franchisor's name and address and the names of its officers and directors. It must state the business experience of the officers and directors; their felony convictions, if any, for fraud, embezzlement, fraudulent conversion, misappropriation of property, or restraint of trade; all of their involvements in civil or administrative agency litigation concerning fraud, dishonesty, or the franchise relationship; and any bankruptcy proceedings in which they have been involved. The document must describe the franchise, including its trademarks, format, the market for its goods or services, and its expected competition. It must disclose the requirements that must be met by franchisees, including initial and recurring payments, obligations to purchase goods from the franchisor or affiliated companies, and personal participation in operating the franchise. It must also disclose the restrictions on franchisee territories, customers, or site selection and describe the financing and training programs made available for the franchisor. Finally, the document must provide information on the grounds for terminating the franchise or denying its renewal, statistics on the number of franchisees terminated in the past year, and balance sheets and income statements for the last three years. The financial statements need not be certified, but they must be prepared in accordance with generally accepted accounting and auditing procedures.

Earning predictions

If the franchisor makes any representations stating a specific level of potential sales, income, or profit for the prospective franchisee, there must be a reasonable basis for the representations, and the material constituting that basis must be made available to prospective franchisees and the FTC. The representations must be made in a separate document containing all bases and assumptions, the number and percentage of franchise outlets known to have at least equaled the predicted record, and the dates on which that record was attained. The document must also contain the following statement in boldface 12-point type:

CAUTION

These figures are only estimates of what we think you may earn. There is no assurance you'll do as well. If you rely upon our figures, you must accept the risk of not doing so well.

Some franchisors do not attempt to predict what prospective franchisees will earn. Instead they advise prospective franchisees of the sales, income, or profits of existing outlets, allowing the prospects to infer that they will do as well. Where earnings of existing outlets are given, similar disclosures must be made. The document in such a case must also contain the following in boldface 12-point type:

CAUTION

Some outlets have (sold) (earned) this amount. There is no assurance you'll do as well. If you reply upon our figures, you must accept the risk of not doing so well.

All such earnings statements must have cover sheets with the following in boldface 12-point type:

INFORMATION FOR PROSPECTIVE FRANCHISEES
ABOUT FRANCHISE (SALES) (INCOME) (PROFIT)
REQUIRED BY THE FEDERAL TRADE COMMISSION

To protect you, we've required the franchisor to give you this information. *We haven't checked it and don't know if it's correct.* Study these facts and figures carefully. If possible, show them to someone who can advise you, like a lawyer or an accountant. Then take your time and think it over.

If you find anything you think may be wrong or anything important that's been left out, let us know about it. It may be against the law.

There may also be laws on franchising in your state. Ask your state agencies about them.

Federal Trade Commission
Washington, D.C.

Violations of the rule

Franchisors who violate the FTC rule are subject to civil fines of up to $10,000. The FTC may also bring actions for damages on behalf of franchisees in federal district court. The FTC's formidable enforcement powers are illustrated by its first enforcement action under the rule. H. N. Singer, Inc., promised investors in Hot Box Products frozen pizza distributorships "$100,000 per Year and More" and further promised to secure in advance such retail accounts as bowling alleys and bars. The accounts did not materialize, and there was no reasonable basis for the earnings claim. The FTC proceeded administratively against H. N. Singer, Inc., and obtained from the U.S. District Court for Northern California a preliminary injunction freezing the assets of the franchisor and its four controlling offices.[4]

SECTION 3 OF THE CLAYTON ACT

Chapter 5 explored the prohibitions of section 3 of the Clayton Act as applied to exclusive dealing arrangements and tie-in devices. These prohib-

---

[4] 976 ATRR (BNA) E–2 (1980).

itions have particular relevance to franchising because the franchisor usually wishes to control much of the franchisee's operations to insure uniform quality. The prohibitions will now be explored in this context.

Exclusive dealing

Significant advantages to both parties are provided by exclusive dealing contracts which obligate the franchisee to purchase all of its requirements for a given product from the franchisor. Such contracts assure the franchisee of a steady supply of goods meeting the franchisor's quality control standards. They assure the franchisor that the franchisee is furthering the uniformity the franchise is built around. These advantages, however, do not necessarily insulate a franchisor-franchisee exclusive dealing contract from antitrust attack. In the following case the Federal Trade Commission relied on the policies underlying section 3 of the Clayton Act to attack Brown Shoe's exclusive dealing contracts under section 5 of the FTC Act.

FTC v. Brown Shoe Co.
384 U.S. 316 (1966)

Brown, one of the world's largest shoe manufacturers, entered into franchise agreements with 650 independent retailers. Under these agreements Brown obligated itself to provide franchisees with services which it did not make available to other retailers. The services included architectural plans, costly merchandising records, assistance from a Brown field representative, and the right to participate in group insurance at rates lower than would have been available to the franchisees individually. In return the franchisee promised to "[c]oncentrate my business within the grades and price lines of shoes representing Brown Shoe Company Franchises of the Brown Division and will have no lines conflicting with Brown Division Brands of the Brown Shoe Company."

The FTC found that the franchise program "effectively foreclosed Brown's competitors from selling to a substantial number of retail shoe dealers." The commission concluded that the program was an unfair method of competition in violation of section 5. The court of appeals reversed, and the Supreme Court reversed the court of appeals.

Mr. Justice Black:

* * * * *

. . . [T]he question we have for decision is whether the Federal Trade Commission can declare it to be an unfair practice for Brown, the second largest manufacturer of shoes in the Nation, to pay a valuable consideration to hundreds of retail shoe purchasers in order to secure a contractual promise from them that they will not purchase conflicting lines of shoes from Brown's competitors. We hold that the Commission has power to find, on the record here, such an anticompetitive practice unfair, subject of course to judicial review.

* * * * *

. . . [I]t is now recognized . . . that the Commission has broad powers to declare trade practices unfair. This broad power of the Commission is particularly well established with regard to trade practices which conflict with the basic policies of the Sherman and Clayton Acts even though such practices may not actually violate these laws. The record in this case shows beyond doubt that Brown, the country's second largest manufacturer of shoes, has a program, which requires shoe retailers, unless faithless to their contractual obligations with Brown, substantially to limit their trade with Brown's competitors. This program obviously conflicts with the central policy of both §1 of the Sherman Act and §3 of the Clayton Act against contracts which take away freedom of purchasers to buy in an open market. Brown nevertheless contends that the Commission had no power to declare the franchise program unfair without proof that its effect "may be to substantially lessen competition or tend to create a monopoly," which of course would have to be proved if the Government were proceeding against Brown under §3 of the Clayton Act rather than §5 of the Federal Trade Commission Act. We reject the argument that proof of this §3 element must be made for as we pointed out above our cases hold that the Commission has power under §5 to arrest trade restraints in their incipiency without proof that they amount to an outright violation of §3 of the Clayton Act or other provisions of the antitrust laws. This power of the Commission was emphatically stated in *F.T.C.* v. *Motion Picture Adv. Co.*

"It is . . . clear that the Federal Trade Commission Act was designed to supplement and bolster the Sherman Act and the Clayton Act . . . to stop in their incipiency acts and practices which, when full blown, would violate those Acts . . . as well as to condemn as 'unfair methods of competition' existing violations of them."

We hold that the Commission acted well within its authority in declaring the Brown franchise program unfair whether it was completely full blown or not.

Case questions

1. Did the Brown Shoe exclusive dealing contracts violate section 3 of the Clayton Act?

2. What was unfair about the Brown Shoe franchise agreement?

3. If Brown Shoe had been a smaller company, would the franchise program have been legal? If Brown Shoe had offered its plan to new dealers rather than existing retailers, would the plan have been legal?

Although *Brown Shoe* found the franchisor-franchisee exclusive dealing contract illegal, courts and the FTC have generally permitted franchisors to require franchisees to stock a representative cross section of the franchisor's products in quantities sufficient to meet the demand for them. This requirement serves the franchisor's legitimate interest in marketing its products without unduly restricting franchisee choice. Thus a Chevrolet dealer can be required to keep a reasonable quantity of General Motors replacement parts on hand. This enables GM to advertise that its parts are available from the local Chevrolet dealer while allowing the dealer to offer competing brands.

Tie-in devices

As discussed in Chapter 5, tie-ins may violate section 3 of the Clayton Act and section 1 of the Sherman Act. Franchisors must therefore exercise caution in assembling packages of goods for their franchisees. If the goods in such packages are not generally sold together, the franchisors may be liable for violating section 3.

Most tie-in liability for franchisors arises under section 1 of the Sherman Act. At one time many franchisors required their franchisees to purchase certain goods only from them. This requirement assured the franchisor of a market for its products and of a uniform quality of product at all outlets. The franchisor's goodwill is dependent upon the assurance of uniform quality. The reputation associated with the trademark is the heart of the franchisor's marketing scheme. If a local outlet is substandard, the negative repercussions will be felt by all franchisees.

Although such purchasing requirements were the subject of several previous challenges, the most significant development in the law was the decision of the Ninth Circuit Court of Appeals in *Siegel* v. *Chicken Delight, Inc.*[5] The franchisees of Chicken Delight, a fast-food franchisor, paid no franchise fees or royalties but were required to purchase their cookers, fryers, packaging supplies, and coating mixes from it. The prices charged by Chicken Delight for these items were higher than those charged for comparable items by other potential suppliers. Siegel, a disenchanted franchisee, sued, alleging that the cookers, fryers, packaging supplies, and coating mixes were illegally tied to the license to use the Chicken Delight trademark.

A trademark license is not a tangible commodity. Consequently, section 3 of the Clayton Act could not apply. Siegel therefore alleged that Chicken Delight's purchasing requirement was per se unreasonable in violation of section 1 of the Sherman Act. Recall from Chapter 5 that a per se illegal tie-in under section 1 must meet these conditions: two distinct products, sufficient power in the tying product to enforce the tie-in, and a not insubstantial amount of commerce affected.

It was agreed that the amount of commerce affected was not insubstantial. The court then held that the trademark license was a separate product, distinct from the items allegedly tied to it. It compared the trademark to a good protected by patent or copyright. It reasoned that because trademark protection conferred a legal monopoly to determine who might use the mark, sufficient economic power to enforce the tie would be presumed as a matter of law. Rejecting Chicken Delight's contention that the tie-in was necessary for quality control, the court noted that by providing specifications, the franchisor could maintain uniform quality without severely restraining competition.

The *Chicken Delight* case raised numerous questions of antitrust policy which have not been definitively resolved by the Supreme Court or Congress. Should a trademark license be considered a tying product separate from the items that the franchisee is required to purchase? Would the answer be the same if Chicken Delight merely requires its franchisees to purchase their chicken from it as it would be if Chicken Delight extended the requirement to paper plates and napkins? The FTC and most circuit courts of appeal have followed the view of the Ninth Circuit expressed in *Chicken*

---

[5] 448 F.2d 43 (9th Cir. 1971).

Delight. Some courts, most notably the Second Circuit, have disagreed. The disagreement can be traced to differing views on the nature of a trademark.

Strictly speaking, a trademark is any arbitrary and fanciful commercial symbol that is affixed to a product to designate its origin. When a trademark is registered with the U.S. Patent Office, it places the entire population on notice of its existence. The use of a symbol confusingly similar to a trademark infringes the trademark and leaves the user liable to the trademark holder. By definition, a trademark cannot be separated from the products it identifies. This view of the trademark has persuaded the Second Circuit that no tie-in exists where a franchisor requires its franchisees to purchase those products from itself. Under this view it is impossible to separate the McDonald's trademark from McDonald's hamburgers. The more remote a product is from a trademark, the easier it is to separate the product from the trademark. It is easier to find a tie-in in required purchases of McDonald's napkins than in required purchases of McDonald's hamburgers, and easier still to find one in required purchases of the sponges used to clean the restaurant tables.

Most courts and the FTC take a broader view of the nature of a trademark. They view trademark licensing, in the context of franchising, as a burgeoning distinct commercial practice. In that context the trademark becomes an emblem of a uniform quality of product and a uniform system of operation. The goodwill of the trademark attaches to the system itself. Under this view the franchisor may require franchisees to purchase items from it only when this is necessary to protect the integrity of the system. Where less restrictive alternatives are available, the items may be distinguished from the trademark license and accordingly found to be tied to it.

The following decision of the Fourth Circuit Court of Appeals takes a middle-of-the-road approach to the problem.

Principe v. McDonald's Corp.
631 F.2d 303 (4th Cir. 1980)

McDonald's principal business is franchising limited-menu fast-food restaurants. McDonald's develops new restaurants according to master plans which utilize demographic data to evaluate potential sites. The most favorable sites are selected, and development of an area is planned three years ahead. The land is acquired, the building is constructed, and a franchisee is approved. The franchisee pays a franchise fee and a periodic royalty and is required to lease the real estate from McDonald's at a rental of 8½ percent of gross sales. The franchise and lease both run for 20 years, and termination of one termi-

nates the other. Neither is available separately. Principe sued McDonald's, claiming that the compulsory lease was a tie-in in violation of the Sherman Act.

Phillips, Circuit Judge:

* * * * *

As support for their position the Principes rely primarily on the decision of the Ninth Circuit in *Siegel* v. *Chicken Delight, Inc.,* one of the first cases to address the problem of franchise tie-ins. Chicken Delight was what McDonald's characterizes as a "rent a name" franchisor; it licensed franchisees to sell chicken under the Chicken Delight name but did not own store premises or fixtures. The company did not even charge franchise fees or realty fees. Instead, it required its franchisees to purchase a specified number of cookers and fryers and to purchase certain packaging supplies and mixes exclusively from Chicken Delight. These supplies were priced higher than comparable goods of competing sellers. . . .

. . . Viewing the essence of a Chicken Delight franchise as the franchisor's trademark, the court sought to determine whether requiring franchisees to purchase common supplies from Chicken Delight was necessary to ensure that their operations lived up to the quality standards the trademark represented. Judged by this standard, the aggregation was found to consist of separate products:

> This being so, it is apparent that the goodwill of the Chicken Delight trademark does not attach to the multitude of separate articles used in the operation of the licensed system or in the production of its end product. It is not what is used, but how it is used and what results that have given the system and its end product their entitlement to trademark protection. It is to the system and the end product that the public looks with the confidence that established goodwill has created.

*   *   *   *   *

The Principes urge this court to apply the *Chicken Delight* reasoning to invalidate the McDonald's franchise lease note aggregation. They urge that McDonald's can protect the integrity of its trademarks by specifying how its franchisees shall operate, where they may locate their restaurants and what types of buildings they may erect. Customers do not and have no reason to connect the building's owner with the McDonald's operation conducted therein. Since company ownership of store premises is not an essential element of the trademark's goodwill, the Principes argue, the franchise, lease and note are separable products tied together in violation of the antitrust laws.

*   *   *   *   *

Without disagreeing with the result in *Chicken Delight,* we conclude that the court's emphasis in that case upon the trademark as the essence of a franchise is too restrictive. Far from merely licensing franchisees to sell products under its trade name, a modern franchisor such as McDonald's offers its franchisees a complete method of doing business. It takes people from all walks of life, sends them to its management school, and teaches them a variety of skills ranging from hamburger grilling to financial planning. It installs them in stores whose market has been researched and whose location has been selected by experts to maximize sales potential. It inspects every facet of every store several times a year and consults with each franchisee about his operation's strengths and weaknesses. Its regime pervades all facets of the business; from the design of the menu board to the amount of catsup on the hamburgers, nothing is left to chance. This pervasive franchisor supervision and control benefits [*sic*] the franchisee in turn. His business is identified with a network of stores whose very uniformity and predictability attracts customers. In short, the modern franchisee pays not only for the right to use a trademark but for the right to become a part of a system whose business methods virtually guarantee his success. It is often unrealistic to view a franchise agreement as little more than a trademark license.

Given the realities of modern franchising, we think the proper inquiry is not whether the allegedly tied products are associated in the public mind with the franchisor's trademark, but whether they are integral components of the business method being franchised. Where the challenged aggregation is an essential ingredient of the franchised system's formula for success, there is but a single product and no tie-in exists as a matter of law.

Applying this standard to the present case we hold the lease is not separable from the McDonald's franchise to which it pertains. McDonald's practice of developing a system of company-owned restaurants operated by franchisees has substantial advantages both for the company and for franchisees. It is part of what make a McDonald's franchise uniquely attractive to franchisors.

First, because it approaches the problem of restaurant site selection systematically, McDonald's is able to obtain better sites than franchisees could select. Armed with its demographic information, guided by its staff of experts and unencumbered by preferences of individual franchisees, McDonald's can wield its economic might to acquire sites where new restaurants will prosper without undercutting existing franchisees' business or limiting future expansion. . . .

Second, McDonald's policy of owning all its own restaurants assures that the stores remain part of the McDonald's system. McDonald's franchise arrangements are not static. Franchisees retire or die. Occasionally they do not live up to their franchise obligations and must be replaced; even if no such contingency intervenes, the agreements normally expire by their own terms after twenty years. If franchisees owned their own stores, any of these events could disrupt McDonald's business and have a negative effect on the system's goodwill. . . .

Third, because McDonald's acquires the sites and builds the stores itself, it can select franchisees based on their management potential rather than their real estate expertise or wealth. Ability to emphasize management skills is important to McDonald's because it has built its reputation largely on the consistent quality of its operations rather than on the merits of its hamburgers. A store's quality is largely a function of its management. McDonald's policy of owning its own stores reduces a franchisee's initial investment, thereby broadening the applicant base and opening the door to persons who otherwise could not afford a McDonald's franchise. . . .

Finally, because both McDonald's and the franchisee have a substantial financial stake in the success of the restaurant, their relationship becomes a sort of partnership that might be impossible under other circumstances. . . .

All of these factors contribute significantly to the overall success of the McDonald's system. The formula that produced systemwide success, the formula that promises to make each new McDonald's store successful, that formula is what McDonald's sells its franchisees. To characterize the franchise as an unnecessary aggregation of separate products tied to the McDonald's name is to miss the point entirely. . . .

Case questions

1. Why did the court decline to follow *Chicken Delight?* Explain the differences between the perceptions of the franchise held by this court and the perceptions held by the court in *Chicken Delight.*

2. What factors led the court to conclude that the franchise and the lease were not separate products?

3. Could the lease arrangement have been attacked as an illegal dealer location restriction?

Not all courts which have agreed with the Ninth Circuit that the trademark license may be a tying product, have also agreed that as a matter of law the franchisor is presumed to have sufficient power to enforce the tie-in. Two different views have emerged. Some courts view the trademark as analogous to the patent or copyright because it also confers a legal monopoly. Without the consent of the franchisor, the franchisee may not use the trademark or operate the franchise. According to this view, in all instances the franchisee will be forced to buy the required items from the franchisor.

Other courts distinguish the trademark from the patent and copyright. Whereas the patent or copyright protect the product itself, guaranteeing that the product is unique, the trademark only protects the symbol affixed to the product. The legally unique name, these courts reason, does not by itself justify a presumption of economic power. These courts require a showing that the franchisor has the power to raise prices or impose burdensome terms on an appreciable number of franchisees. It is usually not difficult to make such a showing. Most franchisees enter the franchise relationship because of their desire to benefit from the success and goodwill associated with the franchise name. Thus the practical effect of the two views on the presumption of economic power is more apparent than real.

All courts and the FTC have recognized that a tie-in may be necessary where the franchisor lacks less restrictive means to effectuate its quality control program. For example, a tie-in may be justified where specifications would be so detailed and cumbersome that they cannot be practicably supplied. This justification is most likely to be accepted for products whose technology has been developed recently or is changing rapidly. As the technology develops further, however, the franchisor will have to require the franchisee to follow specifications.

A second justification that has been accepted for franchise tie-ins is that specifications are impossible because the quality control is subjective. For example, the FTC allowed a restaurant franchisor to tie its coffee to the franchise license because it was impossible to specify a formula for the appropriate blend of coffee beans. The blend depended upon the quality of the different types of beans and the appropriate blend could only be obtained by tasting the coffee.[6]

A strong argument can be made that a tie-in is also justified when the formula for the tied product is a trade secret. To some it seems unreasonable to require a franchisor to divulge secret formulas to competing suppliers. The FTC has rejected this justification, reasoning that the franchisor could grant suppliers licenses to make the items and have them covenant not to disclose the secret formulas as a condition for obtaining the licenses.[7] Although franchisors are prohibited from requiring their franchisees to purchase items from them, they are not prohibited from supplying their franchisees with items pursuant to voluntary contracts. The franchisee may not voluntarily agree to purchase from the franchisor and later attempt to avoid the agreement by alleging a tie-in. In these circumstances courts require franchisees to prove that the franchisor coerced them into purchasing supplies from it.

Franchisors frequently seek to avoid tie-in liability by using specifications

---

[6] Chock Full o' Nuts, [1973–76 Transfer Binder] Trade Reg. Rep. [CCH] ¶20,441.
[7] Id.

or authorized suppliers. Unreasonable specifications, however, may result in franchisor liability under section 1 of the Sherman Act, for they are not justified by quality control considerations. If specifications are reasonably related to quality control, the franchisor will not be liable even if it should turn out that only the franchisor is capable of meeting them in a manner sufficiently efficient to supply the franchisees. There is no requirement that other suppliers be available. What is required is that other suppliers be given an opportunity to compete for the franchisees' business.

If the franchisor wishes, it may require its franchisees to purchase only from authorized suppliers. However, if the franchisor or a company affiliated with it is one of the authorized suppliers, it must be careful to avoid pressuring its franchisees to buy from it rather than its competitors. Courts tend to uphold franchisor-authorized supplier plans where the franchisor adheres to reasonable objective criteria which authorized suppliers must meet and is willing to authorize any supplier able to meet those criteria. The number of authorized suppliers is another factor courts find relevant. The following case presents one major fast-food franchisor's plans for authorized suppliers.

Kentucky Fried Chicken Corp. v. *Diversified Container Corp.*
549 F.2d 368 (5th Cir. 1977)

Kentucky Fried Chicken Corporation, a franchisor of fast-food restaurants, included in its franchise agreements a clause requiring its franchisees to purchase all of their napkins, towelettes, plastic eating utensils, and carry-out chicken boxes from either Kentucky Fried or an approved supplier. Nine independent suppliers received Kentucky Fried's approval. No supplier that requested approval had ever been turned down. The approved suppliers were required to affix the Kentucky Fried "finger lickin' good" trademark to all materials. Diversified never sought Kentucky Fried's approval, but began producing boxes, napkins, towelettes, and utensils with Kentucky Fried's trademark affixed to them.

Kentucky Fried sued Diversified for trademark infringement. Diversified filed a counterclaim alleging that the franchise agreements were illegal tie-ins in violation of section 1 of the Sherman Act. The district court rendered judgment in favor of Kentucky Fried, and Diversified appealed. Only the portion of the opinion dealing with the antitrust issue is reproduced.

Goldberg, Circuit Judge: This case presents us with something mundane, something novel, and something bizarre. The mundane includes commercial law issues now well delimited by precedent. The novel aspects of the case center on intriguing and difficult interrelationships between trademark and antitrust concepts. And the bizarre element is the facially implausible—some might say unappetizing—contention that the man whose chicken is "finger-lickin' good" has unclean hands.

* * * * *

Container's antitrust counterclaim forces us to confront three conclusions: (1) that Kentucky Fried's conduct constitutes a tie-in and thus a per se antitrust violation, (2) that if Kentucky Fried's approved source requirement is not a tie it should nonetheless be held to constitute a new category of per se offense, and (3) that in any event Kentucky Fried's arrangement contravenes the rule of reason. We reject each contention of the triad.

Container's primary contention is that Kentucky Fried has established a tying arrangement in violation of §1 of the Sherman Act. . . .

* * * * *

Tying arrangements comprise one category of behavior that is illegal per se. . . . Here, as elsewhere, however, the per se label can sometimes prove misleading. Per se analysis is susceptible to the unwarranted inference that a plaintiff prevails in a tying case merely by finding some way to characterize the defendant's conduct as a tie. A tie can be generally defined as an arrangement under which a seller agrees to sell one product (the "tying product") only on the condition that the buyer also purchase a second product (the "tied product"). . . .

A plaintiff must show that the challenged arrangement is in fact a tie; that two separate products are involved and that, in addition to complying with the literal terms of the imprecise definition, the seller's behavior follows the general pattern found unacceptable in the earlier tying cases. To measure an arrangement against that general pattern we must take into account the principal evil of tie-ins: they may foreclose the tying party's competitors from a segment of the tied product market, and they may deprive the tie's victims, of the advantages of shopping around.

The problem in the case at bar is to determine whether Kentucky Fried's arrangement is in fact a tie—i.e., whether its behavior follows the general pattern found unacceptable in earlier tying cases. We begin with an analysis of tying in the context of franchise operations. The issue has taken on considerable significance in recent years; franchising has increased while tying structures have grown tighter.

In the commonly recurring situation, the tying product is the franchise itself, and the tied products may be such things as the equipment the franchisees will use to conduct the business, the ingredients of the goods that the franchisee will ultimately sell to consumers, or the supplies the franchisee will distribute to the public in connection with the main product. [A] franchisor who requires franchisees to use trademarked supplies does not escape the impact of tying principles to any extent. The franchisor's right to prevent others from selling supplies bearing its trademarks must yield to the antitrust laws' command to open the tied market to competitors.

*   *   *   *   *

Despite this relatively low threshold for invoking the per se doctrine, however, the franchisor retains a potentially significant defense—one designed to accommodate the franchisor's interests in the franchisee's performance. The franchisor is free to demonstrate that the tie constitutes a necessary device for controlling the quality of the end product sold to the consuming public. Product protection through tying can have a legal legitimacy. As part of this defense, however, the franchisor must establish that the tie constitutes the method of maintaining quality that imposes the least burden on commerce. . . .

With this background we turn to Container's claim that Kentucky Fried's arrangement constitutes a tie. The legal tightrope upon which we walk is very taut. Kentucky Fried does not expressly require franchisees to purchase from it the allegedly tied products. Instead, the franchise agreements permit franchisees to purchase the supplies from any source Kentucky Fried approves in writing. At the time of trial there were ten approved sources for cartons, only one of which was an affiliate of Kentucky Fried. Franchisees were free to recommend additional suppliers for approval, and the franchise agreement mandated that Kentucky Fried's approval "not be unreasonably withheld."

The difference between this arrangement and a traditional tie is readily apparent. Here the franchise agreement does not require franchisees to take the "tied" product (supplies) from Kentucky Fried; they can take their entire requirements from other sources.

*   *   *   *   *

We conclude that this arrangement simply does not constitute a tie. A monolithic tie may bring down the wrath of per se guilt, but not every use of string tangles with the antitrust laws. . . .

That the arrangement is not a tie does not, of course, prevent per se treatment; tying is not the only per se antitrust violation. . . . We are not prepared to say, however, that approved-source requirements are so universally devoid of redeeming virtue that they warrant per se treatment. [T]ies themselves are not as completely objectionable in the franchise context as in the contexts in which tying law originally developed. Moreover, franchise arrangements may sometimes create better competitive markets than would otherwise exist. A system under which an independent franchisee's choices are somewhat restricted may nevertheless prove superior to a system in which retail outlets are owned by the national firm. If, for example, Kentucky Fried had chosen not to franchise local outlets but rather to own them outright, the antitrust laws would leave it relatively free to supply the individual stores solely through the national office. Competition at the national level for Kentucky Fried's supplies business would continue, just as competition to sell Kentucky Fried the supplies it will in turn sell to franchisees is currently unencumbered. But competition at the local level would be as nonexistent under a system of national ownership rather than franchising. We can safely assume, however, that for the most part the application of tying principles to franchise operations will not affect a business's decision whether to engage in franchising.

When we turn from tying to approved-source requirements, however, the situation is somewhat different. We must encourage business ingenuity so long as it is not competitively stifling. We deal here not with tie-ins, whose adverse effects and lack of redeeming virtue are by now quite familiar, but instead with approved-source requirements. When we become more familiar with large-scale franchising and with approved-source requirements, we may discern that the latter are wholly unnecessary to the former. It will be time enough, however, to declare such requirements to be per se violations when that day arrives.

* * * * *

Our conclusion is that Kentucky Fried has not committed a per se antitrust violation: it has not established a de facto tie through coer-

cive tactics, and its approved-source provision is not a per se violation. Container's attack on Kentucky Fried's arrangement is not yet exhausted, however, for the rule of reason remains. An antitrust claimant who unsuccessfully seeks to establish a per se violation may nonetheless prevail by showing that its adversary's conduct unreasonably restrains competition. The burden of proving unreasonable effects rests with the antitrust plaintiff.

In the case at bar Container has failed to carry this burden. First, Container has not demonstrated that Kentucky Fried's arrangement adversely affects competition. Indeed, Container has presented no evidence at all of the actual competitive effect of Kentucky Fried's system. Antitrust claims need not be established by euclidean proof, but they cannot be merely fantasized. For all that appears in this record, competition among suppliers of the franchisees is as open and vigorous as it would be under a system in which Kentucky Fried exerted no control at all over franchisees. Kentucky Fried has excluded not a single supplier from the market; it has narrowed the negotiations between franchisees and their suppliers in not a single respect. The approved-source provision is hardly a boon to competition, but on this record we can only conclude that this approved-source requirement is as innocuous as any could be. Unless we were willing to condemn all approved-source requirements, we could not condemn this one. We have refused, however, to make such provisions per se violations, and Container's failure to adduce evidence of this provision's adverse impact therefore defeats its claim.

* * * * *

Here, Kentucky Fried seeks to justify its approved-source requirement as a device for controlling quality. Kentucky Fried's argument possesses a substantial measure of intuitive appeal. A customer dissatisfied with one Kentucky Fried outlet is unlikely to limit his or her adverse reaction to the particular outlet; instead, the adverse reaction will likely be directed to all Kentucky Fried stores. The quality of a franchisee's product thus undoubtedly affects Kentucky Fried's reputation and its future success. Moreover, this phenomenon is not limited to the quality of the chicken itself. Finger-lickin' good chicken alone does not a satisfied customer make. Kentucky Fried has a legitimate interest in whether cartons are so thin that the grease leaks through or heat readily escapes, in whether the packet of utensils given a carry-out customer contains everything it should and in whether the towelette contains a liquid that will adequately perform the Herculean task of removing Augean refuse from the customer's face and hands.

We therefore conclude that Container has not prevailed on its rule-of-reason contention, both because it has failed to demonstrate adverse competitive impacts and because it has failed to show that Kentucky Fried's system is not a reasonable method for achieving quality control. The district court correctly held for Kentucky Fried with respect to Container's antitrust counterclaim. This knot was not conceived as a loophole in our antitrust statutes.

Case questions

1. How did Kentucky Fried's program differ from a tie-in?

2. What policy considerations led the court to reject Container's argument that approved-source requirements be condemned as per se illegal?

3. What factors led the court to conclude that Kentucky Fried's approved-source requirement did not unreasonably restrain trade?

4. Assume that Kentucky Fried decided not to approve more than 15 independent suppliers. It justified this limitation on the ground that it would be too costly for Kentucky Fried to inspect more than 15 operations to insure that they were complying with its requirements. If Container were rejected as an approved supplier solely on the ground that it would be the 16th such supplier, could it successfully sue Kentucky Fried?

5. Would it be reasonable to impose an approved-supplier requirement for goods and services which the public does not receive directly, such as the services provided by bookkeeping or employment agencies?

OTHER ANTITRUST CONSIDERATIONS

Most of the other antitrust problems faced by franchisors arise under section 1 of the Sherman Act. There is rarely any difficulty in establishing the necessary "contract, combination or conspiracy," as it is usually the franchise contract itself which is challenged. Some of the more common problems that can arise will be discussed.

Covenants not to compete

Chapter 5 related that the Sherman Act's prohibition of "restraints of trade" was enacted with the common law's interpretation of that term in mind. The chapter noted that common-law decisions dealing with restraints of trade involved covenants not to compete. Many franchisors require their franchisees to agree not to operate competing enterprises for the duration of the franchise agreement.

Franchisee covenants not to compete, like all other contract provisions, violate the Sherman Act if they unreasonably restrain trade. The purpose and effect of these covenants are the most important factors to be considered. The typical franchisor may have several legitimate business purposes to justify a franchisee's covenant not to compete.

Where a covenant not to compete is restricted to the area immediately surrounding the city or town of the franchisee's business, the covenant may be justified on the ground that it insures that the franchisee's primary efforts will be devoted to the franchised outlet. The covenant also protects the franchisor against the possibility that the franchisee will use the franchisor's good name to attract customers and then divert those customers to a competing business.

Characteristics of a franchisor's operation may justify more extensive covenants not to compete. For example, Holiday Inns' standard franchise agreement bound its franchisees to avoid operating non–Holiday Inns motels anywhere. The court found this provision by itself to be reasonable because it protected the integrity of the franchisor's Holidex system of nationwide reservations. Were franchisees permitted to operate competing motels even in cities where they did not own Holiday Inns franchises, they could be expected to refer guests to their competing motels rather than to the Holiday Inns in those cities.

Franchise covenants not to compete also insure that information, training, and other services provided by the franchisor will not be used by a franchisee in competition with the franchise. In many cases these covenants may also facilitate exchanges of information and ideas among franchisees.

Even where these or other justifications are present, however, the covenant not to compete may, when combined with other restrictive arrangements, unreasonably restrain trade. For example, although the Holiday Inns' covenant discussed above was justified and reasonable by itself, it was combined with a franchisor policy that singled out specific towns in which all outlets were to be franchisor owned. The court held that this combination amounted to a horizontal territorial division and was consequently per se illegal.[8]

Franchisor-franchisee competition

Many franchisors choose, as Holiday Inns did, to own and operate some outlets themselves. In such instances the franchisor stands in both a vertical and horizontal relationship with the franchisees. Dual distribution systems are not in themselves illegal. They do, however, invite legal troubles if the franchisor gives its own outlets treatment more favorable than that afforded its franchisees.

Much of the law on the antitrust implications of dual distribution systems has come from cases involving automobile dealerships. This is due in part to the dealer enterprise plans used by the major automobile manufacturers

---

[8] *American Motor Inns, Inc.* v. *Holiday Inns, Inc.*, 521 F.2d 1230 (3d Cir. 1975).

to finance new dealers. Originally these manufacturers retailed only through independent dealers. In order to penetrate the market further, the manufacturers established the dealer enterprise plans, which enabled dealers to begin operations without large amounts of capital. Under the plans the dealer owns 25 percent of the dealership's common stock, with the manufacturer owning the remaining 75 percent. The manufacturer controls the dealership's board of directors, while the dealer serves as the president and general manager. The dealer uses the dealership's profits to purchase the manufacturer's stock, gradually buying the manufacturer out.

Chrysler Corporation, finding the dealer enterprise plan insufficient, began a dealer contract program. Under this plan Chrysler advanced all of the initial capital and owned all of the stock. The dealer then used the dealership's profits to purchase the stock. When the dealer had purchased 25 percent of the stock, the dealership converted to the dealer enterprise plan.

Under both plans the dealership had several advantages which independent dealerships lack. First, initial capital costs were eliminated. Second, the manufacturer provided operating loss subsidies which enabled the dealer to operate out of a larger, more attractive showroom and to spend more money on advertising. Finally, the manufacturer provided free services to key managerial employees. The following case is one of several brought by independent dealers alleging that these subsidies violated the Sherman Act.

Coleman Motor Co. v. Chrysler Corp.
525 F.2d 1338 (3d Cir. 1975)

Coleman Motor Co. (plaintiff-appellee), an independent Dodge dealership brought a private anti-trust action against Chrysler Motors Corporation (defendant-appellant). Coleman charged that Chrysler discriminated between its factory and independent dealers "with the intent to destroy independent Dodge dealerships . . ." A jury found in favor of Coleman. The Third Circuit Court of Appeals remanded the case to the district court for a new trial.

Rosenn, Circuit Judge:

* * * * *

It is undisputed that Chrysler financially subsidized factory dealerships. It provided the initial capital for these businesses, thereby eliminating cost of capital. Chrysler also provided significant operating loss subsidies. These funds enabled the factory dealerships to spend signifi-

cantly greater amounts of money than could Coleman on larger, more attractive showrooms and on advertising.

Chrysler contends that the advertising campaign was intended to increase overall sales of Dodge vehicles in Allegheny County. It is fair to state this increase could have been achieved by spreading advertising loss subsidies over all dealers, both independent and factory. Subsidization of Boulevard Dodge's advertising losses in substantial sums cannot be justified over an eight-year period on the basis that Boulevard Dodge was a new entrant in the Dodge retail market in need of assistance in order to survive—in its first year of operation, Boulevard Dodge had cornered 39 percent of the Dodge market.

It is also noteworthy that when plaintiff went out of business, one of its close competitors,

Boulevard Dodge, decreased its advertising expenditures. . . .

There was some testimony that defendants discriminated in favor of the factory dealerships and against the private dealerships in the release of new automobiles. In 1962 when defendants for the first time marketed a full size car which had wide public acceptance, all the Dodge dealers advertised in advance about the release of the car, but only the factory dealership at Boulevard Dodge received immediate delivery of the car.

There was also evidence that Chrysler paid the salaries of key managerial employees of factory dealerships at various times; that Chrysler paid the salaries of accountants and the two Chrysler board members of factory dealerships; and that Chrysler provided free furniture, tools, and equipment to the factory dealership at Cloverleaf Dodge.

When plaintiff lost its used car lot to the redevelopment authority, it arranged to move to a new location four blocks away. Plaintiff's franchise agreement required it to seek permission from Chrysler, which was refused.

Vernon Staley, former president of Boulevard Dodge, testified that he informed Chrysler's regional manager Harris after several months of operation of his concern for the amount of losses his company was sustaining. Staley stated that Harris told him not to worry: "Just roll those cars out. We will make our money at the front end, and, if you can get this somewhere close to a breakeven we will be satisfied." Staley further testified that when Harris was attempting to engage him for the Dodge franchise, Harris indicated that Chrysler intended to reduce the number of Dodge dealers in Allegheny County from 16 to 11, under their new marketing program."

* * * * *

From this evidence, the jury could reasonably have concluded that defendant combined and conspired with managers of factory dealerships. . . . Although the evidence is weak, the jury could have found further that Chrysler's actions were unfairly competitive and that their effect was to force plaintiff out of business. . . . .

Plaintiff's expert, Dr. Rubin E. Slesinger, professor of Economics at Pittsburgh, testified that large infusions of funds to factory dealers, as subsidies to offset losses, and the expenditure for advertising of two to four times the amount spent by independent dealers, and other preferential treatment of factory dealers, would tend to monopolize the Dodge market in Allegheny County. The plain implication of his testimony is that factory dealers would take sales away from independent dealers by these practices.

The jury may also have determined that Chrysler deliberately took advantage of Coleman's financial situation. Plaintiff was in breach of its Direct Dealer Agreement because it had not met its minimum sales requirement between 1962 and 1969, except in 1963. Consequently, Chrysler had the right under the agreement to terminate plaintiff's franchise. Chrysler apparently chose to let plaintiff remain in existence and contribute to overall sales of Dodge vehicles. While plaintiff was losing money, Chrysler was subsiding factory dealer losses. When plaintiff went out of business, Boulevard Dodge lowered its advertising expenses and, after 1971, operated at a profit. Thus, the jury could have concluded that Chrysler had accomplished its purposes of increasing Dodge sales and consolidating retail sales in the hands of several strong Chrysler-controlled dealerships.

The question thus posed is whether the above findings are sufficient to establish an unreasonable restraint of trade under section one of the Sherman Act. The problem is one of restraint *vel non* in intrabrand competition.

* * * * *

While Chrysler's ability to cease doing business with franchisees may generally be restricted only by contractual provisions, the means it chose to accomplish this end here have an anticompetitive effect. If Chrysler had simply ceased doing business with Coleman, Coleman might have been able to seek a franchise from another manufacturer and become an interbrand competitor. However, the continuation of predatory practices for a number of years in the face of Coleman's substantial losses could have so severely damaged Coleman's financial ability that he could not reenter the market as an interbrand competitor. A combination of distributors, which through unfair practices eliminates a competitor and leaves it in such a condition that it lacks the ability to continue business as an interbrand competitor, has an adverse effect on the marketplace.

* * * * *

Case questions

1. What actions taken by Chrysler allowed the jury to infer a conspiracy to unreasonably restrain trade?

2. Does the case hold that all dealer enterprise plans are illegal? That all subsidies to dealer enterprise dealerships are illegal?

3. Would Chrysler have been liable if it had simply terminated Coleman's dealership in order to benefit Boulevard?

Subsequent court decisions have held that automobile manufacturers may subsidize dealer enterprise and dealer contract dealerships when the purpose of such subsidies is market penetration. This is so even if the subsidies force independent dealers out of business. Where, however, the manufacturer's intent is predatory, or where the subsidies effect vertical integration, such subsidies will violate the Sherman Act.

Dealer enterprise and dealer contract dealerships differ from other franchisor-owned outlets. The primary purpose of these dealerships is to finance the initial business costs of future independent dealers. The ultimate goal is for the dealers to independently own and operate the outlets. The more typical franchisor-owned outlet is not designed to be turned over to an independent franchisee. Thus the intent of market penetration is not as easily established in the typical franchise cases as in the cases involving the auto dealer plans. In the typical franchise cases, where more favorable terms are provided to company-owned outlets, a court may infer that the franchisor's motivation is vertical integration.

Territorial and customer restraints

As seen in Chapter 5, horizontal agreements on territorial and customer divisions are per se unreasonable under the Sherman Act. Vertically imposed territorial and customer divisions are not per se illegal, but require a detailed evaluation of their reasonableness. The franchisor has two main problems with regard to territorial restraints: the restraints must not be capable of interpretation as horizontal, and the restraints must be reasonable.

If the franchisor owns and operates outlets and imposes exclusive territories on its franchisees, the territories may be viewed as either vertical or horizontal. In such cases the FTC examines the history and purpose of the exclusive territories. However, other courts have adopted a less flexible approach and have concluded that whenever the franchisor competes with its franchisees, exclusive territories are horizontal and consequently per se unreasonable.

Whether purely vertical exclusive territories or less restrictive horizontal arrangements are employed, the restraints must be justified as reasonable or they will violate the Sherman Act. The restraints may be necessary to attract qualified franchisees, to avoid free rider effects where franchisees are expected to provide customer services or expend money on developing a local market, to facilitate quality control, or for similar purposes. The more established the franchisor, the less severe will be the problems posed by free rider effects and the more difficult it will be to justify territorial restraints.

Promotions and advertising

As has been seen throughout this section, vertical arrangements such as exclusive territories have received more lenient treatment by courts than have similar arrangements agreed to horizontally. The major exception is price-fixing. Vertical price-fixing remains illegal per se. In controlling advertising, a franchisor has considerably more leeway where nonprice advertising is involved.

Advertising or promotional requirements which may result in price-fixing violate the Sherman Act. Franchisors may run promotional discount programs or similar programs but may not require franchisees to participate. Franchisors have generally recognized this, and their giveaways or discount promotions usually read "at participating dealers." Similarly, a franchisor may suggest prices that a franchisee should charge but cannot legally require the franchisee to charge those prices.

Where the franchisor suggests prices or involvement in promotions it may use persuasion but not coercion to get franchisee adherence to the suggestions. The line between persuasion and coercion is sometimes difficult to draw. Offering incentives for participation on a nondiscriminatory basis is not coercion. Thus a franchisor that wishes its franchisees to offer trading stamps may also offer to split the cost of those stamps with each participating franchisee.

A significant case is *Hanson* v. *Shell Oil Co.*[9] Hanson, a Shell franchisee, alleged that Shell was coercing him and other franchisees into lowering prices. Shell maintained a dealer assistance program under which a dealer faced with stiff price competition could request reductions in Shell's wholesale gasoline prices. When Shell granted such requests, it extended the reductions to all Shell dealers in the area. Shell owned and operated two retail outlets in Tucson, Arizona. When it granted dealer assistance requests in Tucson, it frequently also lowered prices at its two retail outlets. Hanson contended that this was an effort by Shell to coerce its franchisees into

---

[9] 541 F.2d 1352 (8th Cir. 1976).

lowering their retail prices. The court, however, held that these activities were persuasion rather than coercion. The court was persuaded by Shell's history of providing dealer assistance regardless of whether the dealer actually lowered prices. The franchisor's strong interest in maintaining the image of the franchise will generally justify reasonable franchisor supervision of and restrictions on the advertising and promotions of individual franchisees.

In this context the line between reasonable restrictions and franchisor price-fixing is often difficult to draw. Illustrative is *Weight Watchers of the Rocky Mountain Region, Inc.* v. *Weight Watchers International, Inc.*[10] The franchisor required franchisees to charge each member a registration fee upon enrollment in a Weight Watchers group, a fee for each class attended, and a missed class fee or a new registration fee if a member stopped attending and later sought to rejoin. Each franchisee was free to independently determine the amount of these fees and to offer discounts. Franchisees, however, were prohibited from offering prepayment or front-loading plans under which a member could receive a discount by paying for a number of meetings in advance.

The court found this prohibition reasonable. Its purpose was not to fix prices, as evidenced by the complete freedom afforded franchisees in setting fees. It was justified as necessary for the success of the Weight Watchers program because members were motivated to join by the understanding that they could leave at any time without any commercial or other pressures to remain. A prepayment plan would place such pressures on the members. It would also detract from the appearance of a noncommercial operation designed to get people to help themselves. This appearance was a central feature of the franchise.

TERMINATION OF THE FRANCHISE RELATIONSHIP

A franchisee may choose to terminate the franchise relationship and sell the business to another party. The franchisor's strong interest in protecting its reputation will usually justify a requirement of franchisor approval prior to sale or transfer of the operation. However, the franchisor cannot unreasonably withhold approval.

If the franchisor terminates the relationship or refuses to renew a franchise agreement which has expired, the termination will not violate the antitrust laws unless it has an anticompetitive motivation. Franchisor refusals to renew are usually protected as unilateral refusals to deal. Where a franchisor terminates one franchisee and replaces it with another, there is usually no anticompetitive effect.

Although termination without predatory intent does not violate the Sherman Act, as a practical matter termination often invites antitrust litigation. Most antitrust franchise litigation has resulted from franchisee terminations.

---

[10] 1976–2 Trade Cas. (CCH) ¶61,157 (E.D.N.Y. 1976).

A frequent reflex reaction by franchisees to termination is to scrutinize all franchisor policies for antitrust violations. The franchisees then allege that they were terminated because they objected to the violations.

POLICY CONSIDERATIONS

Recent developments in the legal regulation of franchising reflect two potentially conflicting trends. One concern expressed by many courts and regulatory agencies is to protect the franchisee. Many franchisees are first-time investors attracted to franchises by the prospect of owning their own businesses. Many have lost their life's savings to promises of profits which never materialized. Those who succeed may still find themselves at the mercy of the franchisor which retains the power to terminate their franchises. Regulations such as the FTC's franchise rule and court decisions such as *Chicken Delight* seek to protect franchisees from fraudulent practices and allow them considerable freedom to act.

A second and potentially conflicting concern is to allow the franchisor sufficient control to insure uniform quality and appearance. Franchisors that are unable to retain sufficient control over their franchisees' operations may vertically integrate, thereby reducing competition. Some have suggested that overregulation could destroy the benefits derived from franchising. This second concern is reflected in court decisions such as *GTE Sylvania* and *McDonald's*. One thing is certain. As franchising continues to expand, it will become increasingly difficult to strike the proper balance between the two concerns.

Review problems

1. A franchisor of hardware stores wishes to use a table which shows potential franchisees what the investor's gross profits will be if a particular number of items are sold in a given period of time from certain retail locations. What liability, if any, might result from the use of the chart?

2. An oil company's agreement with its gasoline retailer franchisees provided for cancellation of the franchise on five days' notice. The franchisor sent a letter to all franchisees asking them to keep prices below a stated maximum in order to increase gasoline sales. Almost all of the franchisees who did not lower their prices were threatened with termination because of their low sales volume. Furthermore, franchisees were prohibited from selling any brand of motor oil other than that produced by the franchisor. What antitrust violations, if any, did the franchisor commit?

3. A manufacturer and retailer of radios and other electronic consumer goods entered into an agreement with an individual to manage one of its stores. The manufacturer supplied the inventory, determined the merchandising policies, and retained title to the goods. The manufacturer set the prices for all goods sold. The individual received a percentage of the store's profits and controlled day-to-day managerial decisions, including hiring and firing. The manufacturer never gave the individual a disclosure statement. Has it violated the FTC or Sherman acts?

4. A franchisor of temporary help agencies restricts the location and territories of its franchisees. It also requires its franchisees to comply with the franchisor's operating manual and to attend annual training sessions. The manual and training sessions cost $1,000.

What antitrust and FTC problems might this franchisor face?

5. A franchisor of ice-cream stores requires its franchisees to purchase their ice cream from it or approved suppliers. Two ice-cream manufacturers produce ice cream for the franchisor, using its secret formula. Their contracts with the franchisor obligate them to sell the ice cream only to the franchisor and to deal with franchisees only through the franchisor. Do these agreements violate section 3 of the Clayton Act?

6. An automobile manufacturer requires its dealers to obtain replacement parts from the manufacturer when performing warranty work on cars. The dealer is paid by the manufacturer for doing the warranty repairs. Does this exclusive dealing requirement violate section 3 of the Clayton Act?

7. A franchisor of "drive-thru" photo processing stores sells franchises to franchisees who operate out of kiosks located in shopping center parking lots. A customer drives up to the side of a kiosk, gives the operator exposed film, may purchase new film and other products, and returns several days later to pick up the finished photos. The franchisor does not conduct any elaborate market research comparing different shopping center locations. It simply leases space in shopping centers, sets up prefabricated kiosks, and requires its franchisees to sublease the property. Is this practice an illegal tie-in?

8. An oil company has numerous retail franchisees who sell gasoline and maintain and service cars. The franchisor has been losing money because its volume of sales has been low. It has decided to change its method of retailing by eliminating maintenance and service operations and restricting overall operations to retail sales of gasoline. The reduced overhead expenses will be passed on to the consumer in the form of price reductions. If the franchisor terminates all of its franchisees for this purpose, will it violate the Sherman Act?

9. Would your answer to question 8 differ if the franchisor terminates only those franchisees who do not agree to convert to gasoline only?

10. Discuss the conflicting policy considerations involved in the regulation of franchising. How do you think the proper balance should be struck?

PART II: REVIEW PROBLEMS

1. Huge Ungainly Grasping Enterprises Ltd. (HUGE) is a large conglomerate which owns, among other corporations, Big Buns, Inc., the second largest supplier of buns, pastries, and condiments to fast-food franchisees. Big Buns currently covers 30 percent of the bun and pastry market and 18 percent of the condiment market. The leading firms in these two markets have shares of 45 percent and 25 percent, respectively. The leading bun and pastry supplier also has 13 percent of the condiment market, ranking fourth behind a condiment supplier which has 16 percent. The leading condiment firm also ranks third in buns and pastries, with 20 percent of the market. The remainder of the buns and pastries and condiments markets are occupied by franchisors which supply their franchisees.

HUGE would like to enter the fast-food restaurant business. Another HUGE subsidiary owns a large number of small parcels of real estate that are notable locations for fast-food enterprises. The parcels are currently vacant. The fast-food restaurant business is highly competitive, with the top 10 firms dividing 98 percent of the market as follows:

Firm	Percent of market share
1	35
2	25
3	10
4	9
5	7
6	4
7	3
8	2
9	2
10	1

HUGE is considering acquiring firm seven or starting a new fast-food franchise. Whichever approach it takes, HUGE will seek new franchisees and require them to lease its currently vacant land parcels and operate from those locations. It will also offer a 20 percent discount to all franchisees who buy their buns and condiments from Big Buns and a 30 percent discount to those who enter into three-year re-quirements contracts with Big Buns. As president of Big Buns, you must react to the proposal.

2. You are the vice president in charge of marketing for Nutwood Furniture, Inc., a large furniture manufacturer based in North Carolina. Your company specializes in manufacturing French provincial–, Danish-, Spanish-, and Mediterranean-style furniture. All of this furniture is made of wood products covered with a veneer. The veneers you use are pecan, walnut, and mahogany. You have decided to expand into retailing. Your staff has studied the potential methods of beginning a retailing operation. It has proposed two alternative plans. They are:

Alternative A. The Nationwide Furniture Company currently has retail stores in 17 states. It is the leading furniture retailer east of the Mississippi River, with 17 percent of the retail market. It is also your best customer, buying 65 percent of its inventory from you. Nationwide began 50 years ago as a partnership between Sam Nation and Oliver Wide. Sam eventually bought Oliver out, incorporated the business, and expanded it to its current size. Six months ago, at age 86, Sam died. His children now own all of the Nationwide stock, but they have no interest in running the business. They would like to sell 75 percent of their stock. We can purchase the stock for a combination of cash and stock in our company.

Alternative B. We can enter the market by franchising Nutwood dealers who will offer the public quality furniture at low prices. We will charge each franchisee a franchise fee. We will specify the location of each franchisee's store and will guarantee that it will be the sole Nutwood store in a given area. We will, of course, require that the store sell only Nutwood furniture. We will provide catalogs free of charge to our franchisees.

We will require franchisees to purchase all of their stationery, business cards, and office furniture from us; however, we will provide a

50 percent discount on all orders of these items from franchisees who purchase their franchise during the first year of our retail operation. We do not make office equipment such as typewriters or adding machines, but the JCN Company has offered us $10,000 for the exclusive right to supply our franchisees with typewriters, adding machines, and similar equipment.

We will open all of our franchised outlets on the same day. We will have a grand opening sale, announced in all local newspapers serving the cities in which our franchisees do business. To insure the success of the campaign, we will require our stores to sell all furniture at 50 percent below the catalog price during the first week of operation. We will also require them to sell at 75 percent of the catalog price for the remainder of the first five months. At that point, we should be somewhat established and can allow each franchisee to set its own price.

Your staff has also presented you with the following assessment of the furniture market:

We are the fifth largest furniture manufacturer in the United States, with 10.1 percent of the market. The top four manufacturers have 12 percent, 13 percent, 15 percent, and 23 percent of the market. Some 60 small manufacturers divide the rest of the market.

Within the past five years the top four manufacturers have all begun large-scale retailing operations. None of them have used mergers; two have used franchises, and two have opened chains of retail stores which they own and operate. It is clear that the small independent store is finding it difficult to compete with these retail arms of the top four manufacturers. Over the past five years 35 percent of the independent stores have failed. The retail stores of Nationwide are among the few independents that remain healthy. It is large enough to compete effectively, as are a few others. However, if we do not get into retailing, we will find that much of the wholesale market for our product will disappear.

You must evaluate the alternatives suggested by your staff. What should Nutwood Furniture, Inc., do? Consider all legal issues.

PART THREE

Consumer law

CHAPTER 10

Product safety

The National Commission on Product Safety revealed in 1970 that 30,000 Americans were killed and 110,000 permanently disabled every year in their home in accidents connected with consumer products. Statistics showed that 20 million people a year fell victim to some injury related to consumer products at a cost of $5.5 billion per year. Excluded from these statistics are injuries and deaths resulting from food, drugs, cigarettes, motor vehicles, and firearms.

Many products which make life more comfortable also present a serious threat to life. Hairdryers, microwave ovens, air conditioners, furnaces, toasters, blenders, and lawn mowers are just a few of the products that are commonly purchased by consumers and used around the house. Normally, these products are used to the satisfaction of the consumer without incident. However, whenever such a product is defective it may cause injury. Product defects and consequent injury account for over 1 million lawsuits per year. Some of the largest money judgments are awarded to injured plaintiffs based on successful product liability suits lodged against manufacturers and distributors. Many of these large awards are highly publicized, and thus provide consumers with incentive to prosecute claims for injury caused by alleged defective products. Consequently, manufacturers have incurred rising costs due to the payment of judgment awards and the defense of suits. Most manufacturers and distributors have shifted their exposure of liability to insurance companies. Insurance companies in turn have, in recent years, increased their rates to reflect the sharp increase in claims payments. Manufacturers and distributors must pass the additional costs on to the consumer. The prices of products naturally reflect these added costs; in the end the consumer pays for the injury.

This chapter concentrates on the remedies afforded to injured consumers and the recent attempts to prevent injuries by government regulation of product safety.

PRODUCT LIABILITY

A product liability action results when a plaintiff seeks damages for an injury sustained because of an alleged defective product. Defects may occur because of a construction, design, or labeling defect. A *construction defect* results when a product falls short of the manufacturer's own established standards and the standards commonly employed within the industry as a whole. Many household products are produced on assembly lines. Quality control becomes very important. Because of human frailty an overcarbonized bottle or a defectively wired television set may go unnoticed. Such manufacturing omissions may result in injury to the consumer and consequent liability to the manufacturer and distributor. A *design defect* occurs when the product meets the manufacturer's standards but the manufacturer's standards are inferior or fall short of the standards commonly employed within the industry. A football helmet or a radial tire may conform to the manufacturer's specifications, yet its incapacity to properly absorb shock may invite injury. A *labeling defect* occurs when the manufacturer fails to provide adequate warning of the proper procedures for using a product. A failure to include a label warning against the hazard to diabetics of ingesting a particular patent medicine would constitute a label defect if the research showed that the drug was hazardous to the health of diabetics. There are several theories of recovery under which a plaintiff may proceed against the party responsible for a defective product that caused injury. The most common theories are negligence, express warranty, implied warranty, and strict liability in tort.

Negligence

Our jurisprudential system is based on the belief that where there is a wrong there should be a remedy. Through the process of the common law, courts have carved out certain recognized wrongs. These wrongs are commonly referred to as *torts.* (A tort is a civil wrong other than a breach of a contract.) One tort recognized in the law is *negligence.* Negligence is conduct that falls short of the standard of care that is imposed by the law to protect persons from unreasonable risk of injury. The standard against which a person's conduct is measured is the reasonable person. The reasonable person always looks both ways before crossing the street, never takes a step in the dark without first ascertaining the condition of the premises, inquires into the habits of a dog before petting it, and never disobeys traffic regulations or any other laws. The reasonable person always acts prudently under the existing circumstances. One whose conduct falls below that of the reasonable person has breached the legal standard. The reasonable person does not really exist but was created by the law. Nonetheless, persons who fail to conform to the reasonable person standard risk liability to plaintiffs who are injured as a result of negligent conduct. As a policy judgment the law has concluded that an innocent victim should prevail against a negligent wrongdoer.

Negligence may result from the commission or omission of an act. An automobile dealer may commit a negligent act by overinflating a spare tire. A manufacturer's failure to test a boiler after assembly is an example of a negligent omission. This is true because a reasonably prudent boilermaker, knowing the potential risk of harm that is associated with a defective boiler, would attempt to eliminate the risk by testing for defects. The test used must be one that is considered effective according to the current state of boiler technology. Testing a boiler for its "explosion potential" by visual inspection would be short of an exercise of reasonable precaution since prudent care demands the use of more sophisticated and reliable tests.

Proximate cause. Under the theory of negligence, in order to recover against another the plaintiff must also prove that the defendant's negligence was the *proximate cause* of the plaintiff's injury. Proximate cause has to do with the likelihood (foreseeability) of injury. If the injury sustained by the plaintiff could not be reasonably foreseen by the defendant at the time of the negligence, then no recovery is available. In *Palsgraf* v. *Long Island Railroad Co.* the railroad's employees helped a passenger jump from a platform onto their moving train.[1] A package that the passenger was carrying contained fireworks that fell to the rails and exploded. The explosion caused a scale on the platform to fall and strike Mrs. Palsgraf. In deciding that "negligence in the air" was not enough, Justice Cardozo reasoned that the company had no duty to Mrs. Palsgraf since her injury was only remotely related to the negligence of the company's agents, and hence not foreseeable. Plaintiff was denied recovery.

Privity. Another impediment to recovery as against a manufacturer was the *privity* doctrine. Early case law required privity between the plaintiff and the defendant before the plaintiff could recover against a defendant for injury based on negligence, i.e., there had to be a contractual relation. Under the privity doctrine the injured plaintiff could only recover from the immediate seller, who was not normally as financially sound as the manufacturer. In reality, intervening distributors of the product insulated the manufacturer from liability, since manufacturers rarely sold directly to the consumer. The apparent rationale for the privity doctrine was that the manufacturer could not be expected to foresee injury past the immediate purchaser. In 1916, in *MacPherson* v. *Buick Motor Co.*,[2] the tide changed in negligence cases. In *MacPherson* an auto manufacturer negligently failed to inspect a defective wheel made by another manufacturer. The car was sold by a dealer to the plaintiff, who was injured when the wooden spokes of a car wheel crumbled. In deciding that the lack of privity between the manufacturer and the plaintiff would not negate the manufacturer's liability based on negligence, Justice Cardozo said:

> If the nature of a thing is such that it is reasonably certain to place life and limb in peril when negligently made, it is then a thing of danger. Its nature

[1] 248 N.Y. 339, 162 N.E. 99 (1928).
[2] 217 N.Y. 382, 111 N.E. 1050 (1916).

gives warning of the consequences to be expected. If to the element of danger there is added knowledge that the thing will be used by persons other than the purchaser, and used without new tests, then, irrespective of contract, the manufacturer of this thing of danger is under a duty to make it carefully.

The sensible rationale in support of the court's holding in *MacPherson* persuaded courts in other jurisdictions to follow the same approach.

Res ipsa loquitur. Of course, not every product defect is caused by a negligent act; some product defects occur even though the manufacturer exercises prudent care. In a highly industrialized society it is often extremely difficult, if not impossible, for a plaintiff to prove that the manufacturer's or seller's negligence was responsible for the defective product that caused injury. The plaintiff is normally not privy to inside information regarding the details of the manufacturer's operation. Moreover, when a manufacturer produces 10,000 "wadgets" a day, it is unlikely that even the manufacturer would know why one wadget proved defective. To aid an injured plaintiff to hurdle the seemingly insurmountable task of establishing negligence, courts developed a rule of evidence referred to as *res ipsa loquitur* ("the thing speaks for itself"). This rule permits the natural inference of negligence to be drawn from the fact that a product is defective. The rule applies when the injury is one that ordinarily does not occur except where someone has been negligent, and where the instrumentality causing the injury was within the defendant's exclusive control. If a rat's tail is found in a pop bottle or poison in baking flour, a commonsense presumption arises that their presence resulted from someone's negligence. Res ipsa loquitur requires the defendant to explain away the inference of negligence. Because of this evidentiary rule many plaintiffs who do not have any direct evidence of negligence are nonetheless able to survive a directed verdict against them and have their cases "go to the jury." Res ipsa loquitur is far from absolute in aiding a plaintiff to recover in negligence. Because the manufacturer is in control of its plant operations it is usually in a good position to dispel the inference created by res ipsa loquitur by presenting evidence to show that it used reasonable quality control standards to guard against product defects. Moreover, it is still the plaintiff's burden to trace the control of the product and show that the product left the defendant's plant in a defective condition. A pop bottle may explode in a consumer's hands because it was overcarbonized at the plant, or because it was rustled in transit by a wholesaler. The plaintiff must present evidence tracing the custody of the product to show that the defect did not occur after it left the hands of the defendant.

Defenses. Even when the plaintiff can successfully prove negligence, affirmative defenses can be raised by a defendant to defeat recovery. Contributory negligence and assumption of the risk are two of the more common defenses.

Contributory negligence. The traditional view is that contributory negligence bars the plaintiff's recovery. This means that a negligent defendant will not be liable if the plaintiff was also negligent and the plaintiff's negligence contributed to his or her injury. Assume, for example, that the defendant negligently designed a refuse bin so that it was unstable and that the plaintiff purchased the bin and negligently placed it on an irregular and inclined surface. Assume further that the plaintiff sustained injury when the bin overturned in a windstorm and that the plaintiff's negligence contributed to the injury. Plaintiff's contributory negligence would preclude recovery. In a state that strictly adheres to the application of contributory negligence, even if plaintiff's contribution to his or her injury was only slight, there would be no recovery. In most states, however, case decision or legislation has overthrown the harshness of the contributory negligence defense in favor of *comparative negligence*. Under principles of comparative negligence the plaintiff's contributory negligence does not completely bar recovery but only causes a reduction in recovery by the percentage that the plaintiff's negligence contributed to the injury. In the above refuse bin case, assume that a jury determines that the plaintiff's damages are $25,000 and that the plaintiff was 50 percent at fault. Plaintiff's recovery would be reduced to $12,500.

Assumption of the risk. Assumption of the risk prevents a plaintiff from recovering against a negligent defendant. Assumption of the risk consists of a voluntary exposure to a known risk. It differs from contributory negligence in that contributory negligence is based on *carelessness,* whereas assumption of the risk is based on voluntary exposure to a risk, or *venturesomeness.* A plaintiff who continues to drive an automobile with full knowledge that it has defective brakes is deemed to have assumed the risk of injury that is likely to result. If a plaintiff continues to drive an automobile that he or she does not know, but should know, has defective brakes, then the plaintiff is guilty of contributory negligence.

Warranties

Negligence derives from tort law. The law of warranty developed alongside the law of tort, and is an attractive alternative to negligence for a plaintiff seeking damages for injury resulting from a defective product. Based on contract law, it frees the purchaser from the burden of proving that the defendant failed to exercise reasonable care. Once the plaintiff proves that the defendant breached a warranty, then liability attaches. However, the same privity requirement that barred recovery under the early negligence case law also barred recovery under warranty theory. Since warranty is based on contract principles, courts were quick to rule that an injured consumer could not recover against a remote manufacturer. However, as the next case demonstrates, in warranty cases even the privity requirement was not sacrosanct.

Express warranty. Often, in an effort to make a product more attractive to the consumer, a seller makes *express warranties* or representations concerning the product. The product will be expected to live up to the representations. Otherwise a plaintiff who sustains injury as a result of the breach of an express warranty may recover damages against the warrantor. A warranty need not be couched in formal language. Section 2–313 of the Uniform

Commercial Code (UCC), adopted in essence by all but one state,[3] reads in part:

(1) Express warranties by the seller are created as follows:

(a) Any affirmation of fact or promise made by the seller to the buyer which relates to the goods and becomes part of the basis of the bargain creates an express warranty that the goods shall conform to the affirmation or promise.

A warranty or representation must be distinguished from a statement of opinion. "[A]n affirmation merely of the value of the goods or a statement purporting to be merely the seller's opinion or commendation of the goods does not create a warranty."[4] It is to be expected by consumers that a car salesperson or any merchant interested in selling a product is prone to make exaggerated claims about the product. A claim couched in terms of a general opinion, such as "This lawn mower is the safest on the market," will normally not be the subject of a warranty. On the other hand, if more specific factual claims are made, such as "The blades in this lawn mower are built to last five years," then a breach of that representation results in liability. There is often a thin line between a representation, to which liability will attach, and an opinion, to which no liability attaches. Sometimes the distinction turns on who makes the statement and on the degree of reliance that a reasonable consumer would be expected to place on the representation. Generally, not much credence should be placed upon a used car salesperson's representation that "this automobile is in A-1 shape." This statement is at most an opinion; it does not constitute an affirmation of fact. (The prudent purchaser will have the automobile checked by an independent mechanic.) However, the result may be different if the used car salesperson had a number of years' experience as an automobile mechanic and represented that fact to the buyer along with this statement: "My examination has proved that this automobile is in A-1 shape." Here the buyer can be expected to place greater reliance upon the statement of the salesperson, and such representation would be elevated to an "affirmation of fact," covered by section 2–313.

One way for manufacturers and sellers to avoid the consequences of breaching an express warranty is not to make any representations. Other limitations precluding plaintiff's recovery are discussed in the next section.

Implied warranty. Under UCC section 2–314, a seller of goods impliedly warrants that those goods "are fit for the ordinary purposes for which such goods are used." In selling a hamburger, the seller impliedly warrants that it is fit for consumption. If the hamburger is rotten, the seller has breached the implied warranty of merchantability and is liable for any injury proximately resulting from the breach. This rule of law is consistent with the expectations of the consumer. It is only reasonable for a consumer to expect that a product placed on the market is safe for its intended use.

---

[3] The Uniform Commercial Code has been adopted, at least in part, by all states plus the Virgin Islands and the District of Columbia. Louisiana has not adopted Article 2.

[4] UCC § 2–313(2).

The implied warranty of merchantability is only applicable when the seller is "a merchant with respect to goods of that kind." A merchant is one who customarily deals in the goods which are the subject of the sale. One who engages in an isolated sale of goods is not a merchant. Such a seller would not normally be versed in the intimacies of the product, and the buyer would not reasonably expect a nonmerchant to imply that the product sold is merchantable.

In addition to the implied warranty of merchantability of section 2–314, the UCC affords an injured plaintiff the protection of section 2–315. This grants the purchaser an implied warranty that goods are *fit for a particular purpose.* The particular purpose warranty is more specific than the merchantability warranty. It involves situations in which the seller has been informed of a particular use as opposed to a customary use. The customary use of shoes would be for normal walking; a particular use of shoes would be for tightrope walking. The purchaser may inform the seller that shoes are to be used for tightrope walking and may rely upon the seller to select shoes appropriate for that use. If the seller then recommends a specific shoe, the implied warranty of fitness for a particular purpose comes into play. Like the implied warranty of merchantability, this warranty is only applicable when the seller is a merchant.

The UCC removes the impediment of privity and, depending upon which UCC alternative a state adopts, extends the warranty to any person "who is in the family or household of his buyer or who is a guest in his home . . ." or to any person "who may reasonably be expected to use, consume or be affected by the goods." (UCC§2–318)

However, limitations have been placed on the implied warranty basis for recovery. These limitations present some of the same problems for a breach of an express warranty theory of recovery. Reasonable notice of the injury must be communicated to the merchant; otherwise the plaintiff cannot recover. Moreover, the UCC imposes a four-year statute of limitations from the time of sale, within which the plaintiff must sue or be barred from recovery. Furthermore, section 2–314 begins with the wording "Unless excluded or modified," and section 2–315 contains similar language. Merchants habitually disclaim warranties, a practice which these words implicitly permit. However, it is not entirely settled that a merchant can disclaim merchantability when it relates to personal safety. There is a division of authority on this question. Some courts conclude that since there is inequality of bargaining power between the merchant and the consumer, it is unfair to permit such disclaimers. (Federal law discussed later restricts disclaimers under certain circumstances.)

Finally, as the UCC makes clear, there is no implied warranty with respect to defects that an inspection could have revealed. An injured purchaser who neglected to inspect the goods may be without warranty protection. In a sense, contributory negligence, a tort concept, has crept into the law of warranty.

Henningsen v. *Bloomfield Motors, Inc.*
32 N.J. 358, 161 A.2d 69 (1960)

Clause Henningsen (plaintiff) purchased a Plymouth automobile for his wife (plaintiff) from Bloomfield Motors, Inc. (defendant). The car was manufactured by Chrysler Corporation (defendant). The purchase agreement contained a clause disclaiming all express and implied warranties except the following: "The manufacturer warrants each new motor vehicle, . . . chassis or parts manufactured by it to be free from defects in material or workmanship under normal use and service." The agreement went on to limit the manufacturer's obligation to replacement of defective parts returned to the manufacturer within 90 days of the original delivery or 4,000 miles, whichever occurred first. The Henningsens drove the vehicle for 10 days without mishap. On the 11th day Mrs. Henningsen was operating the vehicle on a paved, smooth road at 20–22 miles per hour when "[s]uddenly she heard a loud noise 'from the bottom, by the hood.' It 'felt as if something cracked.' " The steering wheel spun and the car veered to the right before crashing into a brick wall. The vehicle was a total loss. Mrs. Henningsen sustained personal injury.

The plaintiffs sued the defendants for damages, on the theories of negligence and breach of express and implied warranties. The case was submitted to the jury on the issue of implied warranty of merchantability. The jury returned verdicts in favor of the plaintiffs against both defendants. Defendants appealed, and the case was certified to the Supreme Court of New Jersey, which affirmed the trial court's decision.

Francis, Judge:

* * * * *

THE CLAIM OF IMPLIED WARRANTY AGAINST THE MANUFACTURER

In the ordinary case of sale of goods by description an implied warranty of merchantability is an integral part of the transaction. . . .

* * * * *

As the Sales Act and its liberal interpretation by the courts threw this protective cloak about the buyer, the decisions in various jurisdictions revealed beyond doubt that many manufacturers took steps to avoid these ever increasing warranty obligations. Realizing that the act governed the relationship of buyer and seller, they undertook to withdraw from actual and direct contractual contact with the buyer. They ceased selling products to the consuming public through their own employees and making contracts of sale in their own names. Instead, a system of independent dealers was established; their products were sold to dealers who in turn dealt with the buyer public, ostensibly solely in their own personal capacity as sellers. In the past in many instances, manufacturers were able to transfer to the dealers burdens imposed by the act and thus achieved a large measure of immunity for themselves. But, . . . such marketing practices, coupled with the advent of large scale advertising by manufacturers to promote the purchase of these goods from dealers by members of the public, provided a basis upon which the existence of express warranties was predicated, even though the manufacturer was not a party to the contract of sale.

* * * * *

The terms of the warranty are a sad commentary upon the automobile manufacturers' marketing practices. Warranties developed in the law in the interest of and to protect the ordinary consumer who cannot be expected to have the knowledge or capacity or even the opportunity to make adequate inspection of mechanical instrumentalities, like automobiles, and to decide for himself whether they are reasonably fit for the designed purpose. But the ingenuity of the Automobile Manufacturers Association, by means of its standardized form, has metamorphosed the warranty into a device to limit the maker's liability.

* * * * *

Chrysler points out that an implied warranty of merchantability is an incident of a contract of sale. It concedes, of course, the making of the original sale to Bloomfield Motors, Inc., but maintains that this transaction marked the terminal point of its contractual connection with the car. Then Chrysler urges that since it was not a party to the sale by the dealer to Henningsen, there is not privity of contract between it and the plaintiffs, and the absence of this privity eliminates any such implied warranty.

* * * * *

. . . The limitations of privity in contracts for the sale of goods developed their place in the law when marketing conditions were simple, when maker and buyer frequently met face to face on an equal bargaining plane and when many of the products were relatively uncomplicated and conducive to inspection by a buyer competent to evaluate their quality. With the advent of mass marketing, the manufacturer became remote from the purchaser, sales were accomplished through intermediaries, and the demand for the product was created by advertising media. In such an economy it became obvious that the consumer was the person being cultivated. Manifestly, the connotation of "consumer" was broader than that of "buyer." He signified such a person who, in the reasonable contemplation of the parties to the sale, might be expected to use the product. Thus, where the commodities sold are such that if defectively manufactured they will be dangerous to life or limb, then society's interests can only be protected by eliminating the requirement of privity between the maker and his dealers and the reasonably expected ultimate consumer. In that way the burden of losses consequent upon use of defective articles is borne by those who are in a position to either control the danger or make an equitable distribution of the losses when they do occur. . . .

* * * * *

Most of the cases where lack of privity has not been permitted to interfere with recovery have involved food and drugs. In fact, the rule as to such products has been characterized as an exception to the general doctrine. But more recently courts, sensing the inequity of such limitation, have moved into broader fields.

We see no rational doctrinal basis for differentiating between a fly in a bottle of beverage and a defective automobile. The unwholesome beverage may bring illness to one person, the defective car, with its great potentiality for harm to the driver, occupants, and others, demands even less adherence to the narrow barrier of privity.

* * * * *

Accordingly, we hold that under modern marketing conditions, when a manufacturer puts a new automobile in the stream of trade and promotes its purchase by the public, an implied warranty that it is reasonably suitable for use as such accompanies it into the hands of the ultimate purchaser. . . .

THE DEFENSE OF LACK OF PRIVITY AGAINST MRS. HENNINGSEN

Both defendants contend that since there was not privity of contract between them and Mrs. Henningsen, she cannot recover for breach of any warranty made by either of them. On the facts, as they were developed, we agree that she was not a party to the purchase agreement. Her right to maintain the action, therefore, depends upon whether she occupies such legal status thereunder as to permit her to take advantage of a breach of defendants' implied warranties. [The court then reasoned that Mrs. Henningsen could recover even though she was a "stranger" to the contract.]

* * * * *

It would be wholly opposed to reality to say that use by such persons is not within the anticipation of parties to such a warranty of reasonable suitablility of an automobile for ordinary highway operation.

* * * * *

Case questions

1. Why did Mr. Henningsen join in the suit with his wife? What losses did he sustain?

2. The cause of action for negligence was dismissed by the court. Why? What doctrine could help to prove negligence in this case. What are the reasons against giving effect to the disclaimer?

3. How did manufacturers over the years convert the warranty of merchantability to their own benefit?

4. How can a manufacturer protect itself? Can it effectively disclaim warranties?

5. Once the requirement of privity is negated, who may recover? Should recovery be confined to members of the purchaser's family? What about pedestrians? Why? What if the Henningsen vehicle had been stolen and the thieves were injured when the steering mechanism faltered? Do you think they could recover?

Strict liability

As society became more industrialized, the relationship between the consumer and the product distributor became more depersonalized. As technology developed and mass production increased, the incidence of product defects and resultant injuries rose sharply. It became very apparent, especially to consumers, that the theories of negligence and warranty had severe limitations. Negligence was difficult to prove, and manufacturers attempted to shield themselves by disclaiming warranties. In addition, some courts still adhered to the privity requirement when an action was based on warranty.

In the interests of injured consumers, courts started chipping away at the impediments posed to recovery by the negligence and warranty theories. Res ipsa loquitur was successfully invoked to compensate for the consumer's inability to pinpoint the producer's negligent act. Courts followed the lead of *Henningsen* in abolishing the necessity for privity in warranty cases. The first cases to extend this help to consumers involved foods and products which contained printed warranties or were widely advertised. Only later did courts extend the same protection to other products. Even then there were still obstacles for the consumer to hurdle. Under negligence theory, contributory negligence and assumption of the risk loomed as a bar to recovery. Under warranty theory, manufacturer disclaimers and limitations further hampered consumer recovery.

Although the concept of strict liability was being developed as early as the 1930s, it was not until 1963, in *Greenman* v. *Yuba Power Products, Inc.*, that it emerged as an independent tort.[5] In *Greenman* plaintiff was seriously injured while using a defective combination power tool. The Supreme Court of

---

[5] 50 Cal.2d 57, 377 P.2d 897 (1963).

California sidestepped the limitations of negligence and warranty theory and recognized the tort of strict liability. In its opinion the court said:

> A manufacturer is strictly liable in tort when an article he places on the market, knowing that it is to be used without inspection for defects, proves to have a defect that causes injury to a human being. . . .

*   *   *   *   *

> . . . The purpose of such liability is to insure that the costs of injuries resulting from defective products are borne by the manufacturers that put such products on the market rather than by the injured persons who are powerless to protect themselves.

Since *Greenman,* courts have followed its lead in developing product liability law along the lines of strict liability independent of negligence or warranty theory. The strict liability standard has been set down in the *Restatement (Second) of Torts,* section 402(A), which imposes liability upon "[o]ne who sells any product in a defective condition unreasonably dangerous to the user or consumer or to his property." Under the *Restatement,* liability for injury exists even if the "seller has exercised all possible care in the preparation and sale of his product" and even if the consumer is not in privity with the seller.

It must be noted that the *Restatement* is a scholarly synthesis and summary of the law as perceived by the American Law Institute. It does not have the force of law, though courts often rely heavily on it and adopt its provisions as the law of their jurisdiction.

Under the strict liability theory the focus is on determining whether the defect makes the product unreasonably dangerous. A plaintiff may recover even if the defendant has neither been negligent nor breached a warranty. It does not matter if the defendant acted reasonably in the manufacture or inspection of the product. A defectively manufactured tire is a classic example of the cases to which strict liability attaches. It is reasonably foreseeable that a defect in a tire would cause the tire to be unreasonably dangerous. Tires support cars that travel at a fast rate of speed. If a tire blows because of a defective tread, there is a reasonable likelihood of injury to the car's occupants. In contrast, a defectively manufactured manual typewriter would not normally present an unreasonably dangerous risk of injury to the user, and hence would not ordinarily be the subject of strict liability.

Under strict liability, recovery for damages due to injury is not limited to the manufacturer. Everyone in the distributive chain that has marketed the product is liable, including the distributor, wholesaler, jobber, and retailer. Their liability, like the manufacturer's, is not dependent on their conduct. Even when a defective component is integrated into a larger product, members in the distributive stream may still be strictly liable as long as the product left the defendants' control in a defective condition.

Strict liability applies only against those regularly engaged in selling the product. Section 402A is not intended to reach the occasional seller, such as the person who makes an isolated sale of a hunting rifle to a friend. The word *seller,* however, has been liberally construed by courts to encompass lessors, bailors, and those performing services.

The *Restatement* has not taken a position as to whether a bystander may recover under strict liability. The trend has certainly been to include family members and those bystanders whose injury is reasonably foreseeable. In an injury caused by an automobile with defective brakes, there is little difference between a pedestrian and the operator of the automobile. In fact, the pedestrian, unlike the operator, lacks the opportunity to inspect the vehicle. The following case involves an injured bystander in embryo.

Sindell v. *Abbott Laboratories*
163 Cal. Rptr. 132, 607 P.2d 924 (1980)

Judith Sindell (plaintiff) sued 11 drug companies (defendants) engaged in the business of distributing diethylstilbestrol (DES), a drug prescribed for use by plaintiff's mother to prevent miscarriages. Plaintiff alleged that she developed a cancerous tumor and suffered from adenosis (precancerous vaginal and cervical growths) as a result of her mother's ingestion of DES. Plaintiff predicated her complaint upon various theories of recovery, including strict liability. She was unable to identify which company manufactured the precise drug that caused the injury. Consequently, the trial court dismissed the action against the defendants. The Supreme Court of California reversed.

Mosk, Justice:

* * * * *

We begin with the proposition that, as a general rule, the imposition of liability depends upon a showing by the plaintiff that his or her injuries were caused by the act of the defendant or by an instrumentality under the defendant's control. . . .

There are, however, exceptions to this rule. Plaintiff's complaint suggests several bases upon which defendants may be held liable for her injuries even though she cannot demonstrate the name of the manufacturer which produced the DES actually taken by her mother. . . .

Plaintiff places primary reliance upon cases which hold that if a party cannot identify which of two or more defendants causes an injury, the burden of proof may shift to the defendants to show that they were not responsible for the harm. This principle is sometimes referred to as the "alternative liability" theory.

The celebrated case of *Summers* v. *Tice,* a unanimous opinion of this court, best exemplifies the rule. In *Summers,* the plaintiff was injured when two hunters negligently shot in his direction. It could not be determined which of them had fired the shot which actually caused the injury to the plaintiff's eye, but both defendants were nevertheless held jointly and severally liable for the whole of the damages. We reasoned that both were wrongdoers, both were negligent toward the plaintiff, and that it would be unfair to require plaintiff to isolate the defendant responsible, because if the one pointed out were to escape liability, the other might also, and the plaintiff-victim would be shorn of any remedy. In these circumstances, we held, the burden of proof shifted to the defendants, "each to absolve himself if he can."

We stated that under these or similar circumstances a defendant is ordinarily in a "far better position" to offer evidence to determine whether he or another defendant caused the injury.

* * * * *

Nevertheless, plaintiff may not prevail in her claim that the *Summers* rationale should be employed to fix the whole liability for her injuries upon defendants, at least as those principles have previously been applied. There is an important difference between the situation involved in *Summers* and the present case. There, all the parties who were or could have been responsible for the harm to the plaintiff were joined as defendants. Here, by contrast, there are approximately 200 drug companies which made DES, any of which might have manufactured the injury-producing drug.

* * * * *

In our contemporary complex industrialized society, advances in science and technology create fungible goods which may harm consumers and which cannot be traced to any specific producer. The response of the courts can be either to adhere rigidly to prior doctrine, denying recovery to those injured by such products, or to fashion remedies to meet these changing needs. . . . Justice Traynor in his landmark concurring opinion in *Escola* v. *Coca Cola Bottling Company* recognized that in an era of mass production and complex marketing methods the traditional standard of negligence was insufficient to govern the obligations of manufacturer to consumer. . . .

* * * * *

From a broader policy standpoint, defendants are better able to bear the cost of injury resulting from the manufacture of a defective product. As was said by Justice Traynor in *Escola,* "[t]he cost of an injury and the loss of time or health may be an overwhelming misfortune to the person injured, and a needless one, for the risk of injury can be insured by the manufacturer and distributed among the public as

a cost of doing business." The manufacturer is in the best position to discover and guard against defects in its products and to warn of harmful effects; thus, holding it liable for defects and failure to warn of harmful effects will provide an incentive to product safety. These considerations are particularly significant where medication is involved, for the consumer is virtually helpless to protect himself from serious, sometimes permanent, sometimes fatal, injuries caused by deleterious drugs.

* * * * *

But we approach the issue of causation from a different perspective: we hold it to be reasonable in the present context to measure the likelihood that any of the defendants supplied the product which allegedly injured plaintiff by the percentage which the DES sold by each of them for the purpose of preventing miscarriage bears to the entire production of the drug sold by all for that purpose. . . .

* * * * *

The presence in the action of a substantial share of the appropriate market also provides a ready means to apportion damages among the defendants. Each defendant will be held liable for the proportion of the judgment represented by its share of that market unless it demonstrates that it could not have made the product which caused plaintiff's injuries. . . .

We are not unmindful of the practical problems involved in defining the market and determining market share, but these are largely matters of proof which properly cannot be determined at the pleading stage of these proceedings. . . . [U]nder the rule we adopt, each manufacturer's liability for an injury would be approximately equivalent to the damages caused by the DES it manufactured.

Case questions

1. Explain the alternative liability theory? Does it place an undue burden upon the defendant? How can the defendant avoid liability?

2. What is the distinction between *Sindell* and *Summers?* Does this case extend the rule of *Summers?* In what way? Should the rule of

this case be confined to drugs and similar inherently dangerous products, or should it be expanded? Explain.

3. What is the reasoning behind the rule of this case? Does this case adopt a no-fault standard? Explain.

4. Assume that the case went to trial and the jury came back with the following findings: *(a)* Verdict in favor of plaintiff against manufacturers A, B, C, and D. *(b)* A had 10 percent of the market; B had 20 percent of the market; C had 15 percent of the market; and D had 20 percent of the market. *(c)* Plaintiff sustained injuries amounting to $500,000. What is the liability of each defendant? Are you bothered by the possibility that none of these defendants were directly responsible for the injury? Why or why not?

Defenses. The *Restatement (Second) of Torts* does not recognize contributory negligence as a defense against strict liability in tort. Economics, not fault is the basis for holding a manufacturer liable for producing a defective product that causes injury. The manufacturer is ordinarily in a better position than the plaintiff to cover the loss for injury. Hence, mere carelessness on the part of the plaintiff will not bar recovery. Misuse of the product, however, is recognized as a bar when such misuse contributes to the plaintiff's injury. Using a power saw as a toenail clipper is an example of misuse. Since this misuse cannot reasonably be foreseen by the seller, no liability will result even if a product defect causes injury. The defense of assumption of the risk is also available to the seller of a defective product. If a plaintiff knows of a dangerous defect in a swimming pool slide but nonetheless proceeds to use the slide, assumption of the risk will prevent recovery for injuries sustained because of the slide's defective condition.

THE MAGNUSON—MOSS WARRANTY ACT

A Task Force on Appliance Warranties and Service established by the president in 1968 concluded that the consumer was unfairly treated and inadequately protected in the area of product servicing, repair, and durability. The prime abuse was found to be in the manufacturer's use of disclaimers to restrict its liability. It was common for the manufacturer to disclaim the product's implied warranty of fitness and merchantability by using a written warranty that appeared to give the consumer something extra. In addition, written warranties were often couched in language imcomprehensible to the average consumer. Many warranties were consciously vague or just downright deceptive. Warrantors frequently failed to honor their warranties. As a result the Magnuson-Moss Warranty Federal Trade Commission Improvement Act was passed by Congress. The stated purpose of the act was to "improve the adequacy of information available to consumers, prevent deception, and improve competition in the marketing of consumer products." Toward those ends the act requires certain disclosures in connection with written warranties, imposes restrictions upon disclaimers of implied warranties, and establishes a procedure through which consumers may more effectively enforce their warranty rights.

Magnuson-Moss covers only consumer products, and it is administered by the FTC. The act defines a consumer product as "any tangible personal property which is distributed in commerce and which is normally used for personal, family, or household purposes." The act is only applicable when a seller offers a written warranty.

Disclosure

The manufacturer or seller does not have to make any warranties. But if a written warranty is made in connection with a consumer product costing over $15, it must "fully and conspicuously disclose in simple and readily understandable language the terms and conditions of the warranty."[6] The specific contents of disclosures under the act, are entrusted to the FTC, which has the power to promulgate rules requiring that the written warranty include such terms as the following: the clear identification of the names and addresses of the warrantors, the products or parts covered, exceptions and exclusions from the terms of the warranty, and a brief, general description of the legal remedies available to the consumer. The FTC has promulgated rules governing these requirements. For example, one FTC rule provides that any exclusion, such as a limitation of liability due to personal or property damage, must be accompanied by the following statement:

> Some states do not allow the exclusion or limitation of incidental or consequential damages, so the above limitation or exclusion may not apply to you.

Another FTC rule deals with warranty registration cards. If a warranty registration card comes with a product and stipulates that the consumer must fill it out and return it to the warrantor in order to be covered by warranty, an FTC rule requires disclosure of this stipulation in the warranty.

Full and limited warranty

Magnuson-Moss also requires that any written warranty involving a product that costs more than $10 must clearly and conspicuously contain the tag "FULL" or "LIMITED." The "FULL" tag is properly employed only if the warranty is consistent with at least the four following federal standards:

1. In case of a defect, malfunction, or failure to conform to the warranty, the warrantor must remedy the product within a reasonable time without charge.
2. The warrantor may not impose any limitation on the duration of an implied warranty on the product.
3. The warrantor may not exclude or limit consequential damages (including personal injury damages) for breach of warranty on the product unless the exclusion appears conspicuously on the face of the warranty.

---

[6] Although the act authorizes the FTC to promulgate rules requiring disclosure on warranties pertaining to products that cost over $5, the FTC thus far by rule has required disclosure only for products costing over $15.

4. After a reasonable number of failed attempts to remedy the defects in the product, the warrantor must permit the customer to elect a refund or replacement of the product without charge.

If a warranty does not meet these federal standards, then it must be conspicuously designated "LIMITED." Note that under the above standards the seller may absolve itself from any personal injury liability resulting from the breach of warranty; confine the remedies to repair, refund, or replacement; and still depict the warranty as "FULL."

The waters are muddied, however, when UCC section 2–719(3) is injected for consideration. This states that a limitation upon consequential damages for personal injury is prima facie unconscionable (unfair), and hence a disclaimer of this nature would appear to be impermissible. This inference is buttressed by a section of the Magnuson-Moss Act which states that "nothing in this title shall invalidate or restrict any right or remedy of any consumer under State law." Since the UCC is state law in the jurisdictions that have adopted it, section 2–719(3) appears to be controlling.

Limitation of disclaimer

Under the Magnuson-Moss Act a supplier is prohibited from disclaiming or modifying any implied warranty. This provision does not preclude a supplier from disclaiming implied warranties of fitness of merchantability when the sale of the product is not connected with a written warranty or a service contract. Consequently, it is possible for a supplier to except all implied warranties by selling "as is." Furthermore, a supplier may limit the duration of implied warranties to the duration of a written warranty as long as such limitation is conscionable and is prominently included in clear language on the face of the warranty. An express warranty that restricts the duration of the implied warranty must be designated "LIMITED."

Remedies

A consumer or class (group) of consumers may bring an action for damages against a warrantor that violates the Magnuson-Moss Act or otherwise breaches an express or implied warranty. A successful plaintiff may recover, in addition to damages, the costs and expenses of the suit, including an award of reasonable attorney fees. However, the warrantor may establish an informal dispute resolution procedure that conforms to FTC rules and may include within the written warranty a requirement that the consumer resort to the dispute procedure before pursuing legal action under the act. The consumer will be bound by this provision. An FTC rule authorizes the informal dispute decision to be admitted into evidence in a civil action; however, the decision is not binding upon the court. The Magnuson-Moss Act also requires that the warrantor be afforded a reasonable opportunity to rectify its failure to comply before a suit may be instituted.

THE CONSUMER PRODUCT SAFETY ACT

In 1967 the National Commission on Product Safety was established to investigate the adequacy of consumer protection against unreasonable risks caused by "hazardous household products." In its report to the president and Congress, the commission observed that "the exposure of consumers to unreasonable consumer product hazards is excessive by any standard of measurement." The commission took particular note of products that were notorious for presenting unreasonable hazards. Those products included color TV sets, fireworks, glass bottles, infant furniture, lawn mowers, and unvented gas heaters. The commission believed that the industries producing these products were too profit conscious to engage in the type of self-regulation that would adequately protect consumers. It recommended the creation of a federal regulatory agency with broad authority to insure the safety of consumer products by imposing mandatory safety standards. In 1972, in response to these recommendations, Congress passed the Consumer Product Safety Act (CPSA), which established the Consumer Product Safety Commission (CPSC).[7]

Structure of the Consumer Product Safety Commission

The CPSC consists of five commissioners appointed by the president—one of whom the president appoints as chairperson—with the advice and consent of the Senate. The commissioners are appointed for seven-years terms. A maximum of three commission members may be affiliated with the same political party. No member of the commission may be financially connected with anyone in the consumer product business or hold outside employment. Commission employees with civil service grades above GS–14 cannot accept a job, within 12 months after leaving the commission's employ, with an employer who was subject to the CPSA.

Consumer product

The commission has jurisdiction over consumer products. A consumer product is defined in the CPSA as

> [A]ny article, or component part thereof, produced or distributed (i) for sale to a consumer for use in or around a permanent or temporary household or residence, a school, in recreation, or otherwise, or (ii) for the personal use, consumption or enjoyment of a consumer in or around a permanent or temporary household or residence, a school, in recreation, or otherwise.

---

[7] The CPSA transferred to the CPSC the administration of several other acts related to consumer safety. These were the Federal Hazardous Substances Act (FHSA), the Poison Prevention Packaging Act (PPPA), the Flammable Fabrics Act (FFA), and the Refrigerator Safety Act (RSA).

The CPSC has expressed its intention of interpreting the term *consumer product* as broadly as possible. Under the definition a product not sold to a consumer may be considered a consumer product as long as it was produced or distributed for consumer use. A product need not be intended for exclusive use by one consumer in order to be classified as a consumer product. Vending machines placed in schools, workplaces, or other public places are deemed consumer products. A serious question exists, however, as to whether a consumer must have exclusive control over a consumer product. This was one of several issues presented in a case involving an amusement park ride.

State of Texas v. CPSC
481 F. Supp. (N.D. Tex. 1979)

The State Fair of Texas (plaintiff) sought an injunction restraining the CPSC (defendant) from conducting an investigation of an accident that involved plaintiff's aerial tramway. The district court denied the injunction. The defendant thereafter obtained an administrative inspection warrant to inspect the tramway, and the district court was called upon to determine whether an aerial tramway was a consumer product within the definition of the CPSA. The court held in favor of the commission.

Higginbotham, District Judge:

*   *   *   *   *

THE AERIAL TRAMWAY'S STATUS AS A "CONSUMER PRODUCT"

In order for § 16(a)(1) of the Consumer Product Safety Act, to authorize an inspection of the aerial tramway at the State Fair, the ride must be a consumer product within the meaning of . . . the Act. . . . The issue of whether an amusement park ride is a consumer product within the meaning of this Act is one of first impression in this circuit. Those courts which have addressed this issue offer different answers. In *Consumer Product Safety Commission* v. *Chance Manufacturing Co.,* the court held that the "Zipper," a ride consisting primarily of a boom which rotates in a 360 degree arc, is a consumer product. In *Walt Disney*

Productions v. *United States Consumer Product Safety Commission,* the court found that the sky rides at Disneyland and Disney World are not consumer products.

Through consideration of the individual elements in the statutory definition of "consumer product," this court concludes that the term covers the aerial tramway here involved.

*   *   *   *   *

The Act . . . provide[s] specific exemptions for a variety of products unrelated to this sort of amusement park ride. Redefined, the question with which we are faced is whether this ride is an "article . . . produced or distributed for the personal use . . . or enjoyment of a consumer . . . in recreation.". . .

The tramway is an "article," being "an object produced or distributed as a distinct article of commerce, rather than any physical entity that might exist only at an intermediate stage of production." That the tramway is large ought not concern us. Were bulk to be considered in determining the boundaries of the term "article," Congress would not have needed to expressly exempt aircraft from designation as a consumer product.

The ride was clearly produced "for the personal use . . . or enjoyment" of consumers "in recreation," as those terms are normally understood. We can dispose of a variety of grounds for challenging this assertion. Given the nature of the site of the tramway, and the expense, speed, and other features of the ride itself, an argument that the ride was not intended for the enjoyment of recreation-minded consumers fails.

*   *   *   *   *

. . . [O]ne might assert that the adjective "personal" incorporates the concept of individual dominion and control with respect to transfers to consumers not involving a sale. But courts simply have not held that the term "personal" imports a control requirement. In *Chance,* the court held that

> [t]hough the riders of the Zipper do not control it, own it, or otherwise possess it, their occupancy of its cars and concomitant exposure to whatever dangers it may present are sufficient to satisfy the "personal use, consumption, or enjoyment" clause.

In addition, the courts asserted that nowhere does the legislative history of the Act suggest that "Congress intended to import a 'control' requirement into the definition of the term 'consumer product.' "

. . . State Fair argues that because the tramway is not being sold to consumers it cannot be considered a consumer product. This argument also fails. Pointedly, the requirement that the product customarily be "produced or distributed for sale" was eliminated prior to enactment. The amended definition only required that the article be produced or distributed for a consumer's use.

*   *   *   *   *

Finally, the ride is not a product which is "not customarily produced or distributed for sale to, or use or consumption by, or enjoyment of a consumer." This exclusion was intended to exclude industrial products, on the premise that industrial purchasers can better protect themselves and are subject to regulation under the Occupational Safety and Health Act of 1970. It can hardly be maintained that aerial tramways are produced for any reason but for the use or enjoyment of a consumer: the ride is simply not an industrial product. Moreover, this ride, though not purchased by consumers, exposes them to possible danger and is not regulated under OSHA.

*   *   *   *   *

The only forceful argument that the ride cannot be considered a "consumer product" lies outside the definition provided by the Act. As the court in *Disney, supra,* pointed out, § 2066(b) authorizes the Commission to obtain "free samples" of any consumer product offered for import into the United States and 2076(f) authorizes the Commission, in the exercise of its functions, to purchase at cost any consumer product it needs. Because of the cost of aerial tramways, it seems unrealistic to speak of acquiring them free or at cost. But were the ability to be sampled required of a consumer product, there would have been no need to expressly exempt aircraft from the Act's coverage. And while acquiring samples of an entire tramway may not be feasible, the Commission may well acquire various components thereof. Given that the tramway fits comfortably within that language in the Act expressly set out as the definition of consumer product, a peripheral appearance of inconsistency ought not affect the outcome. Any inconsistency is peripheral at best because there is nothing in the idea that the Commission is authorized to obtain samples that leads one to the conclusion that where it is impractical to do so, no right of inspection was intended. The Commission is authorized, not required, to sample.

*   *   *   *   *

Case questions

1. Why do you think the CPSC was interested in conducting an investigation of the aerial tramway accident? Would an injured party in such an accident have any recourse against the manufacturer on any theories previously discussed? Explain.

2. Is an amusement park ride includable as a consumer product under a plain reading of the act? Name some products that are not so includable.

3. Why does the "sampling" argument fail to exclude the tramway?

Information gathering

The CPSC maintains an Injury Information Clearinghouse as directed by the act. The purpose of the clearinghouse is to collect and analyze injury information. The National Electronic Injury Surveillance System (NEISS) assists the CPSC in the collection of the data. NEISS is a computerized record compilation system that accumulates injury data from over 100 hospitals located throughout the United States. Any product-related injury treated in these hospitals is immediately transmitted by NEISS to the commission in Washington, D.C. NEISS provides a sampling of product-related injuries to help the commission determine which products pose the most serious risk of injury. The higher the risk of injury posed by a product, the faster the attention it receives from the CPSC. Some of the products which are or have been high on the CPSC's priority list include bicycles, beds, ladders and stools, matches, outdoor grills, television sets, lawn mowers, razors, and snowmobiles. The commission is also authorized to require manufacturers to keep records and supply CPSC with information regarding products. Pursuant to proper procedure CPSC may inspect the premises or records related to the manufacture of consumer products. In addition, it can require a manufacturer to furnish the CPSC with notice of any new consumer product before making the product available for consumption. In furtherance of its information gathering function, the commission may conduct hearings or inquiries relevant to consumer product safety.

Rules and bans

In its attempt to remove products that present unreasonable risks of injury the CPSC is authorized to issue consumer product safety rules or standards. The standards may be in the form of performance composition, design, construction, finish, or packaging requirements. The commission may also adopt standards requiring the manufacturer to give the consumer warnings or instructions about a product. When no safety standard adopted by the commission could adequately protect the public from unreasonable risk of injury, the commission can seek a ban of a product.

Any interested person may petition the commission for the issuance, amendment, or revocation of a consumer product safety rule or a product ban. In reaction to the petition the CPSC may conduct a public hearing investigation. If the petition is granted, the commission places a notice in the *Federal Register*. The notice identifies the product and the risk of injury that the product creates. The notice also invites the public to submit a proposal of an existing standard to remedy the risk of injury or to offer to develop a proposed standard.

In determining whether to grant a petition to develop a standard, the commission's key inquiry is whether the product presents an unreasonable risk of injury. The commission has denied many petitions on the basis that this key inquiry was lacking. The commission, for example, denied a petition requesting a standard to remedy the laceration hazard presented by pull-tab and pull-lid containers. After analyzing the injury data, the commission concluded that the pull-tab and pull-lid containers did not present any greater hazard than conventional cans. Petitions requesting standards for beer kegs, fondue pots, football shoes, and pierced earrings have all met defeat for similar reasons.

A standard must be "reasonably necessary" to mitigate or eliminate the risk of injury. By interpretation, courts deem consideration of the standard's effectiveness and of the standard's effect on the cost of the product relevant in a determination of "reasonably necessary." In reviewing the commission's standards for matchbook covers, the First Circuit Court of Appeals, passing on the "reasonably necessary" issue, said:

> Since the cost of testing to insure compliance with the general requirements geared to meeting the fragmentation hazard will therefore be slight, and the object of the requirements—ensuring a properly functioning product—seems only reasonable, we think that these requirements can be said to be "reasonably necessary" to reduce the risk from fragmentation [of the matchhead.] [8]

When a safety standard for a product is imposed upon a manufacturer, the commission sets an effective date by which time the standard must be implemented. To prevent manufacturers from stockpiling the product before the effective date, the commission is empowered to issue an antistockpiling order banning the manufacturer from increasing its inventory of the product at a rate significantly greater than the rate at which it was increased during a commission-specified period prior to the institution of the standard.

Among the products subject to consumer product safety standards promulgated by the CPSC are the following: swimming pool slides, matchbooks, cellulose insulation, bicycles, baby cribs, fireworks, pacifiers, clacker balls, baby bouncers, and lawnmowers.

An example: the lawn mower. The commission found in the early 1970s about 77,000 injuries to consumers were caused annually by accidents involving the blades of walk-behind power lawn mowers. The annual economic cost to the injured was found to be about $253 million, not including pain, suffering, and lost use of amputated fingers and toes. The commission implemented standards, effective at the end of 1981, for certain consumer walk-behind power lawn mowers. Two performance standards apply to rotary

---

[8] *D. D. Bean & Sons Co.* v. *CPSC* 574 F.2d 643 at 651 (1st Cir. 1978).

walk-behind lawn mowers only, and one label standard applies to both rotary and reel-type lawn mowers. The first performance standard is that a foot probe inserted under the mower at prescribed places be prevented from entering the path of the blade. Shields may be used for this purpose; however, they must be capable of withstanding a minimum tensile force test without damage. The second performance standard requires the use of a blade control system which allows the blade to be activated only while the operator is in continuous contact with a deadman's control and which stops the blade's movement within three seconds after the control is released. The third standard subjects both rotary and reel-type walk-behind lawn mowers to labeling requirements. A label, attached to a specified location on the mower, must contain in large print the words "DANGER: KEEP HANDS AND FEET AWAY" and include a picture of a blade cutting into the finger of an extended hand. The commission estimated that by the end of 1981 implementation of these standards would reduce blade contact injury by 77 percent, resulting in an annual savings of $211 million in injury costs.

Imminent hazards

When the commission determines that a consumer product presents an imminent hazard, there is a need for a quicker mechanism for eliminating the hazard than the normal safety standard and ban procedures. The commission may bring an action in the federal district court seeking seizure of the imminently hazardous product or may seek an injunction against the manufacturer for temporary or permanent relief, or both. An imminently hazardous consumer product is defined as one "which presents imminent and unreasonable risk of death, serious illness or severe personal injury." It poses a more immediate threat than a product that presents an unreasonable risk of harm. When the commission proceeds against the manufacturer of a consumer product that it finds to be imminently hazardous, the district court may grant relief by requiring that the manufacturer notify purchasers of the risk or may otherwise mandate public notice, repair, recall, replacement, or refund for the product.

Sometimes CPSC actions end in consent judgments entered into by agreement of the defendant. In one case the commission instituted an action against the manufacturer of a baseball pitching machine that the commission alleged to be an imminent hazard. The case was terminated when the manufacturer agreed to a decree whereby it would manufacture the machines with a metal screen guard enclosing the trajectory of the arm to prevent "wild pitches" from injuring the consumer.

Substantial product hazard

If manufacturer, distributor, or retailer of a consumer product has reason to believe that the product does not comply with an applicable consumer product safety rule or has a defect which could create a substantial product hazard, it must immediately notify the commission of the fact. A substantial product hazard is one which creates a substantial risk of injury to the public. Failure to comply with this reporting requirement is excused if the manufacturer or other appropriate party knows that the commission has already been adequately informed about the problem.

Normally it is not unduly difficult for a manufacturer, distributor, or retailer of a consumer product to ascertain that a product is in nonconformity with a consumer product safety standard. Presumably any seller of a product covered by a safety standard would be familiar with the details of compliance. It is much more difficult to ascertain whether a product contains a defect which creates a substantial risk of injury to the public. There are, however, certain guidelines connected with that determination. These include a consideration of the risk of injury, need for the product, the population exposed to the product, and the likelihood of injury. In addition to being informed about substantial product hazards by manufacturers, distributors, and retailers, the commission also becomes aware of such hazards through consumer complaints, news media stories, and NEISS data.

Once the commission is satisfied that a substantial product hazard exists, it may require the firm to submit a corrective action plan announcing what steps it intends to take to remedy the hazard. The commission may or may not accept the plan; however, it deems voluntary action to be the most desirable way to proceed since this avoids costly delay while achieving the desired consumer protection. Another form of voluntary compliance is the consent order agreement. If the corrective action plan is unacceptable and a consent order agreement cannot be reached, then the commission can initiate formal enforcement proceedings. Once there is a formal finding that a consumer product constitutes a substantial hazard, the commission may require the firm to give notice to known customers who purchased the product. In addition to notification or in lieu of it the commission may require the manufacturer, distributor, or retailer to elect to remedy the defect or noncompliance with a standard or to repair or replace the product or refund the purchase price. If the "recall procedures" of repair, replacement, or refund are elected, the consumer may not be charged. However, if the product has been in the consumer's possession for at least one year, and the refund remedy is elected, a reasonable deduction for use is permissible.

Remedies

The CPSA authorizes various means of enforcing the act, including product seizure and injunctions. Other remedies include civil and criminal penalties, private suits to enforce the act and private damage actions.

Civil Penalties. A civil penalty of up to $2,000 may be assessed against a person who knowingly violates any CPSA provisions. As defined by the act, "knowingly" is not confined to actual knowledge. It includes knowledge that a reasonable person would possess by exercising reasonable diligence to discover truth. A manufacturer that knowingly sells banned products commits a separate civil offense for each product sold. However, the commission may not impose multiple civil penalties exceeding $500,000 against a violator. In addition, the commission is authorized to exercise its discretion to compromise a penalty (reduce it to less than the prescribed amount). Such exercise of discretion includes consideration of the size of the offender's business and the gravity of the offense.

Criminal penalties.   A person who knowingly and willfully commits an act prohibited by the CPSA, after being notified by the commission of its prohibition, is subject to a criminal penalty of up to $50,000 or one-year imprisonment, or both. A corporate official or agent may also be deemed in criminal violation of the CPSA even in the absence of conscious wrongdoing, as illustrated in the *Park* case in Chapter 19.

Private suits.   Any interested person may sue in order to enforce the CPSA. At least 30 days before actually filing the suit, the individual must notify the CPSC, the attorney general, and the alleged violator of the intention to sue. Such notification affords the commission or the attorney general an opportunity to take appropriate civil or criminal action and gives the alleged offender an opportunity to resolve the complaint. If the commission or the Department of Justice files suit within the 30 days, the individual is barred from suing. A firm that brings such a suit for commercial motives is not deemed an "interested party." Accordingly, a manufacturer of architectural glazing materials that sought to enforce a consumer product safety standard was not deemed an interested party since its motive for prosecuting the suit was to undermine its competitor.

The provision authorizing a private suit to enforce a safety rule or certain commission orders (discussed above) must be distinguished from a private damage suit. An individual who has been injured as a result of a knowing or willful violation of a consumer product safety rule or other commission rule or order may seek damages in a federal district court. The district court has jurisdiction only when the amount in controversy exceeds $10,000. (Otherwise, the injured party is left solely to state remedies.) The aggrieved individual may recover damages, the costs of the suit, and reasonable attorney fees within the sound discretion of the court.

The remedies under the CPSA are not exclusive but are in addition to common-law and statutory remedies provided under state law.

THE NATIONAL HIGHWAY TRAFFIC AND MOTOR VEHICLE ACT

Every year automobiles kill about 60,000 persons. The National Highway Traffic and Motor Vehicle Safety Act (MVS Act) of 1966 created the National Highway Traffic Safety Administration (NHTSA) to regulate the safety and motor vehicle equipment of motor vehicles. NHTSA is authorized by the legislation to establish safety standards for motor vehicles and motor vehicle equipment and to regulate the grading and labeling of tires. NHTSA activity is designed to protect the public from unreasonable risk of injury resulting from the performance of motor vehicles.

The MVS Act makes it unlawful for any manufacturer to sell, offer to sell, or otherwise introduce into interstate commerce a motor vehicle or motor vehicle equipment which is in violation of a motor vehicle safety standard. Under the act the term *manufacturer* includes assemblers, importers, and tire retreaders. The act also imposes certain requirements upon distributors, dealers, and motor vehicle repairpersons.

As in the case of the CPSA, the MVS Act authorizes concerned persons to file petitions requesting standard setting. A petition must be in English, be captioned "Petition," state facts establishing the necessity for a standard, briefly describe the requested standard, and contain the name and address of the petitioner. The proposed standard must be published in the *Federal Register,* and a comment period must be provided.

In entertaining a proposed safety standard, NHTSA must consider the number of accidents and injuries that the standard will reduce, and the practicality and reasonableness of applying the standard. The determination of a standard's reasonableness must include a consideration of the cost of compliance. In addition, the motor vehicle safety standard must either reduce the likelihood of accidents or reduce injuries or deaths from the accidents that do occur.

Pacific Legal Foundation v. *Department of Transportation*
593 F.2d 1338 (D.C. Cir. 1979)

Pacific Legal Foundation (petitioner) challenged Motor Vehicle Safety Standard 208, promulgated by NHTSA. The standard requires all passenger cars sold after September 1, 1983, to possess passive restraints such as automatic seat belts or air bags. The court of appeals upheld the standard.

J. Skelly Wright, Chief Judge:

I

After the "first collision" between an automobile and an external object, passenger restraint systems protect against the "second collision" between vehicle occupants and the interior of the car. In 1967 the Secretary of Transportation issued the original Standard 208, requiring seatbelts in all passenger cars to reduce damages from the second collision. By July 1969, however, the Deparement of Transportation (DOT) concluded that the level of seatbelt use was far too low to reduce traffic injuries to an acceptable level. Consequently, DOT sought to develop "passive restraints" that would protect car occupants automatically. Two currently available systems protect against injuries from the second collision without requiring independent action by motorists. "Passive seatbelts," which function like shoulder belts when in position, deploy around front seat occupants as they enter the car and close the doors, but are largely restricted to use in cars with bucket seats. Airbags are cushions stored under the dashboard that, when triggered by a frontal collision, fill with stored or rapidly generated gas to protect the rider from collision with the car's interior. Both are designed to protect occupants in frontal crashes, so riders must wear lap belts to guard against injury from lateral-impact crashes and roll-overs.

*   *   *   *   *

II

Our review proceeds under both the informal rulemaking provision of the Administrative Procedure Act (APA) and the substantive sections of the Motor Vehicle Safety Act. The latter statute requires that Motor Vehicle Safety Standards "shall be practicable, shall meet the need for motor vehicle safety, and shall be stated in objective terms." In addition, the Secretary must "consider relevant available motor vehicle safety data" and determine the appropriateness of the standard for the type of vehicle covered by it. As applied, these standards can be tested as part of our "thorough, probing, in-depth review" of the record on appeals of informal rulemaking under the APA. Of course, we may not substitute our judgment for the agency's. Still, we must determine that the agency action was consistent with its statutory mandate, rational, and not arbitrary. As this court noted in an earlier Safety Act case, a court must decide "whether the agency has performed in accordance with the Congressional purposes." . . .

III

Petitioners Pacific Legal Foundation et al. offer three major reasons for overturning revised Standard 208: (A) that experimental and real-world data do not support the Secretary's findings on the effectiveness of airbags; (B) that the Secretary violated the Safety Act by failing to consider public reaction to the revised Standard; and (C) that the rule ignores collateral dangers to public safety posed by airbags.

A. Effectiveness of passive restraints

Petitioners concede that seatbelts, including passive belts, are an effective passenger re-

straint system. They challenge, however, DOT's conclusion that laboratory tests and limited field experience establish the reliability of airbags which, given current technology and the rule before us, would probably have to be installed in 75 percent of American cars. After reviewing the record in this case, we find that the Secretary's decision was rational.

Since this rulemaking began in 1969 DOT has conducted over 2,000 crash tests of airbags, including 188 with human volunteers in the vehicles, 274 with dummies, and a handful with cadavers and baboons. Following these experiments, involving collisions at speeds of up to 50 miles per hour, the agency concluded that if airbags were installed in all cars over 9,000 fatalities and over 100,000 injuries would be averted.

*   *   *   *   *

Petitioners also insist that the Secretary's conclusion on airbag effectiveness is contradicted by experience with the 12,000 airbag cars currently in operation in this country. Indeed, there have been more fatalities in frontal accidents involving airbag cars than the statistical projections from experimental data would have indicated. Nevertheless, in view of the relatively small sample involved, and the extraordinary nature of several of the accidents, this variation does not undermine the agency's conclusion that airbags are effective. Moreover, airbags have been very effective in reducing or preventing major injuries.

B. Public reaction

Petitioners assert that the Secretary violated his statutory mandate by refusing to consider public reaction to his decision. The importance of popular response, they contend, can be seen in the Safety Act's requirements that a safety standard be "practicable." The Secretary stated in his order, however, that "public acceptance or rejection of passive restraints is not one of the statutory criteria which the Department is charged by law to apply in establishing standards." Although we agree with petitioners' view of the requirements of the Saftey Act, we believe that the Secretary did take public reaction into account and satisfactorily explained his conclusion that widespread public resistance to passive restraints is unlikely.

* * * * *

Petitioners raise two related points. First, they argue that the Secretary's calculations of expected benefits from passive restraints fail to take into account the possible deactivation of systems by individual motorists, as was common with the ignition interlock. If Secretary Adams correctly anticipates minimal popular resistance to passive restraints, petitioners' argument has no force. In addition, experience with approximately 65,000 cars equipped with passive seatbelts, which are admittedly more intrusive than airbags, indicates a low deactivation rate. We see no basis here for disturbing the DOT rule, especially since the agency's injury-reduction estimates were revised downward by projecting less-than-total compliance with Standard 208.

Second, petitioners contend that installation of passive restraints may deter use of lap belts, noting that even if passive restraints are in place lap belts are needed to protect motorists in non-frontal collisions. A drop in lap belt use would result in higher fatalities and injuries. DOT defends its estimate that lap belt use will continue at the 20 percent level, citing an agency study concluding that with no further need for more intrusive shoulder belts, lap belt use would actually increase to 26 percent. Petitioners point to nothing in the record to refute the agency's estimates.

C. Collateral dangers

Airbags may also present collateral dangers to the public, petitioners argue, which are not justified by the expected benefits from Standard 208. We note at the outset that the Safety Act charges the Secretary with authority to balance present injuries against possible risks posed by safety equipment.

* * * * *

The major danger associated with airbags is inadvertent deployment that might cause the driver to lose control of the car. There is evidence, however, that such deployments do not present a substantial hazard. In road experience three such incidents have occurred, and none caused a collision or injury, while tests with human volunteers have shown little loss of control by drivers. Moreover, the agency is optimistic that the causes of the three inadvertent deployments are understood and can be remedied, so there is some prospect of reducing their likelihood in the future. Even without such improvements, DOT gauges at one in 200 the chance that in a lifetime an individual would experience an inadvertent deployment as an occupant of a car.

Rapidly inflating airbags also may injure out-of-position passengers in the front seat, especially children. New methods of gas generation, however, permit an initially slower inflation, with the aim of more gently moving the occupant back from the dashbord and out of harm's way.

Finally, the chemical used to generate the gas, usually sodium azide, may present a danger in its own right, either during the car's lifetime or upon its demolition for scrap. But placement of the carefully sealed chemical cannister behind the dashboard should be sufficiently remote to prevent most accidents with it, and the cannister could be removed prior to shredding of the car, as is currently done with batteries and gas tanks.

In view of these circumstances, we cannot conclude that the Secretary abused his discretion in assessing the tradeoffs between the expected benefits and the potential dangers of airbags.

Case questions

1. What is the scope of review that is applied to NHTSA's standard?

2. What expectations have been derived from air bag experimentation? What results

have been obtained from actual air bag use? How can you explain the difference? Which should be given more weight, and why?

3. Do you agree with the secretary of transportation's finding that "widespread public resistance to passive restraints is unlikely"?

How would resistance defeat the purpose of the standard?

4. Is a cost-benefit analysis proper in determining the practicality of the standard? How would you go about preparing a cost-benefit analysis of Standard 208?

Remedies

Manufacturers are required to report to NHTSA within five days after discovering that a motor vehicle or replacement part contains a defect connected with motor vehicle safety or is in nonconformity with a federal safety standard. NHTSA also conducts independent investigations to discover safety defects and noncompliance with safety standards. When such a deviation is discovered, appropriate procedures are taken, such as conducting an investigation, publishing the findings in the *Federal Register,* and giving the manufacturer an opportunity to rebut the findings. NHTSA has the power to order the manufacturer to engage in a notification and remedy campaign. Notification is normally accomplished by mailing a letter. Public notice may also be required by NHTSA. The notice must comply with rigid requirements and describe the defect and the plan to remedy the condition without cost to the owner. A manufacturer may elect to repair, replace, or refund the purchase price (less a reasonable depreciation allowance) of a defective or nonconforming motor vehicle.

In 1978 Firestone Tire and Rubber Company entered into an agreement with NHTSA to recall 14 million steel-belted radial tires that were believed to create a safety hazard. The number was increased by 5 million in 1980. Other recalled items during a one-month period in 1980 included 350,000 light-duty trucks because of a brake defect, 6,030 Rolls-Royce autos because the heat generated by the catalytic converters might cause hydraulic brake failures, 155,000 diesel-equipped VWs because of instances of self-acceleration, and 3,860 Harley-Davidson motorcycles because of possible defects in the front fork lock adjusting screw.

The federal district court is invested with jurisdiction to issue a restraining order against anyone who is in violation of the National Highway Traffic and Motor Vehicle Safety Act. Anyone failing to comply with the restraining order may be held in criminal contempt. In addition, any violation of the act subjects the offender to a civil fine of up to $1,000 per offense. Every prohibited action is an offense and exposes the violator to an additional civil penalty. However, the total fine for a series of related offenses may not exceed $800,000. NHTSA is authorized to exercise discretion to compromise a penalty. Such exercise of discretion includes consideration of the size of the offender's business and the gravity of the offense.

POLICY CONSIDERATIONS

Because of the sharp increase in product liability insurance premiums, many small and medium-size firms now cannot afford to obtain liability coverage. This means that these firms are exposed to product liability awards that could bankrupt them. The product liability insurance crisis is acute. Several factors have contributed to the problem. First, firms have not been without fault. Small and medium-size manufacturing firms have failed to institute loss prevention programs to minimize the distribution of unsafe products. Their liability has consequently been greater, thus causing insurance companies to tax them more heavily. Second, insurance companies have traditionally given inadequate attention to ratemaking in the product liability area. They have usually lumped product liability coverage together with comprehensive liability insurance coverage and have thus failed to establish premiums based on sound actuarial data. Consequently, product liability ratemaking is very subjective, and it is not uncommon for a firm to pay a disproportionately high premium given its industry's actual product liability loss experience. Perhaps the biggest reason for the crisis is the inconsistency among the states in applying product liability law. Manufacturers usually distribute their products to wholesalers throughout the country. Because of the variance in the state laws, uncertainty abounds as to the probability of loss. That probability depends upon the law of the state in which the injury occurs. Predictability is low, and this increases the reluctance of insurance companies to underwrite product liability. Because of these factors an unlimited quantity of affordable product liability insurance is unavailable. The supply of risk reduction for a firm is scarce, which means the price is dear.

To help combat the product liability insurance crisis the Department of Commerce has proposed the Model Uniform Product Liability Act (UPLA) for voluntary adoption by the states. It is hoped that introducing uniformity and predictability into the law of product safety will stabilize insurance premiums. The UPLA is a hybrid. It adopts a strict liability standard, similar to that of the *Restatement (Second) of Torts,* to products that possess construction defects or do not conform to an express warranty. It applies a negligence standard to products that possess a defective design or an inadequate warning label. This distinction is made on the basis that the manufacturer is better able to avoid construction defects and nonconforming warranties since these constitute violations of its own preselected standards. Also, the consumer has reasonably great expectations that a product is free from construction flaws and conforms to representations. The criteria for determining that a product has been designed defectively or is inadequately labeled are less objective since these judgments are not based on the company's violation of its own standards but on an ultimate determination that the company has selected the wrong design or label warning based on complex considerations of the existing state of the art.

The UPLA contains features designed to discourage consumers from filing frivolous claims and to cut the costs of litigation. Anyone filing a claim without a legal or factual basis is liable to the opponent for reasonable attorney fees and the costs of the suit. The UPLA adopts nonbinding arbitration for claims of less than $50,000. Presumably, this will result in a lowering of litigation costs.

The UPLA affords the producer several defenses, including contributory negligence, assumption of the risk, misuse of the product, and alteration of the product. At the same time it adopts a comparative responsibility approach, so that these defenses do not bar recovery but merely reduce the award to the extent of the plaintiff's contribution to the injury.

To meet the problem of the insurance industry's tendency to set ad hoc product liability rates, the Commerce Department supports the Risk Retention Act. This act is designed to eliminate the legal restrictions which now prohibit sellers from grouping together to self-insure. It is believed that the advent of private insurance rate setting and risk retention by product seller groups will place pressure upon commercial insurance carriers to set rates in conformity with actual product risk.

Review problems

1. Mary Domany was descending from the second to the first floor of the Sears, Roebuck store when the escalator she was riding came to an abrupt stop. She fell several steps to the floor below. The escalator involved had been purchased from and installed by Otis Elevator Company. The escalator was serviced and maintained by Otis under a contract with Sears which provided that the escalator was under Sears's exclusive control. The place where the escalator mechanism was housed, while not locked, was actually under the exclusive control of Otis. Pursuant to the contract, Otis inspected and serviced the escalator regularly. In addition, Otis responded to calls from Sears for service. Domany, who was severely injured by the abrupt stop of the escalator, wishes to sue to recover damages for her injuries. Whom should she sue? Under what theories may she recover? What are the problems that attach to each of these theories?

2. In 1966 Waddell, a cattle rancher employing natural insemination processes, built up a herd of some 200–250 head of cows and 100–150 yearlings in a cow-calf operation. This represented a 95 percent calf crop. (95 percent of all cows inseminated gave birth). Discussions with an American Breeders Service, Inc. (ABS) representative interested Waddell in the ABS artificial insemination program. To learn more about the program Waddell enrolled in a school sponsored by ABS. During his course Waddell was encouraged to employ the ABS method because, according to ABS: (1) it would increase the uniformity of his calf crop; (2) it would improve his cow herd; (3) it was cheaper than natural breeding services; and (4) under good management it would result in an 80–90 percent calf crop. In 1967, employing the methods he learned from the ABS course, Waddell artificially inseminated 50 of his cows. As a result of this first-year program, his 1968 calf crop was a little above 70 percent. In 1968 he again employed the ABS method; however, this time he noticed that many cows did not become pregnant. In fact, in 1969 his calf crop was only 7 percent. Waddell first complained to ABS in 1969 after he realized that only 7 percent of his artificially inseminated cows had given birth. Having received no satisfaction from ABS, Waddell desired to bring suit against it. Under what theory should Waddell proceed? What are ABS's possible defenses?

3. On August 5, 1971, John Lindsay, a naval aviator, was killed in the crash of an F4B jet aircraft which he was piloting in the course of naval maneuvers. The aircraft was the product of the McDonnell Douglas Corporation, a large supplier of such aircraft to the U.S. government. The aircraft in question crashed in the ocean and was never recovered. Thus an examination of the aircraft was impossible and no conclusive evidence is available regarding the cause of the crash. It is agreed that the aircraft involved was first flown on July 5, 1971, by a McDonnell Douglas test pilot. During that flight the cooling light came on twice, indicating overheating. Overheating also occurred during the second and third flights. Delivery of the aircraft to the government was delayed to correct this and other deficiencies discovered by McDonnell Douglas in the course of a careful inspection of the plane. Lindsay's widow has brought suit against McDonnell Douglas. What is her best theory, and what must she prove in order to recover? McDonnell Douglas contends that it is not liable for any injury caused by the aircraft's crash because of the scrupulously careful examination it conducted. Do you agree? Explain.

4. Bandy Laboratories, Inc., manufactures rabies vaccine. During the processing of the vaccine its employees used surgeon gloves manufactured by the defendant, Travenol Laboratories, Inc. Bandy Laboratories purchased these gloves from Herndon Medical and Surgical Supply, Inc. They were enclosed in sealed packages and marked "sterile latex surgeon's gloves." Bandy maintains that three serials of its rabies vaccine were contaminated. It asserts that the "cause of the contamination of its vaccine was microscopic holes in the gloves which permitted bacteria to pass from the hands of an employee into the vaccine during processing." Bandy desires to sue Travenol Laboratories, Inc., and Herndon Medical and Surgical Sup-

ply, Inc., under negligence, warranty, and strict liability in tort theories. Discuss.

5. Josh Dowell was injured when a defective foil broke while he was fencing. After the accident the weapon was lost, and Dowell could not remember which of two manufacturers produced it. He sued both manufacturers under strict liability and sought the application of *Sindell.* What is the result?

6. Kings Island Amusement Park has a trainlike vehicle that picks up the amusement park patrons in the parking lot at various stops and delivers them to the front gate. Do you think the vehicle is a consumer product under the CPSA? Explain.

7. At Disney World customers may rent baby strollers. These are unlike the baby strollers purchased by consumers in that they are heavy duty and unpadded. Would a stroller of this kind qualify as an article produced or distributed for the enjoyment of a consumer in recreation? Explain.

8. Kaiser Aluminum and Chemical Corporation manufactures aluminum branch circuit wiring systems. These systems conduct electric current from fuses or circuit breakers to terminals within a residence, such as light fixtures and wall plug outlets. Kaiser sells the systems to wholesalers who sell it to contractors for installation in residences.

The Consumer Product Safety Commission, concerned about reports of electrical failures and overheating of the systems, commenced proceedings to adopt a consumer product safety standard regulating the systems. Kaiser objects to the proceedings on the ground that the CPSC has no jurisdiction over industrial products such as these circuit wiring systems. Reread the definition of consumer product, and refute Kaiser's argument.

9. The following NHTSA notice of proposed rulemaking dealing with technical requirements for testing anthropomorphic dummies appeared in the *Federal Register:*

The instrumentation requirements for the 3-year-old test dummy . . . allow the use of single axis or triaxial accelerometers [instruments for measuring acceleration]. The agency is proposing to specify the use of only a triaxial accelerometer in test dummies to eliminate calibration problems caused by single axis accelerometers. The effect of this proposed amendment is to provide more consistent results and to provide child restraint manufacturers with greater certainty about the instrumentation that the agency will use in its compliance testing.

How would you analyze the proposed safety standard in accordance with the requirements of the Motor Vehicle Safety Act and the considerations outlined in *Pacific Legal Foundation* relevant to the scope of review?

10. Discuss the features of UPLA and the Risk Retention Act, and explain why their adoption is expected by many to reduce product liability insurance. Is such a reduction desirable for the firm? The consumer? Why?

CHAPTER 11

Advertising

The earliest advertisements to appear in America may have been those contained in the *Boston Newsletter* in 1704. Most of the early American advertising was local or classified advertising in newspapers. The subsequent development of American advertising has paralleled the development of the American economy.

The building of a nationwide system of railroads during the last 30 years of the 19th-century precipitated the development of magazines with national circulations. These magazines carried a good deal of advertising, most of it for patent medicines.

The development of mass production and mass marketing techniques caused a tremendous expansion in the advertising industry. Brokers who sold space for magazines to advertisers gave way to advertising agencies rendering a wide range of services to the advertiser. Advertising expenditures increased from $5.7 billion in 1950 to $28.2 billion in 1975 to $54.7 billion in 1980.

This chapter explores the manner in which the law regulates advertising. It examines private remedies for false advertising as well as the administrative regulation of advertising by the Federal Trade Commission. The constitutional protections afforded advertisers are discussed in Chapter 4.

PRIVATE REMEDIES FOR FALSE ADVERTISING

False advertising harms consumers by inducing them to purchase goods and services which they might have otherwise avoided. It also harms competitors by deceptively diverting potential customers. It is therefore not surprising that both consumers and competitors have sought relief from false advertising in the courts.

Consumer remedies

Consumer remedies for false advertising are provided both by the common law and by statute. At common law the consumer may seek redress under

301

the law of contracts and the law of torts. The consumer's statutory remedies consist primarily in protection provided by the Uniform Commercial Code's express warranty provision.

Consumer common-law remedies.   The common law does not provide the consumer with much power against deceptive advertisements. Although common-law protections exist in the form of actions for breach of contract and actions for the tort of deceit, the availability of these protections is more theoretical than actual.

Suppose the reader of an advertisement for a certain product goes to the store which placed the ad and asks for the advertised product, only to be told by the seller that the product will be sold at a price higher than the advertised price—or worse yet, that the store has sold out the product. Can the reader of the ad force the advertiser to deliver the product as advertised or be liable for breach of contract? The general answer at common law is an emphatic no.

A contract is defined as an agreement a court will enforce. For an agreement to exist, there must be an acceptance of an offer. The reader who responded to the advertisement was not accepting an offer from the advertiser to sell the product as advertised, but was making an offer to the advertiser which the advertiser did not accept. Advertisements are generally vague; they do not specify quantities available, and often they do not provide specific price information. Courts therefore generally hold that an advertisement is not an offer to enter into a contract. A consumer who responds to an ad merely makes rather than accepts an offer to contract. The advertiser is free to reject that offer if it desires. Consequently, at common law an advertiser generally may with impunity bait the consumer with advertisements of merchandise which it does not intend to sell and switch the consumer to more expensive merchandise at the time of the sale. An advertiser generally may even refuse to sell goods or services at the advertised price and be free of common-law liability.

This is not to say that all advertisements are not offers or that an advertisement cannot be the basis for the understanding between a buyer and a seller of a completed deal. The factual circumstances may lead to a conclusion that a breach of contract claim will be recognized. If an advertisement is complete and reflects contractual intent, it can constitute an offer. For example, an advertisement to sell a limited number of furs for $1 each, and containing the words *first come, first served,* was held to constitute a binding offer to firstcomers.[1] Thus specificity of sale terms, coupled with words of promise, can elevate an advertisement to the level of an offer. Also, advertisements calling upon the reader to undertake some extraordinary responsive act, such as reward offers for dissatisfied users of the product, are held to

---

[1] *Lefkowitz* v. *Great Minneapolis Surplus Store, Inc.,* 251 Minn. 188 86 N.W. 2d 689 (1957).

be offers rather than mere invitations to negotiate. However, these represent the rare exceptions to the rule. Responding to the general common-law approach, some localities have enacted ordinances requiring advertisers to stock sufficient inventories for the reasonably anticipated demand for an advertised product and requiring them to honor their advertisements. As will be seen, the Federal Trade Commission regulations condemn bait and switch selling.

When the advertiser misrepresents the quality of goods or services, the consumer might seek to recover for the common law tort of deceit. To do so, he or she must establish the following:

1. A misrepresentation of fact made by the defendant.
2. Defendant's knowledge of the falsity of the misrepresentation.
3. Defendant's intent that the plaintiff rely on the misrepresentation.
4. Plaintiff's justified reliance on the misrepresentation.
5. Damage to the plaintiff as a result of that reliance.

The action for deceit is very limited in its effectiveness because of the difficulties of proving each of these elements. For example, if the purchaser of a used car whose odometer has been rolled back sues the dealer for deceit, he or she has to prove that the dealer either rolled back the odometer or knew that this had been done. This is difficult to prove because of the possibility that the prior owner rolled back the odometer before delivering it to the dealer.

Frequently statements intended to induce the purchaser's reliance are held to be not actionable because they are expressions of opinion rather than fact. Obvious exaggerations are considered trade puffing on which reliance is not justified. Reliance on the seller's statements is also held unjustified where the purchaser has the opportunity to inspect the goods.

Consumer statutory remedies. In addition to common-law remedies, the consumer has a statutory remedy under the Uniform Commercial Code (UCC), in which a false advertisement constitutes the breach of an express warranty. The UCC governs various commercial transactions. Article 2 of the UCC governs transactions in goods. Section 2–313 provides that any promise, affirmation of fact, description, or sample or model which is part of the basis of a bargain creates an express warranty, and enables the purchaser to sue for breach of warranty where the goods do not conform to the representation. Thus advertising statements may constitute express warranties. However, courts require the consumer to show that he or she reasonably relied upon these statements. Seller's talk, or puffing, will not create an express warranty under the UCC. Furthermore, a seller may in some instances disclaim any express warranties in the sale contract and avoid liability under section 2–313. Thus the puffing defense and clauses excluding warranties have weakened the action for breach of warranty.

Competitor remedies

Competitors, like consumers, may be injured by false advertisements. Injury to a competitor may result either from the distribution of inferior goods falsely represented to be the goods of the competitor or from false statements made about the competitor. Competitors can seek protection in the common law for the torts of palming off and defamation. A federal statute, the Lanham Act, has been interpreted by the courts to provide a limited private remedy for competitors.

Competitor common-law remedies.   Tort law protects competitors' reputations from injuries directly inflicted upon them. Two torts are involved: palming off and defamation.

If an advertiser represents its goods in a manner that would deceive the average customer into believing them to be the goods of a competitor, the advertiser is liable to the competitor for palming off. The representation may involve imitating the trademark, trade name, labels, containers, uniforms, vehicles, appearance of business, or any other distinctive characteristic of the competitor. The competitor may obtain an injunction restraining the advertiser from misrepresenting its goods, and obtain damages for lost customers.

If an advertiser makes false statements that tend to subject a competitor to the contempt or ridicule of the community, the competitor may sue for one of three types of defamation: libel, slander, or disparagement. If the statements attack the competitor personally and are in writing, the competitor may sue for libel. If the same statements are made orally, the competitor may sue for slander. In either case the court will presume that the competitor was damaged. If, however, the statements attack the competitor's trade or business, the competitor's remedy lies in an action for disparagement. In such cases, competitors must prove that the statements induced specific customers to avoid dealing with them, causing pecuniary loss.

False advertising which causes injury to competitors is not limited to statements which defame competitors or palm off goods. Most frequently, false advertisements misrepresent the quality, price, or other characteristics of the advertised merchandise. Such misrepresentations harm competitors by inducing customers away from them. Nevertheless, the common law of torts leaves the competitor powerless against such claims.

This view dates to a 1900 decision, *American Washboard Co.* v. *Saginaw Manufacturing Co.*[2] American, a manufacturer of aluminum washboards, alleged that Saginaw was selling zinc washboards by representing that they were made of aluminum. The Sixth Circuit Court of Appeals affirmed the trial court judgment for Saginaw. The court reasoned that the purpose of the common law was to protect property rights. In the absence of palming off

---

[2] 103 F. 281 (6th Cir. 1900).

or defamation, no property right was infringed. A contrary holding would give American a property right in the use of the word *aluminum.*

A few cases hold that a competitor may recover against an advertiser which represents that its merchandise has qualities which in fact the merchandise does not have, but which the competitor's merchandise does have. The American Law Institute endorsed this position.[3] Nevertheless, most courts continue to follow the view expressed in *American Washboard.*

Competitor statutory remedies. In 1946 Congress enacted the Lanham Trademark Act. Section 43(a) of the act prohibits the use of "any false description or representation" in connection with any goods or services introduced into commerce.[4] It provides a cause of action to any person likely to be damaged by the false description or representation.

Section 43(a) was hailed by many commentators as creating a new federal competitive tort for false advertising. Early decisions, however, refused to interpret the statute to expand the common law. For example, in *Samson Crane Co.* v. *Union National Sales, Inc.,* plaintiff alleged that defendant, by operating a retail store under the name I.A.M. District Lodge 38 Clothing Project, had created the false impression that the store was run by the International Association of Machinists.[5] The court dismissed the action, holding that the alleged misrepresentation was not within the scope of section 43(a). The court restricted the statute's prohibitions to false representations "of the same economic nature as those which involve infringement . . . . of trademarks," or, in other words, to false representations which tend to palm off the goods of the defendant as those of the plaintiff.

More recent decisions have interpreted section 43(a) more liberally. For example, one federal district court held that the manufacturer of Glass Wax violated section 43(a) because the name created the false impression that the product contained wax.[6] In another case, competitors were afforded relief under section 43(a) when a manufacturer labeled its product "potato chips" even though the product was not made from sliced raw potatoes.[7]

Most of the federal circuits now hold that section 43(a) enables one competitor to sue another for false representations concerning the defendant's product. Thus the clear trend and weight of authority is to interpret the Lanham Act to encompass a claim of false advertising, provided that the misrepresentation relates to the defendant's own product or service. As the following case demonstrates, this trend has not affected every federal circuit.

---

[3] ALI, *Restatement of Torts,* sec. 761 (1938).

[4] 15 U.S.C. § 1125(a) (1946).

[5] 87 F. Supp. 218 (D.Mass. 1949), affirmed per curiam, 180 F.2d 896 (1st Cir. 1950).

[6] *Gold Seal Co.* v. *Weeks,* 129 F. Supp. 928 (D.D.C. 1955), affirmed per curiam, 230 F.2d 832, certiorari denied, 352 U.S. 829 (1956).

[7] *Potato Chip Institute* v. *General Mills, Inc.,* 333 F. Supp. 173 (D.Neb. 1971), affirmed per curiam, 461 F.2d 1088 (8th Cir. 1972).

American Consumers, Inc. v. The Kroger Company
416 F. Supp. 1210 (E.D.Tenn. 1976)

American Consumers, Inc. (plaintiff), doing business as Shop-Rite Super Markets, sought an injunction against an advertising campaign conducted by the Kroger Company (defendant).

That campaign, known as the Price Patrol Report, was a form of price advertising. American contended that the advertising was false in various respects and therefore violated the Lanham Act.

Judgment for Kroger.

Wilson, District Judge:

*   *   *   *   *

The plaintiff contends that section 43(a) of the Lanham Act is sufficiently broad in its language and scope as to include false price advertising as allegedly engaged in by Kroger in its grocery merchandising. The defendant, upon the other hand, contends that section 43(a) is but a part of the trademark laws of the United States and is limited in its scope and intent to merchandising practices equivalent to the misuse of trademarks, that is the passing or "palming off" of one's goods as those of a competitor.

Section 43(a) provides in relevant part:

> Any person who shall . . . use in connection with any goods or services . . . any false description or representation . . . tending falsely to describe or represent the same . . . shall be liable to a civil action by any person . . . who believes that he is or is likely to be damaged by the use of any such false description or representation.

. . . Following the passage of the Lanham Act in 1946, the courts did not initially construe that Act as widening the scope of unfair competition claims beyond the. . . . common law precedents. Although some courts continued to interpret section 43(a) as being confined to situations where there had been a "palming off" of goods of the defendant for those of the plaintiff, with the passage of time, a "checkerboard . . . of apparently conflicting decisions" developed in the federal courts in regard to the interpretation to be placed upon section 43(a).

More recent cases have generally recognized that section 43(a) did not simply reenact the common law tort of "palming off," but rather created a new federal statutory tort rendering actionable any false description or misrepresentation by a defendant of his merchandise where that merchandise moves in interstate commerce.

It must be acknowledged that a review of the case law, as hereinabove cited, reveals that most of the false descriptions or representations complained of by a plaintiff have been false descriptions or representations concerning the ingredients or qualities inherent to the defendant's product. This is in contrast to the instant case where the false statements allegedly made by the defendant do not pertain to the inherent ingredients or qualities of the defendant's goods, but rather pertain to the pricing of those goods in relation to the plaintiff's pricing of similar or identical goods. The question thus presented to the Court is whether section 43(a) of the Lanham Act extends to those situations where the alleged false statements are made by a defendant with regard to the prices of its goods in comparison with the prices of the plaintiff's goods.

Focusing on the words of section 43(a) which would be relevant here, it can be seen that the Lanham Act applies to "any false description or representation" used "in connection with any goods" which tends "falsely to describe or represent the same.". . . [I]t would appear to this Court that the price of a particular item would be as much a "false representation" of the item as any representation concerning the goods' inherent ingredients or qualities. This would be especially true where, as here, the only real and material difference between two competitors' goods are their prices and the only real area of competition is price competition. It can hardly be argued in a case such as this that false representations concerning the comparative prices of similar or identical grocery items would be any less damaging to the business of a plaintiff-competitor than false representations made by a defendant concerning the inherent qualities or ingredients of its groceries. Thus it would appear that . . . falsity in price advertising is equally as unfair and damaging as falsity in the designation of the inherent qualities of ingredients of the goods. It would further appear that false price advertising would equally tend to "falsely . . . represent" the goods as would falsity in the description of the inherent qualities or ingredients of the goods.

However, the foregoing reasoning and conclusion in regard to the interpretation of section 43(a) of the Lanham Act would appear to be precluded in this Circuit by the decision in the case of *Federal-Mogul-Bower Bearings, Inc.* v. *Azoff.* Although that case was decided in 1963, it appears to be the most recent, if not the only, decision in this Circuit upon the issue now before the Court. In that case the Court, quoting with approval the following language from *Sampson Crane Co.* v. *Union National Sales, Inc.,* stated:

> The intent of Congress in passing the Act is set forth in the final paragraph of Section 1127. Only one phrase of that paragraph fails to use the word "mark." And that phrase ("to protect persons engaged in such commerce against unfair competition") must in such a context be construed to refer not to any competitive practice which in the broad meaning of the words might be called unfair, but to that "unfair competition" which has been closely associated with the misuse of trademarks, i.e., the passing off of one's goods as those of a competitor. It is clear, both from this statement of the intent and from a reading of the Act as a whole, that the primary purpose of the Act was to eliminate deceitful practices in interstate commerce involving the misuse of trademarks, but along with this it sought to eliminate other forms of misrepresentations which are of the same general character even though they do not involve any use of what can technically be called a trademark. . . ."

This Court accordingly concludes that, as contended by the defendant, section 43(a) of the Lanham Act is limited in its scope and intent to merchandising practices equivalent to the misuse of trademarks, that is the passing or "palming off" of one's goods as those of a competitor.

It is accordingly the opinion of the Court that the complaint in this case fails to allege and the evidence in the case fails to establish any violation of the Lanham Act and that no federal question jurisdiction would accordingly lie.

Case questions

1. There are two views regarding the Lanham Act's application to false advertising claims. What are they? Which view does the district court seem to favor? Which view does it apply? Why?

2. Could a consumer who purchased a Kroger product that had been falsely advertised with regard to price sue Kroger for breach of contract? Could the consumer successfully sue for deceit? Could he or she successfully sue for breach of express warranty?

3. Could American Consumers, Inc., successfully sue Kroger for disparagement?

ADMINISTRATIVE REGULATION OF FALSE ADVERTISING

The ineffectiveness of private remedies for false advertising has placed the burden of regulating advertising primarily on administrative agencies. Although several federal agencies regulate advertising, the Federal Trade Commission (FTC) has been the most active.[8]

Regulation of advertising by the FTC

In 1914 Congress enacted the Federal Trade Commission Act.[9] Section 5 of the act empowered the FTC to initiate actions against respondents and, after hearings and upon proper findings, to order respondents to cease and desist engaging in unfair methods of competition.[10] Although the statute's legislative history indicated that Congress was primarily concerned with more effective enforcement of the antitrust laws, the FTC interpreted the statute as empowering it to proceed against advertisements which deceived consumers.

Four stages in the development of the FTC. One advertisement attacked by the FTC was used by the Raladam Company to promote its product Marmola. Raladam claimed that Marmola would cure obesity. The FTC found that the product could not be used safely without the supervision of a physician, concluded that the advertisement deceived the public, and ordered Raladam to cease and desist making the claim. The Supreme Court, however, held that the commission had exceeded its authority because it had failed to establish that the advertisement injured competition. Consumer protection was not an independent objective recognized by the statute.[11]

The *Raladam* decision left the FTC powerless to act in situations where every competitor in an industry used the same deceptive practice. These cases, however, were the most egregious. If one competitor advertised falsely, there was a chance that other competitors might expose the false claims. No such chance existed if all competitors made similar false claims.

In 1938, seven years after the *Raladam* decision, Congress enacted the Wheeler-Lea Act, which amended section 5. The amendment enlarged the prohibitions of section 5 by including "unfair or deceptive trade practices." Congress made clear that it intended to make the consumer injured by unfair trade practices of equal concern before the law with the merchant or manufacturer injured by the unfair methods of a dishonest competitor.

For 35 years after the passage of the Wheeler-Lea Act the FTC attacked deceptive advertisement on a case-by-case basis. Although the commission asserted that it had rulemaking authority as well, courts were not so certain.

---

[8] The Federal Communications Commission (FCC) and the Food and Drug Administration (FDA) also regulate advertising to some degree.

[9] 15 U.S.C.§§ 41 et seq. (1914).

[10] 15 U.S.C.§ 45 (1914).

[11] *FTC* v. *Raladum Co.,* 283 U.S. 643 (1931).

Congress removed the uncertainty by enacting the FTC Improvements Act of 1975, specifically delegating to the commission rulemaking authority to prevent unfair and deceptive trade practices.

Dissatisfaction soon developed over the commission's exercise of its newly declared rulemaking power. The FTC embarked upon rulemaking proceedings which aroused considerable criticism. Its most controversial action was the proposal of rules that might have banned all television advertising aimed at children. Enactment of the FTC Improvements Act of 1980, among other things, terminated the then pending proceedings regarding children's television advertising and altered the commission's rulemaking procedures.

FTC structure and adjudicatory procedure. The FTC consists of five commissioners appointed by the president with the advice and consent of the Senate for seven-year terms. The FTC staff is divided into three bureaus. The Bureau of Competition is responsible for enforcing the antitrust laws. The Bureau of Consumer Protection is responsible for controlling unfair and deceptive trade practices. The Bureau of Economics gathers data, conducts surveys, and provides expert support services for the other two bureaus.

The commission receives complaints from interest groups, competitors, consumers, and other members of the public. It also monitors national and local advertisements through its regional offices. When a deceptive practice is brought to the attention of the FTC staff, the staff initiates an informal investigation.

The FTC's investigatory powers are formidable. It can require a corporation to provide access to documentary evidence relevant to an investigation and to file a special report answering specific FTC questions. The commission can also subpoena any individual to testify or produce documents related to an investigation.

The commission is prohibited from making public trade secrets or confidential commercial or financial information which it obtains from private sources. It is also forbidden to disclose information provided by a company if the disclosure would result in any significant financial harm to the company. The kind of information that the FTC must keep confidential could include profit and loss statements, balance sheets, financing details and strategies, and marketing and advertising plans. In this way the commission's broad investigatory powers are balanced by a protection against disclosures of confidential commercial or financial information.

During an FTC investigation the company being investigated may take the initiative and provide the FTC with an "assurance of voluntary compliance." If the commission accepts the assurance, the company will avoid the adverse publicity of an FTC complaint. The FTC rarely accepts such assurances; the graver the violation, the less likely the commission will be to settle.

If, following the investigation, the director of the Bureau of Consumer Protection finds reasonable cause to believe a violation exists, he or she will notify the respondent of the director's intent to file a formal complaint.

The responding company is generally allowed 10 days to indicate its willingness to negotiate a consent order. If the negotiations succeed, the consent order is entered by the commission. The FTC also issues a press release announcing the order and identifying the company involved.

If the parties cannot agree to a consent order, the commission staff files the complaint. The respondent files an answer. Following pretrial procedures which are more limited than those employed in federal district court, the issues are tried before an administrative law judge (ALJ). The losing party may appeal to the full commission. If the commission dismisses the complaint, the case ends. If it issues a cease and desist order, the respondent may appeal to the U.S. court of appeals for any circuit in which it resides or does business or in which the advertisement was used. The court of appeals reviews the decision to determine whether it is supported by substantial evidence on the record as a whole.

The FTC issues press releases announcing the filing of the complaint, the filing of the answer, the decision of the ALJ, and the decision of the full Commission. Thus the mere filing of a complaint can subject a company to substantial unfavorable publicity. The practice, however, is a valid means of advising the public to be on guard against the deceptive advertisement described in the release, and it has been upheld by the courts.[12]

Although inducing the FTC to take action against a competitor may be a useful weapon in a company's competitive arsenal, the commission is restricted by statute to undertaking proceedings only where they are in the public interest. The commission is afforded broad discretion in determining whether a proceeding is in the public interest. Rarely will a court overturn its decision. One such case was *FTC* v. *Klesner*.[13] Klesner became involved in a dispute with Sammons, the owner of a store called the Shade Shop. Klesner began his own business, also calling it the Shade Shop. The FTC ordered Klesner to cease and desist, but the Supreme Court viewed Klesner's actions as arising out of an essentially private controversy, and reversed the commission's order.

The public interest requirement can have a profound effect at the administrative level in guiding the commission's decisions on whether to proceed in a given case. In one case FTC complaint counsel challenged an advertisement for Dry Ban deodorant. Counsel alleged, and the administrative law judge found, that the advertisement represented Dry Ban to be a nonwet spray which left no residue when applied to the body. The ALJ further found this representation to be false and deceptive. The full commission reversed the ALJ, finding that the commercial did not represent Dry Ban to be absolutely dry, but only claimed that it was drier than its competitors. The commission refused to remand the case to the ALJ for further proceedings

---

[12] *FTC* v. *Cinderella Career and Finishing Schools, Inc.*, 404 F.2d 1308 (D.C. Cir. 1968).

[13] 280 U.S. 19 (1929).

to determine the validity of the "drier" claim. It concluded that such a remand would not serve the public interest, because no health or safety considerations demanded the further expenditure of public funds, no particularly vulnerable group was affected by the ad, the ad did no significant economic harm to purchasers who found the product to be less dry than anticipated, and the ad had been discontinued four years previously.[14]

Deceptive price advertising. Advertisements dealing with price were among the first to be scrutinized by the FTC during the early days of the commission's existence. Advertisements frequently claim that goods or services are being offered at "one third off" or "two for the price of one" or "25 percent below the suggested retail price."

Frequently an advertiser offers to provide a good or service free to anyone who purchases another good or service. Such ads are deceptive unless the merchant does not immediately recover the cost of the free merchandise by, for example, marking up the price of the merchandise that must be purchased. The goods to be purchased must be sold at the advertiser's regular price, that is, the price at which the advertiser sold the product in the given geographic or trade area prior to the advertisement. Similarly, when ads offer "two for the price of one," the two units must be sold at the regular price of one unit before the ad was run.

At one time the FTC considered deceptive any offer of free merchandise which was subject to such conditions as the purchase of other goods. Its current view, however, is that such giveaways are not deceptive, provided that the conditions are clearly disclosed.

Price comparisons also present a potential for false advertising. When an advertisement claims that prices have been reduced, they must have been reduced from their former regular prices. If they have been reduced from prices that were artificially inflated to facilitate the "reductions," the ad violates section 5.

Comparisons are also made in advertisements which offer "a $10 retail value for $7.50." In such cases the comparable price must be one charged in a substantial number of sales in the area. If only a few small, isolated outlets charge $10, while most other outlets charge between $7 and $8, the advertisement would violate section 5. Frequently manufacturers preticket merchandise or by other means suggest retail prices. If the manufacturer's suggested retail price does not reflect the prevailing price in the area, an advertiser may not lawfully use it as a basis for comparison.

Another deceptive advertising scheme akin to false price comparisons is the bait and switch. Section 5 is violated if one product is advertised in order to lure customers into a store to buy other, usually more expensive, products, and the advertiser has no intention of selling the advertised product.

---

[14] Bristol-Myers Co., 85 F.T.C. 688 (1972).

Tashof v. *FTC*
437 F.2d 707 (D.C.Cir. 1970)

Tashof (appellant) sought a review of a Federal Trade Commission cease and desist order which was issued after the FTC found Tashof guilty of unfair and deceptive advertising practices in violation of the Federal Trade Commission Act. The FTC order was affirmed, and its enforcement was ordered.

Bazelon, Chief Judge: Appellant Leon A. Tashof is engaged in the retail trade as New York Jewelry Co. (NYJC). His store is located in an area that serves low-income consumers, many of whom hold low-paying jobs, and have no bank or charge accounts. About 85 percent of NYJC's sales are made on credit. The Commission found, after a Hearing Examiner had dismissed the charges as unsubstantiated, that NYJC falsely advertised the availability of discount eyeglasses, and misrepresented its prices and credit practices. NYJC claims that the evidence is insufficient to support the Commission's findings, and that in any event the findings do not justify the order entered against it. We affirm the findings, and enforce the order.

A. False Advertising of Eyeglasses

The Commission first found that NYJC employed a "bait and switch" maneuver with respect to sales of eyeglasses. The evidence showed that NYJC advertised eyeglasses "from $7.50 complete," including "lenses, frames and case." The newspaper advertisements, but not the radio advertisements, mentioned a "moderate examining fee." During this period NYJC offered free eye examinations by a sign posted in its store, and through cards it mailed out and distributed on the street. NYJC claimed that it offered $7.50 eyeglasses only to persons with their own prescriptions. But we have no doubt that the record amply supports the Commission's finding that the advertising campaign taken as a whole offered complete eyeglass service for $7.50.

That much shows "bait." There was no direct evidence of "switch"—no direct evidence, that is, that NYJC disparaged or discouraged the purchase of the $7.50 eyeglasses, or that the glasses were unavailable on demand, or unsuited for their purpose. The evidence on which the Commission rested its finding was a stipulation that out of 1,400 pairs of eyeglasses sold each year by NYJC, less than 10 were sold for $7.50 with or without a prescription. NYJC claims that this evidence does not support the finding. We disagree.

It seems plain to us that the Commission drew a permissible inference of "switch" from the evidence of bait advertising and minimal sales of the advertised product. At best only nine sales—$^{64}/_{100}$ of one percent of NYJC's eyeglass sales—were made at $7.50. The record leaves unexplained why NYJC's customers, presumably anxious to purchase at as low a price as possible, would so consistently have bought more expensive glasses if suitable glasses at $7.50 were available. Further, NYJC continued to advertise the $7.50 glasses for a year and a half despite the scarcity of sales, a fact which tends to support a finding of a purpose to bring customers into the store for other reasons. This evidence, we think, was sufficient to shift the burden of coming forward to the respondent. But NYJC offered no evidence to negate the inference of "switch." The relevant facts are in NYJC's possession, and it was in the best position to show, if it could be shown at all that $7.50 glasses were actually available in the store. Yet the most NYJC could produce was its sales manager's denial that the $7.50 glasses were disparaged. NYJC never did point to even a single sale of the advertised product.

B. False Advertising of Discount Prices

There is no dispute that NYJC claimed to be a discount seller of eyeglasses. Nor is there any question that the sales slips introduced by the FTC were sufficient to show NYJC's actual prices.

The Commission's staff presented the only evidence of prevailing prices: the testimony of Dr. Zachary Ephraim, an optometrist. Since optometrists are a major retail outlet for eyeglasses, and perform a service closely comparable to that provided by NYJC—examining eyes and filling prescriptions—Dr. Ephraim was well qualified to testify about prevailing prices. We hold that his uncontradicted testimony was a sufficient basis for the Commission's findings.

The Commission determined the generally prevailing prices of eyeglasses on the basis of Dr. Ephraim's testimony of the usual price charged by most optometrists in the trade area. NYJC first claims that the Commission erroneously ignored the expert's statements that some sellers might charge higher prices. We disagree, because Dr. Ephraim referred only to some extremely high prices that a relatively few sellers might charge. Thus the record as a whole supports the Commission's finding of generally prevailing eyeglass prices, i.e., the prices to which NYJC's must be compared in considering the charge that its representations of discount prices were false. NYJC's second claim concerns the Commission's refusal to include in the prevailing price the amount which the consumer would have had to pay for an eye examination. Since NYJC offered "free" eye examinations, it could be argued that no adjustment for examinations was required. But the Commission did make allowance for NYJC's actual cost of the examination. We cannot say that this treatment was unreasonable. It is worth noting that even if the prevailing prices were computed as NYJC has urged, NYJC's customers still paid a higher than prevailing price more often than not.

. . . The Commission ordered NYJC to cease and desist from representing that it sells "any article of merchandise" at a discount price

. . . unless it first takes a "statistically significant survey" which shows that the prevailing price is "substantially" above NYJC's. The order apparently subjects NYJC to civil penalties if it advertises discount prices without having taken the survey, even if the advertisement is true.

The Commission claims that this remedy constitutes "reasonable action . . . calculated to preclude the revival of the illegal practices." We agree. NYJC was shown to have taken little account of the true level of prices in the trade area. We think the FTC may enter an order to ensure that this is not repeated in the future, without having to determine whether respondent's previous conduct was due to inadvertence, bad faith, or a kind of inattention or negligence involving some intermediate culpability. Where a businessman has wrought a wrong on the public, he may be held to be a reasonable business procedure that will prevent repetition of that wrong, and in view of his past record he will not be permitted to object that his own approaches might also avoid this wrong in the future, perhaps by happenstance and perhaps only on occasion.

NYJC has offered nothing either here or before the Commission to support its assertion that the statistical survey requirement is unduly burdensome. The requirement does not appear onerous on its face. Thus the order must be enforced.

Robb, Circuit Judge (concurring in part, dissenting in part): . . . In my judgment the Commission exceeds its authority when it requires NYJC to conduct a "statistically significant survey" of relevant prices in its trade area before advertising a "discount price." This requirement shifts to NYJC the burden of proving its innocence; and as the majority opinion concedes, might subject NYJC to heavy civil penalties even if its advertisement is true. I would affirm after eliminating this part of the order.

Case questions

1. What inquiries should an advertiser make to insure that it will not violate section 5 when advertising that its goods are being sold at discount prices?

2. What could Tashof have done to avoid being charged with using bait and switch tactics?

3. Suppose Tashof had advertised "easy credit," but pursued a vigorous collection policy that often resulted in the garnishment of a buyer's wages. Would he have been in violation of section 5?

Testimonials, mock-ups, and simulations. Testimonials and endorsements by well-known personalities receive close scrutiny by the FTC. An advertiser violates the Federal Trade Commission Act when it represents that a product is endorsed by a person who does not, in fact, use the product or prefer it. Some advertisements imply falsely that the user has superior experience or training. For example, an athlete could not praise the energy content of a cereal and imply that he or she is an expert in nutrition.

In television advertising, mock-ups and simulations are necessary because the medium cannot effectively transmit the real product. The use of mock-ups and simulations must be disclosed. If the viewing public is led to believe that it is seeing a real product or experiment, the advertisement will violate section 5.

Quality claims. Advertisers frequently make quality claims. Some of these claims are considered trade puffing and do not violate the act. Senator Wheeler expressed this view during the debates on the Wheeler-Lea Act: "If the manufacturer said, 'My car is the best car on the market for the money,' there would be a vast difference of opinion in the general public's mind as to whether it was or not. . . . It would be a very difficult thing to prove that the car was not just what the manufacturer said it was. Those are things which are generally recognized by the courts as not capable of being reached by any law."[15] Where quality claims exceed the bounds of permissible puffing, two issues frequently arise: (1) What claim did the advertiser make? (2) Was the claim false or deceptive?

Quality claims may be expressly made in an advertisement, or they may be implied from the advertisement's language. The burden of proving that a claim is implied in an ad rests on complaint counsel. When the FTC interprets an advertisement to determine its meaning, the commission may rely upon its expertise in the area. If it chooses to do so, it will simply view the ad and, aided by the arguments of counsel, draw its conclusions. The commission frequently supplements its expertise with testimony from experts, with the advertiser's evaluation of the advertisement, and with consumer surveys.

Consumer surveys are considered by the FTC when they are reliable and probative. In determining what weight it will give such surveys, the commission considers the reputation of the organization which ran the surveys, the training and experience of the persons who managed the surveys

---

[15] 80 Cong. Rec. 6592 (1936).

and interviewed the participants, the sampling and interviewing techniques used, the use of controls and validation procedures, and the incentives to bias the results. The weight of surveys is greatly enhanced where two or more independent surveys confirm each other.

From 1964 to 1970, advertisements appeared on national television depicting a child eating Wonder Bread and growing rapidly from a very young child to a 12-year-old. The words *protein, mineral, carbohydrates,* and *vitamins* flashed above the child, while the announcer narrated:

> These are the Wonder Years, the formative years 1 through 12 when your child develops in many ways, actually grows to 90 percent of her adult height.
>
> To help make the most of these Wonder Years, serve nutritious Wonder Enriched Bread. Wonder helps build strong bodies in 12 ways. Carefully enriched with foods for body and mind, Wonder Bread tastes so good, and is so good for growing child, for active adult.
>
> Help make the most of her Wonder Years, her growth years. Serve Wonder Bread. Wonder helps build strong bodies 12 ways.

FTC complaint counsel alleged that this advertisement impliedly claimed that Wonder Bread was unique in providing nutrients far superior to those of all other breads. The commission, however, reviewed conflicting consumer surveys and expert testimony and concluded that complaint counsel had failed to establish the existence of the implied claim.[16] The cautious advertiser should therefore consider previewing advertisements before representative audiences, to evaluate potential audience perceptions.

Once it has been ascertained that a claim is implied in an advertisement, the FTC must determine whether the claim is deceptive. It does this by requiring that advertisers possess adequate substantiation for the claim at the time that they make it. The FTC views as a deceptive advertising practice product claims for which the advertiser posseses no substantiation. Thus all product claims in advertisements must be substantiated.

The FTC arrives at its substantiation requirement by holding that all quality claims imply that the advertiser has a reasonable basis, or substantiation, for making them. What constitutes a reasonable basis will vary greatly with the type of product and the type of claim. The FTC considers the following factors in deciding whether the basis for a claim is reasonable: (1) the type and specificity of the claim made, (2) the type of product, (3) the possible consequences of a false claim, (4) the degree of reliance that consumers place on the claim, and (5) the type of evidence that is available to evaluate the claim. The reasonable basis or substantiation requirement stems from the commission's view that the proliferation of highly technical and complex problems, coupled with an imbalance of knowledge and resources, places the consumer at a distinct disadvantage compared to the advertiser in evaluating product claims.

---

[16] ITT Continental Baking Co., 83 F.T.C. 865 (1973).

As with the burden of proving the existence of a claim, FTC complaint counsel bears the burden of proving that the advertiser lacked a reasonable basis for the claim. Complaint counsel must not only establish that scientific tests did not substantiate the claim but must also show that no other reasonable basis for the claim existed. Complaint counsel failed to carry its burden when it attacked advertisements for Unburn skin cream which claimed that the product stopped sunburn pain fast by anesthetizing nerves. Although complaint counsel demonstrated that no scientific tests substantiated the claim, it failed to consider the relevant medical literature, general medical knowledge, or clinical experience.[17]

An illustration of why advertisers must be careful to avoid making implied claims is provided by the case of *Firestone Tire & Rubber Co.* v. *FTC*, which involved two Firestone product ads.[18]

From December 1967 through May 1968 the Firestone Tire and Rubber Company ran the following ad:

THE SAFE TIRE. FIRESTONE

When you buy a Firestone tire—no matter how much or how little you pay—you get a safe tire.

Firestone tires are custom-built one by one. By skilled craftsmen. And they're personally inspected for an extra margin of safety. If these tires don't pass all of the exacting Firestone inspections, they don't get out.

Every new firestone design goes through rugged tests of safety and strength far exceeding any driving condition you'll ever encounter. We prove them in our test lab. On our test track. And in rigorous day-to-day driving conditions. All Firestone tires meet or exceed the new Federal Government testing requirements. (They have for some time.)

Firestone—The Safe Tire. At 60,000 Firestone Safe Tire Centers. At no more cost than ordinary tires.

Firestone believed that its ad merely assured the average tire user that it had done everything humanly and technically possible to sell tires free of defects. The FTC, however, interpreted the ad to claim that Firestone tires were absolutely safe, regardless of condition, inflation pressure, load, or usage. The Sixth Circuit Court of Appeals affirmed.

When Firestone introduced its Wide Oval Tire, it claimed that the tire would "corner better, run cooler, stop 25 percent quicker." Firestone had tested the tire by comparing it to an ordinary Firestone tire in 10 runs on one day on a wet, smooth concrete surface at 15 miles per hour. The tests showed an average stopping distance of 29.8 percent less for the Wide Oval Tire. Although the tests were properly run and produced accurate results, they were held insufficient to establish a reasonable basis for the claim.

---

[17] Pfizer Corp., 81 F.T.C. 23 (1973).

[18] 481 F.2d 246 (6th Cir. 1973).

Additional tests on different surfaces and with varying pressure, loads, and speeds were held necessary.[19]

Note that in the *Firestone* case the FTC did not attempt to prove that the Wide Oval Tire would not stop 25 percent faster than regular tires. All of the available evidence proved that it would. The commission merely demonstrated that Firestone's own tests were insufficient to give Firestone a reasonable basis for making the claim. To bring the lack of reasonable basis within the prohibition of deceptive practices, the commission found that Firestone had impliedly claimed to have made such tests.

Under *Firestone* it is possible for a product claim to be true and still violate section 5. If that is so, such advertisements are not truly "deceptive." However, section 5 prohibits "*unfair* or deceptive acts." Thus the FTC may be reaching such ads under an "unfairness doctrine." That is to say, since section 5 prohibits unfair as well as deceptive practices, it is possible for the FTC to focus on the unfairness of an unsubstantiated claim and thus to find that the claim is forbidden by section 5 even though the claim may in fact be true.

This raises the issue of whether section 5 empowers the FTC to regulate ads that it finds unfair even in the absence of deception. Proponents of such a power call for a broad interpretation of section 5, noting that the FTC has been allowed much flexibility in adapting to new practices which are contrary to public policy. Opponents argue that Congress never intended the FTC to regulate ads that were not deceptive. They note that the Wheeler-Lea Act was a direct response to the *Raladam* case. They also argue that the regulation of undeceptive advertising would not be a regulation of the time, place, or manner of commercial speech and would therefore violate the First Amendment.[20]

Had the FTC limited the development of the unfairness doctrine to an adjudicatory context, the issue might not have gained much attention. However, after obtaining rulemaking authority in 1975, the FTC sought to give the doctrine broader application by promulgating trade regulation rules on an industry-wide basis. The FTC initiated proceedings to develop rules that might have banned all children's television advertising. Even if such ads are truthful, they may be considered unfair because they are aimed at a particularly vulnerable audience.

The breadth of the unfairness doctrine and its potential for abuse are magnified when the focus is placed on its possible application to other audiences. If the unfairness doctrine can be used against children's advertising, can it not also be used to restrict any commercial advertising solely because that advertising may have consequences that the FTC finds objectionable or because it is otherwise contrary to the Commission's concept of fairness?

It was this thinking that prompted Congress to enact the FTC Improve-

---

[19] Id.

[20] For a discussion of the constitutionality of commercial speech regulation, see Chapter 4.

ments Act of 1980, which included a section terminating the proceedings on children's advertising. Furthermore, the act declared that "unfairness" might not be used as a basis for a trade regulation rule concerning advertisements directed toward children.

The Senate version of the bill would have confined the FTC's rulemaking authority to rules regarding deceptive ads only. However, the 1980 act merely forbids the FTC to use any funds for the years 1980–82 to initiate rulemaking proceedings which may result in rules governing ads on the basis that they constitute unfair acts or practices. Thus, after 1982 the FTC is free to issue industry-wide rules regulating commercial advertising that is unfair although not deceptive. Furthermore, the 1980 act only restricts FTC rulemaking power. The agency remains free to challenge acts or practices, including commercial advertising, that are unfair in an adjudicatory context. It just cannot apply its standard on an industry-wide basis through rulemaking through 1982.

FTC orders. The FTC is authorized to issue cease and desist orders to persons found to have violated section 5. An FTC cease and desist order instructs a person who has been found to have engaged in an unfair or deceptive act or practice to cease and desist from using such a method of doing business.

Since 1970 the FTC has claimed the authority to order affirmative disclosures to dissipate the residual effects of an advertiser's deception. Such disclosures are called "corrective advertising." Because advertising has residual effects, false or unfair claims may be retained in the public mind for a considerable time after they have ceased to be made. Therefore, corrective statements may be needed for a period to dispel these residual effects. In the following case the circuit court of appeals adopts the concept of corrective advertising.

Warner-Lambert Co. v. *FTC*
562 F.2d 49 (D.C. Cir. 1977)

Warner-Lambert (petitioner) sought a review of an FTC order requiring it to cease and desist from advertising that its product Listerine Antiseptic Mouthwash prevented, cured, or alleviated the common cold. The FTC order further required Warner-Lambert to disclose the following in future Listerine advertisements: "Contrary to prior advertising, Listerine will not help prevent colds or sore throats or lessen their severity." Order affirmed, but modified to delete from the required disclosure the phrase "contrary to prior advertising."

J. Skelly Wright, Circuit Judge:

* * * * *

Listerine has been on the market since 1879. Its formula has never changed. Ever since its introduction it has been represented as being beneficial in certain respects for colds, cold symptoms, and sore throats. Direct advertising to the consumer, including the cold claims as well as others, began in 1921.

* * * * *

The first issue on appeal is whether the Commission's conclusion that Listerine is not beneficial for colds or sore throats is supported by the evidence. The Commission's findings must be sustained if they are supported by substantial evidence on the record viewed as a whole. We conclude that they are.

Both the ALJ and the Commission carefully analyzed the evidence. They gave full consideration to the studies submitted by petitioner. The ultimate conclusion that Listerine is not an effective cold remedy was based on six specific findings of fact.

First, the Commission found that the ingredients of Listerine are not present in sufficient quantities to have any therapeutic effect. This was the testimony of two leading pharmacologists called by Commission counsel. The Commission was justified in concluding that the testimony of Listerine's experts was not sufficiently persuasive to counter this testimomy.

Second, the Commission found that in the process of gargling it is impossible for Listerine to reach the critical areas of the body in medically significant concentration. The liquid is confined to the mouth chamber. Such vapors as might reach the nasal passage would not be in therapeutic concentration. Petitioner did not offer any evidence that vapors reached the affected areas in significant concentration.

Third, the Commission found that even if significant quantities of the active ingredients of Listerine were to reach the critical sites where cold viruses enter and infect the body, they could not interfere with the activities of the virus because they could not penetrate the tissue cells.

Fourth, the Commission discounted the results of a clinical study conducted by petitioner on which petitioner heavily relies. Petitioner contends that in a four-year study schoolchildren who gargled with Listerine had fewer colds and cold symptoms than those who did not gargle with Listerine. The Commission found that the design and execution of the "St. Barnabas study" made its results unreliable. For the first two years of the four-year test no placebo was given to the control group. For the last two years the placebo was inadequate: the control group was given colored water which did not resemble Listerine in smell or taste. There

was also evidence that the physician who examined the test subjects was not blinded from knowing which children were using Listerine and which were not, that his evaluation of the cold symptoms of each child each day may have been imprecise, and that he necessarily relied on the non-blinded child's subjective reporting. Both the ALJ and the Commission analyzed the St. Barnabas study and the expert testimony about it in depth and were justified in concluding that its results are unreliable.

Fifth, the Commission found that the ability of Listerine to kill germs by millions on contact is of no medical significance in the treatment of colds or sore throats. Expert testimony showed that bacteria in the oral cavity, the "germs" which Listerine purports to kill, do not cause colds and play no role in cold symptoms. Colds are caused by viruses. Further, "while Listerine kills millions of bacteria in the mouth, it also leaves millions. It is impossible to sterilize any area of the mouth, let alone the entire mouth."

Sixth, the Commission found that Listerine has no significant beneficial effect on the symptoms of sore throat. The Commission recognized that gargling with Listerine could provide temporary relief from a sore throat by removing accumulated debris irritating the throat. But this type of relief can also be obtained by gargling with salt water or even warm water. . . . It was reasonable to conclude that "such temporary relief does not 'lessen the severity' of a sore throat any more than expectorating or blowing one's nose 'lessens the severity' of a cold."

Petitioner contends that even if its advertising claims in the past were false, the portion of the Commission's order requiring "corrective advertising" exceeds the Commission's statutory power. The argument is based upon a literal reading of Section 5 of the Federal Trade Commission Act, which authorizes the Commission to issue "cease and desist" orders against violators and does not expressly mention any other remedies. The Commission's position, on the other hand, is that the affirmative disclosure that Listerine will not prevent colds or lessen their severity is absolutely necessary to give effect to the prospective cease and desist order; a hundred years of false cold claims have built up a large reservoir of erroneous consumer belief which would persist, unless corrected, long after petitioner ceased making the claims.

* * * * *

The Commission has adopted the following standard for the imposition of corrective advertising:

> [I]f a deceptive advertisement has played a substantial role in creating or reinforcing in the public's mind a false and material belief which lives on after the false advertising ceases, there is clear and continuing injury to competition and to the consuming public as consumers continue to make purchasing decisions based on the false belief. Since this injury cannot be averted by merely requiring respondent to cease disseminating the advertisement, we may appropriately order respondent to take affirmative action designed to terminate the otherwise continuing ill effects of the advertisement.

We think this standard is entirely reasonable. It dictates two factual inquiries: (1) did Listerine's advertisements play a substantial role in creating or reinforcing in the public's mind a false belief about the product? and (2) would this belief linger on after the false advertising ceases? It strikes us that if the answer to both questions is not yes, companies everywhere may be wasting their massive advertising budgets. Indeed, it is more than a little peculiar to hear petitioner assert that its commercials really have no effect on consumer belief.

For these reasons it might be appropriate in some cases to presume the existence of the two factual predicates for corrective advertising. But we need not decide that question, or rely on presumptions here, because the Commission adduced survey evidence to support both propositions.

* * * * *

We turn next to the specific disclosure required: "Contrary to prior advertising, Listerine will not help prevent colds or sore throats or lessen their severity." Petitioner is ordered to include this statement in every future advertisement for Listerine for a defined period. In printed advertisements it must be displayed in type size at least as large as that in which the principal portion of the text of the advertisement appears and it must be separated from the text so that it can be readily noticed. In television commercials the disclosure must be presented simultaneously in both audio and visual portions. During the audio portion of the disclosure in television and radio advertisements, no other sounds, including music, may occur.

These specifications are well calculated to assure that the disclosure will reach the public. It will necessarily attract the notice of readers, viewers, and listeners, and be plainly conveyed. Given these safeguards, we believe the preamble "Contrary to prior advertising" is not necessary. It can serve only two purposes: either to attract attention that a correction follows or to humiliate the advertiser. The Commission claims only the first purpose for it, and this we think is obviated by the other terms of the order. The second purpose, if it were intended, might be called for in an egregious case of deliberate deception, but this is not one. While we do not decide whether petitioner proffered its cold claims in good faith or bad, the record compiled could support a finding of good faith. On these facts, the confessional preamble to the disclosure is not warranted.

Finally, petitioner challenges the duration of the disclosure requirement. By its terms it continues until respondent has expended on Listerine advertising a sum equal to the average annual Listerine advertising budget for the period April 1962 to March 1972. That is approximately ten million dollars. Thus if petitioner continues to advertise normally the corrective advertising will be required for about one year. We cannot say that is an unreasonably long time in which to correct a hundred years of cold claims. But, to petitioner's distress, the requirement will not expire by mere passage of time. If petitioner cuts back its Listerine advertising, or ceases it altogether, it can only postpone the duty to disclose. The Commission concluded that correction was required and that a duration of a fixed period of time might not accomplish that task, since petitioner could evade the order by choosing not to advertise at all. The formula settled upon by the Commission is reasonably related to the violation it found.

* * * * *

Case questions

1. Do you agree that the preamble "Contrary to prior advertising" is not necessary?

2. Would evidence of consumer satisfaction provide a reasonable basis for the Listerine ads?

3. What conditions must be present before the FTC will order corrective advertising?

4. Is corrective advertising punitive in nature, and thus is it outside the FTC's authority to order such advertising? Do corrective advertising orders present any constitutional problems?

FTC trade regulation rules. The FTC is empowered to promulgate trade regulation rules. However, by virtue of the FTC Improvements acts of 1975 and 1980 the commission must follow specific procedures in addition to the notice and comment procedures of the Administrative Procedure Act.

The FTC must begin its rulemaking by publishing two notices of proposed rulemaking. An advance notice must be published in the *Federal Register* and filed with the appropriate congressional oversight committees. It must be followed by a second notice of proposed rulemaking, also in the *Federal Register*. Both notices must contain a brief description of the area of inquiry under consideration, describe the possible regulatory alternatives, and invite public comment on the proposals. Interested parties may submit written comments.

The act entitles interested parties to a trial-type hearing before the commission where there are disputed issues of material fact. Interested parties may therefore cross-examine witnesses who come before the commission and provide testimony regarding any proposed rule. The act also provides that all ex parte proceedings become part of the formal record.

After all hearings on the proposed rule have been held, the commission will consider all the submissions as well as its own evidence, apply its expertise, and promulgate a final version of the rule. The FTC's final rule is then published in the *Federal Register*. The final rule may be reviewed by a court of appeals, which applies the substantial evidence test.

POLICY CONSIDERATIONS

The policy implications of advertising regulation involve two issues: (1) Is governmental interference in the marketplace warranted? (2) What form of governmental regulation is needed? The following discussion focuses on these issues.

The role of advertising

For the marketplace to function effectively, consumers must have accurate information regarding the quality and other characteristics of products and services offered for sale. Consumer confidence in the marketplace depends upon the availability of accurate information on these matters. The production of this information is thus of fundamental importance to the effective operation of the marketplace. Where advertising is accurate it optimizes consumer choice and increases consumer confidence in the market system.

The role of advertising can be examined from three perspectives: the consumer's, the industry's, and the government's. The consumer's interest is to be assured of the availability of relevant, accurate, and complete information which he or she may use to choose among alternative offerings. The challenge to industry is to insure that such information is provided as efficiently as possible. From industry's perspective, however, the purpose of marketing communication is to sell the product or service. It is unlikely that the advertiser will voluntarily divulge information if doing so conflicts with the advertiser's ability to sell the product.

The role of government in the American economic system has been oriented toward attempting to insure the effective functioning of the competitive system. This has been done by preventing monopoly or monopolistic practices through the government's antitrust policy and thus insuring the continuation of alternatives for consumer choice. Equally important has been the task of insuring that the consumer has the information needed to enable rational choice among these alternatives.

The need for governmental regulation

Those who oppose governmental regulation of advertising argue that the marketplace is a self-equilibrating mechanism, which, if left alone, will perform the job of satisfying consumer needs better than any alternative involving regulation or control. Freedom of choice is one of the most cherished and fundamental of American values. Historically, freedom of choice has been defined as the seller's right to enter a market and the worker's right to choose an occupation or a specific type of job. Free market philosophers argue that the consumer too should be free to buy what he or she wishes. They also argue that the consumer should be free to spend more or less in making choices. The consumer will purchase from those sellers who provide the needed product or service at the optimum price.

Deterrents to seller fraud exist in the market in the form of consumer knowledge and intelligence (some claims simply will not be believed), the cost to the seller of developing a reputation of dishonesty, and competition (another seller's advertisement may correct a fraudulent claim). And private legal remedies exist. However, there are limits to the ability of market forces to deter fraud. Some consumer groups lack sufficient knowledge or education to judge advertised claims. The costs of developing a reputation for dishonesty are not a deterrent to fly-by-night sellers with no fixed locale or stable clientele. Competitors cannot be expected to discredit all fraudulent claims. Private legal remedies are not attractive to individual consumers of small items.

The market system is in some areas conducive to fraud. The costs of getting product information—what economists call "search costs"—for some low-cost goods may be so prohibitive that buyers are forced to rely upon sellers for product information. Free market economic philosophy assumes that the consumer possesses the ability to accurately appraise the costs and benefits of various purchasing alternatives. In fact the seller has a strong informational advantage over the consumer. Thus the argument can be made that regulation is needed to guide an accommodation between the consumer's need for information and industry's willingness to provide such information.

If regulation is needed, why not allow for a form of self-regulation? A form of self-regulation of advertising already exists. Each major network has a Broadcast Standards Department which reviews all ads for truthfulness, substantiality claims, and conformance with both the network's advertising standards and legal standards. These departments also review ads for compliance with the National Association of Broadcasters (NAB) Television Standards Code. The NAB Code prohibits ads for certain goods and services (e.g., fortune-telling), regulates ads for others (e.g., no beer drinking in beer commercials), and has special standards for ads aimed at children. Ads for some products (e.g., toys and mood drugs) must be presubmitted to the National Advertising Review Board. A procedure exists for the hearing of complaints by the consuming public.

The National Advertising Division (NAD) of the Council of Better Business Bureaus monitors national advertising to uncover possible abuses on its own initiative, and offers guidance to advertising agencies and their clients. It has also established the National Advertising Review Board (NARB) to process consumer complaints. Of the NARB's 50 members, 30 are from advertisers, 10 are from advertising agencies, and 10 are public members. When a complaint is made to the NARB, the chairman convenes a five-member panel of three advertisers, one agency, and one public member to hear the case and render a decision on behalf of the board. The decision is then communicated to the highest corporate level, and if no action is taken, the NARB turns over its file to the appropriate governmental agency.

Many believe that self-regulation can be a useful, flexible, and effective tool. Others are less sanguine about the likely responsiveness of any self-regulatory institution. They point to the lack of public awareness of the existing self-regulatory institutions, the problems of delay that are prevalent in the existing systems, and the lack of specific criteria or standards.

Regulatory reform

Whatever the arguments that can be made for or against governmental regulation of advertising, one fact remains: governmental regulation currently exists. Assuming that it will continue to exist, what reform measures are needed?

As discussed, the substantiation program for product claims requires advertisers to substantiate their claims, whether true or not. Some argue that the substantiation program increases the amount and availability of information to consumers.[21] A prominent critic of the program is Professor Richard Posner of the University of Chicago Law School. He argues:

> The consumer is interested in whether the claim is true, not in the evidence the seller has collected to support it. If a product claim, although unsubstantiated when made, turns out to be true, the consumer who purchased the product on the strength of the claim suffers no harm.[22]

Posner recognizes that the substantiation program may be seen as a method of reducing the FTC's administrative costs. The costs of prosecution are lowered by shifting the burden of proof onto sellers to substantiate their claims. However, Posner contends that this is apt to discourage the advertising of claims that are costly to substantiate, resulting in a reduced flow of information to consumers. He adds that the costs of substantiation will also reduce new market entry by increasing costs to new firms or firms with new products.[23]

However, "the cardinal deficiency in the legislative framework," according to Posner, "is in the area of remedies. Specifically it is the absence of any provision for money damages, compensatory or punitive."[24] Posner points out that the FTC's inability to award monetary reparation to consumers weakens consumer incentive to lodge complaints with the commission, thereby depriving the FTC of substantial private assistance. It also weakens seller incentive to comply with the law since a seller is only obliged to cease and desist and is permitted to keep any profits obtained during the period of violation.

Review Problems

1. On July 31, 1966, Lee Calan Imports advertised a 1964 Volvo station wagon for sale in the *Chicago Sun-Times*. Lee Calan had instructed the newspaper to advertise the price of the automobile at $1,795. However, through an error of the newspaper, the price shown was $1,095. O'Brien visited Lee Calan Imports, examined the automobile, and stated that he wished to purchase it for $1,095. One of Lee Calan's salespeople at first agreed but then refused to sell the car for the erroneous price listed in the advertisement. O'Brien contends that the advertisement represents an offer by Lee Calan Imports which he duly accepted and that the parties thus formed a binding contract. Is O'Brien correct? Has Lee

---

[21] J. Howard and J. Hulbert, *Advertising and the Public Interest: A Staff Report to the Federal Trade Commission,* VIII–6 (1973).

[22] R. Posner, *Regulation of Advertising by the FTC,* 23 (1973).

[23] Id. at 24.

[24] Id. at 15.

Advertising **325**

Calan violated section 5 of the Federal Trade Commission Act?

2. The Seven-Up Company sells a lemon-lime soft drink under the trademark 7up, which it has advertised since 1968 as "the uncola." Seven-Up displays its product in a specific section of supermarkets and in vending machines. It markets 7up nationally. The No-Cal Corporation sells a lemon-lime diet soft drink called "Shape-Up," which it advertises as "the unsugar." At no time has No-Cal advertised Shape-Up without identifying it as a product of No-Cal, and at no time has it used the term *unsugar* without mentioning No-Cal as its source. Although sold in supermarkets, Shape-Up is not sold in vending machines. Seven-Up sues No-Cal under the Lanham Act, seeking to enjoin No-Cal's distribution and advertising of Shape-Up. Who wins?

3. Pussycat Cinema, a theater in New York City, began to show *Debbie Does Dallas,* a movie depicting a fictional high school cheerleader, Debbie, who has been selected to become a "Texas cowgirl." Debbie engages in a variety of sex schemes, sometimes clad or partly clad in a cheerleader's uniform similar to that used by the Dallas Cowboys Cheerleaders, Inc., an entertainment group which performs at the Dallas Cowboys professional football games. Pussycat Cinema advertised the movie with marquee posters depicting Debbie in the cheerleader's uniform and containing such captions as "Starring Ex-Dallas Cowgirl Bambi Woods" and "You'll do more than cheer for this X Dallas Cheerleader." The Dallas Cowboys Cheerleaders, Inc., sued Pussycat Cinema, seeking to enjoin the showing of the movie. Who wins?

4. Mary Carter Paint Company manufactures and sells paint and related products. Mary Carter advertises that for every can of Mary Carter paint purchased, the company will give the buyer a free can of equal quality and quantity. Ever since it started selling paint, Mary Carter has sold its product on a "two-for-the-price-of-one" basis. Its practice has been to establish its price on a per can basis, but to give each customer a second can without further charge for each can purchased. Is Mary Carter in violation of section 5?

5. Parker Pen Company's advertisements of its fountain pen contained the words "Guaranteed for Life." In a less prominent and finer type the following qualification was included: "Pens marked with the Blue Diamond are guaranteed for the life of the owner against everything except loss or intentional damage, subject only to a charge of 35 cents for postage, insurance and handling, provided complete pen is returned for service." Did the company violate section 5?

6. Standard Oil Company of California advertised its product F-310, a gasoline additive, on television commercials from January 9 to June 9, 1970. The commercials were based on a demonstration designed to afford viewers a visual comparison of automobile exhaust before and after F-310 was used. A large, clear balloon was attached to the exhaust pipe of an idling automobile. The balloon was shown inflating with black, opaque vapor while the announcer described it as "filling with dirty exhaust emissions that go into the air and waste mileage." The announcer then stated that "Standard Oil of California has accomplished the development of a remarkable gasoline additive, Formula F-310, that reduces exhaust emissions from dirty engines." He informed the viewers that the same car was run on six tankfuls of Chevron F-310 and the result was "no dirty smoke, cleaner air." To prove the point, a clear balloon was again shown being attached to the car. This time the balloon inflated with transparent vapor. In conclusion the viewers were told: "Chevron F-310 turns dirty smoke into good, clean mileage." The FTC advised Standard that it objected to the ads because these had not made clear that the car depicted in the before segment of each commercial had been driven previously with a gasoline that had been deliberately formulated to accelerate carbon deposits, resulting in an especially dirty engine. Has Standard violated section 5?

7. The Beneficial Corporation was engaged in the business of making loans to creditworthy borrowers. In 1969 it decided to go into the business of preparing income tax returns. The decision was based on the belief that customers of the service who needed funds to pay the tax found to be due would find it convenient to borrow the funds from Beneficial. However, it soon became apparent that most of these customers would actually receive refunds. Beneficial decided to advertise a loan providing for an immediate use of money in anticipation of such tax refunds, thus eliminating the wait for a refund check from the government. The advertisement Beneficial employed used the following text:

Announcer: This year have your taxes prepared a better way . . .

Singers: At Beneficial [toot, toot] . . .

Announcer: At Beneficial Finance. Beneficial's Income Tax Service does your taxes by computer . . . for as little as $5. And listen to Beneficial's "Instant Tax Refund" Plan: if you have a refund coming, you don't have to wait weeks for a government check. The instant you qualify for a loan, Beneficial will lend you the equivalent of your refund, in cash, instantly. It's the "Instant Tax Refund" Plan . . . at Beneficial Finance. The place to have your taxes done this year.

The FTC claimed that the advertising was false and misleading and that the proper remedy was a total prohibition against the use of the term *Instant Tax Refund Plan.* Was the FTC correct?

8. The Colgate-Palmolive Company set out to prove to the television viewing public that its shaving cream Rapid Shave outshaved them all. It used a one-minute commercial designed to show that Rapid Shave could soften even the toughness of sandpaper. The commercial contained a "sandpaper test." The announcer informed the audience that "to prove Rapid Shave's super moisturizing power, we put it right from the can onto this tough, dry sandpaper. It was apply . . . soak . . . and off in a stroke." While the announcer was speaking, Rapid Shave was applied to a substance that appeared to be sandpaper, and immediately thereafter a razor was shown shaving the substance clean. Sandpaper of the type depicted in the commercials could not be shaved immediately following the application of Rapid Shave, but required a substantial soaking period of about 80 minutes. The substance resembling sandpaper in the commercial was in fact a simulated prop, or mock-up, made of plexiglas to which sandpaper had been applied. The FTC claimed that the commercials violated section 5 of the Federal Trade Commission Act. Colgate-Palmolive argued that Rapid Shave could shave sandpaper, even though not in the short time represented by the commercials, and that if real sandpaper had been used in the commercials the inadequacies of television transmission would have made it appear to viewers to be nothing more than plain, colored paper. Who is right?

9. The Campbell Soup Company advertises its soup on television. In its television commercials Campbell's soups appear to be quite rich. This effect is achieved by Campbell's practice of adding marbles to its soups before showing them in the commercials. This ploy displaces the solid ingredients and thereby gives the products a deceptively rich appearance. Campbell has been doing this for years. Should consumers who relied upon the apparently bounteous nature of the soups be informed of Campbell's past deception through corrective advertising?

10. Evaluate the economic costs and benefits of advertising regulation by the FTC.

CHAPTER 12

Debtor-creditor relations

Consumers owe over $1.5 trillion in debts for their homes and other goods and services. "Plastic money" in the form of credit cards has replaced the traditional "green stuff." Americans have more than 600 million credit cards, averaging about three credit cards for every man, woman, and child. In an age of rapid technological advancement and innovative marketing techniques there are a growing number of gadgets for the consumer to buy. For these reasons more consumers are borrowing money or purchasing on credit to realize their "dreams." This creates a debtor-creditor relationship. The debtor is the person who owes money. The creditor is the person to whom money is owed. One might automatically think that it is always better to be a creditor than to be a debtor. However, this is not necessarily true, especially in times of rising interest rates. If a person can borrow money at 12 percent and invest it at 18 percent, that person is better off by 6 percent. Inflationary trends and rising interest rates invite investors to borrow capital in order to realize higher returns on their investments than the cost of the capital. An additional incentive to borrow is provided by the income tax benefits that a debtor derives from the interest deduction permitted by the taxing authorities. It seems that our society places a premium on being a debtor.

There are inherent abuses in a credit system. In the debt collection area, for example, the Senate Committee on Banking, Housing, and Urban Affairs found that collection abuses included "obscene or profane language, threats of violence, telephone calls at unreasonable hours, misrepresentation of a consumer's legal rights, disclosing a consumer's personal affairs to friends, neighbors, or an employer, obtaining information about a consumer through false pretense, impersonating public officials and attorneys and simulating legal process."[1]

Other abuses in the consumer credit industry have also received congressional attention. It was not uncommon for consumer reporting agencies to gather inaccurate or obsolete information about the consumer's credit and

---

[1] S. Rep. No. 382, 95th Cong., 1st Sess. 2 (1977).

personal history and then to disseminate that information to the general public. Married and single women as well as minorities were uniformly discriminated against in the extension of consumer loans. Consumers had great difficulty in resolving billing errors or obtaining additional information on a monthly charge account from dunning computers whose only response to these requests was threatened legal action. Finally, even if consumers could somehow fight their way through the thicket of the abuses listed above, there existed no meaningful way for them to make informed judgments about the cost of credit. Interest rates and charges were computed in nonuniform, often mystifying, ways by loan companies and banks.

To deal with these problems Congress, over the course of a decade, passed the Consumer Credit Protection Act. The various parts (titles) of this legislation deal, respectively, with the various abuses noted above. The Truth in Lending Act encourages the informed use of credit. The Fair Credit Reporting Act regulates the content and use of credit reports. The Fair Credit Billing Act mandates procedures for the resolution of billing errors. The Equal Credit Opportunity Act promotes nondiscrimination in the extension of credit. The Fair Debt Collection Practices Act and federal restrictions on garnishment restrain the deceptive and abusive conduct of overzealous bill collectors and judgment creditors.

These component parts or titles of the Consumer Credit Protection Act will be discussed in this chapter. In addition, all states regulate consumer credit. The Uniform Consumer Credit Code, proposed by the National Conference of Commissioners on Uniform State Law for adoption by all states, merits notice. Finally, the Bankruptcy Reform Act, designed to relieve debtor failures, will be outlined.

THE TRUTH IN LENDING ACT

Congress passed the Truth in Lending Act (TILA) (Title I of the Consumer Credit Protection Act) in 1968, and TILA was most recently amended by the Truth in Lending Simplification and Reform Act.[2] The purpose of TILA is to insure that consumers have adequate information about the cost of credit. To promote cost comparison and the informed use of credit Congress mandated that lenders compute and disclose certain significant credit terms in a standard fashion. The Truth in Lending Act requires disclosure and the uniform expression of credit terms only when the party extending credit is a creditor and the transaction involves consumer credit.

Creditor

As defined by TILA, a creditor is one who regularly extends credit which is payable in more than four installments or for which a finance charge

---

[2] The amended provisions, effective March 31, 1982, have been incorporated into the discussion of TILA in this chapter.

may be required. Assume, for example, that Connie Consumer borrows $20 from John Friend and agrees to repay $22 next payday. John is certainly requiring a finance charge for the extension of the loan. However, unless he regularly extends credit he will not be obliged to make TILA disclosures.

One who regularly arranges from credit for a person or entity that does not regularly extend credit also qualifies as a creditor. Generally, a credit arranger receives a fee for arranging for credit. Assume that Connie Consumer purchases a new Eldorado from TD Cadillac Dealer (TD) for $17,000. TD prepares and processes loan papers supplied by General Motors Acceptance Corporation (GMAC) and receives a fee from GMAC for each loan processed. TD is a credit arranger. GMAC is the credit extender. TD will not be required to give Connie TILA disclosures since TD is arranging for credit from GMAC, which is regularly engaged in the credit extension business. Arrangers are deemed creditors under TILA and are subject to the disclosure requirements only when they arrange for credit from another who is not regularly engaged in the business of credit extension. This rule is intended to avoid duplicity of disclosure. In the above example GMAC must give disclosures to Connie since it is, by definition, a creditor.

Consumer credit

Consumer credit is credit which is extended to natural persons primarily for personal, family, or household purposes. Credit extended to corporations does not qualify as consumer credit because corporations are not natural persons. Credit extended primarily for business, commercial, or agricultural purposes is not deemed consumer credit. Assume that Connie Consumer borrows $1,000 from First Member Bank for the purpose of opening a shoe repair store. Since the purpose of the loan is commercial, First Member Bank will be exempt from disclosure requirements. In carving out this exemption, Congress undoubtedly believed that the types of consumers involved in such transactions are capable of protecting themselves without benefit of the act. Under the same reasoning most credit transactions are exempt when the total amount to be financed exceeds $25,000. Dealings in securities or commodities accounts by a broker-dealer registered with the Securities and Exchange Commission are also exempt, because the SEC and other authorities adequately supervise these transactions.

Disclosure

A creditor must conspicuously disclose to the consumer the key terms of a credit transaction, which generally includes the cash price, the total amount deferred, the finance charges, and the annual percentage rate of interest (APR). The APR is determined by computing the interest paid on the amount of money actually used during a given time. For example, assume that a creditor borrows $1,000 for one year and the lender charges a total interest charge of $100 for the loan. If the borrower has the use of the entire $1,000 for one year, then the APR is 10 percent. But if the $1,100 (principal plus interest) is repaid over the year in equal installments, then the borrower has the average use of about one half of the $1,000. In this case the $100 interest charge is translated into an APR of almost 20 percent. The finance charges used to compute the APR consist of the total of all charges for the loan, including interest, service charges, loan fees, and in most instances fees for credit reports. Since lenders must quote the costs of loans in terms of the APR, consumers can more easily compare the prices among lending institutions. Presumably consumers also benefit from the heightened competition which naturally results from more knowledgeable credit shopping.

The Board of Governors of the Federal Reserve System is required to provide model disclosure forms to facilitate compliance with the disclosure requirements. The forms use simplified, nontechnical language to help the borrower understand the transaction. Although a creditor is not required to use the forms provided, doing so insures compliance.

The enforcement of TILA is specifically committed to various administrative authorities, depending upon the parties involved in the credit transaction. For example, the Civil Aeronautics Board is empowered to enforce the act with respect to any domestic or foreign air carrier subject to the act. The Federal Trade Commission enforces the act with respect to all transactions not specifically delegated to another authority. Where a creditor inaccurately discloses the annual percentage rate or finance charge, the appropriate agency is authorized to require the creditor to adjust the consumer's account to assure that the consumer only pays the lower finance charge or APR actually disclosed.

TILA interpretation

Regulation Z, issued by the Federal Reserve Board, implements TILA and sets out in detail the rules for compliance with TILA. The Board of Governors of the Federal Reserve System explains Regulation Z through official and unofficial publications. Despite the efforts made by Congress and various agencies to crystallize the Truth in Lending Act's requirements, disputes arise as to what information must be disclosed pursuant to TILA.

Ford Motor Credit Co. v. *Milhollin*
444 U.S. 555 (1980)

Milhollin and others (respondents) purchased automobiles from dealers who financed the transactions through standard retail agreements and then assigned (sold) those agreements to Ford Motor Credit Company.

The contracts required the respondents to pay a precomputed finance charge. In accordance with TILA and Regulation Z, certain disclosures were made on the front of each contract. A clause in the body of the contract gave the petitioner the right to accelerate payment of the entire debt if the buyer defaulted on the contract. The respondents sued the petitioner for failure to disclose the acceleration clause on the front of the contract. The district court found for the respondents, and the court of appeals affirmed. The Supreme Court granted certiorari and reversed the decision.

Mr. Justice Brennan: The issue for decision in this case is whether the Truth in Lending Act (TILA) . . . requires that the existence of an acceleration clause always be disclosed on the face of a credit agreement. The Federal Reserve Board staff has consistently construed the statute and regulations as imposing no such uniform requirement. Because we believe that a high degree of deference to this administrative interpretation is warranted, we hold that TILA does not mandate a general rule of disclosure for acceleration clauses.

* * * * *

Respondents have advanced two theories to buttress their claim that the Act and Regulation expressly mandate disclosure of acceleration clauses. In the District Court, they contended that acceleration clauses were comprehended by the general statutory prescription that a creditor shall disclose "default, delinquency, or similar charges payable in the event of late payments," and were included within the provision of Regulation Z requiring disclosure of the "amount, or method of computing the amount, of any default, delinquency, or similar charges payable in the event of late payments." . . .

* * * * *

An acceleration clause cannot be equated with a "default, delinquency, or similar charg[e]," subject to disclosure. . . . The prerogative of acceleration affords the creditor a mechanism for collecting the outstanding portion of a debt on which there has been a partial default. In itself, acceleration entails no monetary penalty, although a creditor may independently impose such a penalty, for example, by failing to rebate unearned finance charges. A "default, delinquency, or similar charg[e]," on

the other hand, self-evidently refers to a specific assessable sum. Thus, within the trade delinquency charges are understood to be "the compensation a creditor receives on a precomputed contract for the debtor's delay in making timely instalment payments." Acceleration is not compensatory; a creditor accelerates to avoid further delay by demanding immediate payment of the outstanding debt.

* * * * *

The prepayment rebate disclosure regulation also fails to afford direct support for an invariable specific acceleration disclosure rule. To be sure, payment by the debtor in response to acceleration might be deemed a prepayment within the ambit of that regulation. But so long as the creditor's rebate practice under acceleration is identical to its policy with respect to voluntary prepayments, separate disclosure of the acceleration policy does not seem obligatory under a literal reading of the regulation. . . .

* * * * *

It is a commonplace that courts will further legislative goals by filling the interstitial silences within a statute or a regulation. Because legislators cannot foresee all eventualities, judges must decide unanticipated cases by extrapolating from related statutes or administrative provisions. But legislative silence is not always the result of a lack of prescience; it may instead be token permission or, perhaps, considered abstention from regulation. In that event, judges are not accredited to supersede Congress or the appropriate agency by embellishing upon the regulatory scheme. Accordingly, caution must temper judicial creativity in the face of legislative or regulatory silence.

* * * * *

Finally, wholly apart from jurisprudential considerations or congressional intent, deference to the Federal Reserve is compelled by necessity; a court that tries to chart a true course to the Act's purpose embarks upon a voyage without a compass when it disregards the agency's views. The concept of "meaningful disclosure" that animates TILA . . . cannot be applied in the abstract. Meaningful disclosure does not mean more disclosure. Rather, it describes a balance between "competing considerations of complete disclosure . . . and the need to avoid . . . 'informational overload.'" And striking the appropriate balance is an empirical process that entails investigation into consumer psychology and that presupposes broad experience with credit practices. Administrative agencies are simply better suited than courts to engage in such a process.

Case questions

1. How did the Supreme Court meet and refute the findings of the district court and the court of appeals?

2. What cogent reasons exist for the judicial policy of deferring to the Federal Reserve Board for interpretation of TILA?

3. Why might most consumers not need disclosure about an acceleration clause? How could the consumers in *Milhollin* have discovered the acceleration clause since it was not mentioned on the disclosure page? Do you think that the average borrower under these circumstances would have inquired about or otherwise discovered the acceleration clause at the time of the financing?

4. What is the proper balance between the competing considerations of full disclosure and the need to avoid "informational overload"?

5. TILA requires disclosure on the face of the contract regarding late fees and delinquency charges. Assume that in *Milhollin* there was a clause in the contract providing for a ¼ percent increase in finance charges in the event of nonpayment and an acceleration clause providing for the payment of the attorney fees and court costs necessary to enforce the clause. Must this information be clearly disclosed on the face of the contract?

Credit advertising

The Truth in Lending Act also regulates credit advertising. Any advertisement that lists any terms of credit must also include other significant terms. Some credit plans are open-ended. They include the common credit cards and revolving charge accounts. Other credit plans are closed-ended. They involve loans for specific amounts, for example, automobile financing. If an open-end credit plan lists a credit term in an advertisement, it must also conspicuously include:

1. Any minimum or fixed sum that could be imposed.
2. The annual percentage rate.
3. Any other term that the Federal Reserve Board may require by regulation.

Any advertisement for *closed-end credit* other than for residential real estate (except as required by board regulation) that states certain credit terms must also include:

1. The cash price or amount of the loan.
2. The down payment.
3. The number, amount, and due dates of the payments scheduled to repay the indebtedness if the credit is extended.

Cancellation of credit agreements

Under certain circumstances a debtor may cancel a credit transaction. Generally, when a principal dwelling is used as security for a loan, the borrower may cancel the transaction within three business days following the completion of the transaction or delivery of the material disclosures. (This right does not apply to a first mortgage given to secure the financing of a dwelling.) The creditor is required to inform the borrower in writing of this right to cancel. Cancellation is accomplished when written notice by mail or telegram is communicated to the creditor. Upon cancellation the borrower is not liable for any finance charges and any security interest given by the borrower becomes void. The creditor has 20 days to refund monies the borrower has paid and cancel the transaction. A homeowner may need money to remedy a structural defect or leaking gutters. Normally, because of the right of the owner to cancel the credit agreement within three days, the contractor hired will not begin work within that period. However, the homeowner may waive the right to cancel the agreement by notifying the contractor in writing that there is a real emergency and credit is needed immediately to finance repairs necessary to avert danger to person or property. In that event the contractor may start the work immediately.

Consumer leasing

The TILA provisions regulating consumer leases are designed "to protect consumers against inadequate and misleading leasing information, and assure meaningful disclosure of lease terms." These provisions, known as the Consumer Leasing Act, apply to consumer leases. A consumer lease is a transaction involving a lessor who leases personal property to a person (lessee) for personal, family, or household use when (1) the leasehold period exceeds four months and (2) the amount of the lease does not exceed $25,000. A lessor is defined as a person or entity that regularly engages in leasing or arranging to lease under a consumer lease. An automobile leased for personal use would be covered under the Truth in Lending Act if it met the other criteria, while an automobile leased for business purposes would be excluded.

Every lessor covered under the act must supply the lessee with a dated written statement identifying the lessor and the lessee and accurately disclosing in a clear and conspicuous manner an identification of the leased property, an itemization of the charges, the express warranties, insurance information and responsibility, periodic payment details, the lessee's liability at the end of the lease term, and the method for determining the conditions and consequences for terminating the lease prior to the end of the lease term.

Penalties

The law provides for both criminal and civil liability for violation of the disclosure provisions of the Truth in Lending Act. Whoever willfully fails to comply with the provisions of the act or gives false or inaccurate information may be fined up to $5,000 or imprisoned up to one year, or both. A creditor who fails to accurately disclose required information may be civilly liable to a consumer. The liability is limited to twice the amount of the finance charge incurred in connection with the transaction, with the further proviso that the liability shall not be less than $100 or more than $1,000. A creditor may avoid civil liability after making an error by notifying the consumer and adjusting the error within 60 days after discovery. A creditor may also escape civil liability by showing that the violation was unintentional and resulted from a bona fide error even though the creditor employed procedures reasonably adapted to avoid the error. An example of a bona fide error would be a mistake resulting from a computer malfunction.

Credit cards

TILA regulates the issuance and use of credit cards. It provides that no credit cards may be issued without a request. This provision effectively prevents unsolicited credit cards.

Under the act, a credit card holder may only be liable for up to $50 if another person uses the credit card without authorization, and then only if:

1. The cardholder accepted the credit card.
2. The card issuer gave adequate notice to the cardholder of the potential liability.
3. The card issuer provided the cardholder with a description of the means for notifying the card issuer in the event of loss or theft of the card.
4. The unauthorized use occurred before the cardholder notified the issuer of the card's loss or theft.
5. The card issuer provided a method for identifying the card user as the authorized user.

A credit card holder who extends credit past the authorized limitations will not be liable for any amount other than the actual amounts charged. Anyone who uses a counterfeit, fictitious, altered, forged, lost, stolen, or fraudulently obtained credit card, however, incurs criminal liability under TILA if:

1. The unauthorized usage was in a transaction affecting interstate or foreign commerce.
2. The obtained goods or services, or both, have a retail value of $5,000 or more.

A violation carries a penalty of up to $10,000 and imprisonment of up to five years, or both. Of course, state laws provide for criminal penalties for using a credit card under similar unlawful circumstances, regardless of the value of the obtained goods or services.

THE FAIR CREDIT REPORTING ACT

Computer technology now permits the storing of enormous quantities of information that may be retrieved instantaneously. When a consumer lender considers a loan application, the logical place to start the investigation is at a credit information storage house termed a *credit bureau.* Credit bureaus compile information to help the potential creditor make intelligent decisions as to the credit risks of applicants. The information that may be contained within the credit files of such a bureau is massive and varied.

Credit bureaus maintain files on over 100 million Americans, and every year they receive over 100 million requests for credit reports. Inherent in this credit system is a propensity for abuse. Because of the increased number of reported abuses, including breach of confidentiality, credit report inaccuracies and irrelevancies, and improper use of credit information, Congress enacted the Fair Credit Reporting Act (FCRA) (Title VI of the Consumer Credit Protection Act).

The FCRA regulates consumer reporting agencies. Under the act a consumer reporting agency is any entity which regularly engages in the practice of assembling or evaluating consumer credit information for the purpose of furnishing consumer reports to third parties, and which uses any means or facility of interstate commerce for the purpose of preparing or furnishing consumer reports. An entity may escape the regulations of the act if its assembly of credit information is for its own use as opposed to use by a third party. Reports which are confined to the disclosure of information regarding transactions between the consumer and the reporter are not consumer reports under the act. Thus information supplied by any business to a third party is outside the act as long as the information is based on transactions between that business and the consumer.

Permissible purposes

A consumer reporting agency may furnish consumer reports only for the purposes specified in the act. It may legitimately supply information:

1. In response to a valid court order.
2. Upon the written request of a consumer to whom it relates.
3. To a person or entity that it has reason to believe intends to use the information as a factor in determining a consumer's eligibility for *(a)* credit or insurance to be used primarily for personal, family, or household purposes; *(b)* employment purposes; *(c)* governmental licenses, or *(d)* an otherwise legitimate business purpose.

Obsolete information

The consumer reporting agency is obliged under the act to keep its files up to date. Generally, the agency may not report bankruptcies of the consumer that occurred more than 14 years prior to the report. Suits, judgments, tax liens, and accounts placed for collection or written off as bad debts may not be included in a consumer report if they are more than seven years old. Similarly, records of arrest, indictment, or conviction for a crime are not properly includable if their date of disposition, release, or parole predates the report by more than seven years. These time limitations are inapplicable if the consumer report is to be used in connection with a credit or life insurance transaction involving $50,000 or more or with the employment of an individual at an annual salary of at least $20,000.

Compliance

Every consumer reporting agency is required to maintain reasonable procedures to avoid violations of the act's obsolete information and permissible purpose requirements. The reporting agency must take measures to insure that the prospective users of the information identify themselves and certify the purposes and the intended exclusive use of the information. It must also make reasonable efforts to verify these statements when a new prospective user requests a consumer report.

The reporting agency is also required to maintain reasonable procedures to assure the maximum possible accuracy of its consumer reports. When information to be reported for employment purposes includes matter of public record likely to adversely affect the consumer, the reporting agency must maintain strict procedures to assure its completeness. Otherwise, the reporting agency must notify the consumer each time it supplies public information for employment purposes. The notification must include the name and address of the person to whom the report was sent.

Investigative consumer reports

Consumer reporting agencies often accumulate information about a consumer's character, reputation, characteristics, or mode of living through personal interviews with neighbors, friends, associates, or anyone else who may possess such information. This information gathering is permissible under the Fair Credit Reporting Act. Although Congress recognized that abuses occurred because of the gathering of irrelevant information, it failed to regulate the types of information that could be gathered and reported. Instead it sharply defined the permissible use of the information.

No adverse nonpublic information based on an investigative report that is three months old or older may be included in a consumer report unless it is reverified. When an investigative consumer report is requested, or prepared by the reporting agency, the consumer must be informed in writing not later than three days after the request for the report. The consumer has a right to a complete and accurate disclosure of the nature and scope of the investigation if a written report has been requested. This right does not apply if the investigative report is to be used to consider the consumer's suitability for a job for which the consumer did not specifically apply.

Disclosure

Under the act consumers who request it are entitled to disclosure of the nature, substance, and source of all information (except medical) on them that is in the files of the reporting agency, except that the agency need not disclose the sources of information used solely to prepare investigative consumer reports. Consumers are also entitled to the names of those to whom the agency supplied consumer reports for employment purposes within the preceding two years and for any other purposes within the preceding six months.

Disputes

A consumer may dispute the accuracy of information discovered in the reporting agency's files. In such case the reporting agency is required to reinvestigate the accuracy of the information unless it has reasonable grounds to believe that the consumer's contention is frivolous or irrelevant. If the reinvestigation fails to confirm the validity of the information, then the reporting agency must delete the information from its files. If the reinvestigation fails to resolve the dispute, the consumer must be permitted to file a brief written statement defining the nature of the dispute. The consumer reporting agency may limit the length of the statement to 100 words as long as it provides the consumer with assistance in writing it. On all subsequent reports containing the information the reporting agency must clearly point out that the information is disputed and supply the consumer's statement or an accurate abstract of it. The consumer may insist that any deleted or disputed information be brought to the attention of specifically designated persons who received a report containing that information for employment purposes within the last two years. If the report was used for any other purposes, the consumer may request that the deleted or disputed information be brought to the attention of anyone who received the report within the last six months.

Requirements on users of reports

An adverse consumer report may result in denial of credit, insurance, or employment or higher finance charges or insurance premiums. In such cases the user of the report is required, under the act, to advise the consumer of the name and address of the consumer reporting agency that supplied the report. Sometimes consumer credit is denied or the charge for consumer credit is increased because of information received from a source other than a consumer reporting agency. When this occurs, the user of the information, upon written request, must inform the applicant of the nature of the information that resulted in the adverse action.

Remedies

Violations of the FCRA are considered unfair or deceptive practices under the Federal Trade Commission Act. The FTC is empowered to enforce the act by cease and desist orders against consumer reporting agencies, users of common reports, and others not committed under the act to another specified governmental agency. Criminal and private civil enforcement are also available.

Criminal. The act provides criminal penalties against persons who obtain information about a consumer from a consumer reporting agency under false pretenses. In addition, officers and employees of consumer reporting agencies who knowingly provide information from agency files about an individual to a person not authorized to receive the information are subject to criminal penalties. In either case violators may be fined up to $5,000 or imprisoned up to one year, or both.

Civil. Civil liability under the act is divided into two categories based on the violator's degree of culpability. First, any consumer reporting agency or user that *willfully* violates the act is liable to the consumer for actual damages incurred by the consumer, punitive damages, costs, and reasonable attorney fees. If no actual damages result from the violation, punitive damages are still assessable against the violator. Second, a reporting agency or user of information that negligently fails to comply with any provision of the act is liable for the actual damages that result to the consumer, the costs of the action, and reasonable attorney fees. Consumer reporting agencies find some protection in the act in sections that expressly state or imply that no liability attaches for violations if the consumer reporting agency maintains reasonable procedures to assure compliance.

THE FAIR CREDIT BILLING ACT

The Fair Credit Billing Act was enacted to protect the consumer against inaccurate and unfair billing practices. The act regulates procedures for resolving billing errors. It is applicable both to creditors that issue credit cards to consumers and creditors that regularly extend credit payable in more than four installments or that require the payment of a finance charge. These creditors must advise consumers of their rights and responsibilities under the act when the consumers open an account and at semiannual intervals thereafter. The act requires that the creditor disclose on the periodic billing statement where to address billing inquiries. To take advantage of the protection afforded to consumers under the act, within 60 days of the receipt of a billing statement the consumer must notify the creditor in writing at the disclosed address that there is a billing error. The consumer must designate the amount of the error and his or her reason for believing that there is an error. The notification must contain data to enable the billing creditor to identify the consumer's name and account number, if any. The consumer may also request documentary evidence concerning charges which are in need of clarification.

Any creditor that receives a written notice in proper form indicating a billing error must respond in writing. If the creditor concludes that an error exists, then it must make appropriate corrections in the consumer's account, and so notify the consumer. If the creditor concludes that the billing statement is correct, then it must give the consumer reasons in support of that conclusion. The creditor must include documentary evidence of the debt if the consumer requests it.

The creditor may not institute any action to collect the debt until it makes the proper response. However, the creditor may continue to send periodic statements reflecting the disputed amount. In that event the creditor must indicate on the bill that the payment of the disputed amount is not required, pending the creditor's response. During this interval period the creditor may not close or otherwise restrict the consumer's account. The creditor, is however, permitted to use the amount of the dispute to determine whether the consumer's credit limit has been exceeded.

A creditor which knows a debt is disputed is prohibited, under the act, from making or threatening to make any adverse credit reports concerning the disputed amount until at least 10 days after the creditor has informed the consumer of its belief in the accuracy of its bill. This allows the consumer time to react to the creditor's response. The consumer may continue to dispute the billing statement—in which event a creditor which reports to a third party that the disputed amount is delinquent must indicate on the report that the delinquency is disputed.

A creditor that violates any of the above requirements forfeits the right to collect the disputed amount and finance charges of up to $50 for each disputed item. For extenders of large amounts of credit this is a small price to pay for noncompliance. In fact, it may be economically justified for large firms to ignore billing complaints and suffer the forfeiture. Ethical considerations, however, are also relevant.

THE EQUAL CREDIT OPPORTUNITY ACT

Market forces proved insufficient to insure that credit was equally available to all creditworthy customers. Stereotypes and prejudices clouded the decision-making process, so that extenders of credit often based their determinations on irrational factors such as race or marital status. The Equal Credit Opportunity Act (Title VII of the Consumer Credit Protection Act) was enacted to insure that an applicant would not be denied credit because of (1) race, (2) color, (3) religion, (4) national origin, (5) marital status, (6) age, or (7) sex or because (8) any of the applicant's income was derived from any public assistance program or (9) the applicant had exercised a right under the Consumer Credit Protection Act. The Equal Credit Opportunity Act prohibits a creditor from discriminating against an applicant on any of the above prohibited bases in any aspect of a credit transaction. A creditor as defined under the act is a person who regularly participates in the decision of whether or not to extend credit. The act prohibits a creditor from making certain inquiries of credit applicants. For example, apart from some carefully defined exceptions, a creditor may not inquire of an applicant as to whether any of the income stated in the application is derived from alimony, child support, or separate maintenance payments. A creditor is also prohibited from requesting the race, color, religion, or national origin of an applicant (except for statistical monitoring purposes) in connection with a credit transaction.

Within 30 days of an application a creditor must notify the applicant for credit of its action on the application. If the application results in adverse action, the applicant is entitled to a statement of the specific reasons for the adverse action or to a notification that such a statement is available upon request. Adverse action includes a denial or revocation of credit or a change in the terms of the existing credit arrangement.

Any violator of the Equal Credit Opportunity Act is civilly liable to the aggrieved applicant in the amount of the actual damages. Any nongovernmental unit is additionally liable for punitive damages not to exceed $10,000. Where members of a discriminated group bring a class action against a creditor, the total recovery for the whole class cannot exceed the lesser of $500,000 or 1 percent of the net worth of the creditor. Costs and reasonable attorney fees are added to the damage award. An aggrieved party may in an appropriate case obtain an injunction prohibiting the creditor from discriminating.

Which of various administrative authorities enforces the act depends upon the applicant, or the subject matter of the credit transaction. For example, the Small Business Administration is empowered to enforce the act with respect to small business investment companies, while the Securities and Exchange Commission enforces it with respect to securities brokers and dealers. The Federal Trade Commission enforces the act with respect to all transactions not specifically delegated to another authority.

DEBT COLLECTION

Some debtors and creditors enter into voluntary relationships with each other for their mutual benefit. The debtor receives goods or money to purchase goods which were otherwise unaffordable. The creditor receives payment in the future and interest on the loan or credit extended. As long as the debtor makes timely payments on the debt, there is no problem. When the debtor defaults on the debt, however, the creditor will naturally make attempts to collect it. Those attempts will probably first take the form of debtor pursuit by letter and phone. Sometimes these communications are extremely harsh and threatening. When such efforts fail, the creditor may employ third parties to collect the debt. Professional collection agencies often invoke novel techniques in attempts to force payment. Sometimes their collection manners become unreasonable. Creditors may not go beyond certain defined permissible limits in pursuing the debtor. Their conduct is circumscribed by the common law and by federal and state statutes.

Common law

Under the common law the most popular protections for debtors against unreasonable creditor collection activities are causes in action for defamation, invasion of privacy, and intentional infliction of mental distress. Although these actions are generally available, they are normally ill suited to the traditional circumstances surrounding creditor hounding.

Defamation is the publication of statements that tend to discredit another's reputation. Since truth is a defense to defamation, this action is generally successful only where allegations of a debt or of unwillingness to pay a debt are in fact false. Privilege is another defense to defamation. If a creditor communicates statements to another who has a legitimate interest in the information, the creditor may take advantage of this defense unless those statements are made with an evil motive. Employers of debtors are popular targets for debt collectors. Some courts hold that employers have a legitimate interest in knowing of their employees' delinquencies and hence deem these communications privileged.

Invasion of privacy may be a basis for recovery for damages against an overenthusiastic bill collector. Some courts grant recovery where the creditor publishes the debt in a newspaper or makes repetitive and harassing calls to the debtor's neighbors or employer or to the debtor. Generally, reasonable communications do not form a basis for an invasion of privacy suit.

Some states recognize a cause of action for *intentional infliction of mental distress*. In most states that recognize this common-law tort, the collection activity must be outrageous and the resulting distress severe.

Because of the inadequate protection provided by the common law against abusive collection tactics, Congress responded with legislation that regulates creditors' collection activities.

The Fair Debt Collection Practices Act

The Fair Debt Collection Practices Act (FDCPA) covers debt collectors who are in the business of collecting debts for another. The act also applies to those who process their own debts when they do so under another name.

Prohibitions. Under the act a covered "debt collector" may contact a person other than the debtor, the debtor's spouse, or the debtor's parents (if the debtor is a minor) only for the purpose of ascertaining "location information" on the debtor. Location information includes the debtor's home telephone number, place of residence, and place of employment. Obviously, if the debt collector knows the debtor's location, then no communication with third parties is necessary or permissible. When talking to a third party, the debt collector is prohibited from volunteering the nature of his or her business, though that information may be supplied if it is expressly requested. Even then, the debt collector is not permitted to inform the third party that a debt is owed. Of course, at this juncture the third party either makes the natural inference or becomes annoyingly curious. The debt collector is not permitted to communicate with the same third party more than once unless the third party so requests or the debt collector reasonably believes that the third party's information was erroneous or incomplete.

There are further restrictions on debt collectors' practices under the act. The debt collector may not contract the debtor at a time or place "which should be known to be inconvenient." In the absence of knowledge as to convenient times or places, the act specifies as convenient the hours between 8:00 A.M. and 9:00 P.M. at the consumer's location. By implication, any other hours are considered inconvenient. If a collector knows that a debtor works other than a daytime shift, the collector may not inconvenience the debtor by calling at a time when the collector should know, the debtor would be caught asleep.

As soon as the collector becomes aware that the debtor is represented by an attorney, further contacts with the debtor must cease. They may be resumed only if the attorney fails to respond to the debt collector's inquiry within a reasonable time or if the attorney permits direct communications with the client. Contacts with the debtor must also cease if the debtor communicates, in writing, a refusal to pay or a request that the contacts end. This communication then normally leads the creditor to pursue legal recourse through a judicial suit.

The collector may not engage in "any conduct the natural consequence of which is to harass, oppress, or abuse any person in connection with the collection of debt." For example, a debt collector may not make repeated phone calls to the debtor or advertise the debt as for sale.

The FDCPA also prohibits the debt collector from using false or misleading misrepresentations in collection efforts. For example, the debt collector may not falsely purport to be an attorney or to be employed by a consumer reporting agency or to be a government official. The collector also may not threaten to take action which the collector cannot legally take or does not intend to take. For example, a creditor may not ordinarily take a debtor's property without legal process. In such a case any threat that the creditor intends to do so violates the Act. In addition, the act prohibits the collector from engaging in unfair or unconscionable practices in connection with debt collection. Such practices include attempting to collect a debt that is not authorized by law and concealing charges for collection. The following case illustrates the application of the FDCPA.

Rutyna v. *Collection Accounts Terminal, Inc.*
478 F. Supp. 980 (N.D.Ill. 1979)

Rutyna (plaintiff), a widow on social security, was 60 years old and suffered from high blood pressure and epilepsy. Plaintiff incurred a debt for medical services which she thought had been paid by insurance. The debt was in fact unpaid and had been turned over to Collection Accounts Terminal, Inc. (defendant). Defendant's agent telephoned the plaintiff and, in response to plaintiff's denial of the indebtedness, said, "You owe it; you don't want to pay, so we're going to have to do something about it."

Thereafter the plaintiff received the following letter from the defendant:

You have shown that you are unwilling to work out a friendly settlement with us to clear the above debt. Our field investigator has now been instructed to make an investigation in your neighborhood and to personally call on your employer. The immediate payment of the full amount, or a personal visit to this office, will spare you this embarrassment.

The envelope contained the name and the return address of the defendant. Plaintiff instituted suit, alleging that upon receipt of the letter she became very nervous and fearful that the defendant would embarrass her by contacting her neighbors. Defendant moved for summary judgment, which the district court denied.

McMillen, District Judge:

* * * * *

Harassment or abuse. The first sentence of §1692d provides: "A debt collector may not engage in any conduct the natural consequence of which is to harass, oppress, or abuse any

person in connection with the collection of a debt." This section then lists six specifically prohibited types of conduct, without limiting the general application of the foregoing sentence. The legislative history makes clear that this generality was intended. . .

* * * * *

Plaintiff does not allege conduct which falls within one of the specific prohibitions contained in §1692d, but we find that defendant's letter to plaintiff does violate this general standard. Without doubt defendant's letter has the natural (and intended) consequence of harassing, oppressing, and abusing the recipient. The tone of the letter is one of intimidation, and was intended as such in order to effect a collection. The threat of an investigation and resulting embarrassment to the alleged debtor is clear and the actual effect on the recipient is irrelevant. The egregiousness of the violation is a factor to be considered in awarding statutory damages. Defendant's violation of §1692d is clear.

Deception and improper threats. §1692e bars a debt collector from using any "false, deceptive, or misleading representation or means in connection with the collection of any debt." Sixteen specific practices are listed in this provision, without limiting the application of this general standard. §1692e(5) bars a threat "to take any action that cannot legally be taken or that is not intended to be taken." Defendant also violated this provision.

Defendant's letter threatened embarrassing contacts with plaintiff's employer and neighbors. This constitutes a false representation of the actions that defendant could legally take. §1692c(b) prohibits communication by the debt collector with third parties (with certain limited exceptions not here relevant). Plaintiff's neighbors and employer could not legally be contacted by defendant in connection with this debt. The letter falsely represents, or deceives the recipient, to the contrary. This is a deceptive means employed by defendant in connection with its debt collection. Defendant violated §1692e(5) in its threat to take such illegal action.

Unfair practice/return address. The envelope received by plaintiff bore a return address, which began "COLLECTION ACCOUNTS TERMINAL, INC." §1692f bars unfair or unconscionable means to collect or attempt to collect any debt. §1692f specifically bars:

(8) Using any language or symbol, other than the debt collector's address, on any envelope when communicating with a consumer by use of the mails or by telegram, except that a debt collector may use his business name if such name does not indicate that he is in the debt collection business.

Defendant's return address violated this provision, because its business name does indicate that it is in the debt collection business. The purpose of this specific provision is apparently to prevent embarrassment resulting from a conspicuous name on the envelope, indicating that the contents pertain to debt collection.

On the subject of the return address on the envelope, defendant cites §1692k(c), which provides:

A debt collector may not be held liable in any action brought under this subchapter if the debt collector shows by a preponderance of the evidence that the violation was not intentional and resulted from a bona fide error notwithstanding the maintenance of procedures reasonably adapted to avoid any such error.

Defendant states that it was "unaware that the return address could be considered a violation of any statute." No affidavit is offered. §1692k(c) does not immunize mistakes of law, even if properly proven (as this one is not). §1692k(c) is designed to protect the defendant who intended to prevent the conduct which constitutes a violation of this Act but who failed even though he maintained procedures reasonably adapted to avoid such an error. Defendant here obviously intended the conduct which violates the Act in respect to the return address, but it simply failed to acquaint itself with the pertinent law. . . .

* * * * *

Case questions

1. Were the words used by the collection agent over the phone violative of the Fair Debt Collection Practices Act? Explain.

2. Does the FDCPA prohibit a collector from making "an investigation in the neighborhood and . . . personally call[ing] on [the debtor's] employer." Why is doing so a violation in this case?

3. Why is a collector prohibited from sending a letter with a return address bearing the name of the collection agency when the name on the envelope indicates that it is in the debt collection business? Are any defenses available to the collector to rebut this charge?

4. Redraft the letter so that it is firm, yet not violative of the FDCPA.

5. Discuss whether Mrs. Rutyna would have had a cause of action at common law.

Penalties. Any debt collector who violates the act is liable to the debtor for actual damages. Actual damages might occur if an employer fires the debtor as a result of having been informed of the debt. The debt collector may be assessed additional damages of up to $1,000, depending upon the nature of the violation. Malicious, repeated violations are more likely to result in upper limit additional damages than are isolated, nonmalicious violations.

Relationship to state laws.   In addition to the FDPCA, state laws have been enacted which protect debtors from the unscrupulous techniques of creditors and their agents. Where a state law sets greater limitations on collection practices than does the federal law, a creditor need only abide by the state law. Otherwise the debt collector must comply with both the state and federal laws in the area of debt collection unless the state law is inconsistent with the federal law. In that case the federal law controls.

The Federal Trade Commission is charged with the administration and enforcement of the FDCP. If the commission determines that a given state has enacted a law which grants adequate protection to the consumer and provides sufficient provision for enforcement, it may exempt the debt collectors in that state from the operation of the act.

Postjudgment collection

When "peaceable" means of debt collection are unsuccessful, a creditor may have to resort to courts to aid in the collection process. After a creditor sues on a debt and receives a court judgment for a specific sum of money, the debtor might still refuse to pay. A court judgment is reflected by an entry signed by a judge acknowledging the amount awarded to the winning party. If the debtor is "judgment proof," that is, has no assets, then the court entry will not aid the creditor. However, if the uncooperative judgment debtor has property, the judgment creditor may cause certain of the debtor's property to be attached. Under attachment a sheriff seizes property of the debtor. The property is sold, and the proceeds are distributed to the creditor to the extent necessary to satisfy the judgment and related expenses. Any excess funds derived from the sale are returned to the debtor.

Garnishment is another remedy available to a judgment creditor. This is a way of reaching debtors' property that is held by third parties. The most commonly garnished property includes bank accounts and wages. (In certain circumstances a creditor may attach or garnishee a debtor's property prior to a judgment; many states permit this when it appears that the debtor intends to leave the jurisdiction to avoid creditors.) Each state has enacted its own statute to regulate the creditor's right to garnishee a debtor's wages. In the past the garnishment process was loosely controlled and subject to abuse. Under many state statutes the ease with which wages could be garnisheed invited lenders to extend credit without adequate inquiry into the borrower's credit background.

In many instances, when a creditor garnisheed a debtor's wages, the employer immediately fired the debtor. This common practice resulted in widespread disruption of employment, production, and consumption. The employers had two primary reasons for firing these debtors. The employer, known as the garnishee, when notified by the court of the garnishment, is required to send a portion of the employee's wages to the court. Failure to do so can result in employer liability to the creditor. Some employers simply did not want to be a party to the court process which necessitated increased administrative expense. Secondly, employees whose wages are being garnisheed are often less motivated to work to their normal capacity because of the reduction in their paycheck. Largely to curb the impact of unrestricted garnishment practices and discharge because of garnishment, Congress passed Title III of the Consumer Credit Protection Act. Title III does not supplant state garnishment statutes but merely places limitations upon them.

A state statute providing for garnishment procedure does not violate Title III as long as it is at least as restrictive as Title III. The act places certain limits upon what percentage of a debtor's disposable earnings is subject to garnishment. Disposable earnings are the wages that an employee receives after statutorily required withholdings are deducted. These withholdings include federal, state, and local taxes; social security payments; and deductions for pension plans required by state law for governmental employees. Under the act, the maximum amount that may be subjected to garnishment for any workweek, is generally (1) 25 percent of an employee's disposable earnings for the week or (2) the amount that the disposable earnings for the week exceeds 30 times the federal minimum hourly wage, whichever is less. Assume, for example, that Rocky Hound receives a court judgment against Ron Debtor in the amount of $500. Ron debtor, a business law professor, earns $400 each week. Assume that the federal minimum hourly wage is $3.50. Deductions from Debtor's pay each week amount to: taxes, $100; social security, $50; credit union, $10; Blue Cross–Blue Shield, $20; and alimony, $50. Although the total deductions are $230, the total statutorily required deductions are only $150, leaving a total disposable income of $250 ($400 − $150). The maximum amount that Hound may garnishee for the week would be $62.50 (25 percent of $250), since this amount is less than the difference between Debtor's disposable income and 30 times the federal minimum hourly wage as given ($250 − $105 = $145). Hound will have to attach or continue to garnishee Debtor's property to satisfy the remaining $437.50 unless satisfactory arrangements can be made for payment. Many state statutes restrict the number of permissible garnishments to one per month.

The act also places restrictions on discharge from employment by reason of garnishment and provides a penalty against employers who violate this section. An employer may not discharge an employee because the employee's earnings have been subjected to garnishment for any one indebtedness. An employer who violates this provision may be subjected to a fine of up to $1,000 or imprisoned for up to one year, or both. Even if a creditor garnishees an employee's wages 12 times in a year, the debtor-employee is afforded protection as long as this is for the same debt. The secretary of labor, acting through the Wage and Hour Division of the Department of Labor, enforces the provisions of Title III.

UNIFORM CONSUMER CREDIT CODE

All states have some regulation in the consumer credit area. The Uniform Consumer Credit Code (UCCC) was proposed by the National Conference of Commissioners on Uniform State Laws in 1968. It is designed to replace existing state laws in the consumer credit area and to provide uniformity of regulation among the states. Ten states have enacted the entire UCCC or a substantial portion of it.[3] Originally consumer advocates severely criticized the UCCC because of its failure to adequately protect the consumer. Recent drafts have adopted a more consumer-oriented posture.

The UCCC covers consumer credit sales and loan extensions by those that regularly engage in such transactions, when the transactions are with consumers whose primary purpose is personal, family, household, or agricultural and when the financed amount does not exceed $25,000. Real estate transactions are covered when they involve an interest rate in excess of 12 percent a year. The UCCC generally excludes charge account transactions which do not require repayment in installments. It also excludes pawnbroker and insurance transactions and short-term credit arrangements, such as charges for professional services.

The UCCC requires certain disclosures and specifically regulates in the area of rate ceilings, creditors' remedies, referral sales, and fine print clauses. The UCCC has been streamlined by incorporating the federal Truth in Lending Act by reference.

Under the UCCC the consumer has the right to cancel a home solicitation credit sale within three days. Most states grant the consumer this right independent of UCCC adoption. Furthermore, a rule of the Federal Trade Commission makes it a deceptive trade practice under section 5 of the FTC Act to fail to afford the consumer the right to cancel such a transaction within three days, upon proper notice. This FTC rule includes cash sales and sales outside the purchaser's home when such sales are not made at the seller's place of business.

Civil and criminal remedies attach to UCCC violations.

THE BANKRUPTCY REFORM ACT

Every day individuals and businesses are confronted with serious financial hardship. This usually boils down to a very simple fact—they cannot meet their creditors' legitimate demands. Business distress means suffering for various members of society. The failure of a business entity translates into

---

[3] The adopting states are Colorado, Idaho, Indiana, Iowa, Kansas, Maine, Oklahoma, South Carolina, Utah, and Wyoming. Several other states are considering adoption.

a loss of jobs for its employees and a financial loss to its creditors. Shareholders and others that have an interest in the business may lose their investment, and customers may lose a supplier. Whatever the reason for the failure, there is a need for debtor relief to mitigate the failure's impact on society by insuring that those affected by it are treated equitably.

In addition to certain state relief available in the form of trusteeships and receiverships, the federal bankruptcy laws afford debtor relief. Bankruptcy laws have been enacted by Congress pursuant to its power to establish uniform laws on the subject of bankruptcies throughout the United States. The first federal Bankruptcy Act was enacted in 1898. The Bankruptcy Reform Act of 1978 repealed all prior bankruptcy legislation. It represented the first major overhaul of bankruptcy legislation in 40 years. The act established a new Bankruptcy Court in each federal district and invested these bankruptcy courts with broad jurisdiction over all cases arising under the act and over all cases related thereto.

The new bankruptcy court system will be "phased in" during a transition period. Although most of the substantive provisions of the act went into effect on October 1, 1979, the actual physical transfer of facilities and cases to the new bankruptcy courts and the introduction of some of the new procedural operations will not take place until April 1, 1984. Commencing on that date, bankruptcy judges will be appointed by the president with the advice and consent of the Senate to serve for 14-year terms. During the transition period the attorney general will appoint U.S. trustees in 18 districts to administer bankruptcy cases and to replace the court-appointed private trustee system now used in those districts. This experimental U.S. trustee system will expire on April 1, 1984, unless Congress acts before that date to permanently incorporate it into the act.

This section is concerned with three types of debtor relief under the Bankruptcy Reform Act. These include liquidation (chapter 7), reorganization (chapter 11), and adjustment of the debts of an individual with regular income (chapter 13).

Liquidation

Liquidation is sometimes referred to as straight bankruptcy or as a chapter 7 proceeding. Generally, a liquidation, as administered by the Bankruptcy courts, involves the sale of the debtor's assets, distribution of the proceeds to creditors, and the discharge of the debtor's remaining liabilities. Liquidation is consistent with the "fresh start" philosophy of allowing an honest debtor to surrender assets for distribution to creditors and thereby be relieved of any further indebtedness. Individuals, partnerships, or corporations that are insolvent may be the subject of a liquidation. Insolvency under the Bankruptcy Act means that the debtor cannot meet financial obligations as they become due. This differs from the ordinary *balance sheet* concept of insolvency under which liabilities exceed assets. It is not uncommon for a debtor to possess assets in excess of liabilities, yet still be unable to meet the liabilities as they mature. The assets might be in the form of unmarketable securities, slow-moving inventory, or real property. The nonliquid state of these assets might prevent the debtor from meeting day-to-day debts.

Voluntary and involuntary petitions. Liquidation may be voluntary or involuntary. In a voluntary liquidation the insolvent debtor files a bankruptcy petition seeking debtor relief. The petition acts as an order for relief by giving the court jurisdiction to proceed with the administration of the liquidation. Railroads, governmental units, banks, insurance companies, and savings and loan associations may not initiate voluntary petitions in bankruptcy. These highly regulated industries are subject to rigid supervision and control by regulatory agencies.

In an involuntary liquidation a debtor may be forced into liquidation by creditors. Farmers and charitable corporations, as well as the industries which may not initiate a voluntary petition in bankruptcy, may not be the targets of involuntary liquidations. In order to force a debtor into liquidation, the creditor(s) must file an involuntary petition. If the debtor has more than 12 creditors, at least 3 must join in the filing of the petition. If there are less than 12 creditors, then at least 1 creditor must file the petition. In either case the petitioning creditors must have unsecured claims totaling at least $5,000. For example, assume that Janet Milestone is doing business as the Corner Drugstore. She has four creditors, as follows:

Blue	$ 5,000
Green	4,000
Hazel	2,000
Rose	1,000
Total	$12,000

Since Milestone has less than 12 creditors, only 1 creditor need sign the involuntary petition. However, since the signing creditor must have at least a $5,000 claim, only Blue qualifies. If Green and Hazel or Green and Rose both sign the involuntary petition, then the $5,000 requirement would also be satisfied. The petitioning creditors are granted an order for relief if they can prove that (1) the debtor is insolvent; or (2) someone was appointed to receive and distribute or to take possession of the debtor's property for the benefit of the creditors within 120 days prior to the filing of the petition.

The voluntary or involuntary debtor is required to file with the court a list of creditors, a schedule of assets and liabilities, and a statement of financial affairs. Each creditor and other interested party is given a notice of the filing of the petition.

Automatic stay. The filing of a petition in bankruptcy causes an automatic stay (suspension) of most attempts by creditors to collect on their indebtedness. Actions by a governmental unit to enforce its regulatory powers are excepted from the stay, as are, for example, creditors pursuing alimony or child support. In some cases a creditor not excepted from the stay may be granted relief upon application to the Bankruptcy Court. If the applicant can show that an interest in specific property held as collateral on a debt is jeopardized by the stay, the court will relieve the applicant unless the applicant can otherwise be afforded "adequate protection," a concept discussed below under the heading "The Trustee's Powers and Responsibilities."

Interim and permanent trustees. After an order for relief has been granted by the court in either a voluntary or involuntary liquidation case, an interim trustee is appointed to take over the debtor's property. This takeover is not usually physical at this stage; however, the interim trustee does possess the legal rights of ownership. The interim trustee conducts the first meeting of creditors. At this meeting the debtor appears and is examined by the creditors and the trustee about assets and other matters. At this stage creditors are generally most concerned about the whereabouts of the debtor's property. The creditors may elect a permanent trustee; otherwise the interim trustee continues to serve. The debtor's property passes to the trustee, who is obliged to reduce the debtor's property to cash to the extent necessary to pay creditors.

Exemptions. An individual debtor is entitled to exempt certain property from distribution to creditors. The debtor may elect to take advantage of the exemptions provided by the state law or by the federal law unless the state law forbids the election of the federal exemptions. Since the federal exemptions are more liberal than the exemptions granted in most of the states, debtors usually choose the federal exemptions where state law does not prohibit them from doing so. The federal exemptions include the following:

1. Up to $7,500 equity in a residential home. (Homestead exemption.)
2. Up to $1,200 equity in a motor vehicle.
3. Every household item, every item of wearing apparel, and other specified property held for personal use whose value is $200 or less. (There is no aggregate monetary limitation for this category.)
4. Up to $500 in jewelry.
5. Property selected by a debtor of up to $400 in value in addition to the value of any unused portion of the homestead exemption mentioned under number 1 above.
6. Trade tools not exceeding $750 in value.
7. Interests in life insurance policies.
8. Health aids.
9. State and federal benefits, such as social security, unemployment, alimony, and pensions, to the extent reasonably necessary for support.

A husband and wife may be joint petitioners, and each may claim his or her applicable exemptions. If they do not own a residence, a husband and wife may, under the federal exemptions, each select $7,900 of otherwise nonexempt personal property to be held exempt from distribution. This means that under 5 above the joint petitioners may retain $15,800 in personal property in addition to the other specified applicable exemptions. Because of the liberality of the federal exemptions some debtors feel that they cannot afford not to go bankrupt.

The trustee's powers and responsibilities. The debtor's estate includes all property in which the debtor has an interest. Entities holding estate property must turn over the property to the trustee. However, any entity having an interest in the property, such as a secured creditor, may insist upon "adequate protection" from the trustee before being required to turn over the property. A secured creditor is one that possesses a security interest in specific property as collateral for a debt. As we shall see, a secured creditor is entitled to satisfaction of indebtedness out of the proceeds of the sale of the secured property. For this reason a secured creditor has a strong interest in protecting the secured property from depreciation or other loss until such time as the property is sold. The trustee may provide such a creditor with "adequate protection" by, for example, agreeing to make cash payments to the creditor in an amount equal to the periodic depreciation of the secured property or by giving the creditor an additional security interest in other property.

Preferential and fraudulent transfer. The trustee has the power to avoid the following types of preferential transfers of property made by the debtor: A *preferential transfer* is (1) a transfer made for the benefit of a creditor (2) to pay a preexisting debt (3) when the debtor is insolvent and (4) made during the 90-day period before the petition is filed (5) which causes a creditor to receive a *greater percentage* of the debt than would have been received under the distribution provision of the act. In addition, trustees may avoid transfers under these circumstances to an "insider" if the transfers were made within one year before the filing of the petition and the insider had reasonable cause to believe that the debtor was insolvent. An insider is one who is in a close relationship to the debtor, e.g., a spouse, relative, partner, corporate officer, or director. Some types of transactions are not voidable by the trustee even if they appear to be preferential. The trustee cannot set aside the payment of a debt incurred within the ordinary course of the debtor's business within 45 days after the debt was contracted.

The trustee may set aside certain fraudulent transfers that were made within one year of the filing of the petition. Fraudulent transfers include those intended to hinder, delay, or otherwise defraud creditors.

Distribution. The trustee is charged with distributing the cash realized from the liquidation to satisfy the allowed claims of creditors. There are three classes of creditors: secured creditors, priority creditors, and general creditors. Secured creditors are paid out of the proceeds of the sale of the collateral in which they have an interest. If those proceeds are insufficient to satisfy the debt, then the secured creditor is relegated to a general creditor status for the balance due.

Certain unsecured claims are entitled to *priority* in distribution—these claims are entitled to be paid before the claims of other unsecured creditors. Priority claims are grouped into the following categories:

1. Administrative expenses, including court costs, trustee and attorney fees, and the costs of preserving the debtor's estate and prosecuting criminal cases related to bankruptcy fraud.
2. Claims that arise against the debtor between the time a petition is filed and the time an order for relief is issued or a trustee is appointed, whichever occurs first.
3. Claims of up to $2,000 per employee for wages earned within 90 days preceding the filing of the petition.
4. Employee claims, arising within 180 days prior to the filing of the petition, for unpaid contributions to employee benefit plans, to the extent of the unused limitation in the preceding priority category.
5. Claims of up to $900 per claimant for deposits made for consumer goods or services never received.
6. Claims of the federal, state, and local governments for taxes.

Each category of priority creditors must be paid in full before the next category of priority creditors is entitled to be paid. If there are insufficient funds to satisfy the claims of all the creditors within a category, then each of the creditors within that category receives a pro rata share.

After the claims of the priority creditors have been satisfied, any remaining nonexempt assets are distributed among the general creditors, who are also referred to as unsecured creditors. Any assets or proceeds remaining after the distribution to the general creditors are delivered to the debtor.

Discharge. An individual debtor may be afforded a discharge in bankruptcy excusing the debtor from the obligation to pay most of the remaining unpaid debts. Unpaid creditors may contest the discharge in bankruptcy on any one of several grounds, including the following: concealment of assets, destruction of financial books and records, commission of a bankruptcy crime, and a prior discharge in bankruptcy within the last six years. Certain claims are nondischargeable, i.e., they must ultimately be paid by the debtor. These include the following:

1. Certain taxes entitled to priority.
2. Claims for property obtained under false pretenses.
3. Debts not listed by the debtor in the schedule of debts so as to permit the creditor to make timely claim.
4. Claims arising from embezzlement or larceny or from a debt for fraud or defalcation of the debtor while the debtor was acting in a fiduciary capacity.
5. Claims for alimony and child support.
6. Claims arising from willful and malicious torts.
7. Claims arising from a prior bankruptcy when the debtor was denied a discharge for grounds other than the six-year limitation.

8. Claims for certain student loans that have been due and owing for less than five years unless repayment would cause undue hardship.

Handsome v. *Rutgers University*
445 F. Supp. 1362 (D.N.J. 1978)

Lynn Handsome (plaintiff) was a student at Rutgers University from 1968 through 1974. During this time she borrowed $4,600 in the form of National Defense Student loans and National Direct Student loans. Health problems necessitated her withdrawal from college in January 1975, and because of large medical bills she was unable to meet the repayment schedule on the loans. Consequently, Rutgers (defendant) obtained a default judgment against the plaintiff for $4,991.75 plus costs and interest.

Plaintiff filed a petition in bankruptcy in April 1977. The liabilities listed in her petition were in excess of $25,000, including the indebtedness to Rutgers University. Her assets totaled $368.75. Plaintiff was adjudicated a bankrupt and was discharged of all indebtedness, including the debt to Rutgers. Thereafter plaintiff attempted to reenroll at Rutgers. Although her admission was approved on scholastic grounds, a "place hold" notice was put upon her records since she was "more than three months delinquent in [her] debts to the university." She was prevented from registering and was unable to obtain a release of her transcripts.

Plaintiff filed a complaint against Rutgers University alleging that its actions violated the Constitution and the Bankruptcy Act. The court granted a temporary restraining order that directed Rutgers to allow plaintiff to register. The court was then presented with the question of whether the restraining order should be made permanent. The court determined that it should be.

Stein, District Judge:

*   *   *   *   *

Plaintiff's principal contention is that defendant's actions impinge upon the policies of the Bankruptcy Act and are, therefore, invalid under the Supremacy Clause. She relies primarily on the Supreme Court's decision in *Perez* v. *Campbell.*

In *Perez*, plaintiffs, two bankrupts whose licenses had been suspended, attacked the constitutionality of a state statute which provided for the suspension of the driver's licenses of persons who had outstanding automobile accident judgments against them, notwithstanding that such judgments may have been discharged in bankruptcy.

*   *   *   *   *

Concluding that the sole purpose of the statute was to provide leverage for the collection of debts, the Supreme Court held the statute unconstitutional under the Supremacy Clause and overruled its decisions to the contrary. The Court stated that the purpose of the Bankruptcy Act is to give the debtor "a new opportunity in life and a clear field for future effort, unhampered by the pressure and discouragement of pre-existing debt." . . . The Court held that the statute "stands as an obstacle to the accomplishment and execution of the full purposes and objectives of Congress" . . . and, thus, was invalid under the Supremacy Clause.

*   *   *   *   *

Inasmuch as defendant, both by withholding plaintiff's transcripts and refusing to permit her to register, has transgressed upon the "fresh start" policies of the Bankruptcy Act, this Court must hold such actions violative of the Supremacy Clause.

The Court next addresses plaintiff's contention that defendant's actions violate her right to equal protection as guaranteed by the Fourteenth Amendment. Since education is not a fundamental right, and since wealth is not a suspect classification, the Court need only determine whether the classification at issue here is reasonably related to a legitimate governmental interest. However, on analysis, it is clear that defendant's actions cannot survive even this less lenient level of scrutiny.

The classification employed by Rutgers includes all persons who are more than three months delinquent in their debts to the school. As applied to persons who are not bankrupts, there is little doubt that this classification is legitimate, for the university has a legitimate interest in seeking repayment of valid debts. However, insofar as this classification includes bankrupts, it necessarily runs afoul of the Equal Protection Clause. The state cannot claim a legitimate interest in securing the repayment of loans discharged in bankruptcy, for, as we have already demonstrated, pursuit of such an interest is foreclosed by *Perez*. Moreover, defendant, as a state university, is under an obligation to treat its citizens alike. While it may, of course, discriminate on the basis of reasonable classifications such as academic performance, a citizen's status as a bankrupt is, per force, an impermissible criterion. This is not to say that defendant

may not in the future validly decline to extend credit to one who has previously discharged his debts in bankruptcy, but it cannot deny a citizen so vital a privilege as an education on the basis of his status as a bankrupt.

* * * * *

In holding defendant's practices unconstitutional, this Court in no way condones the abuse of the bankruptcy laws by students who, with little or no assets, take out loans with one eye on the bankruptcy laws and with no present intention to repay. However, as to students who have already discharged their student loans in bankruptcy—who, it should be noted, have undergone bankruptcy proceedings where the creditor has been given every opportunity to oppose the discharge and the Bankruptcy Judge was empowered to inquire into any allegations of fraud—this Court holds that the state may neither withhold the fruits of their prior education, nor thrwart them in their attempts to seek a "fresh start" through a college education.

Case questions

1. What was the effect of the temporary restraining order that the court initially issued?

2. Do you think decisions such as *Handsome* will encourage students to seek a discharge of their student loans? Why or why not?

3. Does this decision help to destigmatize those who go bankrupt?

4. Would there be a different result in this case if Handsome's sole motive in pursuing bankruptcy was to wipe out her student loans?

If when she took out the loans she had no intention of ever repaying them? Explain.

5. Suppose that, unlike Rutgers, which is a state institution, a private educational institution had refused to release a student's transcripts until that student's loan, which had been discharged in bankruptcy, was repaid. Should there be a different result? What reason can be advanced for the student's right to transcripts?

Reaffirmation. A debtor may agree to pay a creditor whose debt has been discharged through bankruptcy. Often a debtor reaffirms such a debt so that the creditor will continue to deal with the debtor or so that the creditor will not take secured property to satisfy the debt. Because of the potential that exists for creditors to exert undue influence upon unsuspecting debtors, the act places certain restrictions upon these reaffirmation agreements. For a reaffirmation agreement to be valid it must be entered into before the discharge of the debt, and the agreement may be rescinded by the debtor within 30 days after it becomes effective. In addition, the court must warn the debtor about the consequences of reaffirmation at a discharge hearing. Finally, if the reaffirmation is of a consumer debt that is not secured by real property, the court must approve the agreement for it to be enforceable. The court will not approve the agreement unless it is in the best interests of the debtor or in settlement of a good faith objection to dischargeability of the claim.

Reorganization

Except for stockbrokers and commodities brokers, the same individuals and entities that are eligible for a chapter 7 liquidation treatment are also eligible for reorganization (chapter 11). The purpose of reorganization is to allow a financially disturbed business to continue while arrangements for the adjustment of debts are made with creditors of the business. Reorganizations may be voluntary or involuntary. Generally, the same rules that apply to liquidation cases apply to reorganization, including trustee powers, exemptions, preferential transfers, and discharges.

After issuing the order for relief, the court appoints creditors' and stockholders' committees. The committees' task is to represent their respective interest groups. The committees are charged with investigation of the financial condition and activities of the debtor as well as participation in the formulation of a reorganization plan. They may also request the appointment of a trustee to replace the debtor in possession, if no trustee was previously appointed. At the first creditors' meeting a committee may examine the debtor under oath, to elicit information helpful to the interests of the group it represents.

When no trustee has been appointed, the debtor has the exclusive right to submit a reorganization plan for the first 120 days after the order for relief. If a trustee has been appointed or if the debtor fails to submit a timely plan which is accepted by each class of creditors, then any interested party may submit a proposed plan for reorganization. Interested parties include the debtor, the trustee, and the committees.

Creditors are afforded an opportunity to accept or reject reorganization plans. A class of creditors accepts a plan when it is approved by a majority of the creditors within the class that represents at least two thirds of the allowed claims. A class of stockholders accepts a plan when at least two thirds of the shares within the class approve the plan.

The court will confirm a plan which is accepted by the various classes of creditors and stockholders as long as the plan is fair and reasonable. Even if a class has failed to accept the plan, the court may still confirm the plan if the plan treats the nonaccepting class fairly and equitably. A confirmed plan is binding upon all interest holders and discharges all debts not provided for under the plan.

Under certain circumstances a debtor may convert reorganization into a liquidation. The court may at its own option convert a reorganization into a liquidation or dismiss the case in the best interest of the creditors.

Adjustment of debts for individuals with regular income

Individuals with regular income, except stockbrokers and commodities brokers, may file a voluntary petition to adjust their debts (chapter 13). This includes wage earners and individuals engaged in business. For a debtor to qualify for chapter 13 status his or her unsecured debts may not exceed $100,000 and his or her secured debts may not exceed $350,000. A chapter 13 resembles a reorganization; however, it may only be sought by individuals and it is subject to the above monetary limitations as well as possessing other distinctions mentioned below. Unlike the debtor in a liquidation the debtor in a chapter 13 remains in possession of the assets during the administration of the plan and thereafter. Creditors may not force a debtor into a chapter 13. As long as the debtor is complying with the plan, creditors may not compel the conversion of a chapter 13 into a chapter 7 or 11.

The chapter 13 debtor files a plan for repaying creditors. It may be a *composition* plan or an *extension* plan. In a composition plan the creditors receive less than full payment. They receive a percentage of the indebtedness, and the debtor is discharged of the remaining indebtedness. Under an extension plan the creditors receive the entire indebtedness but the payments extend past the due date. The plan must provide for completion within three years unless the court approves a longer period, in no event more than five years.

Unsecured creditors do not have to accept the plan for it to be implemented; however, they must receive at least as much as they would have received under a liquidation. Priority claimants must be paid in full under the plan unless a lesser payment is agreed upon. The plan may be confirmed without the consent of the secured creditors when the secured creditors are permitted to retain a lien on the property at least equal in value to the indebtedness or when the debtor surrenders the secured property to the secured creditor.

Under a chapter 13 a trustee is appointed by the court to administer the plan. The debtor normally pays a monthly sum to the trustee directly or by payroll deduction. The trustee then apportions the payment to creditors in accordance with the plan. Assume, for example, that Joe files a chapter 13 petition for adjustment of his debts. Joe's debts, which are all due, include:

Hi-Rise Bank	$1,500
Lenox Department Store	500
Doctor	1,200
Shell Oil	400
Total	$3,600

Joe earns $1,000 a month but is unable to pay the $3,600 indebtedness now due. Under a chapter 13 extension plan Joe could pay $100 a month to the trustee over 36 months. The trustee would distribute an apportioned share to each of the creditors, and the creditors would be paid in full at the end of 36 months.

Creditors which are distributees under a chapter 13 plan do not have to extend credit to the debtor in the future. In many instances the court order prevents a chapter 13 debtor from incurring further debt without the consent of the court during the administration of the chapter 13 plan.

At the completion of the plan a chapter 13 debtor receives a discharge from all debts covered by the plan. In a case where the debtor has not completed the payments within three years, or some other prescribed period, the court may still extend a discharge to the debtor as long as the failure was due to circumstances beyond the debtor's control.

POLICY CONSIDERATIONS

Originally the barter method of transfer was used to meet the needs of society. From the barter system, which had definite limitations, society moved to a cash system. Because of advances in technology and in order to meet the requirements of demand and convenience, checks and similar instruments became the principal form of payment for goods and services. The institution of the checking system introduced the concept of "float," or the period that intervenes between the time a check is given as payment and the time the check clears the bank. Float gives consumers who are dissatisfied with the product or service purchased an opportunity to stop payment on their checks before these clear the bank. When credit extension and credit cards were widely introduced, the float period was increased and consumers enjoyed the additional advantage of "buying now and paying later." Along with these advantages the credit system opened the way for the various abuses that have been discussed in this chapter. In the 1960s the consumer's cause, championed by Nader's Raiders and other consumer interest groups, made great strides as legislation to protect consumers was introduced and passed. The spirit of consumerism moved into the 1970s as the momentum for additional consumer protection continued.

There is reason, however, to think that consumer protection is in retreat. The credit system and governmental regulation of debtor-creditor relations have been targeted as a prime cause of the inflationary spiral. The recent amendments to the Truth in Lending Act are a retreat from the fuller disclosure requirements provided by its predecessor. There seems to be a move to permit the normal market forces to regulate debtor-creditor relations. Many fear that this move will work to the severe disadvantage of the consumer.

At the same time society continues to become more mechanized as it seeks more efficient ways to operate. Electronic funds transfer (EFT), introduced by the financial industry, is a means for exchanging value which is gaining increased acceptance by consumers. It includes automated teller machines and computerized cash withdrawal, deposit, and payment systems. Some believe that the rapid increase in the use of electronic funds transfer will project us into a cashless society. EFT eliminates float by effecting instantaneous exchanges of value. It also presents possibilities for computer error, to the detriment of the consumer. Because of concern about these possibilities and about various other problems presented by EFT, Congress enacted the Electronic Funds Transfer Act (EFTA) to deal with error resolution and otherwise regulate the use of EFT. A clearer understanding of the impact of EFT and EFTA on the financial industry, the consumer, and society will have to await further experience.

Review problems

1. Linda Glaire purchased a seven-year membership in a health club owned and operated by LaLanne. The price of the membership was $408, regardless of whether the sum was paid in cash at the outset or over a two-year period in monthly installments of $17 each. Glaire elected to pay over time, as do most of LaLanne's customers. She entered into a standard form contract which stated that no finance charge was made for the extension of credit. In accordance with its usual practice LaLanne then sold Glaire's contract to Universal Guardian Acceptance Corporation at a discount of 37.5 percent. LaLanne thus immediately received $255 in cash, and Glaire became obligated to Universal for the full $408, payable over two years. LaLanne and Universal are interlocking corporations with common ownership and control, and Universal regularly assists LaLanne in its financing by accepting contracts at a discount. Upon learning of the arrangement between LaLanne and Universal, Glaire filed suit against LaLanne, alleging violations of the Truth in Lending Act.

Is the act applicable to LaLanne? Why? Has LaLanne violated the act? Who, if anyone, is required to make TILA disclosures to Glaire?

2. Robert Martin gave his American Express credit card to his business associate E. L. McBride. Martin and McBride were involved in a joint business venture, and Martin's intent was to enable McBride to use the card for joint venture purposes. Although Martin gave McBride verbal authorization to charge a maximum of $500 on the credit card, McBride actually charged $5,300. Martin refused to pay, and American Express instituted suit against him. What is the principal issue in this case? Who will win, and why? Would your answer be different if Martin had a $1,000 credit limit on the card?

3. James C. Jenkins, after moving from Washington, D.C., to St. Louis, applied for auto insurance with the Fireman's Fund Insurance Company. Several days after his application was filed, Jenkins was informed by Fireman's that his background would be investigated in connection with the policy. A few days later Jenkins learned that his application for insurance coverage had been rejected because of information contained in a report compiled by Accurate Reports. Jenkins learned that the information was the result of interviews between Accurate's representative and Jenkins's neighbors in Washington. Jenkins requested that he be given an opportunity to see the report and that he be told to whom Accurate's representative had spoken. The Accurate representative in St. Louis denied both requests. Jenkins learned of the

content of the report from Fireman's and thereupon contacted Accurate once again. He disputed the accuracy of the information in the file and requested an explanation of certain statements contained therein. Accurate's representative refused to discuss the matter with Jenkins. Is the refusal justified? Explain.

4. Glen Wood, an executive vice president of SAR Manufacturing Company, checked into the Holiday Inn in Phenix City, Alabama, and tendered a Gulf Oil Company credit card to pay for his room. After an imprint of the card had been made, it was returned to Wood. Gulf Oil Company monitors the accounts of its credit card holders on a continuing basis and cancels a customer's credit upon determining that the customer cannot afford to pay. Gulf furnishes National Data Corporation with a list of all credit cancellations and authorizes it to disburse credit information to inquirers that are authorized to extend credit to holders of Gulf credit cards. Gulf had noticed that Wood had been charging an increasingly large amount in comparison to his income. (Gulf was unaware that Wood had been using the card to charge business expenses.) Although Wood's account was not in arrears, Gulf determined to cancel his credit. Consequently, Gulf directed National Data Corporation to give the following credit report to those inquiring about the approval of Wood's credit card use:

Pick up travel card. Do not extend further credit. Send card to billing office for reward.

When the night auditor at Holiday Inn checked with National Data Corporation he received the above communciation. The auditor then went to Wood's room at 5:00 A.M. and awakened him on the pretense that he needed Wood's credit card since the "imprinting" had not taken. Wood inquired at the front desk when the credit card was not returned. He was told that the card had been "seized upon the authority of National Data." Wood left the motel, but his anger started to build until he had a heart attack due to the stress of reflecting on the incident. Wood sued Gulf, alleging that it had negligently

failed to comply with the Fair Credit Reporting Act as a consumer reporting agency. He also sued National Data Corporation and Holiday Inn, alleging that they had negligently failed to comply with the Fair Credit Reporting Act as users of a consumer report. With what result?

5. Robert Cragin and his wife submitted a written application for a $2,000 property improvement loan to First Federal Savings. Mr. and Mrs. Cragin signed the application as joint applicants. The loan was approved by First Federal, and the Cragins were informed of the approval in a letter from Arthur Barnett, a loan manager of the bank. Thereafter Barnett informed Mr. Cragin that several documents would have to be signed by both Mr. and Mrs. Cragin and notarized. Mr. Cragin informed Barnett that it would be extremely inconvenient for his wife to go before a notary to sign the documents since she took care of two small children and could not get away from the house. Barnett insisted that this procedure had to be followed. Cragin then said, "I want to apply for the loan in my own name." Barnett responded by saying, "You will have to submit a new application in writing as required by the bank's procedure." Cragin refused and sued First Federal, alleging a violation of the Equal Consumer Opportunity Act based on sex and marital status discrimination. Who will prevail?

6. Luella Davis was indebted to Public Finance Corporation. She informed Public Finance that she was no longer employed, was on public aid, and was unable to make payments on the indebtedness. Over an eight-month period, in attempts to collect the debt, employees of Public Finance called Mrs. Davis several times a week, sometimes more than once a day, and frequented her home weekly. On one occasion an agent of Public Finance telephoned Mrs. Davis at the hospital where she was visiting her sick daughter even after Mrs. Davis requested that the agent not contact her there. On another occasion an employee of Public Finance persuaded Mrs. Davis to write a check on the promise that the

check would not be cashed. Thereafter the employee informed an acquaintance of Mrs. Davis that Mrs. Davis was writing bad checks. On still another occasion a Public Finance employee went to Mrs. Davis's home and took an inventory of her household furnishings, refusing to leave her home until her son entered the room. Public Finance was aware that Mrs. Davis suffered from hypertension and a nervous condition. Mrs. Davis's hypertension and nervous condition were aggravated as a result of Public Finance's conduct. Discuss all the possible remedies that Mrs. Davis has against Public Finance. What cause of action affords her the best chance of recovery?

7. Jones is employed in the Dearborn, Michigan, plant of the Ford Motor Company. For his services Jones is paid $235.23 a week (an amount in excess of the federal minimum hourly wage) after all appropriate state and federal taxes are subtracted from his gross pay. Jones made several purchases on credit from Sears. Upon Jones's failure to pay Sears the full amount due according to their charge account agreement, Sears filed a civil action against Jones. Sears was awarded a judgment in the amount of $1,164.89, the unpaid balance due on the account. A month before Sears obtained its judgment, Jones's wife was granted a divorce from Jones and Jones was ordered to pay child support in the amount of $96 a week. Jones contends that he cannot satisfy either judgment and has steadfastly refused to do so. Both Sears and Jones's ex-wife desire prompt satisfaction of their judgments.

What recourse is available to them? Does the ex-wife's judgment limit Sears's ability to collect on its judgment? Can they both collect from Jones? Explain.

8. Bruce Gabriel applied for and was granted a loan by CIT Financial Services, Inc. Gabriel sought the loan so that he could consolidate all of his existing debts. CIT's credit application was designed to allow CIT to determine the applicant's financial position. The application requested that Gabriel list the exact number of the debts he owed and the amount due on each. On the application Gabriel neglected to list several of his creditors. CIT examined the application turned in by Gabriel and granted him a loan on the basis of the information furnished in the application. Gabriel was still unable to meet all of his financial obligations and subsequently filed a voluntary petition in bankruptcy. Gabriel's trustee in bankruptcy maintains that Gabriel's bankruptcy discharged the debt owed to CIT. CIT disagreed and filed suit against Gabriel's trustee in bankruptcy to recover the full amount of the loan.

Is CIT entitled to payment? Why?

9. Robert Girardier applied for and received a National Defense Student Loan with Webster College in September 1978. After he graduated with a bachelor's degree in the summer of 81, he defaulted on the loan. He is now contemplating bankruptcy in the hope of obtaining a discharge of his obligation to pay Webster College $1,500, the amount of the loan. He is aware of Webster's policy of not releasing transcripts to students who have not satisfied their financial obligations to the college. Girardier needs the transcripts in order to obtain a master's degree. What should Girardier do? What should he argue if he files bankruptcy and lists Webster as a creditor?

10. How do you think the credit system of exchange as constituted at present impacts the consumer? What effects do you think the elimination of the credit system would have upon the consumer?

PART III: REVIEW PROBLEMS

1. The Computer Complex, Inc. (CCI), is a manufacturer of small home computers. They range in price from $1,000 to $150,000. CCI offers financing at the maximum rate allowed by state usury laws for consumer transactions. These rates are below the prime rate. CCI has an aggressive collections department which frequently calls delinquent debtors and threatens lawsuits, nasty letters to employers, and general embarrassment. It persists in doing so even if the consumer contests the debt. It frequently ignores letters from consumers claiming billing errors.

CCI's chief electrical engineer recently discovered a defect in the wiring of the most expensive model. The defect could result in electrical shock or fire in 1 out of every 10,000 units. The engineer resigned in protest over CCI's refusal to take corrective action or warn purchasers of the danger.

CCI advertises on television. Its ad shows a happy teenage boy using a home computer. The computer used in the ad is not a CCI model but is manufactured by Competitor Corporation. The narrator says:

> CCI turns computers into child's play. Computers are the way of the future. Your child should be prepared. Buy a CCI home computer. You can use it yourself in tax planning, managing the family budget, playing games, and dozens of other ways. And your children will enjoy it too as you teach them the wonders of computers. Liberal financing is available below the skyrocketing prime rate. Hurry! Act today!

You have just been hired by CCI. Your first assignment is to prepare a report to the president discussing all of the legal concerns raised by the above facts.

2. The Electric Factory manufactures toys for mature children. Its research and development department produced a bicycle that is designed to operate by sprockets, springs, or motor. The bicycle is called the Chameleon. The standard model 10-speed sprocket-control

bike, sells for $149.95. By means of the #666 adaptable spring kit, which sells for $99.99, the bicycle can be made to self-propel. The springs self-wind when the operator peddles the bicycle. If the operator then flicks a switch to engage the springs, they will propel the bicycle. The #777 adaptable motor attachment, which sells for $499, converts the Chameleon into a motorbike.

The Electric Factory markets the Chameleon through 37 exclusive dealerships in various parts of the country. It places all Chameleon advertisements and is running the following advertisement concerning the Chameleon:

THE CHAMELEON
A CHAMPION'S 10-SPEED BICYCLE
FOR RACERS
$149.95
AND IT'S STURDIER, SAFER,
LIGHTER, AND LESS
EXPENSIVE THAN ITS COMPETITORS
EASY TO ASSEMBLE

When customers inquire about the Chameleon they are first made aware of the spring and motor attachments. Most of the dealerships use high-pressure techniques to persuade customers to purchase the attachments. Customers are offered a 10 percent discount if they buy the spring or motor attachment within 30 days after they purchase the standard model. The standard model contains a written warranty, portions of which read:

> The company agrees to fix any movable defective parts within 60 days of sale when said parts are delivered or sent postage prepaid to the plant.

> The company disclaims liability for any injuries sustained as a result of manufacturer's defects.

> This warranty is in lieu of all other warranties, express or implied.

In reality, the standard-model Chameleon without attachments is two pounds heavier than the average weight of its 10-speed competitors, although it is lighter than all of its spring bike and motorbike competitors. The bike comes unassembled in two boxes and includes a booklet for "easy assembly." The standard model is assembled in 47 steps; 26 additional steps are required to assemble the spring attachment, and 34 additional steps are required to assemble the motor attachment. The steps are clearly explained with explicit diagrams. In order to assemble even the standard model, 16 standard-size sprocket wrenches are needed, in addition to Phillips screwdrivers, pliers, a hammer, and a vise.

Swan manufactures a $139.95 bicycle that competes with the Chameleon standard model. Through its legal office, Swan has contacted the Electric Factory and has threatened suit unless the Electric Factory removes or alters its present advertisement. The Federal Trade Commission has already filed a complaint alleging unfair and deceptive advertising against the Electric Company and has stated that it will accept a consent order only if the order includes a corrective advertising order which says, "Contrary to prior advertisements, the Chameleon is not lighter or less expensive than all of its competitors."

Through the National Electronic Injury Surveillance System the Consumer Product Safety Commission has become aware of several injuries sustained on the Chameleon because the sprockets disengage when the operator is peddling, causing the rider to lurch forward and fall off the bike. The Consumer Product Safety Commission may seek a ban of the product because it poses an imminent threat of injury to consumers.

An accident occurred while Jimmy Jones, age 15, was assembling the motor attachment to the Chameleon he had recently purchased. Apparently, while the motor was hanging from an A-frame by a double-strand rope in accordance with the instructions, a sharp edge of the motor mounting sliced through the rope. The motor fell on his brother's chest, fracturing three ribs. There was no warning in the instructions or otherwise of this danger. Jimmy's parents have initiated suit against the Electric Company.

John Moore made $1,200 a month at the Electric Factory. His take-home pay after the normal federal, state, and local deductions was $1,000. He owes $200 to Jan Ross, a lawyer who handled an accident case for him. She called him twice on the job and left messages with his employer for John to return the call. On one occasion she called John at home at 7:30 A.M. and demanded payment. Every week she sends a bill to John's home; the envelope gives her name and address and identifies her as an attorney at law. John also owes Sears department store $500. International Revenue Corporation has been collecting for Sears. John recently moved to get away from his hounding creditors. International conducted an investigation in John's old neighborhood to ascertain his whereabouts. When it found out his new address it phoned his wife and said "Your husband is a deadbeat. If he doesn't pay by tomorrow, we are going to sue him for everything he has." In addition, a $1,000 judgment against John was awarded to Jim McNeil as a result of an auto accident. Jim hired a lawyer who garnisheed John's wages for the months of January, February, and March and obtained the entire indebtedness. As a result, the Electric Factory fired John.

James Auser, a divorced Electric Company employee, is unable to meet his day-to-day debts. His balance sheet looks like this:

Assets

Cash	$ 1,200
Inventory	2,000
Automobile	3,000
House	63,500
Household furnishings	15,000
Jewelry	1,000
Business tools	3,000
Life insurance policies	3,050
	$91,750

Liabilities

Doctors . . . . $ 3,000
Paris Finance Company   56,000
Mastercharge   2,500
Sears   1,000
Food Fast, Inc.   6,000
Taxes   12,000
Payroll   1,000
Alimony   2,500
Student loan   2,500
                                   86,500

Owner's equity   5,250
                                   $91,750

The Paris Finance Company holds a $56,000 mortgage on James's house. The household furnishings consist of 22 pieces of furniture, of which 15 are valued at $200 apiece and the remaining 7 at over $200 apiece. James owes the taxes to the IRS because he failed to pay last year's income tax. He incurred the student loan six years ago. The administrative expenses (court costs) of any bankruptcy proceeding are $200. The state exemptions are: homestead, $5,000; Jewelry, $2,000; motor vehicle, unlimited; and tools of trade, $500. James went to the Electric Company's in-house counsel to discuss the problem.

You are being interviewed for a position with the Electric Company as a general executive manager. The interviewer is aware that you have taken a legal environment of business course that includes product safety, advertising, and debtor-creditor relations. The interviewer asks you to discuss the relevant issues contained in the data presented above.

PART FOUR

Securities law

CHAPTER 13

Issuing securities

The sale of securities is a prime method for raising capital to finance business ventures. Investors buy stocks, bonds, and other securities in the hope of earning a profit or deriving some other benefit from their purchase. Before the nature of securities and the laws that govern their issuance are introduced, a brief examination of business organizations is in order.

BUSINESS ORGANIZATIONS

A business must take on an organizational form in order to operate. Selecting a particular business form normally turns on a careful analysis involving such considerations as management control, risk exposure, and capital needs. Three main types of business organizations are commonly employed: sole proprietorship, partnership, and corporation.

Sole proprietorship

The simplest form of business organization is the sole proprietorship. It involves one person who owns and operates a business. Theoretically, any business, regardless of size, can operate through a sole proprietor. Practically, however, this method of operation is usually confined to small businesses that do not require a large initial capital outlay. The owner usually obtains funding for a sole proprietorship from personal savings and loans.

The sole proprietorship enjoys the advantage, from the owner's perspective, of concentrating management and control in the owner. As the business expands, the owner needs to employ agents to assist in its operation. An agent is one who is authorized to act for another. An employee is a type of agent. Because of the nature of this agency relationship the employer is responsible for the acts of the agents that are committed within the scope of the employment.

A major disadvantage of the sole proprietorship is that its creditors may look to the personal assets of the owner to satisfy their claims. Sometimes this is a high price to pay for being you own boss.

Partnership

The partnership is an association of two or more persons who carry on a business for profit. It is formed by agreement of the parties. Normally each partner contributes money or property to the partnership to initially fund the business. The Uniform Partnership Act (UPA), which has been adopted by most states, specifies the rules of law that govern the operation of partnerships. Although a partnership is not deemed to be a separate legal entity, it does possess certain characteristics that are common to recognized legal entities. For example, a partnership can own and convey property in its own name. It can, in most states, sue or be sued in its own name. However, for other purposes the partnership is not treated as a legal entity. For example, it is not taxed. The individual partners are taxed on the earnings in accordance with their share as defined in the partnership agreement. If the partnership agreement is silent about the share of profits, then each partner is entitled to an equal share. Similarly, in the absence of an agreement to the contrary, each is obligated to bear an equal share of the losses. Each partner has the right to use partnership property for partnership purposes, and each partner possesses equal rights in the management and control of the partnership's affairs unless the partnership agreement specifies otherwise.

Each partner is both an agent for the partnership and for every other partner. This agency relationship places certain fiduciary duties upon each partner. It requires a high standard of good faith and loyalty. A partner may not act against the interests of the partnership to promote his or her own interests. Partners are "held to something stricter than the morals of the market place."[1] Any breach of this fiduciary responsibility results in liability. For example, a partner who fails to inform other partners about a business opportunity, and instead takes advantage of it for his or her own benefit, will be liable to the partnership for the equivalent value of the benefit.

A major disadvantage of the partnership form of business is the unlimited liability to which each partner is exposed. After exhausting the partnership assets, creditors can look to the individual partners for satisfaction. The limited partnership was created to counter this undesirable characteristic. The Uniform Limited Partnership Act (ULPA), adopted by most states, governs the operation of limited partnerships. Limited partnerships must have at least one partner whose liability is unlimited. The other partners, designated limited partners, are shielded from personal liability. In return for this protection the limited partners surrender the right to exercise manage-

---

[1] *Meinhard* v. *Salmon*, 294 N.Y. 458, 164 N.E. 545 (1928).

ment powers. Limited partners are passive investors who contribute capital, expecting to earn a profit.

Corporation

The corporation is the usual organizational form employed by large businesses. It is a statutory creature. Every state has laws that govern the creation, operation, and termination of corporations. A corporation is a separate legal entity; consequently, it is taxed on its earnings and is liable for its debts.

A corporation consists of a board of directors, officers, and shareholders. The board of directors is normally elected by the shareholders and manages the corporation. For assistance in that task the board employs officers and delegates the day-to-day management function to them. Officers are normally authorized to hire employees, to whom they delegate duties. The shareholders are the owners of the corporation. They invest in the corporation by purchasing shares of stock. These shares of stock are known as *equity securities,* since they represent ownership interests in the corporation. One of the main attractions of the corporate form for shareholders is that they enjoy limited liability. The most they can lose is their investment. A corporation's creditors must satisfy their claims out of the corporate assets and may not look to the individual shareholders to satisfy those claims. In addition to issuing stock, corporations often raise money by issuing bonds. Those who invest in bonds are called bondholders. They are really lending money to the corporation. These bonds are known as *debt securities* since they represent a debt of the corporation.

INTRODUCTION TO SECURITIES REGULATION

Securities are different from most of the "merchandise" familiar to the average person. A consumer who purchases a loaf of bread in the grocery store can touch and smell the bread and can evaluate its worth by comparing it with other brands on the shelf. This is not the case with securities. The worth of a share of stock depends on the worth of the entity that issued it. Evaluating this worth requires knowledge of that entity's operations. This is ordinarily beyond the investor's reach. An alternative is for the investor to rely on the issuer's credibility and to believe the issuer's claims about the enterprise. In the past this means of ascertaining value often tempted those issuing stocks and other securities to make exaggerated claims about the financial status and prospects of their enterprises. Unsuspecting investors were frequently enticed with fanciful promises of "pie in the blue sky."[2] This practice made legislators aware of the need for investor protection.

---

[2] The term *blue sky laws* refers to state securities regulations intended to protect investors from "speculative schemes which have no more basis than so many feet of blue sky." *Hall* v. *Geiger Jones, Co.,* 242 U.S. 539 (1917).

At the turn of the century a few states enacted laws designed to protect investors, and by 1933 all but one state were operating under some type of securities regulation.[3] These state laws varied in form. Some contained antifraud provisions prohibiting misrepresentations in the sale of securities. Others contained registration requirements for securities or for those engaged in the securities business. Still others contained a combination of these regulatory devices.

State regulations of securities proved inadequate to protect investors. There was a lack of uniformity among the various state securities laws. Schemers preyed upon consumers in the states that possessed the most permissive securities laws. It was often possible to evade state securities laws by operating on a purely interstate basis, or pursuant to liberal state exemptions.

The 1929 stock market crash shattered American confidence in securities and their markets. Congress recognized that federal intervention was needed to aid in restoring public confidence in securities. The following congressional statement exemplifies the concerns underlying the federal securities laws:

> During the post-war decade some $50 billion of new securities were floated in the United States. Fully half or $25,000,000,000 worth of securities floated during this period have been proven to be worthless. These cold figures spell tragedy in the lives of thousands of individuals who invested their life savings, accumulated after years of effort, in these worthless securities. The flotation of such a mass of essentially fraudulent securities was made possible because of the complete abandonment by many underwriters and dealers in securities of those standards of fair, honest, and prudent dealing that should be basic to the encouragement in investment in any enterprise. Alluring promises of easy wealth were freely made with little or no attempt to bring to the investor's attention those facts essential to estimating the worth of any security.[4]

Since most state securities laws were based on a paternalist philosophy, they generally incorporated the principle of *merit discretion*. This gave the regulatory authority the power to evaluate the merit or worth of securities before qualifying them for issuance. Starting with the Securities Act of 1933, Congress rejected this paternalist philosophy. The federal securities laws are based on the philosophy that the best protection for an investor is access to complete information regarding the contemplated investment. The Securities and Exchange Commission, which administers the federal securities laws, is not empowered to pass on the worth of a security or even to decide whether its issuance would be in the public interest. As long as full disclosure is provided, the securities may "float," regardless of their worth. The final determination of their desirability is left to the investor. Congress did not, however, disturb the states' regulation of securities. As a result state and

---

[3] Nevada was the sole exception.

[4] H.R. Rep. No. 85, 73d, Cong., 1st Sess., (1933).

federal securities laws operate side by side and often necessitate dual compliance.

FEDERAL SECURITIES LAWS

The federal securities laws are administered and enforced by the Securities and Exchange Commission (SEC), an independent administrative agency created in 1934 by the Securities Exchange Act. These laws seek to protect the general public and the investors in securities. The federal securities laws consist of the Securities Act of 1933, the Securities Exchange Act of 1934, and other specialized securities laws.

The Securities Act of 1933

The focus of this chapter is the Securities Act of 1933. This act requires that nonexempt securities be *registered* before they can be offered for sale. It also provides for criminal and civil liability for misstatements or fraudulent practices in connection with the sale of securities and preparation of the registration statements. Before the Securities and Exchange Commission was established in 1934, the Federal Trade Commission was responsible for administering the Securities Act of 1933.

The Securities Exchange Act of 1934

The Securities Exchange Act of 1934 extends the disclosure requirements to securities traded on national exchanges and to securities traded over the counter if they meet a size requirement. Under this act the trading firm is required to file a registration statement with and make periodic reports to the SEC. The act regulates proxy and tender offer solicitations, insider trading, securities brokers, dealers, and exchanges. It also includes antifraud provisions. The details of this act are treated in Chapter 14.

Other securities legislation

The *Public Utility Holding Company Act* of 1935 was designed to correct abuses that existed among the gas and electric public utility holding companies. Many of these companies had built huge empires and had concealed their diversified holdings through complicated corporate and capital structures. The act requires public utility holding companies to register and to simplify and fully disclose their financial, organizational, and operational behavior.

The *Trust Indenture Act* of 1939 regulates the public sale of bonds and other debt securities in excess of $1 million when these are issued pursuant to a trust indenture. A trust indenture is a document whose terms and conditions govern the responsibility of the issuer (seller) and the rights of the bondholders. It designates a trustee who is charged with carrying out the indenture. The Trust Indenture Act imposes high standards of conduct on the trustee to insure that the rights of the bondholders are adequately safeguarded.

The *Investment Company Act* of 1940 regulates publicly owned companies engaged in the business of investing and trading in securities. These companies must comply with registration and disclosure requirements designed to safeguard the public. The *Investment Advisers Act* of 1940 empowers the SEC to regulate persons and firms that are in the business of rendering investment advice to clients. The act requires that investment advisers register with the SEC. It also contains antifraud and other provisions to protect the advisers' clients.

Under chapter 11 of the *Bankruptcy Reform Act* the SEC may render expert advice and assistance to the Bankruptcy courts in connection with the reorganization of certain debtor corporations. The advice is designed to assist these courts in affording fair treatment to creditors and investors while assuring that the corporations emerge from the reorganization in sound financial condition.

The *Securities Investor Protection Act* of 1970 empowers the Securities Investor Protection Corporation (SIPC) to supervise the liquidation of securities firms in financial trouble. SIPC, a nonprofit corporation whose members are brokers, also protect investors from losses due to the financial failure of brokerage firms.

THE SECURITIES AND EXCHANGE COMMISSION

The SEC is an administrative agency which was created by Congress to administer the securities laws. Its five members are appointed by the president and serve five-year terms. No more than three of the members may be affiliated with the same political party. The terms are staggered so that one member's term expires each year. Most of the commission's staff is located in Washington, and the remainder is situated in nine regional and eight branch offices in key cities throughout the country. Every year the commission submits a report to Congress on its activities in connection with the adminstration of the securities laws.

The SEC has broad rulemaking powers. SEC rules have the force of law. The SEC prescribes the disclosures and forms which registrants must file. Informal SEC releases further define the attitudes and policies of the agency, although they do not have the effect of law. In addition, the SEC responds to specific questions by advising the inquirers of its opinion on proposed transactions. These responses are sometimes referred to as *no action* letters because they often state that the SEC will not take any action against the inquirer based on the facts and the intended of action outlined in the inquirer's letter.

Court decisions involving interpretations of the securities statutes and rules set precedents. Under certain sections of the 1933 act such decisions have been sparse since the SEC has issued numerous rules clarifying those sections. However, where SEC rules are scarcer, court cases play a larger role in defining the terms and application of the statutory provisions regarding securities. One such area that required clarification was the definition of a security.

DEFINITION OF A SECURITY

Perhaps one of the greatest tasks that faced Congress when it was drafting securities legislation was to define a security. The definition had to be specific enough for common instruments to be readily identified as securities and yet general enough to allow for the inclusion of new instruments or interests. The Securities Act of 1933 defines a security in section 2(1) by stating:

> Unless the context otherwise requires—the term "security" means any note, stock, treasury stock, bond, debenture, evidence of indebtedness, certificate of interest or participation in any profit-sharing agreement, collateral trust certificate, preorganization certificate or subscription, transferable share, investment contract, voting trust certificate, certificate of deposit for a security, fractional undivided interest in oil, gas, or other mineral rights, or, in general, any interest or instrument commonly known as a "security."

The catchall phrase "or, in general, any interest or instrument commonly known as a 'security'" appears circular. By including that phrase, Congress was incorporating the states' experience and approach to comprehending various transactions that were difficult to categorize.

The definition has been interpreted broadly by courts to elevate the substance of a transaction over its form. In *SEC* v. *W. J. Howey Co.* the Supreme Court adhered to this principle and established the general test for a security.[5] In that case the W. J. Howey Company (Howey), which owned 500 acres of citrus groves in Florida, offered 250 acres to the public. The company sold each purchaser a narrow strip of the grove (one sale, for example, consisted of about two thirds of an acre) on a land installment contract, with the deed to be delivered to the buyer when the last installment was paid. Howey also offered a service contract for maintaining the acreage. This required pooling the proceeds of the whole crop and distributing those proceeds pro rata to the individual investors. The Supreme Court held that the combination of the land sales contract, service contract, and deed as a package constituted an "investment contract," which is specifically named as a security under the section 2(1) definition. In arriving at its findings, the Court included the following three characteristics of a security: (1) A contract, transaction or scheme whereby a person invests money in a common enterprise (2) whose investors have reasonable expectations of profit and (3) whose profits are derived solely from the efforts of persons other than the investors.

[5] 328 U.S. 293 (1946).

Common enterprise

The first characteristic stipulated by the *Howey* definition requires that money be invested in a common enterprise. A common enterprise in this context has been defined as "one in which the fortunes of the investor are interwoven and dependent upon the efforts and success of those seeking the investment." In order to satisfy this prong of the definition it suffices if the success of each investor is tied to the efforts of the promoter. It does not matter that an investor's return is not linked to other investors' participation in the scheme.

Expectation of profit

The second prong of the *Howey* definition requires that investors have reasonable expectations of profit. For example, stock purchased by low-income persons in a low-rent cooperative project has been held not to be a security. Since the stock is not purchased with an expectation of profit but to acquire subsidized low-cost housing, the economic realities of the transaction prefail over its form, and the context of the transaction excludes the stock from being deemed a security.[6]

Derivation of profits

The third ingredient of the *Howey* definition of a security requires that the profits be derived solely from the efforts of the promoter. An investor who is actively involved in the operation of the enterprise from which that investor expects profits is normally in a self-protecting position and does not need the assistance of the securities laws. The question of whether token investor activity will remove an investment from the category of a security was considered in *SEC* v. *Glenn Turner Enterprises.*[7] That case dealt with sales courses offered by Dare to be Great, a wholly owned subsidiary of Turner Enterprises, in which a purchaser paid for the privilege of receiving lessons aimed at self-improvement and sales ability plus the *opportunity to help sell the course to others* in return for a commission. The Ninth Circuit Court of Appeals found that what was being sold was not the usual "business motivation" course; instead, the buyer was purchasing the possibility of deriving profits from the sale of Dare to Be Great courses. The court applied the *Howey* test and found all of its requirements present except the requirement that profits must be derived *solely* from the efforts of others. In examining the remedial nature of the Securities Act, the court recognized the policy of affording broad protection to the investor. In adhering to this policy,

---

[6] *United Housing Foundation* v. *Foreman,* 421 U.S. 837 (1975).
[7] 474 F.2d 476 (9th Cir. 1973).

the court diluted the third prong of the *Howey* test by holding it to be satisfied if:

> the efforts made by those other than the investor are the *undeniably significant* ones, those essential managerial efforts which affect the failure or success of the enterprise. (Emphasis added.)

These concepts were handled by the following court, called upon to interpret a pyramid promotion scheme in the cosmetic industry.

SEC v. *Koscot Interplanetary Inc.*
497 F.2d 473 (5th Cir. 1974)

The Securities and Exchange Commission (SEC) (plaintiff) sought an injunction against Koscot Interplanetary, Inc. (defendant), for violating the federal securities laws by selling unregistered securities. The SEC maintained that Koscot's pyramid promotion scheme constituted a security under the Securities Act of 1933, necessitating registration. The federal district court denied the injunction. It held that the Koscot scheme did not involve the sale of a security since the investors were involved in the promotion of the scheme. The court of appeals disagreed and reversed and remanded the case.

Gewin, Circuit Judge:

The Koscot scheme

The procedure followed by Koscot in the promotion of its enterprise can be synoptically chronicled. . . . Koscot thrives by enticing prospective investors to participate in its enterprise, holding out as a lure the expectation of galactic profits. . . .

The vehicle for the lure is a multi-level network of independent distributors purportedly engaged in the business of selling a line of cosmetics. At the lowest level is a "beauty advisor" whose income is derived solely from retail sales of Koscot products made available at a discount, customarily of 45%. Those desirous of ascending the ladder of the Koscot enterprise may also participate on a second level, that of supervisor or retail manager. For an invest-

ment of $1,000, a supervisor receives cosmetics at a greater discount from retail price, typically 55% to be sold either directly to the public or to be held for wholesale distribution to the beauty advisors. In addition, a supervisor who introduces a prospect to the Koscot program with whom a sale is ultimately consummated receives $600 of the $1,000 paid to Koscot. The loftiest position in the multi-level scheme is that of distributor. An investment of $5,000 with Koscot entitles a distributor to purchase cosmetics at an even greater discount, typically 65%, for distribution to supervisors and retailers. Moreover, fruitful sponsorship of either a supervisor or distributor brings $600 or $3,000 respectively to the sponsor.

* * * * *

The modus operandi of Koscot and its investors is as follows. Investors solicit prospects to attend Opportunity Meetings at which the latter are introduced to the Koscot scheme. Significantly, the investor is admonished not to mention the details of the business before bringing the prospect to the meeting, a technique euphemistically denominated the "curiosity approach." . . . Thus, in the initial stage, an investor's sole task is to attract the individuals to the meeting.

Once a prospect's attendance at a meeting is secured, Koscot employees, frequently in conjunction with investors, undertake to apprise prospects of the "virtues" of enlisting in the Koscot plan. The meeting is conducted in conformity with scripts prepared by Koscot. Indeed, Koscot distributes a bulletin which states: ". . . this program is to be presented by the script. It is strongly recommended that you consider replacing any individual who does not present the program verbatim." The principal design of the meetings is to foster an illusion of affluence. Investors and Koscot employees are instructed to drive to meetings in expensive cars, preferably Cadillacs, to dress expensively, and to flaunt large amounts of money. It is intended that prospects will be galvanized into signing a contract by these ostentations displayed in the evangelical atmosphere of the meetings. . . .

* * * * *

The third element—solely from the efforts of others

* * * * *

The legal standard

A literal application of the *Howey* test would frustrate the remedial purposes of the Act. As the Ninth Circuit noted is *SEC* v. *Turner Enterprises, Inc.,* "[I]t would be easy to evade [the *Howey* test] by adding a requirement that the buyer contribute a modicum of effort."

* * * * *

The Supreme Court admonished against such a rigid and quixotic application, noting . . . that in searching for the meaning and scope of the word *security,* form should be disregarded for substance, and proclaiming in *SEC* v. *W. J. Howey Co.* that "[T]he statutory policy of affording broad protection to investors is not to be thwarted by unrealistic and irrelevant formulae." It would be anomalous to maintain that the Court in *Howey* intended to formulate the type of intractable rule which it had decried. The admitted salutary purposes of the Act can only be safeguarded by a functional approach to the *Howey* test.

* * * * *

Moreover, a significant number of federal courts invoking the *Howey* test have given it a broader, more salutary application in principle. Thus, in several cases where the scheme required or envisioned the possibility of partici-

pation by an investor in the enterprise, courts nevertheless found an investment contract. . . .

In view of these developments and our analysis of the import of the language in and the derivation of the *Howey* test, we hold that the proper standard in determining whether a scheme constitutes an investment contract is that explicated by the Ninth Circuit in *SEC* v. *Glenn W. Turner Enterprises, Inc.,* supra. In that case, the court announced that the critical inquiry is "whether the efforts made by those other than the investor are the undeniably significant ones, those essential managerial efforts which affect the failure or success of the enterprise.". . .

. . . [In this case] an investor's sole contribution in following the script is a nominal one. Without the scenario created by the Opportunity Meetings . . . an investor would invariably be powerless to realize any return on his investment.

We confine our holding to those schemes in which promoters retain immediate control over the essential managerial conduct of an enterprise and where the investor's realization of profits is inextricably tied to the success of the promotional scheme. Thus, we acknowledge that a conventional franchise arrangement, wherein the promoter exercises merely remote control over an enterprise and the investor operates largely unfettered by promoter mandates, presents a different question than the one posed herein. But the Koscot scheme does not qualify as a conventional franchising arrangement.

[The test]—comports with the observation of the Supreme Court in *SEC* v. *W. J. Howey Co.* that the definition of securities "embodies a flexible rather than a static principle, one that is capable of adaptation to meet the countless and variable schemes devised by those who seek the use of the money of others on the promise of profits." We merely endorse a test which is resilient enough to encompass the egregious promotional scheme purveyed by Koscot.

* * * * *

Case questions

1. Did Koscot expand the concept of a security from *Howey?* From *Glenn Turner Enterprises?* If so, in what way?

2. Do you think Congress drafted the securities laws and particularly section 2(1) with the intent of reaching the Koscot type of fraudulent activity? How much, if at all, was the court's decision influenced by the distasteful fraudulent activities of Koscot?

3. How could the promoters in this case have removed the transaction from the realm of a security?

4. What is the danger, if any, of having too flexible a definition of a security?

5. What if all the characteristics of a security are present but one invests work (human capital) instead of money in a common scheme? Should this be classified as a security, and what types of operations would it encompass?

REGISTRATION

The crux of the requirements of the Securities Act of 1933 is full disclosure, which is accomplished by requiring a nonexempt security to be registered with the SEC. The purpose of the registration is to afford the investors full information so that they may appraise the merits of the security and make an informed investment decision based on information contained in the registration statement.

The SEC examines the statement to make sure that there has been full disclosure about the company and about the securities the company intends to offer for sale. The commission, upon approving a registration statement, does not vouch for the financial condition of the company or the fairness of the terms of the securities offering. As long as the registration statement is complete, the commission cannot deny the registration. It is the investor and not the commission that must bear the burden and the risk of evaluating the merit of the security. Neither does the commission guarantee the accuracy of the information contained in the registration statement. There are, however, criminal laws that prohibit a registrant from making false or misleading representations under the pain of imprisonment and/or fine. In addition, any investor who suffers financial injury due to a material misrepresentation in the registration statement may pursue civil remedies, discussed later in this chapter.

The registration statement consists of two parts. One part contains elaborate information about the registrant's business and properties; the management, control, and operation of the business; the securities that are to be offered for sale; and certified financial statements. The second part is the prospectus, which contains much of the same information mandated in the first part. See Figure 13–1. The prospectus must be given to each person to whom a security is offered for sale. Preparation of the registration state-

Figure 13–1: Table of contents—Prospectus

No person is authorized to give any information or to make any representations other than those contained or incorporated by reference in this Prospectus and, if given or made, such information or representations must not be relied upon as having been authorized. This Prospectus does not constitute an offer to sell or a solicitation of an offer to buy any securities other than the securities to which it relates. This Prospectus does not constitute an offer to sell or a solicitation of an offer to buy such securities in any circumstances in which such offer or solicitation is unlawful. Neither the delivery of this Prospectus nor any sale made hereunder shall, under any circumstances, create any implication that there has been no change in the affairs of the Company since the date hereof or that the information herein is correct as of any time subsequent to its date.

Archer-Daniels-Midland Company

$250,000,000
7% Debentures due May 15, 2011

$125,000,000
16% Sinking Fund Debentures
due May 15, 2011

Goldman, Sachs & Co.

Kidder, Peabody & Co.
Incorporated

Merrill Lynch White Weld
Capital Markets Group
Merrill Lynch, Pierce, Fenner & Smith Incorporated

Representatives of the Underwriters

ment is costly. It involves the work of lawyers, accountants, financial analysts, management specialists, and other experts.

The primary objective of the Securities Act of 1933 is to prevent the offering or sale of securities to the public until registration has occurred, so that prospective investors may have the benefit of the information in the registration statement before purchase. The registration process may be divided into the prefiling, waiting, and posteffective periods.

Prefiling period

The statute prevents offers to buy or sell prior to the filing of a registration statement. It does not prohibit preliminary negotiations or agreements between issuers and underwriters. Thus, during this prefiling stage the issuer may begin to set up its network for distribution of the securities in anticipation of its eventual offering. Offers or sales to dealers or investors are prohibited during the prefiling period.

Offers are not confined to formal proposals. The SEC considers unusual publicity about the proposed securities or the issuer's business to be part of a sales effort to condition the public. Offers disguised as speeches or writings are considered "gun jumping" that is prohibited by the act during this stage. An SEC rule does permit an issuer to release news of a proposed offering that contains the name of the issuer and the purpose and terms of a proposed issue. It is forbidden to include the name of the underwriters.

Waiting period

The interlude between filing and the time when the registration becomes effective is called the waiting period. During this period the SEC examines the registration to insure its completeness. Oral offers are permissible at this time. However, written offers are expressly prohibited unless they conform to SEC requirements. The most common form of compliance is the use of a preliminary prospectus which summarizes the information contained in the registration statement. This prospectus is commonly referred to as a *red herring* prospectus because it requires a special legend printed in red which states that the securities may not be sold and offers to buy may not be accepted before the registration statement becomes effective. The SEC further requires that copies of the preliminary prospectus be distributed to persons intending to solicit customers and to any customers requesting such.

During this period the SEC also permits the distribution of notices which include identifying information and legends specifying that they are not an offer to sell or a solicitation of an offer to buy the securities. Such notices often appear in newspapers. Because they are often bordered in black they are termed *tombstone ads*. See Figure 13–2.

Posteffective period

The registration becomes effective 20 days after filing unless the registration process is accelerated or postponed by the commission. This effective date informs the underwriters and dealers that they are free to offer and sell the securities. Generally, the original registration statement, including

Figure 13–2: Tombstone ad

This advertisement is neither an offer to sell nor a solicitation of offers to buy any of these securities.
The offering is made only by the Prospectus.

NEW ISSUE   July 6, 1981

1,500,000 Common Shares

Liebert Corporation

Price $16 Per Share

Copies of the Prospectus may be obtained from such of the under-
writers as are registered dealers in securities in this State.

A. G. Edwards & Sons, Inc.   The Ohio Company

Bache Halsey Stuart Shields   The First Boston Corporation   Bear, Stearns & Co.
        Incorporated
Blyth Eastman Paine Webber   Dillon, Read & Co. Inc.   Donaldson, Lufkin & Jenrette
        Incorporated   Securities Corporation
Drexel Burnham Lambert   Goldman, Sachs & Co.   E. F. Hutton & Company Inc.
        Incorporated
Kidder, Peabody & Co.   Lazard Frères & Co.   Lehman Brothers Kuhn Loeb
        Incorporated   Incorporated
Merrill Lynch White Weld Capital Markets Group   L. F. Rothschild, Unterberg, Towbin
        Merrill Lynch, Pierce, Fenner & Smith Incorporated
Salomon Brothers   Shearson Loeb Rhoades Inc.   Smith Barney, Harris Upham & Co.
                                                                                            Incorporated
Warburg Paribas Becker   Wertheim & Co., Inc.   Dean Witter Reynolds Inc.
        A. G. Becker
Alex. Brown & Sons   F. Eberstadt & Co., Inc.   Hambrecht & Quist

Ladenburg, Thalmann & Co. Inc.   Moseley, Hallgarten, Estabrook & Weeden Inc.

Oppenheimer & Co., Inc.   Thomson McKinnon Securities Inc.   Tucker, Anthony & R. L. Day, Inc.

Robert W. Baird & Co.   William Blair & Company   Blunt Ellis & Loewi   J. C. Bradford & Co.
        Incorporated   Incorporated   Incorporated
Dain Bosworth   First of Michigan Corporation   J. J. B. Hilliard, W. L. Lyons, Inc.
        Incorporated
Edward D. Jones & Co.   Manley, Bennett, McDonald & Co.   McDonald & Company

Newhard, Cook & Co.   Piper, Jaffray & Hopwood   Prescott, Ball & Turben   R. Rowland & Co.
        Incorporated   Incorporated   Incorporated
Stifel, Nicolaus & Company   Bacon, Whipple & Co.   The Chicago Corporation
        Incorporated
B. C. Christopher & Co.   R. G. Dickinson & Co.   Rodman & Renshaw, Inc.

Wm. C. Roney & Co.   Scherck, Stein & Franc, Inc.   I. M. Simon & Co.   Stix & Co. Inc.

Traub and Company, Inc.   Vercoe & Company Inc.   Weinrich·Zitzmann·Whitehead Inc.

the preliminary prospectus, must be amended to contain pricing and other information omitted from it. A prospectus must accompany a written offer to sell a security or a confirmation of its sale.

If a prospectus is used more than 9 months after the effective date, it must be updated so that the information it contains is not more than 16 months old. Any material developments subsequent to the effective date must be reported by amending the registration statement to include them.

MARKETING SECURITIES

Within the normal process of distributing securities there are an issuer, underwriter, dealer, and investor. The issuer is generally the person or entity that issues or proposes to issue the securities. These are ultimately offered and sold to investors. Underwriters and brokers are often employed to aid in the distribution effort. An underwriter is a person or entity other than a dealer that purchases securities from an issuer with a view to selling them or that offers or sells securities on behalf of an issuer. The underwriter's outlet is a dealer who acts as an agent or a principal in the business of buying or selling the securities. Underwriting is of two types: firm commitment and best efforts.

Firm commitment

Under a firm commitment the underwriter purchases securities from the issuer. The underwriter is obligated to purchase a designated number of shares at a specified price. An underwriter that makes such a commitment prearranges to sell the securities through brokers at a markup. The brokers sell the securities at retail to the public. To illustrate this process, assume that an underwriter undertakes a firm commitment to buy 100,000 shares of stock from an issuer, XYZ, Inc., at $31 a share. The underwriter sells the stock at an underwriter's discount to brokers at $32 a share, and the brokers in turn sell the stock to the investing public at $33 a share. The underwriter's gross profit is $100,000, and the brokers enjoy a gross profit of $1 times the number of shares they sell. If the underwriter is unable to sell all or any portion of its undertaking, it must assume the loss, as there is no recourse against the issuer under firm commitment underwriting.

Best efforts

Under a best efforts commitment the underwriter acts for the issuer and expends its best efforts to sell the securities to brokers. In return the underwriter receives a commission on the sales it makes. Under this type of distribution the underwriter is not obligated to sell any designated quantity of securities.

EXEMPTIONS

Section 5 of the Securities Act of 1933 provides that in the absence of an exemption no security may be offered or sold to the public unless it has been registered with the SEC. This registration provides the public with information concerning the securities being offered. The filing of a registration statement is very costly, as it involves careful preparation by accountants, attorneys, and other professionals. For this reason the issuance of securities as a means of raising capital may be discouraged by cost considerations, unless they may be issued under an exemption. Some exemptions are made for securities issued by the government or charitable institutions. The following are the more common exemptions relevant to the businessperson.

Persons other than issuer

Section 4(1) exempts "transactions by any person other than an issuer, underwriter or dealer." Since most transactions by dealers are exempt, under another section, almost all offerings other than the first offering are free from the registration requirements of the 1933 act. The resale, or secondary trading, of a security may, however, be subject to registration under the Securities Exchange Act of 1934, which is treated in the next chapter.

Private placements

Section 4(2) of the Securities Act of 1933 exempts "transactions by an issuer not involving any public offering." About one fourth of all corporate securities are offered under this exemption. In order to qualify for this preferred exempt status, an offering must be confined to selected individuals or entities that have access to the same type of information as is provided by registration and that possess the sophistication necessary to evaluate the merits of the offering. Included within this category are insurance companies, pension funds, and other institutional investors that meet the "access" and "sophistication" criteria. Issuances to such investors pose no threat to the public and are routinely honored as legitimate section 4(2) exemptions by the SEC. In fact, these institutional investors are normally able to command more information from the issuer than registration requires.

The private placement exemption is also used in corporate securities offerings to employees of the corporation. In *SEC* v. *Ralston Purina Co.*[8] the Supreme Court clarified that the validity of a private offering exemption is determined by whether the offerees need the protection of the Securities Act. If the offerees have sufficient information, knowledge, and skill to fend for themselves, then they are not in need of the disclosure afforded by the registration statement. In *Ralston* "key employees" were afforded the option of purchasing

---

[8] 346 U.S. 119 (1953).

treasury stock in the corporation.[9] A key employee was, according to the company, one "who is eligible for promotion, an individual who especially influences others or who advises others, a person whom the employees look to in some special way, an individual, of course, who carries some special responsibility, who is sympathetic to management and who is ambitious and who the management feels is likely to be promoted to a greater responsibility." Employees from a variety of job positions, including artist, bakeshop foreman, electrician, stenographer, and veterinarian, responded to the opportunity to purchase the stock. The Supreme Court, in denying that this constituted a private offering under section 4(2), ruled that Ralston had failed to show that the employees had "access to the kind of information which registration would disclose."

Under section 4(2) and the cases interpreting that section there is no magic formula that will insure the exempt status of a promotional offering, although the following factors are certainly relevant to that status:

1. Number of offerees.
2. Identity of the offerees and their relationship to the issuer and one another.
3. Size of the offering.
4. Manner of the offering.

The following case illustrates the application of these factors and the restrictions on the private placement exemption under section 4(2).

SEC v. Continental Tobacco Co.
463 F.2d 137 (5th Cir. 1972)

The SEC (plaintiff) brought an action against Continental Tobacco Company (defendant) for selling unregistered nonexempt securities. The district court held that the securities were exempt from registration because they did not involve a public offering. The court of appeals reversed.

Continental, a manufacturer of cigarettes, sold unregistered five-year, 6 percent debentures with warrants attached to purchase common stock. The securities were offered at meetings characterized by one purchaser as a "boiler room operation," that is, a room in which numerous telephones are manned with orders for securities continuously taken. The meetings involved high-pressure sales tactics, including presentations about the company's product interrupted frequently by long-

distance phone calls telling of new orders for the product.

Coleman, Circuit Judge:

* * * * *

The District Court concluded as a matter of law that "the offering of securities by the defendant, Continental, from June, 1969 to October, 1970, were transactions not involving any public offering, and are, therefore, exempt from the registration provisions of the Securities Act of 1933 as amended." Apparently the District Court arrived at this conclusion by finding that "from approximately June 1969 until October 1970, the defendant, Continental, offered common stock to 38 persons," that "almost all of these investors executed an agreement with the defendant corporation prior to the pur-

---

[9] Treasury stock is normally stock which has been issued to shareholders and then repurchased by the corporation. Sometimes treasury stock includes authorized but unissued shares of stock. This was the case in *Ralston*.

chase of their common stock ("investment letters") which acknowledged receipt of a brochure concerning the corporation and which included unaudited financial statements"; that "the testimony of the common stock purchasers of Continental, who were called as witnesses by the plaintiff, established that these investors had received both written and oral information concerning the corporation, and that they had access to any additional information which they might have required or requested, and that they had had personal contacts with the officers of the defendant corporation"; that "these witnesses further testified that they knew the risk of their investments, that they knew the stock was not registered, and that they had purchased the stock with the intent to hold the stock for investment and not to resell it"; that "the evidence also showed that the stock has remained in the hands of the original purchasers and that the defendant, Continental, had refused to allow transfer of this unregistered stock"; and that "the experience and background of these investors were such that they were in a position to make an informed investment decision, i.e., they could fend for themselves."

* * * * *

The ultimate test, of course, is whether the particular class of persons affected need the protection of the Act, *S.E.C.* v. *Ralston Purina Company,* supra.

From the evidence recited in the beginning of this opinion we are left with an abiding conviction that Continental failed to carry its burden.

The record does not establish that each offeree had a relationship with Continental giving access to the kind of information that registration would have disclosed. The offers of common stock were to dentists, physicians,

housewives, and businessmen, who had no relationship with Continental other than that of shareholder once the purchases were made. None of the purchasers had an actual opportunity to inspect Continental's records or to verify for themselves statements made to them as inducements for the purchases. Some of the purchasers had never met any officers of the company prior to acquiring the stock.

* * * * *

". . . In order for an offering to fall within the exemption of section 4 two conditions must be met. First, the offeree must have such information as registration would have disclosed or have access to such information and, secondly, the purchasers must take for investment."

* * * * *

There is no evidence that we can find that all of the purchasers of Continental securities had actual access to any additional information concerning Continental which they might have required or requested.

Therefore, we hold that Continental failed to sustain its burden of affirmatively proving that all of the offerees of Continental enjoyed a relationship with Continental making registration unnecessary.

* * * * *

Upon application of the controlling legal principles to the evidence adduced in this record, we are compelled to hold that Continental failed to discharge its burden of establishing a "private offering exemption."

Moreover, applying the *Ralston Purina* standard, Continental failed to sustain its burden of proving that there existed no practical need for the application of § 5 of the Securities Act of 1933 to its 1969–70 offering of securities. Neither did it prove that the public benefits to be derived from registration were too remote.

Case questions

1. What is a boiler room operation? How do you think the use of a boiler room operation influenced the decision of the court?

2. What arguments can be made in support of the transaction as a private offering?

Analyze it in accordance with the four factors listed before the *Continental Tobacco* case.

3. On what basis did the court of appeals reject the district court's finding? What key missing ingredient led the court to conclude that the offering was not exempt under section 4(2)?

4. What should Continental have done in order to insure a private offering exempt status?

5. Does this case seem to be more or less restrictive than *Ralston?* Explain.

The decision in *Continental Tobacco* evoked an outcry from the corporate community. Two years later the SEC responded with Rule 146 in an attempt to provide a more objective standard for determining the validity of a private placement exemption. The rule grants assurance of exemption if all the following criteria are adhered to.

1. The number of purchasers cannot exceed 35. Any purchaser who buys more than $150,000 worth of securities need not be counted.

2. Securities may be offered and sold only to persons who the issuer has reason to believe *(a)* are sufficiently sophisticated to evaluate the merits and risks of the investment or *(b)* are in a position to bear the risks of the investment and have the services of a representative with sufficient knowledge and experience to evaluate the investment.

3. There can be no general advertising, and any solicitation must be confined to eligible purchasers.

4. Each offeree must either have access to the type of information detailed in a registration statement or be furnished that information. One ineligible offeree will destroy the exemption of the entire offering.

5. The issuer must take specified precautions to insure that the securities are bought for investment purposes and are not resold by the purchasers, except in accordance with specific rules governing resales. These precautions include "lettering" the stock certificates with legends setting forth the limitations on resale, obtaining written representations from purchasers that they do not intend to resell, and using stop transfer orders designed to prevent the corporation's recognition of transfers of shares to ineligible purchasers.

Failure to strictly adhere to the above requirements destroys the Rule 146 private placement exemption. Even if there is compliance, if it is "part of a plan or scheme to evade the registration provisions of the Act," the exemption is unavailable. Rule 146 is certainly not the safe harbor it was intended to be for issuers. The limitation on the number of investors severely restricts the issuer's capacity to raise capital. Although Rule 146 was intended to be objective, such terms as *reason to believe* and *sophistication* are subject to differing interpretations. Finally, since each offeree must be provided with the same information as that contained in a registration statement or provided with access to it, compliance with Rule 146 seems no easier or less costly than full-blown registration. Good faith attempted compliance with Rule 146 will not protect the issuer from failure of the exemption.

Rule 146 is not the only means for gaining a private placement exemption. Compliance with section 4(2) under the case law is still available. Although compliance under section 4(2) or Rule 146 exempts a security from the registration requirements, it does not exempt it from the antifraud sections of the securities laws.

Intrastate offerings

The constitutional powers under which Congress acted to pass the securities laws are the interstate commerce clause and the federal government's exclusive jurisdiction over the use of the mails. However, a security offering which uses interstate facilities or the mails may still obtain an exemption as long as it meets the requirements for the intrastate offering exemption. Section 3(a)(11) of the Securities Act provides an exemption for "any security which is part of an issue offered and sold only to persons resident within a single state or territory, where the issuer of such security is a person resident and doing business within, or if a corporation incorporated by and doing business within such state or territory." The exemption is quite narrow, as the SEC and the courts have been very strict in their interpretation of "doing business within the state." To take advantage of this exemption the issuer must do substantial business in the state. In addition, each *offeree* of the securities must be a resident of the same state, and offering the security to any person who is not a resident of the state will cause the exemption for the whole issue to fail. This virtually precludes the use of general advertising in the offering because of the possibility of communicating the offer to an out-of-state resident.

Securities and Exchange Commission v. Truckee Showboat, Inc.
157 F. Supp. 824 (S.D.Calif. 1957)

Truckee Showboat, Inc. (defendant), was charged with issuing unregistered nonexempt securities by the Securities and Exchange Commission (plaintiff). Truckee Showboat sought to prove an intrastate exemption as a defense. Based on the following findings of fact, the district court held that the section 3(a)(11) intrastate exemption was not available to the defendant.

Byrne, District Judge:

* * * * *

FINDINGS OF FACT

1. From June 18, 1957, through September 5, 1957, defendant Truckee Showboat, Inc. offered to sell its common capital stock, $1,000 par value, to residents of the State of California through the use of the United States mails. No sales of securities were made pursuant to said offer.

2. No registration statement with respect to said securities has been filed with plaintiff Securities and Exchange Commission or is in effect. Defendant relied upon the "intrastate exemption" from registration set forth in Section 3(a)(11) of said Act.

3. Said offer was made pursuant to a permit duly granted by the Commissioner of Corporations of the State of California. Defendant filed an application with said Commissioner for extension of its permit which was pending on the date of the hearing herein.

4. Defendant corporation was duly organized in, and keeps its books and records in, the State of California. All its directors and officers are residents of the State of California.

5. Defendant corporation's said offer to sell was made by means of an advertisement inserted in the *Los Angeles Times* issue of June 18, 1957. Copies of said issue containing said advertisement were duly placed in the United States mails by said newspaper to various of its subscribers.

6. Defendant corporation offered to sell, in said advertisement, 4,080 shares at $1,000 per share exclusively to bona fide residents of the State of California. The proceeds from said sales, less a selling commission of 20%, were to be used to acquire, refurbish and operate the El Cortez Hotel in the City of Las Vegas, State of Nevada.

7. Defendant corporation owns a wholesale pharmaceutical business in the City and County of San Francisco. The balance sheet of said pharmaceutical business indicates it had total assets as of August 31, 1957, of $12,629.59. The pharmaceutical business is not related to the primary business of the corporation.

Case questions

1. How much money was Truckee Showboat, Inc., expecting to raise through the offering? For what purpose? Who would benefit? What is the purpose of the intrastate offering exemption.

2. On what basis do you think the court came to the conclusion that the intrastate exemption was unavailable to the defendant? Was defendant a "person resident"? Was defendant "doing business within the state"?

3. Should the fact that the defendant received a permit to issue securities from the state of California automatically exempt it from federal registration requirements?

4. Should the fact that no one purchased the securities exempt the defendant from registration requirements?

5. How could the defendant have legally avoided the necessity of registration?

Rule 147. To vitiate the harsh results and to provide more objective standards for compliance with the intrastate exemption, the SEC adopted Rule 147, which defined some of the terms contained in section 3(a)(11).

Person resident. Rule 147 clarifies that the issuer of the securities is a resident of the state under the laws in which it is incorporated, or organized, or if an individual, the state in which the issuer has its principal residence.

An offeree or purchaser is a resident of the state in which the individual has his or her principal place of residence, or if a corporation, where its principal office is located.

Doing business within. An issuer is deemed to be doing business within the state if (1) it receives at least 80 percent of its gross revenues within the state, (2) at least 80 percent of its assets are within the state, (3) it intends to use at least 80 percent of the net proceeds from the offering within the state, and (4) its principal office is in the state.

Coming to rest. An intrastate exemption is lost in the event that a security comes to rest in a nonresident. Under Rule 147 no part of an issue may be offered or resold outside the state for nine months following the date of the last sale by the issuer. Rule 147 also requires the issuer to take steps to prevent resales outside the state.

Compliance with Rule 147 is not the only way to qualify for the intrastate exemption, but it is the most secure way. Absent compliance with Rule 147 the case law and SEC interpretations prior to Rule 147 must be consulted to ascertain the availability of the exemption. Compliance with the intrastate exemption, though removing the necessity of filing a registration statement pursuant to section 5, does not afford the issuer immunity from the antifraud provisions of the securities laws (discussed later in this chapter and in chapter 14).

Small offerings

Certain small issues are exempt from full registration. Instead, an issuer need only file a short form registration statement and a miniprospectus. Section 3(b) of the Act of '33 authorizes the SEC to exempt offerings not exceeding $2 million when "by reason of the small amount involved or the limited character of the public offering" registration is not necessary.

Regulation A. Pursuant to section 3(b) the SEC adopted Regulation A. To qualify for the limited exemption the issue cannot exceed a total amount of $1,500,000 within a one-year period. The exemption is not available to those who have been convicted of securities offenses.

To comply with Regulation A an issuer must file a notification and an offering circular with the SEC at least 10 days before the proposed offering. The offering circular contains information and a prospectus which are like the registration statements under the act but on a reduced scale. The financial statements may be unaudited. The filings need not be made with the SEC office in Washington, as is required for nonexempt securities. They may be filed at a regional office.

Rule 240. A second exemption for small offerings is provided by SEC Rule 240. Rule 240, enacted pursuant to section 3(b), is designed to provide a simple exemption for small offerings whose issuer desires to be free of Registration A compliance. In order to qualify for the exemption the issuer cannot offer to sell more than $100,000 of securities within any 12-month period. Sales to organizers, directors, executive officers, or full-time employees of the issuer are excluded from the $100,000 aggregate figure and are exempt regardless of their degree of sophistication. The sales of the offering cannot result in the issuer having issued securities, in its lifetime, to more than 100 holders, including the issuer. A husband and wife are considered as one holder for the purpose of calculating the number of owners. No general solicitation, advertising, or sales commissions are permitted if an issuer is to take advantage of the Rule 240 exemption. Resales to purchasers are restricted. A simplified report of the sales made under Rule 240 must be filed with the SEC regional office in any year that such sales are made.

Rule 242. In order to relieve small businesses from the financial burden of registration the SEC has issued Rule 242, which is designed to enlarge the small offering exemption to the statutory limits while still insuring adequate protection for the investor. Rule 242 permits certain corporate issuers to sell up to $2 million in securities within any six-month period without the necessity of registration when certain conditions are met. Sales may be made to an unlimited number of "accredited persons." An accredited person is defined as certain institutional investors, purchasers of at least $100,000 in securities, and the issuer's executive officers or directors. In addition, the corporation may sell to as many as 35 nonaccredited investors. A nonaccredited person is anyone other than an accredited person. If only accredited persons are involved in the sale, the corporation need not furnish them with any information. However, if at least one nonaccredited person is involved in the sale, then all purchasers, regardless of whether they are accredited, must be furnished with a simplified prospectus which need include only certified financial statements for the issuer's most recent fiscal year. A corporation seeking to take advantage of a Rule 242 exemption may not engage in any general advertising or solicitation. Compliance with the requirements of a small offering exemption does not exempt the issuer and others from the antifraud sections.

INTEGRATION

Rules of integration determine the relationship of one security to another. If securities are part of the same issue, they are said to be integrated. If not for the rules of "integration" an issuer could qualify for small offering status or private placement exemption status by dividing a larger issue into smaller components. The following rules are guidelines for determining whether the SEC will require offerings to be integrated or permit them to be separate. Those factors relevant for consideration include whether:

1. The issues are part of a single plan of financing.
2. The issues involve the same class of securities.
3. The issues were made at or about the same time.
4. The issues involve the same type of pricing.
5. The issues were made for the same general purpose.

PRIVATE REMEDIES

In the absence of the remedies provided for under the Securities Act of 1933 an injured purchaser of securities would be left to a common-law action in fraud. Under this theory there were three major impediments to recovery. The plaintiff had to prove that loss occurred as a result of a justifiable *reliance* upon a misrepresentation of a material fact. In addition, plaintiff had the burden of proving *scienter* (that the defendant had knowledge of the misrepresentation). Further, the doctrine of *privity* of contract confined recovery to the purchaser's immediate seller. Generally the Securities Act of 1933 has removed the elements of reliance, scienter, and privity and has to a large degree shifted the burden of proof to the seller, so that *caveat venditor* ("seller beware") has replaced *caveat emptor* ("buyer beware").

Within the act there are sections which impose liability against specified persons who violate the securities laws. These sections offer aggrieved individuals certain private remedies.

Misrepresentation in registration statement

Section 11 of the 1933 act imposes liability upon certain persons if the registration statement contains material untruths or omissions. Section 11 application is only available when a registration statement has been filed. In order to recover in a cause of action under section 11 the purchaser must prove (1) a material misstatement in or omission from the registration statement and (2) monetary damages. Generally it is not even necessary for the purchaser to prove a reliance on the misstatement or omission. A person may recover despite having failed to examine the registration statement. The right of action exists even for secondary purchasers, that is, purchasers who did not buy the security as part of the initial offering.

The omission or untrue statement must concern a material fact. SEC Rule 405 defines *material* as "matters as to which an average prudent investor ought reasonably to be informed before purchasing the security registered." Thus a material fact has been interpreted to mean a fact which if correctly stated or disclosed might have deterred a prudent investor from purchasing the securities in question. Examples of such facts might include impending litigation or new acquisitions, customers' delinquencies, proposed government controls that would affect the company, and loans to corporate officials.

Persons liable.[10]   Section 11 imposes absolute liability on an issuer for violation of its provisions. In addition, the following persons may be liable absent a defense:

1. Every person who signed the registration statement.
2. Every director of the issuer at the time of registration.
3. Every person who consented to being named as a director or a future director.
4. Every accountant, engineer, appraiser, attorney, or other expert who consented to the use of his or her statement and whose statement was used in the preparation of the registration statement.
5. Every underwriter.

Any or all of the above persons may be liable for a violation of section 11. Their liability is joint and several, so that the injured purchaser of the

---

[10] The Securities Act of 1933 imposes vicarious liability on "[e]very person who, by or through stock ownership, agency, or otherwise, . . . controls any person liable under sections [11 or 12] . . . unless the controlling person had no knowledge of or reasonable grounds to believe in the existence of the facts by reason of which the liability of the controlled person is alleged to exist." 15 U.S.C § 77(0) (1976).

security may enforce a judgment against any one or any combination of the above defendants who are adjudged liable.

Defenses. Several defenses are available to defendants civilly prosecuted under section 11. A cause of action under section 11 must be brought within one year after discovery of the untrue statement or omission, or after discovery has been made by the exercise of reasonable diligence. In no event may an action be brought more than three years from the date of the original offer.

If a defendant can prove that the plaintiff knew of the untruth or omission, the claim will be defeated. In addition, before liability attaches, a relationship must be established between the decline in value of the security and the material untruth or omission. If the two are wholly unrelated and the defendant can demonstrate that the reduced value of the security resulted from other causes, such as economic trends, the claim will be defeated.

The most popular defense is the *due diligence* defense. This defense is available to all persons other than the issuer. It is the subject of the following case, which involved plaintiffs who purchased stock in a corporation constructing "bowling centers."

Escott v. BarChris Construction Corp.
283 F. Supp. 643 (S.D.N.Y. 1968)

Escott and other investors (plaintiffs) sued BarChris Construction Corporation, its directors, executive officers, legal counsel, and auditors (defendants) for material misrepresentations contained in the registration statement filed with the SEC. The district court awarded judgment to the plaintiffs.

BarChris, a company which built and sold bowling alleys, was founded by Vitolo and Pugliese, two men of limited education. They employed Russo, an accountant, who became executive vice president; Kircher, a certified public accountant, who first became comptroller and then treasurer; Trilling, who succeeded Kircher as comptroller; and Birnbaum, who was hired as house counsel and became secretary. Early in 1961 BarChris sold debentures because it needed additional working capital. At the same time it was experiencing difficulties in collecting amounts due from some of its customers. It continued to build bowling alleys, but the industry was overbuilt. In May 1967 it made a futile effort to rehabili-

tate its financial condition by the sale of common stock. It then filed a bankruptcy petition and defaulted on the interest due on the debentures.

McLean, District Judge:

* * * * *

It is a prerequisite to liability under Section 11 of the Act that the fact which is falsely stated in a registration statement, or the fact that is omitted when it should have been stated to avoid misleading be "material." The regulations of the Securities and Exchange Commission pertaining to the registration of securities define the word as follows:

The term 'material,' when used to qualify a requirement for the furnishing of information as to any subject, limits the information required to those matters as to which an average prudent investor ought reasonably to be informed before purchasing the security registered.

*   *   *   *   *

What are "matters as to which an average prudent investor ought reasonably to be informed"? It seems obvious that they are matters which such an investor needs to know before he can make an intelligent, informed decision whether or not to buy the security.

Judged by this test, there is no doubt that many of the misstatements and omissions in this prospectus were material. This is true of all of them which relate to the state of affairs in 1961, i.e., the overstatement of sales and gross profit for the first quarter, the understatement of contingent liabilities as of April 30, the overstatement of orders on hand, and the failure to disclose the true facts with respect to officers' loans, customers' delinquencies, application of proceeds, and the prospective operation of several alleys.

*   *   *   *   *

This leaves for consideration the errors in the 1960 balance sheet figures. . . . Current assets were overstated by approximately $600,000. Liabilities were understated by approximately $325,000. [There were other significant misstatements and omissions in the balance sheet.]

*   *   *   *   *

. . . On all the evidence I find that these balance sheet errors were material within the meaning of Section 11.

I turn now to the question of whether defendants have proved their due diligence defenses. The position of each defendant will be separately considered.

[Large portions of the remainder of the opinion are paraphrased.]

Chief executive officer

The court held that Russo, the "chief executive officer" of the corporation, could not successfully invoke the due diligence defenses. As a member of the executive committee with knowledge of all the relevant facts, "he could not have believed that there were no untrue statements or material omission in the prospectus."

Inside directors

Vitolo and Pugliese were directors who were also on the executive committee and very close to the corporation. As such, they were termed inside directors. They were men of limited intelligence, and the prospectus may well have been beyond their comprehension. However, because of their position with the company they knew of the inadequate cash position, of their own large advances to the company which remained unpaid, and of other financial disturbances.

". . . They could not have believed that the registration statement was wholly true and that no material facts had been omitted. And in any case, there is nothing to show that they made any investigation of anything which they may not have known about or understood. They have not proved their due diligence defenses."

Treasurer

"Kircher was treasurer of BarChris and its chief financial officer. He is a certified public accountant and an intelligent man. He was thoroughly familiar with BarChris' financial affairs. . . .

"Kircher worked on the preparation of the registration statement. . . . He supplied information about the company's business. He read the prospectus and understood it. He knew what it said and what it did not say.

"As to the rest of the prospectus, knowing the facts, he did not have a reasonable ground to believe it to be true. On the contrary, he must have known that in part it was untrue. Under these circumstances, he is not entitled to sit back and place the blame on the lawyers for not advising him about it.

"Kircher has not proved his due diligence defenses."

Attorney

Birnbaum, a young attorney, was the house counsel for BarChris. Later he also became secretary and a director, and as such he signed the registration statement. He did not participate in the management of the company and attended to routine legal matters. He did keep the corporate minutes, which informed him about the company's affairs, though he was unaware of many of the inaccuracies in the prospectus.

"As a lawyer . . . he should have known that he was required to make a reasonable investigation of the truth of all the statements in the unexpertised portion of the document which he signed. Having failed to make such an investigation, he did not have reasonable ground to believe that all these statements were true. Birnbaum has not established his due diligence defenses except as to the audited 1960 figures."

Outside director

Auslander was a banker. He was a director of BarChris but not an officer of the corporation. As such, he was termed an outside director.

Auslander signed signature sheets for amendments to the registration statement without seeing a copy of the statement in its final form. He did glance at a copy of the registration statement in its earlier form, but he did not read it thoroughly.

"In considering Auslander's due diligence defenses, a distinction is to be drawn between the expertised and non-expertised portions of the prospectus. As to the former, Auslander knew that Peat, Marwick had audited the 1960 figures. He believed them to be correct because he had confidence in Peat, Marwick. He had no reasonable ground to believe otherwise.

"As to the non-expertised portions, however, Auslander is in a different position. He seems to have been under the impression that Peat, Marwick was responsible for all the figures. This impression was not correct, as he would have realized if he had read the prospec-

tus carefully. Auslander made no investigation of the accuracy of the prospectus.

* * * * *

"I find and conclude that Auslander has not established his due diligence defense with respect to the misstatements and omissions in those portions of the prospectus other than the audited 1960 figures.

Accountant

"Peat, Marwick was the accounting firm that audited BarChris' 1960 figures. The actual work was delegated to Berardi, the senior accountant. Berardi was not versed in the bowling industry, and this particular assignment was an extremely difficult one for someone as uninitiated as he. Berardi asked questions in order to prepare portions of the registration statement, and accepted the answers without independent verification.

"Accountants should not be held to a standard higher than that recognized in their profession. I do not do so here. Berardi's review did not come up to that standard. He did not take some of the steps which Peat, Marwick's written program prescribed. He did not spend an adequate amount of time on a task of this magnitude. Most important of all, he was too easily satisfied with glib answers to his inquiries.

"This is not to say that he should have made a complete audit. But there were enough danger signals in the materials which he did examine to require some further investigation on his part. Generally accepted accounting standards required such further investigation under these circumstances. It is not always sufficient merely to ask questions.

"Here again, the burden of proof is on Peat, Marwick. I find that that burden has not been satisfied. I conclude that Peat, Marwick has not established its due diligence defense."

Case questions

1. What were the material omissions in the *BarChris* registration statement? What is the test of materiality?

2. What is the difference in obligation when relying upon nonexpert portions of the registration statement as compared to relying upon expert portions? What is the reason for the distinction?

3. What is the difference between an "inside director" and an "outside director"?

4. Are you less inclined to become a board member of a corporation after *BarChris?* Why?

5. Do you think the *BarChris* decision affected the cost of malpractice insurance for attorneys and accountants? What effect would an increase in such costs have on the cost of preparing the registration statement? Who pays in the long run?

Failure to file registration statement

Any person who sells a nonexempt security without complying with the section 5 registration requirements is liable to purchasers for rescission under section 12(1).[11] Assume that the Bogus Company makes a public offering of 1 million shares of common stock, advertising such in the *Wall Street Journal* at $3 per share. Bogus Company fails to file a registration statement in accordance with section 5. Mack Donaldson, a resident of Virginia, purchases 500 shares of that stock for $1,500. Bogus Company is incorporated under the laws of the state of Virginia and conducts all of its business in that state. Mack Donaldson is a sophisticated investor who is intimately aware of the operations of Bogus Company. Thereafter, the price of the stock dropped to $1 per share. Mack Donaldson may seek rescission of the transaction and receive a return of the full purchase price under section 12 upon returning the stock. The stock was not exempt from registration since the issue did not qualify as either a private offering or an intrastate offering within the meaning of the act. A cause of action under section 12(1) must be brought within one year of the violation and no more than three years from the date of the original offer.

Misrepresentation and fraud in sale of security

Section 12(2) imposes liability on any person who offers or sells a security by means of any written or oral communication which misstates a material fact or which omits a material fact necessary to make the statements made not misleading.[12] Section 12(2) is applicable whether or not the security was registered. But for liability to attach, the plaintiff must show that the security was offered or sold by means of a communication which contained the misstatement or from which the material fact was omitted.

A cause of action under section 12(2) must be brought within one year after discovery of the untrue statement or omission or after discovery should have been made by the exercise of reasonable diligence. In no event may an action be brought more than three years after the sale.

Section 17 prohibits fraud in the offer or sale of securities and is commonly

---

[11] See note 10.

[12] See note 10.

the basis for criminal sanctions and injunctive relief. In addition, it has been used successfully by aggrieved purchasers to recover against persons who defrauded them in the sale of securities. In this respect it affords a defrauded purchaser an implied remedy free of section 11 and section 12 restrictions, such as the statute of limitations.

PUBLIC REMEDIES

In addition to private actions, persons who violate the Securities Act are subject to public remedies which include administrative stop orders, court injunctions and criminal penalties. These measures are discussed below.

Stop orders

The act provides an administrative remedy against fraudulent offerings or sales of securities. If the registration statement appears to be materially incomplete, inaccurate, or otherwise defective, the SEC will ordinarily inform the registrant of such finding and give the registrant an opportunity to clarify or amend the problematic portions. If the registrant fails to comply, the commission may proceed to a hearing to determine the facts. Upon a finding that material representations are misleading, inaccurate, or incomplete, the commission may suspend the effectiveness of a registration statement by issuing a "stop order." The commission may also issue a stop order, after a hearing, even after the sale of securities has begun. The stop order must be lifted and effectiveness granted when the registration statement has been amended in conformity with the stop order decision.

Injunction

The SEC also has the power to seek an injunction in the federal district courts to prevent violations of the act or rules or regulations. An injunction will be granted to stop persons from using the mails or instruments of interstate commerce to sell nonexempt securities when the proper registration has not been filed or a prospectus supplied pursuant to section 5.

Criminal penalties

Any person who willfully violates any provision of the statute or any rules and regulations promulgated by the commission is guilty of a criminal offense. Similarly, any person who willfully makes an untrue statement about a material fact or omits to state any material fact in connection with the offering or sale of a security is guilty of a crime. The key element is "willfulness." There has been a split in authority as to what constitutes willful conduct? The SEC holds that only a deliberate act is necessary, while other authority contends that this must be coupled with an evil motive.

The SEC does not have the power to adjudicate guilt or impose penalties. It may transmit evidence of a violation to the attorney general, who may prosecute an alleged offender. Conviction of an offense may carry a penalty of up to $10,000 or five years imprisonment, or both. There is a five-year statute of limitations for prosecuting criminal actions against offenders.

STATE LAWS

Federal securities laws do not preempt the states' right to regulate securities, even when those securities are the subject of interstate activity. Since all states and the District of Columbia have laws pertaining to securities, an issuer that floats a new issue of securities on a national level has to contend with 52 distinct bodies of securities laws. This multipronged registration requirement may appear to be a huge obstacle to the offering of public securities. In some instances the cost and complication of the various procedures discourage the issuance of securities among the states. For this reason recent moves to provide uniformity and ease of registration among the states have been gaining some impetus.

In 1956 the commission on Uniform State Laws created a Uniform Securities Act (USA) for adoption by the states. More than 30 states have adopted at least portions of the USA, which includes provisions for securities registration, exemptions, and sanctions for offenders. Of course, the states are free to adopt or not adopt the USA or to adopt it in part or with amendments.

Registration of securities

Most states require registration of securities and information similar to the federal registration requirements. The methods of registration vary from state to state. Most states use one or a combination of the procedures available under the USA.

By qualification. In sharp contrast to the federal securities laws practically all state securities laws contain qualification requirements for registration. Accordingly these laws include standards against which the quality of securities can be measured. Under this approach the states maintain the discretion, based on guidelines, to refuse registration to securities which do not qualify as bona fide and nonfraudulent. The issuer that must register a security files a statement similar to that required under the 1933 act. The statement becomes effective and the security becomes available for sale upon approval by the administrator. The USA authorizes the issuance of a stop order denying effectiveness to the registration if the administrator finds that such an order would be in the public interest and that the offering would tend to work a fraud upon purchasers.

By notification. Registration by notification is a simplified method of registering on the order of a federal Registration A statement. It is available for certain securities that are deemed less risky since they have a proven track record. The specific standards vary from state to state. Registration is effected by supplying a statement that demonstrates eligibility for registration by notification, a description of the security, and other specified information and documents. In most states that permit registration by notification, registration is effective upon filing. Some states have a short waiting period to give the administrator time to stop the effectiveness of the registration if it is found not to be in compliance.

By coordination. In order to register by coordination the registrant simply files the same registration statement and prospectus with the state that was filed with the SEC. The registration, if in full compliance, will take effect at the same time that the federal registration becomes effective. A majority of the states have adopted registration by coordination. This is happy news for issuers and underwriters who "blue-sky" public securities offerings among the several states, as it affords them an efficient way to effect registration in many states at the same time.

Exemptions

Exemptions from registration similar to those afforded by the Securities Act of 1933 also exist in a large number of states. These include exemptions for government securities and for securities issued by companies subject to special regulatory statutes (e.g., banks and common carriers).

More recently states have been adopting a counterpart to the federal exemption afforded to private placements, by providing an exemption for offers directed to less than a specified number of people. In some instances additional qualification tends to mirror Rule 146 by restricting the offers to sophisticated investors.

New York and New Jersey have taken the lead in enacting a novel statute which exempts all offerings registered with the SEC. The effect is to require only nonexempt intrastate securities to register.

Remedies

Like the federal government, the states provide injunctive remedies for violations of their securities laws. Because of the large number of securities transactions and the often too small state staff for enforcement the more meaningful remedies are in the private civil realm. Many states permit investors the right of rescission if the security purchased has not been registered as required or if the sale involved fraud. The USA also permits recovery for damages if the investor sold the security at a loss. The USA expressly limits causes of action to those contained in the Securities Act. Consequently, those states that have adopted the USA in toto do not afford implied remedies.

POLICY CONSIDERATIONS

The securities laws are based on the supposition that the investor who has all of the material information about a security is capable of making an informed decision. The securities laws are intended to give the investor that information by requiring issuers to make disclosures via registration. In recent years the philosophy of mandated disclosure has been sharply attacked. There are a number of persons who advocate the dismantling of the present system. These critics assert that the average investor does not rely upon the disclosures and that the professional analyst demands more and different types of information than the present disclosure system affords. They advocate a market-motivated system, arguing that the normal market forces would do a better job of regulating the type and quantity of disclosure. The theory is that the market forces would be more efficient in producing the information that a particular investor desires. The type of information that the SEC requires is basically firm oriented. However, some experts and surveys indicate that industry influences and market and other macro-economic conditions are significant in determining the prices of securities. Therefore, information about the management and finances of the firm itself should not be the exclusive concern of investors. Opponents of the present system further argue that mandated disclosure places an artificial restraint on the market by imposing costly registration on firms. This results in barriers of entry, diversion of capital, and other anticompetitive effects.

Opponents of deregulation cite surveys of issuers, investors, and others which show a satisfaction with the present level and method of disclosure. They staunchly maintain that full mandated disclosure is necessary to protect the market system and to keep it pure.

While the battle rages, a new securities code now under consideration, and briefly discussed in the next chapter, would revamp the securities laws in an effort to make the present system more efficient.

Review problems

1. The Bangor Punta Corporation was contemplating issuing a block of securities. Bangor prepared to file a registration statement covering the proposed distribution under the Securities Act of 1933. Before the registration statement was filed, Bangor issued a press release stating its intention to issue the securities. The release also stated that "in the judgment of The First Boston Corporation, each share of Bangor Stock has a value of not less than $80." The SEC filed suit against Bangor, claiming that the press release violated section 5 of the Act of '33. What was the result?

2. Ms. Borg, the owner of an Arabian stallion, sold partial undivided interests in the stallion as a means of forming a syndicate of coowners to govern the standing and development of the stallion for breeding purposes. Borg proposed to issue 50 shares, retaining 5 of the shares for herself. The ownership interests were to be sold in conjunction with a syndicate agreement. The syndicate agreement provided that the stallion was to be under the supervision of the syndicate managers at Borg's facility, or such other facility as a majority of the coowners designated. The owners of each fractional interest were required to pay an annual fee of $1,050 for maintenance, conditioning, board, and care of the stallion. Each coowner was also required to pay $550 annually to the syndicate managers for advertising and promotion of the stal-

lion and as compensation for their services. Each interest held by the coowner entitled the holder to breed two Arabian mares to the stallion each breeding season. These breeding rights could be sold or assigned by the coowners. If the stallion was able to service other mares, the stud fee was distributed to the coowners by lot. Was the syndicate required to register its shares under the Act of '33? Explain.

3. Johnson devised a plan whereby his corporation issued notes to investors and purportedly used the proceeds from the notes to import industrial wine. He did not file a registration statement. Johnson sold the notes through intermediaries to sophisticated, wealthy business people. He did not advertise. At no time were the notes held by more than 30 investors. The enterprise turned out to be a fraud. The money Johnson received from investors was used exclusively to pay off other investors who had previously been lured into the scheme. It was not used to import wine. Mower, a sophisticated investor, became interested in the plan and invested large sums of money with Johnson. When it finally became known that Johnson had defrauded his investors, Mower brought suit under the Securities Act of 1933, claiming violations of the antifraud provisions of the act.

In his defense Johnson asserts that the act is inapplicable because the notes (which he concedes to be securities) were issued persuant to a section 4(2) exemption. Is Johnson's assertion valid? Explain.

4. John Marcussi formulated an unusual distribution plan. Because he was uncertain as to whether the SEC would construe the plan as a sale of securities, he requested that the commission study his plan and determine whether a no-action letter would be appropriate. In a letter to the SEC Marcussi explained the plan in the following terms: An individual purchases a list of 10 names and a $25 savings bond for $37.50. The bond is made out in the name of the first person on the list. The individual then delivers the bond and makes two new lists, moving each name on the original list up one place and putting his or her

own name at the bottom of each new list. The individual then purchases two $25 bonds (at $18.75 each) and sells each list for $37.50. The individual thus recovers the $75 investment ($37.50 to buy the original list plus $37.50 for the two bonds) and then simply sits back and ultimately recovers 2,048 bonds worth more than $50,000.

Marcussi stressed that personal distribution is employed and the mail is not used. Furthermore, the plan recommends distribution to close family and friends as a means of assuring its continuation. How will the SEC respond to Marcussi's letter?

5. In 1954 collective bargaining between the Teamsters and Chicago trucking firms produced a pension plan for employees represented by the Teamsters. Employees were required to participate in the plan and did not have the option of demanding that the employer's contribution be paid directly to them as a substitute for pension eligibility. They paid nothing to the plan themselves. Thus the plan was compulsory and noncontributory. The board of trustees of the pension fund, a body composed of an equal number of employer and union representatives, was given sole authority to set the level of benefits. In order to receive a pension an employee had to have 20 years of continuous service, including time worked before the start of the plan. Mr. Daniel retired from one of the trucking firms covered by the plan in 1973 and applied to the plan's administrator for a pension. The administrator determined that Daniel was not eligible because of a break in his service to the firm due to a six-month layoff in 1960. Daniel brought suit against the Teamsters. His complaint alleged that the union misrepresented and omitted to state material facts with respect to the value of a covered employee's interest in the pension plan. Daniel contended that the union's misrepresentations constituted a fraud in connection with the sale of a security and therefore violated the Securities Act of 1933 and the Securities Exchange Act of 1934. The union moved to dismiss the suit on the ground that the acts were inapplicable as no security was involved. Who is right? Explain.

6. T.V. Tempo, Inc., sells *T.V. Tempo* magazine, a small weekly publication that lists television schedules. The magazine is distributed free of charge. Revenues are derived from the sale of advertisements to local merchants. T.V. Tempo, Inc., maintains control over the "composition, quality and printing of the magazines [and] the price to be charged for advertising." Martin and Bridges purchased an exclusive francise to sell T.V. Tempo, Inc., advertisements and to distribute the magazine in specified geographic areas in Georgia and Florida. T.V. Tempo, Inc., provided the initial training to Martin and Bridges and their employees. Martin and Bridges were required to pay for the composition and printing of the magazines distributed in their area and also had to pay their employees. Their profits were derived from the proceeds of advertising sales.

The franchise was unsuccessful, and Martin and Bridges went out of business. They instituted a suit against T.V. Tempo, Inc., alleging that "in offering and selling the franchise agreements [T.V. Tempo, Inc.] knowingly made material misrepresentations of fact on which they relied." They sought damages based on violation of the federal securities laws. The district court granted the defendant's motion for summary judgment. Was the decision correct? Why or why not?

7. Andrew and Mary Tell are real estate developers. They arranged with the Usedco Corporation, through its president, Roghbard, to sell certain lands and buildings to Usedco. It was subsequently agreed that, in lieu of cash, Usedco would issue 93,333 shares of its stock to the Tells. No registration statement was filed under the Securities Act of 1933 with regard to the issuance or sale of the stock.

Bromberg and Cravitz were attorneys for Usedco, and Cravitz's family held all the shares of DJ&M Investment Company. On the advice of Cravitz, DJ&M bought 61,000 of the shares issued to the Tells and subsequently resold them to various brokers, including Murray J. Ross & Company. Ross sold a block of 5,000 shares to Aaron and Ruth Winter. The Winters allege that Ross effected the sale by making material misrepresentations concerning Usedco's profitability and by omitting pertinent facts as to Usedco's financial condition. If the Winters sue to recover damages, what must they prove to succeed? Who may be liable for violating which section of the Securities Act? What damages are possible?

8. Prisco Company sold stock and carefully insured that the offerees were intrastate residents. It was discovered shortly after the offering that 200 shares had been sold by a broker to a relative in another state with the broker acting as a "straw man." The broker kept the shares in his own account. When Prisco found out that a nonresident had purchased shares, it bought back the shares. Do you think the transaction qualified for an intrastate exemption? Explain.

9. McGuire owned oil and gas leases on 300,000–500,000 acres in northern Ohio. In need of cash to pay the rental for the leases, he proposed to raise capital by selling investment interests in them. He organized three Delaware corporations to accomplish this: Asta-King, Tamarac, and Haratine. Each corporation had a board of directors and officers who were McGuire's relatives and employees. All three corporations were controlled by McGuire. Each corporation sold securities amounting to $1 million. The securities were registered with the SEC pursuant to Regulation A. What advantage did McGuire achieve? Were McGuire's actions lawful? Explain.

10. Reread the "Policy Considerations" section, and determine how you would select the securities regulation system that would best accommodate corporate freedom and investor protection.

CHAPTER 14

Trading securities

The Securities Act of 1933 (Act of 1933) was the main subject of the previous chapter. On the whole it was designed to regulate the initial offering of securities by requiring registration of those securities. Until 1934 the Federal Trade Commission was responsible for its enforcement. In that year Congress passed the Securities Exchange Act of 1934 (Exchange Act), which created the Securities and Exchange Commission (SEC) to administer the federal securities laws. In addition, the Exchange Act regulates the secondary trading of securities (as opposed to their original sale) and does this by imposing certain obligations upon the active agents in the securities industry. The areas regulated by the Exchange Act discussed in this chapter include:

1. Stock exchange and over-the-counter markets, which are subject to SEC registration requirements and supervision.
2. Certain issuers of securities, which are subject to SEC registration and periodic reporting requirements.
3. Certain persons who realize profits by trading in corporate securities who are subject to registration, reporting requirements, and liability for short-swing profits.
4. The use of proxies whereby corporate management and others must supply certain information to security holders.
5. Attempts to take over corporate control, which are closely regulated by disclosure requirements.
6. Securities brokers, dealers, and investment advisers, who are subject to SEC registration requirements and sanctions for noncompliance.
7. Fraud in the purchase, sale, or brokering of securities, which is prohibited.

SECURITIES MARKETS

A market is a place where buyers and sellers meet to transact business. There are two types of securities markets in the United States: securities exchanges and over-the-counter markets.

Securities exchanges

The New York Stock Exchange is the largest and most well known securities exchange. It is not unusual for 40 million or more shares of stock to be traded there in one day. The procedure for trading on the New York Stock Exchange is substantially similar to that used on any other national securities exchange. Trading begins when a customer contacts a broker with an order to buy or sell a certain quantity of a specific security. The broker transmits the order to the brokerage firm's order room at the exchange. There the order is communicated to a floor broker who offers to buy or sell as instructed. Upon consummating the purchase or sale, the broker notifies the central office of the brokerage firm, and the customer is then informed of the purchase or sale price, the stock certificates are exchanged, and the transaction is complete.

Securities exchanges are required to register with the SEC unless exempt. A broker-dealer may not effect any transaction in a security on an exchange unless the exchange is registered or exempt from registration. In order to register as a securities exchange, an exchange must be capable of complying with the Exchange Act and rules thereunder and of policing its members and their personnel. Aside from meeting strict reporting requirements concerning market transactions, the exchange must adopt certain self-regulatory rules that promote specified standards regarding, for example:

1. Admission to membership.
2. Prevention of fraud.
3. Protection of investors and promotion of the public interest.
4. Discipline of members and their associates for offenses while affording due process standards to alleged violators.
5. Avoidance of unnecessary burdens on competition.

The SEC may deny registration to an exchange until it determines that the exchange is in conformity with the Exchange Act and regulations thereunder. The commission may also require modifications of an exchange's rules. It may suspend or withdraw the registration of any exchange, expel or suspend a member of an exchange, and suspend the trading of any security listed on an exchange.

The commission has complete authority over the activities of securities exchanges. Any modifications in an exchange's rules must be approved by the commission. The commission also has the power to review disciplinary actions of exchanges against their members.

Over-the-counter markets

An over-the-counter market handles securities transactions that do not take place on an organized exchange. Most over-the-counter trading occurs through the National Association of Securities Dealers Automated Quotations (NASDAQ), a computerized system that collects and stores data on over-the-counter transactions. Up-to-the-minute market data are projected by the system upon video terminal units in each establishment of over-the-counter brokers.

The National Association of Securities Dealers (NASD) supervises the conduct of the over-the-counter market. Established persuant to the Exchange Act, it is the only self-regulatory organization which the commission has approved to supervise this market. Pursuant to the Exchange Act and regulations thereunder, NASD must have self-governing rules that prevent fraudulent and manipulative acts and that promote fair principles of trade in over-the-counter transactions. NASD has adopted rules of fair practice. It regulates the conduct of its broker-dealer members. Most brokerage firms are members of NASD. However, a brokerage firm may deal in over-the-counter securities without belonging to NASD. The SEC imposes rules on NASD nonmembers that are similar to the rules adopted by NASD. Because of dealer discounts that may be withheld from nonmembers, there is an economic incentive for dealers to join NASD if they intend to trade in over-the-counter securities.

REGISTRATION AND REPORTING

Section 12 of the Exchange Act requires that, unless exempt, any equity or debt security be registered by its issuer in order to be traded on a national securities exchange. An *equity security* is any stock or similar security which evidences an ownership interest in the issuing company. A debt security is any bond or similar security which evidences a debt of the issuing company. Under the Exchange Act registration of a security is accomplished by filing a registration statement with the exchange and the commission. Registration becomes effective 30 days after certification that the security has been approved by the exchange unless the date is accelerated.

Section 12 requires the registration of any equity security that is to be traded in the over-the-counter market if (1) the issuer is engaged in a business that affects interstate commerce or uses the mails or interstate facilities for trading in the security, and (2) the issuer has $1 million or more in assets, and (3) the issuer's shareholders number at least 500. Registration must be filed with the commission. It becomes effective 60 days after the filing unless the date is accelerated.

The contents of the registration required under the Exchange Act depend upon whether the registrant must file the general form for registering a security or qualifies for the simplified form. The general form requires detailed information about the registrant's business holdings, securities, finances, management, and relationship to all parent companies and subsidiaries. The information it requires is very similar to that required under the Act of 1933. A company qualifies for a short-form registration if it has previously registered under the Exchange Act or the Act of 1933. The contents of this registration include a description of the class and character of the securities to be registered and a list of the exhibits incorporated into the registration, such as specimens of the securities and any related instruments affecting the security holders' rights, copies of the charter and the bylaws, and financial reports. Registration contents are available for public inspection.

Registration pursuant to the Act of 1933 does not excuse an issuer from registering pursuant to the Exchange Act. The Act of 1933 registration permits the initial sale of the security, while the Exchange Act registration permits the security to be traded in certain markets.

The Exchange Act was designed to assure the continuing availability of adequate information about publicly traded securities, since trading is ongoing. To further that design the registrant must update its registration periodically with annual, quarterly, and current reports. Generally, Form 10–K must be filed within 90 days after the end of the fiscal period. It includes current audited financial statements and information regarding the operations of the business and the status of the business and its securities. Form 10–Q must be filed quarterly to cover the first three quarters of the fiscal year. It includes an unaudited financial summary of the financial changes that have occurred in the registrant's finances, management, and securities since the preceding report was made. Form 8–K must be filed in order to disclose materially important events such as a change in the control of the registrant, a change in the registrant's certifying accountants, bankruptcy, or the resignation of a director. A materially important event is one about which a reasonable prudent investor should be informed in order to decide whether to buy or sell the registered security.

As previously noted, a company that makes a nonexempt securities offering need only comply with the registration requirements of the Act of 1933. Once the company desires that the securities be traded on a national stock exchange, or over-the counter, (when applicable) it must comply with the registration and reporting requirements of the Exchange Act. Duplication is involved in the dual registration now required. Congress is currently considering a new securities code that would revamp the existing securities laws. The purposes of the proposed code are to (1) simplify the federal securities laws, (2) eliminate the duplicative provisions of these laws, and (3) protect the investor while keeping interference with honest business to a minimum. In order to eliminate the duplicative efforts required by the present registrations, the proposed code provides for the registration of companies on a registration statement. Registration triggers disclosure and continuous reporting requirements similar to 10–K, 10–Q, and 8–K reporting. Under the proposed code, when a registered company desires to make a public securities offering it must file an offering statement with the commission. The SEC is given broad latitude as to the content requirements of the offering statement: it may require no disclosure or a great quantity of disclosure. Although the proposed code appears to be an improvement, many critics do not think it has gone far enough to maximize the efficiency of the securities registration process.

Registration of a security under section 12 not only subjects the registrant to reporting requirements but also subjects certain insiders of the issuer to requirements and to liability for *short-swing profits.*

CONTROL OF CORPORATE INSIDERS

By reason of their position, insiders within a corporation may acquire information that, when made public, will affect the value of the corporation's securities. Because of the delay between the time such information is available to these insiders and the time it becomes public, insiders familiar with the ultimate market impact of the information may trade accordingly to realize profits. For example, as a result of attending a board meeting, a corporate director may learn that a particular stock is about to split. By purchasing that stock before the information becomes public, the director will realize profits.

The Exchange Act seeks to prevent such uses of inside information. Under section 16 of the act an insider is liable to the corporation that issued the securities for any profits realized from the sale or purchase of nonexempt securities within a six-month period. These short-swing profits are conclusively presumed to be an outcome of inside advantage. Thus the fact that they did not result from inside information is no defense. The profits can only be recovered by or on behalf of the corporation. Neither the SEC nor the Justice Department has any standing to prosecute a claim for violation of section 16. To facilitate the section's enforcement by the corporation and by shareholders on behalf of the corporation, insiders are required to file periodic reports with the commission, disclosing their portfolio of corporate holdings. Insiders, by definition, are directors, officers and 10 percent beneficial owners of an issuer which has section 12 securities.

Director

A director of a corporation is a person who sits on its board of directors and participates in its affairs. The term *director* also applies to persons who perform similar functions, regardless of their assigned titles. The weight of authority is that directors are liable for short-swing profits even if the purchase or sale by which the profits were realized occurred after they were no longer directors, as long as one of the transactions occurred while they were. The same holds true for corporate officers.

Officer

An officer of a corporation enjoys a position of responsibility and authority and normally has access to confidential information. Common titles of corporate officers are president, vice president, treasurer, and secretary. However, the title is inconclusive. Any person, regardless of title, who performs the same functions as those who hold the above titles is an insider subject to SEC registration and reporting, unless exempt. In contrast a person in a merely honorary position who possesses an officer's title would not be subject to registration, as the following case illustrates.

Merrill Lynch, Pierce, Fenner & Smith v. *Livingston*
566 F.2d 119 (9th Cir. 1978)

Merrill Lynch, Pierce, Fenner & Smith, Inc. (appellee), sued its employee, Livingston (appellant), seeking $14,836.37, which represented the profit he made on the short-swing transactions in the appellee's securities. The district court found that the appellant was an officer of his employer with access to inside information not generally available to members of the investing public and thus was liable under section 16(b) of the Securities Exchange Act of 1934. The court of appeals reversed.

Hufstedler, Circuit Judge:

* * * * *

From 1951 to 1972, Livingston was employed by Merrill Lynch as a securities salesman with the title of "Account Executive." In January, 1972, Merrill Lynch began an "Account Executive Recognition Program" for its career Account Executives to reward outstanding sales records. As part of the program, Merrill Lynch awarded Livingston and 47 other Account Executives the title "Vice President." Livingston had exactly the same duties after he was awarded the title as he did before the recognition. Livingston never attended, nor was he invited or permitted to attend, meetings of the Board of Directors or the Executive Committee. He acquired no executive or policy making duties. Executive and managerial functions were performed by approximately 350 "Executive Vice Presidents."

Livingston received the same kind of information about the company as an Account Executive both before and after he acquired his honorary title. As an Account Executive, he did obtain some information that was not generally available to the investing public, such as the

growth production rankings on the various Merrill Lynch retail offices. Information of this kind was regularly distributed to other salesmen for Merrill Lynch. Livingston's supervisor, a branch office manager, testified that he gave Livingston the same kind of information that he gave other salesmen about the company, none of which was useful for purposes of stock trading.

In November and December, 1972, Livingston sold a total of 1,000 shares of Merrill Lynch stock. He repurchased 1,000 shares of Merrill Lynch stock in March, 1973, realizing the profit in question.

* * * * *

The district court used an incorrect legal standard in applying Section 16(b). Liability under Section 16(b) is not based simply upon a person's title within his corporation; rather, liability follows from the existence of a relationship with the corporation that makes it more probable than not that the individual has access to insider information. Insider information, to which Section 16(b) is addressed, does not mean all information about the company that is not public knowledge. Insider information within the meaning of Section 16(b) encompasses that kind of confidential information about the company's affairs that would help the particular employee to make decisions affecting his market transactions in his employer's securities.

Strict liability to the issuer is imposed upon any "beneficial owner, director, or officer" for entering into such a short-swing transaction "[f]or the purpose of preventing the unfair use of information which may have been obtained by such . . . officer by reason of his relationship to the issuer." "The purpose of the statute was to take 'the profits out of a class of transactions in which the possibility of abuse was believed to be intolerably great' and to prevent the use by 'insiders' of confidential information, accessible because of one's corporate position or status, in speculative trading in the securities of one's corporation for personal profit."

To achieve the beneficial purposes of the statute, the court must look behind the title of the purchaser or seller to ascertain that person's real duties. Thus, a person who does not have the title of an officer, may, in fact, have a relationship to the company which gives him the very access to insider information that the statute was designed to reach. . . .

* * * * *

The title "Vice President" does no more than raise an inference that the person who holds the title has the executive duties and the opportunities for confidential information that the title implies. The inference can be overcome by proof that the title was merely honorary and did not carry with it any of the executive responsibilities that might otherwise be assumed. The record in this case convincingly demonstrates that Livingston was simply a securities salesman who had none of the powers of an executive officer of Merrill Lynch.

Livingston did not have the job in fact which would have given him presumptive access to insider information. Information that is freely circulated among nonmanagement employees is not insider information within the meaning of Section 16(b), even if the general public does not have the same information. Employees of corporations know all kinds of things about the companies they work for and about the personnel of their concerns that are not within the public domain. Rather, insider information to which Section 16(b) refers is the kind of information that is commonly reserved for company management and is thus the type of information that would "aid [one] if he engaged in personal market transactions."

* * * * *

Case questions

1. What information was accessible to Livingston but not to the general public? Why was Livingston's access to that information insufficient to consider him an insider?

2. What test is used to determine whether an "officer" is an insider? What questions would you ask the employee to determine whether the test has been satisfied?

3. Can an employee who is not an officer, director, or 10 percent beneficial owner be liable under section 16(b)? Discuss.

4. Assume that two months after Livingston purchased stock in his employer's company he was promoted to Executive Vice President and that two months thereafter he sold the stock and realized a profit. Would he be liable for short-swing profits?

5. Assume that Livingston was "deputized" by Merrill Lynch to seek an executive position with Sperry Rand, Inc. Could Merrill Lynch be liable for short-swing profits in Sperry Rand's stock? Under what circumstances? Discuss.

Ten percent beneficial owner

Anyone who owns at least 10 percent of the beneficial interest of a class of securities of a corporation subject to section 12 registration is required to register with the SEC and is liable for short-swing profits. The rationale is that a person who controls 10 percent of a corporation's shares undoubtedly has access to nonpublic information on that corporation which is vital to investment decision making. Treasury stock is not included for purposes of computing ownership interests. Treasury stock is stock which has been repurchased by the corporation. Assume that a corporation issues 1 million shares of stock and repurchases 100,000 shares which it holds in its treasury. Any person owning 90,000 or more shares of that corporation's stock must register with the commission as an insider, since that person owns at least 10 percent of the corporation's nontreasury stocks.

A 10 percent owner's liability for short-swing profits attaches only if both the sale and purchase occur while the security holder owns at least 10 percent of the outstanding shares. A purchase that makes a security holder a 10 percent owner cannot be matched with sales made by that security holder after becoming a 10 percent owner. Once a sale reduces the ownership interest to below 10 percent, then the security holder is no longer classified as a 10 percent owner. Assume that a stockholder acquires 90,000 of the outstanding shares (10 percent) in the above-mentioned corporation on February 1. On March 1 the stockholder purchases 27,000 more shares (3 percent). The stockholder then sells 36,000 shares (4 percent) on April 1 and the remaining 81,000 shares (9 percent) on August 1. When the first purchase was made, the shareholder was not a 10 percent owner. But when the second purchase and the first sale were made, the stockholder was a 10 percent owner. Thus the 27,000 shares purchased can be matched against the 36,000 shares sold, and the shareholder would be liable to the corporation for any realized profits. When the second sale was made, the shareholder was no longer a 10 percent owner and consequently was free form section 16(b) liability and the registration requirements.

Beneficial ownership is acquired over a security when all arrangements are completed for its purchase. Even before the stock certificates are delivered, a purchaser may be their beneficial owner. Beneficial ownership over a security is similarly divested. The purchase and selling dates are often crucial in determining short-swing profits. A person may be classified as the beneficial owner of a security even if the security is not in his or her name. For example, a person is classified as the benefical owner of securities in the name of a spouse, minor child, or other relatives as long as the person has control over those securities.

Filing

An officer or director of a section 12 corporation, or a 10 percent owner of its equity securities, must file Form 3 with the SEC within 10 days after acquiring that status. In addition, one signed copy of the form must be filed with the national exchange on which the corporation's securities are listed. However, any corporation that lists its securities on more than one exchange may designate a single exchange to receive the copy. After Form 3 has been filed, any changes in beneficial ownership must be filed on Form

4 within 10 days after the end of any month in which there has been a change in such ownership.

The information contained in Forms 3 and 4 includes:

1. The state of incorporation of the company whose securities are being reported.
2. Ownership interest or transaction in a put,[1] a call,[2] or an option.
3. The date of the original statement, if amended.
4. The insider's tax identification number.
5. A special number that identifies the reported securities.

The SEC provides for registering a disclaimer upon filing if the filer does not believe that he or she is the beneficial owner of the securities named in the statement. This permits a person to avoid possible liability for nonfiling and to deny beneficial ownership in an action made against the person for recoupment of short-swing profits.

Recovery of profits

It is very unlikely that an insider will voluntarily surrender short-swing profits. The issuer, normally a corporation, may sue the insider to recover the profits. Any security holder may request that the corporation commence such a suit. If the corporation fails to initiate suit within 60 days of the request, the security holder may sue on behalf of the corporation. If the insider is in control of the corporation, a security holder may commence suit without the necessity of first making a demand upon the corporation.

Valuation of profits

Short-swing profits are calculated by matching the lowest purchase price for a class of securities against the highest sale price. This results in the highest profit realization possible. An example of the computations follows:

On February 1 Insider purchases 300 shares of Megaton stock at $25 a share.

On March 1 Insider sells 100 shares of Megaton stock at $50 a share.

On April 1 Insider purchases 100 shares at $20 a share.

On May 1 Insider sells 200 shares at $30 a share.

On June 1 Insider purchases 200 shares at $80 a share.

On July 1 Insider sells 100 shares at $60 a share.

---

[1] Contracts whereby a person purchases the right to sell stock at a fixed price within a definite period of time.

[2] Contracts whereby a person purchases the right to purchase stock at a fixed price within a definite period of time.

Sold 100 shares at $60 per share	$6,000	
Purchased 100 shares at $20 per share	2,000	
		$4,000
Sold 100 shares at $50 per share	$5,000	
Purchased 100 shares at $25 per share	2,500	
		2,500
Sold 200 shares at $30 per share	$6,000	
Purchased 200 shares at $25 per share	5,000	
		1,000
Total realized profit		$7,500

Defense

The statute of limitation for recovery of short-swing profits is two years. This means that a suit must be commenced within two years after the profits are realized. Otherwise the corporation is barred from recovery. If the insider fails to register or to disclose the profit by report, the statute is suspended until the date on which the fact of the profit realization has been discovered.

PROXY RULES

The Exchange Act regulates the common corporate practice of proxy solicitation. A *proxy* is a document that grants an agent authority to vote for a security holder. Voting by proxy is the principal method of voting corporate shares in the United States. Specific SEC rules govern the content of proxies. Figure 14–1 is an example of a proxy form that conforms with these rules.

Proxy solicitation is the battleground for control of the corporate enterprise. Inherent in its use are the possibilities of abuse. The Exchange Act and the commission rules regulate proxy solicitation in order to prevent management and others from obtaining or maintaining corporate control through deception or inadequate disclosure.

Under the commission's rules governing proxy solicitation, no proxies may be solicited unless the solicitor furnishes 22 items of prescribed information to the shareholders in the form of a *proxy statement.* Eight of these are general items dealing with, for example, the revocability of the proxy, the persons making the solicitation, the interests of the solicitors regarding the matters to be considered at the shareholders' meeting, and the vote required on specific matters. The remaining 14 items concern specific proposals, such as information about nominees and directors when an election of board members is on the agenda of the shareholders' meeting.

Even if no proxies are solicited, SEC rules require a section 12 corporation to make the disclosures to its shareholders that would be required if they were solicited. These disclosures are made in the form of an *information statement.* The statement includes a notice of the date, time, and place of the shareholders' meeting and says that proxies are not being solicited. It also discloses the interests of certain persons involved in a matter to be voted on and presents the proposals of security holders.

Figure 14–1

ISELDORF, INC.

This Proxy Is Solicited on behalf of Management.

The undersigned hereby designates Alexander Rubin and Marianne Hite, or either of them in the absence of the other, with power of substitution to act as my lawful authorized attorney and proxy to act in my stead to attend the shareholder's meeting of ISELDORF, INC., to be conducted at 124 West Ninth Avenue, Cincinnati, Ohio, at 9:30 A.M. on March 15, 1981, and there to vote the shares of ISELDORF, INC., which I own, with all powers which I would possess if present at such meeting regarding:

    _____   1.   The election of directors.

    _____   2.   A merger with Amalgum, Inc.
                      ☐   For   (Management recommends
                      ☐   Against   a vote for this
                                               proposal.)

    _____   3.   For every other matter that may come before the meeting to vote in the best interest of the company.

IN THE EVENT THAT NO SPECIFIC DIRECTION IS GIVEN ON ITEMS 1 AND 2, THE PROXY WILL VOTE FOR THE SLATE OF CANDIDATES NAMED IN THE PROXY STATEMENT AND FOR THE MERGER.

Date:

                                                      _____
                                                          Signature

Any stockholder who wishes to revoke this proxy and vote in person may do so by written instrument or as modified by state law.

At least 10 days before mailing the proxy or information statement to the shareholders, the issuer is required to send the SEC a preliminary copy of its inspection. The SEC reviews it for completeness. The commission may issue a letter of comment requiring changes before the mailing is made. Conforming copies of the proxy or information statement actually mailed must be filed with the commission and the securities exchanges upon which the securities are registered.

When a proxy or information statement relates to voting for directors, stockholders must be supplied with an annual report, including financial statements for the last two years, along with other prescribed information. An agenda of the proposals that are expected to be considered at the shareholders' meeting must also be included in the statement, as well as a place for the shareholder's approval or disapproval for each proposal.

Proxy contests necessitate the filing of additional information, and special procedures govern the fight. The insurgents are required to file a proxy statement and information about those participating in the fight. Management must provide the insurgents with a list of the shareholders or mail the proxy material to the shareholders at the insurgents' expense. Since management is reluctant to surrender the shareholders' list, for obvious reasons, it usually opts to comply with the alternative requirement. However, the corporate law of many states gives shareholders the right to inspect shareholders' lists for legitimate purposes, upon reasonable notice to management.

Liability

An issuer that supplies a misleading proxy statement may be criminally liable. In addition, the SEC maintains the power to force compliance with the proxy rules by seeking injunctive relief. In a proper case the injunction may be invoked to prevent the solicitation or use of proxies or, if necessary, to postpone an election. Private actions are also available both to aggrieved members of management and to shareholders. The following case illustrates the basis of an available private remedy after a shareholders' meeting resulted in the election of a board.

Gladwin v. *Medfield Corp.*
540 F.2d 1266 (5th Cir. 1976)

The Gladwins own voting stock in Medfield Corporation, a company engaged in operating hospitals and other health facilities. In preparation for the March 1 annual shareholders' meeting, at which directors were to be elected, Medfield sent shareholders an annual report and proxy solicitation material, including a proxy statement. A rival group known as the Medfield Shareholders Committee nominated its own slate of candidates in opposition to the management slate and also solicited proxies.

At the annual meeting the slate endorsed by management received 56 percent of the votes cast, while the slate endorsed by the Medfield Shareholders Committee received

44 percent. The Gladwins, who were aligned with the Medfield Shareholders Committee, alleged that misstatements and material omissions in the Medfield Corporation proxy material were in violation of section 14(a) of the Securities and Exchange Act of 1934 and the applicable SEC proxy rules. The district court found six violations of section 14(a) and ordered a new election. The court directed that proxy solicatation material for the new election include "corrections of all illegal misstatements and omissions, a statement that the prior solicitations were in violation of the 1934 Act and the proxy rules, and an explanation that the resolicitation was the result of this suit." The court order was suspended pending appeal. *The court of appeals affirmed the district court's decision with modification not material to our consideration.*

Godbold, Circuit Judge:

I. Disclosure of Medicare liabilities

Medfield and its wholly-owned subsidiary, Palms of Pasadena Hospital, are participants in the Medicare program of the U.S. Department of Health, Education and Welfare. HEW pays for services and products provided to Medicare beneficiaries. Funding is done through "fiscal intermediaries." Reimbursement to a provider of services is made through interim payments based upon estimated costs of the services and products furnished, as defined in Medicare regulations. The fiscal intermediary audits the provider's costs on an annual basis, and adjustments are made depending upon whether the audit indicates that interim payments to the provider have resulted in excessive or insufficient reimbursement. In June 1973 Blue Cross of Florida, Medfield's "fiscal intermediary," notified Medfield that Blue Cross had reached a "tentative final settlement" for fiscal 1969 of $253,553 in overpayments and requested payment within 30 days. In July 1973 Medfield requested a 24-month repayment plan and was advised by the fiscal intermediary that a request for a repayment plan exceeding 12 months must be forwarded to the Regional Office of the Bureau of Health Insurance, a branch of HEW, and must include the first payment under the proposed payout period. During December 1973 Blue Cross informed Medfield of its determinations that it had been overpaid for the years 1970, 1971 and 1972 in the amounts of $367,243, $327,609, and $419,097, respectively.

On January 15, 1974, the fiscal intermediary told Medfield that the total amount "due and owing" from it was $1,836,272, consisting of the above amounts for 1969 through 1972, plus $163,783 for 1973 and current amounts of $304,987. Blue Cross also told Medfield that current Medicare funds were being withheld because of Medfield's non-payment.

* * * * *

. . . While disputing the Blue Cross figures, Medfield asked for a ten-year repayment plan.

In the proxy solicitation the only information provided by Medfield to its stockholders concerning this controversy was in the form of a footnote to the consolidated financial statement in the 1973 annual report. . . .

We agree with the district court that this footnote did not sufficiently describe the overpayment controversy as it then existed. It did not reveal the amount of the claim as asserted on January 15, the cessation of HEW payments, or the subsequent arrangements agreed to between Blue Cross and Medfield. . . . No rational argument can be mounted that the omissions which we have described were not material.

* * * * *

II. Management turnover

Medfield did not reveal in its proxy material that between January 23, 1973, and February 4, 1974, a number of high-level management changes occurred in the company, that its president intended to resign, and that it had been seeking for six months to employ someone to operate the company on a day-to-day basis. . . .

Medfield's response, that the stockholders learned of the actual changes in personnel from the materials distributed by the Shareholders Committee, is unavailing. While a proxy is not normally required to contain matter contained in other materials which are furnished and which are clearly referred to in the proxy, a company soliciting proxies may not obviate violation of the disclosure requirements by referring to materials furnished by its opponents in a proxy contest. . . .

III. Disclosure of stock purchases

During 1973 Medfield's nominees purchased an aggregate of 34,972 shares of Medfield common stock. . . . The purchases were not disclosed in Medfield's proxy material.

* * * * *

. . . While the district court made no finding on materiality we think that there was a substantial likelihood that knowledge of these purchases "would have assumed actual significance in the deliberations of the reasonable shareholder." . . . Although the total number of shares purchased by the nominess in 1973 represented only 4.9% of the voting stock, the great majority of those shares were purchased by a single nominee, the president of Medfield. A shareholder, being advised of this fact, might believe that this officer-nominee was attempting to acquire a degree of influence or control. . . .

IV. Disclosure of self-dealing

The district court found a material omission in Medfield's failure to disclose full details of an arrangement whereby a professional corporation, partially owned by a Medfield director and nominee [Dr. Willey], provided all laboratory, pathology and diagnostic services for Medfield. The contract between the professional corporation and Medfield was described in Medfield's proxy statement. . . .

The following facts concerning this contractual arrangement were not revealed to the shareholders:

1. In return for its services, the professional corporation was guaranteed $208,500 per year.
2. Medfield provided the group with all necessary expendable and non-expendable equipment, supplies, furniture and fixtures, offices and laboratories, and all technologists, technical aides, secretaries, clerks and other non-medical employees.

* * * * *

We agree with the district court that neither the true extent of the economic benefit conferred on Dr. Willey nor its concomitant cost to the corporation was fully disclosed.

V. Disclosure of the sale of major assets

Medfield did not reveal in its proxy materials that it had been attempting to sell two nursing homes. In fact the materials stated that Medfield was hopeful that the profitability of these two major facilities would increase.

Medfield urges that these attempts to sell need not be disclosed because neither the proxy rules nor Florida law requires shareholder approval of the sale of these facilities. This misses the issue, which is not stockholder consent to a sale but disclosure of matters important to stockholders in voting at the annual meeting.

VI. Impugning the character of a committee nominee

Medfield disseminated a letter pointing out the involvement of a Committee nominee in an unrelated patent infringement suit. The letter quoted from a lower court opinion that described the person as having infringed upon the patent of another. The case had been reversed on appeal and eventually settled. The settlement expressly avoided an admission of liability.

The district court found that the reference in the letter implied that the nominee was of bad moral character because he was a patent infringer. We affirm this point. . . .

Case questions

1. The court ordered a new election as the corrective remedy. How do you think the proxy material which must be included in the new solicitations will affect the slate of the Medfield Shareholders Committee?

2. Would any one of the six misstatements and omissions have been sufficient to result in a new election, or was it the aggregate of these misstatements and omissions that influenced the court? Explain.

3. Were the omissions and the misstatements willful? How do you know? Would the outcome have been different if they were not willful?

4. Under what circumstances should a new election be considered a proper remedy?

5. Assume that all of the material omissions in a proxy statement are available to the shareholders through other sources which a reasonably prudent shareholder should discover? Would this affect the ruling of the court?

Proposals by security holders

The Exchange Act affords a security holder the right to make a proposal at the shareholders' meeting. The security holder must tender timely notice of the proposal to management, which must include the proposal in the proxy statement, affording the shareholders a right to cast their vote either for or against the proposal. If management opposes the proposal, then the security holder who advanced it is entitled to include a statement of up to 200 words concerning the proposal within the proxy statement.

Management may exclude the proposal from consideration if:

1. It does not involve legal subject matter for the action of security holders or its inclusion or passage would violate laws or commission rules or regulations.
2. It is a personal, political, social, or similar claim or grievance not in the benefical interest of the security holders and not significantly related to the issuer's business.
3. It relates to ordinary business operations.
4. It is moot.
5. It relates to elections.
6. It is similar to a proposal offered within the last five years which was last defeated within three years by a specified margin.
7. It relates to specific amounts of dividends.

In *Medical Committee for Human Rights* v. *SEC* the plaintiff, having acquired several shares of Dow Chemical Company stock, sought to include a shareholder proposal in management's proxy materials that would have had the effect of restricting Dow from selling napalm for use against humans.[3] Dow refused to include the proposal, and the SEC issued a "no action" letter stating that it would not raise any objections if Dow omitted the proposal. Plaintiff instituted an action in the court of appeals seeking review of the SEC's position. The SEC adopted Dow's argument that the proposal was improper for inclusion because it related to the conduct of Dow's ordinary business operations and was submitted primarily in order to promote political and social causes. In remanding the case to the commission for further treatment, the court of appeals indicated that Dow's rationale was a subterfuge tending to undermine corporate suffrage. The court also said "What is of

---

[3] 432 F.2d 659 (D.C. Cir. 1970).

immediate concern, however, is the question of whether the corporate proxy rules can be employed as a shield to isolate such managerial decisions from shareholder control." The case was appealed to the Supreme Court. Meanwhile, Dow included the proposal in its proxy materials and at the shareholders' meeting the proposal was soundly defeated. Consequently, the Supreme Court dismissed the case as moot.

Since the decision in *Medical Committee* the SEC has more closely reviewed shareholder objections to the refusals of management to include within its proxy materials the proposals of security holders, and has adopted a more liberal policy toward inclusion.

TAKEOVER BIDS

Various techniques may be used to acquire a controlling interest in a company. A proxy contest may result in divesting current management of its control. But proxy contests are expensive and have a low incidence of success. An alternative strategy involves publicly offering cash or securities to stockholders in return for their stockholdings. Applications of this strategy are termed takeover bids or tender offers. The subject of the takeover attempt is called the *target company*. The entity attempting the takeover is referred to as the *tender offeror*. Takeover attempts often result in bitter contests between the tender offeror and the target company. A target company faced with the threat of a takeover may deploy a host of defensive tactics to neutralize the outside threat. Shareholders may be warned of the takeover attempt and solicited not to sell their shares. The target company may buy up its own shares on the open market or may effect a dividend increase or a stock split to increase the market price of the stock, thus making the expense to the tender offeror prohibitive. To resist tender offerors, the managements of target companies have also issued additional shares of stock to management or other persons aligned with management or have effected mergers with other companies. Often the shareholders are the pawns of takeover contests, courted with inflated purchase offers for their stock. The tender offeror may or may not be interested in the welfare of the target company, and in many cases it engages in highly sophisticated industrial espionage. The target company may have fallen prey to the tender offeror because of its own mismanagement, and perhaps the new management may prove better for the target company's shareholders and market. In any case, market manipulation, coercion, and confusion are natural by-products of takeover contests.

If a tender offeror attempts to take over a target company by making a public offer to exchange its own securities for the stock of the target company, the Act of 1933 requires that the tender offeror comply with the registration requirements. However, until 1964 the federal securities laws did not regulate the acquisition of control by cash tender offers. In that year Congress passed the Williams Amendment to the Exchange Act, which regulates tender offers.

Under section 13(d) of the Williams Act, a person or group that acquires more than 5 percent of a class of securities registered under section 12 is required to file a statement with the SEC and the issuer of the securities. The statement must include:

1. The background of the person or entity.
2. The number of shares owned.
3. The source of the funds for the acquisition.
4. The purpose of the acquisition.
5. The tender offeror's plans for the target company (if major changes are contemplated).
6. Information as to any agreements by the tender offeror with any person relevant to the target company.

The target company that is attempting to ward off its attacker must also comply with the filing and disclosure provisions.

The Williams Amendment also regulates certain terms of the tender offer, These are mentioned in the following case, in which the court was faced with the definition of a tender offer.

Kennecott Copper Corp. v. *Curtiss-Wright Corp.*
584 F.2d 1195 (2d Cir. 1978)

Curtiss Wright Corporation (defendant-appellant), a diversified manufacturing company, wanted to acquire an interest in Kennecott Copper Corporation (plaintiff-appellee), the largest copper producer in the United States. Appellant purchased 9.9 percent of Kennecott's shares of stock at a cost of about $77 million. Practically all of this stock was purchased on national exchanges. One of the appellant's brokers solicited 50 of the appellee's shareholders off the exchange floor; however, the sales were consummated on the floor. The solicitation of about 12 institutional stockholders by another broker resulted in sales off the floor. Potential sellers were simply asked whether they desired to sell. They were offered the market price and were not given a deadline within which to respond. The district court held that the transactions did not constitute a tender offer. The court of appeals affirmed on that finding. (There were other issues, but they are not the subject of our present discussion.)

VanGraafeiland, Circuit Judge:

* * * * *

THE WILLIAMS ACT CLAIM

Section 3 of the Williams Act amended section 14 of the Securities Exchange Act of 1934, by adding subsections (d), (e), and (f). Subsection (d) prohibits the making of a tender offer for any class of a registered stock if, after consummation thereof, the offeror would own more than five percent of the class, unless a Schedule 13D form is first filed with the SEC. If ownership of more than five percent is obtained through more customary modes of stock acquisition, the Schedule 13D form must be filed within ten days after the five percent figure is reached. Curtiss-Wright filed its Schedule 13D on March 17, 1978, which was within ten days of the time it had acquired five percent of Kennecott's stock. Accordingly, unless it had acquired this stock by means of a tender offer, it was not in violation [of the Act].

*   *   *   *   *

Although the Williams Act does not define the term "tender offer," the characteristics of a typical offer are well-recognized. They are described in the House Report of the Committee on Interstate and Foreign Commerce, which held hearings on the proposed Act.

The offer normally consists of a bid by an individual or group to buy shares of a company—usually at a price above the current market price. Those accepting the offer are said to tender their stock for purchase. The person making the offer obligates himself to purchase all or a specified portion of the tendered shares if certain specified conditions are met.

This definition of a conventional tender offer has received general recognition in the courts. Several courts and commentators have taken the position, however, that other unique methods of stock acquisition which exert pressure on shareholders to make uninformed, ill-considered decisions to sell, as is possible in the case of tender offers, should be treated as tender offers for purposes of the statute.

Although broad and remedial interpretations of the Act may create no problems insofar as the antifraud provisions of subsection (3) . . . are concerned, this may not be true with regard to subsections (d)(5) – (d)(7). Subsectoin (d)(5) provides that securities deposited pursuant to a tender offer may be withdrawn within seven days of the publication or delivery to shareholders of the tender offer or at any time after sixty days from the date of the original tender offer. Subsection (d)(6) requires offerors to purchase securities on a pro rata basis where more are tendered than the offeror is bound or willing to take. Subsection (d)(7) provides that where

the offeror increases the offering price before the expiration of his tender offer, those tenderers whose stock has already been taken up are entitled to be paid the higher price. It seems unlikely that Congress intended "tender offer" to be so broadly interpreted as to make these provisions unworkable.

In any event, we know of no court that has adopted the extremely broad interpretation Kennecott urges upon us in this case. Kennecott's contention, as we understand it, is that whenever a purchaser of stock intends through its purchases to obtain and exercise control of a company, it should immediately file a Schedule 13D. Kennecott conceded in the trial court that no pressure was exerted on sellers other than the normal pressure of the marketplace and argued there and here that the absence of pressure is not a relevant factor. Kennecott also conceded in the trial court that no cases supported its argument and that it was asking the court to "make new ground." The district court did not err in refusing to do so.

Kennecott's interpretation would render the five percent filing provisions . . . meaningless except in cases where the purchaser did not intend to obtain a controlling interest. It would also require courts to apply the withdrawal, pro rata, and increased price provisions . . . to ordinary stock purchases, a difficult if not impossible task.

The fact that several of Curtiss-Wright's purchases were negotiated directly with financial institutions lends no force to Kennecott's contentions.

If this Court is to opt for an interpretation of "tender offer" that differs from its conventional meaning, this is not the case in which to do it.

*   *   *   *   *

Case questions

1. Under what circumstances must a 13D form be filed? When must a 13D be filed for tender offers as opposed to "more customary modes of stock acquisition"? Why the difference?

2. What are the characteristics of a tender offer? Why was the Curtiss-Wright offer not considered a tender offer?

3. What three provisions does the Williams Amendment require in tender offers? What is the reason behind each? Why do these provisions not fit well into a *Curtiss-Wright* type of offer?

Under section 14(e) of the Williams Amendment it is a crime to make any untrue or misleading statements of material facts or omissions or to engage in "fraudulent, deceptive or manipulative acts or practices" in extending or opposing a tender offer. An implied civil cause of action is predicated upon this section. The remedy is available to either an injured target company and its shareholders or a defeated tender offeror.

In an effort to provide local business with greater protection from "foreign raiders," some states have enacted takeover statutes that are more restrictive than their federal counterpart. These statutes tend to favor management and to make it more difficult for a tender offeror to take over a target company. The constitutionality of state takeover statutes is considered in *Great Western United Corp.* v. *Kidwell,* found in Chapter 4.

BROKER-DEALER REGISTRATION

The Exchange Act prohibits any person from engaging in the brokerage, dealer, or investment adviser business, absent an exemption, unless registered with the commission. A broker, for purposes of the act, transacts business in securities for the account of others. A dealer regularly transacts business in securities for his or her own account.

Broker-dealers are held to high standards of professional conduct. The commission may suspend or revoke a broker-dealer's registration or otherwise penalize a broker-dealer who is in violation of the federal securities laws or is guilty of other misconduct. Fraudulent activity will subject a broker-dealer to criminal penalties.

Churning

A broker is entitled to a commission on every transaction performed for a customer, whether the transaction involves a gain or a loss to the customer. The more transactions a broker completes for a customer, the greater are the commissions. A broker may influence a customer to engage in excessive trading. The purpose may be to boost the broker's commissions. This practice is called *churning.* Churning is fraudulent and subjects the broker to liability.

Scalping

A broker appears to the public as an expert. By "hanging a shingle," the broker impliedly represents that there is an adequate basis for his or her opinions regarding stock transactions. A broker is prohibited from offering opinions about a security unless these are based on reliable information. A broker may recommend the purchase of a stock for the purpose of inflating its value so that the broker, who had purchased the same stock previously, may capitalize on its sale. This practice is termed *scalping*. Scalping subjects the broker to liability based on fraud.

Disclosure

Even absent willful fraud or an intent to injure another, civil liability may attach. One area on which the SEC has focused is the possible conflict of interest between the broker-dealer and the customer. Where such a possibility is present, the broker-dealer is required to make full disclosure to the customer or run the risk of violating antifraud provisions. In fact, a broker is required to supply customers with a written confirmation of each transaction, which includes a disclosure of whom the broker represented in the transaction (customer, dealer for own account, or broker for another). These full disclosure requirements are designed to reduce the number of duped customers.

Financial responsibility

All broker-dealers are subject to the SEC net capital rule. Net capital equals assets minus liabilities. A broker or dealer is required to maintain a net capital of at least $25,000, with some exceptions. Other rules are intended to assure the financial responsibility of broker-dealers.

In 1970 Congress passed the Securities Investor Protection Act (SIPA), which created the Securities Investor Protection Corporation (SIPC), a nonprofit entity, and required all registered broker-dealers to become members. The purpose of SIPC is to indemnify the customers of broker-dealers for losses that result from broker-dealer failures. To fund the corporation each member pays an annual fee. If the fund proves insufficient to satisfy SIPC's responsibility, SIPC is further authorized to borrow up to $1 billion from the U.S. Treasury. Though procedural problems in the administration of the act abound, customer confidence has been buttressed by SIPC.

REMEDIES[4]

Willful violations of most provisions of the Exchange Act carry a penalty of up to $10,000 in fines and up to five years' imprisonment. Civil liabilities imposed under the Exchange Act are of two kinds. First the Securities and

[4] The Exchange Act imposes vicarious statutory liability on "[e]very person who, directly or indirectly, controls any person liable under any provision of this [Act] . . . unless the controlling person acted in good faith and did not directly or indirectly induce the act or acts constituting the violation or cause of action" 15 U.S.C. § 78t (1976).

Exchange Commission may enforce the act and rules or regulations thereunder by taking administrative action or by instituting an action in a federal district court to compel compliance or enjoin violations. Second, purchasers or sellers of securities that have been injured as a result of an Exchange Act violation may institute suit in the federal courts. The complaint may demand equitable relief in the form of an injunction to prevent the defendant from initiating or continuing prohibited conduct. The aggrieved plaintiff may also seek damages for injury incurred. These private civil remedies are predicated upon the antifraud provisions in the Exchange Act and rules or regulations thereunder. The antifraud provisions may create an 'express or implied cause of action.

Express remedies

The Securities Exchange Act contains several sections which provide for express civil remedies. We have already examined the section 16(b) liability of an insider who acquires a short-swing profit. In addition, section 9 of the Exchange Act prohibits the manipulation of security prices and gives an express remedy against the manipulator to any person who purchases or sells a security which is the subject of such manipulation. Similarly, under section 18(a) anyone who, in purchasing or selling a security, has been injured through reliance upon a false or misleading statement made in any filing with the commission required by the Exchange Act possesses an express civil cause of action for damage against the maker of the statement, unless the statement was made in good faith without knowledge of its falsity. These express remedies are rarely invoked because of the restrictions imposed upon the plaintiff's potential to recover. These restrictions include a short statute of limitations and placing the burden of proof upon the plaintiff to show causation between the act complained of and the changed price of the security. Resort to implied remedies sidesteps these impediments, and thus such remedies are more commonly invoked.

Implied remedies

The basis of an implied remedy is a finding that a legislative act which does not recognize an express right nonetheless implies a cause of action in favor of an injured party. A cause of action for a violation of a statute is often implied if the harm that the plaintiff incurs is the type of harm that the statute was intended to prevent and if the plaintiff falls within the class of persons that the statute was intended to protect. A great majority of securities cases involving implied causes of actions are brought under Rule 10b–5.

Rule 10b–5. Section 10(b) of the Exchange Act makes it unlawful "to use or employ in connection with the purchase or sale of any security . . . any manipulative or deceptive device or contrivance in contravention of such rules and regulations as the Commission may prescribe." Under this section the commission is authorized to promulgate rules and regulations to combat fraud in connection with the purchase or sale of securities. The securities laws contain other sections prohibiting fraud. For example, section 17 of the Act of 1933 prohibits fraud in the sale of securities. But section 17 could not reach a situation that was troubling an assistant solicitor for the SEC, in 1942. The situation involved the president of a corporation who was purchasing stock from shareholders at a low price by misrepresenting the corporation's financial condition. Section 17 only extended to defrauded purchasers. The young assistant solicitor borrowed language from section 17, added "in connection with the purchase or sale of any security" to the appropriate section 10(b) language, and proposed that the statement be adopted as Rule 10b–5. The rule, which was adopted, reads:

> It shall be unlawful for any person, directly or indirectly, by the use of any means or instrumentality of interstate commerce, or of the mails, or of any facility of any national securities exchange,
>
> 1. To employ any device, or scheme, or artifice to defraud,
> 2. To make any untrue statement of a material fact or to omit to state a material fact necessary in order to make the statements made, in the light of the circumstances under which they were made, not misleading, or
> 3. To engage in any act, practice, or course of business which operates or would operate as a fraud or deceit upon any person,
>
> in connection with the purchase or sale of any security.

The rule was invoked successfully to issue a stop order against the corporate president who had been fraudulently purchasing stock. But its applicability since the occasion that precipitated its adoption has been extended to a myriad of situations. In an early case Rule 10b–5 was invoked against defendants who were charged with fraudulently inducing plaintiffs to sell corporate stock for less than its true value.[5] In the 1960s and 70s the rule was expanded even further to include liability for negligent conduct. That line of cases has since been reversed.

Ernst & Ernst v. *Hochfelder*
425 U.S. 185 (1976)

Ernst & Ernst (appellant), an accounting firm, was retained by First Securities Company of Chicago, a small brokerage firm, to periodically audit its books. Ernst & Ernst conducted the audits and also prepared the reports that

First Securities was required to file with the SEC. Hochfelder and others (respondents) were customers of First Securities. They invested money in a fraudulent scheme contrived by the president of First Securities,

---

[5] *Kardon* v. *National Gypsum Co.*, 69 F. Supp. 512 (E.D.Pa. 1946).

Leston B. Nay, who owned 92 percent of its stock.

From 1942 through 1966 the respondents invested funds in "escrow" accounts which Nay represented would earn high interest rates. No such accounts actually existed. Nay appropriated the funds for his own use. The escrow accounts did not appear on either the books of First Securities or on its periodic accountings to the respondents in connection with their other investments. They were not included in First Securities' filings with the commission or the Midwest Stock Exchange.

In 1968 Nay committed suicide. He left a note describing First Securities as bankrupt and revealed the escrow fraud. The respondents subsequently filed a complaint against Ernst & Ernst, charging that Nay's escrow scheme violated section 10(b) and commission Rule 10b–5, and that Ernst & Ernst "aided and abetted" Nay's violations by failing to discover the fraud. The respondents contended that if Ernst & Ernst had used proper auditing procedures, it would have discovered Nay's mail rule—that only he could open mail addressed to him or to his attention, even if the mail arrived at First Securities in his absence. The respondents further contended that had Ernst & Ernst become aware of Nay's mail rule, it would have reported this irregular procedure to the commission and the stock exchange. This would have led to an investigation and an exposure of Nay's fraudulent scheme.

The district court granted Ernst & Ernst's motion for summary judgment and dismissed the action. The court of appeals reversed and remanded, reasoning that Ernst & Ernst had a common-law and statutory duty of inquiry into the adequacy of First Securities' internal control system and that the respondents were beneficiaries of that duty.

The Supreme Court granted certiorari to resolve the question and reversed the court of appeals decision.

Mr. Justice Powell: The issue in this case is whether an action for civil damages may lie under section 10(b) of the Securities Exchange Act of 1934 . . . and Securities and Exchange Commission Rule 10b–5 . . . , in the absence of an allegation of intent to deceive, manipulate, or defraud on the part of the defendant.

* * * * *

II

* * * * *

Although section 10(b) does not by its terms create an express civil remedy for its violation, and there is no indication that Congress or the Commission when adopting Rule 10b–5, contemplated such a remedy, the existence of a private cause of action for violations of *the statute and the Rule is now well established . . . .*

A

Section 10(b) makes unlawful the use or employment of "any manipulative or deceptive device or contrivance" in contravention of Commission rules. The words "manipulative or deceptive" used in conjunction with "device or contrivance" strongly suggest that section 10(b) was intended to proscribe knowing or intentional misconduct. . . .

In its *amicus curiae* brief, however, the Commission contends that nothing in the language "manipulative or deceptive device or contrivance" limits its operation to knowing or intentional practices. . . .

In addition to relying upon the Commission's argument with respect to the operative language of the statute, respondents contend that since we are dealing with "remedial legislation," it must be construed " 'not technically and restrictively, but flexibly to effectuate its remedial purposes.' " They argue that the "remedial purposes" of the Acts demand a construction of section 10(b) that embraces negligence as a standard of liability. But in seeking to accomplish its broad remedial goals, Congress did not adopt uniformly a negligence standard even as to express civil remedies. In some circumstances and with respect to certain classes of defendants, Congress did create express liability predicated upon a failure to exercise reasonable care. . . . But in other situations good faith is an absolute defense. . . . And in still other circumstances Congress created express liability regardless of the Defendant's fault. . . .

B

Although the extensive legislative history of the 1934 Act is bereft of any explicit explanation of Congress' intent, we think the relevant portions of that history support our conclusion that section 10(b) was addressed to practices that involve some element of scienter and cannot be read to impose liability for negligent conduct alone. . . .

*   *   *   *   *

. . . The section was described rightly as a "catchall" clause to enable the Commission "to deal with new manipulative [or cunning] devices." It is difficult to believe that any lawyer, legislative draftsman, or legislator would use these words if the intent was to create liability for merely negligent acts or omissions. Neither the legislative history nor the briefs supporting respondents identify any usage or authority for construing "manipulative [or cunning] devices" to include negligence.

*   *   *   *   *

D

We have addressed, to this point, primarily the language and history of section 10(b). The Commission contends, however, that subsections (b) and (c) of Rule 10b–5 are cast in language which—if standing alone—could encompass both intentional and negligent behavior. These subsections respectively provide that it is unlawful "[t]o make any untrue statement of a material fact or to omit to state a material fact necessary in order to make the statements made, in the light of the circumstances under which they were made, not misleading . . ." and "[t]o engage in any act, practice, or course of business which operates or would operate as a fraud or deceit upon any person. . . ." Viewed in isolation the language of subsection (b), and arguably that of subsection (c), could be read as proscribing respectively any type of material misstatement or omission, and any course of conduct, that has the effect of defrauding investors, whether the wrongdoing was intentional or not.

We note first that such a reading cannot be harmonized with the administrative history of the Rule, a history making clear that when the Commission adopted the Rule it was intended to apply only to activities that involved scienter. More importantly, Rule 10b–5 was adopted pursuant to authority granted the Commission under section 19(b). The rulemaking power granted to an administrative agency charged with the administration of a federal statute is not the power to make law. Rather it is " 'the power to adopt regulations to carry into effect the will of Congress as expressed by the statute.' ". . . Thus, despite the broad view of the Rule advanced by the Commission in this case, its scope cannot exceed the power granted the Commission by Congress under section 10(b). . . . When a statute speaks so specifically in terms of manipulation and deception, and of implementing devices and contrivances—the commonly understood terminology of intentional wrongdoing—and when its history reflects no more expansive intent, we are quite unwilling to extend the scope of the statute to negligent conduct.

*   *   *   *   *

Case questions

1. Do you think that the plain wording of Rule 10b–5 is broad enough to encompass liability for negligent conduct?

2. How much weight did the Court attach to the legislative history of section 10(b)? Do you agree with the Court's rationale?

3. Is any other remedy available to the security holders who have been injured?

4. May accountants be grossly negligent or reckless and still avoid Rule 10b–5 liability? When does scienter exist?

5. What if, given facts similar to those in the case, the SEC had sought an injunction to prevent Ernst & Ernst from using "improper auditing procedures and disclosure principles in the preparation of First Securities reports to be filed with the SEC"? Would the result have been different? Discuss.

Going private. Rule 10b–5 applies to fraud in connection with any sale or purchase of securities, which includes, among other transactions, exchanges of stock and mergers. The rule has been invoked to impose liability on deceptive tender offerors and target companies. However, one relatively unsuccessful application of Rule 10b–5 has been in the area of going private.

In going private transactions an inside group of a public corporation is able to freeze out the equity interest of minority shareholders by requiring them to accept payment for the surrender of their shares. Most states facilitate such transactions by authorizing a company that owns a sizable percentage of another company to acquire the remaining minority interest by a short-form merger prescribed by statute. Normally this type of merger only requires the directors' approval and does not necessitate prior notice to the minority shareholders. This was the case in *Santa Fe Industries* v. *Green.*[6]

Sante Fe Industries acquired 95 percent of the stock of Kirby Lumber Company. It then acquired the remaining 5 percent under Delaware state law. Delaware law permitted a short-form merger of a subsidiary into a parent corporation which held at least 90 percent of the stock. The minority shareholders were "squeezed out" without a vote and forced to accept $150 per share or to seek compensation based on a judicial appraisal of the value of the shares. The plaintiff, a minority shareholder, sought relief under Rule 10b–5, alleging that the merger lacked a valid business purpose and that the price was grossly inadequate, and hence fraudulent. The district court dismissed the complaint. The Second Circuit Court of Appeals reversed the district court's decision, finding that the Rule 10b–5 violation arose from a breach of a fiduciary duty which management owed to the minority stockholders. The breach was purportedly grounded on an unfair price and lack of notice and a valid business purpose. The case was appealed to the Supreme Court, which reversed the court of appeals and held that the breach of a fiduciary duty was not elevated to a Rule 10b–5 fraud. Relying on *Hochfelder*, Justice White reasoned that conduct must be manipulative or deceptive to constitute a Rule 10b–5 violation and that since the transaction was in conformity with state law, it lacked those essential elements.

Inside trading. Rule 10b–5 has also been applied to the area of inside trading. The prohibition against trading in stock by insiders based on inside information has been extended to include sanctions against *anyone* trading based on inside information, unless full disclosure of the information is

---

[6] 430 U.S. 462 (1977).

made. In the landmark case of *SEC* v. *Texas Gulf Sulphur* officers and employees of the company purchased stock after learning that exploratory drilling on the company's property gave evidence of a significant ore discovery.[7] They failed to disclose this information to the sellers of the stock and were found in violation of Rule 10b–5. An insider for purposes of Rule 10b–5 thus extends beyond the traditional definition of insiders to include anyone receiving inside information from a corporate informant.

In *Shapiro* v. *Merrill Lynch, Pierce, Fenner & Smith, Inc.* the stock brokerage firm, while preparing an offering of stock for Douglas Aircraft Company, learned from some Douglas officers, directors, and employees of unfavorable conditions which would affect Douglas' earnings.[8] The information was not yet public. Merrill Lynch disclosed the information to some of its customers. These customers sold their holdings in Douglas, or otherwise improved their positions, without disclosing the information to the purchasers. The court held that both Merrill Lynch, the "tipper," and the favored customers, the "tippees," were liable not only to the specific purchasers of the shares sold on the basis of Merrill Lynch's information but to all those who purchased Douglas stock without benefit of the material information in the defendants' hands. *Shapiro* sounds a warning not only to "nontrading tippers" but also to "trading tippees," as long as those tippees trade upon information they know or have reason to know is not public and was wrongfully obtained.

State laws. The Uniform Securities Act incorporates the wording of Rule 10b–5. Even the states which have not adopted the act have a general anti-fraud provision authorizing criminal sanctions against violators and granting government officials the power to enjoin fraudulent acitivtes. In addition, violation of the antifraud provision may be a basis for civil remedies by injured parties.

POLICY CONSIDERATIONS

Over the years the role of Rule 10b–5 has increased to an extent that its drafter probably never contemplated. Originally the scope of liability for nondisclosure was confined to officers and directors of corporations who traded their securities on inside nonpublic information. Now it has evolved to encompass anyone, insider or not, who has access to and trades on material nonpublic information, without making disclosure.

The intent of the expansion has been to promote the federal regulatory policy of insuring that everyone has equal access to material information necessary for informed decision making. Equal access presumably means equal opportunity and equal profits. In reality, of course, profits often depend on how the investor acts upon the information to which he or she has access. A skillful investor does have an advantage over an ordinary investor.

[7] 401 F.2d 833 (2d Cir. 1968).
[8] 495 F.2d 228 (2d Cir. 1974).

If the two are given the same information about a company, the skillful investor can presumably convert that information into greater profits. Few would deny that there is a justification for rewarding such an investor for his or her skills. Similarly, an argument could be made that an outsider cunning enough to obtain inside information deserves the reward of greater profits. However, this rationale neglects an overriding concern for fairness in the marketplace. Investors will be less inclined to participate in market trading if they feel that others have a strategic advantage because of access to information generally unavailable. And from the perspective of these investors it makes little difference whether the advantaged persons are insiders or outsiders. When privileged information is in the hands of a few, the masses feel victimized—investors develop a feeling of helplessness if information likely to affect the market value of an issuer's securities is within the exclusive possession of the "elect." When this occurs, investors lose confidence in the market and the market is undermined.

Review problems

1. On May 23, 1972, Designcraft made a public offering of 300,000 shares of its common stock. The total outstanding common stock of Designcraft, including the 300,000 newly issued shares, was 817,500 shares. William Norton and Company, a broker-dealer in securities, was counderwriter of the public offering, distributing 250,000 shares itself. The underwriting was made on a firm commitment basis requiring Norton to buy the shares from Designcraft and to resell them to the public, a process completed within a few days. At all material times Designcraft was registered pursuant to section 12 of the Exchange Act. There was no relevant connection between Norton and Designcraft before the underwriting transaction took place. H. Perine, a stockholder of Designcraft, brought an action against Norton under section 16(b) of the Exchange Act to recover the short-swing profits earned by Norton in its underwriting of the distribution.

Do you think the relationship between Norton and Designcraft is sufficient to establish liability for Norton under section 16(b)? Explain.

2. Mergenthaler Linotype Company owned over 50 percent of the outstanding shares of stock in Electric Autolite Company (EAC) and was in control of EAC. American Manufacturing owned about one third of the outstanding shares of Mergenthaler and controlled Mergenthaler and through it, EAC. In 1963 EAC merged with Mergenthaler. The proxy statement announcing the proposal for merger to the shareholders had informed the shareholders that EAC's board of directors was in favor of the merger. The statement had failed, however, to inform the shareholders that all 11 of EAC's board members were under the direct control of Mergenthaler.

An affirmative vote of two thirds of the EAC shares was needed in order to approve the merger. Approximately 54 percent of EAC's shares were owned by Mergenthaler and American Manufacturing. About 950,000 shares out of 1,160,000 shares voted in favor of the merger. Included within the favorable votes were 317,000 votes secured by proxy from the minority shareholders. A group of the minority shareholders now protest on the basis that the proxy statement was misleading. They seek corrective measures. Are the minority shareholders entitled to a remedy, and if so, what would be the appropriate remedy? What if Mergenthaler had 67 percent of the outstanding shares of stock? Would your answer be different? Why?

3. What basis do you think is behind each of the grounds, listed in this chapter under *Proposals by security holders,* for management exclusion of a shareholder proposal?

4. The Take Over Chalmers Group acquired in excess of 5 percent of the stock of Chalmers corporation through over-the-counter transactions. The group then obtained a shareholders' list and proceeded to solicit shareholders personally. In this way it acquired another 4.9 percent of Chalmer's stock. The group filed a Schedule 13D five days after having made its last purchase of Chalmers' shares. What are the arguments in favor of labeling these transactions tender offers?

5. Elyria Corporation made a cash tender offer to purchase up to 1 million shares of ABC, Inc., for $30 a share. The tender offer provided that if less than 1 million shares were tendered within 30 days of the offer, then Elyria would not be obligated to purchase any. It also provided that Elyria maintained the right to purchase all shares tendered in excess of 1 million shares. Assume that the market price was $20 a share at the time of the tender offer and that after the tender offer the market price increased to $25 a share. If you had 1,000 shares of ABC, Inc., what would you have done, and why?

6. Fred Lowenschuss is a shareholder of Great Atlantic & Pacific Tea Co., Inc. (A&P) He tendered A&P shares to Gulf & Western Industries, Inc. (G&W), in response to G&W's tender offer for A&P shares. The tender offer announced that G&W was willing to purchase up to 3,750,000 shares of A&P common stock (15 percent of A&P's outstanding shares) at $20 per share. G&W held extensive investments in other food processors and distributors, and its acquisition of A&P stock would probably result in a violation of the antitrust laws. Furthermore, there was evidence to indicate that G&W intended to acquire a controlling position in A&P or at least to exercise influence over A&P's management and policies. Neither G&W's holdings nor its intentions regarding control over A&P were disclosed in the tender offer. Lowenschuss

brought suit against G&W in an attempt to prevent G&W from gaining control of A&P. What must Lowenschuss allege and prove? What is G&W's rebuttal?

7. Cargill Incorporated announced an offer to purchase all the outstanding common stock of Missouri Portland Cement Company (MPC). MPC opposed the tender offer. In an attempt to muster shareholder support MPC issued a proxy statement explaining its position. Cargill brought suit against MPC because of allegedly misleading and false statements in the proxy statement. The parties agree that: (1) MPC failed to disclose the seven-year employment contract for MPC's board chairman, approved by the directors of MPC within hours after they learned of the tender offer; (2) MPC told its shareholders that their stock was worth much more than the $30 per share offered by Cargill, although MPC had made $30 the upper limit in authorizing repurchase of its stock on the market; and (3) MPC advised its shareholders that an increase in the price of the stock during the term of the tender offer would not inure to the benefit of those shareholders who had already tendered their shares, when in fact the terms of the tender offer clearly stated otherwise.

Under what section or sections of the Exchange Act will Cargill sue? Which, if any, of the statements or omissions of MPC violate the act? What relief will be granted to Cargill if it proves its contentions?

8. On June 23 Financial Industrial Fund (FIF), a mutual fund, purchased a large block of the securities of McDonnell Douglas Corporation (MD). In making its investment decision, FIF relied upon information published by independent market analysts. Shortly after FIF purchased MD's stock in the open market, MD issued a press release in which it noted that its earnings were down from the prior year more than had been previously announced by the company. The press release was based on information on incidents that had occurred between May 27 and June 15. As a result of the press release, the price of

MD stock fell sharply. After conducting its own investigation, FIF sold its shares in MD at a substantial loss. FIF commenced an action against MD, claiming that MD's delay in disseminating information known to it had caused the information upon which FIF had originally relied to be misleading.

Under what section or sections of the Exchange Act should FIF bring suit? What must FIF prove in order to succeed in its suit? How might MD justify the delay?

9. Alex Campbell, a financial columnist for the *Los Angeles Herald Examiner,* wrote a column containing a highly favorable description of American Systems, Inc. (ASI). The *Herald Examiner* published the column. Campbell had obtained the information presented in the column from an interview with ASI directors. These directors made material misrepresentations and omissions during the interview in the hope that the false information would be printed and would cause an inflation of ASI stock prices. Just before the column was published, Campbell bought 5,000 shares from ASI at a substantial discount. The price of ASI stock rose swiftly after the column appeared. Campbell sold 2,000 shares and recouped his entire investment. Richard Zweig and Muriel Bruno merged their company with ASI in return for inflated ASI stock. They claim injury and allege that Campbell violated Rule 10b–5 by publishing his column without fully informing his readers of the fact that he bought ASI stock at a discount and intended to sell it at a profit after the column was published and the price rose. Is Campbell liable for the damages sustained by Zweig and Bruno? Explain.

10. What "domino effect" might be expected if the bulk of investors lose faith in the securities market due to a perceived unfairness? What consequences for business, consumers, and the economy might result from such a domino effect?

PART IV: REVIEW PROBLEMS

1. Your friend Ben Z. Drive, a sophomore chemistry major, claims to have invented a liquid which when added to the gas tank of a typical automobile will triple the gas mileage. Ben has never impressed you as being very bright. His grades in school are mediocre. Nevertheless, he claims that he has tested the additive in his own car and that it works.

Ben believes that with the proper development and marketing the additive can produce millions of dollars in income. He lacks two things to carry out his dream: money and business expertise. He has asked you to supply the business expertise. Another friend of Ben's, Mike Finneran, a wealthy peanut farmer, has agreed to contribute $100,000 to the project in exchange for being named vice president of any resulting enterprise.

Ben requires $1 million to further develop and test the additives. If it proves marketable, it will cost another $1.5 million to mass-produce and market it. Ben would like to establish a corporation with Finneran, him, and you as officers. The corporation would raise the $2.5 million by selling stock. Ben believes that $1 million can be raised from the following people, contacted by him and Finneran, who have expressed interest in the operation:

Two chemistry professors at your school.

Ten members of his father's investment club.

His family doctor.

His brother, who is a CPA, and six members of his firm.

His neighbor, who is a bank president, and seven bank employees.

Five farmhands who work for Finneran.

Finneran's neighbor, who is a rich widow with little business experience.

The remaining $1.5 million will be raised by advertising the stock in newspapers and magazines. Milhouse offered to take care of the stock sale, but Ben is concerned about Finneran's past. Ten years ago Finneran was indicted for securities fraud, but the charges were mysteriously dropped after Finneran contributed $100,000 to the incumbent president's reelection campaign. Ben has asked you to become the company's secretary-treasurer and guide it through its formation. How will you respond?

2. E. Turner Brite developed a scheme which he believed would either put him in the poorhouse or make him a South Sea retiree within two years. He started a company named Eternity Enterprises. The company sold "fountain of youth" packages. For $2,000 a purchaser received "three words" and a money-back guarantee to live 20 years (Bronze Plan). For $5,000 a purchaser received "two words" and a money-back guarantee to live 40 years (Silver Plan). For $10,000 a purchaser received "one word" and a money-back guarantee to live forever (Gold Plan). Eternity Enterprises marketed the "words" to persons who demonstrated a real knowledge of and interest in the spiritual. It sold:

1. Bronze plans to 20 elderly members of an investment club and 2 salesmen in a stock brokerage firm.
2. Silver plans to the widow of one of Brite's former business associates and to seven upper-echelon employees of an investment advisors' firm.
3. Gold plans to 150 sophisticated investors and to an accountant, a lawyer, and three veterinarians.

Along with the words the purchasers received a handbook on how to use them and a script on how to organize "eternity youth-ins" to sell the plans to others. Portions of the handbook read:

Always look energetic and alive; think young, talk young, dress young, act young, and expound on the virtues of the "words" and how they transformed your life. You are the living proof of the value of the "words." You are the product. Market yourself.

Any deviation from the approved script will result in revocation of permission to sell the plans.

Eternity Enterprises provided all of the marketing materials used to sell the plans as well as the physical facilities for the youth-ins. A Bronze Plan purchaser could sell only Bronze plans; a Silver Plan purchaser could sell Silver and Bronze plans; and a Gold Plan purchaser could sell all three plans. For each sale the salesperson received 50 percent of the sales price.

There was no media advertising of the plans. Brite failed to file a registration statement covering the scheme with the SEC. The SEC sought an injunction against the further marketing of the scheme. In addition, 13 representatives of the estates of purchasers who died instituted a suit to rescind the transactions.

While those cases were pending, Brite developed plans to automate diamond cutting. He produced a working scale model of a mechanical diamond cutter, which he insured for $1,500,000. Brite incorporated Diamond Cutters International (DCI) in the State of Confusion, which had adopted the Uniform Securities Act. The corporation was approved by the secretary of the State of Confusion. In need of raising $20 million in capital to pursue the venture, DCI sold $20 million in stock. The corporation has 5,000 shareholders. It filed a registration statement under the Act of 33. DCI shares are traded over-the-counter.

James Malcolm, a sales representative of DCI, owned 1,500,000 shares of its stock. On April 1, 1983, he acquired 250,000 shares at $10 per share; on May 1, 1983, he acquired an additional 250,000 shares at $20 per share; on June 1, 1983, he sold 250,000 shares at $10/share; and on December 1, 1983, he sold the remaining shares at $50/share.

Of the 15,000,000 outstanding shares of DCI the Brite Faction controlled 41 percent while the Take Over Brite and Corporate Freedom groups, which sought control of the corporation, controlled 21 percent and 19 percent, respectively. In anticipation of an upcoming annual shareholders' meeting all three groups sought proxies and filed proxy statements. The Brite Faction omitted to mention that one of

the persons whom it was supporting for a position on the board of directors had been charged with embezzling company funds, though the charges had been dismissed. In its proxy statement the Take Over Brite group failed to say that it intended to eliminate dividends for two years in order to improve the corporation's capital position. In fact, Bill Mellow, a shareholder, aware of that capital position and fearful of the consequences to the shareholders if the Take Over Brite group prevailed, gave notice to management of a proposal he desired to have included in its proxy statement. The proposal read, "Be it resolved that the present policy of issuing dividends annually will continue as long as there is a capital surplus." Management refused to include the proposal in its proxy materials.

At the shareholders' meeting the incumbents won by the following margin:

Brite Faction	51%
Take Over Brite	42
Corporate Freedom	7

The Take Over Brite and Corporate Freedom groups instituted suit and sought to have the election set aside. That action is pending.

Meanwhile, DCI has been threatened from the outside by Precious Jewels Hand Cutters, Inc. (PJ-HI), which has waged a campaign offering to purchase DCI stock at $40 per share, or $7 above the current market price. Of the 15,000,000 outstanding shares it has acquired 637,500 shares thus far. In addition, PJ-HI is offering two shares of its stock in exchange for one share of DCI stock. As part of its campaign it has sought to undermine the Brite Faction by exposing its "financial improprieties." DCI has retaliated by raising the DCI dividend and enlisting the Sway Mouth Universal Times (SMUT) advertising agency to aid it in its campaign. In reckless disregard of the truth SMUT characterized several PJ-HI officers and directors as "Marxist oriented" in their economic philosophy. Although PJ-HI has failed to file a registration statement under the Williams Act, it has been delivering its prospectus to the shareholders it has solicited. It has failed to inform them that its true motivation for the takeover is to demechanize DCI and return DCI to the traditional hand diamond-cutter mold.

Brite has been in communication with Fran Bingham PJ-HI's chief executive officer and chairman of the board. His discussions with her have convinced him that PJ-HI's takeover strategy will be successful. That strategy is to continue offering inflated prices to DCI share-holders, gradually increasing the offer to $75 per share over the next six months. Consequently, Brite has purchased several thousand shares of DCI stock at $60 per share, $5 above the current PJ-HI offer, in the hope of reselling them to PJ-HI for $75 per share in the future.

Discuss fully all of the relevant issues contained in this problem.

PART FIVE

Labor law

CHAPTER 15

Labor-management relations

Between the Civil War and World War I, an era known as America's Age of Industrialization, a number of social developments fostered a labor movement in the United States. A dramatic increase in capital investment in manufacturing transformed America from a nation of farmers into a nation of urban wage earners. The growth of large corporations put an end to the personal employer-employee relationship that existed in smaller enterprises. Urbanization, which made possible greater social intercourse among workers in different companies, and an influx of immigrants, which threatened the economic security of skilled craftsmen, strengthened skilled workers' awareness of the need for solidarity. Labor organizations, such as the Knights of Labor and the American Federation of Labor, came into existence during this period. Social conditions were ripe for the rise of unions in America, but the law was unreceptive.

Although no statute declared concerted worker activity to be unlawful, the courts applied the common-law doctrine of criminal conspiracy to such activity, holding that a combination of workers constituted a criminal conspiracy where the goals sought and the means used were improper. Concerted worker activity to achieve economic gains was generally considered improper. The first American case to apply the conspiracy doctrine in this way was the *Philadelphia Cordwainers* case of 1806. Several cordwainers (shoemakers) were convicted of conspiracy after engaging in a strike for higher pay. The trial judge instructed the jury that "a combination of workers to raise wages may be considered in a twofold point of view: one is to benefit themselves, the other is to injure those who do not join their society. The rule of law condemns both."

By 1880, criminal prosecutions of trade unionists had become politically unpopular with prosecutors. Thus employers used the civil courts to combat unions through injunctions. An injunction is a court order commanding someone to do something or to refrain from doing something. Disobedience of an injunction is punishable by fine or imprisonment for contempt of court.

The widespread use of injunctions as an antilabor weapon during the 1890s led to the characterization of U.S. labor law as "law by injunction." By the turn of the 20th century, the labor movement had nevertheless gained momentum. Its political power was finally felt in 1932, when Congress passed the Norris–La Guardia Act, which restricted the availability of federal court injunctions in labor disputes. The statute, which is still in effect, removed the power of federal courts to enjoin concerted union activity that did not involve violence. Along with several state statutes enacted shortly thereafter, the act permitted unions to exert effective economic power against employers. However, it did not obligate employers to negotiate with unions.

Congress created the obligation of employers to bargain with unions in 1935, when it passed the Wagner Act, also known as the National Labor Relations Act (NLRA). This statute recognized the legitimacy of collective employee efforts; made it obligatory for employers to deal in good faith with unions; designated certain employer conduct as "unfair labor practices"; and created the National Labor Relations Board (NLRB) as the administrative agency to administer the act, granting it the power to declare that employers had engaged in unfair labor practices. The statute contained no protections for management.

Following World War II, the economic balance of power tipped in favor of unions. Union membership grew significantly. National strikes took place in several industries at times of peak consumer demand. Public opinion then shifted against unions, and in 1947 Congress passed the Taft-Hartley Act, also known as the Labor-Management Relations Act, which was an amendment to the NLRA. The statute added union unfair labor practices to the NLRA's list of unlawful activities. It also recognized that collective bargaining did not always resolve disputes and therefore made available the alternative processes of mediation and "cooling off" injunctions. The act created the Federal Mediation and Conciliation Service to assist in collective bargaining. It also gave the federal government power to intervene in strikes that threatened the national welfare and to seek an 80-day injunction from a federal court to serve as a cooling-off period.

As a result of Senate investigations into union corruption in the 1950s, Congress enacted the Labor-Management Reporting and Disclosure Act of 1959, usually referred to as the Landrum-Griffin Act. The statute amended the NLRA to extend into internal union affairs, establishing an "employee's bill of rights" for union members. It also placed restrictions on the use of secondary union activity and picketing during a union's efforts to gain the right to represent an employer's work force.

In 1974 Congress enacted the health care amendments to the NLRA. These brought health care facilities under the act.

This capsule history of labor relations law reveals that federal regulation of labor-management relations has been the result of piecemeal legislative reponses to particular labor relations problems. Although patchwork in character, the laws reflect a national labor policy of promoting industrial peace through collective bargaining. To this end, federal labor law recognizes the right of employees to organize, requires and assists collective bargaining, and prohibits the use of unfair labor practices.

THE NATIONAL LABOR RELATIONS BOARD

As the previous discussion points out, several federal statutes pertain to the regulation of labor-management relations. However, the federal labor code is usually referred to as the National Labor Relations Act, which may be viewed as having been enacted in three phases: the Wagner Act, the Taft-Hartley Act, and the Landrum-Griffin Act. The National Labor Relations Board administers the NLRA. The board has two principal functions: (1) to prevent and remedy unfair labor practices and (2) to conduct secret ballot elections in which employees decide whether unions will represent them in collective bargaining. The following discussion focuses on the board's jurisdiction, organization, procedures, and powers.

Board jurisdiction

The NLRB derives its authority from Congress by way of the National Labor Relations Act. The NLRA generally covers employers engaged in interstate commerce and employees in a business or industry where a labor dispute would affect interstate commerce. Congress extended the NLRA's coverage to the full limit of its constitutional power under the Commerce Clause, but excluded certain classes of employers and employees and granted the board discretion to limit the exercise of its jurisdiction.

Excluded employers. The NLRA does not apply to railroads and airlines, which are covered by other legislation. Furthermore, the board, as a policy matter, does not exercise jurisdiction over all the employers theoretically covered by the NLRA.

Congress provided in section 14(c) of the NLRA that the board, "in its discretion, may . . . decline to assert jurisdiction over any labor dispute involving any class or category of employers, where, in the opinion of the Board, the effect of such labor dispute on commerce is not sufficiently substantial to warrant the exercise of its jurisdiction." The board has adopted certain requirements for exercising its jurisdiction, called "jurisdictional standards." These standards are based on the yearly amount of business done by an enterprise or on the yearly amount of its sales or its purchases. They are stated in terms of total dollar volume of business and are different for different kinds of enterprises. An enterprise that does the total annual volume of business listed in the standard is considered to be engaged in activities that affect interstate commerce.

Excluded employees. Certain classes of employees are not covered by the NLRA and thus are not within the board's jurisdiction. The act specifically excludes the following types of employees from its provisions: agricultural laborers, domestic servants, employees of a parent or spouse, government employees, employees of railroads and airlines, and independent contractors.

Supervisors are also excluded from the act's coverage. Whether an individual is a supervisor depends on his or her authority over employees and not merely on job title. Section 2(11) of the NLRA defines a supervisor as "any individual having authority, in the interest of the employer, to hire, transfer, suspend, lay off, recall, promote, discharge, assign, reward, or discipline other employees, or responsibly to direct them, or to adjust their grievances, or effectively to recommend such action, if in connection with the foregoing the exercise of such authority is not of a merely routine or clerical nature, but requires the use of independent judgment."

In addition, the board has excluded managerial employees, who are defined as those who formulate and effectuate management policy by expressing and making operative their employer's decisions and as those who have discretion in performing their jobs which is independent of their employer's established policy. Supervisors and managers are excluded from the act to assure their single-minded loyalty to the employer by not involving them in a conflict of interest between the employer and their union representative. The following case shows the Supreme Court's present approach to these exclusions.

NLRB v. Yeshiva University
444 U.S. 672 (1980)

Full-time faculty at Yeshiva University (appellee), a private institution, petitioned the NLRB (appellant) to conduct an election to determine whether a majority of the faculty wished to be represented by a labor union. Yeshiva claimed that its faculty were managerial employees. The NLRB concluded that they were professional employees and conducted the election. Yeshiva appealed to the Second Circuit Court of Appeals, which reversed, holding faculty to be managers. The NLRB petitioned the Supreme Court for review. The Court affirmed the Second Circuit.

Yeshiva's faculty participated in university-wide governance through representatives on elected committees. The university was divided into relatively autonomous schools, whose faculty met to decide matters of institutional and professional concern. They determined curriculum, grading systems, admission

standards, academic calendars, course schedules, hiring, promotion, tenure, and sabbatical leaves. All faculty decisions were in the form of recommendations to the central administration, but these recommendations were usually followed.

Mr. Justice Powell:

* * * * *

Yeshiva does not contend that its faculty are not professionals under the statute. But professionals, like other employees, may be exempted from coverage under the Act's exclusion for "supervisors" who use independent judgment in overseeing other employees in the interest of the employer, or under the judicially implied exclusion for "managerial employees" who are involved in developing and enforcing employer policy. Both exemptions grow out of the same concern: that an employer is entitled to the undivided loyalty of its representatives. . . .

Managerial employees are defined as those who "formulate and effectuate management policies by expressing and making operative the decisions of their employer." These employees are "much higher in the managerial structure" than those explicitly mentioned by Congress, which "regarded [them] as so clearly outside the Act that no specific exclusionary provision was thought necessary." . . . Managerial employees must exercise discretion within or even independently of established employer policy and must be aligned with management. . . . Although the Board has established no firm criteria for determining when an employee is so aligned, normally an employee may be excluded as managerial only if he represents management interests by taking or recommending discretionary actions that effectively control or implement employer policy.

The Board . . . contends that the managerial exclusion cannot be applied in a straightforward fashion to professional employees because those employees often appear to be exercising managerial authority when they are merely performing routine job duties. The status of such employees, in the Board's view, must be determined by reference to the "alignment with management criterion." The Board argues that the Yeshiva faculty are not aligned with management because they are expected to exercise "independent professional judgment" while participating in academic governance, and because they are neither "expected to conform to management policies [nor] judged according to their effectiveness in carrying out those policies." Because of this independence, the Board contends there is no danger of divided loyalty and no need for the managerial exclusion. In its view, union pressure cannot divert the faculty from adhering to the interests of the university, because the university itself expects its faculty to pursue professional values rather than institutional interests. . . .

The controlling consideration in this case is that the faculty of Yeshiva University exercise authority which in any other context unques-

tionably would be managerial. Their authority in academic matters is absolute. They decide what courses will be offered, when they will be scheduled, and to whom they will be taught. They debate and determine teaching methods, grading policies, and matriculation standards. They effectively decide which students will be admitted, retained, and graduated. On occasion their views have determined the size of the student body, the tuition to be charged, and the location of a school. When one considers the function of a university, it is difficult to imagine decisions more managerial than these. To the extent the industrial analogy applies, the faculty determines within each school the product to be produced, the terms upon which it will be offered, and the customers who will be served. . . .

* * * * *

The problem of divided loyalty is particularly acute for a university like Yeshiva, which depends on the professional judgment of its faculty to formulate and apply crucial policies constrained only by necessarily general institutional goals. The University requires faculty participation in governance because professional expertise is indispensable to the formulation and implementation of academic policy. It may appear, as the Board contends, that the professor performing governance functions is less "accountable" for departures from institutional policy than a middle-level industrial manager whose discretion is more confined. Moreover, traditional systems of collegiality and tenure insulate the professor from some of the sanctions applied to an industrial manager who fails to adhere to company policy. But the analogy of the university to industry need not, and indeed cannot, be complete. It is clear that Yeshiva and like universities must rely on their faculties to participate in the making and implementation of their policies. The large measure of independence enjoyed by faculty members can only increase the danger that divided loyalty will lead to those harms that the Board traditionally has sought to prevent.

We certainly are not suggesting an application of the managerial exclusion that would sweep all professionals outside the Act in derogation of Congress' expressed intent to protect them. The Board has recognized that employees whose decisionmaking is limited to the routine discharge of professional duties in projects to which they have been assigned cannot be excluded from coverage even if union membership arguably may involve some divided loyalty. Only if an employee's activities fall outside the scope of the duties routinely performed by similarly situated professionals will he be found aligned with management. We think these decisions accurately capture the intent of Congress, and that they provide an appropriate starting point for analysis in cases involving professionals alleged to be managerial. . . .

Case questions

1. What was the "independent professional judgment" test that the NLRB used in determining the managerial status of the Yeshiva faculty? Why did the Court reject this approach? What standard did the Court fashion in determining whether university faculty members were professional or managerial employees? When will a professional employee not be excluded from the NLRA's protections as a managerial employee?

2. Is the Court's industrial analogy appropriate?

3. If the Yeshiva faculty are exempt from the NLRA, what Yeshiva employees are protected by the act?

4. Could the associates of a major CPA firm organize a union under the NLRA's protections? What facts would be helpful in deciding this?

Board organization

The NLRB consists of the board itself, which has five members, each appointed by the president with Senate approval; the general counsel, who is charged with investigating and prosecuting complaints; and the regional offices located in major cities across the country, which assist in administering the NLRA.

The board. The five-member board functions as an adjudicatory body, deciding unfair labor practice cases and representation cases (cases involving the certification of a union as the bargaining representative of an employer's work force). The board's adjudicatory functions have been delegated to administrative law judges (ALJs) located in the regional offices. An ALJ holds judicial hearings and makes a decision which, if appealed, serves as a recommendation to the board.

The general counsel. To guarantee the separation of enforcement and adjudicatory functions, the NLRA has established the office of general counsel. The general counsel, who is appointed by the president with Senate approval for a four-year term, serves as the agency's enforcement arm. The general counsel, located in Washington, D.C., and his staff, located in the regional offices, investigate charges of unfair labor practices, decide whether to issue complaints, and if a complaint is issued, prosecute the complaint before the board. The general counsel also represents the board in court actions to enforce or review board decisions.

The regional offices.   Assisting the board and the general counsel is a staff, divided between the Washington office and the regional offices. The regional offices, located in major cities in various states, are under the general supervision of the general counsel. Each office is under the direction of a regional director, who is assisted by a regional attorney. The staff consists of field executives, who conduct investigations of charges and conduct representation elections, and attorneys, who prosecute complaints before administrative law judges.

Board procedure

As noted, the NLRB's two principal functions are: (1) to conduct secret ballot elections in which employees decide whether unions will represent them in bargaining and (2) to prevent and remedy unfair labor practices. The NLRB can act only when it is formally requested to do so. Individuals, employers, or unions may initiate cases by filing petitions for employee representation elections or charges of unfair labor practices with the NLRB regional office serving the area in which the case arises. The following discussion explains the procedures followed by the board in representation and unfair labor practice cases.

Representation cases.   The board has delegated to its regional directors the authority to make decisions in employee representation cases. This allows the NLRB regional directors to conduct hearings, determine the appropriateness of employee bargaining units, direct that employee elections be held, and conduct the elections. Actions by the regional directors are subject to review by the board on restricted grounds.

The jurisdiction of the NLRB can be invoked in a representation proceeding only by filing a petition. Election petitions are filed in the regional office in the area where the employee's unit is located. Petitions may be filed by an employer whose recognition as the bargaining representative of its employees has been demanded by a union, or by a union seeking representation status and demonstrating a showing of interest from 30 percent of the employees in the bargaining unit—usually evidenced by signed cards authorizing the union to serve as the bargaining representative.

The regional staff then investigates the petition to determine whether the board has jurisdiction over it. If there is reasonable cause to believe that a question of representation affecting interstate commerce exists, a hearing will be conducted before a hearing officer. The hearing transcript is then transferred to the regional director, who decides such issues as whether board jurisdiction exists or whether the bargaining unit is appropriate. If the regional director finds that a question of representation exists, he or she directs an election by secret ballot and certifies the results. If a union receives a majority of the votes cast, it is certified; if no union gets a majority, that result is certified. A union that has been certified is entitled to recognition from the employer as the exclusive bargaining agent for the employees in the unit. An employer that fails to bargain with that union is committing an unfair labor practice.

Unfair labor practice cases. The procedure in an unfair labor practice case is begun by filing a charge. A charge may be filed by an employee, an employer, a labor organization, or any other person. Like petitions, charge forms, which are available at regional offices, must be signed, sworn to or affirmed under oath, and filed with the appropriate regional office—that is, the regional office in the area where the alleged unfair labor practice was committed. Section 10 provides for the issuance of a complaint stating the charges and notifying the charged party of a hearing on them. Such a complaint is issued only after investigation of the charges through the regional office indicates that an unfair labor practice has in fact occurred.

An unfair labor practice hearing is conducted before an NLRB administrative law judge in accordance with the rules of evidence and procedure that apply in the U.S. district courts. Based on the hearing record, the administrative law judge makes findings and recommendations to the board. All parties to the hearing may appeal the administrative law judge's decision to the board. If the board considers that the party named in the complaint has engaged in or is engaging in the unfair labor practice charged, the board is authorized to issue an order requiring such person to cease and desist from such practice and to take appropriate affirmative action.

Section 10(b) provides that "no complaint shall issue based upon any unfair labor practice occurring more than six months prior to the filing of the charge with the Board and the service of a copy thereof upon the person against whom such charge is made." If the regional director refuses to issue a complaint, the person who filed the charge may appeal the decision to the general counsel in Washington. Section 3(d) places in the general counsel "final authority, on behalf of the Board, in respect of the investigation of charges and issuance of complaints." If the general counsel reverses the regional director's decision, a complaint will be issued. If the general counsel approves the decision, there is no further appeal.

If an employer or a union fails to comply with a board order, section 10(e) empowers the board to petition the U.S. court of appeals for a court decree enforcing the board's order. Section 10(f) provides that any person aggrieved by a final order of the board granting or denying in whole or in part the relief sought may obtain a review of the order in any appropriate circuit court of appeals. When the court of appeals hears a petition concerning a board order, it may enforce the order, remand it to the board for reconsideration, change it, or set it aside. If the court of appeals issues a judgment enforcing the board order, failure to comply may be punishable by fine or imprisonment for contempt of court.

In some cases the U.S. Supreme Court may be asked to review the decision of a circuit court of appeals, particularly where different courts have conflicting views on the same important problem.

Board powers

The NLRA is not a criminal statute. It is intended to prevent and remedy unfair labor practices, not to punish the persons responsible for them. The board is authorized by the act not only to issue cease and desist orders but to take such affirmative action as will effectuate the act's policies.

Court enforcement of board orders. If an employer or union fails to comply with a board order, the board may petition a U.S. court of appeals for a decree enforcing the order. The court of appeals may enforce the order, remand it to the board for reconsideration, change it, or set it aside. If the court of appeals issues a decree enforcing the board order, failure to comply may be punishable by a fine or imprisonment for contempt of court.

ESTABLISHING THE COLLECTIVE BARGAINING RELATIONSHIP

When a group of employees feel that their working conditions are inadequate, they may seek to have a union represent them in bargaining with their employer. They usually begin by approaching an existing union, which will send a union organizer to talk with the employees who wish to unionize. The organizer will generally attempt to convince these employees of the advantages of becoming a local of the union. If they are convinced, they will form an organizing committee of employees who will work with the union organizer to convince the rest of the work force of the need to unionize.

Although most organizing efforts are initiated at the local level, national union organizing campaigns sometimes occur. These campaigns usually take place when a unionized company establishes a new plant whose employees are not organized. The union representing the rest of the company's plants may send organizers to the new plant to bring its employees into the organization. Sometimes national organizational campaigns start when a union targets a particular employer for unionization. This frequently occurs when a nonunion employer exists in a predominantly unionized industry.

After establishing the organizing committee, the union supporters seek to obtain their co-workers' signatures on cards authorizing the union to act as their collective bargaining agent. In order to obtain a representation election the union must obtain the signatures of 30 percent of the employees in the unit. It may use a majority of signatures to obtain representation rights without an election.

If the union obtains the signatures of 30 percent of the employees, it may petition the board to conduct an election. If a majority of employees sign, it sends a recognition letter to the employer, seeking recognition of the union as the empoyees' exclusive bargaining agent. The employer may respond by challenging the union's claim of majority status and insisting that the union win an election before bargaining begins. The union would then file a petition for a representation election with the board.

Before the election the union and the employer wage a campaign to win the workers over to their position. This campaign is regulated by the board. The board has stated that such elections must be conducted under laboratory conditions; that is, the election proceedings must be conducted under conditions which make it possible to determine the uninhibited wishes of the employees. If the proceedings fall below these standards, the board will set aside an election and conduct a new one.

If the losing party feels that the board's campaign rules have been violated, it may file objections with the board, setting forth the violations. If the objections are valid, the board sets aside the election and orders a new one. A party may also file an unfair labor practice charge, claiming that the other side is interfering with the employees' rights to bargain collectively through representatives of their own choosing. If the board finds that the charge is valid, it may issue a cease and desist order against the prohibited practice. If it finds employer interference with employee choice so serious that a fair election cannot be conducted, it may order the employer to bargain with the union even when the union has lost the election. This is known as a board bargaining order.

Protection of campaign laboratory conditions

As mentioned, the NLRA and the board's decisional rules prescribe laboratory conditions for conducting representation elections. These conditions are a specific environment which the board insists that the parties maintain from the time that the election petition is filed to the time that the regional director certifies the election results. During this critical period both sides, but especially the employer, must be careful not to upset the laboratory conditions.

Section 8(a)(1) of the NLRA provides that it is an unfair labor practice to interfere with, restrain, or coerce employees in the exercise of their right to organize themselves; to form, join or, assist labor organizations; to bargain collectively; and to engage in concerted activities for the purpose of collective bargaining or other mutual aid or protection. The following discussion concentrates on the conduct that may constitute an unfair labor practice and the conduct that will result in a cease and desist order, a new election, or a bargaining order.

Employer interference, restraint, or coercion. As noted, section 8(a)(1) provides that it is an unfair labor practice for an employer "to interfere with, restrain or coerce employees" in the exercise of their self-organizational rights. However, the act does not prohibit employer activities that tend to obstruct organizational efforts but do not amount to interference, restraint, or coercion. Section 8(c) provides that the mere "expressing of any views, argument or opinion . . . shall not constitute an unfair labor practice . . . if such expression contains no threat of reprisal or force, or promise of benefit." The act thus attempts to balance the self-organizational rights of employees with the property rights of their employer.

The self-organizational rights of employees come into conflict with the property rights of their employer when organizing activity is attempted on company property. Frequently employers have rules forbidding solicitation and the distribution of literature. Employers are permitted to have nondiscriminatory rules prohibiting the distribution of union literature or the solicitation of union membership during an employee's work time or in work areas. However, any absolute ban on employee solicitation, such as a rule forbidding the distribution of literature in nonwork areas (e.g., lunchrooms and parking lots) or during an employee's nonwork hours, is an unfair labor practice. Although employees may thus use company property for organizational purposes within certain limits, nonemployee organizers may use the employer's property only when there is no other practical method of reaching the employees. Furthermore, the employer may prohibit solicitation for purposes not related to labor organizing. The following case deals with the limits of employees' rights to solicit.

Eastex, Inc. v. *NLRB*
437 U.S. 556 (1978)

Eastex (petitioner) prohibited its employees from distributing on its property literature opposing a proposal to incorporate the Texas right-to-work law (which prohibited union shop agreements) into the state constitution and protesting a presidential veto of a minimum wage increase. The NLRB (respondent) held that Eastex violated section 8(a)(1). The court of appeals and the Supreme Court affirmed.

Mr. Justice Powell:

* * * * *

Section 7 provides that "[e]mployees shall have the right . . . to engage in . . . concerted activities for the purpose of collective bargaining or other mutual aid or protection. . . ." Petitioner contends that the activity here is not within the "mutual aid or protection" language because it does not relate to a "specific dispute" between employees and their own employer "over an issue which the employer has the right or power to affect." . . . Petitioner rejects the idea that § 7 might protect any activity that could be characterized as "political," and suggests that the discharge of an employee

who engages in any such activity would not violate the Act.

We believe that petitioner misconceives the reach of the "mutual aid or protection" clause. The "employees" who may engage in concerted activities for "mutual aid or protection" are defined by § 2(3) of the Act, to "include any employee, and shall not be limited to the employees of a particular employer, unless the Act explicitly states otherwise. . . ." This definition was intended to protect employees when they engage in otherwise proper concerted activities in support of employees of employers other than their own. . . .

We also find no warrant for petitioner's view that employees lose their protection under the "mutual aid or protection" clause when they seek to improve terms and conditions of employment or otherwise improve their lot as employees through channels outside the immediate employee-employer relationship. The 74th Congress knew well enough that labor's cause often is advanced on fronts other than collective bargaining and grievance settlement within the immediate employment context. It recognized this fact by choosing, as the language of § 7 makes clear, to protect concerted activities for the somewhat broader purpose of "mutual aid or protection" as well as for the narrower purposes of "self-organization" and "collective bargaining." . . .

It is true, of course, that some concerted activity bears a less immediate relationship to employees' interests as employees than other such activity. We may assume that at some point the relationship becomes so attenuated that an activity cannot fairly be deemed to come within the "mutual aid or protection" clause. It is neither necessary nor appropriate, however, for us to attempt to delineate precisely the boundaries of the "mutual aid or protection" clause. That task is for the Board to perform in the first instance as it considers the wide variety of cases that come before it. . . .

The Board determined that distribution of the second section, urging employees to write their legislators to oppose incorporation of the state "right-to-work" statute into a revised state constitution, was protected because union security is "central to the union concept of strength through solidarity" and "a mandatory subject of bargaining in other than right-to-work states." The newsletter warned that incorporation could affect employees adversely "by weakening Unions and improving the edge business has at the bargaining table." . . . We cannot say that the Board erred in holding that this section of the newsletter bears such a relation to employees' interests as to come within the guarantee of the "mutual aid or protection" clause. . . .

The Board held that distribution of the third section, criticizing a presidential veto of an increase in the federal minimum wage and urging employees to register to vote to "defeat our enemies and elect our friends," was protected despite the fact that petitioner's employees were paid more than the vetoed minimum wage. It reasoned that the "minimum wage inevitably influences wage levels derived from collective bargaining, even those far above the minimum," and that "concern by [petitioner's] employees for the plight of other employees might gain support for them at some future time when they might have a dispute with their employer." We think that the Board acted within

the range of its discretion in so holding. . . .

In sum, we hold that distribution of both the second and the third sections of the newsletter is protected under the "mutual aid or protection" clause of § 7.

The question that remains is whether the Board erred in holding that petitioner's employees may distribute the newsletter in nonworking areas of petitioner's property during nonworking time. . . .

* * * * *

Petitioner contends that the Board must distinguish among distributions of protected matter by employees on an employer's property on the basis of the content of each distribution. . . .

We hold that the Board was not required to adopt this view in the case at hand. . . . Here, petitioner's employees are "already rightfully on the employer's property," so that in the context of this case it is the "employer's management interests rather than [its] property interests" that primarily are implicated. As already noted, petitioner made no attempt to show that its management interests would be prejudiced in any way by the exercise of § 7 rights proposed by its employees here. Even if the mere distribution by employees of material protected by § 7 can be said to intrude on petitioner's property rights in any meaningful sense, the degree of intrusion does not vary with the content of the material. Petitioner's only cognizable property right in this respect is in preventing employees from bringing literature onto its property and distributing it there—not in choosing which distributions protected by § 7 it wishes to suppress.

On the other side of the balance, it may be argued that the employees' interest in distributing literature that deals with matters affecting them as employees, but not with self-organization or collective bargaining, is so removed from the central concerns of the Act as to justify application of a different rule. Although such an argument may have force in some circumstances, the Board to date generally has chosen not to engage in such refinement of its rules regarding the distribution of literature by employees during nonworking time in nonworking areas of their employers' property. We are not prepared to say in this case that the Board erred in the view it took.

It is apparent that the complexity of the Board's rules and the difficulty of the Board's task might be compounded greatly if it were required to distinguish not only between litera-

ture that is within and without the protection of § 7, but also among subcategories of literature within that protection. . . .

. . . This is a new area for the Board and the courts which has not yet received mature consideration. . . . For this reason, we confine our holding to the facts of this case

* * * * *

Case questions

1. How did the literature in this case differ from the literature in union organizing campaigns? Was this difference significant? Explain.

2. Does the Court hold that an employer may never prohibit the distribution of political literature by its employees on its property? Explain.

3. If the NLRB had resolved the issues in Eastex's favor and the union had appealed, would the Court have reversed the NLRB? Explain.

4. Could Eastex prohibit nonemployees from distributing the same literature on its property? Explain.

Although employers may within limits have no-solicitation/no-distribution rules for employees and outsiders, they may wish to violate their own rules by using company property and time to address employees and distribute antiunion literature. In determining whether such employer efforts constitute employer free speech under section 8(c) or an unfair labor practice under section 8(a)(1), the board has been cognizant of the enormous economic power employers have over their employees. Thus the employer may not make any statement containing threats against union supporters or promising benefits to those who do not support the union. An employer's predictions of adverse economic consequences following unionization are considered coercive unless the predictions are reasonably based on objective facts over which the employer has no control.

Although an employer has a captive audience when addressing employees on company property and time, the employer need not offer the union an equal opportunity to respond, so long as the employer's speech is not coercive. However, the board forbids even noncoercive speeches to captive audiences during the 24-hour period before a representation election. This election eve rule does not ban speeches where attendance is voluntary and on the employee's own time.

The board generally does not police campaign propaganda to assure its accuracy, relying on the opponent to rebut exaggerated or erroneous statements and on the ability of workers to determine who is telling the truth. However, in certain cases the board does concern itself with the truthfulness of preelection propaganda. If substantial misstatements are made in a campaign and the opponent does not have time to respond, the board will set aside the election results and order a new election. The more flagrant the misstatements and the more limited the opponent's opportunity to rebut, the more likely it is that the board will set aside the election results.

The board's policy regarding election campaign misrepresentations has oscillated rapidly in recent years. In 1962 it established the above rule in the case of *Hollywood Ceramics*.[1] In 1977, it reversed the *Hollywood Ceramics* doctrine in the case of *Shopping Kart Food Market, Inc.*, holding that elections would no longer be set aside solely because of misleading campaign statements.[2] However, it maintained this position for only one year. In *General Knit of California* the board overruled *Shopping Kart* and readopted its prior standard of reviewing allegations of election campaign misrepresentatives.

General Knit of California
99 LRRM 1687 (1978)

A certification election was conducted of the employees of General Knit of California, Inc. (employer). 134 ballots were cast in favor of representation by the United Steelworkers of America, AFL-CIO (petitioner), and 104 ballots were cast against the petitioner. The employer filed objections to the union's campaign conduct with the NLRB's regional director, charging that the union distributed leaflets which falsely listed the employer's net worth and its profits from the previous year. The figures in the leaflet made it appear that the employer had gathered considerable profits, when in fact it had sustained a $5 million loss. The regional director issued a report recommending that General Knit's objections be overruled and that the union be certified as the bargaining agent of the employer. General Knit filed exceptions with the Board to the regional director's report, and the union responded. The Board reversed.

Opinion of the Board:

*   *   *   *   *

. . . After much deliberation, we have decided that the principle expressed in the majority and concurring opinions in *Shopping Kart* is inconsistent with our responsibility to insure fair elections. Accordingly, we hereby overrule *Shopping Kart Food Market, Inc.*, and return to the standard of review for alleged misrepresentations most cogently articulated in *Hollywood Ceramics Company, Inc.* That standard indicates that:

"[A]n election should be set aside only where there has been a misrepresentation or other similar campaign trickery, which involves a substantial departure from the truth, at a time which prevents the other party or parties from making an effective reply, so that the misrepresentation, whether deliberate or not, may reasonably be expected to have a significant impact on the election.

In *Shopping Kart*, which itself overruled *Hollywood Ceramics*, a Board majority determined that elections would no longer be set aside solely because of misleading campaign statements.

In disagreeing with the principles of *Hollywood Ceramics*, the *Shopping Kart* majority, in essence, disagreed with the general proposition that misrepresentations may, in fact, affect the way employees vote and thereby undermine the integrity of our electoral processes. As support for its view, the *Shopping Kart* majority relied on certain findings of one empirical

---

[1] *Hollywood Ceramics Company, Inc.*, 140 NLRB 221 (1962).
[2] *Shopping Kart Food Market, Inc.*, 228 NLRB 1311 (1977).

study and what that study purported to prove. In that study, its authors attempted to verify empirically certain assumptions which they believed underlay the Board's regulation of election conduct—most importantly, the Board's assumption that electioneering by the employer and union affects the employee's decision as to how to cast his or her ballot. They concluded that this assumption was not supported by voter behavior in the 31 elections they studied. Rather, the authors found, on the basis of interviews with voters both before and after the elections involved, that the parties' electioneering had not affected the decision of 81 percent of the voters. Thus, 81 percent voted in accordance with the intent they expressed to interviewers prior to the bulk of the union-management campaign. From this finding, the authors concluded that the voters' decisions seemed to be determined by their attitudes toward unions and toward their jobs, both of which had been established prior to the campaign, and which for 81 percent of the voters remained unchanged during the campaign. Of the remaining 19 percent, 6 percent were undecided at the first interview, while 13 percent voted contrary to the intent they had expressed to interviewers immediately after the filing of a petition for an election. Interestingly, in at-tempting to determine how voters in these two groups made their voting decisions, the authors found that the votes of the undecided 6 percent correlated with their "familiarity" with the unions' campaigns. Thus, those employees who voted for a union recalled significantly more issues raised by the union than did those who voted against the union. A similar pattern existed for the 13 percent who switched their votes. Finally, the authors found that the votes of the undecided and switchers were determinative in 9 of the 31 elections; that is, in 29 percent of the elections they studied.

In evaluating the findings summarized above, the authors speculated that the campaign itself had had little effect on voting decisions, but that the extent of familiarity with and reaction to each side's campaign was determined by a voter's initial attitude toward unions in general. However, the study was not de-signed to investigate the actual reasons for the reaction of voters to the campaigns, and theirs is by no means the only possible conclusion to be drawn from the data. The results of 43 years of conducting elections, investigating objections, and holding hearings at which employees testify concerning their recollection of campaign tactics convince us that employees are influenced by certain union and employer campaign statements. Even the authors acknowledged that, of the 19 percent, those who ultimately voted against the union may have been influenced by the employer's campaign, even though they did not recall specific issues.

The authors' final recommendations, including the suggested deregulation of misrepresentations, were based on their findings vis-à-vis the 81 percent of voters rather than the 19 percent. Such a narrow focus might have been warranted if the authors had concluded either that the votes of the 19 percent had not affected the results of a significant number of elections or that the 19 percent, in deciding how to vote, had not based that decision on information provided during the campaign. But where, as this study indicates, not only are a substantial minority of employees influenced by the campaign, but their votes also affected the outcome of over a quarter of the elections, we find this persuasive evidence for maintaining reasonable procedures to insure that the employees exercise their franchise in an atmosphere free from substantial and material misrepresentations.

Even if this particular study were clearly supportive of all of the authors' conclusions, however, we would still not find it an adequate ground for rejecting a rule which had been well established for 15 years. While we welcome research from the behavioral sciences, one study of only 31 elections in one area of the country—although it may provide food for thought—is simply not sufficient to disprove the assumptions upon which the Board has regulated election conduct, especially since, in our experience, statements made by either side can significantly affect voter preference.

. . . In returning to the rule of *Hollywood Ceramics,* we are convinced that the rule better enhances employee free choice and the fairness of Board elections than did *Shopping Kart*. The *Hollywood Ceramics* rule further assures the public that the Board will not tolerate substantial and material misrepresentations made in the final hours of an election campaign and thereby gives stability to any bargaining relationship resulting from the election. The aims of insuring employee free choice, fairness of elections, and bargaining stability are high, but they are achievable under *Hollywood Ceramics*. It is for the foregoing reasons that we now return to the rule of that case.

Case questions

1. The empirical study mentioned in the instant case as being instrumental in the *Shopping Kart* decision is Getman and Goldberg, "The Behavioral Assumptions Underlying NLRB Regulation of Campaign Misrepresentations: An Empirical Evaluation," 28 *Stanford Law Review* 263 (1976); see also J. Getman, S. Goldberg, and J. Herman, *Union Representation Elections: Law and Reality* (1976), for the authors' final report on the study. Should such studies be the basis for NLRB decisions?

2. Will the board's return to the *Hollywood Ceramics* rule provide a vehicle for delaying the ultimate results of certification elections?

3. Does the board's present posture assume that workers are not mature adults capable of recognizing and evaluating campaign propaganda?

Besides forbidding threats and promises, the board prohibits employers from conferring benefits upon their employees for the purpose of affecting the election outcome. Such unilateral changes in employment conditions by an employer are an unfair labor practice where (1) the employer knew or should have known that a union was organizing when the changes were made and (2) the benefits appear to have been granted in order to interfere with the employees' decision to unionize.

Sometimes an employer will want to gauge the union's strength by interrogating employees. An employer's questioning of employees will be evaluated in the context of the whole campaign. Isolated interrogations are generally not regarded as sufficiently coercive to set aside an election, but, depending on the closeness of the election, may constitute illegal interference. If an employer desires to determine how many employees support the union, a secret poll of the employees may be conducted, provided the employer observes the following safeguards: (1) the poll's purpose must be to test the validity of the union's claim of majority status; (2) the employees are made aware of this purpose; (3) assurances against reprisals are given; and (4) the employer has not previously committed any unfair labor practices or created a coercive atmosphere.

Company domination of or assistance to unions

An employer commits an unfair labor practice if it dominates a union, interferes with a union's formation or administration, or contributes financial or other support to a union. For example, an employer may take an active part in organizing a union or a committee to represent its employees, bring pressure upon employees to join a particular union, or play favorites with one of two or more unions which are competing to represent its employees. These would all constitute unfair labor practices.

In remedying such practices, the board distinguishes between domination of a labor organization and conduct which amounts to no more than illegal interference. When a union is found to be dominated by an employer, the board will order the organization completely disestablished as a representative of employees. But if the union is found to have been supported by employer assistance amounting to less than domination, the board usually orders the employer to stop such support and to withhold recognition from the organization until it has been certified by the board as a bona fide representative of employees.

Employer discrimination. Section 8(a)(3) forbids employers to discriminate against employees for the purpose of encouraging or discouraging membership in any labor organization. For example, employers cannot demote or discharge an employee for urging fellow workers to join or organize a union.

This section does not limit the employer's right to discharge, transfer, or lay off an employee for genuine economic reasons or for just cause, such as disobedience or bad work. This applies equally to employees who are active union advocates and to those who are not. However, the fact that a lawful reason for the discharge or disciplining of any employee may exist does not entitle an employer to discharge or discipline an employee when the true reason is the employee's union activities or other activities protected by the law.

Union misconduct. Section 8(b) prohibits a union from restraining or otherwise coercing employees in the exercise of their self-organizational rights. The protections and restrictions upon free speech applicable to employers also apply to unions. Thus expressions of union opinion are protected, but coercive statements constitute an unfair union labor practice. Examples of union misconduct include mass picketing in such numbers that nonstriking employees are physically barred from entering the plant, and threats to employees that they will lose their jobs unless they support the union's activities.

Section 8(b)(7) bans recognitional and organizational picketing but permits informational picketing. Thus a union that is not certified to represent an appropriate unit of employees cannot picket, or threaten to picket, the employer to force recognition by the employer or to force the employees to accept the union as their representative. Such recognitional or organizational picketing violates the NLRA where: (1) another union has already been recognized by the employer as the employees' representative and the board will not conduct an election because of an existing contract with another union; (2) the employees voted in a valid board representation election within the preceding 12 months; or (3) the union pickets for more than 30 days without filing a normal petition for an employee representation election.

A union's informational picketing is, however, protected. Informational picketing is picketing for the purpose of truthfully advising the public that an employer does not employ union members or have a contract with a labor organization. The protection accorded to informational picketing is lost where its effect is to induce individuals employed by others to refuse to pick up or deliver goods or perform other services.

REGULATION OF COLLECTIVE BARGAINING

Once the union has been certified as the representative of the employees, the business of bargaining with the employer begins. The union and the employer must now negotiate a collective bargaining contract establishing the wages, hours, and working conditions of the employees. The process of collective bargaining is examined in two phases: the negotiation of the collective contract and the administration of the agreement.

Negotiating the collective bargaining contract

Section 1 of the NLRA expresses the national labor policy as follows:

> It is hereby declared to be the policy of the United States to eliminate the causes of certain circumstances obstructing the free flow of commerce . . . and to mitigate and eliminate these obstructions when they have occurred . . . by encouraging the practice and procedure of collective bargaining.

This policy is promoted in other sections of the act. Section 8(a)(5) requires an employer to bargain collectively with the certified bargaining representative of the employees. Section 9(a) confers exclusive representation status upon the certified union. Section 8(d) imposes an obligation of good faith bargaining upon both parties. The following materials examine these sections by looking first at the duration and scope of the union's representative authority, the duty to bargain in good faith, and the subjects of bargaining.

Duration and scope of union authority.   Because a newly elected union needs time to establish itself and implement its programs, it is permitted a "reasonable period" to achieve its promised goals through collective bargaining. The board interprets a "reasonable period" as one calendar year from the certification date. Thus the union is presumed to represent a majority of the employees for one year, and an employer cannot refuse to bargain during that time because it believes that the union no longer commands the confidence of the majority of its employees. This is true even if the employees no longer want the union as their representative. The rationale for not permitting the employees to switch representatives for one year is that to permit such switches to occur so easily would contradict the NLRA goal of promoting industrial stability.

Once the union has been certified as the choice of a majority of employees, it is given exclusive representation status for all employees. The employer may not negotiate individual contracts with individual employees. The certification binds all members of the bargaining unit to the act's policy of majority rule. The employer must bargain directly with the exclusive representative that the employees have selected.

Duty to bargain in good faith. Section 8(d) defines the type of collective bargaining that is required as follows:

> [T]o bargain collectively is the performance of the employer and the representative of the employees to meet at reasonable times and confer in good faith with respect to wages, hours, and other terms and conditions of employment. . . . [B]ut such obligation does not compel either party to a proposal or require the making of a concession.

Collective bargaining usually begins with the union making a request for a meeting of the parties. It is common practice for the union to request in writing, shortly after certification, that the employer meet with it for the purpose of negotiating a contract.

Section 8(d) requires that both parties "meet at reasonable times." The act contains no precise requirements regarding the time and place of negotiations. A reasonableness standard is used. However, an employer cannot use excessive delays or other dilatory tactics to avoid negotiating with a union.

Under the act it is an unfair labor practice for either party to refuse to bargain in good faith. The act does not require the parties to reach an agreement, but it prohibits bad faith bargaining designed to avoid a contract.

The board uses two standards to assess the bargaining faith of parties. Some practices are held to be per se violations of good faith bargaining; and some practices are viewed as evidencing bad faith but are considered in light of other practices to see whether the total circumstances add up to bad faith bargaining. Examples of per se violations are: refusing to bargain at all; insisting on an illegal provision in the contract; refusing to execute a written contract; for an employer, unilaterally changing some aspect of wages, hours, and working conditions during negotiations without consulting the union; for an employer, refusing to negotiate because the employees are out on a lawful strike; and for a union, refusing to enter into a written contract of reasonable duration.

As noted, Section 8(d) does not require the parties to arrive at an agreement. Frequently the parties in good faith bargaining simply cannot agree. The act is not interpreted to require endless discussion when an agreement is not possible. Thus, if the parties reach a valid impasse, after good faith bargaining, negotiations may be stopped. This usually results in a strike.

Subjects of bargaining. There are three categories of bargaining subjects: mandatory subjects, permissive subjects, and prohibited subjects. The classification of a subject into one of these categories determines whether the parties must discuss it or be held to having committed an unfair labor practice, whether they may decide to discuss it voluntarily, or whether they should not waste time discussing it because any agreement on the subject would not be binding.

If either party makes a proposal on a mandatory subject during negotiations, the other party cannot refuse to bargain on the proposal. Section 8(d) requires bargaining on "wages, hours, and other terms and conditions of employment," but the NLRA does not define what subjects can be classified as falling under these headings. However, by its decisions the board has developed what may be described as an exhaustive list of mandatory subjects. These include retirement benefits, vacations, rest periods, and work assignments.

Permissive subjects are those that either party may refuse to bargain on without committing an unfair labor practice. Among permissive subjects are corporate organization, the size of the supervisory force, and the location of plants.

Neither the board nor the courts will enforce agreements on prohibited subjects. Illustrations of prohibited subjects are: provisions for a closed shop (requiring that the employer hire only union members) and hot cargo clauses (stating that workers will not be required to handle goods of a nonunion employer).

The following case reveals the complexity of these classifications.

Fibreboard Paper Products Corp. v. *NLRB*
379 U.S. 203 (1964)

The employees of Fibreboard (appellant) were represented by Steelworkers Local 1304. Fibreboard, concerned with the increasing costs of its maintenance operations, decided to contract out this work to an independent company and lay off its maintenance employees. It refused to bargain with the union over the decision to contract out. The NLRB held that Fibreboard had violated section 8(a)(5), and the D.C. Circuit Court of Appeals affirmed. The Supreme Court also affirmed.

Mr. Chief Justice Warren:

* * * * *

. . . We are concerned here only with whether the subject upon which the employer allegedly refused to bargain—contracting out of plant maintenance work previously performed by employees in the bargaining unit, which the employees were capable of continu-

ing to perform—is covered by the phrase "terms and conditions of employment." . . .

The subject matter of the present dispute is well within the literal meaning of the phrase "terms and conditions of employment." A stipulation with respect to the contracting out of work performed by members of the bargaining unit might appropriately be called a "condition of employment." The words even more plainly cover termination of employment which, as the facts of this case indicate, necessarily results from the contracting out of work performed by members of the established bargaining unit.

The inclusion of "contracting out" within the statutory scope of collective bargaining also seems well designed to effectuate the purposes of the National Labor Relations Act. One of the primary purposes of the Act is to promote the peaceful settlement of industrial disputes by subjecting labor-management controversies to the mediatory influence of negotiation. The Act was framed with an awareness that refusals to confer and negotiate had been one of the most prolific causes of industrial strife. To hold, as the Board has done, that contracting out is a mandatory subject of collective bargaining would promote the fundamental purpose of the Act by bringing a problem of vital concern to labor and management within the framework established by Congress as most conducive to industrial peace.

The conclusion that "contracting out" is a statutory subject of collective bargaining is further reinforced by industrial practices in this country. . . . Experience illustrates that contracting out in one form or another has been brought, widely and successfully, within the collective bargaining framework. Provisions relating to contracting out exist in numerous collective bargaining agreements, and "[c]ontracting out work is the basis of many grievances. . . .

* * * * *

The facts of the present case illustrate the propriety of submitting the dispute to collective negotiation. The Company's decision to contract out the maintenance work did not alter the Company's basic operation. The mainte-

nance work still had to be performed in the plant. No capital investment was contemplated; the Company merely replaced existing employees with those of an independent contractor to do the same work under similar conditions of employment. Therefore, to require the employer to bargain about the matter would not significantly abridge his freedom to manage the business.

The Company was concerned with the high cost of its maintenance operation. It was induced to contract out the work by assurances from independent contractors that economies could be derived by reducing the work force, decreasing fringe benefits, and eliminating overtime payments. These have long been regarded as matters peculiarly suitable for resolution within the collective bargaining framework, and industrial experience demonstrates that collective negotiation has been highly successful in achieving peaceful accommodation of the conflicting interest . . . although it is not possible to say whether a satisfactory solution could be reached, national labor policy is founded upon the congressional determination that the chances are good enough to warrant subjecting such issues to the process of collective negotiation. . . .

* * * * *

Case questions

1. What factors led the Court to conclude that contracting out is a mandatory subject of collective bargaining?

2. May the employer never unilaterally decide to contract out bargaining unit work?

3. Is there a difference between bargaining about the effects a decision will have on the employees and bargaining about the decision itself? Explain.

Administering the collective bargaining contract

Although many issues affecting employment may be resolved in the collective bargaining contract, controversies will continue to arise after the parties have entered into the contract. The parties are obligated to bargain in good faith over its interpretation. The settlement of contract interpretation disputes is often left to an arbitrator.

Arbitration.   Arbitration is a process in which the parties submit issues for decision by a mutually agreed upon third party. It differs from mediation, a process in which the third party attempts to persuade the parties to reach an agreement. Most collective contracts contain an arbitration clause, providing for certain grievance and arbitration procedures to resolve contract interpretation disputes. The clause generally outlines a grievance procedure, and it establishes a method for choosing an arbitrator if the issue cannot be resolved in the early stages of the grievance procedure.

The arbitrator's authority is governed by the contract's arbitration clause. Most contracts contain broad arbitration clauses, authorizing the arbitrator to decide all disputes regarding the interpretation and application of the contract. Sometimes controversy arises over whether a dispute is arbitrable or whether it must be decided by a court. The presumption is that the dispute is arbitrable. This means that if the parties do not wish to have disputes decided by arbitration, they must explicitly withdraw arbitration from their contract.

The arbitrator's authority is confined to deciding disputes under the contract. That is, the arbitrator decides disputes involving the contract's application by using the contract as the governing document. Where contract interpretation is the issue, the arbitrator uses the law of the shop, meaning that the past practice of the parties will be examined to give meaning to the contract's wording.

Board deferral to an arbitrator's award.   Some disputes involve issues of both contract interpretation and possible unfair labor practices. Where a dispute involves both an arbitrable issue and a possible unfair labor practice, and an arbitrator has made an award, the board generally does not exercise its discretionary jurisdiction.

Judicial deferral to an arbitrator's award.   In three cases decided on the same day by the Supreme Court, the Court established a policy favoring judicial deferral to arbitration awards. These cases, involving the United Steelworkers and collectively called the Steelworkers Triology, held that the merits of an arbitration award are irrelevant when a federal court is asked to enforce it. If a claim comes within an arbitration clause, the court must order the matter to be resolved by arbitration. Once the arbitrator has made an award, judicial review is limited to whether the award was within the authority conferred upon the arbitrator by the collective contract. The Court's decision to defer to the arbitrator on the merits of the case rests on the recognition that arbitration is part of a system of industrial self-government, that there is a law of the shop in which an arbitrator has special expertise that courts generally lack.

Court enforcement of collective contracts.   If a dispute is not governed by an arbitration clause, the NLRA permits a party to bring suit for breach of contract in federal court. This generally occurs with violations of a no-strike clause.

A no-strike clause manifests the union's agreement not to strike during the duration of the collective contract. It is agreed to in return for the company's agreement to submit contract disputes for arbitration. If a strike occurs while the contract is still in effect, the company may sue in federal court for an injunction against the strike and for an order to submit the dispute to arbitration.

REGULATION OF UNION CONDUCT AND COUNTERVAILING EMPLOYER ACTION

Although the national labor policy promotes industrial peace through collective bargaining, occasionally bargaining efforts fail to produce agreement and the parties resort to their economic weapons. The economic weapon of labor is the strike; the economic weapon of employers is the lockout. Both are work stoppages. The following discussion examines strikes, with focus on the legal alternatives that employers have when picket lines go up.

Regulation of strikes

The NLRA regulates strike activity. Section 7 provides that workers may engage in concerted activity. Section 13 grants workers the right to strike, subject to certain limitations. What follows is a look at unlawful strikes, against which an employer may seek an injunction; the regulation of picketing; and how employers may treat strikes.

Unlawful strikes. Although the NLRA protects the worker's right to strike, certain strikes are nevertheless unlawful. Any violent strike may be enjoined, and any striker guilty of violence may be discharged.

Secondary strikes are also unlawful. A secondary strike is a strike against an employer for doing business with a nonunionized employer. Under section 8(b)(4) a hot cargo agreement is illegal. Thus any strike designed to accomplish the goal of such an agreement is illegal.

Regulation of picketing. Most strikes involve picketing, which consists of patrolling a particular locality, usually outside the employer's business premises, with signs expressing the workers' opinions about their employer. The purposes of picketing are to encourage workers to continue striking, to discourage others from replacing them on the job, and to win public sympathy and support. Mass picketing which disrupts deliveries to the employer may be enjoined. Secondary picketing may also be enjoined.

Secondary picketing—sometimes called a secondary boycott—is the application of union pressure against a party with which the union has no dispute, with the goal of persuading that party to stop dealing with the employer and thus inducing the employer to acquiesce in the union's demands. If an employer reserves a plant entrance for the exclusive use of outside contractors, the union violates the secondary boycott provisions of the act if it pickets that entrance. This is known as the reserve gate rule.

Problems arise in distinguishing primary from secondary picketing. They are exemplified by the following case.

Sailor Union of the Pacific (Moore Dry Dock)
92 NLRB 547 (1950)

The union (respondent) had a dispute with Samsoc Corporation, the owner of the S.S. Phopho, a shipping vessel. The Phopho was undergoing repairs at Moore Dry Dock, an independent company. While at Moore Dry Dock, the Phopho was training sailors aboard ship.

The union picketed the entrance to Moore Dry Dock, carrying signs saying that the Phopho was unfair. Moore employees refused to work on the Phopho. Moore filed secondary boycott charges.

Opinion of the board:

* * * *

Section 8(b)(4)(A) is aimed at secondary boycotts and secondary strike activities. It was not intended to proscribe primary action by a union having a legitimate labor dispute with an employer. . . . The difficulty in the present case arises therefore, not because of any difference in picketing objectives, but from the fact that the Phopho was not tied up at its own dock, but at that of Moore, while the picketing was going on in front of the Moore premises.

In the usual case, the *situs* of a labor dispute is the premises of the primary employer. Picketing of the premises is also picketing of the *situs;* . . . But in some cases the *situs* of the dispute may not be limited to a fixed location; it may be ambulatory. . . . We hold in the present case, that, as the Phopho was the place of employment of the seamen, it was the *situs* of the dispute between Samsoc and the Respondent over working conditions aboard the vessel.

. . . Essentially the problem is one of balancing the right of a union to picket at the site of its dispute as against the right of a secondary employer to be free from picketing in a controversy in which it is not directly involved.

When a secondary employer is harboring the *situs* of a dispute between a union and a primary employer, the right of neither the union to picket nor of the secondary employer to be free from picketing can be absolute. The enmeshing of premises and *situs* qualifies both rights. In the kind of situation that exists in this case, we believe that picketing of the premises of a secondary employer is primary if it meets the following conditions: *(a)* The picketing is strictly limited to times when the *situs* of dispute is located on the secondary employer's premises; *(b)* at the time of the picketing the primary employer is engaged in its normal business at the *situs; (c)* the picketing is limited to places reasonably close to the location of the *situs;* and *(d)* the picketing discloses clearly that the dispute is with the primary employer. All these conditions were met in the present case.

(a) During the entire period of the picketing the Phopho was tied up at a dock in the Moore shipyard.

(b) Under its contract with Samsoc, Moore agreed to permit the former to put a crew on board the Phopho for training purposes during the last two weeks before the vessel's delivery to Samsoc. . . . The various members of the crew commenced work as soon as they reported aboard the Phopho. . . . The crew were thus getting the ship ready for sea. . . . We find, therefore, that during the entire period of the picketing, the Phopho was engaged in its normal business.

(c) Before placing its pickets outside the entrance to the Moore shipyard, the Respondent

Union asked, but was refused, permission to place its pickets at the dock where the Phopho was tied up. The Respondent therefore posted its pickets at the yard entrance which, as the parties stipulated, was as close to the Phopho as they could get under the circumstances.

(d) Finally, by its picketing and other conduct the Respondent was scrupulously careful to indicate that its dispute was solely with the primary employer, the owners of the Phopho. . . .

*   *   *   *   *

. . . Accordingly, we shall dismiss the complaint in its entirety.

*   *   *   *   *

Case questions

1. On whose premises was the labor dispute located? Why did this create problems?

2. What four factors must be present for common situs picketing to be legal? How were they present in this case?

3. Would the result have changed if there had been no crew members aboard ship at the time of the picketing?

4. Assume that the union's dispute was with Moore, and that the crew of the *Phopho* refused to board the ship because to do so it would have to cross the union's picket line. Is the union's picketing legal?

Employer treatment of strikers. Economic strikers retain their employee status unless they are permanently replaced. An employer therefore may discharge economic strikers. If a collective bargaining contract is signed after a strike, the union and the company generally agree to the retention of workers who struck the employer. However, frequently the employer bargains for the discharge of certain strikers whom it believes to have engaged in violent behavior during the strike.

Because strikers retain their employee status, they continue to accumulate seniority during a strike. The employer may, however, lawfully discontinue disability payments to employees on sick leave at the start of a strike if it can reasonably conclude that they support the strike.

POLICY CONSIDERATIONS

American labor policy is based on an adversarial model. Federal labor legislation balances labor organizations against management in a symbiotic relationship to achieve the best mix of the interests of each. Thus institutionalized conflict, which is viewed as essential for maintaining the integrity of free collective bargaining, accentuates any natural dichotomy between the two groups.

American labor policy may be reconciled with other governmental policy promoting a free enterprise economy. Labor is simply another cost of doing business, and just as management must be prepared to negotiate the cost of supplies with suppliers, it must be prepared to negotiate the cost of labor with employee representatives. Federal labor policy seeks to promote balanced, fair, and peaceful bargaining by insuring employees' freedom to engage in concerted activity with employers while protecting both employers and employees against unfair labor practices.

The adversarial model of labor relations in the United States differs from the labor policies of other capitalist countries, most notably the countries of Western Europe. In most Western European countries cooperation, not conflict, is the thrust of labor relations policy. Perhaps the most striking example of this is the concept of codetermination.

Under codetermination, sometimes called "industrial democracy" or "participatory management," workers share in management decision making by participating on corporate boards of directors and plant works councils. Thus employee representatives may have voting seats or sit in a consultative capacity on corporate boards of directors and participate in the formulation of corporate policy. Employee representatives may also sit on works councils, plant-level committees consisting of management and labor representatives. The works council implements policy at the plant level. For example, it may decide such matters as plant production schedules and employee discipline cases. The objective of codetermination is to instill a spirit of cooperation into labor-management relations from the top levels of corporate policy determination to policy implementation on the shop floor.

The existence of codetermination on the Continent and its absence in the United States suggest that labor-management relations in the two areas are developing in different directions, or at least that they are at different stages of development. The existence abroad of alternative forms of labor relations may spur American management to experiment with such forms. This raises the issue of whether section 8(a)(2) of the NLRA prevents experimentation of this kind. That is, would the creation of employee-employer management teams and the placing of worker representatives on corporate boards constitute employer domination and interference with the formation or administration of labor organizations? If so, then to what extent should American labor policy preclude experimentation with new forms of labor relations? To what extent should federal labor policy be predicated on protecting and promoting collective bargaining? To what extent should labor-management cooperation be considered a part of federal labor policy? To some, the innovative forms of labor relations signify enlightened management. To others, they are tokenist alternatives to the extension of collective bargaining, means of appeasing workers in order to keep unions out. The direction of American labor relations law will depend on which view dominates.

Review problems

1. The Cabot Carbon Company operated a number of plants in Texas and Louisiana for the purpose of manufacturing and selling carbon black and oil field equipment. Pursuant to a suggestion of the War Production Board in 1943, Cabot decided to establish an

Employee Committee at each of its plants. Cabot prepared, in collaboration with employee representatives from its plants, a set of bylaws stating the purposes, duties, and functions of the Employee Committees for transmittal to and adoption by the employees. The bylaws were adopted by a majority of employees at each plant, and thus the Employee Committees were established. According to the bylaws, the committees' purposes are to provide a procedure for considering employees' ideas and problems of mutual interest to employees and management, provide a fixed term of committee members, provide for regular elections of employees to the committees, and handle grievances at nonunion plants. The International Chemical Workers Union, AFL–CIO, filed with the NLRB an unfair labor practice charge against Cabot, alleging that Cabot was unlawfully dominating, interfering with, and supporting labor organizations. Has Cabot violated the NLRA?

2. The United Automobile, Aerospace, and Agricultural Implement Workers, Local 588, represents the employees of an automobile parts stamping plant operated by the Ford Motor Company. For many years Ford has provided in-plant food services to the employees. These services, which include both cafeterias and vending machines, are managed by ARA Services, Inc., under a contract with Ford whereby ARA provides the food services in exchange for reimbursement of costs and a 9 percent surcharge on receipts. Over the years Ford and the union have negotiated about food services. Their local contract has included provisions covering the staffing of service lines, the restocking and repair of vending machines, and menu variety. Ford, however, has always refused to bargain about the prices of food items. Ford notified the union that cafeteria and vending machine prices would be increased by unspecified amounts. The union requested bargaining over prices and services and asked for information regarding Ford's involvement in food services. These requests were refused by Ford. The union filed an unfair labor practice charge with the NLRB. Will the union succeed in obtaining an NLRB order to bargain on the union requests? Explain.

3. Safeco Title Insurance Company does business with several title companies that derive over 90 percent of their gross income from the sale of Safeco insurance policies. When contract negotiations between Safeco and the Retail Store Employees Union Local 1001, the bargaining representative of certain Safeco employees, reached an impasse, the employees went on strike. The union picketed each of the title companies, urging customers to support the strike by canceling their Safeco policies. Safeco and one of the title companies filed complaints with the NLRB charging that the union had engaged in an unfair labor practice. Will the board order the union to cease and desist picketing?

4. Without notice to its employees' bargaining agent, an employer closes its restaurant and lays off the staff. About a week later the restaurant reopens as a self-service cafeteria, the kitchen staff is recalled, and the waitresses are notified that they cannot expect to return to work. Has the employer violated the NLRA?

5. The XYZ Corporation manufactures widgets at seven different plants scattered throughout the country. It has decided to close one plant entirely. Must it bargain about the decision with the union?

6. Grossinger's, Inc., is a resort hotel. Its employees, primarily waiters, waitresses, kitchen workers, lifeguards, and camp counselors, live in housing provided by Grossinger's. They eat all of their meals on the grounds. They are allowed to use the hotel's recreational facilities on their time off. Consequently, many rarely leave the premises. The Hotel and Restaurant Workers Union is trying to organize Grossinger's employees. Can Grossinger's prohibit the union from distributing its literature on Grossinger property? Why or why not?

7. Wallace Widget Work's work force is 57 percent white and 43 percent black. Wallace has never discriminated on the basis of

race in hiring or layoffs. There have been some recent layoffs in which employees with the least seniority were let go. About half of these employees were black and half white. During an election campaign the International Widget Workers distributed leaflets which stated, among other things: "If all blacks don't vote together in a group and the union loses the election, all blacks will be fired. Wallace is already using the slow period as an excuse to fire blacks." About a week before the election Wallace placed in each employee's pay envelope a leaflet entitled "The Truth about Layoffs" which provided a breakdown by race of all employees laid off. The union won the election. Will the NLRB set it aside?

8. Prior to an election the employer showed the film *And Women Must Weep*, which depicts an illegal strike accompanied by picket line violence and the shooting of the newborn baby of an employee who crossed the picket line. The union showed the film *Anatomy of a Lie*, which responds to the first film. Both films claim to be based on real incidents. Both contain distortions and falsehoods. Should the board set the election aside if the union wins? If the union loses?

9. General Motors operated a leasing division which leased GM trucks. It decided to sell the division to an independent franchisee. The franchisee was given a license to use GM's trademarks and to lease GM trucks. The decision forced GM to lay off several hundred employees represented by the UAW. Did GM violate section 8(a)(5) by not bargaining about the decision with the UAW?

10. What economic, political, and social differences may account for the differences between American and Western European labor relations policies?

CHAPTER 16

Labor standards and employee safety

During the first century of U.S. history, employment practices were established and regulated by the individuals involved. There was little need for governmental intervention, as the employment relationships that existed then were relatively simple. As the U.S. economy expanded and became more complex, employment relationships became more impersonal and the need for regulation emerged. The industrial revolution drastically altered traditional work conditions and employment practices. In response to these changes Congress sought to enact legislation aimed at protecting the rights of workers.

Early attempts by Congress to regulate employment practices were frustrated by successful constitutional challenges. Such legislation was deemed to infringe upon the freedom to contract as guaranteed by Article 1, Section 10, of the Constitution and by the Due Process clauses of the 5th and 14th amendments. Gradually, however, judicial interpretation began to view contractual freedom as a limited right which could be abrogated by Congress under the power of the Commerce Clause and by the states under their police powers.

With the regulatory powers of government thus firmly established, Congress and state legislatures moved to enact much-needed social legislation designed to provide minimum labor standards and safety for the American worker. This chapter will examine some of that legislation.

FAIR LABOR STANDARDS

In 1938 Congress enacted the Fair Labor Standards Act (FLSA) in an attempt to combat the devastating effects of the Great Depression. The intent of Congress was to stimulate and stabilize the economy. Toward that end the FSLA regulates minimum wages, maximum hours, and child labor practices. In addition, the act provides for the administrative apparatus necessary to insure compliance and enforcement.

Wage and hour laws

By far the most important provisions of the FLSA are concerned with the regulation of wages and hours. Initially the act stipulated a minimum wage of 25 cents per hour and a maximum standard workweek of 44 hours. Any employee who fell under the act's coverage was guaranteed a wage of not less than the minimum wage for every hour worked up to 44 hours per week. For every hour over 44, a wage of not less than 1½ times the worker's regular wage was to be paid. Since their enactment in 1938 the wage and hour provisions have been amended many times. As of January 1, 1981, the minimum wage under the FLSA was $3.35 per hour and the standard workweek was 40 hours.

Effect on employment relations. The primary effect of the FLSA's wage and hour provisions has been to establish certain standards by which employment practices are measured. The act does not regulate the method, means, or system by which wages or other compensation is paid. The provisions of the FLSA explicitly deny giving employers grounds to break or alter existing, valid employment contracts, except as necessary to bring wages and hours into line with the act's minimum standards. However, nothing in the act forbids employers from modifying noncontractual wage and hour levels, so long as the minimum standards are not violated.

Factors determining coverage. A comprehensive examination of the factors which determine the act's coverage is beyond the scope of this book. In general, however, coverage of employees under the wage and hour provisions of the FLSA can be divided into two categories. The first category comprises the traditional or individual coverage. As originally enacted, the FLSA covered only employees who were personally "engaged in commerce or in the production of goods for commerce." However, in 1961 Congress extended the act's coverage by adding the category of enterprise coverage. Under this category the act covers *all* the employees of a firm that engages in commerce. Thus, under the enterprise coverage category, the employer's activities, and not those of the individual employee, are determinative. The enterprise coverage extension ended a situation in which some employees of a particular employer were covered by the FLSA's wage and overtime laws, while other employees, because of their job tasks, were not covered.

Exemptions. Application of the act's standards to certain groups of employees and employers engaged in interstate commerce would be impracticable, inequitable, or impossible. To meet the needs of these groups Congress has explicitly exempted various occupations from some or all of the FLSA's provisions.

The occupations exempt from coverage have not remained constant since the initial enactment of the FLSA. Congress has tended to gradually remove exemptions and thus broaden coverage. Among the categories of workers who are currently exempt from some or all of the act's provisions are workers employed in certain phases of agriculture, commercial fishing operations, casual domestic service, and certain retail service positions. Executive, administrative, and professional personnel, outside salespersons, and child actors and performers are also exempt. These employees do not really need the wage and hour protection that the act affords, as they are normally able to protect themselves.

Minimum wage computation. The FLSA provides that in calculating wages paid, the reasonable cost of board, lodging, or other facilities furnished to employees shall ordinarily be included. For example, an employer could credit toward wages of waiters and waitresses the reasonable cost of the meals it regularly provides them.

The act also allows employers to pay apprentices, handicapped workers, and students wages below the applicable minimum hourly rate, provided that permission is granted by the secretary of labor. It permits an employer to pay a "tipped" employee as little as one half of the minimum wage as long as certain conditions are met. A tipped employee regularly receives more than $20 a month in tips. An employer may credit the tips received by a tipped employee to up to 50 percent of the applicable minimum. The employer must inform tipped employees of the FLSA's credit provisions.

Determination of overtime compensation. The calculation of overtime wages can be complicated. One source of difficulty is the fact that two formulas exist for determining how much overtime compensation is due. Applicable law treats employees engaged entirely in private business differently from those engaged in selling goods or services to the government.

The FLSA governs minimum wage and overtime standards for private employment. A parallel law, the Walsh-Healey Act, governs minimum wage and overtime standards for all employees on all government contracts exceeding $10,000 in value. As previously stated, the FLSA requires that at least 1½ times the regular wage be paid for each hour worked over 40 hours per workweek. The Walsh-Healey Act, by contrast, sets a series of minimum wages for each occupation, based on comparable wages in private industry for similar jobs. The Walsh-Healey Act requires that 1½ times the regular wage be paid for every hour worked *over 8 hours per workday* as well as every hour worked over 40 hours per workweek. Thus employers on government contracts may be required to pay overtime even though their employees are not on the job more than 40 hours a week. The distinction between the two laws can cause considerable confusion to employers, especially to those that engage simultaneously in providing goods and services to both the government and the private sector. For such employers, each employee's activity determines which regulatory act applies. However, unless separate employment records are kept, there is a presumption that everyone in a plant with a government contract is working on it.

Another source of difficulty in calculating overtime wages arises whenever compensation other than the employee's regular wage is paid. An employee's regular wage is the basis for computation of overtime payments. However, the regular wage may include some forms of nonstandard compensation, such as an incentive bonus or a profit-sharing plan. If such a nonstandard form of compensation is paid, it must be included in the employee's regular wage for purposes of overtime computation. This provision can cause a good deal of confusion. Fortunately for employers, many forms of nonstandard payments are statutorily excluded from the provision. The excluded payment forms include Christmas bonuses, reimbursements for expenses, and completely discretionary bonuses. However, nondiscretionary awards objectively based on performance are not excluded and must be taken into account in overtime wage computation.

The following case illustrates some of the basic principles involved in calculating overtime pay under the FLSA.

Mumbower v. *Callicott*
526 F.2d 1183 (8th Cir. 1975)

Loraine Mumbower (plaintiff) brought suit against her former employers, H. R. Callicott and others (defendants), charging violations of the maximum hour and overtime provisions of the FLSA and seeking recovery of unpaid overtime compensation. The district court entered judgment for defendants. The court of appeals reversed and remanded the case, with instructions to the district court to award plaintiff her unpaid overtime compensation.

Gibson, Chief Judge: Prior to July 26, 1968, plaintiff worked with three other women as a part-time switchboard operator for the answering service, then partly owned by her ex-husband, defendant Callicott. On that date Callicott and others purchased the business from the joint owners. . . . At the time of the purchase by Callicott, plaintiff agreed to operate the switchboard by herself for $80 per week, maintaining the same hours as before, 8:00 A.M. to 6:00 P.M., six days per week, with one hour for lunch. Up to the time of her discharge in August, 1973, her hours gradually decreased and pay increased.

*   *   *   *   *

. . . Plaintiff testified that Callicott determined the hours the switchboard was to be open. However, no employment records were maintained. She testified that she arrived early on a regular basis and usually received a call from Callicott at 7:30 A.M. with instructions for the day. He requested her to perform duties such as admitting the janitor, opening the mail, posting checks, maintaining a record of accounts in Callicott's office, obtaining the appointment book of a customer, Dr. Walter, from his nearby office to take the day's appointments, reviewing customers' daily itineraries, and meeting with customers who picked up their packages and messages. These duties she performed regularly between 7:30 a.m. and 8:00 a.m. with Callicott's knowledge and "tacit" approval before the switchboard opened. . . .

Plaintiff also testified that she was instructed by Callicott to remain on duty after the switchboard officially closed to transmit daily messages to customers calling in. Her hours thus extended fifteen to thirty minutes beyond the official closing. . . . She further testified that she had complained of her inability to take lunch periods because no one was available to replace her. . . .

[The District Court] held she was not entitled to additional overtime compensation for the reason that her overall pay was in excess of the current minimum wage of $1.60 per hour. . . .

Section 7(a) of the FLSA requires an employee to be paid overtime compensation for hours worked in excess of forty per week "at a rate not less than one and one-half times the *regular rate* at which he is employed." This provision has been uniformly interpreted to require the fifty percent overtime premium to be added to the actual wage paid, not to the statutory minimum wage for hours up to forty, with the "intended effect" of requiring extra pay for overtime even for employees whose hourly wages exceed the statutory minimum. This principle applies to employees hired on a weekly as well as an hourly basis.

* * * * *

. . . For employees paid weekly, absent explicit proof of a mutual agreement for a rate of pay capable of delineation in hourly terms, the court must infer that the "regular rate" is substantially that calculated by dividing the total weekly compensation by the number of hours scheduled in the workweek. In the instant case no explicit agreement was made, stipulating a weekly wage inclusive of regular and overtime compensation for a workweek in excess of forty hours, from which the appropriate "regular" hourly rate can be derived by formula. Consequently, on remand plaintiff's actual "regular rate" of pay must be recalculated by dividing her weekly salary by the number of scheduled hours worked and her overtime compensation reassessed at time and a half her regular rate for the period embraced by the complaint.

On remand it will also be necessary to reassess the number of hours actually worked by plaintiff for the reason that the District Court's computation was apparently induced by an erroneous view of the law defining hours worked. The court held that the plaintiff was not entitled to be paid for her lunch hours spent at the switchboard, nor for the time she performed duties before and after the scheduled switchboard hours, because such work was not part of "her arrangement as to when she would keep the board open." However, liability under the Act depends not upon formal or agreed arrangements between employer and employee limiting work hours but upon the number of hours the employee is actually permitted to work for the employer's benefit.

The term "work" is not defined in the FLSA, but it is settled that duties performed by an employee before and after scheduled hours, even if not requested, must be compensated if the employer "knows or has reason to believe" the employee is continuing to work, and the duties are an "integral and indispensable part" of the employee's principal work activity. . . .

* * * * *

. . . Defendants' contention that plaintiff agreed to the conditions of her scheduled workweek is no defense. . . . The employer's obligation to pay premium overtime compensation, whatever the regular rate of pay, is statutory and cannot be waived or substituted by an agreement to work for less.

Case questions

1. What is meant by an employee's "regular rate" of compensation?

2. How is overtime compensation computed when an employee is paid a weekly wage and not on an hourly basis?

3. Why is Loraine Mumbower entitled to overtime compensation?

Child labor laws

In addition to governing minimum wage and maximum hour standards, the FLSA regulates the use of child labor in private employment. The first congressional attempts to restrict child labor were found unconstitutional by the Supreme Court. With judicial evolution, regulation of child labor practices, like wage and hour standards, was eventually held to be within the power of Congress under the Commerce Clause.

Generally, the child labor provisions of the FLSA prohibit the shipment in interstate commerce of any goods produced in an establishment where any oppressive child labor has been employed. In addition, the FLSA empowers the secretary of labor or representatives to conduct investigations of all child labor practices and to require proof of age for all employees.

Determination of "oppressive child labor." Congress desired to eliminate wage exploitation of children and to eliminate child labor in industrial manufacturing plants, while encouraging school attendance. Notwithstanding these goals, the child labor laws apply uniformly to all child labor practices, whether or not they are exploitative or oppressive.

The particular employment practices that constitute "oppressive child labor" are determined by the secretary of labor and vary according to type of occupation. The child labor provisions of the FLSA do not apply to employees over 17 years old. Employment of minors 16 or 17 years old is restricted, but not entirely prohibited, in industries declared by the secretary of labor to be hazardous. The hazardous industries include coal mining, logging, roofing, explosive work, and excavating work. Employment of 16- and 17-year-olds is not restricted in nonhazardous occupations. Children 14 and 15 years old may only be employed in certain approved jobs. These approved jobs are primarily in retail, food, and gasoline service establishments and in school-supported or -administered work experience and career exploration programs. Subject to explicit exceptions, employment of children 13 years old or younger is prohibited.

Exemptions. To meet the special requirements of certain occupations the FSLA exempts them from compliance with its child labor provisions. These exemptions relate largely to agricultural employment. Subject to regulations regarding hours, school obligations, and the job task, children may generally be employed in agriculture at an earlier age than would otherwise be allowed. For example, even children under the age of 12 may be employed on a farm if parental consent is given and other conditions are met. Child actors and performers are similarly exempt from the child labor laws.

Administration and enforcement

To insure compliance and provide for enforcement of the FLSA's regulations, Congress established an elaborate new bureaucratic agency.

The Wage and Hour Division. The agency created to oversee enforcement of the FLSA is the Wage and Hour Division of the Employment Standards Administration, which is part of the Department of Labor. The Wage and Hour Division is headed by an administrator who is appointed by the president with the advice and approval of the Senate. The administrator is charged with promulgating rules and regulations pertaining to the act's interpretation and enforcement, employment regulations and restrictions, and the record-keeping and notice-posting requirements of employers. The administrator and his or her representatives are empowered to conduct investigations into alleged violations and to initiate inspections of employers' premises and employment records. If the administrator or the secretary of labor feels that such action is warranted, suit may be brought under the direction and control of the attorney general to restrain violations of the act. Though the powers of the Wage and Hour Division's administrator are broad, his or her actions are always subject to review by the courts and by Congress.

Judicial proceedings. Legal action against employers allegedly in violation of the wage and hour laws can be brought both by the injured employees and by the secretary of labor on behalf of the injured employees. Generally, injured employees can collect unpaid minimum wages, overtime compensation, and liquidated damages (a sum equal to twice the amount of unpaid compensation). The secretary of labor may sue and collect the same on behalf of injured employees. In addition, the secretary may seek an injunction restraining an employer from failing to pay the required minimum or overtime wage or violating any other provision of the FLSA.

Both federal and state courts have jurisdiction to hear suits concerning violations of the FLSA's provisions. In addition to civil suits, criminal proceedings may be brought against employers who willfully violate the act. As used by the courts, willfulness does not require evil intent. It is instead defined as a deliberate or purposeful failure to comply. Mere mistake or oversight is not enough to constitute willful violation.

UNEMPLOYMENT COMPENSATION

In 1933, at the height of the Great Depression, 25 percent of the American work force was unemployed. The vast majority of these 13 million workers had little or no outside income with which to support themselves and their families. The resulting hardship so severely suffered by so many gave great impetus to the creation of governmental unemployment compensation plans, a form of social insurance taken for granted today.

The federal law

Congress could not constitutionally force the states to adopt unemployment compensation plans. It could, however, use the federal taxing power to pressure state legislatures into complying with congressional wishes. Through the use of a tax offset procedure, Congress accomplished its goal. Though only Wisconsin had an unemployment insurance (UI) plan in 1935, by 1937 all the states and several territories had established such plans.

Under the tax offset procedure, a federal unemployment tax was imposed on all covered employers. If, however, the employers made contributions to a federally approved state UI system, they could be relieved of paying to the federal government an amount equal to their state contributions, up to 90 percent of the federal tax. Thus, enacting an approved state UI plan provided benefits for the state's unemployed without putting in-state employers at a competitive disadvantage. If a state did not enact an approved plan, employers in that state would pay the same amount anyway, but unemployed workers would receive no benefits. In addition, federal provisions allowed state plans to collect less from employers with good unemployment records than from employers with poor unemployment records. This gave employers an incentive to maintain a stable work force. Given the choices provided by the tax offset procedure, it is easy to see why all the states quickly adopted UI systems.

Coverage. Though the basic structure of the federal UI system has remained the same since 1935, Congress has expanded the system's coverage by taxing a greater number of employers and by bringing new categories of workers within the system. For example, beginning in 1956 the federal unemployment tax was assessed on all employers of four or more employees in at least 20 different weeks of the year, as opposed to only those with eight or more employees, as originally enacted. In 1970 coverage was extended further to include employers of at least one employee who works a minimum of 20 weeks of the year and employers who had a quarterly payroll of at least $1,500.

In 1955 Congress extended coverage to employees of the federal government, and in 1958 unemployed ex-servicemen were included. A 1960 amendment added employees working in commercial and industrial activities of nonprofit organizations, and a 1970 law extended coverage to workers in the charitable, educational, and scientific areas of such organizations.

As initially enacted, the federal unemployment tax applied to an employer's entire payroll. However, this generated more funds than were needed. At present, the federal unemployment tax applies to the first $6,000 of each employee's annual wages.

Congress has varied the net federal percentage in accordance with revenue needs. While the tax offset percentage has remained at 2.7 percent of total taxable wages since 1938, the net federal portion of taxable wages has varied. Employers are currently subject to federal unemployment tax rate of at least 3.4 percent (states may adopt higher tax rates) of the first $6,000 of each employee's annual wages. Of this amount, 0.7 percent must go to the federal government, and, ignoring experience-rating rebates, 2.7 percent to an approved state UI plan.

State unemployment insurance programs

Though no two state systems are identical, certain generalizations can be made about state benefit plans. Eligibility for state unemployment benefits is usually based on having earned at least a specified, average minimum income during a base period, which is usually 52 weeks. The required minimum earnings range from $300 to $1,000. The minimum earnings requirement is designed to insure that benefits go to workers newly unemployed and not to people who have not recently been gainfully employed. Generally, individuals may not receive benefits if they voluntarily leave employment without cause. Employees who quit work, are fired for misconduct, or are out of work as a result of a labor dispute are usually not eligible for benefits.

Beneficiaries are often made to wait a period of time before receiving payments, are usually not compelled to accept work drastically different from their former employment, and are generally required to actively seek employment while receiving benefit payments.

Most states set a maximum duration for the payment of benefits. However, both the federal government and the state can extend the duration of benefit payments if economic conditions warrant such action. Published economic indicators, such as the national unemployment level, sometimes trigger extension of the payment duration when a predetermined level has been reached.

The amount of unemployment compensation received weekly is generally some percentage of average base period earnings. To determine a given benefit percentage of a worker's full-time earnings, most states compute the weekly benefit by using the worker's average earnings during the highest one or two quarters, thus reflecting most closely the worker's full-employment earning levels.

From the worker's standpoint, the most important benefit provisions are often those pertaining to minimum and maximum allowable payments. In most states the maximum weekly payments range from $100 to $150, though these levels vary greatly and tend to increase as wage levels rise. The minimum levels of most states are about $10 to $25.

Experience-rating provisions. Experience-rating provisions allow an employer whose work force has historically experienced low unemployment to pay less tax than is paid by an employer whose work force experiences recurrent high unemployment. Depending upon the particular experience-rating method used, an employer with a good record can substantially reduce the tax (in some states, no tax at all is required of employers with the best rating), while an employer with a bad rating may have to pay the entire tax. In any case the net federal tax must be paid. It is only the contribution to the state plan that can be reduced.

An obvious effect of the experience-rating provisions is that employers have an incentive to keep unemployment to a minimum. It is financially advantageous for employers to keep their former employees off the unemployment rolls. If an employer can prove that the employee quit or was dismissed with cause, unemployment benefits will be denied and the employer's experience rating maintained.

A less obvious and somewhat detrimental effect of the experience-rating provisions is that the aggregate taxes which the business sector must pay are highest when unemployment is high and lowest when unemployment is low. This means that employers bear a greater tax burden during economic downturns, which are almost always accompanied by high unemployment.

SOCIAL SECURITY

The Social Security Act of 1935 created a federal social insurance system designed to prevent the severe financial hardship that so many elderly persons suffer upon entering retirement. Under the system employees are compelled to pay a certain percentage of their annual income to the government during their entire working lifetime. Upon attaining retirement age, the contributors become eligible to receive various benefit payments from the general social security fund.

At first, the social security system was narrow in scope, providing only limited retirement benefits and covering only individuals in certain occupations. Its coverage burgeoned, however, until today virtually every employed person in America is protected by some form of social security. Though benefits are conditioned on the actual contributions of employees, benefit formulas are now heavily weighted to favor the lower-income worker. In addition, since the system's medicare provisions were enacted, elderly beneficiaries have received protection from the skyrocketing costs of medical care.

Old-age, Survivors, and Disability Insurance

In common usage, when people refer to social security, what they are talking about is Old-age, Survivors, and Disability Insurance (OASDI). The OASDI program is a compulsory retirement plan. All except a very few working Americans contribute to, and are covered by, OASDI. Persons not covered by OASDI are generally protected by similar plans, such as those created by the Railroad Retirement Act and the Civil Service Retirement Act.

Payment of social security taxes.   Taxes paid into the social security fund are governed by the provisions of the Federal Insurance Contributions Act. The collection of these taxes is handled by the Internal Revenue Service in much the same way as the collection of income taxes. Social security taxes on employees are withheld on a pay-as-you-go basis. In addition, each employer is required to contribute a matching amount to the social security fund.

The social security tax rate applies only to the wage base, or all gross income earned up to a statutory maximum. The wage base has been increased constantly over the years, and recently it has grown rapidly. From 1978 to 1981 it rose nearly 68 percent, from $17,700 to $29,700.

The social security tax rate is the same for all contributing workers, regardless of annual income. Thus the rate structure is regressive, as the tax paid by someone earning $100,000 per year is currently the same as that paid by someone earning less than a third of that amount. Like the wage base, the social security tax rate has been increased over the years. The rates for the years 1980 through 1982 are, respectively: 6.13 percent, 6.65 percent, and 6.70 percent.

Benefit provisions of OASDI. Unlike the public programs of old-age social insurance which exist in some countries, OASDI is not based on the principle of universal coverage, that is, coverage of the entire population. Rather, coverage is conditioned upon having substantially participated in the active work force, though the minimum requirements for eligibility are not stringent. Coverage for employed persons is compulsory and immediate. Thus the OASDI system can be viewed as a device by which currently employed persons are forced by law to contribute to the maintenance of retired and disabled workers. Financial need is not generally a condition of eligibility for benefits under OASDI.

Eligibility conditions. Eligibility is based on the number of quarters of coverage an individual has been credited with during employment. One quarter of credit is earned for each calendar quarter in which at least $50 in income was earned ($100 for self-employed individuals).

There are three categories of insured status. Fully insured status grants eligibility for all types of old-age and survivor benefits. In most cases, for an individual to achieve fully insured status his or her quarters of coverage must equal or exceed the number of years elapsing after 1950 or since the attainment of age 21. Currently insured status yields eligibility for some survivor benefits. It is achieved by having at least six quarters of coverage in the 13-quarter period ending with death, disability, or the attainment of age 62. Disability status gives eligibility for disability benefits and is usually achieved by having at least 20 quarters of coverage in the 40 quarters preceding disablement. (There are special provisions for young disabled workers who have been in the labor force for less than 20 quarters.) An individual's insured status is used to determine his or her benefits and beneficiary category.

Benefit formulas. Benefit amounts are calculated from a complicated formula which is modified from year to year to account for cost-of-living increases. As mentioned, the benefit formulas are heavily weighted in favor of lower-income contributors. Thus the benefits for those on the bottom of the wage scale are likely to be greater than their actual average monthly wage, while the benefits for upper-income contributors are certainly less than their average monthly wage.

Recipient earnings test. The earnings test is generally used to screen out individuals who are still gainfully employed. Benefits are not paid to retirees or survivors who are still engaged in substantial employment. Benefit payments are adjusted downward for every dollar the beneficiary earns over a statutory minimum. However, as the adjustment is less than 100 percent of earnings above the minimum, there is still some incentive to remain employed past the attainment of retirement age. Moreover, the earnings test is not applicable to beneficiaries over 71 years old.

Medicare

In addition to the OASDI system, the Social Security Act governs an extensive health and medical care insurance program for old and disabled persons. Enacted in 1965, the program is officially entitled Health Insurance for the Aged and Disabled, though it is more commonly referred to as medicare.

Medicare coverage consists of two distinct insurance plans. The first, Hospital Insurance (HI), provides hospital and related benefits to all persons who are at least 65 years old and are entitled to receive OASDI or Railroad Retirement benefits. The second medicare plan is Supplementary Medical Insurance (SMI), which covers all persons over age 65 and all disabled persons covered by HI. This plan provides benefits for physicians' services and related medical services. SMI coverage is provided only on a voluntary basis. Unlike HI and OASDI benefits, which are provided as a matter of entitlement once eligibility has been established, SMI coverage must be elected by its beneficiaries, who pay a premium in partial financial support of the plan. If an eligible person elects SMI, the federal government will pay an amount at least equal to the person's premium. SMI closely resembles private health insurance plans; but the coverage is partly subsidized by the government.

PRIVATE PENSION PLANS

Private pension plans were introduced over a century ago, but they have become important to retirement planning only in the last 50 years. Very few employers offered pension plans prior to 1900, and in the early 20th century the development and acceptance of such plans were slow. Pension benefits were almost universally recognized as being gratuitous rewards from grateful employers to faithful employees. Benefit payments were largely discretionary, as few employers assumed any legal obligation to make them. Many early pension plans stated specifically that no employee rights were created thereunder and that the employer could terminate the plans or reduce their benefits at any time. Gradually, however, the pension movement gained acceptance. By the end of World War II, the private pension plan had become a significant means of combating financial hardship in old age.

Until recently private pension plans were left largely unencumbered by federal regulation. They were subject only to provisions of the Internal Revenue Code, which had limited regulatory objectives, and to a few scattered, rather specific federal laws. Before 1974 there was no all-inclusive law or body of law designed to control the formation and operation of pension plans. The diversity of the practices and pension provisions which developed during this period ultimately served as the catalyst in the movement toward a uniform, regulatory law.

The Employee Retirement Income Security Act

In 1974 Congress passed a comprehensive and complex new law designed to effect sweeping reforms in private pension plans. Officially entitled the Employee Retirement Income Security Act, the law is more commonly known by its acronym, ERISA. Several hundred pages in length, ERISA ambitiously attempted to bring uniformity to pension planning by prescribing acceptable and prohibiting unacceptable practices for pension plans. In general, pension plans must meet ERISA's requirements. One of its more important provisions involves the time within which benefits must vest.

Under ERISA, employers implementing pension plans must affirmatively select one of three vesting schedules, ranging from 100 percent vesting after 10 years of service to partial or graduated vesting beginning at an earlier date. Prior to ERISA, many pension plans did not vest accrued benefits. Thus an employee who was discharged after 24½ years of service would not receive any pension at all under a plan requiring 25 years of service. The outrage generated by such abusive practices was instrumental in the movement for pension reform.

There is no doubt that prior to ERISA's enactment the regulatory laws governing private pension plans did not adequately protect employees from various abuses. Many of the reforms instituted by ERISA were much needed and have been successful. However, the impact of ERISA has not been entirely positive. ERISA remains highly controversial and much criticized. Though originally written to crystallize and protect the rights of pension plan beneficiaries, ERISA threatens the very existence of the pension movement. Its requirements are so stringent and costly that many employers would rather not offer a pension plan than comply with its provisions. As a practical matter, however, most employers that now offer plans are unable to terminate them and are therefore obliged to conform to ERISA's requirements.

STATE WORKERS' COMPENSATION STATUTES

Workers' compensation statutes at the state level protect workers and their families from the risks of injury, disease, or death resulting from the workers' employment. These statutes were a response to the harshness of certain common-law concepts which made employee recovery from employers extremely difficult. This section discusses the common law background and origin of workers' compensation statutes. It also examines the scope of coverage and benefits of current statutes and some of the more common issues that arise in determining whether coverage should be afforded in a particular case.

Common-law background

At common law an employee injured in the course of employment could sue the employer whose negligence caused the injury. Negligence is the failure to exercise ordinary care in such a way as to injure another person whom it is one's duty to protect against harm. Ordinary care is that degree of care which a reasonable person would exercise under the circumstances. The reasonable person is a mythical figure who serves as the legal standard against which one's actions or nonactions are measured. An employer whose conduct falls short of that expected from a reasonable person has breached the standard of ordinary care. If that breach results in injury to an employee, the employer may be liable. (Negligence is discussed at greater length in Chapter 10.)

At common law, however, three legal defenses barred the employee from successful recovery against an employer in a negligence suit. The practical effect of these defenses was that the employer's liability was defeated and the employee was often forced to shoulder the economic loss of impaired earning power. This was true even though the employer was normally in a better position to assume the loss. These three employer defenses were the fellow servant doctrine, assumption of the risk, and contributory negligence.

The fellow servant doctrine. The fellow servant doctrine states that an employer is not liable to an employee who is injured as a result of a coemployee's negligence. The fellow servant defense prevented an employee from recovering against an employer for an injury if that injury resulted from a coemployee's negligence. The defense first emerged in 1837 in the English case of *Priestley* v. *Fowler* as an exception to the doctrine of *respondeat superior.*[1]

Respondeat superior is based on the relationship existing between master (employer) and servant (employee). Because of that relationship the negligent acts which an employee commits in the course of employment are imputed to the employer even though the employer was not directly involved in those acts. Under this doctrine of respondeat superior an employer is liable to a third party for the negligent acts of its employee if those acts were committed within the scope of the employment. The doctrine is grounded on the policy judgment that the employer has vouched for its employee and is normally in a better financial position than the employee to assume the loss.

In *Priestley* the employer, a butcher, was held not liable for the injury to one of his employees which resulted from the negligent overloading of a van by a second employee. Lord Abinger based this exception to respondeat superior on a "parade of horribles" argument which depicted the alarming consequences of extending the master's responsibility to indemnifying employees for injuries resulting from the negligent acts of "fellow servants."

This exception, which came to be known as the fellow servant doctrine, was quickly imported into the United States. The first state court to adopt the doctrine reasoned that an implied contract between the employer and

---

[1] (1837) M&W 1, 150 Reprint 1030.

the employee relieved the former of liability. At a time when a laissez-faire economic philosophy prevailed and courts desired to spur industrial enterprise by mitigating its economic burdens, the fellow servant doctrine caught on rapidly and was soon extended throughout the states.

Assumption of the risk. Another prong of the *Priestley* decision was based on the observation that "the servant is not bound to risk his safety in the service of his master, and may, if he thinks fit, decline any service in which he reasonably apprehends injury to himself."[2] Accordingly, an employee is charged with appreciating the risk of injury that a particular job entails. If in the face of the normal dangers of a job, the employee nonetheless continues to work at it, then that employee is barred from recovery for injury under the doctrine of assumption of the risk. This doctrine was also imported into the United States.

Contributory negligence. The employer's responsibility to exercise ordinary care to protect employees against injury was further diminished by the defense of contributory negligence. This defense exonerated the employer of all liability where the employee's negligence contributed to bringing about the injury. Just as the common law recognized an employer's responsibility to exercise reasonable care to protect its employees from injury, the common law also recognized that the employees were obligated to exercise reasonable care for their self-protection. Thus the contributory negligence defense was available if an employer could demonstrate that an employee's breach of a standard of care contributed to an injury. If, for example, the employer negligently failed to warn an employee of a dangerous crevice in a mine, the employee would nevertheless be barred from recovery if the employee fell into the crevice while negligently ignoring the obvious danger. It should be noted that the contributory negligence defense was a complete bar to recovery by the employee. This was true even though the employee's negligence was slight compared to that of the employer.

Origin

With the advent of the industrial revolution and the consequent increase of industrial accidents there was an inclination to afford a remedy to employees who were handicapped by the common-law defenses.

Some courts mitigated the impact of the fellow servant and the assumption of the risk defenses by the *vice principal* and *nondelegable duty* rules.

The vice principal rule excluded from the fellow servant category all employees vested with supervisory authority over the injured employee. Under the vice principal rule an employee who was injured when a superior negligently assigned work on a defective machine would not be barred from recovery by the fellow servant doctrine. In such cases the doctrine of respondeat superior was applicable.

---

[2] Id.

The nondelegable duty rule held that the employer had a duty to provide a reasonably safe place to work which could not be negated by delegation. Inherent in this duty was a responsibility to instruct employees as to the safe use of the devices entrusted to them. An employer could not escape responsibility for injury sustained by an employee as a result of a coemployee's negligence if that negligence was due in part to the employer's failure to properly instruct the coemployee in safety conduct. The nondelegable duty rule was even expanded to require the employer to select employees with reasonable regard for their competence. Employees did not assume the risk for an employer's breach of a nondelegable duty. Because courts were reluctant to do more than soften the harsh results of the defenses, state legislatures began to act. The Georgia Act of 1855, for example, abolished the fellow servant defense for railway companies. Other states followed Georgia's lead, and some abolished the defense altogether.

A few states modified the severity of contributory negligence by legislating comparative negligence statutes under which the cost of the damages or injury incurred is borne by the two negligent parties on the basis of their comparative contribution. Such statutes generally provide for apportionment of damages according to degree of fault, so that although the contributory negligence of an injured employee will not bar recovery, it will reduce recovery in proportion to the employee's negligence.

Another method by which a few states sought to mitigate the harshness of the contributory negligence and assumption of the risk defenses was to abrogate those defenses in cases where injury resulted from an employer violation of a safety statute.

In 1903 the Federal Employers' Liability Act (FELA) was enacted. It was a pivotal event in the development of a workers' compensation employee protection system. FELA applied its coverage to employees of common carriers engaged in interstate or foreign commerce. It incorporated the best of the state modifications of the common law by legislating that:

1. Contributory negligence would only reduce damages but not completely bar recovery.
2. Neither contributory negligence nor assumption of the risk would apply in the event of employer safety statute violations.
3. A railroad employer was liable for the negligence of all officers and agents causing injury to employees.

In 1884 Germany became the first country to adopt a comprehensive modern workers' compensation system. In 1897 Britain adopted a national workers' compensation act. These early precedents provided impetus, inspiration, and illustration to the states. Maryland, in 1902, and Montana, in 1909, enacted compensation acts covering miners. By 1920 only eight states were without some type of workers' compensation law. By 1949 every state had some such law to cover specified employees. Although these laws vary from state to state, they possess some common features.

Coverage

The objective of workers' compensation laws is to provide assistance to injured employees, or to dependents in case of the employees' death, where injury or death results from an on-the-job injury. Fault is immaterial. Injured employees are entitled to benefits whether or not they were negligent and whether or not their employer was free from fault. In most states an injured employee cannot pursue an employer for damages beyond those allowed by the statute unless the employer has not complied with the workers' compensation law. The injured employee can still sue third parties who cause injury such as negligent coemployees or manufacturers of defective machines. However, the employer or the state workers' compensation insurance fund is usually indemnified from the recovery up to the amount that it paid out to the injured employee pursuant to the workers' compensation statute.

Coverage is granted by statute to employees as opposed to independent contractors. The basic distinction between an employee and an independent contractor turns on the degree of the employer's control over the worker. An employer controls the method and manner with which employees perform the work. If the employer does not retain control of these details of the work but is merely interested in its ultimate results, the worker is not an employee but an independent contractor. For example, a salesperson who sells magazines door to door on a solely commission basis is usually considered an independent contractor. Here the employer does not normally dictate the details of the work, such as its hours and methods. However, a magazine salesperson would probably be considered an employee if he or she were required as part of the job to attend sales meetings, to canvass a specified area, and to put in specified working hours. Often the distinction between an employee and an independent contractor is subtle, turning on particular facts of the contractual relationship.

Many states mandate that an employer provide coverage for its employees. In other states coverage is discretionary and an employer may elect to be under the umbrella of the workers' compensation law or to opt out. In almost all of the elective jurisdictions, both employer and employee have the right to reject coverage, but acceptance is presumed in the absence of express rejection. Normally some workers, such as agricultural and casual employees, are excluded from workers' compensation statutes.

Benefits

Although the benefits to covered employees vary from state to state, they normally include payment for hospital and medical expenses, including artificial appliances and rehabilitation services. They also include compensation for loss of wages. The amounts vary from one half to two thirds of the employee's average weekly wage. Some states require that an employee be out of work for a specified period of time, such as a week, before qualifying for loss-of-income benefits. Loss-of-income benefits may be divided into four categories: temporary total disability, temporary partial disability, permanent partial disability, and permanent total disability.

Temporary total disability is present when a work injury prevents an employee from returning to work for a specific time. As a result of some work injuries, employees return to lower-paying jobs for a specific time. Thus a textile mill threader whose threading finger and thumb were injured on the job might be able to return to lower-paying work. Here the wage impairment disability benefits are designated temporary partial and are computed on the basis of the diminution in wages. When disability is permanent but partial, many states provide for a determination of the percentage of permanent partial disability. That percentage is, by statutory guidelines, translated into a monetary award. An incurable occupational skin disease and an on-the-job neck injury which causes permanent loss of full rotational movement are examples of permanent partial injury. These injuries, though permanent, are partial since they do not bar the employee from all forms of gainful employment. A permanently and totally disabled employee is one who will never again be able to do any work at all. Some state statutes set up a presumption of permanent total disability when an employee loses any two limbs or eyes. In the absence of such a presumption the employee would have to show that the injury in fact caused permanent incapacity to work.

In addition to these four forms of loss-of-income disability, many states provide for a loss-of-member compensation according to a statutory schedule for losses. For example, in Ohio the loss of a thumb is compensated by 60 weeks of benefits to the injured employee in a weekly amount equal to two thirds of the employee's average weekly wage. Most states also pay death awards to the employee's dependents or survivors.

Administration

Workers' compensation systems are usually administered by an agency which is referred to as an industrial commission or a workers' compensation bureau. A typical arrangement for the administration of compensation claims is used in Ohio.

In Ohio administrative control over the workers' compensation program is exercised by the Bureau of Workers Compensation. The bureau has two primary administrative functions: adjudication of claims and control of the general business management of the workers' compensation system.

A typical claim process begins when an injured employee fills out an application for workers' compensation benefits furnished to the employer by the administrator of the bureau. When the application is received by the bureau, it is checked for completeness and correctness, numbered, indexed, and docketed, so that it is ready for adjudication by a claims examiner. If the employer verifies the facts contained in the employee's claim, the claim is referred to as certified. Generally, the claims examiners allow all claims that the employer has certified. Certified claims constitute 85 percent of the total claims filed, and certification waives the employer's right to a formal hearing.

Claims examiners consider the proper payment of benefits in all certified claims, and the remaining claims are sent for investigation to the district office nearest the claimant's residence. About two thirds of the claims sent to the district office are accepted and processed without a formal hearing, so that only 5 percent of the total claims filed are contested and formally heard in the district office. The district hearing officer hears these cases.

The hearing is informal, and rules of evidence and procedure are substantially relaxed. Legal representation is optional. After the hearing officer's decision either the employer or the employee may file an application for a reconsideration hearing, which is almost routinely conducted in the central office by members of the administrator's staff. If a party is dissatisfied with the outcome of the reconsideration hearing, an appeal to the regional board is proper. The administrator, represented by the attorney general, becomes a party at this stage. A pretrial conference is held. This is followed by a hearing at which a decision is rendered. Either party may appeal the decision of the regional board to the Industrial Commission, which may hear the case or decline to hear it and thus let the regional board decision stand. A party who is still dissatisfied with the outcome may seek review in the court of common pleas, the trial court of general jurisdiction. Once the validity of an employee's claim is finally established, the employer must satisfy the award.

Funding

There are generally three accepted methods employed by state workers' compensation statutes by which an employer can provide funds for compensation benefits. These are private insurance, self-insurance, and payment into a state fund.

The amount paid by the employer is determined by various factors, including the type of industry and prior accident experience. Most states have official rating systems which are designed to determine the premiums necessary to pay all accepted claims. Rate determination is an administrative function and differs among the states. Many states have a merit rating system whereby an employer with a history of fewer injuries will receive a premium concession.

Compensable injuries

Injuries which arise out of the employment and happen in the course of the employement are normally compensable under workers' compensation acts. Determining whether an injury arose out of the employment often requires an examination of the relationship between the injury and the particular employment. Is the risk or hazard which resulted in injury peculiar to the type of work that the employee performed? If the answer is yes, then the injury arose out of the employment. For example, a bulldozer operator who is injured when th bulldozer overturns on an embankment has obviously sustained injury as a result of a risk peculiar to the job. But if a bulldozer operator is struck and killed by a low-flying plane, there is a serious question of whether the death arose out of the employment. The risks created by the plane appear to be no greater to the bulldozer operator than to the public at large. They are not peculiar to the job. However, many states grant recovery in such a case because but for the particular employment the injury would not have occurred.

Sometimes the relationship between the employment and the injury is amorphous. A serious question of compensability occurs when, for example, an employee suffers an epileptic seizure while working and as a result falls to the floor and sustains a head injury. Most courts today would probably deny recovery because the employee's preexisting epileptic condition was a contributory cause of the injury and was personal to the employee. The courts that deny recovery in such cases hold that the injury does not arise out of the employment because there is no causal connection between the epileptic attack and the job. More liberal courts allow recovery in these circumstances. They reason that the injury was caused by the impact with which the employee's head struck the floor and that such contact is a risk or hazard incident to the employment and hence compensable.

In addition to arising out of the employment, an injury must have occurred in the course of the employment. Here courts examine the time, location, and circumstances of the accident in relationship to the employment.

Courts have exhibited a liberal tendency in awarding compensation on a finding that an accident both arose out of and was in the course of employment. In *Minor* v. *U.S. Fidelity & Guaranty Insurance Co.* a police lieutenant accidently discharged his revolver and injured his hand while at home. The court found this to be an injury arising out of and within the course of his employment because the employee was always "on call," was normally armed with a revolver, and had gone home to change to his uniform pursuant to a departmental requirement.[3] In another case the Supreme Court of New Jersey upheld a workers' compensation award to an employee who was robbed and shot during his lunch break as he was returning to his place of employment after purchasing a soda and sandwich "to go."[4]

Going and coming rule. Among the most familiar and troublesome course of employment problems are those which involve the *going and coming rule.* Under this rule employees with a fixed place of employment and fixed hours of work are generally not compensated for injuries sustained while

---

[3] 356 S.2d 1049 (La. Ct. App. 1977).

[4] *Wyatt* v. *Metropolitan Maintenance Co.*, 74 N.J. 167, 376 A.2d 1222 (1977).

they are going to and from the actual site of employment. The reason for noncompensation in such instances is that these employees are not deemed to be within the course of employment. The converse of the going and coming rule is that employees usually recover for injuries if they have arrived on the job or have not yet departed from the job. It is not always easy to discern when an employee has actually arrived at or departed from work. In *Lee* v. *Cady* an employee on his way to work, in the act of reaching for the door handle of his place of work, slipped on the ice on the public sidewalk and was injured.[5] Even though the employee had actually crossed the employer's boundary, recovery was denied, as the employee was still "subject to the common risks" of the street.

Most courts apply the premises rule as a criterion for determining whether an employee is excluded from recovery under the going and coming rule. Under the premises rule an employee injured while on the employer's premises is not barred from recovery though going to or coming from the work site.

Employees whose work entails travel away from the employer's premises do not fit easily under the going and coming rule. Most jurisdictions find such employees to be continuously within the course of employment during a trip, except where a distinct deviation from the course of employment occurs.

It is generally agreed that carrying work-related items while going to and from work does not automatically negate the going and coming rule. An accountant carrying papers to work on at home in the evening would not normally be protected if injury resulted from a slip on the icy steps leading to his or her home. Normally an accountant could remain at the office to do the work, and taking the work home is only for the accountant's convenience. However, protection is afforded if on the way home an employee is performing a service to an employer which needs to be accomplished outside the employment situs. For example, where an employee mails letters in a postbox on the way home, the trip possesses a business purpose which would have caused someone to make it even if it had not coincided with the employee's personal journey home. Hence, notwithstanding the going and coming rule, most courts would permit recovery for injuries incurred on the way to the postbox.

Horseplay. Engaging in horseplay may remove an employee from the course of employment category. However, the innocent victim of horseplay is not automatically deemed outside the course of employment and will normally be compensated. For example, in *Burns,* v. *Merritt Engineering Co.* a coemployee offered the injured party a drink from a bottle purported to contain gin.[6] It actually contained carbon tetrachloride, and the worker be-

---

[5] 294 Mich. 460, 293 N.W. 718 (1940).
[6] 303 N.Y. 131, 96 N.E.2d 739 (1951).

came violently ill and disabled after drinking the contents. Despite a rule in his employment contract that forbade drinking alcohol on company property, the court determined that the injury occurred in the course of employment and was compensable.

The factors which courts consider in determining whether a participant should be compensated for injury in horseplay cases include the extent of the deviation from employment, the seriousness of the deviation, and whether some horseplay is normally expected in the course of the employment involved. Some states permit recovery even to instigators of horseplay.

Mental injury.   In recent years courts have been faced with an increased number of cases in which employees seek recovery for mental injury. Courts have taken varied approaches to such cases, and three distinct categories of cases have emerged. The first category comprises cases in which a physical injury sustained at work results in mental illness or injury. A worker who receives an electric shock while working on an electric wire may, in addition to incurring physical harm, experience psychic injury such as a phobic reaction to electric wires or a hysterical paralysis. Here courts have had little difficulty in compensating the full injury, including the mental portion. The second category comprises cases in which a mental impact or mental stimulus encountered on the job results in distinct physical injury. For example, fright due to a sudden noise or an electric flash may result in a cerebral hemorrhage or heart failure. Compensation is generally awarded in such cases. Other cases in this category involve physical injuries which result, not from a single traumatic episode, but from the cumulative effect of mental pressure over a period of time. An employee may sustain a heart attack because of years of on-the-job mental strain. In most jurisdictions workers' compensation coverage in such cases turns on the connection between the work and the injury. If the strain or exertion caused by employment contributed to the injury, it will be compensable regardless of other contributing factors. The third category is the most troublesome. It involves mental injury absent physical impact. The jurisdictions split regarding the compensability of such injuries.

Occupational disease.   All states provide coverage for occupational diseases, though compensation in this area has lagged behind compensation for occupational accidents. Generally coverage is granted for any disease arising out of exposure to harmful conditions of employment when those conditions are present in a greater degree than exists in employment generally. Hence lung and skin disorders, allergies of all types, and even loss of hearing have been the subject of compensation awards for occupational diseases. Some courts have even gone so far as to compensate the aggravating effect of "compensationitis," a psychological disorder which causes symptoms of an injury to continue past the normal recovery period.

In the following case, the court was confronted with the issue of whether psychological problems resulting from a buildup of stress over time is a compensable occupational disease.

Transportation Insurance Co. v. Maksyn
567 S.W.2d 845 (Tex.Civ.App. 1978)

Transportation Insurance Company (plaintiff-appellant) filed suit to set aside an award granted to Joe Maksyn (defendant-appellee) by the Texas Industrial Accident Board. Maksyn sought to recover workers' compensation benefits from Transportation Insurance on the basis of an occupational disease sustained in the course of his employment. He claimed that the pressures of his employment had caused him to suffer from anxiety depression, which culminated on September 4, 1974. He asserted that this disorder had caused numbness of his hands and feet, high blood pressure, and vertigo. A jury returned a verdict in favor of Maksyn. It found (1) that Maksyn had an occupational disease as a result of traumatic repetitious physical activities extending over a period of time; (2) that the occupational disease sustained by Maksyn arose out of and in the course of his employment; (3) that the occupational disease was a cause of his total incapacity, which began on September 4, 1974; and (4) that the total incapacity was permanent. Judgment was entered for 40 weekly payments of $70 each for total permanent incapacity, attorney fees, and interest. The Texas Court of Civil Appeals affirmed the judgment of the trial court.

Klingman, Justice:

* * * * *

Defendant, at time of suit, was 62 years old. He began working with the Express-News Publishing Company in 1932 when he was 17 years of age, as a copy boy. He was later promoted to assistant merchandise manager, to display advertising salesman, to production manager, to administrative executive, and finally to advertising service manager, a position that he held for approximately 28 years.

Defendant testified that he never worked less than 55 hours a week and frequently worked for 65 hours a week. His work schedule ran from Monday through Saturday and he generally worked some time on Sunday. He stated that at night he would receive phone calls from the office and many times had to return to work at night and that he frequently took work home.

Defendant testified that during the week before September 4, 1974, he worked 87½ hours, and that on the evening of September 4, 1974, he started feeling bad, that he felt pressure in his head and felt like he was going to black out. He then went home and went to bed and the next morning when he tried to get up, he felt weak and dizzy and later that day he went to his family physician. He thereafter returned to his office and advised his superiors of his illness and requested that he be given vacation time, which was granted. He remained on vacation for three weeks. On the fourth week, he began working approximately three to four hours a day. The following week, he worked approximately four to five hours a day, and the following week approximately seven to eight hours a day. On October 28, 1974, he was retired by his employer. At that time, he was sixty years of age.

* * * * *

In 1971, the Texas Legislature amended the section of the Workmen's Compensation Act relating to the definition of "injury" and "occupational diseases," which new provision is as follows:

. . . Whenever the term "Occupational Disease" is used in the Workmen's Compensation Laws of this State, such [terms] shall be construed to mean any disease arising out of and in the course of employment which causes damage or harm to the physical structure of the body and such other diseases or infections as naturally result therefrom. An "Occupational Disease" shall also include damage or harm to the physical structure of the body occurring as the result of repetitive physical traumatic activities extending over a period of time and arising in the course of employment; provided, that the date of the cumulative injury shall be the date disability was caused thereby.

* * * * *

Plaintiff argues vigorously that it was not the intent of the Legislature to include mental traumatic activities and discusses in some detail the legislative background in connection with such amendment to [the Act], and points out that the House version of the amendment omitted the word "mental" from that of the Senate version. However, it is noteworthy that the amendment as adopted provides in Section 5, as follows:

It is the express intent of the Legislation in enacting this Act that nothing contained in this Act shall ever be deemed or considered to limit or expand recovery in cases of mental trauma accompanied by physical trauma.

* * * * *

We have found no Texas cases holding that recovery will never be permitted for mental injury or mental disease, and, as we construe the applicable cases, the court seems to be saying not that there can never be a recovery for a mental injury or mental illness, but that the claimant must produce sufficient probative evidence to convince the jury.

There is a conflict of authorities in out-of-state jurisdictions with some out-of-state jurisdictions holding that a disabling mental condition brought about by a gradual buildup of emotional stress over a period of time and not by one exceptional injury causing event, is not compensable unless accompanied by physical force or exertion.

* * * * *

Other out-of-state jurisdictions have reached a contrary result. . . .

* * * * *

Plaintiff argues that the disability here involved results purely from mentally traumatic activities and as such is not compensable under the Workmen's Compensation Act. The record here shows that the disability resulted from a combination of physical and mental activities including exceedingly long working hours, nerve racking working schedule, continuous pressure, strain, overwork, and physical exhaustion culminating in high blood pressure, numbness in some parts of the body, dizziness, vertigo and, ultimately, inability to work. There was ample evidence of a combination of physical and mental activities that produced the occupational disease here involved, and it is clear that the claimant has suffered damage or harm to the physical structure of his body.

Case questions

1. Do you think the court violated the plain meaning of the statute when it considered the term *physical structure* to include injury to mental faculties?

2. Is there a line of demarcation between physical and mental injury? What is it?

3. Do you see a valid distinction between a psychic injury that results from a single traumatic event and one that results from a slow buildup of stressful activities? Explain.

OCCUPATIONAL SAFETY AND HEALTH PROTECTION

Until recently the federal government's provision for safety protection extended to only very limited classes of workers. These included railroad employees, coal miners, maritime workers, and workers under certain federal construction and service contracts. Consequently, the states were left with the responsibility of assuring safe working conditions for the bulk of the labor force. Death, disability, and disease resulting from on-the-job conditions reached epidemic levels in the third quarter of the 20th century. Each year about 14,000 workers died, 2¼ million were disabled, and 400,000 contracted occupational diseases. During the entire period no less than 25 million workers, including those who sustained nonserious injuries suffered from industrial accidents. The prospects for a healthy future for the American worker were dim. Every 20 minutes a new potentially lethal chemical was introduced into the industrial environment. In the 1950s and 1960s, with the advent of atomic energy, laser beams, microwave equipment, and other technological innovations, concern about industrial health reached new heights.

Yet even in the late 1960s the states were not insuring adequate protection for the labor force. Eight states made no provision for health or safety, and the remaining states averaged less than 35 inspectors to enforce health and safety standards. In the wake of these somber conditions and of pressure from various labor-oriented groups, Congress passed the Occupational Safety and Health Act (OSH Act) in 1970. The act marked a new era in safety and health protection for about 60 million members of the work force.

Coverage

Congress passed the OSH Act under its constitutional authority to regulate interstate commerce. Any employer that is "engaged in a business affecting commerce" and has at least one employee is covered by the act, unless specifically exempted. Virtually any effect on interstate commerce is sufficient to bring a business within the "affecting commerce" provision.

Excluded from compliance with the OSH Act are employers that fall within its scope but are exempted from its requirements because they are regulated by federal agencies created under other acts which exercise statutory authority to prescribe or enforce safety or health standards or regulations. These acts include the Coal Mine Safety Act, Railway Safety Act, and Nuclear Regulatory Act, all of which involve extrahazardous industries. Also excluded from OSH Act compliance are employers of domestic household employees and religious organizations whose employees are engaged in religious activities.

Administration

The secretary of labor administers the OSH Act. The act established three federal administrative agencies: the Occupational Safety and Health Administration, the National Institute of Occupational Safety and Health, and the Occupational Safety and Health Review Commission. The Occupational Safety and Health Administration (OSHA), which is within the Department of Labor, is charged with conducting inspections and enforcing compliance with the OSH Act. OSHA is also responsible for formulating and enacting safety and health standards and is assisted by the National Institute of Occupational Safety and Health (NIOSH) toward those ends. NIOSH, which is housed in the Department of Health and Human Services, makes safety standard recommendations to the secretary of labor based on its research into occupational diseases and health-related problems in the workplace. NIOSH is also responsible for developing programs designed to educate and train employers and employees to recognize and avoid unsafe working conditions. Finally, the Occupational Safety and Health Review Commission (OSHRC) is an independent agency created by the act, whose duties are to hear appeals from OSHA citations, abatement period determinations, and proposed penalties. OSHRC has three members who are appointed by the president for staggered six-year terms. When an employer, an employee, or a union files an appeal to OSHRC, an administrative law judge assigned to a regional office will normally hear the case. The decision of the administrative law judge is appealable to the full commission, which may review the judge's decision. OSHRC's final order is appealable to a U.S. court of appeals by any adversely affected party. The final possible step is an appeal to the U.S. Supreme Court, which reviews these decisions by certiorari.

Duties

The OSH Act imposes standards upon the employer and the employee. It contains a general duty clause which requires the employer to provide a place of employment free from "recognized hazards causing or likely to cause death or serious physical harm to employees" and to comply with all OSHA health and safety standards. Employees, in addition, must comply with all the OSHA rules.

Courts generally agree on four criteria that must be present to trigger the general duty under the OSH Act. First, the hazard must be from a condition arising from employment. Second, the condition must be generally recognized in the industry as a hazard, and the employer must or should know this. For example, although carbon monoxide fumes cannot be perceived by the senses, an employer in a chemical processing industry would be charged with recognizing the hazard through the use of monitoring devices. In addition, NIOSH published pursuant to the act a list of over 64,000 toxic substances. Any of the substances listed is a recognized hazard since employers are on notice of the list. Third, there must be a causal connection between the condition and the likelihood of serious physical harm. Since the recognized hazard must cause or be likely to cause death or serious physical harm, its effect must be substantial. A hazard which would probably result in dizziness or a minor abrasion would not qualify as a recognized hazard. However, recognized hazards would include hazards that result in injuries which cause temporary disablement requiring in-hospital care. Finally, the hazard must be preventable in the course of business. If these four criteria are met, the employer has an absolute duty to remove the hazard.

The OSH Act further requires employers to comply with specific occupational safety and health standards promulgated under the act. OSHA standards adopted by the secretary of labor pursuant to the act, require employer compliance with specific conditions, methods, operations, or processes. The specific standards are printed in an easily available OSHA publication. As previously stated, NIOSH is charged with recommending to the secretary of labor the adoption of such standards. Specific standards have been adopted by the secretary in connection with asbestos, carcinogens, vinyl chloride, and coke oven emissions. In addition, the secretary has adopted standards from federal safety requirements imposed on contractors under the Walsh-Healey Act as a condition of their contracts with the federal government. The Longshoremen's Act, National Service Contract Act, and Arts and Humanities Act, as well as national consensus standards recommended by concerned private organizations, were additional sources from which the secretary extracted and adopted standards.

The act also requires workers to comply with the health standards, rules, regulations, and orders issued pursuant to it. Although an employer may be cited for a violation of the act and be fined, or in a proper case imprisoned, the act does not specifically impose penalties upon an employee in violation. The secretary of labor is empowered to seek in federal district court an injunction prohibiting "any conditions or practices . . . which are such that a danger exists which could reasonably be expected to cause death or serious physical harm." The secretary may seek an injunction against an employee whose activities are creating a safety hazard. In addition, an employer may discipline an employee who is in breach of an OSHA standard (for example, by refusing to wear protective headgear). The disciplinary measures taken may include fine, suspension, or termination from employment, but the penalty must be commensurate with the violation.

Inspection and procedure

In order to enforce the OSH Act's safety requirements OSHA officials are authorized to inspect work premises. However, there are far too few compliance officers to cover all the workplaces. About 800 OSHA inspectors are authorized to inspect about 5 million business establishments. As a result inspection priorities are assigned generally as follows:

1. Investigation of safety hazards where workers may be killed or seriously injured if corrective action is not taken immediately.
2. Catastrophe or fatality investigation.
3. Complaints investigation.

4. Target industry inspection emphasizing high-hazard industries and operations.
5. General random inspection.

In most instances advance notice of inspection is prohibited and fines and imprisonment are penalties that may be imposed against a person who gives unauthorized advance notice of an OSHA inspection to an employer. Where advance notice is permitted, usually not more than 24 hours' notice may be given.

A compliance officer's inspection of an employer's premises begins when the compliance officer presents his or her official credentials to the employer and requests permission to inspect the premises. The employer or a designated representative is entitled to accompany the officer during the walkaround, and a representative authorized by the employees may also be present. At the termination of the walkaround, OSHA provides for a closing conference between the officer and the employer or the designated representative to "informally advise [the employer] of any apparent safety or health violations disclosed by the inspection."

Employees or their representatives may request an inspection of their employer's premises if they believe a violation of a safety or health standard exists which threatens physical harm. The complaint should be in writing. Under most circumstances the identity of employees who have requested inspections will be protected. An inspection will be conducted if the secretary determines that there are reasonable grounds for believing that a condition exists which violates the act. After it has been decided that an inspection should be made, the employer will be provided with a copy of the complaint with the employee's name deleted.

The OSH Act also empowers the secretary or designated agents to enter a workplace and inspect the premises without notice "during regular working hours and at other reasonable times, and within reasonable limits and in a reasonable manner." In *Marshall* v. *Barlow's, Inc.*, the Supreme Court declared unconstitutional the section of the act which authorized an inspection without a warrant.[7] The Court reasoned that the section was contrary to the Fourth Amendment to the Constitution, which prohibits unreasonable searches. (See Chapter 4 for a fuller treatment of *Barlow's, Inc.*) There was a great fear after *Barlow's, Inc.*, that the warrant requirement would hamper the effectiveness of the act. However, that fear has proved unfounded since most employers do not demand a warrant from the OSHA inspector, but readily consent to a search. Less than 1 employer out of 20 refuses inspection without a warrant. Although a judicial officer may issue a warrant only upon probable cause, *Barlow's, Inc.*, made it clear that probable cause in the criminal law sense was not required. To obtain a warrant the secretary must demonstrate a reasonable basis for selecting the workplace in question for inspection. Employee complaints, high accident rates, a history of employer

---

[7] 436 U.S. 307 (1978).

noncompliance with the OSH Act, a large number of employees in a large business place, and the passage of a long interval since the last inspection may all be neutral criteria that constitute the necessary reasonable basis for obtaining an administrative search warrant.

In cases where a hazard presents imminent danger of death or serious physical harm, the secretary is empowered to seek injunctive relief in the federal district court, by requesting that the hazard be abated. In fact, under the emergency exception, where there is reasonable cause to believe that an "imminent danger" exists, a warrantless inspection would be permitted.[8] The OSHA Act defines "imminent danger" as a condition "which could be reasonably expected to cause death or serious physical harm immediately or before the imminence of such danger can be eliminated through the enforcement procedures otherwise provided by this Act."

Upon a finding by the secretary or an authorized representative that an OSH Act violation exists, the secretary must issue a written citation to the employer with reasonable promptness. The citation must (1) contain a detailed description of the violation, (2) state which standard has been violated, and (3) provide a reasonable time for abatement of the violation. An employer may receive a citation at the worksite immediately following an inspection or thereafter by mail, in no event more than six months after the inspection. After 15 workdays from the service of the citation it becomes final, unless contested.

Employer retaliation

The OSH Act forbids discharge or any other discrimination against an employee who exercises rights under the act. An employee who believes that he or she has been discriminated against may within 30 days thereafter lodge a complaint with the secretary of labor. The secretary is required to conduct an investigation, and if it is determined that a violation has occurred, appropriate relief may be sought in a U.S. district court. Such relief may include rehiring the employee and reinstating the employee to a former position with back pay. In the following case the secretary sought appropriate relief under the OSHA Act, on behalf of two employees who were suspended when they refused to work under conditions which posed an imminent threat to their safety.

Whirlpool v. *Marshall*
445 U.S. 1 (1980)

The secretary of labor (respondent) filed suit against Whirlpool (petitioner), alleging that Whirlpool's act of reprimanding and suspending two employees for refusing to work *under what they believed were unsafe conditions violated a regulation promulgated under the Occupational Safety and Health Act by the secretary. The secretary sought to have*

---

[8] *Michigan* v. *Tyler,* 436 U.S. 499 (1978).

Whirlpool ordered to expunge the reprimands from the employees' personnel files and to compensate the employees for the time they lost as a result of the disciplinary suspensions. The district court denied the requested relief, holding that the secretary's regulation was inconsistent with the act. The court of appeals reversed. The U.S. Supreme Court affirmed the judgment of the court of appeals.

Mr. Justice Stewart:

*   *   *   *   *

The petitioner company maintains a manufacturing plant in Marion, Ohio, for production of household appliances. Overhead conveyors transport appliance components throughout the plant. To protect employees from objects that occasionally fall from these conveyors, the petitioner has installed a horizontal wire mesh guard screen approximately 20 feet above the plant floor. This mesh screen is welded to angle-iron frames suspended from the building's structural steel skeleton.

Maintenance employees of the petitioner spend several hours each week removing objects from the screen, replacing paper spread on the screen to catch grease drippings from the material on the conveyors, and performing occasional maintenance work on the conveyors themselves. To perform these duties, maintenance employees usually are able to stand on the iron frames, but sometimes find it necessary to step onto the steel mesh screen itself.

In 1973 the company began to install heavier wire in the screen because its safety had been drawn into question.

On June 28, 1974, a maintenance employee fell to his death through the guard screen in an area where the newer, stronger mesh had not yet been installed. Following this incident, the petitioner effectuated some repairs and issued an order strictly forbidding maintenance employees from stepping on either the screens or the angle-iron supporting structure. An alternative but somewhat more cumbersome and less satisfactory method was developed for removing objects from the screen. This procedure required employees to stand on power-raised mobile platforms and use hooks to recover the material.

On July 7, 1974, petitioner's maintenance employees, Virgil Deemer and Thomas Cornwell, met with the plant maintenance superintendent to voice their concern about the safety of the screen. The superintendent disagreed with their view, but permitted the two men to inspect the screen with their foreman and to point out dangerous areas needing repair. Unsatisfied with the petitioner's response to the results of this inspection, Deemer and Cornwell met on July 9 with the plant safety director. At that meeting, they requested the name, address, and telephone number of a representative of the local office of the Occupational Safety and Health Administration (OSHA). Although the safety director told the men that they "had better stop and think about what [they] were doing," he furnished the men with the information they requested. Later that same day, Deemer contacted an official of the regional OSHA office and discussed the guard screen.

The next day, Deemer and Cornwell reported for the night shift at 10:45 p.m. Their foreman, after himself walking on some of the angle-iron frames, directed the two men to perform their usual maintenance duties on a section of the old screen. Claiming that the screen was unsafe, they refused to carry out this directive. The foreman then sent them to the personnel office, where they were ordered to punch out without working or being paid for the remaining six hours of the shift. The two men subsequently received written reprimands, which were placed in their employment files.

*   *   *   *   *

. . . The Secretary is obviously correct when he acknowledges in his regulation that, "as a general matter, there is no right afforded by the Act which would entitle employees to walk off the job because of potential unsafe conditions at the workplace." By providing for prompt notice to the employer of an inspector's intention to seek an injunction against an imminently dangerous condition, the legislation obviously contemplates that the employer will normally respond by voluntarily and speedily eliminating the danger. And in the few instances where this does not occur, the legislative provisions authorizing prompt judicial action are designed to give employees full protection in most situations from the risk of injury or death resulting from an imminently dangerous condition at the worksite.

As this case illustrates, however, circumstances may sometimes exist in which the employee justifiably believes that the express statutory arrangement does not sufficiently protect him from death or serious injury. Such circumstances will probably not often occur, but such a situation may arise when (1) the employee is ordered by his employer to work under conditions that the employee reasonably believes pose an imminent risk of death or serious bodily injury, and (2) the employee has reason to believe that there is not sufficient time or opportunity either to seek effective redress from his employer or to apprise OSHA of the danger.

Nothing in the Act suggests that those few employees who have to face this dilemma must rely exclusively on the remedies expressly set forth in the Act at the risk of their own safety. But nothing in the Act explicitly provides otherwise. Against this background of legislative silence, the Secretary has exercised his rulemaking power . . . and has determined that, when an employee in good faith finds himself in such a predicament, he may refuse to expose himself to the dangerous condition, without being subjected to "subsequent discrimination" by the employer.

The question before us is whether this interpretative regulation constitutes a permissible gloss on the Act by the Secretary. . . . Our inquiry is informed by an awareness that the regulation is entitled to deference unless it can be said not to be a reasoned and supportable interpretation of the Act.

The regulation clearly conforms to the fundamental objective of the Act—to prevent occupational deaths and serious injuries. The Act, in its preamble, declares that its purpose and policy is "to assure so far as possible every working man and woman in the Nation safe and healthful working conditions and to preserve our human resources. . . ."

To accomplish this basic purpose, the legislation's remedial orientation is prophylactic in nature. The Act does not wait for an employee to die or become injured. It authorizes the promulgation of health and safety standards and the issuance of citations in the hope that these will act to prevent deaths or injuries from ever occurring. It would seem anomalous to construe an Act so directed and constructed as prohibiting an employee, with no other reasonable alternative, the freedom to withdraw from a workplace environment that he reasonably believes is highly dangerous.

Moreover, the Secretary's regulation can be viewed as an appropriate aid to the full effectuation of the Act's "general duty" clause. That clause provides that "[e]ach employer . . . shall furnish to each of his employees employment and a place of employment which are free from recognized hazards that are causing or are likely to cause death or serious physical harm to his employees.". . . Since OSHA inspectors cannot be present around the clock in every workplace, the Secretary's regulation ensures that employees will in all circumstances enjoy the rights afforded them by the "general duty" clause.

The regulation thus on its face appears to further the overriding purpose of the Act, and rationally to complement its remedial scheme. . . . [T]he Secretary's regulation must, therefore, be upheld, particularly when it is remembered that safety legislation is to be liberally construed to effectuate the congressional purpose.

Case questions

1. Under what authority did the secretary promulgate the regulation relied upon by the two employees? Is the regulation derived from any express provisions of the act? Is it implied? How?

2. Aside from Whirlpool's violation of the secretary's regulation, what else did Whirlpool violate?

3. Will this decision result in many employees walking off their jobs and consequently increase work stoppages? What should management do to insure that this does not happen?

4. As a result of *Whirlpool,* could a fireman refuse to enter a burning building because of the unsafe conditions and successfully seek the protection of the secretary's regulation? Explain.

Variance

Any employer may request a temporary or permanent variance from an OSHA standard. An employer that needs additional time to comply with a standard will request a temporary variance. A temporary variance will be granted only if the employer can show that all the necessary steps will be taken to adequately protect the employees until compliance has been attained. Employees are entitled to a hearing to contest the variance. If the temporary variance is granted, it may not continue any longer than necessary to permit the employer time to effect compliance with the standard. A permanent variance may be granted to an employer only if it is shown that under the variance the employer will provide an environment as safe as would have been obtained if the standard were followed.

Employer defenses

An employer in violation of the general duty clause or the specific standard clause is subject to citation. The common-law defenses that the employee assumed the risk or was guilty of contributory negligence are not available to the employer. An employer's duties are not absolute, however, and there are procedural and substantive defenses that will successfully refute a citation.

Procedural. A citation must be issued within six months of the alleged violation. The success of this statute of limitations defense depends simply upon how much time has elapsed between the date of the violation and the issuance of the citation. The act also requires that the secretary with "reasonable promptness [from the time of forming a belief as to the offense] issue a citation to the employer." The requirement of reasonable promptness necessitates inquiry into the reason for delay in issuing a citation and into the effect of the delay on the employer's ability to prepare a defense. If the delay is unreasonable, the citation will be dismissed.

An employer may contest a citation by filing a notice of contest with OSHA. Regulations require that the secretary transmit the notice of contest and copies of the relevant documents to OSHRC within seven days after receipt of the notice. Failure of the secretary to comply with this provision may result in vacation of the original citation.

Under the act the secretary must notify the employer of the citation and the proposed penalty within a reasonable time after an inspection or investigation. Service must be obtained upon the employer. Service over an employee that lacks the authority to abate the violation, contest the citation, or pay the penalty is insufficient. The citation must describe in detail the nature of the offense so as to afford the employer an opportunity to prepare and defend. Failure to comply with this provision is a denial of procedural due process which results in dismissal of the complaint. Due process standards also require the application of fundamental fairness throughout the administrative and judicial proceedings. The opportunity to present and examine witnesses is essential to a fair trial. If that opportunity is denied, an appellate review would result in victory for the employer.

Substantive.   The isolated incident defense has been successfully raised in cases where the alleged violation resulted exclusively from an employee's misconduct that was in breach of the employer's express safety rules. For this defense to be successful the employer must have provided an adequate safety and training program for the employees, must have actually enforced the safety rules, and must have been ignorant of the employee's noncompliance.

In some rare cases the hazard involved in complying with an OSHA safety standard is greater than the hazard involved in noncompliance. In such cases compliance is excused. Similarly, if the nature of the physical plant or of the work in process make it impossible to comply with a standard, compliance may be excused. For example, if expert engineering opinion confirms that the noise in a plant cannot be reduced to the level prescribed by the OSHA standard, this defense would be available. This, of course, would not excuse the employer from requiring that employees wear earplugs to reduce the harmful effects of the noise. If compliance renders the performance of the work impossible or unfeasible, then the employer's defense is apt to be sustained. Where, for example, guardrails required by an OSHA standard damage the work in process and prevent further work, strict compliance is excused.

Penalities

The OSH Act authorizes the secretary of labor to issue penalties for safety violations. In the assessment of a penalty the compliance officer will take into consideration the severity of the condition, the size of the business, and the employer's good faith and previous safety record. Violations may result in no penalties, fines, imprisonment, or both fines and imprisonment. The gravity of violations are graduated as follows.

De minimis violation.   This violation is deemed to have no direct or immediate relationship to job safety. The employer may be notified of the violation, but no citation will be issued and no penalty imposed. Failure to provide a receptacle for disposal of used paper cups was held to be de minimis.

Nonserious violation.   This violation relates to job safety, but it presents no substantial probability of death or serious harm. Failure to comply with a standard requiring that instructional charts be posted on machinery was held to be a nonserious violation. It was reasoned that their presence was only a warning and that their absence would not create a substantial probability of death or serious harm. Under the act the compliance officer possesses discretion to level a penalty of up to $1,000 for a nonserious violation.

Serious violation.   For a serious violation to exist the employer must know or should have known of a hazard which is likely to result in death or serious injury. A penalty of up to $1,000 is mandatory for such a violation.

Willful or repeated violation.   When a willful violation results in the death of a worker, a penalty of up to $10,000 and/or up to six months in jail is mandatory. A second offense exposes an employer to a fine of up to $20,000 and one-year imprisonment.

Record-keeping notification, and posting requirements

To effectuate the act employers are required to file reports as prescribed by the secretary of labor. Only recordable incidents need be reported. Such incidents include occupational injuries or illnesses which result in fatalities, lost workdays, job transfers, job termination, medical treatment other than first aid, loss of consciousness, and restriction of work or motion.

The employer must maintain a detailed log of all recordable incidents and enter each incident in the log no later than six work days after having acquired knowledge thereof. In addition, each establishment must complete an annual summary of all injuries and illnesses within one month after the close of the calendar year. The summary is a numerical breakdown of injuries and illnesses in various prescribed categories.The log and the summary must be available for OSHA inspection. An employer that employs fewer than 11 employees is exempt from the above record keeping.

Within 48 hours of any fatality or any accident that results in the hospitalization of more than four employees, an employer must notify OSHA of the incident by telephone or telegraph. The notification must include an account of the circumstances surrounding the incident, the extent of the injuries, and the number of fatalities.

Employers are required to post information telling employees of their protections and obligations under the OSH Act and applicable standards. The information must be posted conspicuously in close proximity to the employees' place of work.

Failure to comply with record-keeping and posting requirements may result in citations and fines.

Common law

Although the OSH Act repesents a significant step in regulating on-the-job safety and health conditions, and although it has been criticized by industry as an example of too much government regulation, the act provides workers with limited redress. Several problems arise with an employee's use of the OSH Act to enforce his or her rights. An employee can report violations and be protected from discharge for doing so, but no private cause of action exists to enforce the act. Only the Department of Labor has such enforcement power. Further, problems with bureaucratic machinery and OSHA staff size cut into the act's practical uses. For private redress the worker must resort to the common law.

In most jurisdictions employers have a duty at common law to provide employees with a reasonably safe place to work. Employee redress is in the form of a civil action for negligence. Such action also has limited practical application because the employer may resort to the defenses of assumption of risk, contributory negligence, and the fellow servant doctrine. The following case, however, shows a state court using common law to protect a non-smoking employee from the dangers of "sidestream smoke," smoke that comes from the lighted end of a cigarette or is exhaled by smokers.

Shimp v. *New Jersey Bell Telephone Company*
368 A.2d 408 (N.J. Super. Ct. 1977)

Ms. Shimp (plaintiff) sued the New Jersey Bell Telephone Company (defendant) to enjoin cigarette smoking in her work area. The Superior Court granted the injunction.[9]

Gruccio, J. S. C.: This case involves a matter of first impression in this State: whether a non-smoking employee is denied a safe working environment and entitled to injunctive relief when forced by proximity to smoking employees to involuntarily inhale "second hand" cigarette smoke.

Plaintiff seeks to have cigarette smoking enjoined in the area where she works. She alleges that her employer, defendant N.J. Bell Telephone Co., is causing her to work in an unsafe environment by refusing to enact a ban against smoking in the office where she works. The company allows other employees to smoke while on the job at desks situated in the same work area as that of the plaintiff. Plaintiff contends that the passive inhalation of smoke and the gaseous by-products of burning tobacco is deleterious to her health. Therefore her employer, by permitting employees to smoke in the work area, is allowing an unsafe condition to exist. The present action is a suit to enjoin these allegedly unsafe conditions, thereby restoring to plaintiff a healthy environment in which to work.

. . . Plaintiff's affidavit clearly outlines a legitimate grievance based upon a genuine health problem. She is allergic to cigarette smoke. Mere passive inhalation causes a severe allergic

---

[9] The case is discussed in Blackburn, "Legal Aspects of Smoking in the Workplace," 31 *Labor Law Journal* 564 (1980).

reaction which has forced her to leave work physically ill on numerous occasions.

Plaintiff's representations are substantiated by the affidavits of attending physicians who confirm her sensitivity to cigarette smoke and the negative effect it is having upon her physical well-being. Plaintiff's symptoms evoked by the presence of cigarette smoke include severe throat irritations, nasal irritation sometimes taking the form of nosebleeds, irritation to the eyes which has resulted in corneal abrasion and corneal erosion, headaches, nausea and vomiting. It is important to note that a remission of these symptoms occurs whenever plaintiff remains in a smoke-free environment. Further, it appears that a severe allergic reaction can be triggered by the presence of as little as one smoker adjacent to plaintiff. . . .

It is clearly the law in this State that an employee has a right to work in a safe environment. An employer is under an affirmative duty to provide a work area that is free from unsafe conditions. This right to safe and healthful working conditions is protected not only by the duty imposed by common law upon employers, but has also been the subject of federal legislation. In 1970 Congress enacted the Occupational Safety and Health Act (OSHA) which expresses a policy of prevention of occupational hazards. The act authorizes the Secretary of Labor to set mandatory occupational safety and health standards in order to assure safe and healthful working conditions. Under the general duty clause, Congress imposed upon the employer a duty to eliminate all foreseeable and preventable hazards. OSHA in no way preempted the field of occupational safety. Specifically, 29 U.S.C.A. §653(b)(4) recognizes concurrent state power to act either legislatively or judicially under the common law with regard to occupational safety. . . .

Where an employer is under a common law duty to act, a court of equity may enforce an employee's rights by ordering the employer to eliminate any preventable hazardous condition which the court finds to exist. . . .

The authority of this court has not been affected by the Workmen's Compensation Act. The provisions of N.J.S.A. 34:15–8 cover the presumptively elective surrender by the parties of "their rights to any other method, form or amount of *compensation* or determination thereof . . ." (emphasis supplied). This provision bars only the common law action in tort for damages resulting from work-related injury and makes the workmen's compensation system the exclusive method of securing *money recoveries.* The act is silent with respect to the question of injunctive relief against occupational hazards. There is no provision in the act making it the exclusive method of protecting the worker against an occupational hazard. The act becomes the exclusive remedy for the employee when the hazard has ripened to injury. . . .

The evidence is clear and overwhelming. Cigarette smoke contaminates and pollutes the air, creating a health hazard not merely to the smoker but to all those around her who must rely upon the same air supply. The right of an individual to risk his or her own health does not include the right to jeopardize the health of those who must remain around him or her in order to properly perform the duties of their jobs. The portion of the population which is especially sensitive to cigarette smoke is so significant that it is reasonable to expect an employer to foresee health consequences and to impose upon him a duty to abate the hazard which causes the discomfort. I order New Jersey Bell Telephone Company to do so.

In determining the extent to which smoking must be restricted the rights and interests of smoking and nonsmoking employees alike must be considered. The employees' right to a safe working environment makes it clear that smoking must be forbidden in the work area. The employee who desires to smoke on his own time, during coffee breaks and lunch hours, should have a reasonably accessible area in which to smoke. In the present case the employees' lunchroom and lounge could serve this function. Such a rule imposes no hardship upon defendant New Jersey Bell Telephone Company. The company already has in effect a rule that cigarettes may not be smoked around the telephone equipment. The rationale behind the rule is that the machines are extremely sensitive and can be damaged by the smoke. Human beings are also very sensitive and can be damaged by cigarette smoke. Unlike a piece of machinery, the damage to a human is all to [*sic*] often irreparable. If a circuit or wiring goes bad, the company can install a replacement part. It is not so simple in the case of a human lung, eye or heart. The parts are hard to come by, if indeed they can be found at all.

A company which has demonstrated such concern for its mechanical components should have at least as much concern for its human beings. Plaintiff asks nothing more than to be able to breathe the air in its clear and natural state.

Accordingly, I order defendant New Jersey Bell Telephone Company to provide safe working conditions for plaintiff by restricting the smoking of employees to the nonwork area presently used as a lunchroom. No smoking shall be permitted in the offices or adjacent customer service area.

It is so ordered.

Case questions

1. What circumstances in *Shimp* limit the case's application? Would New Jersey Bell be required to prevent the health hazard presented to Ms. Shimp under the OSH Act's general duty clause?

2. How did Judge Gruccio reconcile Ms. Shimp's claim with the New Jersey Workmen's Compensation Act? Explain.

3. Minnesota and Utah have statutes restricting or prohibiting smoking in all workplaces "where the close proximity of workers or the inadequacy of ventilation causes smoke pollution detrimental to the health [and/or] comfort of nonsmoking employees." Do you favor such legislation at either the state or federal level? Explain.

POLICY CONSIDERATIONS

At the time of their enactment, a number of the labor laws discussed in this chapter were novel and extremely controversial. Controversy still surrounds many of these laws. Much of this controversy centers on concern that the laws have outlived their original purpose.

The Fair Labor Standards Act was an attempt to combat the devastating effects of the Great Depression. The act was intended to achieve several goals. First, Congress hoped to further social equality by insuring a fair wage for workers. It sought to close the channels of interstate commerce to goods produced under conditions detrimental to the health, efficiency, and general well-being of workers. It also expected to spread employment among a greater number of workers by providing employers with a financial incentive to avoid overtime. A related goal was to strengthen the bargaining power of labor by forbidding wages below the stated minimum and by exerting financial pressure on employers that would gain an unfair advantage through substandard wage and employment practices. Finally, Congress wished to promote economic recovery and stability by increasing the purchasing power of workers.

Current critics of the FLSA question its continuation during inflationary times. One effect of establishing a minimum wage floor and a maximum hour ceiling is to greatly increase the labor costs of employers. During the Great Depression inflation was not a problem; the problems were unemployment and depressed wages and prices. Does it make sense to emphasize FLSA compliance when inflation is the major social problem? On the other hand, do other purposes underlie the FLSA that warrant its continuation?

The FLSA's child labor provisions have also come under attack. Some critics claim that the FLSA's child labor and wage and hour provisions discourage employers from hiring younger workers. At a time when teenage unemployment is rampant, many critics see the FLSA as creating a new class of unemployed.

Public unemployment compensation exists in this country to shield the unemployed worker against the economic effects of job loss. Elsewhere, most notably in European countries, a different approach is taken to unemployment compensation. Instead of relying upon a public program, many countries require employers to provide reasonable notice of discharge and reasonable serverance pay to their workers. What notice and severance pay are viewed as reasonable often varies with the length of time that an employee has worked for the employer.

Different cultural, political, and social climates have dictated the divergence between the European and American approaches to providing protection for the unemployed. This country's current system of unemployment insurance is perhaps too firmly rooted to be abandoned for the European alternative. However, the existence of other approaches permits comparison and analysis to ascertain which is best.

In recent years the social security system has been criticized because of its weakened financial footing. As the number of recipients increased, and as inflation increased the amounts paid out to recipients, Congress has sought to meet the increased outlays by increasing the wage base. Some have proposed that social security be financed out of the federal government's general revenues rather than operated as a separate insurance fund. Others have argued that the age of retirement should be raised to reflect increases in life expectancy.

The major recent issue in the area of workers' compensation has been whether to federalize it. Various bills have been introduced into Congress to create a system whereby the states would administer a comprehensive federal law applicable to all employers engaged in interstate commerce. All of these bills have failed to meet with congressional approval. The need for federal involvement has waned as state laws have been upgraded in the areas of coverage, benefits, rehabilitation, and administration. Nevertheless, support for federalizing workers' compensation persists. However, until the pressing concerns of energy and economics have been effectively dealt with, the states will probably be left unfettered in their administration of workers' compensation programs.

OSHA has had its share of critics. Its numerous regulations impose substantial hardship upon employers. The paperwork required to comply with OSHA has been mounting. Many are wondering whether the benefits are worth the costs.

Review problems

1. The Copper Cellar Restaurant paid its waitresses $1.10 per hour in 1977 and $1 per hour in 1978. The applicable minimum wage per hour in 1977 was $2.30 and $2.65 per hour in 1978. Copper Cellar regularly furnished meals to its waitresses at half price. For this it claimed a credit of 5 cents and 32½ cents per hour toward payment of the minimum wage in 1977 and 1978, respectively. Copper Cellar also claimed a credit toward the minimum wage payment, based on tips received by waitresses, of $1.15 per hour in 1977 and $1.32½ per hour in 1978. The waitresses pooled their tips in a common fund, and at the end of each day 15 percent of all waitresses' tips was shared equally among bartenders, busboys, and kitchen personnel. Copper Cellar never explained the provisions of the minimum wage law to its waitresses. The waitresses filed suit to recover unpaid wages, alleging that Copper Cellar violated the Fair Labor Standards Act when it failed to pay them the applicable minimum wage for 1977 and 1978. Copper Cellar argued that it paid the waitresses in compliance with the FLSA. Who is right?

2. A union negotiates a collective bargaining contract requiring the employer to pay twice the hourly rate to an employee who works more than 40 hours per week. Will such a provision be enforceable? Suppose the contract provides that any employee who works more than 40 hours per week will be paid time and a quarter instead of time and a half. Will such a provision be enforceable?

3. Edwin H. Browder, Jr. (appellant), appealed an order of the Florida Department of Labor and Employment Services assessing him with tripled unemployment compensation rates. The increase was imposed because of the unemployment of an employee who had worked for and been terminated by a former corporate employer. The department concluded that the appellant's acquisition of the corporate employer's assets in lieu of the mortgage foreclosure made the appellant responsible for the corporate employer's experience rate. Do you think the department is correct? Explain.

4. Vincent Martin was employed as a laborer by the Bonclarken Assembly. During his lunch hour he went swimming in a lake on the assembly's grounds, which he had permission to do. The lake had a swimming area enclosed by a rope, and within the swimming area a smaller section was enclosed by a chain. When Vincent entered the lake, the lifeguard had left to eat lunch. When the lifeguard left, he removed some buoys from the water and locked them up. No sign said that the pool was closed. This sign was posted by the lake entrance at a place where Vincent could have read it:

LAKE REGULATIONS

MONDAY–SATURDAY: Swimming and boating under supervision of lifeguard until 4:30 P.M.

MONDAY–SATURDAY: Swimming *only* 5:00 P.M.–7:00 P.M. AT YOUR OWN RISK.

SUNDAY ONLY: Lake open from 2:00 P.M.–5:00 P.M. under supervision of lifeguard.

SWIMMING TEST BY LIFEGUARD
REQUIRED FOR SWIMMING
BEYOND CHAINED AREA

Vincent drowned in the lake. He was within the rope area outside the chain when he drowned. His parents filed a claim to recover death benefits under the state workers' compensation statute. Bonclarken Assembly contended that the accident which caused Vincent's death was not one "arising out of and in the course of" his employment. Who is right? Suppose that Vincent had been struck and killed by a meteorite while swimming in the lake under the same circumstances. Would the parents have been entitled to death benefits? Suppose that the parents had sued Bonclarken Assembly for negligence. What common-law defenses would have been available to the employer? On what factual basis?

5. Lois High, an elevator operator, was stuck between floors with a dying person for about half an hour. As a result, psychological problems prevented her from returning to her job. She filed a workers' compensation claim for loss of wages and psychiatric counseling expenses. Should she recover?

6. Two workmen were on a scaffold when the supporting cables broke. One fell to his death, but the other landed safely on the roof of an adjacent building. Thereafter he was unable to work in high places and suffered from a nervous disorder evidenced by temporary paralysis, troubled sleep, nightmares, eyelid tremors, and other symptoms. He filed a workers' compensation claim for loss of wages as well as medical and psychiatric expenses. Should he recover?

7. Makeshift Muffler, Inc., is in the business of replacing and repairing automobile mufflers. It has 20 employees. Wally Worker is employed as a welder for Makeshift. He was specially trained by Makeshift in the procedures and safety precautions applicable to installing replacement mufflers on cars. One rule of which he was aware involved a prohibition against installing a muffler on any car which had heavily congealed oil or grease or which had any leaks. Wally disregarded

this rule, and as a result a car caught fire, causing extensive injury to Wally. Assuming that Makeshift has workers' compensation insurance pursuant to a state workers' compensation statute, what are Wally's rights and Makeshift's liability? Explain. Assuming the same facts except that Makeshift has no workers' compensation insurance, which is in violation of state law, what are the legal implications to Makeshift and to Wally? Explain.

8. Old Bridge Chemical, Inc. (Old Bridge), was charged with a serious OSHA violation for having failed to abide by a safety standard and for having failed to adequately train employees who had been engaged in the rescue of other employees from a railroad tank car. An employee had been assigned to collect chemical samples from the bottom of a railroad tank car. The employee passed out after having been manually lowered through a hatch at the top of the car. A second employee jumped in to rescue the first and was also overcome by fumes. A third employee, who was lowered into the tank in an attempt to rescue the second, also succumbed to fumes. The employees had never been instructed in the hazards of confined entry space and emergency rescue procedures. The employer had admonished its employees not to enter the tank car without authorization.

An OSHA standard requires that employers provide rescuers with air respirators. Old Bridge failed to do this on the ground that air respirators were not needed since the chemical in the tank did not form a vapor, dust, or fumes. Was Old Bridge in violation? Explain. Would the result be different if the employees received safety instruction procedures but ignored them? What if the employees were provided with air respirators but refused to use them? What should employers do to insure employee compliance with health and safety instructions?

9. An employer and its employees negotiate a collective bargaining agreement which includes a provision prohibiting strikes during the contract term. As a result of what several employees believe to be unsafe working conditions, the employees strike and refuse to return until the employer agrees to render the working conditions safe. Was the employee conduct legal? Explain.

10. Select one of the employment regulation areas discussed in this chapter. What are the objectives of the law in the area you selected? Are the objectives being met? Explain. How would you improve the law which governs the area you selected?

CHAPTER 17

Equal employment opportunity

Federal laws prohibit employment discrimination based on race, color, religion, national origin, sex, and age. Virtually all employers, as well as employment agencies and labor unions, are affected by the requirements of these laws. This chapter surveys the coverage under these laws and the discrimination that they prohibit. It also highlights selected developments in equal employment opportunity (EEO) laws. The federal EEO laws discussed in this chapter are:

1. Title VII of the Civil Rights Act of 1964, which prohibits employment discrimination based on race, color, religion, national origin, and sex. Employers with 15 or more employees, as well as employment agencies and unions, are covered by Title VII. The Equal Employment Opportunity Commission (EEOC) enforces its provisions.

2. The Equal Pay Act of 1963, which prohibits pay differentials based on sex. Until 1979 this act was enforced by the Department of Labor (DOL), Wage and Hour Division. Currently the EEOC is vested with the enforcement responsibility. The Equal Pay Act was enacted as an amendment to the Fair Labor Standards Act (FLSA), discussed in Chapter 16. Its coverage is similar to the basic FLSA coverage.

3. The Age Discrimination in Employment Act of 1967 (ADEA), which outlaws discrimination against individuals between the ages of 40 and 70. The ADEA applies to employers with 25 or more employees, as well as to unions and employment agencies. As with the Equal Pay Act, enforcement of the ADEA has been transferred from the DOL to the EEOC.

4. Sections 503 and 504 of the Vocational Rehabilitation Act of 1973, which prohibit discrimination against handicapped persons by federal contractors. These contractors are also required to take affirmative action in hiring qualified handicapped persons. The DOL enforces this legislation.

5. The Civil Rights Act of 1866, which has been held to apply to racial discrimination in private employment and to entitle workers to sue directly in federal courts.

6. Various executive orders which not only ban discrimination in employ-

504

ment by federal contractors but require affirmative action. The Office of Federal Contract Compliance Programs (OFCCP) is charged with administering the executive order program.

In addition to the federal laws discussed in this chapter, most states have enacted laws prohibiting discrimination on the basis of race, color, religion, national origin, sex, and physical disability. Many of these laws reach farther than comparable federal legislation.

TITLE VII OF THE CIVIL RIGHTS ACT OF 1964

During the Reconstruction Period Congress passed several civil right acts in order to protect the newly freed slaves. These acts were soon forgotten as segregation and discrimination became widespread in America's social institutions. The Civil Rights Act of 1964 was a comprehensive assault upon these practices. Title VII of the Civil Rights Act prohibits discrimination in employment based on race, color, religion, national origin, or sex. It covers employers and labor unions engaged in industries affecting commerce and employment agencies which serve such employers. Employers and unions must have 15 or more employees or members. Any union maintaining a hiring hall is covered regardless of the size of its membership.

Under Title VII an employer cannot discriminate on the basis of race, color, religion, national origin, or sex with regard to hiring, firing, compensation, and terms, conditions or privileges of employment. Neither can an employer limit, segregate, or classify employees on any of these five bases in any way that tends to deprive any individual of employment, apprenticeship, or training program opportunities, or adversely affects his or her employment status. Unions and employment agencies are prohibited from similar discrimination with regard to their membership criteria or their referral activity. Liability for discrimination under Title VII may result from disparate treatment of an individual based on race, sex, religion, or national origin; from a pattern or practice of discrimination; or from the disparate impact an employment practice has on a race, sex, religion, or nationality.

Disparate treatment

An employer that treats one employee less favorably than another because of race, sex, religion or national origin is subject to liability for the disparate treatment. The typical disparate treatment case is an alleged discriminatory refusal to hire. A plaintiff may establish a prima facie case of disparate treatment by showing that he or she belonged to a protected class (i.e., racial minority, nationality, sex, religion), applied and was qualified for a job for which the employer was seeking applicants, and was rejected despite his or her suitability for the job, after which the position remained open and the employer continued seeking applicants with the plaintiff's qualifications. This approach requires complainants to establish on a comparative basis that they have been denied an employment opportunity which they are qualified to perform. Similar comparisons may establish a prima facie case of disparate treatment with regard to matters other than initial hire.

When a prima facie case of disparate treatment has been established, the defendant must provide a legitimate, nondiscriminatory explanation for the disparate treatment. The plaintiff may then establish that the reason given is a pretext for discrimination. The plaintiff may demonstrate this by using statistics which show the defendant's general policy and practice with respect to minority employment or by showing that the defendant's rationale was not uniformly applied. The ultimate issue is a factual one: Is the defendant's apparently valid reason a cover-up for discrimination?

Pattern or practice of discrimination

In a pattern or practice case the plaintiff attempts to demonstrate that the defendant's policy has been to treat minorities less favorably than other employees. The pattern or practice case attempts to establish a general policy of discrimination, whereas the disparate treatment case attempts to estabish a specific instance of discrimination. Rarely, however, will an employer advertise "Blacks [or Jews, or Women, or Hispanics] need not apply." The policy of discrimination must therefore be proved by circumstantial evidence.

The strongest circumstantial evidence of an employer's policy of discrimination is provided by a statistical comparison between the percentage of minorities in the employer's work force and the percentage of minorities in the relevant labor market. Where the percentage of a minority group in the employer's work force is two or three standard deviations less than what would be expected had the employer hired randomly, a strong inference is raised that the employer discriminated against members of the minority group. This inference may be strengthened with direct evidence of specific instances of disparate treatment or direct evidence of a policy of discrimination. Such evidence may consist of statements made by officials or supervisors of the employer.

The employer faced with a pattern or practice charge may attempt to rebut the inference in several ways. The employer may argue that the statistical comparison is not valid because the plaintiff failed to select the appropriate relevant labor market. The appropriate relevant labor market depends upon the skill required for the job. If the job requires little specialized skill, general population figures would provide an appropriate basis of comparison. If the job is highly specialized, the relevant labor market must be restricted to those who are qualified. For example, the work force of an employer charged with discriminating in hiring messengers may be compared to the general population, whereas the work force of an employer charged with discriminating in hiring certified public accountants must be compared to CPAs generally.

The employer's location may also influence the composition of the relevant labor market. Commuting patterns in a given metropolitan area may be significant in determining the relevant labor market of an employer located in the central city or in a suburb.

Besides attacking the validity of the statistical comparison, the defendant may also attack its probative value. For example, the employer might show that its work force has experienced little turnover and little expansion since the effective date of Title VII. The employer might also offer nondiscriminatory explanations for statistical disparities.

Finally, the employer may rebut the evidence offered by the plaintiff to corroborate the statistical evidence. It may offer nondiscriminatory explanations for individual cases of disparate treatment. It may also attack the credibility of those testifying to statements made by supervisors or company officials and may show that those persons making the statements were not in positions to influence hiring policy or know what the hiring policies were.

When a pattern or practice of discrimination has been established, it is presumed that all minority applicants who were refused employment are entitled to relief. Each individual is not required to establish a prima facie case of disparate treatment. The employer has to show that a specific individual's rejection was due to reasons other than race, sex, religion, or national origin. Even persons who did not apply for positions may be entitled to relief. If they can establish that they would have applied but were deterred from doing so because of the employer's policy of discrimination, they will have the same presumption as the rejected applicants.

Disparate impact

Employment discrimination is not limited to overt acts of discrimination. Today discrimination is often covert and unintentional. Title VII litigation typically results from the use of what at first glance appear to be neutral and objective job criteria. Closer examination, however, may reveal that applying a facially neutral job criterion adversely affects the employment opportunities of a disproportionate number of women or minorities. For example, consider an employer that requires security guards to be at least six feet tall. Initially the requirement appears nondiscriminatory. However, if scrutinized, it may prove to have an adverse impact upon women, Latinos, and Orientals. The average height of such persons is less than six feet, so that they would be systematically excluded form consideration for the security guard jobs.

In cases challenging the use of neutral criteria, courts require the plaintiff to prove that a criterion disproportionately affects the employment opportunities of a protected group, classified by race, color, religion, sex, or national origin. Once the disparate impact of the criterion has been shown, the defendant must establish that the criterion is job related or required by a business necessity. If this is done, the plaintiff must establish the availability of a less discriminatory alternative which would also meet the employer's needs. Therefore, the employer that requires security guards to be at least six feet tall will have to show that protection of the property requires not just a tall, strong person, but persons at least six feet tall.

The disparate treatment, pattern or practice, and disparate impact approaches may be used to attack discrimination based on race, sex, religion, or national origin. Each category of discrimination has also produced specific issues peculiar to itself. These issues are considered below.

Race discrimination against whites and affirmative action

For a considerable time, the question of whether Title VII protected whites from disparate treatment on the basis of race was unresolved. In *McDonald v. Santa Fe Trail Transportation Co.* the Supreme Court held that Title VII applied to racial discrimination in employment directed against whites.[1] In *Santa Fe* several white employees were discharged for misappropriating their employer's property, but their black accomplice was not dismissed. The Court stated that "Title VII . . . prohibits the discharge of 'any individual' because of such 'individual's race.' . . . Its terms are not limited to discrimination against members of any particular race."[2] *Santa Fe* left open the issue of the legality of voluntary affirmative action programs. That issue was addressed in the following case.

Kaiser Aluminum & Chemical Corp. v. *Weber*
443 U.S. 193 (1979)

Kaiser and the United Steelworkers of America (petitioners) entered into a collective bargaining agreement which established training programs to teach unskilled production workers the skills necessary to become craft workers. The program reserved 50 percent of the openings for black employees. This aspect of the program was to continue until the percentage of blacks in the craft work force approximated the percentage of blacks in the local labor force. Before the program began, Kaiser hired only experienced craft workers, almost all of whom were white.

Weber (respondent) brought a class action alleging that junior black employees were accepted into the program ahead of more senior whites. The trial court held that this violated

Title VII, and the Fifth Circuit Court of Appeals affirmed. The Supreme Court reversed.

Mr. Justice Brennan: The only question before us is the narrow statutory issue of whether Title VII *forbids* private employers and unions from voluntarily agreeing upon bona fide affirmative action plans that accord racial preference in the manner and for the purpose provided in the Kaiser-USWA plan. That question was expressly left open in *McDonald* v. *Santa Fe Trail Trans. Co.*

Respondent argues that Congress intended in Title VII to prohibit all race-conscious affirmative action plans. Respondent's argument rests upon a literal interpretation of §§ 703(a) and (d) of the Act. Those sections make it un-

---

[1] 427 U.S. 273 (1976).
[2] Id. at 278–79.

lawful to "discriminate . . . because of . . . race" in hiring and in the selection of apprentices for training programs. Since, the argument runs, *McDonald* v. *Santa Fe Trail Trans. Co.,* *supra,* settled that Title VII forbids discrimination against whites as well as blacks, and since the Kaiser-USWA affirmative action plan operates to discriminate against white employees solely because they are white, it follows that the Kaiser-USWA plan violates Title VII.

Respondent's argument is not without force. But it overlooks the significance of the fact that the Kaiser-USWA plan is an affirmative action plan voluntarily adopted by private parties to eliminate traditional patterns of racial segregation. In this context respondent's reliance upon a literal construction of §§ 703(a) and (d) and upon *McDonald* is misplaced. It is a "familiar rule, that a thing may be within the letter of the statute and yet not within the statute, because not within its spirit, nor within the intention of its makers." The prohibition against racial discrimination in §§ 703(a) and (d) of Title VII must therefore be read against the background of the legislative history of Title VII and the historical context from which the Act arose. Examination of those sources makes clear that an interpretation of the sections that forbade all race-conscious affirmative action would "bring about an end completely at variance with the purpose of the statute" and must be rejected.

Congress' primary concern in enacting the prohibition against racial discrimination in Title VII of the Civil Rights Act of 1964 was with "the plight of the Negro in our economy." Before 1964, blacks were largely relegated to "unskilled and semi-skilled jobs."

It plainly appears from the House Report accompanying the Civil Rights Act that Congress did not intend wholly to prohibit private and voluntary affirmative action efforts as one method of solving this problem. The report provides:

No bill can or should lay claim to eliminating all of the causes and consequences of racial and other types of discrimination against minorities. There is reason to believe, however, that national leadership provided by the enactment of Federal legislation dealing with the most troublesome problems will create an atmosphere conducive to voluntary or local resolution of other forms of discrimination.

Given this legislative history, we cannot agree with respondent that Congress intended to prohibit the private sector from taking effective steps to accomplish the goal that Congress designed Title VII to achieve. The very statutory words intended as a spur or catalyst to cause "employers and unions to self-examine and to self-evaluate their employment practices and to endeavor to eliminate, so far as possible, the last vestiges of an unfortunate and ignominious page in this country's history," cannot be interpreted as an absolute prohibiton against all private, voluntary, race-conscious affirmative action efforts to hasten the elimination of such vestiges. It would be ironic indeed if a law triggered by a Nation's concern over centuries of racial injustice and intended to improve the lot of those who had "been excluded from the American dream for so long," constituted the first legislative prohibition of all voluntary, private, race-conscious efforts to abolish traditional patterns of racial segregation and hierarchy.

Our conclusion is further reinforced by examination of the language and legislative history of § 703(j) of Title VII. . . . The section provides that nothing contained in Title VII "shall be interpreted to *require* any employer . . . to grant preferential treatment . . . to any group because of the race . . . of such . . . group on account of" a *de facto* racial imbalance in the employer's work force. The section does *not* state that "nothing in Title VII shall be interpreted to *permit*" voluntary affirmative efforts to correct racial imbalances. The natural inference is that Congress chose not to forbid all voluntary race-conscious affirmative action.

The reasons for this choice are evident from the legislative record. Title VII could not have been enacted into law without substantial support from legislators in both Houses who traditionally resisted federal regulations of private business. Those legislators demanded as a price for their support that "management prerogatives and union freedoms . . . be left undisturbed to the greatest extent possible." Section 703(j) was proposed by Senator Dirksen to allay any fears that the Act might be interpreted in such a way as to upset this compromise. The section was designed to prevent § 703 of Title VII from being interpreted in such a way as to lead to undue "Federal Government interference with private businesses because of some Federal employee's ideas about racial balance or imbalance." Clearly, a prohibition against all voluntary, race-conscious, affirmative action efforts would disserve these ends. Such a prohibition would augment the powers of the Federal Government and diminish traditional man-

agement prerogatives while at the same time impeding attainment of the ultimate statutory goals. In view of this legislative history and in view of Congress' desire to avoid undue federal regulation of private businesses, use of the word "require" rather than the phrase "require or permit" in § 703(j) fortifies the conclusion that Congress did not intend to limit traditional business freedom to such a degree as to prohibit all voluntary, race-conscious affirmative action.

We therefore hold that Title VII's prohibition in §§ 703(a) and (d) against racial discrimination does not condemn all private, voluntary, race-conscious affirmative action plans.

Case questions

1. What is the basis for the Court's conclusion that the Kaiser affirmative action plan did not violate Title VII?

2. Can *Weber* be reconciled with *McDonald* v. *Santa Fe Trail Transportation Co.?*

3. What is the line of demarcation between permissible and impermissible affirmative action plans?

4. Would the Kaiser plan have been legal if it had limited the training program to whites?

5. Does *Weber* support the legality of government-mandated affirmative action plans?

Sex

Sexual discrimination in employment is not a new phenomenon. The concepts of "men's work" and "women's work" have been ingrained in society since civilization began. Today the typical work roles of the sexes in our society are being altered. Yet the notion of sex-type jobs remains a threat to the freedom of persons to work and retain employment regardless of sex.

Many of the problems peculiar to sex discrimination result from industry practice, stereotyped social roles, and erroneous beliefs. For example, many employers that would not think of asking a man whether he has young children will not hire a woman who has young children. This and similar problems are discussed below.

Sex-plus discrimination. Sex-plus discrimination denotes the imposition of a constraint or requirement on members of one sex but not on members of the other sex. For example, if an employer hires men regardless of their educational background but hires only women with at least high school diplomas, the employer is practicing sex-plus discrimination. Although the employer hires both men and women, it requires a plus factor for women.

Another example of sex-plus discrimination is a requirement that female employees be single while males may be married or single. Formerly this policy prevailed in the airline industry, where female flight attendants (stewardesses) were generally required to be single, while males in the same category (stewards) could be married. EEOC guidelines now prohibit this policy, and courts agree.

Women have been subjected to a number of discriminatory employment policies resulting from their status as mothers. In *Phillips* v. *Martin Marietta Corp.* an employer's refusal to hire women with preschool-age children was considered.[3] This hiring practice did not appear to discriminate against women, because 70–75 percent of the job applicants were women and 75–80 percent of those hired for the position were women. Hence no question of bias against women as such was presented. The Court ruled, however, that since men with preschool-age children were hired but women were not, the practice violated Title VII.

Pregnancy. Another concern of working women is the manner in which employers deal with a pregnant employee. In 1978, Congress enacted the Pregnancy Discrimination Act as an amendment to the definitional section of Title VII. The terms *because of sex* or *on the basis of sex*, as used in Title VII, were modified to include "because of or on the basis of pregnancy, childbirth or related medical conditions." The act further provides:

> [W]omen affected by pregnancy, childbirth, or related medical conditions shall be treated the same for all employment-related purposes, including the receipt of benefits under fringe benefit programs, as other persons not so affected but similar in their ability or inability to work.[4]

A number of interesting questions are suggested by the Pregnancy Discrimination Act. For example, suppose that an employer gives maternity leave to women workers. Must that employer grant a "paternity leave" to male employees when their wives or girl friends are pregnant? Does the act's statement that *"women* affected by pregnancy . . . shall be treated the same" restrict its application to maternity leaves? Or, does the denial of paternity leave discriminate against men in the terms and conditions of their employment?

Sexual harassment. Only in recent years have the courts begun to address the issue of sexual advances in employment situations. This may be because such advances were deemed "personal matters" that employers should handle.

Sexual harassment may violate Title VII in several ways. An employee who is required to have sexual relations with a supervisor to secure, maintain, or advance in employment is subjected to conditions which are not imposed upon employees of the opposite sex. An employee who is promoted as a

---

[3] 400 U.S. 542 (1971).
[4] Title VII, section 701 (1978).

reward for having relations with a supervisor is given an opportunity which employees of the opposite sex do not have. Even where submission to sexual advances is not used as a basis for employment decisions, the existence of sexual harassment in the workplace may create a hostile, intimidating, or offensive atmosphere. An employee who quits because of that atmosphere may file a Title VII claim alleging that the quit amounted to a "constructive discharge."

Pensions and life insurance. It is an established fact that as a class, women live longer than men. Consequently, it has been a common practice of insurance and annuity companies to classify life expectancy tables by sex. Thus women generally receive lower annual pension payments and greater life insurance benefits than similarly situated men. In *City of Los Angeles* v. *Manhart* the Supreme Court held that Title VII was violated by the use of such tables in benefit plans provided by employers.[5] The Court emphasized that Title VII protects individuals from sex discrimination. Employees must be treated as individuals rather than as members of a class of men or women. Thus distinction in benefits must be based on individual characteristics rather than sex.

The duty to accommodate religion

Title VII prohibits discrimination in employment based upon religion. Section 701(j) states:

> The term "religion" includes all aspects of religious observance and practice, as well as belief, unless an employer demonstrates that he is unable to reasonably accommodate to an employee's or prospective employee's religious observance or practice without undue hardship in the conduct of the employer's business.

This definition obliges the employer to demonstrate that it is unable to "reasonably accommodate" to an employee's or prospective employee's religious observance, practice, or belief without undue hardship to its business.

Since religious discrimination has been a far less frequent topic of litigation than other forms of forbidden discrimination, the law regarding what constitutes "reasonable accommodation" and what constitutes an "undue hardship" to the employer's business is not well developed. The most frequent charges of religious discrimination dealt with by courts and the EEOC have involved, not raw prejudice against an employee's religion, but instances in which a work rule of the employer, innocent in intent, conflicts with a religious belief of an employee. Such conditions trigger the employer's duty to accommodate the employee's religious beliefs. The nature of that duty is the subject of the following case.

---

[5] 435 U.S. 702 (1978).

Trans World Airlines, Inc. v. Hardison
432 U.S. 63 (1977)

Hardison (respondent), a Sabbatarian, was employed by Trans World Airlines petitioner as a clerk in TWA's maintenance and overhaul base in Kansas City. The base was required to operate 24 hours per day, 365 days per year. Under the applicable collective bargaining agreement, employees received shift assignments according to seniority, with the most senior employees receiving first choice. Hardison advised the employer of his religious convictions, which prevented Saturday work. TWA agreed that the union steward would seek a job swap or change of days off for Hardison and that Hardison would have his religious holidays off whenever possible if he agreed to work traditional holidays when asked. Hardison was initially employed in one building on the late night shift, where he had sufficient seniority to avoid working on his Sabbath. He then transferred to another building and the day shift, where he was second from the bottom of the seniority list. When a fellow employee went on vacation, Hardison was asked to work Saturdays. He refused. TWA asked the union to seek a change of work assignments, but the union refused to waive the seniority provision. When Hardison failed to report for work on Saturdays he was fired.

Hardison brought suit, alleging that TWA's failure to accommodate his religious beliefs violated Title VII. The district court entered judgment for TWA, but the Eighth Circuit Court of Appeals reversed. The Supreme Court reversed the court of appeals.

Mr. Justice White: The emphasis of both the language and the legislative history of [Title VII] is on eliminating discrimination in employment; similarly situated employees are not to be treated differently solely because they differ with respect to race, color, religion, sex, or national origin.

The prohibition against religious discrimina-

tion soon raised the question of whether it was impermissible under § 703(a) (1) to discharge or refuse to hire a person who for religious reasons refused to work during the employer's normal workweek. In 1966 an EEOC guideline dealing with this problem declared that an employer had an obligation under the statute "to accommodate to the reasonable religious needs of employees . . . where such accommodations can be made without serious inconvenience to the conduct of the business."

In 1967 the EEOC amended its guidelines to require employers "to make reasonable accommodations to the religious needs of employees and prospective employees where such accommodations can be made without undue hardship on the conduct of the employer's business." . . .

This question—the extent of the required accommodation—remained unsettled when this Court, in *Dewey* v. *Reynolds Metals Co.,* affirmed by an equally divided Court the Sixth Circuit's decision. The discharge of an employee who for religious reasons had refused to work on Sundays was there held by the Court of Appeals not to be an unlawful employment practice because the manner in which the employer allocated Sunday work assignments was discriminatory in neither its purpose nor effect; and consistent with the 1967 EEOC guidelines, the employer had made a reasonable accommodation of the employee's beliefs by giving him the opportunity to secure a replacement for his Sunday work.

In part "to resolve by legislation" some of the issues raised in *Dewey,* Congress included the following definition of religion in its 1972 amendments to Title VII:

The term "religion" includes all aspects of religious observance and practice as well as belief, unless an employer demonstrates that he is unable to reasonably accommodate to an employee's or prospective employee's religious observance or practice without undue hardship on the conduct of the employer's business.

* * * * *

. . . [T]he employer's statutory obligation to make reasonable accommodation for the religious observances of its employees, short of incurring an undue hardship, is clear, but the reach of that obligation has never been spelled out by Congress or by EEOC guidelines. With this in mind, we turn to a consideration of whether TWA has met its obligation under Title VII to accommodate the religious observances of its employees.

* * * * *

. . . In summarizing its more detailed findings, the District Court observed:

TWA established as a matter of fact that it did take appropriate action to accommodate as required by Title VII. It held several meetings with plaintiff at which it attempted to find a solution to plaintiff's problems. It did accommodate plaintiff's observance of his special religious holidays. It authorized the union steward to search for someone who would swap shifts, which apparently was normal procedure.

It is also true that TWA itself attempted without success to find Hardison another job. The District Court's view was that TWA had done all that could reasonably be expected within the bounds of the seniority system.

* * * * *

We are convinced . . . that TWA itself cannot be faulted for having failed to work out a shift or job swap for Hardison. Both the union and TWA had agreed to the seniority system; the union was unwilling to entertain a variance over the objections of men senior to Hardison; and for TWA to have arranged unilaterally for a swap would have amounted to a breach of the collective-bargaining agreement.

. . . Collective bargaining aimed at effecting workable and enforceable agreements between management and labor, lies at the core of our national labor policy, and seniority provisions are universally included in these contracts.

Without a clear and express indication from Congress, we cannot agree with Hardison and the EEOC that an agreed-upon seniority system must give way when necessary to accommodate religious observances. . . .

Any employer who, like TWA, conducts an around-the-clock operation is presented with the choice of allocating work schedules either in accordance with the preferences of its employees or by involuntary assignment. Insofar as the varying shift preferences of its employees complement each other, TWA could meet its need through voluntary work scheduling. . . .

Whenever there are not enough employees who choose to work a particular shift, however, some employees must be assigned to that shift even though it is not their first choice. Such was evidently the case with regard to Saturday work. . . .

* * * * *

. . . Allocating the burdens of weekend work was a matter for collective bargaining. In considering criteria to govern this allocation, TWA and the union had two alternatives: adopt a neutral system, such as seniority, a lottery, or rotating shifts; or allocate days off in accordance with the religious needs of its employees. TWA would have had to adopt the latter in order to assure Hardison and others like him of getting the days off necessary for strict observance of their religion, but it could have done so only at the expense of others who had strong, but perhaps nonreligious, reasons for not working on weekends. There were no volunteers to relieve Hardison on Saturdays, and to give Hardison Saturdays off, TWA would have had to deprive another employee of his shift preference at least in part because he did not adhere to a religion that observed the Saturday Sabbath.

Title VII does not contemplate such unequal treatment. . . . It would be anomalous to conclude that by "reasonable accommodation" Congress meant that the employer must deny the shift and job preference of some employees, as well as deprive them of their contractual rights, in order to accommodate or prefer the religious needs of others, and we conclude that

Title VII does not require an employer to go that far.

*   *   *   *   *

The Court of Appeals also suggested that TWA could have permitted Hardison to work a four-day week if necessary in order to avoid working on his Sabbath. Recognizing that this might have left TWA short-handed on the one shift each week that Hardison did not work, the court still concluded that TWA would suffer no undue hardship if it were required to replace Hardison either with supervisory personnel or with qualified personnel from other departments. Alternatively, the Court of Appeals suggested that TWA could have replaced Hardison on his Saturday shift with other available employees through the payment of premium wages. Both of these alternatives would involve costs to TWA, either in the form of lost efficiency in other jobs or higher wages.

To require TWA to bear more than a *de minimis* cost in order to give Hardison Saturdays off is an undue hardship. Like abandonment of the seniority system, to require TWA to bear additional costs when no such costs are incurred to give other employees the days off that they want would involve unequal treatment of employees on the basis of their religion. By suggesting that TWA should incur certain costs in order to give Hardison Saturdays off the Court of Appeals would in effect require TWA to finance an additional Saturday off and then to choose the employee who will enjoy it on the basis of his religious beliefs. While incurring extra costs to secure a replacement for Hardison might remove the necessity of compelling another employee to work involuntarily in Hardison's place, it would not change the fact that the privilege of having Saturdays off would be allocated according to religious beliefs.

*   *   *   *   *

Case questions

1. What efforts did TWA make to accommodate Hardison's religious beliefs?

2. How did the Court define *undue hardship?* What reasoning supports this definition?

3. What amount do you think TWA would have had to spend annually to accommodate Hardison's religious beliefs? What does this amount suggest about the de minimis standard?

National origin

Although discrimination on the basis of national origin is forbidden by Title VII, the act does not define the term. An initial issue thus presented by the term *national origin* is whether it includes aliens or whether it is restricted to citizens who are discriminated against on the basis of their ancestry. The Supreme Court considered this issue in *Espinoza* v. *Farah Mfg., Inc.*[6] It held that Title VII's prohibiton against national origin discrimination does not prohibit discrimination on the basis of alienage. Aliens, however, are entitled to the same protection from discrimination on the basis of national origin as citizens. In accordance with Title VII's prohibition against discrimination and EEOC guidelines, employment differentials applied against employees or applicants based on the following factors would constitute unlawful national origin discrimination:

[6] 414 U.S. 86 (1973).

1. Language requirements, i.e., the use of tests in the English language where English is not the individual's first language or mother tongue, *and* where English language skill is not a requirement of the work to be performed.
2. Marriage or association with persons of a particular national origin.
3. Membership in a lawful organization identified with or seeking to promote the interests of a given nationality or ethnic group.
4. Attendance at a school or church commonly utilized by persons of a particular national origin.
5. Having a surname indicative of a particular national origin.

Exceptions

The above prohibitons are subject to some important exceptions, namely, the exception accorded to bona fide occupational qualifications, the exception made for professionally developed ability tests, and the seniority exception.

The bona fide occupational qualification. The bona fide occupational qualification, or bfoq, is a statutory exception to employment practices which might otherwise violate Title VII. This exception allows an employer to discriminate in its hiring where religion, national origin, or sex is a "bona fide occupational qualification" reasonably necessary to the normal operation of a particular business or operation. The exception excuses sexual, religious, and national origin discrimination in some hiring situations, but it extends no such excuse to racial discrimination.

To establish a bfoq the employer must show that it is a business necessity to have employees of a given sex, religion, or national origin because hiring persons of another sex, religion, or national origin would "undermine the essence of" the business operation. This may be done by showing that certain qualifications possessed by persons of a given sex, religion, or national origin are essential to the employer's business and that it is impracticable to find members of the excluded class who also possess these qualifications.

The bfoq is interpreted narrowly, and the employer bears a heavy burden of proof. Thus an employer hiring tour guides to lead a trip to Spain cannot restrict its hiring to persons of Spanish origin. Although Spanish-speaking employees are essential, it is relatively easy for the employer to test the ability of non-Spanish persons to speak Spanish. Similarly, an airline may not restrict its hiring to female flight attendants even if it can establish that women are generally far better able than men to provide courteous service and set anxious passengers at ease and that it is impracticable to test such abilities in advance of hire. Courtesy, or the lack of it, does not seriously affect the airline's ability to transport passengers safely. In the preceding instances it was convenient for the employer to require that employees be of a particular sex or national origin, but the requirement was not necessary to the business.[7] In the following case the employer was able to establish sex as a bfoq.

---

[7] *Diaz* v. *Pan American World Airways,* 442 F.21 385 (5th Cir. 1971).

Fernandez v. Wynn Oil Co.
26 FEP Cases 815 (9th Cir. 1981)

Fernandez (plaintiff-appellant) was employed by the Wynn Oil Company (defendant-appellee) from February 1968 to February 4, 1977. During that time she held various positions, including that of administrative assistant to the vice president of Wynn's International Operations division. She sued Wynn, alleging that it discriminated against her on the basis of sex in violation of Title VII. She claimed discrimination in that Wynn failed to promote her from her position to that of Director of International Operations (DIO) because she was female, and in fact terminated her for that reason. Wynn defended on the ground that Fernandez' lack of qualifications for the job, rather than her sex, prompted its decision. Alternatively, Wynn argued that male sex is a bona fide occupational qualification (bfoq) for a job performed in foreign countries where women are barred from business.

The U.S. District Court for the Central District of California entered judgment for Wynn on both alternative grounds, finding that Fernandez had failed to establish a prima facie case of sex discrimination, and, alternatively, that sex was a bfoq for the position of DIO.

In holding that sex was a bfoq for the position of Wynn's DIO, the District Court stated:

. . . Much of defendant's business . . . takes place in Latin America and Southeast Asia. Louis Dashwood, an executive of the defendant, testified that he would not consider plaintiff or any other woman for the position of Director of International Operations because of the feeling among defendant's customers and distributors that it would be less desirable to deal with a woman in a high-level management position. Dashwood testified that many of Wynn's South American distributors and customers, for instance, would be offended by a woman conducting business meetings in her hotel room. The offensive nature of this apparently innocuous conduct stems

from prevailing cultural customs and mores in Latin America.

. . . Whatever view Americans may hold regarding business and social customs in South America and Southeast Asia, it was not merely for the convenience of itself or its customers that Wynn Oil refused to consider a woman for that position. To have hired Ms. Fernandez—regardless of her qualifications—would have totally subverted any business Wynn hoped to accomplish in those areas of the world. . . . South American customs and mores would, for example, prohibit a woman from conducting business from her hotel room. As quaint as that notion appears to the American mind, it is a very real and formidable obstacle to the success of any business enterprise in South America. The Court finds that it was necessary that Wynn hire a male for the position. . . . Accordingly, Wynn was entitled to discriminate on the basis of sex. . . .

Fernandez appealed to the Ninth Circuit Court of Appeals, which affirmed the District Court's holding that Fernandez had not established a prima facie case of sex discrimination, but reversed the District Court's discussion of the bfoq defense.

Ferguson, Circuit Judge: Wynn Oil Company is an international petro-chemical manufacturer located in Orange County, California. It hired Fernandez in 1968. From 1972 through 1973, Fernandez served as administrative assistant to Louis Dashwood, the vice president of Wynn's International Operations division.

Dashwood testified, as a witness for Fernandez, that during this time Fernandez performed many functions of his job but he chose not to promote her because she was so valuable to him as an administrative assistant. He also testified that he felt Latin American clients would react negatively to a woman vice president on International Operations.

Joseph Borrello was subsequently appointed Director of International Operations (DIO). In October 1975, Dashwood's employment terminated and Borrello informed Fernandez of plans to terminate her administrative assistant position. In March 1976, Borrello hired Arturo Matthews to fill the position of DIO, although Fernandez had requested consideration for the job. In April, Fernandez accepted an assignment as manager of a different division. She was discharged in February 1977.

* * * * *

. . . [A] party complaining of discrimination by disparate treatment establishes a prima facie case by showing that (1) she was within a protected group; (2) she applied and was qualified for a job for which the company was seeking applicants; (3) she was rejected; and (4) after her rejection, the employer continued to seek applicants. . . .

The district court in the instant case found that Fernandez failed to prove a prima facie case. . . .

The record supports the district court's findings. Testimony was presented that Fernandez was not proficient in the English language and had difficulty with articulation. She had no secondary education. Borrello testified that he did not seriously consider Fernandez because she had a drinking problem and erratic work habits. He also testified that she was indiscreet in her criticism of him and in infringing on the job authority of others. Finally, she had refused an assignment to address a group of listeners and there was testimony that she had exhibited poor supervisory and marketing skills.

Fernandez has therefore failed to demonstrate that the district court erred in failing to find her qualified for the DIO position. If an applicant is not qualified for the job in question, she has failed to establish a prima facie case.

The district court found masculine gender a bona fide occupational qualification for the position in question. It based this conclusion on testimony that Wynn's South American clients would refuse to deal with a female DIO.

The district court erred in its factual findings and legal conclusions.

Testimony in the record indicated that a female would have difficulty in conducting business in South America from a hotel room. No proof was adduced, however, that the position required work of this nature. Nor does the record provide any basis for the district court's findings that hiring Fernandez would "destroy the essence" of Wynn's business or "create serious safety and efficacy problems." There is, in short, no factual basis for linking sex with job performance. The bfoq finding is accordingly factually erroneous.

Even if the record supported the district court's factual conclusion, we would be compelled to reject the bfoq finding in this case because it is based on an erroneous interpretation of Title VII. The district court found that sex discrimination must be compelled by business considerations in order to qualify as a bfoq. It also stated that customer preferences should not be bootstrapped to the level of business necessity. Nevertheless, it held that customer preferences rise to the dignity of a bona fide occupational qualification if "no customer will do business with a member of one sex either because it would destroy the essence of the business or would create serious safety and efficacy problems." On this basis, the district court found the customer preferences of Wynn's clients a bfoq.

That conclusion cannot stand. Title VII . . . permits hiring decisions to be based on gender if gender is a bona fide occupational qualification reasonably necessary to the normal operation of that particular business. However, stereotypic impressions of male and female roles do not qualify gender as a bfoq. . . . Nor does stereotyped customer preferences justify a sexually discriminatory practice. . . . Furthermore, the Equal Employment Opportunity Commission has held that the need to accommodate racially discriminatory policies of other nations cannot be the basis of a valid bfoq exception. The EEOC has promulgated regulations stating that the only customer preferences allowed as a bfoq exception is one necessary for the purpose of genuineness or authenticity.

* * * * *

Diaz . . . held that customer preferences based on sexual stereotype cannot justify discriminatory conduct. The court below relied on [Diaz], yet found that customer preference which prevents customers from dealing with the employer does qualify as a bfoq. Nothing in [Diaz] justifies this distinction.

Wynn attempts to distinguish Diaz by asserting that a separate rule applies in international contexts. Such a distinction is unfounded. Though the United States cannot impose standards of nondiscriminatory conduct on other nations through its legal system, the district court's rule would allow other nations to dictate discrimination in this country. No foreign nation can compel the non-enforcement of Title VII here.

Case questions

1. What standard does the court apply to determine whether sex is a bfoq?

2. Was it necessary to Wynn's business operations that the International Marketing Director conduct business from a hotel room when in Southeast Asia or South America? Explain.

3. Does the court hold that customer preference will never serve as a bfoq? Explain.

Professionally developed ability tests. Title VII permits the use of any "professionally developed ability test," provided that the test is not designed or used to discriminate. In *Griggs* v. *Duke Power Co.* the Supreme Court held that Title VII prohibits an employer from requiring that applicants have a high school education or attain a minimum score on a standardized general intelligence test as a condition of employment when (1) both requirements operate to disqualify black applicants at a substantially higher rate than white applicants and (2) neither requirement is shown to be significantly related to successful job performance.[8]

In *Albemarle Paper Co.* v. *Moody* the Court further required that any employment test adversely affecting minorities be validated.[9] The EEOC has issued

---

[8] 401 U.S. 424 (1971).
[9] 422 U.S. 405 (1975).

guidelines detailing the validation processes that it approves for establishing the job relatedness of any selection procedure which has an adverse impact on a protected group. Under the guidelines a test is considered discriminatory if it results in a selection rate for one race, sex, religion, or national origin which is less than four fifths of the selection rate for another. The burden is then on the user of the test to validate the test by one of three methods.

Criterion validity establishes a statistical relationship between performance on the test and an objective indicator of job performance. Content validity establishes that the test representatively samples a function of the job. A typing test for a typist is content valid. Construct validity establishes that the test indicates a psychological trait required for the job. A test indicating leadership ability is construct valid for a police commander.

Seniority systems. Section 703(h) permits an employer to apply different standards of employment pursuant to a bona fide seniority system provided that the system is not the result of an intention to discriminate. Seniority is the cornerstone of many collective bargaining agreements. From organized labor's perspective, a seniority system provides employment security to workers because it eliminates favoritism and gives senior workers preference in any promotion or layoff. From the employer's perspective, a seniority system is justified because it adds to the safety and efficiency of the employer's place of business. The theory is that a more experienced worker will be safer and more efficient than a less experienced worker. What constitutes a bona fide seniority system is the subject of the following case.

Teamsters v. United States
431 U.S. 324 (1977)

The United States (respondent) alleged that the Teamsters Union and T.I.M.E.–D.C., Inc. (petitioners), engaged in a pattern or practice of discrimination against blacks and Spanish in the hiring, assignment, transfer, and promotion of line (i.e., intercity) truck drivers. The government further alleged that the petitioners' seniority system locked in the effects of this discrimination and was therefore not bona fide. The lower courts granted relief. The Supreme Court reversed.

The seniority system maintained separate seniority lists for line drivers. An individual who transferred to another job with the company was not credited with seniority accumulated in the previous job for purposes of lay-

offs, promotions, and bidding for assignments. The government established that petitioners discriminated against blacks and Spanish both before and after the effective date of Title VII.

Mr. Justice Rehnquist: . . . Because the company discriminated both before and after the enactment of Title VII, the seniority system is said to have operated to perpetuate the effects of both pre- and post-Act discrimination. Post-Act discriminatees, however, may obtain full "make whole" relief, including retroactive seniority . . . without attacking the legality of the seniority system as applied to them. . . . [R]etroactive seniority may be awarded as relief from an employer's discriminatory hiring and assignment policies even if the seniority system agreement itself makes no provision for such relief. . . .

What remains for review is the judgment that the seniority system unlawfully perpetuated the effects of *pre-Act* discrimination. . . .

The primary purpose of Title VII was "to assure equality of employment opportunities and to eliminate those discriminatory practices and devices which have fostered racially stratified job environments to the disadvantage of minority citizens." To achieve this purpose, Congress "proscribe[d] not only overt discrimination but also practices that are fair in form, but discriminatory in operation." . . .

One kind of practice "fair in form, but discriminatory in operation" is that which perpetuates the effects of prior discrimination. . . .

Were it not for § 703(h), the seniority system in this case would seem to fall under the *Griggs* rationale. The heart of the system is its allocation of the choicest jobs, the greatest protection against layoffs, and other advantages to those employees who have been line drivers for the longest time. Where, because of the employer's prior intentional discrimination, the line drivers with the longest tenure are without exception white, the advantages of the seniority system flow disproportionately to them and away from Negro and Spanish-surnamed employees who might by now have enjoyed those advantages had not the employer discriminated before the passage of the Act. This disproportionate distribution of advantages does in a very real sense "operate to 'freeze' the status quo of prior discriminatory employment practices." But both the literal terms of § 703(h) and the legislative history of Title VII demonstrate that Congress considered this very effect of many seniority systems and extended a measure of immunity to them.

Throughout the initial consideration of H.R. 7152, later enacted as the Civil Rights Act of 1964, critics of the bill charged that it would destroy existing seniority rights. The consistent response of Title VII's congressional proponents and of the Justice Department was that seniority rights would not be affected, even where the employer had discriminated prior to the Act. . . .

. . . Section 703(h) was enacted as part of the Mansfield-Dirksen compromise substitute bill that cleared the way for the passage of Title VII. The drafters of the compromise bill stated that one of its principal goals was to resolve the ambiguities in the House-passed version. As the debates indicate, one of those ambiguities concerned Title VII's impact on existing collectively bargained seniority rights. It is apparent that § 703(h) was drafted with an eye toward meeting the earlier criticism on this issue with an explicit provision embodying the understanding and assurances of the Act's proponents, namely, that Title VII would not outlaw such differences in treatments among employees as flowed from a bona fide seniority system that allowed for full exercise of seniority accumulated before the effective date of the Act. . . .

In sum, the unmistakable purpose of § 703(h) was to make clear that the routine application of a bona fide seniority system would not be unlawful under Title VII. As the legislative history shows, this was the intended result even where the employer's pre-Act discrimination resulted in whites having greater existing seniority rights than Negroes. . . . Accordingly, we hold that an otherwise neutral legitimate seniority system does not become unlawful under Title VII simply because it may perpetuate pre-Act discrimination. . . .

* * * * *

The seniority system in this litigation is entirely bona fide. It applies equally to all races and ethnic groups. To the extent that it "locks" employees into non-line-driver jobs, it does so for all. The city drivers and servicemen who are discouraged from transferring to line-driver jobs are not all Negroes or Spanish-surnamed Americans; to the contrary, the overwhelming majority are white. The placing of line drivers in a separate bargaining unit from other employees is rational, in accord with the industry practice, and consistent with National Labor Relation Board precedents. It is conceded that the seniority system did not have its genesis in racial discrimination, and that it was negotiated and has been maintained free from any illegal purpose. In these circumstances, the single fact that the system extends no retroactive seniority to pre-Act discriminatees does not make it unlawful.

Case questions

1. Why does the perpetuation of postact discrimination not defeat the bona fides of the seniority system?

2. Why does the perpetuation of preact discrimination not defeat the bona fides of the seniority system?

3. What factors did the Court consider in holding this seniority system to be bona fide?

Title VII administration and enforcement

The Equal Employment Opportunity Commission administers Title VII. Its principal methods of enforcement are the voluntary compliance efforts of conciliation and mediation. If these efforts fail, the commission is authorized to initiate litigation in a federal district court on behalf of aggrieved persons.

Filing the charge. EEOC involvement is triggered when an aggrieved person—the charging party—files a written charge in one of the commission's regional offices, claiming to have been the victim of unlawful discrimination. Normally the written charge must be filed within 180 days of the alleged discriminatory act. Although a form for the written charge is specified, the charge must be submitted under oath.

Sixty-day state deferral. To give state and local agencies responsible for fair employment practices a chance to resolve the dispute, the EEOC is required to defer its activity until 60 days after state or local proceedings commence. If a charging party goes to the EEOC first, the EEOC generally requires that both an EEOC and a state or local charge form be completed. The state or local form is forwarded to the proper agency, and the EEOC waits 60 days before initiating its investigation.

Investigation. After the 60-day deferral period the EEOC begins an investigation. A notice of the charges is delivered to the respondent. Title VII protects the charging party from any retaliatory acts by the employer. Thus, if an employer innocent of the charges initially filed undertakes any retaliatory acts against the charging party, it may become liable to the charging party for violating Title VII's antiretaliation provision.

The EEOC investigation may take a variety of forms. Interrogatories (written questions) may be sent to the respondent, or a respondent's plant may be visited. Interrogatories are usually sent along with the copy of the notice of the charge. Plant visits are usually made only after the employer has been sent a copy of the notice of the charge. Upon presenting proper identification, an EEOC investigator may conduct an investigation of the respondent's records and ask questions of employees. The EEOC is given the power to subpoena any relevant documents.

Determination of reasonable cause. The EEOC's investigation culminates in a determination of whether or not there is reasonable cause to believe that a Title VII violation occurred. If the commission finds that no reasonable cause exists, then the charge is dismissed. If, however, there is a finding of reasonable cause, then the EEOC issues a determination letter notifying the respondent that the commission seeks to eliminate the alleged unlawful practice by the informal method of conciliation.

The conciliation process. Parties to the conciliation process, which is a confidential proceeding, are the charging party and the respondent. In practice, however, the charging party is rarely present at the conciliation conference. His or her interests are represented by an EEOC representative. The commission may also send its attorney to the conciliation conference, in anticipation of a court proceeding. The respondent is entitled to legal representation at all stages of the proceeding. At this stage, however, the charging party is generally not permitted private counsel, as the EEOC assumes this role.

The conciliation process results either in the execution of a conciliation agreement or in an impasse in the negotiations. The conciliation agreement, which is binding, must be signed by the parties and approved by the EEOC director of the region in which the charge has been filed. The agreement may bar most civil actions which the charging party could bring against the respondent because of the matters complained of.

If conciliation fails, one of two things may happen. The EEOC regional office may refer the case to one of its litigation centers for possible direct EEOC action against the respondent, or the commission may send the charging party a notice that conciliation has been fruitless and that the charging party has a right to sue in federal court within 90 days. If the charging party elects to sue, the court may, at its discretion, appoint counsel. Successful litigants may be awarded costs and attorney fees.

Records. Title VII requires all covered employers, unions, and employment agencies to make and keep records relevant to determining whether unlawful discriminatory practices have been or are being committed. The commission's regulations require employers to keep all personnel records for six months. These include records relating to job application, hiring, promotion, demotion, transfer, layoff, pay rates, and selection for apprenticeship and training programs. In addition, if a discrimination charge has been filed or a lawsuit brought, the commission requires that all records relevant to the charge be preserved until the final disposition of the case.

Reporting requirements. The EEOC mandates that employers, unions, and employment agencies audit their minority population annually. All employers covered by Title VII that have 100 or more employees and government contracts of $50,000 or more must file Employer Information Report Form EEO–1, which details the composition of the employer's workforce.

Posting requirement. The EEOC requires that employers, unions, and employment agencies post a prescribed notice summarizing pertinent provisions of Title VII. The notice is available in both English and Spanish. It must be conspicuously posted where employment notices are customarily displayed. Willful violation of this requirement is punishable by a fine of up to $100 for each offense.

THE EQUAL PAY ACT OF 1963

Sex discrimination in wages is specifically forbidden by the Equal Pay Act of 1963. Essentially, the Equal Pay Act, a short amendment to the Fair Labor Standards Act of 1938 (the Wage-Hour law, which provides for payment of the federal minimum wage and overtime pay), requires the payment of equal wages for equal work between the sexes. Until 1979 it was enforced by the Wage-Hour Division of the Labor Department. After 1979 enforcement responsibility was transferred to the EEOC.

Equal pay for equal work

The Equal Pay Act prohibits differences in pay between the two sexes for employees who are performing work that requires "equal skill, effort and responsibility" and is "performed under similar working conditions." If even one male (or female) is paid at a higher rate than members of the opposite sex who are doing equal work, a violation of the act may be found.

The term *equal* in the phrase *equal skill, effort and responsibility* is, however, subject to varying interpretations. In *Wirtz* v. *Wheaton Glass Co.*, the first equal pay case to reach a federal court of appeals, male glass packers performed extra menial tasks not done by female glass packers.[10] The employer argued that men were paid more than women because of this "difference" in work. The court, however, rejected this argument and held that the work of men and women workers need not be identical, but only substantially equal, to justify equal pay. Thus small differences in job descriptions will not make jobs so unequal as to justify a higher pay scale for one sex where both sexes perform essentially the same tasks.

In writing the Equal Pay Act, Congress referred to equality of "skill," "effort," and "responsibility" exercised "under similar working conditions" primarily because these are the criteria by which industry evaluates jobs for classification purposes. Like the term *equal,* however, the other terms may have more than one meaning. The Supreme Court has held that equal

[10] 427 F.2d 259 (3d Cir. 1970).

skill, effort, and responsibility, will be defined according to industrial usage. For example in *Corning Glass* v. *Brennan* the Supreme Court considered whether the differences between the day and night shifts were sufficient to determine that female day-shift employees were working under conditions similar to those of males on the night shift.[11] The Court rejected the employer's argument that different shifts constituted different working conditions and therefore a reason to pay male night-shift workers a higher rate. The Court said that in the glass industry the term *working conditions* commonly did not refer to the time of day during which work was performed.

Exceptions

There are several exceptions to the equal work–equal pay standard. These include situations in which pay differentials arise due to a seniority system, a merit system, a system which bases earnings on the quantity or quality of work, or a system which bases differentials on a factor other than sex. The first two exceptions are self-explanatory. The third exception is illustrated by systems in which employees are paid an individual production piece rate. Here there would be no equal pay violation even though male and female workers performed identical work on an assembly line but received different wages. However, it is difficult to prove that a wage disparity is based on a factor other than sex. Although wage differentials based on day-night shifts are not working conditions, higher pay to a male can be legitimately based on a factor other than sex if the male's extra rate is paid because of a night-shift differential.

No sex-based wage discrimination exists where a wage disparity arises out of a bona fide training program which rotates males in management training through all departments and therefore requires them to work temporarily with females who receive a lower rate than the trainees. However, training programs which are available only to employees of one sex will be carefully scrutinized to determine whether the programs are, in fact, bona fide exceptions. The following case illustrates the judicial posture toward training programs.

Schultz v. *First Victoria National Bank*
420 F.2d 648 (5th Cir. 1969)

Secretary of Labor Schultz (petitioner) alleged that First Victoria National Bank and the American Bank of Commerce (respondents) paid female bookkeepers and tellers substantially less than they paid male employees performing the same work. The district court found that the pay differential was based on bona fide training programs which were "a factor other than sex." The court of appeals reversed.

---

[11] 417 U.S. 188 (1974).

Brown, Chief Judge: . . . The training programs that the District Court found to exist and to be the justification for the unequal pay were informal, unwritten, and if not imaginary, consisted of little more than the recognition of the ability of employees to work their way up the ranks. The training program was supposed to provide rotation for the "trainee" through the various departments of the bank so the employee would more fully comprehend the banks' operations. Such rotation of the male "trainees" was, however, not distinguishable from the normal course of employment for the female employees. The rotation of the "trainee" has apparently been unpredictable, sporadic, and unplanned. The time spent in each department varied widely and was in fact based not upon any concept of training but upon the banks' personnel needs.

Moreover, there was no definite understanding or agreement between the banks and their male employees concerning a training program. Mr. Sheffield, Vice President of First Victoria in charge of personnel, testified that when he hired an employee he did not know if that employee would be "trained" to be an officer. Yet, the male employees were started at substantially higher salaries than female employees performing the same task. . . .

Thus it is apparent that the training programs that the District Court found to exist and be the motivation for the discrimination were not specific and their metes and bounds were at best poorly surveyed. As structured and oper-

ated it was [sic] little more than a post-event justification for disparate pay to men and women from the commencement of employment up through advancement. The training was essentially the acquiring of skills, and experience and knowledge of the business through continued performance of regular tasks. In this sense every job in every type of business would be training. . . .

Moreover, such imprecise programs are outside the scope of the broad statutory exception—"a factor other than sex"— because they are not in harmony with the Congressional purpose: The elimination of those subjective assumptions and traditional stereotyped misconceptions regarding the value of women's work. These programs are inconsistent since in actual operation the work and role of the male employees–"trainees" cannot be distinguished from the female workers who do the same jobs and who are likewise learning and growing in the business but without the title of trainee.

*   *   *   *   *

. . . Since the commencement of this proceeding both banks made female employees officers. Both banks thus obviously recognized that some of their women employees had the capacity and the drive to become officers. Both banks, nevertheless, included none of these women in the "training programs." Thus the system starts with discrimination on sex with no showing yet that any exception would justify it.

Case questions

1. Describe the training programs and their operation and effect.

2. Why were the training programs not "a factor other than sex"?

3. After the case was commenced, the

banks altered their employment practices. What effect did this have on the court?

4. If the training programs had been formalized in an employment manual, would they have justified the pay disparities?

THE AGE DISCRIMINATION IN EMPLOYMENT ACT OF 1967

The manifest purpose of the Age Discrimination in Employment Act (ADEA) is to promote the employment of older workers on the basis of their ability rather than their age. The ADEA prohibits discrimination against older workers by employers, employment agencies, and labor organizations. The secretary of labor was originally charged with its enforcement and administration, but these functions have been transferred to the EEOC. ADEA guidelines and interpretative bulletins developed by the Labor Department remain available to employers and courts.

The protected group

When the ADEA was enacted, it protected only persons between the ages of 40 and 65. In 1978, however, Congress extended the act's protection to all nonfederal employees up to age 70 who are covered by the act. Thus, under the act it may be unlawful for an employer to discriminate in its hiring practices by giving individuals 30 years of age a preference over individuals 40-to-70 years of age. The same employer, however, would not be prohibited by the act from refusing to hire applicants between the ages of 30 and 39, since these are not within the protected age range. Similarly, an employer could indicate a preference for individuals who are at least 40 but less than 70 years of age, since those excluded do not fall within the protected class. If, however, an employer indicates a preference for persons between the ages of 40 and 50, the employer may be violating the act because it is unlawful to discriminate on the basis of age between persons within the protected group.

Covered employers

Notwithstanding the limitations on the ADEA's protection outside the designated age range, all nonseasonal employers with 20 or more employees whose businesses affect commerce fall within the act.

Firms engaged in international commerce may also qualify as regulated employers under the ADEA. Thus domestic contractors working abroad must conform their local hiring practices to the ADEA, even though their principal effort may be overseas. Similarly, U.S. subsidiaries of foreign firms are covered if they meet the statutory requirements. Under the DOL guidelines, if the total number of a firm's foreign and domestic personnel totals 20 or more, the enterprise constitutes an "employer" under the act.

Covered employment agencies

Employment agencies fall within the act and are prohibited from referring prospective employees on the basis of age. If an employment agency regularly finds employees for at least one covered employer, it is subject to the ADEA with regard to all its clients. Thus a covered agency can be subject to the act's provisions even when it is acting on behalf of a noncovered employer. It is also a violation of the act to indicate an age preference in a published notice or advertisement.

ADEA's prohibitions and requirements

ADEA's prohibitions generally parallel those contained in Title VII. Employers are prohibited from discriminating against persons between the ages of 40 and 70 in hiring, compensation, or other conditions of employment. Any segregation or classification of employees is unlawful if it is based on age. Furthermore, the prohibitions ban retaliatory action against individuals for having participated in proceedings or pursued rights granted under the ADEA.

Employers are required to maintain a conspicuously posted notice explaining the act's provisions. Record-keeping requirements have also been imposed on all covered entities in order to effectuate the administration of the act. If there has been discrimination in the payment of wages, a reduction in the higher wage rate will not cure the violation. The older employee earning the lower rate must be brought up to the higher rate.

Exceptions

Certain exceptions to the ADEA are permitted, which, if established, will exonerate an employer's actions. Thus it is permissible for an employer to discriminate on the basis of age "where age is a bona fide occupational qualification reasonably necessary to the normal operations of a particular business." Practices based on reasonable factors other than age, and discharges or other discipline of individuals for cause, are also allowed. Further allowance is made for discriminatory practices which are pursuant to a bona fide seniority system or an employee benefit plan. In addition to these exceptions, the EEOC is authorized to establish any others which are necessary to the public interest.

THE REHABILITATION ACT OF 1973

Sections 503 and 504 of the Vocational Rehabilitation Act of 1973 prohibit discrimination against handicapped persons by federal contractors and require federal contractors to take affirmative action in hiring qualified handicapped persons. A qualified handicapped person is anyone who has (or had a record or history of) a physical or mental impairment that substantially limits one or more of life's major activities. This includes such diverse impairments as blindness, diabetes, epilepsy, heart disease, and alcoholism. Conceivably, a person with a history of cancer or mental disease, a mentally retarded person, or a deaf individual could also be included. The law applies to any job that, with "reasonable accommodation" for his or her handicap, a worker can perform at the minimum level of productivity expected of a normal person in that job.

Sections 503 and 504 of the act do not require employers to hire persons unqualified to do the job. In *Davis* v. *Butcher*[12] a federal district court concluded that persons with histories of drug use, including present participants in methadone maintenance programs, were handicapped. However, the court noted that "if, in any individual situation, it can be shown that a particular addiction, or prior drug use, prevents successful performance of a job, an applicant need not be provided the employment opportunity." A 1978 amendment to the Rehabilitation Act supports this position. Employment decisions, therefore, must be based on ability to perform a task rather than on stereotypes of handicapped people.

The Labor Department enforces this legislation. The department has issued regulations forbidding discrimination against handicapped persons and requiring employers having federal contracts for more than $2,500 to take affirmative action to hire the handicapped. The regulations provide that such a contractor "must attempt to make a reasonable accommodation to the physical and mental limitations of an employee or applicant" unless the contractor can establish that this would impose undue hardship on the conduct of the contractor's business. The regulations provide for consideration of business necessity, financial expense and cost, and resultant personnel problems in determining the extent of a contractor's accommodation responsibilities. Contractors that are in noncompliance may be liable for breach of contract and may be barred from entering into future federal contracts. A current issue is whether in addition to authorizing governmental action, the act provides a private cause of action by a handicapped individual against an employer. Courts have divided on this issue.

THE CIVIL RIGHTS ACT OF 1866

In the Civil War the issues of freedom and the relative rights of governments were joined. Following the war the 13th Amendment to the U.S. Constitution was ratified. It provided that slavery and involuntary servitude should not exist in the United States and gave Congress power to enforce this by appropriate legislation.

The Civil Rights Act of 1866 (42 U.S.C. section 1981) sought to implement the 13th Amendment and to eliminate the incidence of servitude. The act provides that all persons in the United States "shall have the same right . . . to make and enforce contracts . . . and to the full and equal benefit of all laws . . . as is enjoyed by white citizens."

In 1975 the Supreme Court held in *Johnson* v. *Railway Express Agency, Inc.,* that section 1981 provided a federal remedy against racial discrimination

---

[12] 451 F. Supp. 791 (E.D.Pa. 1978).

in employment.[13] Although the phrase "as is enjoyed by white citizens" seemed to limit the act's application to racial discrimination directed against nonwhites, the Supreme Court in *McDonald* v. *Santa Fe Trail Transportation Co.* relied upon the act's language and legislative history to conclude that section 1981 also applied to racial discrimination in employment against white persons. Sex discrimination has been excluded from the act's coverage. Courts have applied section 1981 to discrimination against aliens. Thus, although an alien has no remedy under Title VII, he or she can sue in federal court under section 1981. Courts are divided over whether section 1981 covers national origin discrimination.

Section 1981 applies only to racial discrimination, whereas Title VII includes other forms of discrimination. Title VII provides assistance in investigation, conciliation, and counsel, which are unavailable under section 1981. In litigation under section 1981, employers do not have available the bfoq defense that is available under Title VII in cases of national origin discrimination. Under Title VII a back pay award is limited to two years of unpaid wages, whereas section 1981 does not restrict the plaintiff's remedy.

THE EXECUTIVE ORDER PROGRAM

Various executive orders not only ban discrimination in employment by federal contractors but also require that federal contractors undertake affirmative action plans. The Office of Federal Contract Compliance Programs (OFCCP) of the Labor Department administers the executive order program.

The concept of affirmative action originated through a series of executive orders. The most important of these, Executive Order 11246, requires that government contractors take affirmative action to insure that their employees are hired and promoted on a nondiscriminatory basis.

Executive Order 11246 requires that all government contracts include a clause which states the contractor's agreement not to discriminate on the basis of race, creed, color, or national origin (a later executive order added sex as a category). The clause also states the contractor's agreement to take affirmative action to insure that no discrimination occurs. Thus, under the executive order program the duties of nondiscrimination and affirmative action are conditions included in every federal contract. Contractors wishing to do business with the federal government must agree to these terms or take their business elsewhere. Executive Order 11246 provides that contracts may be canceled or suspended in part and that contractors may be declared ineligible for further government contracts.

Revised Order No. 4

To supplement the affirmative action programs required of all government contractors, the OFCCP issued Revised Order No. 4 for use as a guide in

---

[13] 421 U.S. 454 (1975).

developing and judging the affirmative action programs of contractors outside the construction industry. Revised Order No. 4 states that a covered contractor will be in noncompliance with Executive Order 11246 unless it has developed an acceptable affirmative action plan by using the standards and guidelines set forth in the revised order. Revised Order No. 4 requires that an affirmative action plan with realistic goals and timetables be prepared by each employer with 50 or more employees and a contract or subcontract of $50,000 or more. It offers a comprehensive statement of the steps required to develop and implement such a plan. First, the employer must perform a utilization analysis, including evaluation of the size of the minority and female population and labor force in the area, the requisite skills among minorities and women in the area and the available training programs and facilities. Having completed this analysis, the employer must identify the deficiencies in its work force. It must then establish attainable goals for correcting and eliminating those deficiencies and a timetable for achieving the goals. The employer must develop methods for implementing the plan which is calculated to achieve the goals. Such methods include wide internal and external dissemination of the employer's policy, making a high-level official responsible for implementation, utilizing minority and female sources to seek personnel, and utilizing minority and female employees as recruiters.

An employer is not in violation of its plan if it fails to meet its goals, provided the employer has made good faith efforts to do so. This is the principal difference between goals and quotas. If a contractor is required by law to meet the goals, they become quotas.

POLICY CONSIDERATIONS

As already noted, in enforcing equal employment opportunity laws, heavy reliance is placed on statistics. Statistics are the essence of prima facie cases of disparate impact and of cases of pattern or practice of discrimination. Statistics are also used to show that an employer's rebuttal to a disparate treatment case is pretextual. Statistics were intended as a means to an end— determining whether an employer's practices discriminated against a particular group of individuals. Critics contend that for many employers they have become an end in themselves.

Consider, for example, the disparate impact case. The goal of Title VII in this area is to have employers use racially neutral and job-related criteria for employment and promotion. It seems logical that an employer will seek to validate its practices if it knows it will be liable for job requirements that have not been validated. Validation, however, is expensive, time consuming, and imprecise. There is no guarantee that it will be accepted by the EEOC and courts. Consequently, many employers have sought to avoid the problem of validation by insuring that their statistics demonstrate no disparate impact. Thus, instead of being racially or sexually neutral, the employment process becomes race- or sex-conscious. The result is that institutionalized impediments to minority employees remain unvalidated while majority employees resent what they view as favoritism in the hiring and promotion of minorities.

Supporters of validation respond to these criticisms by challenging the critics to devise a more workable method of enforcement. They argue that as long as validation is carried out by generally accepted professional methods, employers need not fear challenges to their job requirements. They characterize statistic-conscious employers as shortsighted.

Review problems

1. Prior to 1975 an employer refused to hire blacks or women. After 1965 the employer dropped this policy but failed to attract many qualified black or female employees except at the low levels. Consequently, the employer and the union agreed to implement an affirmative action program designed to eliminate a perceived racial imbalance in the employer's work force. The program called for a special apprenticeship program, with the graduates guaranteed employment. Preference for entry to the program was given to current low-level employees according to seniority. Seventy-five percent of the slots were reserved for blacks. When the program began, there were 20 slots. Ten whites and 30 blacks applied. Five of the whites were male, and five were female. All of the blacks were male. The white males had worked for the employer since 1963. Because they had far greater seniority than the white females they received the five white slots in the program. The 15 black slots went to 15 black males, 10 of whom had less seniority than the 5 white females. Has Title VII been violated?

2. Your company has decided to close an obsolete plant. The plant employs 15 supervisors. The company has room to transfer 12 to other plants, but must lay off 3. The ages of the three oldest supervisors are 61, 60, and 58. These supervisors are eligible for early retirement, whereas the remaining 12 are not. They have been with the company longest and therefore receive the highest salaries. If you force them to take early retirement, you will save a substantial sum in salaries and retirement contributions and benefits. If you do so, will you violate ADEA?

3. A state requires prison guards to be at least 5 feet 2 inches tall and to weigh at least 120 pounds. Although an equal percentage of the male and female job applicants meet these qualifications, statistics compiled by the Census Bureau show that nationally 41 percent of the female population does not meet the height requirement, as compared to 1 percent of the male population. Does the requirement violate Title VII?

4. An employer pays its secretaries an average of $2 per hour less than it pays its manual laborers. Although both jobs are open to both sexes, all of the employer's manual laborers are male while all of its secretaries are female. Is the employer violating either Title VII or the Equal Pay Act?

5. A seniority system requires anyone who is promoted to sacrifice all accrued seniority. The employees in the lowest job classifications are 95 percent black, while those in the highest classifications are 100 percent white. The employer maintained separate lunchroom, rest room, and locker facilities for blacks and whites for several years after the effective date of Title VII. Is the seniority system bona fide?

6. Brown is an assembly line worker for General Motors Corporation (GM). GM operates six days per week, with all employees given Sunday off. The employees bid by seniority for their second day off. Brown, a Sabbatarian with low seniority, is required to work Saturdays. GM employs "extraboard men" who are on call to work in case of unscheduled absences. Must GM accommodate Brown's religious beliefs?

7. Seventh-Day Adventists are prohibited by their religion from joining labor unions. May an employer legally terminate a Seventh-Day Adventist who refuses to abide by a union shop agreement which requires all employees to join the union within 30 days of starting work?

8. A restaurant hires only female waitresses and cashiers. It features "businessmen's lunches" and "stag dinners." All waitresses and cashiers work topless. Is the restaurant violating Title VII?

9. An employer obtains all of its employees from the union-run hiring hall. The agreement between the employer and the union provides for job referrals based on seniority. Employees are classified as permanent or temporary, with permanent employees given preference over temporaries. To be classified permanent, an employee must work at least 45 weeks in a year. Before Title VII became effective, the employer refused to hire blacks. After 1965 the employer dropped its whites-only policy, but because black employees lack seniority, few of them have been able to accumulate the 45 work weeks needed to become permanent employees. Does this violate Title VII?

10. Discuss the use of statistics in employment discrimination enforcement, and evaluate the policy considerations which favor or disfavor their continued use.

PART V: REVIEW PROBLEMS

1. You are the vice president in charge of labor relations for Ace Building Company (ABC). ABC is nonunion. Prior to 1965 ABC refused to hire blacks. After 1965 it dropped its whites-only policy, but few blacks sought jobs with it. By 1975, only 17 of its 200 employees were black despite the fact that 25 percent of the general population in the surrounding area and 18 percent of all members of building trades unions were black. In 1975 ABC began an affirmative action program under which it actively recruited black workers. Today ABC employs 220 workers, of whom 37 are black.

lunch break. The leaflet charged that ABC had become "a black man's operation," that this had caused the death of a white foreman, and that ABC planned to lay off white workers. It urged employees to join the White Workers Union and secure "white rights" through collective bargaining. Osbourn Poverty, a black employee, objected to the leaflet distribution. White punched Poverty in the face, breaking his jaw.

ABC's president has called a meeting of all vice presidents to discuss the company's deteriorating employee relations. In preparation for the meeting, consider these questions:

1. Are the widows Macho, Careless, and Poverty entitled to workers' compensation benefits?
2. What can OSHA be expected to do?
3. Can ABC fire Careless?
4. **Can ABC fire White? Poverty?**
5. Can ABC lay off 20 employees according to seniority even though that will result in a layoff of 20 blacks?
6. Can ABC lay off the 20 least senior white employees?
7. Can ABC prohibit White and his supporters from soliciting for their union on company property?

Last week several ABC employees were excavating a pit. I. M. Careless, a black hired under the affirmative action program, was operating a front-end loader up and down ramps leading into the pit. In violation of company rules several other employees were riding the running board of the front-end loader. On one occasion I. M. Macho, the site foreman, was riding the running board when the front-end loader skidded off the ramp. Both Careless and Macho jumped. Carless landed clear of the front-end loader but hurt his back. He will miss work for six weeks. Macho was killed when the front-end loader landed on top of him. Carless has filed a compliant with OSHA.

Work has fallen off in the past year, and ABC will have to lay off 20 employees shortly. Rumors of layoffs have been circulating among the employees. The day after the front-end loader accident Willie White, a white employee, began distributing a leaflet during the

2. The Gregarious Gizmo Company (GGC) is a major manufacturer of gizmos. Employees who work on the assembly line are represented by Local 1 of the Gizmo Employees International Union. The collective bargaining agreement is silent concerning whether employees are permitted to smoke while on duty. The past practice has been to allow smoking.

Recently two groups of employees have written letters to the president of GGC complaining about a petition signed by 10 percent of the line employees who claimed that their health was being harmed because they were being forced to inhale the fumes of cigarette smoke. A second group submitted a petition signed by all the female line employees (about 20 percent of all the line employees) who claimed that inhaling the fumes from cigarette smokers endangers the life of a fetus and urged that cigarette smoking be banned in light of the fact that 10 line employees were pregnant.

534

The president of GGC has read much of the available literature on the effects of smoking on nonsmokers and is concerned about the threat of smoking to the health of nonsmokers and to the fetuses of pregnant employees. Prepare a report for the president which considers the following:

1. Can we ban smoking without discussing it with the union?
2. Can we discuss the question of a smoking ban with representatives of the two petitioning groups?
3. If we do not ban smoking, can we expect trouble from OSHA?
4. If we do not ban smoking, can we require all pregnant employees to take maternity leave as soon as we learn of their pregnancy?

PART SIX

Social environment of business

CHAPTER 18

Environmental law

Statistical evidence, substantiated by dramatic events, made American legislators of the 1960s and 1970s acutely aware of their dependence upon a protected environment. Evidence that emissions of sulfur dioxide increased from 22 million to 33 million tons annually between 1940 and 1970, for example, was punctuated by reports of deaths in Los Angeles caused by photochemically activated smog. Acid rain from fossil fuel combustion in the Northeastern United States destroyed 200 lakes in the New York Adirondack Mountains alone; the fish in those lakes had been killed, and the aquatic vegetation had dwindled severely. Floating wastes in the Great Lakes around Ohio self-ignited.

During the 1970s state and federal legislators responded to these hazards and other problems of balancing civilization's growth with stewardship of the environment. Common-law environmental protections still served to settle some individual disputes, but broader environmental policy concerns had to be addressed by statutes. This chapter explains the nature and limitations of common-law environmental protections, details governmental policies, and describes some federal and state programs for pollution control, land use, and resource management.

COMMON-LAW PROTECTIONS

Under common law, landholders can use a range of responses to keep their land free of encumbrances, their water free of obstructions, and their air free of debris. Depending upon the interests they have at stake, landholders can sue under the theories of trespass, nuisance, negligence, or strict liability.

Note: This chapter was written by Carol D'Laine Ditzhazy Vogel, Assistant Director Legal Writing and Research, IIT/Chicago-Kent College of Law.

Trespass

The trespass action protects landholders' interests in the exclusive possession of their properties. Under this common-law theory, any intrusion onto land without permission or lawful right gives the possessor of the land the right to sue the intruder for damages.

Single trespass.   If a worker were to begin a construction project on one lot but drive a truck across a second lot to bring in supplies, the owner of the second lot would have the right to sue the worker for trespass. The worker's accounting for interference with the owner's right to exclusive possession of the second lot would include the costs of repairing any damage done to the owner's sod.

If the worker had not damaged the sod at all, or even left tracks across lot 2, the worker would still be liable for nominal damages. The common law awarded damages in name, though many times only $1 in amount, because it greatly favored interests in land.

Continuing trespass.   So long as workers set events in motion that cause a physical invasion of owners' properties, they trespass those properties even if they do not personally set foot on them. If in excavating the foundation for a house on lot 1, a worker were to dump dirt and trees on lot 2, the owner of lot 2 could sue for trespass. Trespass in this case, however, is not a simple, completed act. The presence of dirt and trees on lot 2 makes this a continuing trespass.

The common law did not settle on a simple remedy for continuing trespass. Some courts allowed landholders to maintain successive actions, recovering periodically as long as the offending objects remained. Other courts, dissatisfied with the inconvenience this caused landholders, allowed them to dispose of these matters in a single action. By awarding in a single suit all damages, past and prospective, these courts made recovery more convenient. Still, damages were often speculative and trespasses were sometimes terminated long after judgments.

Invasions by particles.   Continuing trespasses were further complicated where the offending objects were particulate matter sent onto the owner's lot by a worker in a factory on a neighboring lot. Historically, the trespass action depended upon proving a direct physical invasion of the land as clear as a worker's dumping debris from a wheelbarrow. For hundreds of years the invasion of land by particles smaller than the eye could see was an insufficient ground for finding a trespass. Direct invasion was impossible to prove. This limitation was a significant drawback to the use of trespass actions to fight fine dusts emanating from factories, which, slowly but surely, might cover the ground as effectively as would depositing debris from a wheelbarrow all at once.

In this century, scientific capacity to peer into the atomic world has overcome the problem of proving direct invasion by particulates. Advances in atomic physics provided means of tracking particulates from their sources to their destinations. Thus, where gases and particles from fluoride compounds escaped from an aluminum reduction plant and made people's land unfit for raising livestock, owners were able to recover for losses of affected animals.[1]

Statutes of limitations. Difficulties remain, however, in providing a general remedy for continuing trespass. Since states set limitations on the time in which suits could be brought, some landholders found that they lost the right to object to trespass offenses if they waited too long. This was not a problem in areas were the offenses were suable in successive actions, because the right to sue renewed continually. In areas with single-action provisions, however, the time to sue began with the initiation of the trespass. Once the time to sue ran out, courts in these areas barred landholders from taking action to have the offending materials removed, even though interference with the exclusive possession of their properties continued.

Limited rights to airspace. Some 20th-century developments have changed even simple trespass actions in a way that has left landholders without this effective private remedy. Common-law land rights were long considered to extend down into the earth and up into the sky. Thus, if an airplane pilot took off from lot 1 and flew over lot 2, the owner of lot 2 could sue the pilot for trespass. The exercise of this option to keep airplane noise and vibrations away from landholders' properties had to give way with the progress of aviation.

Some courts drew the line on landholders' rights to sue for trespass at the limit of their effective possession. Only where they would effectively use the airspace, as for trees that would grow to a certain height, could they sue for trespass.[2] Some courts went further, allowing suit only where actual use was made of the airspace. Many states reacted to these limitations by passing laws which recognized landholders' rights to all airspace above their land, limited only by a privilege of flight similar to the public right to make use of a navigable stream.

Although this problem has not been definitely settled, one modern trend avoids problems of air ownership completely by allowing suits only where flights result in actual interference with the use of land. Under this approach, flight directly over land is irrelevant; thus trespass is not the theory under which to sue. Liability for actual interference must be found under nuisance or negligence.

Nuisance

The nuisance action protects landholders' interests in the use and enjoyment of their properties. All landholders' rights to use and enjoy their properties are necessarily subject to the rights of other landholders to do the same,

---

[1] *Martin* v. *Reynolds Metal Co.*, 221 Ore. 86, 342 P.2d 790 (1959), certiorari denied, 362 U.S. 918 (1960).

[2] *Smith* v. *New England Aircraft Co.*, 270 Mass. 511, 170 N.E. 385 (1930).

so the courts weigh the utility of the conduct of one landholder against the gravity of the harm caused another. Generally, if the harm caused by the conduct outweighs its utility, the courts deem the conduct a nuisance.

Gravity of harm. The gravity of the harm that one landholder's conduct causes another depends upon several factors. The greater the extent and duration of the harm, the more likely it is that the harm will be taken seriously. Occasional puffs of smoke from factory chimneys, for example, are not as grave as clouds of smoke that are always present. The greater the physical damage caused by the harm, the graver is its character. Fumes carrying chemicals that destroy lung tissue, for instance, are graver than clouds carrying dust that makes people sneeze.

Harm will not be considered grave if complaining landholders can avoid the harm by taking simple precautions against it. Thus, landholders may reasonably be expected to close their windows to keep out occasional noise.

The gravity of harm may also vary with the use complaining landholders make of their own properties. Runoff water from another's land, for example, poses a potentially graver problem if the land is used by the complainer for a residence than it does if the land is used to graze cattle.

Utility of conduct. Although certain conduct causes harm, still it may have utility. The utility of the conduct a landholder complains of depends upon several factors. The social value of the conduct is a very important factor; landholders may be required to tolerate moderate blasting noise, airplane vibrations, or refinery smells due to their place in furthering the progress demanded by society. Motives for the conduct may be considered too; the utility of drilling a well may be voided, for instance, by the driller's intention of cutting off another's access to underground water.

Means to prevent harm. If landholders have reasonably practical means to avoid causing harm to their neighbors, they may be liable for nuisance even if the harm of their conduct is shown to be slight and its social utility great. Thus, if adding coolants could reduce the temperature of power plant effluents discharged into fishing waters, failure to use the coolants would make power plant owners responsible for causing reductions in fishers' catches. Liability would not follow if implementing the means would be very expensive or difficult. If incorporating coolants into the discharge process at the power plant required redesign and reconstruction of portions of the plant, the owners would probably not be required to undertake those projects.

Property locations. Whether parties have legitimate claims or defenses to nuisance actions may depend upon where their properties are located. Courts recognize that friction among landholders has been reduced in many areas divided into residential, industrial, and agricultural districts. Therefore, courts are not likely to act on complaints about noise from a homeowner who has built on property in the middle of a business district. Neither are they likely to heed pleas from a sawmill owner to allow expanded operations in a residential district.

Injunctions. In the final determination of whether conduct amounts to a nuisance, courts factor general community concerns in with the special interests of the parties. Especially where courts may order heavy fines or enjoin further operations at plants, the impact on local community growth and citizens' jobs has to be considered.

The case that follows illustrates how state courts have limited the application of injunctions in the face of substantial investments by companies in the community.

Boomer v. Atlantic Cement Company
26 N.Y.2d 219, 257 N.E. 2d 870 (1970)

Atlantic is the operator of a cement company near Albany, New York. Boomer and other neighboring landowners sought an injunction against Atlantic to stop dirt, smoke, and vibrations emanating from the plant that were injuring their property. The trial court found that these conditions were a nuisance. However, because techniques to eliminate annoying by-products of cementmaking were unlikely to be developed by any research that Atlantic could undertake within any short period and because the plant represented an investment of more than $45 million and had 300 employees, the trial court would not grant an injunction. Rather, it allowed temporary damages to compensate for harm done to the properties of Boomer and others and granted the landowners the right to sue for damages suffered in the future. An intermediate appellate court affirmed, and the landowners appealed to the highest state court, which reversed the lower courts and granted permanent damages.

Bergan, Judge:

* * * * *

The public concern with air pollution arising from many sources in industry and in transportation is currently accorded ever wider recognition accompanied by a growing sense of responsibility in State and Federal Governments to control it. Cement plants are obvious sources

of air pollution in the neighborhoods where they operate.

* * * * *

It seems apparent that the amelioration of air pollution will depend on technical research in great depth; on a carefully balanced consideration of the economic impact of close regulation; and of the actual effect on public health. It is likely to require massive public expenditure and to demand more than any local community can accomplish and to depend on regional and interstate controls.

A court should not try to do this on its own as a by-product of private litigation and it seems manifest that the judicial establishment is neither equipped in the limited nature of any judgment it can pronounce nor prepared to lay down and implement an effective policy for the elimination of air pollution. This is an area beyond the circumference of one private lawsuit. It is a direct responsibility for government and should not thus be undertaken as an incident to solving a dispute between property owners and a single cement plant—one of many—in the Hudson River valley.

* * * * *

The ground for the denial of injunction, notwithstanding the finding both that there is a nuisance and that plaintiffs have been damaged substantially, is the large disparity in economic consequences of the nuisance and of the injunction. This theory cannot, however, be sustained without overruling a doctrine which has been consistently reaffirmed in several leading cases in this court and which has never been disavowed here, namely that where a nuisance has been found and where there has been any substantial damage shown by the party complaining an injunction will be granted.

* * * * *

Although the court at Special Term and the Appellate Division held that injunction should be denied, it was found that plaintiffs had been damaged in various specific amounts up to the time of the trial and damages to the respective plaintiffs were awarded for those amounts. The effect of this was, injunction having been denied, plaintiffs could maintain successive actions at law for damages thereafter as further damage was incurred.

The court at Special Term also found the amount of permanent damage attributable to each plaintiff, for the guidance of the parties in the event both sides stipulated to the payment and acceptance of such permanent damage as a settlement of all the controversies among the parties. The total of permanent damages to all plaintiffs thus found was $185,000. This basis of adjustment has not resulted in any stipulation by the parties.

This result at Special Term and at the Appellate Division is a departure from a rule that has become settled; but to follow the rule literally in these cases would be to close down the plant at once. This court is fully agreed to avoid that immediately drastic remedy; the difference in view is how best to avoid it.

One alternative is to grant the injunction but postpone its effect to a specified future date to give opportunity for technical advances to permit defendant to eliminate the nuisance; another is to grant the injunction conditioned on the payment of permanent damages to plaintiffs which would compensate them for the total economic loss to their property present and future caused by defendant's operations. For reasons which will be developed the court chooses the latter alternative.

If the injuction were to be granted unless within a short period—e.g., 18 months—the nuisance be abated by improved methods, there would be no assurance that any significant technical improvement would occur.

The parties could settle this private litigation at any time if defendant paid enough money and the imminent threat of closing the plant would build up the pressure on defendant. If there were no improved techniques found, there would inevitably be applications to the court at Special Term for extensions of time to perform on showing of good faith efforts to find such techniques.

Moreover, techniques to eliminate dust and other annoying by-products of cement making are unlikely to be developed by any research the defendant can undertake within any short period, but will depend on the total resources of the cement industry nationwide and throughout the world. The problem is universal wherever cement is made.

For obvious reasons the rate of the research is beyond control of defendant. If at the end of 18 months the whole industry has not found a technical solution a court would be hard put to close down this one cement plant if due regard is given to equitable principles.

On the other hand, to grant the injunction unless defendant pays plaintiffs such permanent damages as may be fixed by the court seems to do justice between the contending parties. All of the attributions of economic loss to the properties on which plaintiffs' complaints are based will have been redressed.

* * * * *

The present cases and the remedy here proposed are in a number of other respects rather similar to *Northern Indiana Public Service Co. v. W. J. & M. S. Vesey,* decided by the Supreme Court of Indiana. The gases, odors, ammonia and smoke from the Northern Indiana company's gas plant damaged the nearby Vesey greenhouse operation. An injunction and damages were sought, but an injunction was denied and the relief granted was limited to permanent damages "present, past, and future."

Denial of injunction was grounded on a public interest in the operation of the gas plant and on the court's conclusion "that less injury would be occasioned by requiring the appellant (Public Service) to pay the appellee (Vesey) all damages suffered by it . . . than by enjoining the operation of the gas plant; and that the maintenance and operation of the gas plant should not be enjoined."

The Indiana Supreme Court opinion continued: "When the trial court refused injunctive relief to the appellee upon the ground of public interest in the continuance of the gas plant, it properly retained jurisdiction of the case and awarded full compensation to the appellee. This is upon the general equitable principle that equity will give full relief in one action and prevent a multiplicity of suits."

It was held that in this type of continuing and recurrent nuisance permanent damages were appropriate. *See, also, City of Amarillo* v. *Ware,* where recurring overflows from a system of storm sewers were treated as the kind of nuisance for which permanent depreciation of value of affected property would be recoverable.

* * * * *

Thus it seems fair to both sides to grant permanent damages to plaintiffs which will terminate this private litigation. The theory of damage is the "servitude on land" of plaintiffs imposed by defendant's nuisance. *See United States* v. *Causby,* where the term "servitude" addressed to the land was used by Justice Douglas relating to the effect of airplane noise on property near an airport.

The judgment, by allowance of permanent damages imposing a servitude on land, which is the basis of the actions, would preclude future recovery by plaintiffs or their grantees.

* * * * *

Jasen, Judge (dissenting):

* * * * *

I see grave dangers in overruling our long-established rule of granting an injunction where a nuisance results in substantial continuing damage. In permitting the injunction to become inoperative upon the payment of permanent damages, the majority is, in effect, licensing a continuing wrong. It is the same as saying to the cement company, you may continue to do harm to your neighbors so long as you pay a fee for it. Furthermore, once such permanent

damages are assessed and paid, the incentive to alleviate the wrong would be eliminated, thereby continuing air pollution of an area without abatement.

It is true that some courts have sanctioned the remedy here proposed by the majority in a number of cases, but none of the authorities relied upon by the majority are analogous to the situation before us. In those cases, the courts, in denying an injunction and awarding money damages, grounded their decision on a showing that the use to which the property was intended to be put was primarily for the public benefit. Here, on the other hand, it is clearly established that the cement company is creating a continuing air pollution nuisance primarily for its own private interest with no public benefit.

* * * * *

I would enjoin the defendent cement company from continuing the discharge of dust particles upon its neighbors' properties unless, within 18 months, the cement company abated this nuisance.

It is not my intention to cause the removal of the cement plant from the Albany area, but to recognize the urgency of the problem stemming from this stationary source of air pollution, and to allow the company a specified period of time to develop a means to alleviate this nuisance.

I am aware that the trial court found that the most modern dust control devices available have been installed in defendant's plant, but, I submit, this does not mean that better and more effective dust control devices could not be developed within the time allowed to abate the pollution.

Moreover, I believe it is incumbent upon the defendant to develop such devices, since the cement company, at the time the plant commenced production (1962), was well aware of the plaintiffs' presence in the area, as well as the probable consequences of its contemplated operation. Yet, it still chose to build and operate the plant at this site.

In a day when there is a growing concern for clean air, highly developed industry should not expect acquiescence by the courts, but should, instead, plan its operations to eliminate

contamination of our air and damage to its neighbors.

Case questions

1. Before this case was decided, what was the prevailing New York rule on issuing injunctions where nuisances were found? Why did the majority say they had to change this rule?

2. Both the majority and the dissent would issue an injunction in the future if certain conditions were not met. How do the conditions imposed by the majority and the dissent differ?

3. How do the majority and the dissent differ in their views of how far the courts should

go to make policy for the elimination of air pollution generally?

4. A pulp mill that has invested $1 million in a small community discharges its pulp into a stream that flows by a local farmer's land. The farmer finds that he cannot irrigate his crops with water from the stream without severely stunting their growth. How would the majority and dissent of the court in *Boomer* decide the farmer's complaint for an injunction?

Negligence

The negligence action redresses injuries to body or property caused when one person breaches a legal duty to act reasonably toward another person. Since all persons have a legal duty to prevent unreasonably great risks of harm to others whenever they act, landholders using their properties without heed for the risks posed may be liable to others for negligence.

Liability for negligence may result from the failure of landholders to take precautions to protect their neighbors. If the owners of a rendering plant bury the carcasses of animals near underground water sources, neighbors can object to the owners' failure to seal the animals in appropriate containers or to bury them elsewhere. If the owners' actions cause their neighbors' sources of fresh drinking water to be polluted, the owners will be liable to their neighbors in negligence for their actions.

Foreseeability of consequences. If landholders plan to bring about the harms foreseeable in their actions, they are faced with more serious claims than negligence. They may even be charged with crimes against the public. On the other hand, landowners may not be charged with anything if the risks of harmful consequences from their actions are so remote that society would not make it necessary to burden human actions with precautions against them. The risk of a flash flood causing barrels to roll off the grounds of a chemical plant and crush a farmer's nearby corn plants is likely to be considered an unavoidable accident insufficient to require the plant to tie down all the barrels on its property.

If the risk of harm is appreciable, however, and if the possible consequences are serious, courts are more likely to find negligence. If untied barrels on the lands of a chemical plant are capable of exploding into flames as they roll, the strong possibility that flash floods will result in the burning of crops or barns may prompt courts to compel the plant's owners to pay for those consequences when they occur.

Burden of taking precautions. The burden that taking adequate precautions would pose to landholders is considered in determining whether they have been negligent. Tying barrels down to keep them from rolling away may be required, whereas building a structure to house them may be considered an unduly expensive alternative. Public interest in the operation of an enterprise may support the running of greater risks in doing so where costly precautions would otherwise prohibit its operation. Thus, although construction companies might be able to build bridges which would be safe against any anticipated accident, they are not required to incur the ruinous expense necessary to do so.

The probability and the extent of the harm to a complainer's interests are thus weighed against the expediency of the actor's course. Both parties' claims are finally judged by their social value.

Strict liability

The theory of strict liability generally protects landholders from harm by abnormally dangerous activities that their neighbors carry on voluntarily. Abnormally dangerous activities are those which involve a serious risk of harm to the persons, lands, or chattels of others that cannot be eliminated even if the actor exercises great care. Where landholders engage in abnormally dangerous activities, they bear responsibility for the injuries they cause despite all the precautions they take to prevent harm.

Activities are usually dangerous because they are out of place in their locality. Blasting operations are abnormally dangerous activities when they are conducted in cities, and in the same settings the storage of explosives or flammable gases in large quantities is an abnormally dangerous condition. Such activities and conditions are abnormally dangerous because they pose serious threats to human life and the integrity of property. These activities and conditions would not necessarily be considered unnatural on an uninhabited mountainside; for this reason, imposing liability for harm done requires a showing of some fault, often negligence.

ENVIRONMENTAL POLICIES

Federal environmental legislation before the 1970s was generally designed to fund research projects and assist states in handling problems of pollution control and resource management. During the 1970s Congress took a more aggressive part in setting and enforcing standards for assuring environmental quality. Declaring a national environmental policy was the first major step Congress took in this direction.

National Environmental Policy Act (NEPA)

Under Title I of NEPA Congress made the encouragement of a productive harmony between Man and nature national policy. Furthermore, it mandated consideration of this policy in all federal actions taken after January 1, 1970. Under Title II, Congress created a Council on Environmental Quality (CEQ) to monitor and report annually on the status and condition of the nation's resources. The council also reviews programs affecting the conservation and utilization of natural resources and proposes legislation to remedy their deficiencies.

Environmental impact statement (EIS). Under NEPA Congress made it clear that all federal agencies would have to address environmental concerns along with economic and technical considerations when planning or making decisions. Furthermore, those agencies undertaking "major Federal actions significantly affecting the quality of the human environment" are each responsible for preparing an environmental impact statement.

An environmental impact statement must reveal any adverse environmental effects which could not be avoided if a proposal were implemented, irreversible commitments of resources that would be involved, the relationship between the short-term uses of the environment and the long-term enhancement of productivity, and possible alternative actions. The statement must be circulated to the president, the CEQ, and the public for comments.

"Major federal actions." As NEPA has been interpreted, activities wholly undertaken by federal agencies are not the only federal actions subject to EIS preparation. Activities also require an EIS if they are supported by federal funding assistance or by Federal entitlement for land use. Private enterprise thus may be consulted on information for EIS preparation when it carries on business under federal contracts, grants, subsidies, or loans. Private companies may also become involved where they need federal leases, permits, licenses, or certificates to operate.

Though many federal actions consist solely of granting private enterprise papers of entitlement to operate, these activities are generally considered to be "major." Major federal action occurs in the licensing of electric, nuclear, or hydraulic power plant operations. It also occurs in Bureau of Indian Affairs approval of leases permitting companies to commerically develop Indian lands. Authorizing the development of highways or the abandonment of railways is also major federal action, unless it concerns small, insignificant stretches in relationship to large-scale ongoing projects.

"Significantly affecting the human environment." Some consider the use by Congress of the terms *major* and *significantly affecting* the environment to have been solely for the purpose of emphasis in describing actions requiring an EIS. Others maintain that while a project may be considered a major federal action, its effects on the human environment may not be significant.

Whether major federal actions significantly affect the "human environment" depends upon the types of impacts those actions have. The following case expresses the predominant view on whether the human environment is implicated when impacts are economic or sociological, as opposed to simply physical.

Breckinridge v. *Rumsfeld*
537 F.2d 864 (6th Cir. 1976)

In November 1974 the secretary of defense announced 111 actions involving the realignment of units and closures of particular Army bases. One of these actions affected the Lexington-Bluegrass Army Depot (LBAD). The action was to eliminate 18 millitary jobs and 2,630 civilian jobs in the Lexington area, with personnel transferred to depots in California and Pennsylvania. The Army prepared an environmental assessment which concluded that because there would be no significant effect on the human environment, a formal environmental impact statement was not required. A nongovernmental research institution studied the possible socioeconomic impact of the action and concluded that the Lexington area would suffer only minimal short-term unemployment as a result of the partial closure. In August 1975, four Kentucky congressmen, two U.S. senators, two county judges, the city of Richmond, the Lexington-Fayette Urban County Government, the Greater Lexington Chamber of Commerce, three property and business owners in the vicinity of LBAD, and four civilian employees of LBAD all sued to block the proposed action. The U.S. district court granted a preliminary injunction against the U.S. Army and the Department of Defense; it did not, however, rule on the dispositive question of whether the scope of the term human environment *in NEPA extended to the closing of a military base and the transfer of personnel and functions by the U.S. Army. The court of appeals dissolved the injunction and reversed the U.S. district court.*

Phillips, Chief Judge:

* * * * *

Appellants [the Army and Defense Department] assert that this is not an environmental lawsuit. They argue that Congress did not intend that NEPA be a statutory cure-all for the temporary economic ills of Lexington, Kentucky. The appellees [complainants] counter by stating that the term "human environment" means environment which directly affects human beings, including unemployment and loss of revenue. The appellants argue that NEPA is directed only to the preservation of those resources needed to sustain present and future generations and that personal and economic interests are not in and of themselves sufficient to bring the statute into play. In the present case there is no long-term impact, no permanent commitment of a national resource and no degradation of a traditional environmental asset, but rather short-term personal inconveniences and short-term economic disruptions. We conclude that such a situation does not fall within the purview of the Act.

The contention that NEPA goes beyond what might be stated to be the "physical environment" is not in dispute. Environmental impact statements have been mandated in such diverse instances as construction of a federal jail in the back of the United States Court House in Manhattan, and railroad abandonment proceedings.

Although factors other than the physical environment have been considered, this has been done only when there existed a primary impact on the physical environment.

In discussing the breadth of NEPA, the District of Columbia Circuit has stated:

Not all deviations from local zoning will necessarily rise to the level of affecting the "quality of human environment" within the fair meaning of that term. The "overriding" issue underlying MNCPC's recommended rejection of this project was "social and economic" and as we observed, rooted in the prospective loss of real and personal property taxation. A secondary, and related factor, was the prospect of an influx of low-income workers into the County. Concerned persons might fashion a claim, supported by linguistics and etymology, that there is an impact from people pollution on "environment," if the term be stretched to its maximum. We think this type of effect cannot fairly be projected as having been within the contemplations of Congress.

We conclude that the facts of the present case likewise do not come "within the contemplation of Congress."

In discussion of NEPA on the floor of the Senate, Senator Jackson provided insight into the breadth of the statute:

> What is involved is a congressional declaration that we do not intend, as a government or as a people, to initiate actions which endanger the continued existence or the health of mankind: That we will not intentionally initiate actions which will do irreparable damage to the air, land, and water which support life on earth.

*   *   *   *

An environmental policy is a policy for people. Its primary concern is with man and his future. The basic principle of the policy is that we must strive in all that we do, to achieve a standard of excellence in man's relationships to his physical surroundings.

*   *   *   *

Taken together, the provisions of section 102 directs [*sic*] any Federal agency which takes action that it must take into account environmental management and environmental quality considerations.

In seeking to define the crucial term "the human evnironment," Senator Jackson stated:

> Mr. President, there is a new kind of revolutionary movement underway in this country. This movement is concerned with the integrity of man's life support system— the human environment.

To extend the meaning of "the integrity of man's life support system" to apply to the factual situation involved in this case would distort the congressional intent. Since the case before us is primarily concerned with the effects of unemployment, an analogy drawn by Senator Jackson is of significance:

> In many respects, the only precedent and parallel to what is proposed in S. 1075 is in the Full Employment Act of 1946, which declared an historic national policy on management of the economy and established the Council of Economic Advisers. It is my view that S. 1075 will provide an equally important national policy for the management of America's future environment.

NEPA is not a national employment act. Environmental goals and policies were never intended to reach social problems such as those presented here. We, therefore, dissolved the injunction and reverse the judgment, remanding the case to the District Court for dismissal.

*   *   *   *

Case questions

1. Why does the partial closing of a military base, which reduces jobs in one area and transfers them to another area, not affect the "human environment" within the meaning of NEPA?

2. Why does the court not believe that Congress contemplated including the facts of this case within the scope of the term *human environment?*

3. Are socioeconomic interests ever considered in determining whether actions significantly affect the human environment?

4. Would the court's decision in this case have been different if long-term unemployment in the Lexington, Kentucky, area was expected to result from the partial closure of the base?

EIS contents. Agency activities which can be connected as part of one action must be reported in one EIS. Regulations require agencies to "scope," or search for related activities, early in agency planning and decision making. Fragmenting correlated activities is prohibited, to prevent breaking an action down into component parts and thereby thwart a finding of significance sufficient to trigger EIS mandates.

An agency proposal may suggest the proper scope of action for EIS contents. Where the proposal is part of a larger project, however, the impacts of the entire project may have to be discussed. If one small part of a highway is being constructed, for example, and it is part of a bigger highway development, the impact of the construction of the entire highway must be included in one EIS unless the small road segment can be shown to have independent utility.

Every agency action causes a range of impacts. As *Breckinridge* v. *Rumsfeld* illustrated, an action causing primarily physical harm to the environment may cause socioeconomic harms secondarily. An EIS need only discuss the probable secondary consequences. Thus, where changes in surrounding land use patterns were possibilities only remotely associated with the construction of the Teton Dam, an EIS prepared without reference to those changes was considered complete.

Every agency action suggests alternatives whose impacts may be different. In the EIS, agencies must discuss and assess the reasonable alternatives. Developing case law has followed Council on Environmental Quality guidelines in encouraging opportunities for public review and comments on the desirability of every action and its alternatives.

EIS timing. The underlying policies of NEPA favor timely reporting on the effects of agency action. When planning is in its first stages, little may be known about the effects of the technologies being researched or the actions being considered. To speculate then on environmental impacts in order to formally fulfill NEPA's requirements would go against the spirit of informed analysis encouraged by the act. Much later on, however, when technologies have been applied or actions have been taken, considerable time and energy may have been spent in decisions that compromise environmental concerns. To delay the preparation of environmental impact statements until this late date would undermine the act's emphasis on broad input into the decision-making process.

Four factors have been suggested for determining how to strike a balance between these extremes when preparing an EIS for technology development programs. First, agencies should consider how likely the technology is to prove commercially feasible and how soon commercial feasibility might occur. Second, they should consider the information already available on the effects of applying the technology; then they should compare that with the available information about alternatives and their effects. Third, they should note to what extent irretrievable commitments are being made and options precluded as the development program progresses. Finally, they should consider how severe the environmental effects will be if the technology does prove commercially feasible.

These factors were weighed in favor of requiring an EIS for the government's Liquid Fast Metal Breeder Reactor Program in 1973. The deciding court took into account the magnitude of the ongoing federal investment in this program and the controversial environmental effects from future widespread deployment of breeder reactors. It referred to the rapidity with which the program had moved beyond pure scientific research toward the creation of a viable breeder reactor electrical energy industry and to the manner in which investment in this new technology was likely to restrict future alternatives. These considerations prompted it to require a program statement.[3]

Lead agencies. Where many agencies are involved in conducting or funding actions, other factors are required to determine when an EIS must be prepared. The Council on Environmental Quality suggests that agencies pool their resources and prepare one impact statement, designating a single "lead" agency to assume supervisory responsibility. Factors relevant to the selection of an appropriate lead agency include the sequence in which the agencies become involved, the respective magnitudes of their involvement, and their relative expertise with regard to the project's environmental effects. All of the agencies involved should contribute their expertise to the preparation of the EIS, and the EIS should be prepared before any of the participating agencies takes major or irreversible actions.

A federal agency may seek industry contributions in preparing an EIS. This is particularly true where an agency is seeking information on the commercial feasibility of developing technology. Although businesses may further the progress of the EIS, it is unlawful for any agency to rely on a private concern to write the impact statement.

Little NEPAs

Many states followed NEPA's design in statutes of their own requiring state and local agents to prepare environmental documents similar to the EIS. Private groups which planned to take actions that would significantly affect the environment had to undergo two reviews if federal and state authorizations or money were required for their projects. This dual review process increased paperwork and caused many delays. The two-review procedure is still being used, but federal and state officials have issued guidelines standardizing documents and synchronizing review and comment procedures to cut down on private costs.

---

[3] *Scientists' Institute for Public Information, Inc.* v. *Atomic Energy Commission,* 481 F.2d 1079 (D.C. Cir. 1973).

POLLUTION CONTROL MEASURES

Measures against pollution are designed to eliminate or carefully control the diffusion of waste particles through the air, water, and land. In the 1970s major antipollution measures were passed by legislatures in response to decades of studies showing that waste particles in natural resources had many devastating effects on the public health. Congress created the Environmental Protection Agency (EPA) to oversee many of the federal pollution control programs, and states formed similar agencies.

The Federal Water Pollution Control Act (FWPCA)

Congress passed this act with two stated goals. It sought to make the nation's water safe for swimming and fishing by 1984, and it sought to eliminate the discharge of all pollutants into navigable waters by 1985.

To achieve these goals Congress set up a nationwide program called the National Pollutant Discharge Elimination System. Permits must be obtained under this system whenever pollutants are to be discharged. Permits can only be granted by EPA or state pollution control agencies to which EPA has delegated authority.

Discharges. Discharges under the act include waste which may seep or overflow into public waters. They also include the more obvious "point source" discharges, involving conduits such as pipes, ditches, and canals. Point-source discharges cover the discharge of oil or hazardous substances, whether accidental or otherwise, and the discharge of dredged or fill material.

Publicly owned treatment works. Discharges into publicly owned treatment works, though also point-source discharges, require no permit from the system. Still, industrial users must meet certain pretreatment standards before they make such discharges. The standards are designed to assure that the pollutants in industrial discharges will be compatible with the processes used by the treatment works. Treatment works which are receiving federal grants must charge industrial users for their treatment services.

New Source Performance Standards. The treatment of pollution discharges requiring a permit depends upon the source of the discharges. If the source is a new plant, the plant must meet New Source Performance Standards set by the EPA. Food processing, paper and paperboard manufacturing, and petroleum processing are just a few of the industries for which the EPA has already developed New Source Performance Standards. For industries not covered the EPA will develop standards in the course of considering a permit application for the process involved.

Performance standards for existing sources. Plants already in operation when FWPCA was passed had to meet other EPA standards. By 1977, existing plants had to discharge in accordance with standards based on the best practicable control technology then available (BPT). By 1987, all plants will have to comply with standards based on the best available technology economically achievable in their categories (BAT).

Clean Air Act (CAA)

Congress passed this act as evidence accumulated showing that airborne particulates could cause disease and death. CAA was intended to motivate the states to control the local sources of harmful airborne particles.

National ambient air quality standards. Congress required the EPA to determine concentrations of various particles that would be consistent with human health. In addition to these primary standards, Congress required the EPA to determine secondary concentrations acceptable to animals, vegetation, property and scenic valuations. In 1971 the EPA set standards for relatively common pollutants such as dust, sulfur dioxide, carbon monoxide, nitrogen dioxide, and ozone. Later the EPA related its ozone standards to hydrocarbon measurements and set standards for lead.

State implementation plans. Once the EPA set these National Ambient Air Quality Standards, states were responsible for controlling and cleaning up areas that did not comply with them. States had to detail the measures they would use to achieve the National Ambient Air Quality Standards and to submit their plans to the EPA. The EPA could withhold federal funds, prohibit the construction of new air pollution sources, or intercede with its own plan if a state's implementation plan was inadequate.

Many states developed programs to control effluents from mobile sources of pollution. Automobile inspection and monitoring curbed the production of carbon monoxide and reduced the smog generated by the breakdown of hydrocarbons. Airborne leads diminished with reductions in gasoline lead content.

The problems caused by stationary sources of pollution were more intractable. States developed some methods for reducing local industrial pollution, including the installation of filters and brushes in plant smokestacks. Tall smokestacks were a less satisfactory solution. While these decreased local pollution, they increased regional problems. In fact, large numbers of particles released into higher strata of air seem to have contributed to the international problem of acid precipitation. This results largely when drops of moisture mix with residues of high-sulfur coals burned in power plants and smelting operations.

Emissions offset policy. Many state regions, including virtually all urban areas, failed to attain the National Ambient Air Quality Standards by 1977, the act's first deadline. The EPA published a special "emissions offset" ruling to permit growth in nonattainment areas while still assuring progress toward statutory goals. A new source of air pollution could not operate in a nonattainment area unless the operator of the new source made provision for a larger corresponding decrease of pollution. In other words the operator of the new pollution source had to install improvements or cut production in its own plant or in the plant of another operator.

Lowest achievable emission rate.   CAA amendments in 1977 extended the emissions offset policy until July 1979, when states were to have completed revising their state implementation plans (SIPs). So long as revised plans are not in place, no new pollution sources can locate in nonattainment areas. Moreover, once a revised plan is submitted, the proposed new source must comply with the lowest achievable emission rate. This rate equals the most stringent limitation possible in any SIP or as achieved in practice.

Prevention of significant deterioration.   In the 1977 CAA Amendments, Congress dictated the special protection of areas whose air quality is higher than that designated by the national ambient standards. Congress accordingly made the EPA responsible for monitoring the prevention of significant deterioration (PSD) in the air quality of these areas. States must now submit PSD programs for EPA review as part of their revised state implementation plans for meeting required air quality standards.

The preconstruction review program is the major enforcement mechanism which the EPA uses to monitor the potential for deterioration in clear air areas. A new or modified source of pollution with the potential to emit a designated tonnage of pollutants must submit to a review before it is granted a construction permit. Part of the review is a check to see whether the best available control technology has been applied for each pollutant regulated by the act.

The bubble concept.   The EPA's concern with modified sources has been focused on those which cause net increases in pollution output due to their modifications. Exempt from PSD review are modified plants which replace old equipment with new equipment producing equivalent or lower emissions. Plants whose emissions from new equipment are offset by adjustments in old equipment are also exempt. These exemptions have been likened to putting a bubble over the plant and allowing adjustments within so long as the net effect is no change. Industry favors the bubble concept and would like to see it implemented across multiple facilities, towns, and even greater areas.

Offsets under the bubble concept must be instituted "contemporaneously," or PSD review will apply. How long credit for measures to reduce emissions may be carried forward to offset planned increases is not clear.

The Resource Conservation and Recovery Act (RCRA)

To help states and local governments develop resource recovery and solid waste disposal programs, Congress enacted the Solid Waste Disposal Act (SWDA) in 1965 and amended it in 1970. States and municipalities addressed waste disposal problems in various ways. Certain states granted tax breaks to companies recycling waste materials. Other states enacted "bottle bills," which were essentially designed to encourage the use of recoverable containers. Many municipalities began to provide for sanitary landfills in disposing of waste.

In 1976 Congress led the states to address the special problems of hazardous waste sites by passing the Resource Conservation and Recovery Act amendment to SWDA. Under RCRA, handlers of hazardous wastes are required to conform with specified standards. Handlers include those who generate, transport, treat, or store hazardous wastes. Hazardous wastes are wastes that significantly contribute to a serious, irreversible illness or pose a hazard to human health when improperly managed. According to EPA regulations, hazardous wastes are characterized by ignitability, corrosivity, reactivity, and toxicity.

Generators and transporters. Generators and transporters of wastes with these characteristics must notify the EPA of the location and general description of their activities. They must also specify what wastes they are handling. The EPA will issue identification numbers to each handler.

Generators of waste must keep records on their hazardous wastes. If waste generators transport the wastes off site, they must package and label the wastes and ship the packages with a manifest. The manifest identifies the persons originating, carrying, and receiving the wastes and states the nature and quantity of the wastes. If a generator does not receive a signed copy of the manifest from the intended receiver within 45 days of the time it transports its wastes, it must report to the EPA regional administrator. In any event, generators must report to the regional administrator yearly.

Transporters must comply with the terms of the manifests they receive from generators and must keep a copy of each manifest. If waste discharge occurs during carriage, transporters must take appropriate immediate action to protect human health and the environment. They may have to clean up the discharge or notify authorities, depending upon what action is officially approved for them.

Owners or operators. Owners or operators of a hazardous waste treatment, storage, or disposal facility (TSDF) have to apply for permits allowing them to dispose of their hazardous wastes. Permits will not be issued unless certain performance standards are met. These standards have not yet been detailed by EPA regulations, but they will cover record keeping, monitoring and inspection, facility location and design, contingency plans to keep down damage from operations, personnel training, and showings of financial responsibility.

TSDFs in operation when the act was passed are in "interim status" until their application for permits can be considered for disposition. These TSDFs have to comply with EPA regulations that have already been promulgated.

Present owners or operators of TSDFs must obtain an identification number from the EPA. In running their facilities, they must analyze representative samples of waste before storing or treating them. They must act to prevent unknown entries and to minimize unauthorized ones. They must also provide training for personnel and inspect facilities to discover malfunctions. Where discharges occur, they must take necessary remedial action. Regulations are in process to provide for financial assistance for plant closings and postclosure monitoring for maintenance and liability claims.

EPA employees are authorized to enter facilities at reasonable times. They may inspect and obtain samples, and they may copy records. If violations of the hazardous waste provisions are found and not corrected, violators may ultimately be liable for a civil penalty of $25,000 per day. Knowingly making a false statement in required documents is a crime punishable by fines and by imprisonment for up to one year.

Toxic Substances Control Act (TSCA)

Congress passed this act in 1976 to generally regulate hazardous chemical substances and mixtures. Manufacturers, processors, and distributors were initially required to make reports to the EPA so that it could compile an inventory of all chemical substances and mixtures handled in the United States.

After the inventory was published, all persons seeking to manufacture any new substance or to process a present substance for a significant new use had to notify the EPA of their intention.

Congress gave the EPA administrator the power to make rules necessary to protect personal health and the environment against unreasonable risks posed by all substances and mixtures. The administrator must apply the least burdensome rule that will be effective, but the possible rules range from requiring notice of the unreasonable risk of injury to entirely prohibiting the manufacture of the substance or mixture. Intermediate options include limiting its scope of distribution or its concentration for certain uses. The EPA may also mandate that adequate warnings or instructions be given or that continuous testing and record keeping be done. TSCA also established an Interagency Testing Committee. The committee's function is to inform the administrator of substances and mixtures which he should test immediately in order to propose rules.

The administrator may issue rules upon review of a premanufacturing notice. If the information the proposed manufacturer has given is sufficient for the administrator to evaluate the risk of harm posed by the substance to be manufactured, the administrator may propose an order to prohibit its manufacture. The administrator would then go to court only if the manufacturer or processor filed an objection to the proposed order. Where threatened with the imminent production of a substance hazardous to the public, however, the administrator may directly seek an injunction in a U.S. district court to stop the manufacturing process.

Federal Environmental Pesticide Control Act (FEPCA)

Pesticides are not covered by the Toxic Substances Control Act. Since 1947 they have been regulated by the Federal Insecticide, Fungicide, and Rodenticide Act (FIFRA). That act provides that pesticides in interstate shipments be adequately labeled and unadulterated. The Federal Environmental Pesticide Control Act, passed in 1972, extended the control of FIFRA to interstate manufacturing and actual misuse of pesticides.

Pesticides are classified for general or restricted use. Restricted pesticides may be applied only by persons certified to use them. States certify pesticide applicators under the approval of the EPA.

The use of any registered pesticide in a way inconsistent with its labeling instructions is prohibited. Knowing violations of FEPCA's provisions by farmers or private applicators may lead to $1,000 in fines or 30 days in jail. More severe penalties apply to commercial applicators, dealers, or distributors who purposely violate the law. Pesticide manufacturing plants must register with the EPA. The plants must report annually on types and amounts of pesticides produced and sold. EPA agents may inspect the plants and take samples.

When a pesticide violates FEPCA provisions, the EPA administrator may issue an order to stop its sale or use. Pesticides violating the law may also be seized.

LAND USE AND RESOURCE MANAGEMENT

Energy demands in the highly industrialized United States prompted strip mining, wetlands filling, and other activities which destroyed virgin lands and spoiled scenic places. Animals displaced by these activities rarely survived. In the 1970s federal and state legislators passed laws to allow development to continue in critical areas such as virgin lands and scenic places while minimizing environmental damage. Critical areas include parks, forests, tidelands, wetlands, and continental shelves.

Approximately one third of the land area in the United States is owned by the federal government, which preserves part of its critical areas for natural beauty and develops part of them through permits granted to private industry. The U.S. government regulates both federal and state lands when licensing nuclear power plants. Federal regulations cover both nuclear power plant operations and the nuclear by-products that pose waste storage problems for the entire country.

Nuclear power development

Congress passed the Atomic Energy Act of 1946 in the belief that the government would monopolize the development of nuclear power. In the early 1950s, however, Congress concluded that development might proceed more rapidly if competitive pressures of the private sector were brought to bear on researching and applying nuclear power. Thus, in the Atomic Energy Act of 1954, Congress created the Atomic Energy Commission to oversee the private construction, ownership, and operation of commercial nuclear power reactors.

Experimenting under the 1954 act, private industry discovered that prospects for profit making in atomic energy development were uncertain, while risks of operations were substantial. The most significant risk of operation was catastrophic nuclear accident. Although such a disaster was considered remote, the potential liability overwhelmed the pooled resources of industry and private insurance companies.

Concerned that the private sector would have to withdraw from the nuclear power field, Congress passed the 1957 Price-Anderson Act. Under this act, the nuclear power industry would have to buy the maximum available amount of privately underwritten public liability insurance; then, if damages from a nuclear disaster exceeded the amount of insurance available, the act provided that the federal government would indemnify the licensee by up to $500 million. Since $60 million of private insurance was available in 1957, this effectively put a ceiling on the liability for a single nuclear disaster at $560 million.

A 1966 amendment to the act essentially required that those indemnified under the act waive all legal defenses in the event of a substantial nuclear accident. This insured a common, strict liability standard for nuclear accidents in all jurisdictions, rather than a patchwork quilt of liability standards that might be created under varying state laws.

A 1975 amendment to the act provided that those owning nuclear reactors would have to contribute $2–$5 million toward the cost of compensating victims in the event of a nuclear disaster. The intended effect of this deferred premium provision was to reduce the federal government's contribution to the liability pool. While Congress extended the act's coverage to 1987, it also provided that if damages exceeding the $560 million ceiling of liability occurred in any nuclear accident, Congress itself would review the incident and take whatever action was deemed necessary and appropriate to protect the public from the consequences of such a disaster.

The Price-Anderson Act and its $560 million limitation on liability for nuclear incidents was challenged in the 1970s. The case that follows details the Supreme Court's final position on why the act is constitutional.

Duke Power Co. v. *Carolina Environmental Study Group, Inc.*
438 U.S. 59 (1978)

In 1973 the Carolina Environmental Study Group, the Catawba Central Labor Union, and 40 individuals who lived within close proxim- *ity of planned nuclear power plants in North and South Carolina sued Duke Power Company, the investor-owned public utility which* *was constructing them. The district court found: (1) that the operations of the plants had "immediate" adverse effects upon the complainants, including thermal pollution of local lakes and emissions of nonnatural radiation into the local environment, and (2) that there was a "substantial likelihood" that Duke would not be able to complete construction and maintain operation of the plants "but for" the protection provided by the act. Thus, the district court held that the complainants had standing to challenge the act's constitutionality. The complainants chose to attack the provisions for a $560 million liability ceiling for nuclear incidents. The district court later agreed with the complainants that these provisions violated the constitutional mandate that neither human life nor property should be taken without due process of law because: (1) the $560 million amount was not rationally related to the potential losses; (2) the act tended to encourage irresponsibility in matters of safety and environmental protection; and (3) the act's protections did not provide a quid pro quo for state law provisions that the act superseded. Duke Power Company appealed to the Supreme Court, which disagreed with the district court's holding.*

Mr. Chief Justice Burger:

*   *   *   *   *

A

Our due process analysis properly begins with a discussion of the appropriate standard of review. Appellants, portraying the liability-limitation provision as a legislative balancing of economic interests, urge that the Price-Anderson Act be accorded the traditional presumption of constitutionality generally accorded economic regulations and that it be upheld absent proof of arbitrariness or irrationality on the part of Congress. Appellees, however, urge a more elevated standard of review on the ground that the interests jeopardized by the Price-Anderson Act "are far more important than those in the economic due process and business-oriented cases" where the traditional rationality standard has been invoked.

An intermediate standard like that applied in cases such as *Craig v. Boren* (equal protection challenge to statute requiring that males be older than females in order to purchase beer) or *United States Trust Co. of New York* v. *New Jersey* (Contract Clause challenge to repeal of statutory covenant providing security for bondholders) is thus recommended for our use here.

As we read the Act and its legislative history, it is clear that Congress' purpose was to remove the economic impediments in order to stimulate the private development of electric energy by nuclear power while simultaneously providing the public compensation in the event of a catastrophic nuclear incident. The liability-limitation provision thus emerges as a classic example of an economic regulation—a legislative effort to structure and accommodate "the burdens and benefits of economic life." "It is by now well established that [such] legislative Acts . . . come to the Court with a presumption of constitutionality, and that the burden is on one complaining of a due process violation to establish that the legislature has acted in an arbitrary and irrational way." That the accommodation struck may have profound and far-reaching consequences, contrary to appellees' suggestion, provides all the more reason for this Court to defer to the congressional judgment unless it is demonstrably arbitrary or irrational.

B

When examined in light of this standard of review, the Price-Anderson Act, in our view, passes constitutional muster. The record before us fully supports the need for the imposition of a statutory limit on liability to encourage private industry participation and hence bears a rational relationship to Congress' concern for stimulating the involvement of private enterprise in the production of electric energy through the use of atomic power; nor do we understand appellees or the District Court to be of a different view. Rather their challenge is to the alleged arbitrariness of the *particular figure* of $560 million, which is the statutory ceiling on liability. The District Court aptly summarized its position:

The amount of recovery is not rationally related to the potential losses. Abundant evidence in the record shows that although major catastrophe in any particular place is not certain and may not be extremely likely, nevertheless, in the territory where these plants are located, damage to life and property for this and future generations could well be many, many times the limit which the law places on liability.

Assuming, *arguendo,* that the $560 million fund would not insure full recovery in all conceivable circumstances—and the hard truth is that no one can ever know—it does not by any means follow that the liability limitation is therefore irrational and violative of due process. The legislative history clearly indicates that the $560 million figure was not arrived at on the supposition that it alone would necessarily be sufficient to guarantee full compensation in the event of a nuclear incident. Instead, it was conceived of as a "starting point" or a working hypothesis. The reasonableness of the statute's assumed ceiling on liability was predicated on two corollary considerations—expert appraisals of the exceedingly small risk of a nuclear incident involving claims in excess of $560 million, and the recognition that in the event of such an incident, Congress would likely enact extraordinary relief provisions to provide additional relief, in accord with prior practice.

*   *   *   *   *

Given our conclusion that, in general, limiting liability is an acceptable method for Congress to utilize in encouraging the private development of electric energy by atomic power, candor requires acknowledgment that whatever ceiling figure is selected will, of necessity, be arbitrary in the sense that any choice of a figure based on imponderables like those at issue here can always be so characterized. This is not, however, the kind of arbitrariness which flaws otherwise constitutional action. When appraised in terms of both the extremely remote possibility of an accident where liability would exceed the limitation and Congress' now statutory commitment to "take whatever action is

deemed necessary and appropriate to protect the public from the consequences of" any such disaster, we hold the congressional decision to fix a $560 million ceiling, at this stage in the private development and production of electric energy by nuclear power, to be within permissible limits and not violative of due process.

This District Court's further conclusion that the Price-Anderson Act "tends to encourage irresponsibility . . . on the part of builders and owners" of the nuclear power plants simply cannot withstand careful scrutiny. We recently outlined the multitude of detailed steps involved in the review of any application for a license to construct or to operate a nuclear power plant; nothing in the liability-limitation provision undermines or alters in any respect the rigor and integrity of that process. Moreover, in the event of a nuclear accident the utility itself would suffer perhaps the largest damages. While obviously not to be compared with the loss of human life and injury to health, the risk of financial loss and possible bankruptcy to the utility is in itself no small incentive to avoid the kind of irresponsible and cavalier conduct implicitly attributed to licensees by the District Court.

The remaining due process objection to the liability-limitation provision is that it fails to provide those injured by a nuclear accident with a satisfactory *quid pro quo* for the common-law rights of recovery which the Act abrogates. Initially, it is not at all clear that the Due Process Clause in fact requires that a legislatively enacted compensation scheme either duplicate the recovery at common law or provide a reasonable substitute remedy. However, we need not resolve this question here since the Price-Anderson Act does, in our view, provide a reasonably just substitute for the common-law or state tort law remedies it replaces.

The legislative history of the liability-limitation provisions and the accompanying compensation mechanism reflects Congress' determination that reliance on state tort law remedies and state-court procedures was an unsatisfactory approach to assuring public compensation for nuclear accidents, while at the same time providing the necessary incentives for private development of nuclear-produced energy. The remarks of Chairman Anders of the NRC before the Joint Committee on Atomic Energy during the 1975 hearings on the need for renewal of the Price-Anderson Act are illustrative of this concern and of the expectation that the Act would provide a more efficient and certain vehicle for assuring compensation in the unlikely event of a nuclear incident:

> The primary defect of this alternative [nonrenewal of the Act], however, is its failure to afford the public either a secure source of funds or a firm basis for legal liability with respect to new plants. While in theory no legal limit would be placed on liability, as a practical matter the public would be less assured of obtaining compensation than under Price-Anderson. Establishing liability would depend in each case on state tort law and procedures, and these might or might not provide for no-fault liability, let alone the multiple other protections now embodied in Price-Anderson. The present assurance of prompt and equitable compensation under a pre-structured and nationally applicable protective system would give way to uncertainties, variations and potentially lengthy delays in recovery. It should be emphasized, moreover, that it is collecting a judgment, not filing a lawsuit, that counts. Even if defenses are waived under state law, a defendant with theoretically "unlimited" liability may be unable to pay a judgment once obtained. When the defendant's assets are exhausted by earlier judgments, subsequent claimants would be left with uncollectable awards. The prospect of inequitable distribution would produce a race to the courthouse door in contrast to the present system of assured orderly and equitable compensation.

Appellees, like the District Court, differ with this appraisal on several grounds. They argue, *inter alia,* that recovery under the Act would not be greater than without it, that the waiver of defenses required by the Act is an idle gesture since those involved in the development of nuclear energy would likely be held strictly liable

under common-law principles; that the claim-administration procedure under the Act delays rather than expedites individual recovery; and finally that recovery of even limited compensation is uncertain since the liability ceiling does not vary with the number of persons injured or amount of property damaged. The extension of short state statutes of limitations and the provision of omnibus coverage do not save the Act, in their view, since such provisions could equally well be included in a fairer plan which would assure greater compensation.

We disagree. We view the congressional *assurance* of a $560 million fund for recovery, accompanied by an express statutory commitment, to "take whatever action is deemed necessary and appropriate to protect the public from the consequences of" a nuclear accident, to be a fair and reasonable substitute for the uncertain recovery of damages of this magnitude from a utility or component manufacturer, whose resources might well be exhausted at an early stage. The record in this case raises serious questions about the ability of a utility or component manufacturer to satisfy a judgment approaching $560 million—the amount guaranteed under the Price-Anderson Act. Nor are we persuaded that the mandatory waiver of defenses required by the Act is of no benefit to potential claimants. Since there has never been, to our knowledge, a case arising out of a nuclear incident like those covered by the Price-Anderson Act, any discussion of the standard of liability that state courts will apply is necessarily speculative. At the minimum, the statutorily mandated waiver of defenses establishes at the threshold the right of injured parties to compensation without proof of fault and eliminates the burden of delay and uncertainty which would follow from the need to litigate the question of liability after an accident. Further, even if strict liability were routinely applied, the common-law doctrine is subject to exceptions for acts of God or of third parties—two of the very factors which appellees emphasized in the District Court in the course of arguing that the risks of a nuclear accident are greater than generally admitted. All of these considerations belie the suggestion that the Act leaves the potential victims of a nuclear disaster in a more disadvantageous position than they would be in if left to their common-law remedies—not known in modern times for either their speed or economy.

Appellees' remaining objections can be briefly treated. The claim-administration procedures under the Act provide that in the event of an accident with potential liability exceeding the $560 million ceiling, no more than 15% of the limit can be distributed pending court approval of a plan of distribution taking into account the need to assure compensation for "possible latent injury claims which may not be discovered until a later time." Although some delay might follow from compliance with this statutory procedure, we doubt that it would approach that resulting from routine litigation of the large number of claims caused by a catastrophic accident. Moreover, the statutory scheme insures the equitable distribution of benefits to all who suffer injury—both immediate and latent; under the common-law route, the proverbial race to the courthouse would instead determine who had "first crack" at the

diminishing resources of the tortfeasor, and fairness could well be sacrificed in the process. The remaining contention that recovery is uncertain because of the aggregate rather than individualized nature of the liability ceiling is but a thinly disguised version of the contention that the $560 million figure is inadequate, which we have already rejected.

*　*　*　*　*

. . . The Price-Anderson Act not only provides a reasonable, prompt, and equitable mechanism for compensating victims of a catastrophic nuclear incident, it also guarantees a level of net compensation generally exceeding that recoverable in private litigation. Moreover, the Act contains an explicit congressional commitment to take further action to aid victims of a nuclear accident in the event that the $560 million ceiling on liability is exceeded. This panoply of remedies and guarantees is at the least a reasonably just substitute for the common-law rights replaced by the Price-Anderson Act. Nothing more is required by the Due Process Clause.

Case questions

1. In the Court's opinion, the $560 million limit on liability is not irrational and not violative of due process. Why not?

2. What incentive does the Court believe that utilities have for avoiding irresponsibility in building and operating nuclear power plants?

3. Why does the Court think that Price-Anderson provides a reasonably just substitute for the common-law or state-law remedies it replaces?

Under the Atomic Energy Act the full responsibility for nuclear power development in the United States was initially with the Atomic Energy Commission (AEC). The Energy Reorganization Act of 1974 divided the AEC's former jurisdiction between two new agencies whose duties to conduct research on and develop nuclear power would not conflict with their duties to protect the public health and safety. The Nuclear Regulatory Commission (NRC) assumed the licensing and regulatory activities of the AEC with respect to the siting and operation of nuclear power plants; the Energy Research and Development Agency (ERDA) took control over all major federal research and development programs, including nuclear weapons testing.

Nuclear plant licensing procedure. The Nuclear Regulatory Commission inherited its basic framework for the licensing of nuclear power plants from the AEC. The AEC followed a two-stage licensing process for nuclear power plants, the first authorizing the plant to be built, the second authorizing it to operate.

Persons seeking to build a nuclear power plant must make an application for a construction permit. A major portion of the application is devoted to a Preliminary Safety Analysis Report. The report must include a description of the proposed site, the plant's unusual design features, the equipment for controlling normal emissions of radioactive materials, the procedures for coping with emergencies, possible accidents and their potential consequences, the applicant's technical and financial qualifications, and the provisions for off-site shipment of waste.

Two reviews of the Preliminary Safety Analysis Report take place after it has been prepared. The NRC reviews the application and contacts the applicant, questioning the applicant until it is satisfied enough to conclude in a safety evaluation report why the facility can be safely constructed and operated.

Concurrently with the NRC staff review, the 15-member Advisory Committee on Reactor Safeguards (ACRS) holds hearings and reviews the applications as it exchanges documents with the applicant and other experts. ACRS reports discuss health and safety issues surrounding the facility.

If the NRC and the ACRS agree that a construction permit can be issued, the three-member Atomic Safety and Licensing Board conducts a hearing. Notice must be given at least 30 days before the hearing; time must be allowed for interventions by persons interested in the proceedings.

If a construction permit is issued, the initial application to build is carried over to the operational licensing stage. The application is adjusted by new facts that emerge during the course of construction; at the end the preliminary safety analysis report becomes the final analysis report. Unless good cause can be shown as to why an operating license should not be issued, the license is awarded when the facility has been completed.

NRC criteria for plant siting. The suitability of an applicant's site is determined by comparing the design and operating characteristics of the proposed reactor with the physical characteristics of the site. The human environment of the site is also considered, with particular regard for population density in the surrounding area.

Otherwise unacceptable sites can become acceptable if compensating engineering safeguards are included in reactor designs. Special design concerns include withstanding vibrations from earthquakes and high winds from tornadoes. High waters from floods require special precautions also, since significant quantities of radioactive effluents might accidentally flow into nearby streams or rivers or find access to underground water tables.

A hypothetical accident releasing fission products from the reactor core is the basis used for determining whether a site is suitable in relation to the population distribution in the surrounding area. The site must permit room for three zones based on radiation dosages acceptable for persons residing in the vicinity of the plant should such an accident occur. The applicant must provide for an exclusion zone over which it can exercise power to exclude or remove personnel and property. Surrounding the exclusion zone must be a low population zone from which residents can be readily evacuated. Population centers must be at least 1⅓ times as far away from the low population zone 's outer boundary as that outer boundary is from the nuclear reactor. The Supreme Court has affirmed the NRC's position that the distance to the population center is based on the distance to a population concentration rather than to the political boundaries of the population center.

Management of high-level radioactive waste

The by-products of nuclear power plant operation are highly radioactive. Highly radioactive material presents problems of permanent storage and disposal because of its long half-life. Plutonium found in fuel manufacturing waste, for example, has a half-life of 24,000 years.

Most nuclear power plants store spent fuel in cool water pools on their own property. ERDA has warned, however, that 23 nuclear power plants will run out of storage space in the next decade and may have to shut down. This problem has been aggravated by official decisions to halt the development of commercial reprocessing plants which could reclaim usable fuel and solidify reactor fuel wastes.

ERDA has managed some commercial, high-level radioactive wastes, converting them from liquid to solid form by evaporation. It has stored the resulting salt cubes in geologic repositories. ERDA's predecessor, AEC, did not consider salt cubes acceptable for long-term storage; salt cubes were water dispersible. ERDA's successor in waste management, the Department of Energy, is considering the conversion of the salt cubes to silicate glass for ultimate disposal.

The United States has accumulated more than 80 million gallons of high-level wastes in the past 30 years. Its nuclear weapons program alone continues to produce about 7½ million gallons of high-level wastes annually. The storage of radioactive wastes will continue to be a significant problem, as the Environmental Protection Agency estimates that 1 billion cubic feet of these wastes will have been generated by the year 2000.

Wildlife preservation

Many wildlife species are protected by acts that limit rights to hunt or fish for them. When the killing of rare species is known to continue, the sale or possession of the hides, feathers, bones, or other parts of these species is prohibited.

The Endangered Species Act protects many rare species from activities which would harm them or their habitats. Under the act a $78 million dam project was halted in order to save the habitat of a three-inch fish called the snail darter.[4] Although the project was nearing completion, the Supreme Court ruled that it be halted because Congress had made saving endangered species one of the highest federal priorities. Congress later specially deliberated to allow the dam project to proceed, finding that the fish could be transported to new habitats.

POLICY CONSIDERATIONS

Governmental regulation is generally attacked because of the burdens it adds to private enterprise. The expense of Environmental regulation is particularly prone to attack by industry because many of its rules are based on tenuous scientific grounds. Determining what causes of air pollution create effects inimical to the public health, for instance, requires assessing studies from areas as diverse as inhalation toxicology, hematology, neurology, epidemiology, and psychiatry. Scientific knowledge of human biology is incomplete, and controversy surrounds the medical studies that have been made.

Environmentalists believe that the laws controlling pollution must be strengthened in the face of uncertainty. They maintain that action must be taken to prevent serious environmental harm before it occurs, rather than wait until it manifests itself in the diseased and dying. Industry claims that Man will not progress without increased technological growth supported by expanded energy production. It objects to policies that allow plants to be closed because they cannot meet the costs of complying with environmental regulations.

Polarization of these positions can be expected as the United States attempts to ease its dependence upon imported oil.

Review problems

1. Dustin Company allows its employees to spray-paint company cars on its back lot. The spray occasionally drifts to Mrs. Perkin's garage, leaving specks of blue, yellow, and brown on the walls and door. If Mrs. Perkins sues to make the Dustin Company stop authorizing this activity, what is the court likely to decide?

2. A power company's operations raise the level of water in a stream that flows by a couple's vacation property. Half of the rocks the couple uses to dive into the stream are covered up in the process. The couple sues to enjoin the power company's operations. What result and why?

3. Kramer Food Service, Inc., plans to build a small cafeteria and beachhouse in a popular federal park along the Atlantic Ocean. Kramer believes its new facility will provide jobs for eight people. Supplying the facility will require three visits weekly by trucks bringing fresh food and clean towels. Is Kramer Food's planned construction likely to require the preparation of an EIS?

4. Ohio has been found to produce twice as much sulfer dioxide as all the New England

---

[4]*TVA* v. *Hill,* 437 U.S. 153 (1978).

states combined. The EPA administrator attempted to implement a plan to clean up Ohio's air when Ohio could not produce a satisfactory state implementation plan to achieve national clean air standards. The administrator found that the EPA was without sufficient money or political power to control the local situation effectively. By what authority could the administrator provide a plan for Ohio? What alternative actions could the administrator have taken, and how effective were those actions likely to be?

5. Harry Zimmerman and his son run a small, independent trucking company carrying flammable materials for short trips within states. They make informal agreements to carry these materials for companies which are recommended to them by their business friends. Recently one of their business friends warned them that they might be running their business illegally and suggested that they check with a lawyer. What will the lawyer tell them they must do? What might happen to them if they do not follow the lawyer's advice?

6. Donegal's Power Company is planning to build a nuclear power plant along the Pacific Ocean. Donegal's scientists have determined that earthquake activity is not significant in the area in which they want to build, but that tremors in the region may cause vibrations sufficient to cause occasional flooding. Will Donegal's be able to build its plant in the place the scientists have chosen?

7. Steelworkers residing in the Youngstown, Ohio, area allege that they will be threatened with unemployment from shutdowns in their area if U.S. Steel builds a new plant in Conneaut, Ohio, about 50 miles from Youngstown. They sue to challenge the sufficiency of an EIS issued by the Corps of Engineers, allowing the construction of the complex facility. The steelworkers live in the area that will experience the environmental impacts of the proposed operation. They agree with the members of the Lake Erie Alliance, persons who depend on Lake Erie for drinking, fishing, and swimming, that the lake will be adversely affected by the new plant. Will the court recognize all of their concerns, including the threatened loss of their jobs, and grant them the right to challenge the sufficiency of the EIS as it addresses the impact on the human environment?

8. The core of Nuclear Power Plant XIII has melted down, releasing radioactive wastes, water, and air at 50 times acceptable levels as far as 20 miles away. The countryside for 10 miles is thoroughly poisoned, and vegetation for 15 miles has become wilted or diseased. Increased levels of cancer have been detected among populations formerly located near the plant. Losses by farmers in land, livestock, and private residences have already been estimated at $500 million. If the farmers sue immediately, will victims of radiation poisoning or cancer suing later have to split the remaining $60 million available under Price-Anderson's liability limit?

9. The design of Commons Nuclear Power Plant proves to be faulty. Water used in cooling the power plant becomes contaminated and seeps into water holes used by grazing animals in nearby low-population zones. How much of its own money would the utility company have to pay out to livestock owners? Indicate the utility company's maximum responsibility.

10. Should a small business that cannot afford expensive water or air pollution prevention equipment required by environmental regulations have to shut down? Should the costs of environmental regulations be compared with the benefits to the public?

CHAPTER 19

Business ethics and corporate social responsibility

In the early 1960s the public was shocked when 20 indictments charged 29 electrical equipment manufacturers and 45 corporate executives with criminal violations of the antitrust laws, including price-fixing, bid rigging, and allocating customers. The prosecutions resulted in pleas of guilty and nolo contendere.[1] Seven corporate officials served jail sentences.

Ten years later, investigations into the burglary of the Democratic National Committee's office in the Watergate Hotel in Washington led to the discovery of numerous illegal corporate domestic political campaign contributions. Further inquiry uncovered that bribing officials of foreign governments was a common business practice.

The exposures of the electrical equipment conspiracy and the prevalence of large-scale illegal corporate political activity were two of the most spectacular business scandals of the past 30 years. Unfortunately, similar activities commonly occur on a smaller scale. An even larger number of practices which are not illegal but are arguably unethical take place daily.

This chapter explores problems that fall under the general headings of business ethics and corporate social responsibility. It examines ethical dilemmas involved in the conduct of business.

BUSINESS ETHICS

Managers frequently face decisions that present perplexing ethical dilemmas. A particular course of conduct may prove financially lucrative but may also conflict with personal standards of morality. Certain situations may present ethically unappealing alternatives which compel the decision maker to choose the lesser of two evils. The following paragraphs discuss issues of business ethics. Much of the material consists of readings. This is the authors' way of avoiding sermonizing about truth with a capital *T.*

---

[1] A plea of nolo contendere means that the defendant does not not admit his or her guilt but chooses not to contest the government's case.

It is also the authors' hope that the readings will spur students to think through for themselves the important ethical issues confronting business. The readings are not intended to serve as the final word on their subjects, but as catalysts for class discussion. They should be read critically. The readings focus first on defining ethics, then examine the ethical climate of the business community, and finally explore two proposals for institutionalizing business ethics.

Defining Business Ethics

Most people have difficulty in defining business ethics. Like other fundamental concepts, such as truth and love, the term *ethics* seems to defy definition. Yet some attempt to grasp its meaning must be made before ethical problems and their solutions are explored. The following reading attempts to define ethics. It suggests that corporate or organizational ethics may differ from individual ethics.

C. McCoy et al., Ethics in the Corporate Policy Process: An Introduction 2–4 (1975). Reprinted with permission of the Center for Ethics and Social Policy, Graduate Theological Union, Berkeley, California.

WHAT IS ETHICS?

Ethics is reflection on the moral meaning of action. Ethics does not reveal suddenly a new reality of right and wrong totally invisible to us before. Ethics does not offer a single, absolute right way of behavior. Rather, much like economics or political science, ethics assists us to see more clearly and understand with greater precision what we were already aware of but saw only dimly or inadequately. Ethics is the process by which individuals, social groups, and societies evaluate their actions from the perspective of moral principles and values. This evaluation may be on the basis of traditional convictions, of ideals sought, of goals desired, of moral laws to be obeyed, of an improved quality of relations among humans and with the environment. When we speak of "ethics" and ethical reflection, we mean the activity of applying these various yardsticks to the actions of persons and groups.

For some, morality may mean utilizing only a single yardstick by which to measure and evaluate action. One such set of criteria is the Ten Commandments. Another is the Golden Rule. Persons are taught some form of morality in their home and immediate childhood community. Similar guides may be discovered in other major religions —Hindu, Buddhist, Muslim, and in the philosophical traditions—Kantian, utilitarian, hedonist, and others.

For most of us in this society, ethics includes more than a single set of ideals or moral principles. We feel the pull of divergent loyalties and desires within ourselves as individuals. In an even more complex way, the actions of organizations are based on many different interests, values, and convictions. Ethics works within this diversity and develops criteria to evaluate and guide actions related to specific situations.

In our pluralistic world of complex social organizations, ethical issues arise in situations where persons from differing perspectives meet and share in shaping policy. Rigid moral judgments based on one individual's views are inadequate. Ethical issues arise also because groups affected by policy are not represented in policy making. Ethics applicable to corporations or other social organizations must take account of diverse perspectives and seek for criteria inclusive of divergent interests, goals, and beliefs.

CORPORATE ETHICS

Corporate ethics is concerned not with individual, private behavior but with the moral meaning of organizational action and purpose. Corporate ethics evaluates and guides the actions, policies, and decision-making processes of social groups. In *Moral Man and Immoral Society*, Reinhold Niebuhr insists that "a sharp distinction must be drawn between the moral and social behavior of individuals and of social groups." He attacks a naive confidence in the moral capacities of human collectives and demonstrates that power, rather than goodwill or reasonableness alone, is necessary in overcoming social injustice.

Individual ethics remains important for the ethics of an organization. Decisions made by individuals have a significant bearing on organizational decisions and policy. One person's errors or dishonesty can destroy the reputation of an entire group. And a single individual's moral courage at a crucial juncture may stem a wave of disastrous decisions or enlarge the visions of the group's responsbility and action.

Yet corporate ethics is more than the sum of the ethics of individuals within the group. No matter how important individual actions may be, an organization involves more than the collection of actions and views of the individuals who participate in it. An organization has an existence of its own: its own history and traditions, its own rules and ways of operating derived from its constituting character and its customs, its own patterns of informal understandings, its own purposes and goals, its own particular network of influence and factions within it, its own relations to other organizations, its own particular place in a nexus of social and cultural functions. An individual thinks and acts differently in family relationships, in recreational activities, in professional/vocational groups; in each different group, he or she takes on the social patterns, expectations, and responsibilities which belong to each distinctive organization and group relation. Writing of President Truman's decision to drop the atomic bomb on Japan in 1945, Robert Batchelder comments on the power of organizational process:

> Social institutions appear to take on an independence and a power of their own which defy the attempts of individual men to control them. General Groves has said of President Truman's decision to use the bomb: "Truman did not so much say yes as not say no. It would indeed have taken a lot of nerve to say no at that time."

Though the president has great power, it is exercised within an organizational policy process even more powerful.

It is important to develop discussion of organizational ethics among those people primarily responsible for shaping policy. Persons as individuals frequently exhibit greater awareness of the ethical implications of policy when apart from the policy-making process than when operating within that process. In organizational situations caution, prudence, and "group think" may triumph over innovation and individual awareness. Discussions of corporate ethics must therefore occur with the processes of organizational interaction, raise the consciousness of the policy-making group, and seek change, not only of individual perception, but also of the organization's policy process.

Corporate ethics may focus on particular aspects of organizational action: on its adherence to law and organizational standards, on purposes, priorities, and consequences, or on relationships; on the overall shape of policy, on the processes by which policy is formulated, or on issues of legitimacy. A comprehensive corporate ethic will integrate the widest possible spectrum of organizational action for analysis and evaluation.

Ethical dilemmas in business affairs

The typical corporate official does not identify with criminals or unethical or immoral persons. Most corporate officials who have engaged in questionable business practices would say that they did so for the benefit of the corporation. It is difficult to turn down a $50 million—$5 million profit—contract with a foreign government simply because in order to obtain the contract an official of that government has to be hired as a consultant for a fee of $200,000. The corporate reflex is to take action designed to maximize earnings. It is not difficult to lose sight of basic values in doing so.

Unethical corporate activity is more often a result of failures to consider ethical consequences than of conscious decisions to act improperly. The following article from the *Harvard Business Review (HBR)* reports the results of a survey of its readers regarding ethical dilemmas that they faced in their business affairs. The survey reveals that 43 percent of the respondents believed that competitive pressures forced them to resort to shady practices necessary for business survival; that is, many executives were blinded to ethical considerations by the balance sheet. The survey also reveals that such blindness was not restricted to the upper levels of the corporate structure. Half of the persons responding believed that their superiors' only concern was to have them achieve desired outcomes and that those superiors were not interested in how the outcomes were obtained. The article is excerpted to illustrate the ethical dilemmas reported by managers.

Brenner and Molander, "Is the Ethics of Business Changing?" 55 *Harvard Business Review* 57 (1977). Reprinted with permission of the publisher.

What would you do if . . .

. . . the minister of a foreign nation where extraordinary payments to lubricate the decision-making machinery are common asks you for a $200,000 consulting fee? In return, he promises special assistance in obtaining a $100-million contract which would produce at least a $5-million profit for your company. The contract would probably go to a foreign competitor if your company did not win it.

. . . as the president of a company in a highly competitive industry, you learn that a competitor has made an important scientific discovery that will substantially reduce, but not eliminate, your profit for about a year? There is a possibility of hiring one of the competitor's employees who knows the details of the discovery.

. . . you learn that an executive earning $30,000 a year has been padding his expense account by about $1,500 a year?

These questions were posed as part of a lengthy questionnaire on business ethics and social responsibility completed by 1,227 *Harvard Business Review* readers—25% of the cross section of 5,000 U.S. readers polled. . . .

Our study was prompted by the same concern that Raymond C. Baumhart had in 1961 when he conducted a similar study for *HBR:* the numerous comments on business ethics in the media contained little empirical evidence to indicate whether large numbers of business executives shared the attitudes, behavior, and experience of those whose supposedly unethical and illegal conduct was being represented (or denied) as typical of the business profession.

COMMON DILEMMAS

Of course, the ethics of business includes not only the moral values and duties of the profession itself, but also the existing values and expectations of the large society. Because ethical systems are created by fallible people, they generally have some inherent contradictions. Further, the values and ethics of various organizations differ from those of other sectors of society in which business people participate (such as the family, church, and political parties). For these reasons executives inevitably face some ethical dilemmas in their daily work.

To learn how chronic a problem such ethical dilemmas are in the contemporary business environment, we asked our respondents if they had ever experienced a conflict between what was expected of them as efficient, profit-conscious managers and what was expected of them as ethical persons. Four of every seven of those who responded (399 of 698) say they have experienced such conflicts, compared with three of four respondents in 1961 (603 of 796)—a substantial decrease of 19%.

One possible explanation for this decrease is that the internal pressures for profit and efficiency are not as great as they once were. Since we can find no evidence of such a change, two other possible explanations must be considered: ethical standards have declined from what they were, or situations that once caused ethical discomfort have become accepted practice.

. . . [W]e did find that the nature of compromising circumstances has changed. Honesty in communication is a significantly greater problem in 1976 than it was in 1961. This includes honesty in advertising and in providing information to top management, clients, and government agencies. We found number manipulation to have become a particularly acute problem.

Dilemmas associated with firings and layoffs are significantly less of a problem in 1976. Either terminations and their related problems are becoming accepted as routine in today's business world, or they are being handled more equitably when they occur. Undoubtedly because of government prosecutions, price collusion is also far less of a problem.

We feel it particularly noteworthy that relations with superiors are the primary category of ethical conflict. Respondents frequently complained of superiors' pressure to support incorrect viewpoints, sign false documents, overlook superiors' wrongdoing, and do business with superiors' friends. Either superiors are expecting more than subordinates in 1976, or subordinates are less willing to do their bosses' bidding without questions, at least to themselves. Both possibilities suggest a weakening in the corporate authority structure and an attendant impact on ethical business conduct that deserves future study. The following examples demonstrate ethical dilemmas being faced in busines today:

The vice president of a California industrial manufacturer "being forced as an officer to sign corporate documents which I knew were not in the best interests of minority stockholders."

A Missouri manager of manpower planning "employing marginally qualified minorities in order to meet Affirmative Action quotas."

A manager of product development from a computer company in Massachusetts "trying to act as though the product [computer software] would correspond to what the customer had been led by sales to expect, when, in fact, I knew it wouldn't."

A manager of corporate planning from California "acquiring a non-U.S. company with two sets of books used to evade income taxes—standard practice for that country. Do we (1) declare income and pay taxes, (2) take the 'black money' out of the country (illegally), or (3) continue tax evasion?"

The president of a real estate property management firm in Washington "projecting cash flow without substantial evidence in order to obtain a higher loan than the project can realistically amortize."

A young Texas insurance manager "being asked to make policy changes that produced more premium for the company and commission for an agent but did not appear to be of advantage to the policy-holder."

ACCEPTED PRACTICES

Clearly, that ethical dilemmas do exist and are too often resolved in ways which leave executives dissatisfied seems to be a matter of substantial concern for today's business people. And too often unethical practices become a routine part of doing business. To determine just how routine, we asked: "In every industry there are some generally accepted business practices. In your industry, are there practices which you regard as unethical?"

If we eliminate those who say they "don't know," we see . . . that two-thirds of the responding executives in 1976 indicate that such practices exist, compared with nearly four-fifths who so responded in 1961.

Could this decrease be a sign of improvement in ethical *practices?* Perhaps, but it is also possible that such practices are now less visible than they once were. Even more disturbing is the possibility which we raised earlier—that ethical *standards* have, in fact, fallen in business, so that practices once considered unethical are now not viewed as such. Further, these figures say nothing about the conduct that all agree is both unacceptable and unethical.

Nearly half (540) of all respondents and 84% of those indicating the existence of such practices were willing to tell us which practice or practices they would most like to see eliminated. . . . Both the changes and similarities in these "most unwanted" practices in the past 15 years are interesting.

As in 1961, the practice that most executives want to eliminate involves "gifts, gratuities, bribes, and 'call girls.'" Typical examples given by the 144 respondents in this category are:

"Payoffs to a foreign government to secure contracts." [The vice president of an Oklahoma oil exploration company]

"Egg carton contracts with grocery chains can only be obtained by kickbacks—the egg packers do not have the freedom of choice in buying, thus stifling competition." [A young southern consumer goods executive vice president]

"Loans granted as favors to loan officers." [An Indiana bank vice president]

"Dealings with travel agencies that involve kickbacks, rebates, or other pseudonyms for 'bribes.'" [A Florida transportation industry executive]

Of the 80 respondents who mentioned practices which included cheating customers, unfair credit practices, or overselling, typical comments are:

"Substitution of materials without customer knowledge after the job has been awarded." [A young New York salesman]

"Misrepresenting the contents of products." [A Texas vice president of engineering]

"Scheduled delivery dates that are known to be inaccurate to get a contract." [A California director of engineering]

Both the sharp drop from 1961 to 1976 . . . in concern over "price discrimination and unfair pricing" and "dishonest advertising" and the increase in concern over "unfairness to employees in prejudice in hiring" and "creating customers" are probably attributable to government enforcement and higher legal standards.

Questions

The following questions were included in the questionnaire given to the *HBR* readers who participated in the survey described in the above article. How would you answer these questions? How do you think the average executive would answer them?

Case 1. An executive earning $30,000 a year has been padding his expense account by about $1,500 a year. I think that this is: *(a)* acceptable if other executives in the company do the same thing, *(b)* unacceptable regardless of the circumstances, *(c)* acceptable if the executive's superior knows about it and says nothing.

Case 2. Imagine that you are the president of a company in a highly competitive industry. You learn that a competitor has made an important scientific discovery which will give him an advantage that will substantially reduce, but not eliminate, the profits of your company for about a year. If there were some hope of hiring one of the competitor's employees who knew the details of the discovery, would you try to hire him? I *(a)* probably would hire him, *(b)* probably would not hire him.

Case 3. The minister of a foreign nation where extraordinary payments to lubricate the decision-making machinery are common asks you as a company marketing director for a $200,000 consulting fee. In return, he promises special assistance in obtaining a $100 million contract which should produce at least $5 million in profit for your company. What would you do? *(a)* pay the fee, feeling it was ethical in the moral climate of the foreign nation; *(b)* pay the fee, feeling it was unethical but necessary to ensure the sale; *(c)* refuse to pay, even if the sale is thereby lost.

Case 4. At a board meeting of High Fly Insurance Company (HFI), a new board member learns that HFI is the "officially approved" insurer of the Private Pilots Benevolent Association (PPBA), which has 200,000 members. On joining PPBA, members automatically subscribe to HFI's accident insurance for a premium included in the standard dues assessment. In return, HFI pays PPBA a fee tied to the value of business PPBA members generate and gets use of the PPBA mailing list, which it uses to sell aircraft liability policies (its major source of revenues). PPBA's president sits on HFI's board of directors, and the two companies are both located in the same office building. In this situation, the average new director *who is a recently promoted HFI employee: (a)* would do nothing; *(b)* would privately and delicately raise the issue with the chairman of the board; *(c)* would express opposition in a directors' meeting, but would go along with whatever position the board chose to take; *(d)* would express vigorous opposition and resign if corrective action were not taken. Using the same choices, what would the average new *outside* director do in this situation?

Institutionalizing ethics

Ethical codes have been most persistently suggested as a solution to the business ethics issue. Many trade and professional associations have employed such codes as a means of self-regulation. Self-regulation by such organizations is frequently suggested as an alternative to government regulation.

Codes of ethics are not new. As early as 1340 a British *Manual for Confessors* defined "evils of trade" to include:

1. Selling as dear as one may or buying as cheaply as one may.
2. Lying or forswearing to sell wares.
3. Using false weights or measures.
4. Selling on time.
5. Failing to comply with the sample.

6. Hiding the truth about latent defects.
7. Making a thing look better than it is.[2]

Since that time many persons have wrestled with the task of institutionalizing business ethics. Some of those efforts are detailed in the two following articles.

Brown, "Ethics and Earnings: Profit-Minded Chief at Bendix Tries to Set a Businessmen's Code," *The Wall Street Journal,* November 18, 1975, pp. 1, 35. Reprinted with permission of the publishers.

Southfield, Mich.—When W. Michael Blumenthal joined Bendix Corp. in 1967 to run its international operations, many wondered how long he would stay. Could a former economics professor and U.S. ambassador find happiness in the everyday world of big business?

Eight years later, 49-year-old "Mike" Blumenthal is still at Bendix. He is chairman and president, running the diversified $2.6-billion-a-year supplier to the auto, aerospace and housing industries—and doing much more. Among other things, the cigar-puffing chief executive heads a committee trying to find ways to bail the State of Michigan out of its economic woes, participates in several foreign trade and economic groups, and serves as a trustee of the Rockefeller Foundation and Princeton University.

"What we don't need around here is for Mike to take on another extracurricular activity," a Bendix vice president says only half-jokingly. But that is exactly what the scholar-turned-businessman plans to do.

Last month, Mr. Blumenthal met me in New York with several top executives of major companies to "talk through" the idea of establishing a professional watchdog group that would devise and police an ethical code for American businessmen. It's an idea that a disheartened Mr. Blumenthal first floated in a Detroit speech last May after a wave of corporate crimes and scandals began rolling in the wake of Watergate.

"The response was so great that I have an obligation to follow through with it," he says.

Exactly how far the project will go isn't clear. Indeed, considering the meager results of past attempts to devise broad codes in business ethics, skeptics think Mr. Blumenthal and his associates will be wasting their time. But others who know the Bendix chief say that if anyone has a chance of making it work, he does.

Mike Blumenthal is one of a small though growing number of corporate leaders who seem willing to plunge voluntarily into the nebulous subject of the social and moral responsibilities of big business. In recent years, of course, many executives have found themselves publicly grappling with such issues, but often not without prodding from consumer activists, theologians, environmentalists or other gadflies. And action has often been slow to follow, in part because changes often conflict with traditional profit-making goals.

Changes Seen Needed

As Mr. Blumenthal sees it, changes are needed. "We're operating in a much more complicated environment, and business leaders are confronted with more difficult choices than ever before," he says. "You used to be able to make decisions on the basis of the greater return for the least dollars. But now you must

---

[2] Stone, "The History of Ethics in American Business," in *Ethics in Business 25* (Bureau of Business Research Monograph No. 111, The Ohio State University, Bartels ed. 1978).

spend time and money on things that don't seem efficient in terms of profits. The old ways don't work anymore. Today, a guy like Henry Ford [the rough-minded founder of Ford Motor Co.] would either be in jail or his company would be on strike."

To some people, perhaps, such comments might sound like the excuses of an executive trying to explain away shrinking profits, or the bleatings of a muddled altruist. But any such suppositions would be ill founded. For the fiscal year ended Sept. 30, as in each of the four years of Mr. Blumenthal's tenure at the top, Bendix reported record earnings—a feat one Wall Street analyst terms "remarkable" in view of the slump that gripped two of the company's major markets, autos and housing. And ironically, one of the complaints by Mr. Blumenthal's detractors is that he is so hard-nosed about turning a profit that, in their view, he tramples on parts of his own social-responsibility philosophy.

Mr. Blumenthal himself contends that the stakes in the growing debate over business ethics are nothing short of corporate survival.

"If businessmen are ethically strong and morally clean, why should they not be the first to denounce the abuses and malpractice which—far more than our critics in the media— threaten the survival of the free enterprise system?"

Not a New Idea

The idea of a code of business ethics isn't new, of course. For instance, the electrical-equipment price-fixing scandals of the early 1960s triggered a barrage of criticism from the press and public, and soon afterward an ethics advisory council of top business leaders was set up under the Commerce Department. In 1962 the group presented a proposed code to President Kennedy. But after his assassination, the Johnson administration, seeking business support, let the code die.

What, if anything, Mr. Blumenthal's effort will produce remains to be seen. He speculates, for example, in terms of "a black book that would show what a panel of experts on business ethics says about a particular problem."

Foreign bribes might be a topic about which a consensus on proper conduct could be reached, he suggests. He also mentions political contributions and the handling of sensitive issues as layoffs, pensions and safety.

"There's nothing in business life which corresponds to the bar associations, the American Medical Association or the American Institute of Architects," he notes. "Business people should set up an association dedicated to defining and maintaining the standards of their profession." An ethical code devised by this group, he says, could correspond to the standards of other such associations and could be enforced by some type of censure.

Theologians and academic experts applaud the idea and believe many top executives agree. But even some sympathetic observers wonder how many corporations are really ready to embrace a code of ethics and make it stick. Many of them remain optimistic, however.

"Many companies are getting more defensive as the social and moral pressures increase," says Charles W. Powers, director of public responsibility for Cummins Engine Co., Columbus, Ind. "Some will emerge to provide leadership, and hopefully that group will be powerful."

Some question whether codes of ethics do much good. "Canons of ethics generally end up being canons of profit," argues Mark Green, an attorney with Ralph Nader's Corporate Accountability Research Group. "You end up with self-policing codes that are inadequate. We need stricter criminal penalties."

And a few regard the whole idea as foolish. Ultimately a businessman has to have his own set of standards, "so why set up a body to tell you what's right and wrong?" asks an executive with an Ohio-based auto parts concern that competes with Bendix. "It's a grandstand play that had to come from a former government bureaucrat."

Many trade and professional association codes of ethics are the product of cooperation with the government. Violations may lead to government sanctions. For example, an attorney may be disbarred for violating the bar association's code of ethics.

Purcell, "Institutionalizing Ethics on Corporate Boards,"
36 *Review of Social Economy* 41 (1978). Reprinted
with permission of the publisher.

* * * * *

WILL CODES HELP ETHICAL BEHAVIOR?

Many professional associations have not found ethics so subjective or so fuzzy that they were afraid to set up their own ethical standards. The American Institute of Certified Public Accountants describes its code of professional ethics "as a voluntary assumption of self-discipline above and beyond the requirements of the law." It further states that in general usage the word ethics means "the philosophy of human conduct, with emphasis on right and wrong, which are moral questions." The AICPA then cites many examples and applications of ethics in the accounting and auditing professions.

The American Psychological Association drew up its ethical code for psychologists from practical problem cases drawn from professional-client relationships.

The American Bar Association (1971) has a detailed code and canons. Of course, we know that Watergate brought the legal profession into serious self-questioning and subjected it to public skepticism; yet it is also true that some Watergate lawyers have been disbarred.

Especially, it is not easy to draw up an ethical code for doing international business among countries with very different values and customs. Yet the Organization for Economic Cooperation and Development (OECD) has recently drawn up such a code. Time will tell how much it helps.

It is important to stress, however, that ethical codes are not a panacea, even when they can be enforced on association members, something not too common. Though they often merely relate the profession to individual clients rather than to the collective public, codes nonetheless can help clarify ethical thinking and encourage ethical behavior.

* * * * *

ETHICS VERSUS THE LAW

Some people say ethical motivation and profit motivation are incompatible. Therefore: "forget about ethics and social responsibility. Just talk about the law." Laws are necessary, of course. The Civil Rights Act of 1964, to take one example, was absolutely essential. But there is a danger in all this. Some years ago, Douglass Brown's presidential address for the Industrial Relations Research Association (1971) warned that excessive legalism was harming industrial relations.

We now find the field of equal employment opportunity going this same route of legalism and litigiousness. We cannot have laws, government agencies, lawyers and courts involved in every management decision. The country would soon be bogged down by a legal bureaucracy and could ultimately produce a contempt for law. We may be seeing something of this now in the medical malpractice mess.

Furthermore, many management decisions involve social issues about which no laws provide guidance and probably no viable laws can be written. What then? Social awareness and conscience can be the only guides.

* * * * *

THE NEED FOR CORPORATE ETHICS SPECIALISTS

. . . Is it not time to appoint a small number of directors and also perhaps officers to be the corporations' ethical "devil's advocates" or better yet, their ethical "angel's advocates"?

We should institutionalize ethical expertise at the board of directors and top management levels, perhaps focusing on one director but with responsibilities shared by a committee of the board. These director/ethical advocates need not be philosophers in the field of ethics, but they should keep up to date on the extensive literature of ethics as applied to business. A number of companies such as General Mills and General Electric already have public responsibility committees. Could not such committees also take on an explicitly ethical function? According to Fred T. Allen (1975) of Pitney Bowes: "A moral dimension should be added to the board's criteria for judging a CEO (chief executive officer) and his principal subordinates."

About 28 large companies now have on their boards of directors committees that are explicitly designated as ethics committees: [Among them are] the Norton Company of Massachusetts, the world's largest manufacturer of abrasives, and the Consolidated Natural Gas Company, Headquartered in Pittsburgh.

The director/ethical advocates proposed here might also include corporate officers, perhaps the general counsel, as suggested by William Gossett, former President of the American Bar Association and Vice-President of Ford Motor Company. Such an appointment admittedly would be controversial. One top management team of a major corporation warns: "Any officer with marketing, financial, legal, staff or whatever responsibilities can scarcely be expected to step back in complete objectivity and to perform the role you envisage."

They may be right. But a firm could well have ethical advocates on its board if not among its officers. However, there is no neat formula here. Much depends on the top management personalities of a given company, their management styles, the structure of the corporation and related characteristics.

A principal function of the ethics committee would be to identify generic questions of an ethical nature that should be asked routinely along with the usual legal, financial and marketing questions. For example, a strategic planner might ask, "If we take certain actions, what would our market share be and will we run afoul of antitrust laws? What would our discounted cash flow be?"

The ethics advocates might want to know how a given decision will affect the rights of employees versus the rights of the corporation. Or will an action help or hurt the long-run general welfare of the cities or countries (South Africa, for instance) where our plants are located? Or, how shall the firm balance the public's right to know about minority hiring with the company's right to keep competitive information confidential? Or will a new product help or hurt the environment, the conservation of energy, the quality of life or the safety of consumers?

The corporate ethics advocates would need to be socially sensitive enough to phrase such questions in generic terms but still keep them sufficiently practical and thus manageable for specific top management decisions. It would be up to this committee to cooperate where necessary with ethics committees from other firms for that watchdog committee that Secretary of the Treasury Michael Blumenthal suggests. They might help develop an ethical code for their company and encourage ethics seminars for top, middle and lower managers in their mid-careers, when their experience will lead them to see more clearly the ethical implications of their decisions. They might encourage the study of ethical principles and cases in schools of business administration, some of which could perhaps help them and their industry with the ethical problems that they face.

If the committee is entirely composed of corporate officers, its secretary will need to be a strong and able manager who has the backing of the chief executive officer. The CEO will be a prime force in the success or failure of the ethical advocacy idea. But a board committee is better.

The committee and its secretary should expect to encounter strong resistance. They will have to win over operating managers—no small assignment when ethical considerations compete with immediate profits or personal power. Their policies may have to persuade managers, not by talking ethics, but by focusing on long-range business problems. (For example, an inner-city plant may have to hire and promote minorities if it is going to have any work force at all. Furthermore, if it makes a consumer product, the inner-city could provide an important market.) But at times the ethics committee should also appeal to a sense of ethics, because operating managers may turn out to be more receptive than one might expect. In any case, the problems of the ethics advocates may be only a little more difficult or different from the problems of any other corporate officers, such as the equal employment director, who has to deal with managers in the field. At the start at least, the main function of the ethics committee will be to ask questions rather than to impose answers.

* * * * *

Questions

1. Do you favor ethical codes for industry? If so, would you prefer a code dealing with general precepts or one delineating specific practices? Would you expect an ethical code to help executives *(a)* raise the ethical level of their industry, *(b)* define the limits of acceptable conduct, or *(c)* refuse unethical requests? Or do you think that such a code is incapable of changing executive conduct in these areas? Do you feel that people would violate the code whenever they thought they could avoid detection?

2. How should ethical codes be enforced? Would such a code be easy to enforce? Should the code be enforced *(a)* at the company level, *(b)* by a combined group of industry executives and members of the community, *(c)* at the industry level by either a trade association or a group of industry executives, or *(d)* by a government agency? What are some advantages and disadvantages of each of the above forms of enforcement?

3. What are the merits and demerits of the ethical advocacy idea proposed by Purcell? Would Purcell's proposal amount to mere tokenism? Would the proposal remove ethical issues from consideration by shifting them onto specialists—convert what is everybody's business into the business of a few specialists? On the other hand, would not the institutionalization of corporate ethics specialists be just as desirable as the institutionalization of corporate functional experts in other areas, such as law, finance, marketing, public relations and research?

CORPORATE SOCIAL RESPONSIBILITY

It has become fashionable in recent years to speak of the social responsibility of the corporation as an institution. Concerns relating to social responsibility are frequently intertwined with concerns about individual ethics. For example, assume that a company manufactures a food additive which has been proven to be carcinogenic. The Food and Drug Administration prohibits the sale of the substance in the United States, but the substance remains legal in Mexico. Should the company continue to manufacture the substance and distribute it in Mexico? Your answer to this question will depend upon your views of the role of the corporation in society and upon your personal values. Your personal beliefs about ethics will influence how you view the social responsibility of corporations.

Some experts assert that a corporation's sole responsibility is to maximize earnings, provided the corporation abides by the law. They argue that the corporation cannot be separated from the shareholders who own it. All nonprofit activities in which the corporation engages and all opportunities for profit which the corporation forgoes represent diminutions in corporate profits which would otherwise become the property of the shareholders in the form of dividends or of increases in the value of their shares. Thus the use of corporate resources for any activity other than profit maximization may be viewed as forcing the shareholder to subsidize the ideals of corporate management.

Historically, the corporation has not always been regarded as a profit maximizer. Initially each corporation received a charter from the legislature and the charter frequently included such privileges as government-guaranteed monopolies. It was granted on the theory that the corporation was designed to serve a specific public purpose, such as the operation of a canal or a turnpike. Thus the corporation's function was to meet a mixture of public and private needs.

During the late 19th century the corporation came to be viewed as an institution operated solely for the benefit of its shareholders. Thus profit maximization came to be seen as its only function. This change in attitude coincided with a period of major industrial expansion and economic development which was spearheaded by corporations. Consequently, having corporations devoted exclusively to profit maximization was seen as consistent with the national interest.

The law's treatment of corporate activity has reflected continually changing perceptions of the role of the corporation. The earliest U.S. corporations were chartered by special legislative action. Then, beginning in 1795, state statutes began to provide for general incorporation without special legislative charter. The first such statutes limited general incorporation procedures to enterprises serving a public purpose. In 1795 North Carolina provided such procedures for companies digging canals. In 1799 Massachusetts established similar procedures for companies operating aqueducts.

In 1837 Connecticut became the first state to adopt procedures permitting incorporation for any lawful purpose. Other states were slow to follow. New York did not adopt such procedures until 1866. However, the drive for economic development during the latter half of the 19th century furnished the necessary incentive for wide-scale reform of the incorporation process. By 1900 almost all jurisdictions prohibited incorporation by legislative charter and provided general incorporation procedures.

Thus the method of establishing corporations changed to reflect society's changed perceptions of their role. With the corporation serving exclusively private purposes, there was no need for legislatures to consider each incorporation individually.

The profit maximization view of corporate purpose also influenced the development of the law controlling managerial discretion. The most famous case involved a dispute between the Dodge brothers and Henry Ford.

The Ford Motor Company was organized in 1903 with a capital stock of $150,000. By 1916 its surplus of assets over liabilities and capital stock totaled almost $112 million. Ford paid dividends of 5 percent per month to its shareholders. It also paid special dividends which had totaled $41 million through 1915. In 1916 Henry Ford announced that the company would cease paying special dividends indefinitely and would use its profits to expand its plant, produce more cars, and lower its prices. The declared ambition of Henry Ford was "to spread the benefits of this industrial system to the greatest possible number, to help them build up their lives and their homes."

The Dodge brothers were shareholders in Ford. They sued to prohibit the expansion and compel the further declaration of special dividends. The trial court granted the relief requested. The Michigan Supreme Court vacated the trial court's order enjoining the expansion, on the ground that the expansion was in the best interest of the company. The Supreme Court, however, affirmed the trial court's order that $19 million in dividends be paid, explaining:

> A business corporation is organized and carried on primarily for the profit of the stockholders. The powers of the directors are to be employed for that end. The discretion of directors is to be exercised on the choice of means to attain that end, and does not extend to a change in the end itself, to the reduction of profits, or to the non-distribution of profits among stockholders in order to devote them to other purposes.[3]

The *Ford* decision did not serve as a complete bar to nonprofit corporate activities. Such activities were not set aside where they were reasonable and in the best interests of the corporation. For example, a corporation's contribution to a charity could be justified as improving its image and thereby promoting goodwill. Similarly, numerous corporate grants to educational institutions have been justified as designed to insure a sufficient supply of trained employees.

Constrained by the profit maximization view of corporate purpose, courts and corporate managers grasped for farfetched justifications for upholding corporate nonprofit activities as valid exercises of business judgment. A particularly interesting case is *Shlensky* v. *Wrigley,* in which shareholders challenged the decision made by the Chicago Cubs management not to install lights in Wrigley Field.[4] Philip K. Wrigley, the president and majority shareholder of the club, considered baseball to be a day game and believed that night games ruined its flavor. He also expressed concern that night baseball would contribute to the decay of the surrounding neighborhood. The court accepted the "decay of neighborhood" argument. It upheld the decision of the Chicago Cubs management on the ground that neighborhood decay could result in reduced attendance.

In recent decades many business relationships have been depersonalized by such developments as automation, mass production, and large-scale meth-

---

[3] *Dodge* v. *Ford Motor Co.,* 204 Mich. 459, 170 N.W. 668 (1919).
[4] 96 Ill. App. 2d 173, 237 N.E. 2d 776 (1968).

ods of distribution. Consequently, many people now believe that the corporation must serve not only the interests of its shareholders but also the well-being of employees, consumers, suppliers, creditors, and the community. This view is shared by many modern managers. The Committee for Economic Development has aptly summarized it:

> The modern professional manager . . . regards himself, not as an owner disposing of personal property as he sees fit, but as a trustee balancing the interests of many diverse participants and constituents in the enterprise, whose interests sometimes conflict with those of others. The chief executive of a large corporation has the problem of reconciling the demands of employees for more wages and improved benefit plans, customers for lower prices and greater values, vendors for higher prices, government for more taxes, stockholders for higher dividends and greater capital appreciation—all within a framework that will be constructive and acceptable to society.[5]

The law has also changed to accommodate the changing view of the role of the corporation in society. The modern view is that corporate nonprofit activity is justified for reasons of public policy. The New Jersey Supreme Court expressed the underlying rationale as follows:

> When the wealth of the nation was primarily in the hands of individuals, they discharged their responsibilities as citizens by donating freely for charitable purposes. With the transfer of most of the wealth to corporate hands and the imposition of heavy burdens of individual taxation, they have been unable to keep pace with increased philanthropic needs. They have therefore, with justification, turned to corporations to assume the modern obligations of good citizenship in the same manner as humans do.[6]

Many states have amended their corporation statutes to authorize nonprofit activities. In these states such activities of management are shielded from shareholder attack unless the activities are arbitrary or in bad faith.

Corporate social responsibility and the individual employee

The discussion so far has focused on the corporation's social responsibility as it relates to the corporation's responsibility to society. However, the corporation's conception of its social responsibility is formulated and implemented by individuals. Hence, it is helpful to consider the question of corporate social responsibility from the perspective of the individual employee's involvement in the corporation.

What is the individual employee's relation to the corporate employer's social responsibility? That is, what responsibility does a corporate employee have with regard to the corporation's conduct? Furthermore, what right does an individual corporate employee have to launch his or her corporate

---

[5] Committee for Economic Development, *Social Responsibilities of Business Corporations* 22 (1971).
[6] *A. P. Smith Mfg. Co.* v. *Barlow*, 13 N.J. 148, 98 A.2d 581 (1953).

employer on a course of action that the employee considers to be socially responsible? Can an employee engage in activity designed to promote the corporation's social responsibility and be protected against retaliation by higher corporate officials who are less socially responsible or who see the corporate social responsibility differently? The following two cases and article examine these issues.

In *United States* v. *Park* the responsibility of the individual employee is presented. In *Park* the employee is the company's chief executive officer. The case illustrates the evolving criminal liability of corporate executives. The *Park* decision reflects a serious current philosophical and legal debate regarding the accountability (and liability) of individuals for the actions they take or do not take while they are serving in positions of authority.

At issue in *Geary* v. *United States Steel* is the right of an employee to engage in socially responsible behavior without fear of retaliation from corporate superiors. The court's conclusion is surprising but not unusual. The case represents the majority view on such matters in America.

United States v. Park
421 U.S. 658 (1975)

Park (respondent), the president of a large national food store chain, was convicted of causing the adulteration of food which had been transported in interstate commerce and was held for sale in violation of the Federal Food and Drugs Act. He appealed, and the court of appeals reversed. The Supreme Court reversed the court of appeals.

Mr. Chief Justice Burger: Acme Markets, Inc., is a national retail food chain with approximately 36,000 employees, 874 retail outlets, 12 general warehouses, and four special warehouses. Its headquarters, including the office of the president, respondent Park, who is chief executive officer of the corporation, are located in Philadelphia, Pennsylvania. In a five-count information . . . the Government alleged that the defendants had received food that had been shipped in interstate commerce and that, while the food was being held for sale in Acme's Baltimore warehouse, . . . they caused it to be held in a building accessible to rodents and to be exposed to contamination by rodents . . .

Acme pleaded guilty to each count of the information. Respondent pleaded not guilty.

The evidence at trial demonstrated that in April 1970 the Food and Drug Administration (FDA) advised respondent by letter of insanitary conditions in Acme's Philadelphia warehouse. In 1971 FDA found that similar conditions existed in the firm's Baltimore warehouse. An FDA consumer safety officer testified concerning evidence of rodent infestation and other unsanitary conditions discovered during a 12-day inspection of the Baltimore warehouse in November and December 1971. He also related that a second inspection of the warehouse had been conducted in March 1972. On that occasion the inspectors found that there had been improvement in the sanitary conditions, but that "there was still evidence of rodent activity in the building and in the warehouse and we found some rodent-contaminated lots of food items." . . .

The Government also presented testimony by the Chief of Compliance of FDA's Baltimore office, who informed respondent by letter of the conditions at the Baltimore warehouse after the first inspection. There was testimony by Acme's Baltimore division vice president, who had responded to the letter on behalf of Acme and respondent and who described the steps taken to remedy the insanitary conditions discovered by both inspections. The Government's final witness, Acme's vice president for legal affairs and assistant secretary, identified respondent as the president and chief executive officer of the company and read a bylaw prescribing the duties of the chief executive officer. He testified that respondent functioned by delegating "normal operating duties," including sanitation, but that he retained "certain things, which are the big, broad, principles of the operation of the company," and had "the responsibility of seeing that they all work together." . . .

Respondent was the only defense witness. He testified that, although all of Acme's employees were in a sense under his general direction, the company had an "organizational structure for responsibilities for certain functions" according to which different phases of its operation were "assigned to individuals who, in turn, have staff and departments under them." He identified those individuals responsible for sanitation and related that upon receipt of the January 1972 FDA letter, he had conferred with the vice president for legal affairs, who informed him that the Baltimore division vice president "was investigating the situation immediately and would be taking corrective action and would be preparing a summary of the corrective action to reply to the letter." Respondent stated that he did not "believe there was anything [he] could have done more constructively than what [he] found was being done."

On cross-examination, respondent conceded that providing sanitary conditions for food offered for sale to the public was something that he was "responsible for in the entire operation of the company," and he stated that it was one of many phases of the company that he assigned to "dependable subordinates." Respondent was asked about and, over the objections of his counsel, admitted receiving, the April 1970 letter addressed to him from FDA regarding insanitary conditions at Acme's Philadelphia warehouse. He acknowledged that, with the exception of the division vice president, the same individuals had responsibility for sanitation in both Baltimore and Philadelphia. Finally, in response to questions concerning the Philadelphia and Baltimore incidents, respondent admitted that the Baltimore problem indicated the system for handling sanitation "wasn't working perfectly" and that as Acme's chief executive officer he was responsible for "any result which occurs in our company." . . .

The jury found respondent guilty on all counts of the information, and he was subsequently sentenced to pay a fine of $50 on each count.

The Court of Appeals reversed the conviction and remanded for a new trial. That court viewed the Government as arguing "that the conviction may be predicated solely upon a showing that . . . [respondent] was the President of the offending corporation," and it stated that as "a general proposition, some act of commission or omission is an essential element of every crime." . . .

* * * * *

The rule that corporate employees who have "a responsible share in the furtherance of the transaction which the statute outlaws" are subject to the criminal provisions of the Act was not formulated in a vacuum. . . . Cases under the Federal Food and Drugs Act of 1906 reflected the view both that knowledge or intent were not required to be proved in prosecutions under its criminal provisions, and that responsible corporate agents could be subjected to the liability thereby imposed. . . . Moreover, the principle had been recognized that a corporate agent, through whose act, default, or omission the corporation committed a crime, was himself guilty individually of that crime. The principle had been applied whether or not the crime required "consciousness of wrongdoing," and it had been applied not only to those corporate agents who themselves committed the criminal act, but also to those who by virtue of their managerial positions or other similar relation to the actor could be deemed responsible for its commission.

In the latter class of cases, the liability of managerial officers did not depend on their knowledge of, or personal participation in, the act made criminal by the statute. Rather, where the statute under which they were prosecuted dispensed with "consciousness of wrongdoing," an omission or failure to act was deemed a sufficient basis for a responsible corporate agent's liability. It was enough in such cases that by virtue of the relationship he bore to the corporation, the agent had the power to have prevented the act complained of. . . .

The rationale of the interpretation given the Act . . . , as holding criminally accountable the persons whose failure to exercise the authority and supervisory responsibility reposed in them by the business organization resulted in the violation complained of, has been confirmed in our . . . cases. Thus, the Court has reaffirmed the proposition that "the public interest in the purity of its food is so great as to warrant the imposition of the highest standard of care on distributors." . . . In order to make "distributors of food the strictest censors of their merchandise," . . . the Act punishes "neglect where the law requires care, or inaction where it imposes a duty." "The accused, if he does not will the violation, usually is in a position to prevent it with no more care than society might reasonably expect and no more exertion than it might reasonably exact from one who assumed his responsibilities." Similarly, . . . the Courts of Appeals have recognized that those corporate agents vested with the responsibility, and power commensurate with that responsibility, to devise whatever measures are necessary to ensure compliance with the Act bear a "responsible relationship" to, or have a "responsible share" in, violations.

Thus . . . the cases . . . reveal that in providing sanctions which reach and touch the individuals who execute the corporate mission—and this is by no means necessarily confined to a single corporate agent or employee—the Act imposes not only a positive duty to seek out and remedy violations when they occur but also, and primarily, a duty to implement measures that will insure that violations will not occur. The requirements of foresight and vigilance imposed on responsible corporate agents are beyond question demanding, and perhaps

onerous, but they are no more stringent than the public has a right to expect of those who voluntarily assume positions of authority in business enterprises whose services and products affect the health and well-being of the public that supports them. . . .

The Act does not . . . make criminal liability turn on "awareness of some wrongdoing" or "conscious fraud." The duty imposed by Congress on responsible corporate agents is, we emphasize, one that requires the highest standard of foresight and vigilance, but the Act, in its criminal aspect, does not require that which is objectively impossible. The theory upon which responsible corporate agents are held criminally accountable for "causing" violations of the Act permits a claim that a defendant was "powerless" to prevent or correct the violation to "be raised defensively at a trial on the merits." If such a claim is made, the defendant has the burden of coming forward with evidence, but this does not alter the Government's ultimate burden of proving beyond a reasonable doubt the defendant's guilt, including his power, in light of the duty imposed by the Act, to prevent or correct the prohibited condition. Congress has seen fit to enforce the accountability of responsible corporate agents dealing with products which may affect the health of consumers by penal sanctions cast in rigorous terms, and the obligation of the courts is to give them effect so long as they do not violate the Constitution.

We cannot agree with the Court of Appeals that . . . the Government had the burden of establishing "wrongful action." . . . The concept of a "responsible relationship" to, or a "responsible share" in, a violation of the Act indeed imports some measure of blameworthiness; but it is equally clear that the Government establishes a prima facie case when it introduces evidence sufficient to warrant a finding . . . that the defendant had, by reason of his position in the corporation, responsibility and authority either to prevent in the first instance, or promptly to correct, the violation complained of, and that he failed to do so. The failure thus to fulfill the duty imposed by the interaction of the corporate agent's authority and the statute furnishes a sufficient causal link. The considerations which prompted the imposition of this duty, and the scope of the duty, provide the measure of culpability.

*   *   *   *   *

We are satisfied that the Act imposes the highest standard of care and permits conviction of responsible corporate officials who, in light of this standard of care, have the power to prevent or correct violations of its provisions.

Case questions

1. Was Park found guilty simply because he was the chief executive officer of Acme?

2. What actions did Park take to alleviate the problem at the Baltimore warehouse? What should he have done? What are the lessons and implications of the *Park* decision for organizational communication structures and decision-making processes?

3. You are a buyer employed by Acme. On two visits to the Baltimore warehouse you notice the presence of rat infestation. You advise the vice president for the Baltimore division of the problem. The vice president does nothing. Are you legally or ethically obligated to advise the president?

Geary v. *United States Steel Corporation*
456 Pa. 171, 319 A.2d 174 (1975)

George Geary (appellant) was employed by the U.S. Steel Corporation (appellee) to sell tubular steel products to the oil and gas industry. Believing that a product was unsafe, Geary advised his immediate superior of the problem. When Geary's immediate supervisor proved unresponsive, Geary presented his misgivings to the vice president in charge of the product's sales. Apparently the management of U.S. Steel recognized the dangerousness of the product, since it was later withdrawn from the market. Nevertheless, Geary was discharged. He sued his former employer for the tort of wrongful discharge. The trial court dismissed the complaint on the basis that Pennsylvania did not recognize the tort. Geary appealed to the Pennsylvania Supreme Court, which affirmed.[7]

Mr. Justice Pomeroy:

*   *   *   *   *

Appellant candidly admits that he is beckoning us into uncharted territory. No court in this

Commonwealth has ever recognized a nonstatutory cause of action for an employer's termination of an at-will employment relationship. What scant authority there is on the subject points the other way. . . .

The Pennsylvania law is in accordance with the weight of authority elsewhere. Absent a statutory or contractual provision to the contrary, the law has taken for granted the power of either party to terminate an employment relationship for any or no reason. . . .

*   *   *   *   *

Appellant's final argument is an appeal to considerations of public policy. Geary asserts in his complaint that he was acting in the best interests of the general public as well as of his employer in opposing the marketing of a product which he believed to be defective. Certainly, the potential for abuse of an employer's power of dismissal is particularly serious where an employee must exercise independent, expert judgment in matters of product safety, but Geary does not hold himself out as this sort

---

[7] For a discussion of the *Geary* decision, see Blackburn, "Restricted Employer Discharge Rights: A Changing Concept of Employment at Will," 17 *Am. Bus. L.J.* 467 (1980).

of employee. So far as the complaint shows, he was involved only in the sale of company products. There is no suggestion that he possessed any expert qualifications, or that his duties extended to making judgments in matters of product safety. In essence, Geary argues that his conduct should be protected because his intentions were good. No doubt most employees who are dismissed from their posts can make the same claim. We doubt that establishing a right to litigate every such case as it arises would operate either in the best interest of the parties or of the public.

* * * * *

Of . . . concern is the possible impact of such suits on the legitimate interests of employers in hiring and retaining the best personnel available. The ever-present threat of suit might well inhibit the making of critical judgments by employers concerning employee qualifications.

The problem extends beyond the question of individual competence, for even an unusually gifted person may be of no use to his employer if he cannot work effectively with fellow employees. Here, for example, Geary's complaint shows that he by-passed his immediate superiors and pressed his views on higher officers, utilizing his close contacts with a company vice president. The praiseworthiness of Geary's motives does not detract from the company's legitimate interest in preserving its normal operational procedures from disruption. In sum, while we agree that employees should be encouraged to express their educated views on the quality of their employer's products, we are not persuaded that creating a new non-statutory cause of action of the sort proposed by appellant is the best way to achieve this result. On balance, whatever public policy imperatives can be discerned here seem to militate against such a course.

Case questions

1. If Geary had been an engineer involved in designing the unsafe product, would the Pennsylvania Supreme Court have decided the case differently?

2. If Geary believed that selling his employer's unsafe product was unethical, what recourse does the Pennsylvania Supreme Court give him?

3. *Geary* involved the termination of an employee who felt that he had a moral and

ethical obligation to undertake the action that resulted in his discharge. He attempted to protect society from a danger brought on by a large corporation. Geary sought protection through the courts of the society he wanted to protect. How well was Geary's interest in society protected? Should the court have provided him with a similar measure of protection?

Ewing, "Manager's Journal: Multiple Loyalties," *The Wall Street Journal,* May 1, 1978, p. 18. Reprinted with permission of the publisher.

"It is not the lofty sails but the unseen wind that moves the ship," wrote W. MacNeile Dixon. His observation explains a major change that is taking place in the corporate world. Management textbooks and training programs focus on the "sails" of management-marketing, control, finance, and the rest. Important as these

functions are, they are not the "unseen wind" that moves many corporations in a fresh direction. That force is a new attitude toward authority, and it results from the dramatic growth of professional and technical employes.

Numbers don't tell the story but, like a wind speed indicator, they suggest rapidity and direction. Between 1950 and 1975, according to the U.S. Bureau of Census, the number of managers and administrators in the United States increased by about one-third (from 6.4 million to 8.6 million); the number of salesworkers increased by almost one-half (from 3.8 million to 5.5 million); and the number of clerical workers doubled (from 7.6 million to 15.2 million). The number of professional and technical employes, however, almost *tripled* (from 4.5 million to 12.8 million) during that period.

Professionals bring to the corporation not one but multiple loyalties. Traditionally, management has demanded the exclusive allegiance of an employe. As the U.S. Supreme Court put it in 1953, in a decision that is becoming as outmoded as the manual typewriter, "There is no more important cause for discharge of an employe than disloyalty to the employer." The professional takes a different view. He (or she) says he must share his loyalty to the company with loyalty to society and his profession.

Dr. Frank von Hippel of Princeton University points to the code of the National Society of Professional Engineers, which states that the engineer "will use his knowledge and skill for the advancement of human welfare." When this duty brings the engineer into conflict with the demands of an employer, the code instructs him to "regard his duty to the public welfare as paramount."

When Marvin Murray, an engineer employed by Microform Data Systems in California, alleged that a new computer console developed by the company failed to meet the state safety codes, he voiced his objections even though management did not want to hear them. He was fired. He went to court and last year was awarded damages by the Superior Court in Santa Clara.

Although Mr. Murray fared better than do most dissidents in court, his willingness to challenge management typifies a growing tendency in the ranks of engineers and scientists. One result is to reduce the unilateral character of management decisions. Another is to reduce the speed and ease of decision making.

Professionals are more interested in effectiveness than in efficiency. They prefer to see an employer corporation doing the right thing inefficiently than the almost right or wrong thing efficiently.

In 1972 three engineers who had worked on the development of the San Francisco Bay Area Rapid Transit System lost their jobs when, after plans had been approved and the work had got under way, they disclosed information about safety defects in the braking system to members of the BART Board of Directors. No executive steeped in the traditional management culture would question management's decision in this case. On the other hand, professionals would.

In fact, among professionals there is a growing conviction that actions of the sort taken by the BART engineers are not only permissible but obligatory. In 1975, an ad hoc committee of the American Association for the Advancement of Science reported on the changing requirements of scientific freedom and responsibility. The committee concluded that more than a right is involved in the release of facts that are in the public interest, regardless of timing. Experts possessing such information *should* release it, the committee stated, "even though they might prefer to remain silent."

This philosophy is incompatible with the textbook philosophy of management control, with its corollaries of secrecy and obedience once the organization commits itself to a course. It destroys the notion of competition and the pursuit of profit as a "game" with rules that must be honored by all participants. Whatever its positive implications for the public interest, it means that, at least in the short run, corporations sometimes will find it harder to meet budgeted costs and deadlines.

Professionals reject the notion of total commitment to the enterprise. They consider after-hours activities as strictly their own affair. Louis V. McIntire, a veteran chemist employed by Du Pont Co. in Orange, Texas, was fired after writing (with his wife) a novel satirizing corporate management. Soon after publication of the novel, Du Pont fired him.

Mr. McIntire claims the discharge was in retaliation for his book and is suing his former employer in federal district court. (Du Pont declines to comment on the reasons for his dismissal.) While the discharge meets with approval among many traditional managers, many of Mr. McIntire's colleagues in the American Chemical Society have expressed support for him. (The society's weekly magazine, incidentally, frequently cites employers for "unprofessional dismissal.")

"Where it is a duty to worship the sun," said Viscount Morley, "it is pretty sure to be a crime to examine the laws of heat." For the traditional manager, the corporation is the sun, and there is such a duty. But for the professional there is no sun to worship, unless possibly it be the scientific method.

Questions

1. David Ewing's article focuses on the multiple loyalties of professionals working for corporations and the impact these loyalties have on corporate managerial decision making. What effects does Ewing see from such multiple loyalties? Did the Pennsylvania Supreme Court recognize these effects in *Geary*? Should only professional engineers and scientists maintain such multiple loyalties? Should the concept of the "professional executive" or "professional manager" be applied so as to foster such multiple loyalties in managers? Are managers professionals? What distinguishes managers from other recognized professionals, such as physicians and attorneys?

2. Do you favor a legally implied "discharge for cause" standard for professionals but not for others within the corporate organization? Do you favor such a standard for discharge for all corporate employees regardless of status? How would you define a "discharge for good cause"? Explain. Give examples of discharges for cause.

3. If the law were to protect all employees against unjust discharge, to what remedies should the wrongfully discharged employee be entitled? Should he or she be entitled to reinstatement to the job in addition to damages? Should damages be reduced by any earnings from subsequent employment? Explain.

Current proposals for change

Two recent proposals advanced by advocates of corporate social responsibility deserve attention. The first is a proposal to change the corporate structure to assure additional inputs into the corporate decision-making process from various constituencies affected by corporate activity. Under this proposal consumers, employees, and the local community would be represented on the corporate board of directors. The second proposal requires disclosure by the corporation of its social responsibility undertakings. Such disclosure would take the form of a social report, similar to the annual report given to shareholders, that would be preceded by a social audit, similar to audits conducted by accountants in other areas, in which corporate attorneys and accountants would audit the corporation's social performance.

The original impetus for these proposals came from West Germany, which pioneered in including worker representatives on corporate boards, and from France, where corporations provide a social balance sheet to their workers.

Although the Western European nations seem to be ahead of the United States in these areas, it should be noted that corporate social responsibility in Western Europe translates into the corporation's responsibility to its workers only, rather than to the public at large. In this country, some movement has taken place to change the corporate structure and provide reports of corporate social performance. In 1979 the Chrysler–United Auto Workers (UAW) collective bargaining contract provided for the inclusion of the UAW president on the Chrysler board of directors. Furthermore, since the mid-70s, among the committees of Aetna Life & Casualty Company's board of directors has been a Committee on Corporate Responsibility. This committee is supported by a Corporate Social Responsibility Staff of Aetna employees. It issues an annual *Report on Social Responsibility*, which includes reports regarding Aetna's minority employment, investment practices, and community involvement.

Changing the corporate structure. As was seen in the Purcell proposal, changing the corporate structure need not be confined to placing workers on corporate boards. Some have argued that consumers and community members should also be represented. However, only in Europe is there a legal requirement for constituency representation on corporate boards, and there the requirement applies only to employee representation. The concept is called "codetermination," and it includes the creation of works councils at the plant level. Works councils are committees consisting of management and employee members. The works council makes plant-level decisions, such as decisions regarding production schedules, disciplinary measures, and discharges.

Codetermination legislation has been enacted in most of the nations of Western Europe. Of these nations only Italy, Belgium, and Great Britain have no legislation giving workers a right to representation on supervisory boards, the European counterpart to the American board of directors. Codetermination originated in postwar West Germany. After World War II the Allies required worker participation on German corporate boards as a safeguard against the militaristic inclinations of German industry. The following excerpts describe how codetermination at the board level works in West Germany.

Blackburn, "Worker Participation on Corporate Directorates: Is America Ready for Industrial Democracy?"
18 *Houston Law Review* 349 (1981). Reprinted with permission of the publisher.

*   *   *   *   *

[A] two-tier board [of directors] has been the vehicle for worker imput into corporate policy making in West Germany for over a quarter of a century. . . . [A] "supervisory board" consisting of both shareholder and employee representatives is charged with supervision of company operations. Until recently, employees comprised one-third of the supervisory board, except in the iron, coal, and steel industries, where, since 1951, half of the supervisory board has consisted of employee representatives. The supervisory board elects members of a "management board," which is responsible for the day-to-day operation of the company. No employees sit on the management board.

Although a study done by the Biedenkopf Commission has suggested that cooperation between employees and shareholders has been fruitful, it has been suggested that in practice the functions of the supervisory board are so limited that it has very little real influence over policy making in the corporation. As an illustration of the supervisory board's limited influence, the Stock Company Law of 1965 contains a general prohibition against the assumption of management powers by the supervisory board in order to protect the management board from interference by the supervisory board. Thus, although the employees are represented in the company structure, their power has been limited not only by their minority representation, but also by the fact that they sit on a board with little muscle in the company.

Partially in response to the recommendations of the Biedenkopf Commission, and partially in response to political pressures from parties forming the coalition government in West Germany, a co-determination bill designed to give parity representation to employees was enacted in 1976. Although maintaining the two-tier structure, and therefore subject to the same criticisms previously made, the introduction of parity representation is seen as a significant advancement of the employee's position in the company. The law applies to "limited liability" companies—roughly parallel to closed corporations in the United States—which employ over 2,000 workers. An estimated 650 companies in West Germany are thus affected. The supervisory board consists of an equal number of employee and shareholder representatives, plus a chairman and a deputy-chairman, who are elected by a two-thirds majority vote of the board. Also by two-thirds majority vote, the board may additionally grant to the chairman the power to resolve any impasses which may occur between the two groups. Election of the members of the managing board also requires a two-thirds majority vote of the supervisory board. For each of the above-mentioned elections, complicated alternative voting methods are provided where a two-thirds majority cannot be obtained.

Criticism has been leveled at the Co-determination Law by both labor and management groups. Labor argues that numerical equality will not offset the dominance of capital in the corporation. Management argues that the bill will lead to dominance of companies by unions. Aside from these somewhat ideologically based arguments, concrete practical problems are posed by the possibility of deadlock under the scheme and by its technical complexity.

* * * * *

Social disclosure. The disclosure of corporate social responsibility undertakings has been suggested as a way of institutionalizing corporate social performance. So far several corporations in the United States have voluntarily instituted social reports. Only in France is social reporting required in the form of a legislatively mandated *bilan social* ("social balance sheet").

In the United States the Securities and Exchange Commission (SEC) has imposed requirements for limited social disclosure. These requirements stemmed from a petition submitted in 1971 by the Nader Project on Corporate Responsibility and the Natural Resources Defense Council that the SEC hold hearings about requiring disclosure on corporate involvement in litigation over civil rights and environmental issues. The hearings were denied, but the SEC later imposed limited disclosure requirements on corporations involved in legal proceedings on the environment and equal employment opportunity. The denial of the National Resources Defense Council's petition resulted in litigation, and the SEC was ordered to hold public hearings regarding its authority to require disclosure of corporate social responsibility data. The outcome of the hearings was a refusal by the SEC to require further social disclosure, because the SEC found that the costs and burdens of such disclosure would be grossly disproportionate to the benefits it would bring to investors. The SEC's chilling tone strongly suggests its reluctance to be a conduit for change in this area. However, the SEC conceded that social information might be economically significant to investors. Thus it is arguably within the SEC's authority to require social disclosure to some extent.

Because France is the only nation that requires corporate social disclosure, the following excerpts illustate what forms social disclosure can take.

Blackburn and Newman, "The French Social Balance Sheet," 48 *Cincinnati Law Review* 972 (1981). Reprinted with permission of the publisher.

II. SOCIAL ACCOUNTING

*　*　*　*　*

The French legislation is based upon the assumption that corporate social performance can be measured. The idea is not new to the United States or to France. American federal agencies have long required corporate gathering of what can be viewed as social information, and French management had already compiled a great deal of the information that the French balance sheet now requires. The innovation of social accounting, however, is its transformation of raw social statistics into a measurement of the social impacts of business actions on various environments. This transformation involves application of traditional financial accounting techniques to the social implications of corporate business actions in order to monitor what the corporation is doing in the area of social responsibility. This process, called the social audit in the United States, has as its unifying principle the qualification of the social efforts taken, or the social effects created, by a corporation in the pursuit of its business.

A social audit, or social balance sheet, necessarily includes some value judgments about social performance. Therefore, a means of comparing different aspects of a corporation's social performance is needed. Social accounting authorities suggest a number of techniques, such as monetization (assignment of money values) of various social assets and liabilities, application of a cost-benefit analysis to determine the opportunity cost of various social programs, and the tabulation of points to measure positive or negative variations from a base performance fixed in different social areas.

The approach taken by the French legislation has been to assemble various indicators of social performance into social credits and debits, to measure them against each other, and then to compare the performance of one year with that of previous years. For example, the number of accidents at the plant in one year, a social debit, would be compared with those occurring during previous years. The legislation itself makes no attempt to give correlative values to different types of social performance in order to evaluate the allocation of resources in social efforts at any one time. This type of judgment is left to the recipients of the balance sheet, particularly the employee committee, which issues an opinion on each balance sheet. The legislation does not preclude more sophisticated systems of social accounting, however, and management and labor are free to modify the balance sheet as long as they fulfill the requirements of the legislated indicators.

The social balance sheet is intended to fulfill three functions. First, it is designed to be an informational tool, providing its recipients (the works committee, union representatives and shareholders) with data concerning the social performance of the plant. Second, it will form a basis for negotiation between labor and management on improving working conditions, including a mutual attempt at fixing a hierarchy of goals in the social environment of the plant. Third, the balance sheet is designed to further corporate planning of social programs. The pursuit of these goals undoubtedly heightens the sensibility of management and individual employees to the social responsibility of the enterprise.

The social audit has been described as "an attempt to define the moving target called social responsibility." This characterization emphasizes the definitional requirements involved in the institution of a social audit. Before setting up a system for measuring the social impact of business actions on a given environment, the drafters must decide what impacts and business actions to measure, as well as which environments to consider. These parameters of social accounting are called the dimensions of the social audit.

The French Legislation

* * * * *

B. The contents of the social balance sheet. According to the text of the French legislation, the social balance sheet "sums up in a single document the principal numerical data that will facilitate an appraisal of the social situation of the plant, the recording of results achieved and the measurement of changes that have occurred during the preceding year and during the two years prior thereto." The legislation requires the compilation of information in seven general areas: employment, salary and benefits, health and safety, other conditions of work (such as organization and type of work performed), training, professional relations and "the living conditions of the employees and their families to the extent that these conditions depend upon the corporation." Implementing decrees and regulations issued by the Council of State and various ministries have afforded considerable specificity to these general categories. The Council of State has the power to determine the information required in the balance sheet for the whole enterprise and for each individual establishment. In order to accommodate differences in the social environments of the sectors of the economy, individual ministries have issued rulings (*arrêtés*) governing information to be included in the balance sheets of companies under their jurisdictions. The content requirements vary according to the level of the reporting body (enterprise or establishment), its size and the activity of the entity. The last factor allows the indicators of the balance sheet to reflect individual characteristics of the sector of industry in which a company operates. Ministries have either issued or are in the process of drafting rulings concerning industry and agriculture, commerce, and services, building and public works, land and air transport and shipbuilding.

It is noteworthy that the legislation requires only measurement of the workplace's internal social environment and not measurement of a corporation's effects on the external environment, such as the amount of pollution generated by an industrial plant. Indeed, examination of the external environment only occurs when the enterprise compiles statistics on "other conditions of the work to the extent that these conditions depend upon the corporation." Such statistics, for example, old-age and sickness benefits, touch only the enterprise's employees. The limited content of the legislation was intentional and reflects a desire to define more precisely the responsibility of management to labor, and not necessarily management's responsibility to society as a whole. In contrast, the little social accounting attempted in the United States has dealt almost entirely with corporations' effect on the external environment.

Notwithstanding its limited examination of

an enterprise's external environment, the balance sheet is intended to be a flexible document. Its contents are susceptible to modification in response to the opinions of the works council and to the recommendations put forth in collective bargaining between unions and management. In addition to ensuring some responsiveness to employee judgments concerning improvement of the plant environment, this flexibility introduces the potential for expanding the contents of the balance sheet. By pressing demands through collective negotiation or the works council, socially conscious workers may be able to force measurement of the impact of business actions on the external environment as well as on the plant's internal environment. In this manner the French balance sheet may eventually embrace many of the areas of corporate activity that have been monitored in the United States, such as the effects of pollution, quality of products produced and compliance with consumer legislation.

C. The recipients of the balance sheet. The potential for effectiveness of the French social accounting concept lies in the availability of an employee forum to which management can report and be held responsible. That forum is the works council, a factory committee consisting of representatives of several unions, elected by the employees, and a management representative of the plant. The council advises management on employees' concerns regarding the work environment. Although its decisions are not binding on the corporation, the council has a consultative role in the policymaking of the corporation. The French legislation requires each enterprise to furnish its council with a copy of the balance sheet to aid the council in its advisory role.

The works council meets to examine the sheet for compliance with the government regulations and may confer on the relative importance of the indicators the sheet includes. Following this examination, the council issues an opinion on the company's progress in improving the social environment. The opinion may include proposals for modifications in the composition of the balance sheet itself. Once the opinion of the factory committee has been issued, it becomes a part of the balance sheet and the entire document is made available to the labor inspector, the shareholders, company employees and union representatives.

That the works council has input concerning factors relied on to measure corporate social performance raises the possibility that workers' values will determine part of what constitutes a good performance in the social sphere. Because the council has only an advisory role, its advice is unlikely to have any concrete effect without management's cooperation.

Review Problems

1. Competitor Corporation filed an antitrust action against Conglomocorp, Inc., seeking $10 million in damages. The case was tried without a jury. The trial judge had the matter under advisement. He wrote an opinion finding in favor of Competitor Comporation and awarding that company $9 million in damages. Three days before releasing the opinion, he called the lawyers into his chambers and advised them of his decision. The case had received a large amount of publicity, and the judge wished to allow the parties time to prepare for the public announcement. He informed them that his decision would be announced in three days.

Your spouse, the secretary to the president of Competitor Corporation, typed a memorandum which explained the impending decision to the Competitor board of directors. Your spouse disclosed its contents to you. You realized that when the decision was released, the price of Competitor's stock would rise and that of Conglomocorp stock would fall. You also realized that you could make a large profit by purchasing puts in Conglomocorp and calls in Competitor. (A put allows the purchaser to sell a specified number of shares in a stock at a specified price at any time for a specified duration. If the price then falls, the purchaser can buy the stock at its new price and resell it at the higher specified price. A call allows the purchaser to buy a specified number of shares of a stock at a specified price at any time for a specified duration. If the price rises, the purchaser can buy the stock at the specified price and resell it at its higher current price.)

Would it be unethical for you to do this? Would your answer be different if instead of learning of the decision from your spouse, you learned of it in your capacity as president of Competitor? Would it be different if instead of trading for your own account, you were a stockbroker advising a client on investments? How would you answer a client who owned stock in both Competitor and Conglomocorp, needed to raise cash, and asked you which to sell?

Now place yourself in the position of the sellers of the puts and calls. Do you think they would feel cheated if they learned that you were aware of the impending decision when you or your client entered into the transaction? If a substantial number of persons traded stock upon receiving such information, what would be the impact of their transactions upon the credibility of the securities markets?

2. You and your partner were the founders and sole shareholders of Publicorp, Inc., a small corporation. During the 1960s, when stock prices were generally high, you each sold some of your stock publicly at $15 per share. The stock rose to $20 per share, and you sold additional shares. Approximately 18 percent of the stock of Publicorp is held by outsiders.

Recently the stock market has been depressed, and Publicorp has dropped to $3 per share. Many of the outside shareholders voiced concern about this at the company's annual meeting. The company's bylaws provide for cumulative voting, and the outsiders narrowly missed electing one of their people to the board of directors. You are concerned that next year they will succeed.

You have tried to repurchase some Publicorp stock on the open market and have succeeded in obtaining 8 percent by offering to pay $4.50 per share. The remaining 10 percent is owned by five individuals who refused to sell because they believed the stock had bottomed out and would be rising soon.

Your partner has suggested the following plan to freeze out the remaining outsiders. The two of you will form Privatecorp, Inc., a new corporation, and then sell your shares in Publicorp to Privatecorp. Publicorp would thus be a 90 percent–owned subsidiary of Privatecorp.

A state statute permits a parent corporation to merge with a subsidiary at least 90 percent of whose stock it owns and to eliminate the equity interests of the outside shareholders. (The outsiders' sole remedy is an independent appraisal of the value of their stock and payment of that value in cash.) This procedure would enable you to regain complete control of the company. Should you use it?

3. You are a male middle-level manager in EEO Corporation, a large diversified company. Your boss, Sam Superior, is the vice president in charge of your division. Your division is by far the most profitable in the company, due in large part to Sam's talents. Recently you recommended hiring two female applicants to fill two openings in the division. Sam admitted to you that the women were the most qualified applicants for the jobs but explained his reasons for not hiring them: "Women have only two functions in business—typing and keeping important customers happy. This is a man's division, and I expect you to find the right man for the job."

Would you advise the president of the company that Sam is discriminating against women? If the president refuses to take any action, would you complain to the Equal Employment Opportunity Commission? If the women filed a lawsuit against EEO Corporation, would you volunteer to testify on their behalf? How would you react if you were subpoenaed to testify?

4.   You are an officer of a medium-sized manufacturer, Suburban Corporation. You operate two large plants in the suburbs of a city whose population exceeds 500,000. The city has been deteriorating for some time. Its unemployment rate is about 15 percent, while the unemployment rate in the surrounding suburbs is about 5 percent. The city's revenues have been declining for some time. In an effort to increase revenue the city has imposed an income tax of 2 percent on all residents and a tax of 0.5 percent on the income that nonresidents earn in the city. The worst blight in the city has been on the east side, where over 15 percent of the residential property lies vacant and condemned. The crime rate is quite high; insurance is almost impossible to obtain. The mayor has said on many occasions that the east side can come back only if there is a large influx of private capital and jobs.

Suburban Corporation has prospered, and the demand for its products continues to expand. It is clear that the company must build another plant to meet this rising demand. Plans have already been drafted for the new plant, which will employ about 1,000 persons. Where should the new plant be located? If you conclude that the socially responsible choice would be to locate on the city's east side, how will your decision affect the community? How will it affect shareholders? Employees? Consumers?

5.   Consider the position of large institutional investors that must decide whether to retain their holdings in companies operating in South Africa. In making this decision, should such investors consider the South African government's practice of apartheid? Should they consider whether the companies in question have formally subscribed to the Sullivan Principles which call for companies to follow nondiscriminatory employment policies in South Africa? Should the institu-

tional investors consider the companies' actual practices in South Africa? Should they consider whether selling their holdings in these companies is likely to persuade the companies to pull out of South Africa? Should they consider whether such a pullout is likely to influence South Africa's policies? Finally, should they consider the effect that selling large blocks of stock will have on the stock market?

6.   You are marketing director for an insurance company, responsible for the sale of property insurance in a major metropolitan area. Almost all the houses of the north, south, and east sides of the city and the southern suburbs are occupied by blacks, while the houses on the west side and in the remaining suburbs are occupied largely by whites. The average market value of houses in the black neighborhoods is $20,000 below that of houses in the white neighborhoods. Your experience shows you that blacks are more likely to buy property insurance from black salespersons and that whites are more likely to buy it from white salespersons. Should you assign all or most of your black personnel to your offices serving black neighborhoods and all or most of your white personnel to your offices serving white neighborhoods?

7.   You are the publisher of a newspaper serving a small town. The town's population can support only one newspaper. Recently your printers went on strike, forcing the paper to close. The publisher of a newspaper serving another town decided to seize the opportunity to win your market away. It began publishing a competing paper at your town. When your strike ended and you resumed operations, your competitor hired union officials to endorse its paper and brand yours as antiunion. It also offered secret rebates to local businesspersons who refused to advertise in your paper and additional rebates to those who persuaded other local businesspersons to cease dealing with you. Should you respond in kind?

8. The complainant had been an executive engineer for General Motors from 1947 to 1973. At his termination he was head of GM's Mechanical Development Department. He alleged that he had been discharged for refusing to give the government false information at his employer's behest, for undertaking to correct alleged misrepresentations made to the government, and for legitimately complaining about certain allegedly deceptive GM practices. The defendant, General Motors, moved for summary judgment, arguing that even if all that the complainant alleged were true and could be proved, the discharge did not concern a sufficient breach of public policy to state a cause of action. How should the court rule? Explain.

9. David W. Ewing has proposed a constitutional amendment, calling it "an employee bill of rights." In pertinent part, it provides:

> No public or private organization shall discriminate against an employee for criticizing the ethical, moral, or legal policies and practices of the organization; nor shall any organization discriminate against an employee for engaging in outside activities of his or her choice, or for objecting to a directive that violates common norms of morality.[8]

Do you favor Ewing's proposal? Would you favor the proposal if it called for a statute rather than a constitutional amendment?

10. You have been asked to speak to the local chamber of commerce. Your speech is to be entitled "Corporate Social Responsibility: Theoretical Framework and Practical Application." Outline your remarks.

---

[8] Ewing, "Freedom inside the Organization," in *Individual Rights in the Corporation: A Reader on Employee Rights* 67 at 69 (Westin and Salisbury, eds. 1980).

PART VI: REVIEW PROBLEMS

1. You are a vice president of Ace Aircraft, Inc., which manufactures jet passenger airplanes. Ace developed the enormously profitable ACE-000 (otherwise known as the "ace-in-the-hole"). Recently Ace entered into several contracts to supply the leading commercial airlines with planes over the next 10 years. In addition, it has a contract to supply the U.S. Army with 100 modified ACE-000s for use as troop transports. The environmental consequences of using the modified ACE-000s are unclear.

You have undertaken a review of Ace's existing production facilities to ascertain whether its productive capacity is sufficient to meet its present contractual commitments and the anticipated growth in demand for the ACE-000. A preliminary report by your staff indicates that some plant facilities and equipment will need to be expanded and modernized and that entirely new plants will need to be built.

The report reveals that the company's two factories for building the ACE-000, located in Newark, New Jersey, and Cleveland, Ohio, are rapidly becoming outdated. State and local taxes are relatively high. Both cities have deteriorated over the past decade. They have high unemployment and crime rates, and their population has declined. These facts, coupled with the high cost of living in these cities, make it difficult for Ace to attract top-quality engineers and executives to work at these two factories.

Both facilities have also experienced labor unrest. The Newark plant is unionized. Negotiation of its last three contracts has resulted in lengthy strikes. At these times the company was able to rely on the nonunionized Cleveland facility. However, a recent election at the Cleveland plant resulted in the certification of the same international union that represents the Newark plant as the bargaining representative of the Cleveland plant's employees.

At your request your staff has prepared the following preliminary proposals for Ace's expansion:

Alternative A. Ace will improve its existing facilities in both Newark and Cleveland. This will require expanding the existing plants and building one new plant in each city. Obtaining the land for this expansion is no problem because Ace owns the property adjacent to its facilities in both cities. The adjacent property at both locations consists of deteriorated residential buildings. The land is zoned for both residential and industrial purposes. Ace's expansion effort will displace the residents of its buildings.

The new factories, like the present factories, will have toxic by-products. The pollution of the rivers on which Ace's present factories are located is already at a toxic level. The plants would also emit noxious but not toxic airborne pollutants.

Alternative B. Ace will close its Newark and Cleveland plants and relocate on the outskirts of Connersville (population 17,000), in east-central Indiana. Connersville is situated on the Whitewater River, which is as clean as its name suggests. Connersville is an hour's drive from both Indianapolis and Cincinnati, and thus offers the pleasures of a small-town environment while being close to the shopping and cultural attractions of these larger communities. Closing Ace's Newark and Cleveland facilities will result in the unemployment of 5,000 workers, and Ace will incur certain expenses in relocating its facilities. However, labor costs will be lower in Connersville and Connersville's location will make it easier to attract engineers and executives who are looking for a small-town lifestyle. If Ace makes the move, Connersville's population will increase substantially, resulting in increased traffic congestion and related problems.

After reviewing the proposals, you decide to confer with your staff to discuss the implications of each alternative and to ascertain what additional information, if any, you will need before you present a report to the board of directors. Explain the legal and social responsibility implications that you see in the staff's suggestions, and make a list of the questions that you would ask your staff to answer as a follow-up to its proposals.

2. Dump Services, Inc., is a company that operates landfills for the reception of hazardous wastes. It purchased a site three years ago on 130 acres of land located over an abandoned mine and surrounded by farmland. The site is covered with a gob pile whose contents are similar to those of the gob piles spread over much of the nearby acreage by mines that operated between 1917 and 1954.

Under the 130 acres purchased by Dump are strata of tight clay. The top stratum extends to a depth of 10 to 12 feet. Beneath that is a very thin layer of more permeable saturated clay called the Sangamon Paleosal. This layer is continuous under Dump's 130 acres. An additional clay stratum more than 10 feet deep lies under the Paleosal. The mine spoil contains much of this clay, and the company uses it as a sealing agent in its landfill.

The company applied to the state EPA for a landfill permit. The application contained extensive information on groundwater, soil permeability, soil subsidence, subsurface, and hydrogeologic conditions. Dump was granted a permit in May of the year in which it acquired the site. It dug trenches in the clay to a depth of 10–12 feet, a width of 50 feet, and a length of 75–350 feet, with a space of 10 feet between the trenches. Hazardous substances were placed in the trenches and covered with soil from the gob piles.

Previously, however, the hazardous substances were dissolved in a solvent. If the solvent contains no PCBs or other hydrocarbons, it will tend to remain in the soil in which it is deposited. This process for keeping hazardous substances in place is known as attenuation. Dump's permit application included a request for permission to bury PCBs, herbicides, and paint sludge. Because PCBs are soluble in paint thinner and water, Dump's application stated that it would not combine PCBs with paint thinner and would keep groundwater and surface water free from PCBs.

To eliminate the possibility that hazardous substances might interact and pollute the air by causing chemical explosions, fires, or emissions of poisonous gas, Dump's application stated that it would not store incompatible substances together, that it would use materials tending to prevent incompatible hazardous substances from coming into contact with each other (e.g., it would place lime on certain substances to prevent them from combining with other substances to form poisonous gases), and that it would store many substances whose inherent qualities deterred their migration. Two years ago the state EPA renewed Dump's permit after an on-site inspection of Dump's operations.

A study of the landfill's operations undertaken by Dr. Dirt, one of Dump's geologists, indicates that the following conditions have occurred:

1. Oxidized spots extending to a depth of 25 feet exist in the undersurface. These oxidized spots are more permeable than the surrounding matter. Dr. Dirt explains that the oxidation occurred because these areas came into contact with the atmosphere in some way, for example, when roots pushed through the soil and then decayed, leaving an air space. He reports that in inspecting the trenches, he found root holes and other channels as large in diameter as a finger.

2. The clay undersurface indicates silty and sandy loesses whose porosity is greater than that of the clay.

3. Water from an artesian source has entered several trenches. The pressure on the water has caused it to rise through the landfill to the top of several trenches instead of being absorbed through the sides of these trenches. Thereby hazardous substances have been transported out of the trenches and to the surface. Dr. Dirt doubts whether the landfill can be restored to its former tightness.

4. The ability of the undersurface to adequately contain hazardous substances has been jeopardized by a collapse that occurred in the underlying abandoned mine. As a result, subsidence of the surface with accompanying cracks in the soil has been taking place and will continue to do so. Dr. Dirt believes that a subsidence crack extending to the top of the mine might de-

velop. The existence of an underground crack indicates the possibility of cracks that would give no warning of their presence and of their need to be repaired. As the burial trenches at the site are only 10 feet apart, a crack of 100–150 feet long could severely impair the ability of the trenches to contain liquid.

5. Paint thinner has been deposited in the same trenches as PCBs.

a. You are the vice president in charge of operations, and you have received Dr. Dirt's report. What will you do? Discuss the legal, ethical, and social responsibility implications of your response to the report.

b. You are Dr. Dirt. What will you do if the vice president in charge of operations fails to act on your report?

c. If Dr. Dirt does not have an employment contract with a stated period of duration, what are his rights if Dump terminates his employment.

d. Suppose that the neighboring landowners and residents of a village located less than a mile away file an action in a state court seeking an injunction to close the landfill. Using common-law principles, discuss the suit's probability of success.

e. Suppose that the state EPA calls a meeting attended by representatives of the state development department, the state department of health, the state department of natural resources, the state planning office, and the office of the governor, as well as you and other Dump officers, officers of other hazardous waste disposal companies, and representatives of the state's hazardous waste disposal trade association. What is at issue is the future disposal of hazardous wastes in a busy industrial state. The state officials are concerned about providing industry and its employees with a necessary service and at the same time protecting the public health. The hazardous waste disposal industry is interested in lawful economic survival. The purpose of the meeting is to explore possibilities. Because of your reputation as a brilliant, incisive, wide-ranging innovative thinker, you have been asked to make opening remarks in which you explore the possible legal alternatives. Justify your reputation.

APPENDIX A

The Constitution of the United States of America (excerpts)

ARTICLE I, SECTION 8

The Congress shall have Power to lay and collect Taxes, Duties, Imposts and Excises, to pay the Debts and provide for the common Defense and general Welfare of the United States; but all Duties, Imposts and Exercises shall be uniform throughout the United States;

To borrow Money on the credit of the United States;

To regulate Commerce with foreign Nations, and among the several States, and with the Indian Tribes;

To establish an uniform Rule of Naturalization, and uniform Laws on the subject of Bankruptcies throughout the United States;

To coin Money, regulate the Value thereof, and of foreign Coin, and fix the Standard of Weights and Measures;

To provide for the Punishment of counterfeiting the Securities and current Coin of the United States;

To establish Post Offices and post Roads;

To promote the Progress of Science and useful Arts, by securing for limited Times to Authors and Inventors the exclusive Right to their respective Writings and Discoveries;

To constitute Tribunals inferior to the supreme Court;

To define and punish Piracies and Felonies committed on the high Seas, and Offences against the Law of Nations;

To declare War, grant Letters of Marque and Reprisal, and make Rules concerning Captures on Land and Water;

To raise and support Armies, but no Appropriation of Money to that Use shall be for a longer Term than two years;

To provide and maintain a Navy;

To make rules for the Government and Regulation of the land and naval Forces;

To provide for calling forth the Militia to execute the Laws of the Union, suppress Insurrections and repel Invasions;

To provide for organizing, arming, and disciplining, the Militia, and for governing such Part of them as may be employed in the Service of the United States, reserving to the States respectively, the Appointment of the Officers and the Authority of training the Militia according to the discipline perscribed by Congress;

To exercise exclusive Legislation in all Cases whatsoever, over such District (not exceeding ten Miles square) as may, by Cession of particular States, and the Acceptance of Congress, become the Seat of the Government of the United States, and to exercise like Authority over all Places purchased by the Consent of the Legislature of the State in which the Same shall be, for the Erection of Forts, Magazines, Arsenals, dock-Yards, and other needful Buildings;—And

To make all Laws which shall be necessary and proper for carrying into Execution the foregoing Powers, and all other Powers vested by this Constitution in the Government of the United States, or in any Department or Officer thereof.

ARTICLE III

Section 1

The judicial Power of the United States, shall be vested in one supreme Court, and in such inferior Courts as the Congress may from time to time ordain and establish. The Judges, both of the supreme and inferior Courts, shall hold their Offices during good Behaviour, and shall, at stated Times, receive for their Services, a Compensation, which shall not be diminished during their Continuance in Office.

Section 2

The judicial Power shall extend to all Cases, in Law and Equity, arising under this Constitution, the Laws of the United States, and Treaties made, or which shall be made, under their Authority;—to all Cases affecting Ambassadors, other public Ministers and Consuls;—to all Cases of admiralty and maritime Jurisdiction;—to Controversies to which the United States shall be a party;—to Controversies between two or more States;—between a State and Citizens of another State;—between Citizens of different States;—between Citizens of the same State claiming Lands under Grants of different States, and between a State, or the Citizens thereof, and foreign States, Citizens or Subjects.

In all Cases affecting Ambassadors, other public Ministers and Consuls, and those in which a State shall be Party, the supreme Court shall have original Jurisdiction. In all the other Cases before mentioned, the supreme Court shall have appellate Jurisdiction, both as to Law and Fact, with such Exceptions, and under such Regulations as the Congress shall make.

The Trial of all Crimes, except in Cases of Impeachment, shall be by Jury; and such Trial shall be held in the State where the said Crimes shall have been committed; but when not committed within any State, the Trial shall be at such Place or Places as the Congress may by Law have directed.

AMENDMENT 1 [1791]

Congress shall make no law respecting an establishment of religion, or prohibiting the free exercise thereof; or abridging the freedom of speech, or of the press; or the right of the people peaceably to assemble, and to petition the Government for a redress of grievances.

AMENDMENT 4 [1791]

The right of the people to be secure in their persons, houses, papers, and effects, against unreasonable searches and seizures, shall not be violated, and no Warrants shall issue, but upon probable cause, supported by Oath or affirmation, and particularly describing the place to be searched, and the persons or things to be seized.

AMENDMENT 5 [1791]

No person shall be held to answer for a capital, or otherwise infamous crime, unless on a presentment or indictment of a Grand Jury, except in cases arising in the land or naval forces, or in the Militia, when in actual service in time of War or public dangers; nor shall any person be subject for the same offence to be twice put in jeopardy of life or limb; nor shall be compelled in any criminal case to be a witness against himself, nor be deprived of life, liberty, or property, without due process of law; nor shall private property be taken for public use, without just compensation.

AMENDMENT 14 [1868]

Section 1. All persons born or naturalized in the United States, and subject to the jurisdiction thereof, are citizens of the United States and of the State wherein they reside. No State shall make or enforce any law which shall abridge the privileges or immunities of citizens of the United States; nor shall any State deprive any person of life, liberty, or property, without due process of law; nor deny to any person within its jurisdiction the equal protection of the laws.

Section 5. The Congress shall have power to enforce, by appropriate legislation, the provisions of this article.

APPENDIX B

The Sherman Act (excerpts)

1. Trusts, etc., in restraint of trade illegal; penalty. Every contract, combination in the form of trust or otherwise, or conspiracy, in restraint of trade or commerce among the several States, or with foreign nations, is declared to be illegal. Every person who shall make any contract or engage in any combination or conspiracy declared by sections 1 to 7 of this title to be illegal shall be deemed guilty of a felony, and, on conviction thereof, shall be punished by fine not exceeding one million dollars if a corporation, or if any other person, one hundred thousand dollars, or by imprisonment not exceeding three years, or both said punishments, in the discretion of the court.

2. Monopolizing trade a felony; penalty. Every person who shall monopolize, or attempt to monopolize, or combine or conspire with any other person or persons, to monopolize any part of the trade or commerce among the several States, or with foreign nations, shall be deemed guilty of a felony, and, on conviction thereof, shall be punished by fine not exceeding one million dollars if a corporation, or, if any other person, one hundred thousand dollars, or by imprisonment not exceeding three years, or by both said punishments, in the discretion of the court.

APPENDIX C

The Clayton Act (excerpts)

3. Sale, etc., on agreement not to use goods of competitor. It shall be unlawful for any person engaged in commerce, in the course of such commerce, to lease or make a sale or contract for sale of goods, wares, merchandise, machinery, supplies, or other commodities, whether patented or unpatented, for use, consumption, or resale within the United States or any Territory thereof or the District of Columbia or any insular possession or other place under the jurisdiction of the United States, or fix a price charged thereof, or discount from, or rebate upon, such price, on the condition, agreement, or understanding that the lessee or purchaser thereof shall not use or deal in the goods, wares, merchandise, machinery, supplies, or other commodities of a competitor or competitors of the lessor or seller, where the effect of such lease, sale, or contract for sale or such condition, agreement or understanding may be to substantially lessen competition or tend to create a monopoly in any line of commerce.

6. Antitrust laws not applicable to labor organizations. The labor of a human being is not a commodity or article of commerce. Nothing contained in the antitrust laws shall be construed to forbid the existence and operation of labor, agricultural, or horticultural organizations, instituted for the purposes of mutual help, and not having capital stock or conducted for profit, or to forbid or restrain individual members of such organizations from lawfully carrying out the legitimate objects thereof; nor shall such organizations, or the members thereof, be held or construed to be illegal combinations or conspiracies in restraint of trade, under the antitrust laws.

7. Acquisition by one corporation of stock of another. No corporation engaged in commerce shall acquire, directly or indirectly, the whole or any part of the stock or other share capital and no corporation subject to the jurisdiction of the Federal Trade Commission shall acquire the whole or any part of the assets of another corporation engaged also in commerce, where in any line of commerce in any section of the country, the effect of such acquisition may be substantially to lessen competition, or to tend to create a monopoly.

No corporation shall acquire, directly or indirectly, the whole or any part of the stock or other share capital and no corporation subject to the jurisdiction of the Federal Trade Commission shall acquire the whole or any part of the assets of one or more corporations engaged in commerce, where in any line of commerce in any section of the country, the effect of such acquisition, of such stocks or assets, or of the use of such stock by the voting or granting of proxies or otherwise, may be substantially to lessen competition, or to tend to create a monopoly.

This section shall not apply to corporations purchasing such stock solely for investment and not using the same by voting or otherwise to bring about, or in attempting to bring about, the substantial lessening of competition. Nor shall anything contained in this section prevent a corporation engaged in commerce from causing the formation of subsidiary corporations for the actual carrying on of their immediate lawful business, or the natural and legitimate branches or extensions thereof, or from owning and holding all or part of the stock of such subsidiary corporations, when the effect of such formation is not to substantially lessen competition.

8. Interlocking directorates and officers.   . . .

No person at the same time shall be a director in any two or more corporations, any one of which has capital, surplus, and undivided profits aggregating more than $1,000,000, engaged in whole or in part in commerce, other than banks, banking associations, trust companies, and common carriers subject to the Act to regulate commerce approved February fourth, eighteen hundred and eighty-seven, if such corporations are or shall have been theretofore, by virtue of their business and location or operation, competitors, so that the elimination of competition by agreement between them would constitute a violation of any of the provisions of any of the antitrust laws. The eligiblity of a director under the foregoing provision shall be determined by the aggregate amount of the capital, surplus, and undivided profits, exclusive of dividends declared but not paid to stockholders, at the end of the fiscal year of said corporation next preceding the election of directors, and when a director has been elected in accordance with the provisions of this Act it shall be lawful for him to continue as such for one year thereafter.

APPENDIX D

The Federal Trade Commission Act (excerpts)

5. Unfair methods of competition unlawful; prevention by Commission—declaration.

Declaration of unlawfulness; power to prohibit unfair practices.

(a) (1) Unfair methods of competition in or affecting commerce, and unfair or deceptive acts or practices in or affecting commerce, are declared unlawful. . . .

Penalty for violation of order, injunctions and other appropriate equitable relief.

(b) Any person, partnership, or corporation who violates an order of the Commission to cease and desist after it has become final, and while such order is in effect, shall forfeit and pay to the United States a civil penalty of not more than $5,000 for each violation, which shall accrue to the United States and may be recovered in a civil action brought by the Attorney General of the United States. Each separate violation of such an order shall be a separate offense, except that in the case of a violation through continuing failure or neglect to obey a final order of the Commission each day of continuance of such failure or neglect shall be deemed a separate offense.

APPENDIX E

The Robinson-Patman Act
(excerpts)

2. Discrimination in price, services, or facilities.

(a) Price; selection of customers.

It shall be unlawfur for any person engaged in commerce, in the course of such commerce, either directly or indirectly, to discriminate in price between different purchases of commodities of like grade and quality, where either or any of the purchasers involved in such discrimination are in commerce, where such commodities are sold for use, consumption, or resale within the United States or any Territory thereof or the District of Columbia or any insular possession or other place under the jurisdiciton of the United States, and where the effect of such discrimination may be substantially to lessen competition or tend to create a monopoly in any line of commerce, or to injure, destroy, or prevent competition with any person who either grants or knowingly receives the benefit of such discrimination, or with customers of either of them: *Provided,* That nothing herein contained shall prevent differentials which make only due allowance for differences in the cost of manufacture, sale, or delivery resulting from the differing methods or quantities in which such commodities are to such purchasers sold or delivered: *Provided, however,* That the Federal Trade Commission may, after due investigation and hearing to all interested parties, fix and establish quantity limits, and revise the same as it finds necessary as to particular commodities or classes of commodities, where it finds that available purchasers in greater quantities are so few as to render differentials on account thereof unjustly discriminatory or promotive of monopoly in any line of commerce; and the foregoing shall then not be construed to permit differentials based on differences in quantities greater than those so fixed and established: *And provided further,* That nothing herein contained shall prevent persons engaged in selling goods, wares, or merchandise in commerce from selecting their own customers in bona fide transactions and not in restraint of trade: *And provided further,* That nothing herein contained shall prevent price changes from time to time where in response to changing conditions affecting the market for or the market-ability of the goods concerned, such as but not limited to actual or imminent deterioration of perishable goods, obsolescence of seasonal goods, distress sales under court process, or sales in good faith in discontinuance of business in the goods concerned.

(b)   Burden of rebutting prima-facie case of discrimination.

Upon proof being made, at any hearing on a complaint under this section, that there has been discrimination in price or services or facilities furnished, the burden of rebutting the prima-facie case thus made by showing justification shall be upon the person charged with a violation of this section, and unless justification shall be affirmatively shown, the Commission is authorized to issue an order terminating the discrimination: *Provided, however,* That nothing herein contained shall prevent a seller rebutting the prima-facie case thus made by showing that his lower price or the furnishing of services or facilities to any purchaser or purchasers was made in good faith to meet an equally low price of a competitor, or the services or facilities furnished by a competitor.

(c)   Payment or acceptance of commission, brokerage or other compensation.

It shall be unlawful for any person engaged in commerce, in the course of such commerce, to pay or grant, or to receive or accept, anything of value as a commission, brokerage, or other compensation, or any allowance of discount in lieu thereof, except for services rendered in connection with the sale or purchase of goods, wares, or merchandise, either to the other party to such transaction or to an agent, representative, or other intermediary therein where such intermediary is acting in fact for or in behalf, or is subject to the direct or indirect control, of any party to such transaction other than the person by whom such compensation is so granted or paid.

(d)   Payment for services or facilities for processing or sale..

It shall be unlawful for any person engaged in commerce to pay or contract for the payment of anything of value to or for the benefit of a customer of such person in the course of such commerce as compensation or in consideration for any services or facilities furnished by or through such customer in connection with the processing, handling, sale, or offering for sale of any products or commodities manufactured, sold, or offered for sale by such person, unless such payment of consideration is available on proportionally equal terms to all other customers competing in the distribution of such products or commodities.

(e)   Furnishing services or facilities for processing, handling, etc.

It shall be unlawful for any person to discriminate in favor of one purchaser against another purchaser or purchasers of a commodity bought for resale, with or without processing, by contracting to furnish or furnishing, or by contributing to the furnishing of, any services or facilities connected with the processing, handling, sale, or offering for sale of such commodity so purchased upon terms not accorded to all purchasers on proportionally equal terms.

(f)   Knowingly inducing or receiving discriminatory price.

It shall be unlawful for any person engaged in commerce, in the course of such commerce, knowingly to induce or receive a discrimination in price which is prohibited by this section.

3. Discrimination in rebates, discounts, or advertising service charges; underselling in particular localities; penalties.   It shall be unlawful for any person engaged in commerce, in the course of such commerce, to be a party to, or assist in, any transaction of sale, or contract to sell, which discriminates to his knowledge against competitors of the purchaser, in that, any discount, rebate, allowance, or advertising service charge is granted to the purchaser over and above any discount, rebate, allowance, or advertising service charge available at the time of such transaction to said competitors in respect of a sale of goods of like grade, quality, and quantity; to sell, or contract to sell, goods in any part of the United States at prices lower than those exacted by said person elsewhere in the United States for the purpose of destroying competition, or eliminating a competitor in such part of the United States; or, to sell, or contract to sell, goods at unreasonably low prices for the purpose of destroying competition or eliminating a competitor.

Any person violating any of the provisions of this section shall, upon conviction thereof, be fined not more than $5,000 or imprisoned not more than one year, or both.

APPENDIX F

Restatement of Torts, Second
(excerpts)

402 A. *Special liability of seller of produce for physical harm to user or consumer.*

(1) One who sells any product in a defective condition unreasonably dangerous to the user or consumer or to his property is subject to liability for physical harm thereby caused to the ultimate user or consumer, or to his property, if

(a) the seller is engaged in the business of selling such a product, and

(b) it is expected to and does reach the user or consumer without substantial change in the condition in which it is sold.

(2) The rule stated in Subsection (1) applies although

(a) the seller has exercised all possible care in the preparation and sale of his product, and

(b) the user or consumer has not bought the product from or entered into any contractual relation with the seller.

402 B. *Misrepresentation by seller of chattels to consumer.*

One engaged in the business of selling chattels who, by advertising, labels, or otherwise, makes to the public a misrepresentation of a material fact concerning the character or quality of a chattel sold by him is subject to liability for physical harm to a consumer of the chattel caused by justifiable reliance upon the misrepresentation, even though

(a) it is not made fraudulently or negligently, and

(b) the consumer has not bought the chattel from or entered into any contractual relations with the seller.

APPENDIX G

Uniform Commercial Code (excerpts)

2–302. *Unconscionable contract or clause.*

(1) If the court as a matter of law finds the contract or any clause of the contract to have been unconscionable at the time it was made the court may refuse to enforce the contract, or it may enforce the remainder of the contract without the unconscionable clause, or it may so limit the application of any unconscionable clause as to avoid any unconscionable result.

(2) When it is claimed or appears to the court that the contract or any clause thereof may be unconscionable the parties shall be afforded a reasonable opportunity to present evidence as to its commercial setting, purpose and effect to aid the court in making the determination.

2–313. *Express warranties by affirmation, promise, description, sample.*

(1) Express warranties by the seller are created as follows:

(a) Any affirmation of fact or promise made by the seller to the buyer which relates to the goods and becomes part of the basis of the bargain creates an express warranty that the goods shall conform to the affirmation or promise.

(b) Any description of the goods which is made part of the basis of the bargain creates an express warranty that the goods shall conform to the description.

(c) Any sample or model which is made part of the basis of the bargain creates an express warranty that the whole of the goods shall conform to the sample or model.

(2) It is not necessary to the creation of an express warranty that the seller use formal words such as "warrant" or "guarantee" or that he have a specific intention to make a warranty, but an affirmation merely of the value of the goods or a statement purporting to be merely the seller's opinion or commendation of the goods does not create a warranty.

2–314. *Implied warranty: merchantability; usage of trade.*

(1) Unless excluded or modified (Section 2–316), a warranty that the goods shall be merchantable is implied in a contract for their sale if the seller is a merchant with respect to goods of that kind. Under this section the serving for value of food or drink to be consumed either on the premises or elsewhere is a sale.

(2) Goods to be merchantable must be at least such as

612

(a) pass without objection in the trade under the contract description; and

(b) in the case of fungible goods, are of fair average quality within the description; and

(c) are fit for the ordinary purpose for which such goods are used; and

(d) run, within the variations permitted by the agreement, of even kind, quality and quantity within each unit and among all units involved; and

(e) are adequately contained, packaged, and labeled as the agreement may require; and

(f) conform to the promises or affirmations of fact made on the container or label if any.

(3) Unless excluded or modified . . . , other implied warranties may arise from course of dealing or usage of trade.

2–315. *Implied warranty: fitness for particular purpose.*

Where the seller at the time of contracting has reason to know any particular purpose for which the goods are required and that the buyer is relying on the seller's skill or judgment to select or furnish suitable goods, there is unless excluded or modified under the next section an implied warranty that the goods shall be fit for such purpose.

2–318. *Third party beneficiaries of warranties express or implied.*

A seller's warranty whether express or implied extends to any natural person who is in the family or household of his buyer or who is a guest in his home if it is reasonable to expect that such person may use, consume or be affected by the goods and who is injured in person by breach of the warranty. A seller may not exclude or limit the operation of this section.

A P P E N D I X   H

National Labor Relations Act
(excerpts)

DEFINITIONS

Section 2.   When used in this Act—

(2) The term "employer" includes any person acting as an agent of an employer, directly or indirectly, but shall not include the United States or any wholly owned Government corporation, or any Federal Reserve Bank, or any State or political subdivision thereof, or any person subject to the Railway Labor Act, as amended from time to time, or any labor organization (other than when acting as an employer), or anyone acting in the capacity of officer or agent of such labor organization.

(3) The term "employee" shall include any employee, and shall not be limited to the employees of a particular employer, unless the Act explicitly states otherwise, and shall include any individual whose work has ceased as a consequence of, or in connection with, any current labor dispute or because of any unfair labor practice, and who has not obtained any other regular and substantially equivalent employment, but shall not include any individual employed as an agricultural laborer, or in the domestic service of any family or person at his home, or any individual employed by his parent or spouse, or any individual having the status of an independent contractor, or any individual employed as a supervisor, or any individual employed by an employer subject to the Railway Labor Act, as amended from time to time, or by any other person who is not an employer as herein defined.

(11) The term "supervisor" means any individual having authority, in the interest of the employer, to hire, transfer, suspend, lay off, recall, promote, discharge, assign, reward, or discipline other employees, or responsibly to direct them, or to adjust their grievances, or effectively to recommend such action, if in connection with the foregoing the exercise of such authority is not of a merely routine or clerical nature, but requires the use of independent judgment.

(12) The term "professional employee" means—

(a) any employee engaged in work (i) predominantly intellectual and varied in character as opposed to routine mental, manual, mechanical, or physical work; (ii) involving the consistent exercise of discretion and judgment in its performance; (iii) of such a character that the output produced or the result accomplished cannot be standardized in relation to a given period of time; (iv) requiring knowledge of an advanced type in a field of science or learning customarily acquired by a prolonged course of specialized intellectual instruction and study in an institution of higher learning or a hospital, as distinguished from a general academic education or from an apprenticeship or from training in the performance of routine mental, manual, or physical processes; or

(b) any employee, who (i) has completed the courses of specialized intellectual instruction and study described in clause (iv) of paragraph (a), and (ii) is performing related work under the supervision of a professional person to qualify himself to become a professional employee as defined in paragraph (a).

RIGHTS OF EMPLOYEES

Section 7. Employees shall have the right to self-organization, to form, join, or assist labor organizations, to bargain collectively through representatives of their own choosing, and to engage in other concerted activities for the purpose of collective bargaining or other mutual aid or protection, and shall also have the right to refrain from any or all of such activities except to the extent that such right may be affected by an agreement requiring membership in a labor organization as a condition of employment as authorized in section 8(a)(3).

UNFAIR LABOR PRACTICES

Section 8. (a) It shall be an unfair labor practice for an employer—

(1) to interfere with, restrain, or coerce employees in the exercise of the rights guaranteed in section 7;

(2) to dominate or interfere with the formation or administration of any labor organization or contribute financial or other support to it: *Provided,* That subject to rules and regulations made and published by the Board pursuant to section 6, an employer shall not be prohibited from permitting employees to confer with him during working hours without loss of time or pay;

(3) by discrimination in regard to hire or tenure of employment or any term or condition of employment to encourage or discourage membership in any labor organization: *Provided,* That nothing in this Act, or in any other statute of the United States, shall preclude an employer from making an agreement with a labor organization (not established, maintained, or assisted by any action defined in section 8(a) of this Act as an unfair labor practice) to require as a condition of employment membership therein on or after the thirtieth day following the beginning of such employment or the effective date of such agreement, whichever is the later, (i) if such labor organization is the representative of the employees as provided in section 9(a), in the appropriate collective-bargaining unit covered by such agreement when made, and (ii) unless following an election held as provided in section 9(e) within one year preceding the effective date of such agreement, the Board shall have certified that at least a majority of the employees eligible to vote in such election have voted to rescind the authority of such labor organization to make such an agreement: *Provided further,* That no employer shall justify any discrimination against an employee for nonmembership in a labor organization (A) if he has reasonable grounds for believing that such membership was not available to the employee on the same

terms and conditions generally applicable to other members, or (B) if he had reasonable grounds for believing that membership was denied or terminated for reasons other than the failure of the employee to tender the periodic dues and the initiation fees uniformly required as a condition of acquiring or retaining membership;

(4) to discharge or otherwise discriminate against an employee because he has filed charges or given testimony under this Act;

(5) to refuse to bargain collectively with the representatives of his employees, subject to the provisions of section 9(a).

(b) It shall be an unfair labor practice for a labor organization or its agents—

(1) to restrain or coerce (A) employees in the exercise of the rights guaranteed in section 7: *Provided,* That this paragraph shall not impair the right of a labor organization to prescribe its own rules with respect to the acquisition or retention of membership therein; or (B) an employer in the selection of his representatives for the purposes of collective bargaining or the adjustment of grievances;

(2) to cause or attempt to cause an employer to discriminate against an employee in violation of subsection (a)(3) or to discriminate against an employee with respect to whom membership in such organization has been denied or terminated on some ground other than his failure to tender the periodic dues and the initiation fees uniformly required as a condition of acquiring or retaining membership;

(3) to refuse to bargain collectively with an employer, provided it is the representative of his employees subject to the provisions of section 9(a);

(4) (i) to engage in, or to induce or encourage [the employees of any employer] an individual employed by any person engaged in commerce or in an industry affecting commerce to engage in, a strike or a refusal in the course of his employment to use, manufacture, process, transport, or otherwise handle or work on any goods, articles, materials, or commodities or to perform any services; or (ii) to threaten, coerce, or restrain any person engaged in commerce or in an industry affecting commerce, where in either case an object thereof is—

(A) forcing or requiring any employer or self-employed person to join any labor or employer organization or to enter into any agreement which is prohibited by section 8(e);

(B) forcing or requiring any person to cease using, selling, handling, transporting, or otherwise dealing in the products of any other producer, processor, or manufacturer, or to cease doing business with any other person, or forcing or requiring any other employer to recognize or bargain with a labor organization as the representative of his employees unless such labor organization has been certified as the representative of such employees under the provisions of section 9: Provided, That nothing contained in this clause (B) shall be construed to make unlawful, where not otherwise unlawful, any primary strike or primary picketing;

(C) forcing or requiring any employer to recognize or bargain with a particular labor organization as the representative of his employees if another labor organization has been certified as the representative of such employees under the provisions of section 9;

(D) forcing or requiring any employer to assign particular work to employees in a particular labor organization or in a particular trade, craft, or class rather than to employees in another labor organization or in another trade, craft, or class, unless such employer is failing to conform to an order or certification of the Board determining the bargaining representative for employees performing such work:

Provided, That nothing contained in this subsection (b) shall be construed to make unlawful a refusal by any person to enter upon the premises of any employer (other than his own employer), if the employees of such employer are engaged in a strike ratified or approved by a representative of such employees whom such employer is required to recognize under this Act: Provided further, That for the purposes of this paragraph (4) only, nothing contained in such paragraph shall be construed to prohibit publicity, other than picketing, for the purpose of truthfully advising the public, including consumers and members of a labor organization, that a product or products are produced by an employer with whom the labor organization has a primary dispute and are distributed by another employer, as long as such publicity does not have an effect of inducing any individual employed by any person other than the primary employer in the course of his employment to refuse to pick up, deliver, or transport any goods, or not to perform any services, at the establishment of the employer engaged in such distribution:

(5) to require of employees covered by an agreement authorized under subsection (a)(3) the payment, as a condition precedent to becoming a member of such organization, of a fee in an amount which the Board finds excessive or discriminatory under all the circumstances. In making such a finding, the Board shall consider, among other relevant factors, the practices and customs of labor organizations in the particular industry, and the wages currently paid to the employees affected;

(6) to cause or attempt to cause an employer to pay or deliver or agree to pay or deliver any money or other thing of value, in the nature of an exaction, for services which are not performed or not to be performed; and

(7) to picket or cause to be picketed, or threatened to picket or cause to be picketed, any employer where an object thereof is forcing or requiring an employer to recognize or bargain with a labor organization as the representative of his employees, or forcing or requiring the employees of an employer to accept or select such labor organization as their collective bargaining representative, unless such labor organization is currently certified as the representative of such employees:

(A) where the employer has lawfully recognized in accordance with this Act any other labor organization and a question concerning representation may not appropriately be raised under section 9(c) of this Act;

(B) where within the preceding twelve months a valid election under section 9(c) of this Act has been conducted, or

(C) where such picketing has been conducted without a petition under section 9(c) being filed within a reasonable period of time not to exceed thirty days from the commencement of such picketing: Provided, That when such a petition has been filed the Board shall forthwith, without regard to the provisions of section 9(c)(1) or the absence of a showing of a substantial interest on the part of the labor organization, direct an election in such unit as the Board finds to be appropriate and shall certify the results thereof: Provided further, That nothing in this subparagraph (C) shall be construed to prohibit any picketing or other publicity for the purpose of truthfully advising the public (including consumers) that an employer does not employ members of, or have a contract with, a labor organization, unless an effect of such picketing is to induce any individual employed by any other person in the course of his employment, not to pick up, deliver or transport any goods or not to perform any services.

Nothing in this paragraph (7) shall be construed to permit any act which would otherwise be an unfair labor practice under this section 8(b).

(c) The expressing of any views, argument, or opinion, or the dissemination thereof, whether in written, printed, graphic, or visual form, shall not constitute or be evidence of an unfair labor practice under any of the provisions of this Act, if such expression contains no threat of reprisal or force or promise of benefit.

(d) For the purposes of this section, to bargain collectively is the performance of the mutual obligation of the employer and the representative of the employees to meet at reasonable times and confer in good faith with respect to wages, hours, and other terms and conditions of employment, or the negotiation of an agreement, or any question arising thereunder, and the execution of a written contract incorporating any agreement reached if requested by either party, but such obligation does not compel either party to agree to a proposal or require the making of a concession: Provided, That where there is in effect a collective-bargaining contract covering employees in an industry affecting commerce, the duty to bargain collectively shall also mean that no party to such contract shall terminate or modify such contract, unless the party desiring such termination or modification—

(1) serves a written notice upon the other party to the contract of the proposed termination or modification sixty days prior to the expiration date thereof, or in the event such contract contains no expiration date, sixty days prior to the time it is proposed to make such termination or modification;

(2) offers to meet and confer with the other party for the purpose of negotiating a new contract or a contract containing the proposed modifications;

(3) notifies the Federal Mediation and Conciliation Service within thirty days after such notice of the existence of a dispute, and simultaneously therewith notifies any State or Territorial agency established to mediate and conciliate disputes within the State or Territory where the dispute occurred, provided no agreement has been reached by that time; and

(4) continues in full force and effect, without resorting to strike or lock-out, all the terms and conditions of the existing contract for a period of sixty days after such notice is given or until the expiration date of such contract, whichever occurs later:

The duties imposed upon employers, employees, and labor organizations by paragraphs (2), (3), and (4) shall become inapplicable upon an intervening certification of the Board, under which the labor organization or individual, which is a party to the contract, has been superseded as or ceased to be the representative of the employees subject to the provisions of section 9(a), and the duties so imposed shall not be construed as requiring either party to discuss or agree to any modification of the terms and conditions contained in a contract for a fixed period, if such modification is to become effective before such terms and conditions can be reopened under the provisions of the contract. Any employee who engages in a strike within [the sixty-day] any notice periods specified in this subsection, or who engages in any strike within the appropriate period specified in subsection (g) of this section, shall lose his status as an employee of the employer engaged in the particular labor dispute, for the purposes of sections 8, 9, and 10 of this Act, but such loss of status for such employee shall terminate if and when he is reemployed by such employer. Whenever the collective bargaining involves employees of a health care institution, the provisions of this section 8(d) shall be modified as follows:

(A) The notice of section 8(d)(1) shall be ninety days; the notice of section 8(d)(3) shall be sixty days; and the contract period of section 8(d)(4) shall be ninety days.

(B) Where the bargaining is for an initial agreement following certification or recognition, at least thirty days' notice of the existence of a dispute shall be given by the labor organization to the agencies set forth in section 8(d)(3).

(C) After notice is given to the Federal Mediation and Conciliation Service under either clause (A) or (B) of this sentence, the Service shall promptly communicate with the parties and use its best efforts, by mediation and conciliation, to bring them to agreement. The parties shall participate fully and promptly in such meetings as may be undertaken by the Service for the purpose of aiding in a settlement of the dispute.

(e) It shall be an unfair labor practice for any labor organization and any employer to enter into any contract or agreement, express or implied, whereby such employer ceases or refrains or agrees to cease or refrain from handling, using, selling, transporting, or otherwise dealing in any of the products of any other employer, or to cease doing business with any other person, and any contract or agreement entered into heretofore or hereafter containing such an agreement shall be to such extent unenforcable and void: Provided, That nothing in this subsection (e) shall apply to an agreement between a labor organization and an employer in the construction industry relating to the contracting or subcontracting of work to be done at the site of the construction, alteration, painting, or repair of a building, structure, or other work: Provided further, That for the purposes of this subsection (e) and section 8(b)(4)(B) the terms "any employer," "any person engaged in commerce or any industry affecting other producer, processor, or manufacturer," "any other employer," or "any other person" shall not include persons in the relation of a jobber, manufacturer, contractor, or subcontractor working on the goods or premises of the jobber or manufacturer or performing parts of an integrated process of production in the apparel and clothing industry: Provided further, That nothing in this Act shall prohibit the enforcement of any agreement which is within the foregoing exception.

(f) It shall not be an unfair labor practice under subsections (a) and (b) of this section for an employer engaged primarily in the building and construction industry to make an agreement covering employees engaged (or who, upon their employment, will be engaged) in the building and construction industry with a labor organization of which building and construction employees are members (not established, maintained, or assisted by any action defined in section 8(a) of this Act as an unfair labor practice) because (1) the majority status of such labor organizations has not been established under the provisions of section 9 of this Act prior to the making of such agreement, or (2) such agreement requires as a condition of employment, membership in such labor organization after the seventh day following the beginning of such employment or the effective date of the agreement, whichever is later, or (3) such agreement requires the employer to notify such labor organization of opportunities for employment with such employer, or gives such labor organization an opportunity to refer qualified applicants for such employment, or (4) such agreement specifies minimum training or experience qualifications for employment or provides for priority in opportunities for employment based upon length of service with such employer, in the industry or in the particular geographical area: Provided, That nothing in this subsection shall set aside the final proviso to section 8(a)(3) of this Act: Provided further, That any agreement which would be invalid, but for clause (1) of this subsection, shall not be a bar to a petition filed pursuant to section 9(c) or 9(e).

(g) A labor organization before engaging in any strike, picketing, or other concerted refusal to work at any health care institution shall, not less than ten days prior to such action, notify the institution in writing and the Federal Mediation and Conciliation Service of that intention, except that in the case of bargaining for an initial agreement following certification or recognition the notice required by this subsection shall not be given until the expiration of the period specified in clause (b) of the last sentence of section 8(d) of this Act. The notice shall state the date and time that such action will commence. The notice, once given, may be extended by the written agreement of both parties.

REPRESENTATIVES AND ELECTIONS

Section 9. (a) Representatives designated or selected for the purposes of collective bargaining by the majority of the employees in a unit appropriate for such purposes, shall be the exclusive representatives of all the employees in such unit for the purposes of collective bargaining in respect to rates of pay, wages, hours of employment, or other conditions of employment: Provided, That any individual employee or a group of employees shall have the right at any time to present grievances to their employer and to have such grievances adjusted, without the intervention of the bargaining representative, as long as the adjustment is not inconsistent with the terms of a collective-bargaining contract or agreement then in effect: Provided further, That the bargaining representative has been given opportunity to be present at such adjustment.

(b) The Board shall decide in each case whether, in order to assure to employees the fullest freedom in exercising the rights guaranteed by this Act, the unit appropriate for the purposes of collective bargaining shall be the employer unit, craft unit, plant unit, or subdivision thereof: Provided, That the Board shall not (1) decide that any unit is appropriate for such purposes if such unit included both professional employees and employees who are not professional employees unless a majority of such professional employees vote for inclusion in such unit; or (2) decide that any craft unit is inappropriate for such purposes on the ground that a different unit has been established by a prior Board determination, unless a majority of the employees in the proposed craft unit vote against separate representation or (3) decide that any unit is appropriate for such purposes if it includes, together with other employees, any individual employed as a guard to enforce against employees and other persons rules to protect property of the employer or to protect the safety of persons on the employer's premises; but no later organization shall be certified as the representative of employees in a bargaining unit of guards if such organization admits to membership, or is affiliated directly or indirectly with an organization which admits to membership, employees other than guards.

(c)(1) Whenever a petition shall have been filed, in accordance with such regulations as may be prescribed by the Board—

(A) by an employee or group of employees or an individual or labor organization acting in their behalf alleging that a substantial number of employees (i) wish to be represented for collective bargaining and that their employer declines to recognize their representative as the representative defined in section 9(a), or (ii) assert that the individual or labor organization, which has been certified or is being currently recognized by their employer as the bargaining representative, is no longer a representative as defined in section 9(a); or

(B) by an employer, alleging that one or more individuals or labor organizations have presented to him a claim to be recognized as the representative defined in section 9(a); the Board shall investigate such petition and if it has reasonable cause to believe that a question of representation affecting commerce exists shall provide for an appropriate hearing upon due notice. Such hearing may be conducted by an officer or employee of the regional office, who shall not make any recommendations with respect thereto. If the Board finds upon the record of such hearing that such a question of representation exists, it shall direct an election by secret ballot and shall certify the results thereof.

(2) In determining whether or not a question of representation affecting commerce exists, the same regulations and rules of decision shall apply irrespective of the identity of the persons filing the petition or the kind of relief sought and in no case shall the Board deny a labor organization a place on the ballot by reason of an order with respect to such labor organization or its predecessor not issued in conformity with section 10(c).

(3) No election shall be directed in any bargaining unit or any subdivision within which, in the preceding twelve-month period, a valid election shall have been held. Employees engaged in an economic strike who are not entitled to reinstatement shall be eligible to vote under such regulations as the Board shall find are consistent with the purposes and provisions of this Act in any election conducted within twelve months after the commencement of the strike. In any election where none of the choices on the ballot receives a majority, a run-off shall be conducted, the ballot providing for a selection between the two choices receiving the largest and second largest number of valid votes cast in the election.

(4) Nothing in this section shall be construed to prohibit the waiving of hearings by stipulation for the purpose of a consent election in conformity with regulations and rules of decision of the Board.

(5) In determining whether a unit is appropriate for the purposes specified in subsection (b) the extent to which the employees have organized shall not be controlling.

(d) Whenever an order of the Board made pursuant to section 10(c) is based in whole or in part upon facts certified following an investigation pursuant to subsection (c) of this section and there is a petition for the enforcement or review of such order, such certification and the record of such investigation shall be included in the transcript of the entire record required to be filed under section 10(e) or 10(f), and thereupon the decree of the court enforcing, modifying, or setting aside in whole or in part the order of the Board shall be made and entered upon the pleadings, testimony, and proceedings set forth in such transcript.

(e)(1)Upon the filing with the Board, by 30 per centum or more of the employees in a bargaining unit covered by an agreement between their employer and a labor organization made pursuant to section 8(a)(3), of a petition alleging they desire that such authority be rescinded, the Board shall take a secret ballot of the employees in such unit, and shall certify the results thereof to such labor organization and to the employer.

(2) No election shall be conducted pursuant to this subsection in any bargaining unit or any subdivision within which, in the preceding twelve-month period, a valid election shall have been held.

APPENDIX I

Title VII of Civil Rights Act of 1964 (as amended) (excerpts)

Section 701. . . .

(j) The term "religion" includes all aspects of religious observance and practice, as well as belief, unless an employer demonstrates that he is unable to reasonably accommondate to an employee's or prospective employee's religious observance or practice without undue hardship on the conduct of the employer's business.

(k) The terms "because of sex" or "on the basis of sex" include, but are not limited to, because of or on the basis of pregnancy, childbirth or related medical conditions; and women affected by pregnancy, childbirth, or related medical conditions shall be treated the same for all employment-related purposes, including receipt of benefits under fringe benefit programs, as other persons not so affected but similar in their ability or inability to work, and nothing in Section 703(h) of this title shall not be interpreted to permit otherwise. This subsection shall not require an employer to pay for health insurance benefits for abortion, except where the life of the mother would be endangered if the fetus were carried to term, or except where medical complications have arisen from an abortion: Provided, That nothing herein shall preclude an employer from providing abortion benefits or otherwise effect bargaining agreements in regard to abortion.

DISCRIMINATION BECAUSE OF RACE, COLOR, RELIGION, SEX, OR NATIONAL ORIGIN

Section 703. (a) It shall be an unlawful employment practice for an employer—

(1) to fail or refuse to hire or to discharge any individual, or otherwise to discriminate against any individual with respect to his compensation, terms, conditions, or privileges of employment, because of such individual's race, color, religion, sex, or national origin; or

(2) limit, segregate, or classify his employees or applicants for employment in any way which would deprive or tend to deprive any individual of employment opportunities or otherwise adversely affect his status as an employee, because of such individual's race, color, religion, sex, or national origin.

(b) It shall be an unlawful employment practice for an employment agency to fail or refuse to refer for employment, or otherwise to discriminate against, an individual because of his race, color, religion, sex, or national origin, or to classify or refer for employment any individual on the basis of his race, color, religion, sex, or national origin.

(c) It shall be an unlawful employment practice for a labor organization—

(1) to exclude or to expel from its membership, or otherwise to discriminate against, any individual because of his race, color, religion, sex, or national origin;

(2) to limit, segregate, or classify its membership or applicants for membership or to classify or fail or refuse to refer for employment any individual, in any way which would deprive or tend to deprive any individual of employment opportunities, or would limit such employment opportunities or otherwise adversely affect his status as an employee or as an applicant for employment, because of such individual's race, color, religion, sex, or national origin; or

(3) to cause or attempt to cause an employer to discriminate against an individual in violation of this section.

(d) It shall be an unlawful employment practice for any employer, labor organization, or joint labor-management committee controlling apprenticeship or other training or retraining, including on-the-job training programs to discriminate against any individual because of his race, color, religion, sex, or national origin in admission to, or employment in, any program established to provide apprenticeship or other training.

(e) Notwithstanding any other provision of this title, (1) it shall not be an unlawful employment practice for an employer to hire and employ employees, for an employment agency to classify, or refer for employment any individual, for a labor organization to classify its membership or to classify or refer for employment any individual, or for any employer, labor organization, or joint labor-management committee controlling apprenticeship or other training or retraining programs to admit or employ any individual in any such program, on the basis of his religion, sex, or national origin in those certain instances where religion, sex, or national origin is a bona fide occupational qualification reasonably necessary to the normal operation of that particular business or enterprise, and (2) it shall not be an unlawful employment practice for a school, college, university, or other educational institution or institution of learning to hire and employ employees of a particular religion if such school, college, university, or other educational institution or institution of learning is, in whole or in substantial part, owned, supported, controlled, or managed by a particular religion or by a particular religious corporation, association, or society, or if the curriculum of such schoool, college, university, or other educational institution or institution of learning is directed toward the propagation of a particular religion.

(f) As used in this title, the phrase "unlawful employment practice" shall not be deemed to include any action or measure taken by an employer, labor organization, joint labor-management committee, or employment agency with respect to an individual who is a member of the Communist Party of the United States or of any other organization required to register as a Communist-action or Communist-front organization by final order of the Subversive Activities Control Act of 1950.

(g) Notwithstanding any other provision of this title, it shall not be an unlawful employment practice for an employer to fail or refuse to hire and employ any individual for any position, for an employer to discharge an individual from any position, or for an employment agency to fail or refuse to refer any individual for employment in any position, or for a labor organization to fail or refuse any individual for employment in any position, if—

(1) the occupancy of such position, or access to the premises in or upon which

any part of the duties of such position is performed or is to be performed, is subject to any requirement imposed in the interest of the national security of the United States under any security program in effect pursuant to or administered under any statute of the United States or any Executive order of the President; and

(2) such individual has not fulfilled or has ceased to fulfill that requirement.

(h) Notwithstanding any other provision of this title, it shall not be an unlawful employment practice for an employer to apply different standards of compensation, or different terms, conditions, or privileges of employment pursuant to a bona fide seniority or merit system, or a system which measures earnings by quantity or quality of production or to employees who work in different locations, provided that such differences are not the result of an intention to discriminate because of race, color, religion, sex, or national origin; nor shall it be an unlawful employment practice for an employer to give and to act upon the results of any professionally developed ability test provided that such test, its administration or action upon the results is not designed, intended, or used to discriminate because of race, color, religion, sex, or national origin. It shall not be an unlawful employment practice under this title for any employer to differentiate upon the basis of sex in determining the amount of wages or compensation paid or to be paid to employees of such employer if such differentiation is authorized by the provision of Section 6(d) of the Fair Labor Standards Act of 1938 as amended (29 U.S.C. 206(d)).

(i) Nothing contained in this title shall apply to any business or enterprise on or near an Indian reservation with respect to any publicly announced employment practice of such business or enterprise under which a preferential treatment is given to any individual because he is an Indian living on or near a reservation.

(j) Nothing contained in this title shall be interpreted to require any employer, employment agency, labor organization, or joint labor-management committee subject to this title to grant preferential treatment to any individual or to any group because of the race, color, religion, sex, or national origin of such individual or group on account of an imbalance which may exist with respect to the total number or percentage of persons of any race, color, religion, sex, or national origin employed by any employer, referred or classified for employment by any employment agency or labor organization, admitted to membership or classified by any labor organization, or admitted to, or employed in, any apprenticeship or other training program, in comparison with the total number or percentage of persons of such race, color, religion, sex, or national origin in any community, State, section, or other area, or in the available work force in any community, State, section, or other area.

OTHER UNLAWFUL EMPLOYMENT PRACTICES

Section 704.   (a) It shall be an unlawful employment practice for an employer to discriminate against any of his employees or applicants for employment, for an employment agency, or joint labor-management committee controlling apprenticeship or other training or retraining, including on-the-job training programs, to discriminate against any individual, or for a labor organization to discriminate against any member thereof or applicant for membership, because he has opposed any practice, made an unlawful employment practice by this title, or because he has made a charge, testified, assisted, or participated in any manner in an investigation, proceeding, or hearing under this title.

(b) It shall be an unlawful employment practice for an employer, labor organization, employment agency, or joint labor-management committee controlling apprenticeship or other training or retraining, including on-the-job training programs, to print or cause to be printed or published any notice or advertisement relating to employment by such an employer or membership in or any classification or referral for employment by such a labor organization, or relating to any classification or referral for employment by such an employment agency, or relating to admission to, or employment in, any program established to provide apprenticeship or other training by such a joint labor-management committee indicating any preference, limitation, specification, or discrimination, based on race, color, religion, sex or national origin, except that such a notice or advertisement may indicate a preference, limitation, specification, or discrimination based on religion, sex or national origin when religion, sex, or national origin is a bona fide occupational qualification for employment.

APPENDIX J

Equal Pay Act of 1963 (excerpts)

Section 3. Section 6 of the Fair Labor Standards Act of 1938, as amended (29, U.S.C. et seq.), is amended by adding thereto a new subsection (d) as follows:

(d)(1) No employer having employees subject to any provisions of this section shall discriminate, within any establishment in which such employees are employed, between employees on the basis of sex by paying wages to employees in such establishment at a rate less than the rate at which he pays wages to employees of the opposite sex in such establishment for equal work on jobs the performance of which requires equal skill, effort, and responsibility, and which are performed under similar working conditions, except where such payment is made pursuant to (i) a seniority system; (ii) a merit system; (iii) a system which measures earnings by quantity or quality of production; or (iv) a differential based on any other factor other than sex: Provided, That an employer who is paying a wage rate differential in violation of this subsection shall not, in order to comply with the provisions of this subsection, reduce the wage rate of any employee. . . .

(3) For purposes of administration and enforcement, any amounts owing to any employee which have been withheld in violation of this subsection shall be deemed to be unpaid minimum wages or unpaid overtime compensation under this Act.

626

GLOSSARY

Acceleration clause   A provision in a credit agreement which allows the creditor to demand full payment of the debt if the debtor does not make timely payments or otherwise fails to comply with the terms of the agreement.

Action   A suit brought in a court.

Actionable   A term used to show that acts provide a basis or legal reason for a lawsuit.

Adjudication   The determination of a controversy and pronouncement of a judgment or decree in a case.

Administrative agency   An agency of the government charged with administering particular legislation.

Administrative law judge   An officer who presides at the initial hearing on matters litigated before a federal agency. He or she is chosen by civil service exam and is independent of the agency staff.

Administrative Procedure Act   A statute establishing the procedural rules governing how federal agencies operate.

Affidavit   A written declaration or statement of facts, sworn before a person who has the authority to administer such an oath.

Affirm   To agree with. An appellate court affirms a lower court decision when it declares the decision valid.

Affirmative action   An obligation undertaken by federal contractors to undertake special efforts to hire women and minorities. It is also a remedy which a court may decree under Title VII of the Civil Rights Act of 1964 and which the National Labor Relations Board is authorized to take under the National Labor Relations Act to effectuate the policies of those statutes.

Affirmative defense   An assertion which, if true, relieves a defendant of liability or limits a plaintiff's recovery.

Allegation   In a pleading, a declaration or statement by a party to a suit.

Allege   To make a statement of fact, an assertion, or a charge.

Amicus curiae   Latin, "Friend of the court." An individual or corporation that, because of strong interest in a case, petitions the court for permission to file a brief.

Appeal The process by which a party asks a higher court to review alleged errors made by a lower court or an agency.

Appellant The party that takes an appeal from one court to another.

Appellate court A court having jurisdiction of appeal and review.

Appellee The party in a case against which an appeal is taken; that is, the party with an interest adverse to setting aside or reversing a judgment.

Arbitrary and capricious A description of a decision or action taken by an administrative agency which clearly disregards facts or principles of law.

Arbitration A process wherein a dispute is submitted to a mutually acceptable person or board, each party to the dispute having agreed beforehand to comply with the decision.

Arraignment A proceeding wherein the accused is formally informed of the charge(s) and is asked to plead guilty, not guilty, or nolo contendere.

Articles of Confederation The name of the document embodying the compact made between the 13 original states of the Union, before the adoption of the present Constitution.

Assumption of the risk An affirmative defense raised by the defendant that defeats the plaintiff's recovery because the plaintiff knowingly and voluntarily exposed himself or herself to the danger that caused the injury.

Attempt In criminal law, an effort to accomplish a crime, amounting to more than mere preparation or planning for it, which, if not prevented, would have resulted in the full consummation of the attempted act, but which, in fact, does not bring to pass the party's ultimate design. In civil matters, an attempt ordinarily means an intent combined with an act falling short of the thing intended.

At-will employee An employee who may be discharged by the employer for any reason without liability.

Aver To set out, assert, or allege in a formal complaint before a court of law.

Bailment A delivery of goods by one person (bailor) to another (bailee) in trust for the accomplishment of a specific purpose involving the goods (e.g., repair) upon an express or implied contract to carry out such trust and subsequently return the goods to the bailor.

Bailor One who entrusts goods to another under a bailment.

Bait and switch advertising A method of selling in which a seller advertises at a low price a product that the seller does not intend to sell (the bait) and then disparages that product to the prospective buyer and directs the buyer to a higher-priced product (the switch) which the seller intended to sell all along.

Banc French, "The full court." A court sits *en banc* when all the judges making up the court hear the case in contradistinction to having the case decided by one judge or a portion of the judges of the court.

Barred Obstructed; subject to a hindrance that will prevent legal redress or recovery.

Beneficiary One for whose benefit a trust is created.

Bill The draft of an act of the legislature before it becomes law.

Bill of information A formal accusation of the commission of a crime made by a prosecutor in place of a grand jury indictment.

Bona fide Latin, "In good faith." Honestly, sincerely.

Bond (security) A certificate issued by a governmental body or a corporation to represent a debt owed to the bondholder as well as a promise to pay interest.

Boycott A conspiracy or confederation to prevent anyone from carrying on business, or to injure anyone's business, by preventing potential customers from doing business with him or her.

Broker An agent who bargains, carries on negotiations, and makes contracts on behalf of his or her employer for compensation; also, a dealer in securities issued by others.

Brokerage The compensation of a broker, including wages and commission.

Burden of proof The necessity or duty of affirmatively proving the fact or facts in dispute on an issue raised between the parties to a suit in court.

Canons of ethics Standards for the professional conduct expected of a lawyer, comprising the Code of Professional Reponsibility. Initially adopted by the American Bar Association, it has been enacted into law in most states.

Case law The law as developed or laid down in decided cases, as opposed to statutes.

Cause of action The facts which evidence a civil wrong, thereby giving rise to a right to judicial relief.

Cease and desist order An order by an agency or a court directing someone to stop doing something.

Certiorari A means of obtaining appellate review; a writ issued by an appellate court to an inferior court commanding the record to be certified to the appellate court for judicial review.

Churning Abuse of a customer's confidence by a broker who initiates excessive transactions for the customer for personal gain.

Circumstantial evidence Evidence of an indirect nature; evidence from which the existence of a fact is inferred.

Civil law That body of law which is concerned with civil or private rights. Contrast *Criminal law*.

Claim A cause of action.

Class action An action brought by one or more persons as representatives of a large group of similarly situated persons.

Codetermination A process of management in which employers and employees share in the decision making.

Collateral Property which is pledged as security for the satisfaction of a debt.

Collusion An agreement between two or more persons to commit a wrongful act.

Commerce The exchange of goods, products, or property of any kind.

Commercial speech A term used in constitutional law to refer to economic speech, such as new political advertising.

Commodity A movable article of commerce, especially merchandise.

Common carrier One that transports persons or property for compensation, providing such services to the general public.

Common law   As distinguished from law created by the enactment of legislatures, the common law comprises the principles and rules which derive solely from custom or from the judgments and decisions of courts. It is judge-made law.

Comparative negligence   The doctrine under which a plaintiff's negligence as a factor in his or her own injury is assigned a percentage value, and his or her recovery from the defendant is reduced proportionately. Contrast with *Contributory negligence*.

Compensable   Capable of being compensated.

Compensable damages   Damages which compensate the victim for a loss; damages that put the victim in the position he or she was in before the injury occurred.

Compensable injury   Within workers' compensation statutes is one which results in compensation to an employee for injury arising out of and in the course of employment.

Compensatory damages   Damages that will compensate an injured party for the injury sustained, and nothing more; such compensation as will simply make good or replace the loss caused by a wrong or injury.

Complaint   The first pleading by the plaintiff in a civil case. Its purpose is to give the defendant the information on which the plaintiff relies to support its demand. In a complaint, the plaintiff sets out a cause of action, consisting of a formal allegation or charge presented to the appropriate court.

Concerted action   Action that has been planned, arranged, adjusted, agreed on, or settled between parties acting together pursuant to some design or scheme.

Conciliation   The proceeding in which litigants are brought together by a third party.

Concur   To agree.

Concurring opinion   A printed opinion in which a judge agrees with the decision of the majority of the court for a different reason. With reference to appellate court opinions, a concurring opinion is one written by a judge who may agree with the majority opinion's conclusion, but for different reasons, and therefore writes a separate opinion.

Confederation   A league or compact for mutual support, particularly of nations or states. Such was the colonial government during the American Revolution.

Consent decree   A decree entered by consent of the parties. It is not a judicial sentence, but is an agreement of the parties made under the sanction of the court.

Consent order   An agreement by the defendant to cease activities which the government asserts are illegal. Also known as consent decree.

Consequential damages   Damage or injury which is not a direct, immediate, or predictable result of a party's act, but is nevertheless shown to be a consequence of it.

Consignee   One to whom goods are consigned for sale or safekeeping.

Consignment   Property delivered by a consignor to an agent for sale where title is held by the consignor until the property is sold.

Consignor   One who delivers goods to another on consignment.

Conspiracy   A combination or confederation between two or more persons formed for the purpose of committing, by their joint efforts, some unlawful or criminal act.

Construction defect   In a product liability action, a defect which results from the negligent manufacture of a particular item rather than from a defect in its design.

Contempt A willful disregard or disobedience of a public authority.

Contempt of court An act which disturbs or obstructs a court or is intended to detract from its authority or dignity.

Contract An agreement that a court will enforce.

Contributory negligence Conduct by the plaintiff which is a contributing factor in his or her injury, thus barring any recovery against the defendant. Contrast *Comparative negligence.*

Conversion An unauthorized assumption and exercise of ownership over goods belonging to another, to the alteration of their condition or the exclusion of the owner's rights.

Conviction The result of a criminal trial which ends in a judgment or sentence that the prisoner is guilty as charged.

Corporate takeover bid An attempt to assume control or management of a corporation by purchasing a controlling portion of its stock.

Corrective advertising A remedy of the Federal Trade Commission by which one found guilty of violating the Federal Trade Commission Act with regard to unlawful advertising is ordered to correct the lasting impression of the advertising upon the public by engaging in advertising that repudiates the earlier advertising.

Counterclaim A claim presented by a defendant which, if successful, defeats or reduces the plaintiff's recovery.

Creditor A person to whom a debt is owed.

Criminal law That body of law, commonly codified into penal codes, which declares what conduct is criminal and provides punishment for such conduct in order to protect society from harm. Contrast *Civil law.*

Cross claim A claim made in the course of an action by a defendant against a codefendant or by a plaintiff against a coplaintiff.

Cross-examination The examination of a witness at a trial or hearing, or upon taking a deposition, by the party opposed to the one that produced said witness, upon his or her evidence given in chief, to test its truth, to further develop it, or for other purposes.

Data Facts from which to draw a conclusion.

De minimis Something small or trifling.

De novo Latin, "To begin anew." Usually refers to the necessity of a new hearing on the same facts and law previously litigated.

Debt security Bonds, notes, debentures, and any other corporate securities which represent a debt owed to the holder.

Deceit A fraudulent misrepresentation used by one person to deceive or trick another, who is ignorant of the facts, to the damage of the latter.

Declaratory judgment A judgment which simply declares the rights of the parties or expresses the opinion of the court on a question of law without ordering anything to be done.

Defamation The disparagement of one's reputation; the offense of injuring a person's character, fame, or reputation by false and malicious statements.

Default Failure; omission to perform a legal or contractual duty; the failure of a party to appear in court after being properly served with process.

Defendant   The party against which an action is brought in a civil case; the accused in a criminal case.

Defense   An assertion offered by a defendant which, if successful, relieves him or her of liability, reduces the plaintiff's recovery, or defeats a criminal charge.

Deposition   Pretrial testimony of a witness taken orally and under oath before an officer of the court (but not in open court), subject to cross-examination, reduced to writing, and intended to be used at trial.

Design defect   In the law of product liability, a defect in a product resulting from its design, so that every one produced is similarly defective. Contrast with *Construction defect.*

Dicta   Plural of *dictum.* Opinions of a judge that do not embody the resolution or determination of the court.

Dictum   The word is generally used as an abbreviated form of *obiter dictum* ("a remark by the way"). An observation or remark made by a judge in pronouncing an opinion in a case, concerning some rule, principle, or application of law, or the solution of a question suggested by the case, but not necessarily involved in the case or essential to its determination.

Discovery   Devices that may be used by one party, as part of its preparation for trial, to obtain information about the case from the other party.

Disparagement   An untrue or misleading statement about a competitor's business or goods which is made to influence or tends to influence the public not to buy from the competitor.

Dissenting opinion   An opinion wherein a judge disagrees with the result reached by the majority of the court. Contrast *Concurring opinion.*

Distress sale   A "going out of business" sale in which the seller receives less for the goods than would be received under normal conditions.

Diversity jurisdiction   The jurisdiction of the federal courts to hear cases in which the parties are citizens of different states or one of the parties is an alien and the amount in controversy exceeds $10,000.

Dividend   The share allotted to each of several persons entitled to participate in a division of profits or property. Dividends are what a shareholder earns from the stock owned in a corporation.

Eminent domain   The power of a sovereign to take private property for public use.

Enabling legislation   A term applied to any statute that enables agencies, corporations, or persons to do something they could not do before. Such statutes confer a lawful power upon an agency to act on a given matter.

Equitable relief   Injunction, specific performance, restraining orders, and the like, as opposed to money damages.

Equity security   A share in a corporation, usually referred to as stock.

Escrow   A writing, deed, stock, or property delivered to a third person, to be held by that person until the fulfillment of a condition and then delivered to its owner.

Ex parte   On the application of one party only. A judicial proceeding is ex parte when it is taken or granted at the request of or for the benefit of one party only, and without notice to, or contestation by, any person adversely interested.

Exclusive dealing agreements   Contracts on which the buyer is obligated to purchase all of its requirements of a given commodity from the seller.

Executive order   An order by the chief executive of a government affecting the administration of the executive branch of government.

Exhaustion   A doctrine requiring that a party utilize remedies provided within an agency before seeking review by a court.

Exonerate   To exculpate; to remove a responsibility or duty.

Express warranty   A warranty which the seller creates by making a representation or a promise relating to goods or by showing the buyer a sample or model of them, regardless of whether such words as *guaranty,* or *warranty* are used.

Expunge   To destroy; to strike out wholly. "Expungement of the record" refers to the process whereby a record of a criminal conviction is sealed or destroyed after a designated period of time.

Federal question jurisdiction   The jurisdiction of the federal courts to hear cases arising under the U.S. Constitution, acts of Congress, or treaties.

Federal Register   A federal publication providing notice of federal rulemaking by federal agencies.

Fellow servant doctrine   A common-law doctrine, now abrogated by all workers' compensation acts, that an employee injured by the negligent act of a fellow employee cannot recover damages from his or her employer.

Fiduciary   A person having a duty, created by his or her undertaking, to act primarily for another's benefit.

Fiduciary duty   The duty which arises whenever one person is in a special relationship of trust to another, such as the duty an attorney owes to a client.

Foreign corporation   A corporation doing business in any state other than the one in which it is incorporated.

Forum non conveniens, doctrine of   The power of a court to decline jurisdiction when the convenience of the parties and the ends of justice would be better served by bringing the action in another court.

Franchise   A special privilege conferred upon someone.

Franchisee   A holder of a franchise.

Franchisor   A party granting a franchise.

Fungible goods   Goods of any type which are by nature considered to be the equivalent of any other goods of that type.

Garnishee   The person on whom a garnishment is served; one who has in his or her possession the property of someone who owes a debt to another person.

Garnishment   A proceeding in which money, property, or credits of a debtor in possession of a third person, the garnishee, are applied to the payment of debts. The process is available only where it is authorized by statute.

General intent   An intention, purpose, or design, either without a specific plan or without a particular object.

Good faith   An intangible quality encompassing honesty, sincerity, and the lack of intent to defraud or take advantage of another.

Gratuity A gift.

Gross negligence A conscious or intentional act or omission which is likely to result in harm to a person or property; a higher level of culpability than simple negligence.

Impeach To challenge the credibility of a witness.

Impleader A procedure whereby a defendant brings a new party into an action on the basis that the new party may be liable to that party.

Implied contract A contract not explicitly created by the parties, but inferred, as a matter of reason and justice, from the circumstances.

Implied warranty A warranty which arises by operation of law although the seller does not express it, e.g., that a good is fit for the purpose for which it is intended.

In camera In chambers; in private. A cause is said to be heard in camera either when the hearing is held before a judge or agency official in his or her private office or when all spectators are excluded from the courtroom or agency hearing room.

In personam jurisdiction The power which a court has over the defendant's person as opposed to the power of a court over property.

Incidental damages Damages resulting from a buyer's breach of contract, such as the costs of stopping delivery and reselling the goods; damages resulting from a seller's breach, including the expenses incurred in returning rightfully rejected goods and procuring a replacement.

Indictment A formal accusation made by a grand jury which charges that a person has committed a crime.

Information See Bill of Information.

Injunction An order of the court directing someone to do or not to do something.

Intent A state of mind with which a person acts.

Interrogatories A discovery device consisting of a series of written questions directed by one party to another party.

Interstate commerce Commercial trading, traffic, or the transportation of persons or property from a point in one state to points in other states.

Instrastate commerce Commerce that is carried out wholly within the limits of a single state.

Judgment non obstante verdicto (judgment n.o.v.) See *Judgment notwithstanding the verdict.*

Judgment notwithstanding the verdict A judge's judgment that is contrary to the verdict of the jury.

Jurisdiction The power of a court or a judicial officer to decide a case; the geographic area of a court's authority.

Jurisprudence The philosophy of law; the science which studies the principles of law and legal relations.

Labeling defect In the law of product liability, a defect in a product resulting from inadequate labeling.

Laissez-faire economics A policy whereby government takes a hands-off posture toward economic planning.

Legal relief Money damages. Contrast *Equitable relief.*

Legislation The act of enacting laws; the making of laws by express decree. Sometimes used as a noun to mean a statute or statutes.

Legislative history The background and events leading up to the enactment of a statute, e.g., committee reports and floor debates. Courts use the legislative history of a statute in determining the legislature's intent in enacting it.

Legislator One who makes laws; a member of a legislative body.

Legislature The department, assembly, or body of government that makes laws for a state or nation.

Libel To defame or injure a person's reputation by a published writing.

Lien A security interest in another's property, usually exercisable upon the nonpayment of a debt.

Liquidation The act or process by which a party settles his or her debt by converting all assets into cash and making distribution to creditors. The term is also used in connection with a Chapter 7 straight bankruptcy proceeding.

Long arm statute A state statute which subjects a nonresident or a foreign corporation to the state's jurisdiction if the person or corporation has committed a tortious wrong or conducted business within the state, or has otherwise had "minimal contacts" within the state.

Magistrate A term for a public officer. Commonly, however, the term is used to apply to judicial officers with limited authority, such as justices of the peace.

Mediation The act of a third person who attempts to persuade disputing parties to adjust their positions so as to resolve their dispute.

Merchantable Of good quality; of the quality fit for the purpose for which the good is intended.

Merger The fusion or absorption of one thing or right into another. For example, a merger occurs when one corporation becomes a part of another corporation.

Misrepresentation An untrue statement that justifies the rescission of a contract.

Modification A change.

Monopoly The ownership or control of so large a part of the market supply of a given commodity as to stifle competition and insure control over prices and competition.

Moot A question which is no longer a controversy because the issue involved is no longer in dispute.

Mortgage A pledge or security of particular property for the payment of a debt.

Motion A request to a court or judge for a rule or order favorable to the requesting party, generally made within the course of an existing lawsuit.

Motion for directed verdict A request that the judge order the entry of a verdict for one party on the grounds that the opposing party has failed to present sufficient evidence for any other verdict.

Necessary and Proper Clause   Clause in U.S. Constitution which authorizes Congress to make all laws necessary and proper to carry out the enumerated powers of Congress and all other powers vested in the federal government.

Negligence   The omission to do something that a reasonable and prudent person, guided by those considerations which ordinarily regulate human affairs, would do, or the doing of something that a reasonable and prudent person would not do.

Nolo contendere   Latin, "I will not contest it." A plea in a criminal action often having the same effect as a guilty plea, except that it may not be used against the defendant in a subsequent civil action. Also known as a no-contest plea.

Nuisance   A class of torts that arise from the unreasonable, unwarrantable, or unlawful use by a person of his or her property, or from unlawful personal conduct, which obstructs or injures the right of another.

Offer   An act on the part of one person whereby he or she gives to another the legal power of creating a contract.

Offeror   Someone who makes an offer.

Open-end credit   Revolving charges and credit cards which permit the consumer to pay a part of what is owed.

Palming off   To impose by fraud; to pass off a product as another product by unfair means.

Parent corporation   A company which owns over 50 percent of the voting stock of another company, known as its subsidiary.

Parliament   The supreme legislative assembly of Great Britain.

Per curiam   Latin, "By the court." Used to indicate an opinion by the entire court rather than a single judge. Sometimes refers to a brief statement of the court's decision unaccompanied by any written opinion.

Per se   Latin, "By itself." Inherently.

Petitioner   A party that files a petition with a court, applying in writing for a court order; a party that takes an appeal from a judgment; a party that initiates an equity action.

Plaintiff   A person who brings an action or complaint against a defendant; the party who initiates a suit.

Plea   An answer to a complaint or to a material allegation of fact therein. In criminal procedure, the answer of the accused in response to the criminal charge.

Pleadings   The formal allegations by the parties of their respective claims and defenses; the complaint, answer and reply.

Plenary   Full; entire; complete; absolute; perfect.

Police power   The inherent power of a state over persons and property which enables the state to regulate the health, safety, and welfare of society.

Positive Law   Law actually or specifically enacted or adopted by proper authority for the government of a society.

Possession   The control or custody of property, for one's use and enjoyment, to the exclusion of all others.

Post hoc   Hereafter; after this time.

Precedent   A previously decided court case which serves as authority for a subsequent similar case.

Predatory intent   An attempt to drive competitors out of business by sacrificing present revenues in the hope of recouping losses through future high prices.

Prejudicial error   An error made during a trial which materially affects the rights of a party and thus may be ground for a reversal of judgment or a new trial.

Price discrimination   Selling to one at a price and refusing to sell to another at the same price by one engaged in interstate commerce, in the absence of reason for the refusal.

Price fix   The act of establishing a price.

Prima facie   Latin, "At first sight." A fact presumed to be true unless disproved by evidence to the contrary.

Prima facie case   A case which has proceeded upon sufficient proof to that stage at which it will support a judicial finding if evidence to the contrary is disregarded. A litigating party is said to have a prima facie case when the evidence in its favor is sufficiently strong for its opponent to be called on to answer it. A prima facie case, then, is one which is established by sufficient evidence and which can be overthrown only by rebutting evidence adduced on the other side.

Private law   As used in contrast to public law, the term means that part of the law which is administered between citizen and citizen or which is concerned with the definition and enforcement of rights in cases where both the person in whom the right inheres and the person upon whom the obligation is incident are private individuals.

Privilege   A right or advantage particular to an individual or a class.

Privity   A mutual or successive relationship, for example, the relationship between the parties to a contract.

Pro rata   Proportionately.

Probable cause   Reasonable grounds for belief in the existence of facts. In criminal procedure, reasonable grounds for the belief that a person should be arrested or a warrant issued.

Procedural law   That part of law which concerns the method or process of enforcing rights.

Prosecution   A criminal action. The term is also frequently used with respect to civil litigation, and includes every step in action, from commencement to its final determination.

Proximate cause   Event(s) or action which, in natural and unbroken sequence, produce an injury that would not have occurred absent the event(s) or action.

Proxy   Written authorization given by a shareholder to vote his or her shares at a shareholders' meeting.

Public law   The branch of law which is concerned with administrative and constitutional law.

Punitive damages   Damages awarded to a plaintiff which are greater than the amount necessary to compensate his or her loss. Generally granted where the wrong involved intent, violence, fraud, malice, or other aggravated circumstances.

Quid pro quo   The giving of one valuable thing for another.

Reconstruction period   Period following the Civil War during which the states of the former Confederacy were reintegrated into the Union.

Redress   The receiving of satisfaction for an injury sustained.

Remand   To send back. The sending of a case back to the same court out of which it came, for the purpose of having some action taken on it.

Res ipsa loquitur   Latin, "The thing speaks for itself." Rule of evidence whereby negligence of the defendant is inferred from the circumstances as the result of a reasonable belief that the injury could not have happened without such negligence.

Res judicata   Latin, "A matter adjudged." A thing judicially acted upon or decided; a rule that a final judgment or decree on the merits by a court of competent jurisdiction is conclusive of the rights of the parties or their privies in all later suits on points and matters determined in the former suit.

Respondeat superior   Latin, "Let the master answer." Doctrine which provides that an employer or master is responsible for the acts of an employee or servant committed within the scope of the employment.

Respondent   The party that contends against an appeal.

Restraining order   An injunction; a court order prohibiting a party from doing something.

Restraint of trade   Contracts or combinations which tend or are designed to eliminate or stifle competition, effect a monopoly, artificially maintain prices, or otherwise obstruct commerce as it would be carried on if left to the control of natural or economic forces.

Reverse   To overthrow, vacate, set aside, make void, annul, repeal, or revoke, as to reverse a judgment.

Revocation   The recall of some power, authority, or thing granted.

Rulemaking   A function of most federal agencies that allows interested parties to comment upon proposed binding rules of an agency before their promulgation.

Scienter   Knowledge; intent to deceive or defraud.

Security   A stock, bond, note, investment contract, or other interest involving an investment in a common enterprise with the expectation of a profit to be derived from the efforts of someone other than the investor; an obligation given by a debtor to assure payment of the debt by providing the creditor with a resource that the creditor can use if the debtor defaults on the debt.

Security interest   A type of interest held by a creditor in a debtor's property such that the property could be sold upon the debtor's default in order to satisfy the debt.

Seniority   Represents in the highest degree the right to work. By seniority, the oldest worker in point of service, ability, and fitness for the job is the first to be given a choice of jobs, is the first to be promoted within a range of jobs subject to seniority, and is the last to be laid off. This proceeding is followed down the line to the youngest worker in point of service.

Shareholder   A person who owns stock in a corporation.

Situs   Situation or location.

Social audit   A report of a company's social behavior.

Social balance sheet   A report, required by French law, in which a company shares information on its social behavior with its workers.

Sovereign An independent body or state; a chief ruler with supreme power, such as a king.

Specific intent Exercise of intelligent will to commit a crime.

Standing A stake in a controversy sufficient to entitle a person to sue and obtain judicial resolution of the controversy.

Stare decisis Latin, "Let the decision stand." Doctrine under which courts stand by precedent and do not disturb a settled point. Under this doctrine, once a court has laid down a principle of law as applied to a certain state of facts, the court will adhere to that principle and apply it to all future cases in which the facts are substantially the same. (Stare decisis does *not* mean "The decision is in the stars.")

State right-to-work statute A state statute authorized by the Taft-Hartley Act whereby an employee may lawfully refuse to join a union that has been certified as the bargaining representative of the employer's employees.

Status quo ante Latin, "The state of things before."

Statute An act of a legislature declaring, commanding, or prohibiting something; a particular law enacted by the legislative department of government. Sometimes the word is used to designate codified law as opposed to case law.

Statute of limitations A statute prescribing the length of time after an event in which a suit must be brought or a criminal charge filed.

Stay To stop, arrest, or forbear. To stay an order or decree means to hold it in abeyance or to refrain from enforcing it.

Stop order The name of a Securities and Exchange Commission order directing that the effectiveness of a registration statement be suspended. The order also suspends a security issuer's license to use the mails and warns the investing public that the SEC has found the registration statement to be unreliable.

Strict liability Liability without fault. A case is one of strict liability when neither care nor negligence, neither good nor bad faith, neither knowledge nor ignorance will exonerate the defendant.

Subject matter jurisdiction A court's authority to hear a particular type of case.

Subpoena A writ ordering a person to appear and give testimony or to bring documents which are in his or her control.

Subsidiary corporation A corporation at least a majority of whose shares are owned by another corporation, which thus has control over it.

Substantive law That part of law which creates, defines, and regulates rights, as opposed to procedural law, which prescribes the methods for enforcing the rights.

Summary judgment A pretrial decision reached by a trial court, after considering the pleadings, affidavits, depositions, and other documents, on the ground that no genuine issue of fact has been raised.

Summons An instrument served on a defendant in a civil proceeding to give the defendant notice that he or she has been sued.

Sunset legislation A statute which provides that an agency's authority shall expire on a given date unless the legislative body acts to extend it.

Supremacy Clause   A clause in the U.S. Constitution which provides that all laws made by the federal government pursuant to the Constitution are the supreme law of the land and are superior to any conflicting state law.

Tender offer   An offer to purchase shares of stock, usually made in an attempt to obtain a controlling interest in a corporation.

Tort   A civil wrong or injury, other than a breach of contract, committed against the person or property of another.

Treble damages   Three times actual damages. The remedy provided to a successful plaintiff in certain actions, including antitrust suits.

Trespass   A tort action affording redress for injury committed to the plaintiff by the immediate force and violence of the defendant.

Trust   A legal arrangement whereby property or other assets are secured for beneficiaries by placing legal title and usually management responsibility in a trustee.

Trustee   The person appointed to execute a trust.

Unconscionable   So unfair or one-sided as to oppress or unfairly surprise a party.

Uniform Commercial Code   A comprehensive code, drafted by the National Conference of Commissioners on Uniform State Laws, which has been enacted in all of the states.

Union certification   The process by which the National Labor Relations Board certifies a union as the exclusive bargaining representative of a unit of employees in the employer's work force.

Variance   Permission to depart from the literal requirements of an administrative regulation.

Venue   The particular county or geographic location in which a court with jurisdiction may hear a case.

Veto   Latin, "I forbid." The refusal of assent by the executive officer whose assent is necessary to perfect a law which a legislative body has passed.

Warrant   A writ from a competent authority in pursuance of law which directs the doing of an act, is addressed to an officer or person competent to do the act, and affords that officer or person protection from damage if he or she does it. In particular, writs are issued by a magistrate or justice, and addressed to a sheriff, constable, or other officer, requiring the latter to arrest someone or to search someone's person or property and seize items of evidence.

Warranty   A promise that a statement is true. In contracts, a written or verbal undertaking or stipulation that a certain statement in relation to the subject matter of the contract is or shall be as it is stated or promised to be.

Work-product doctrine   The doctrine by which certain material prepared by an attorney in anticipation of litigation is protected from discovery.

Works councils   Plant-level committees consisting of supervisory personnel and workers, which decide plant-level matters.

Writ   A court order directing a person to do something.

INDEX OF COURT CASES

641

SUBJECT INDEX

645

*This book has been set CAP VideoComp, in 10 and 9
point Compano, leaded 2 points. Part numbers and titles
are 24 point Palatino Semi-Bold, Chapter numbers are
18 point Palatino Semi-Bold. The size of the type page
is 31 by 47 picas.*